UNDERSTANDING THE

SIGNS

OF THE TIMES

UNDERSTANDING THE

$\mathcal{S}$IGNS

OF THE TIMES

DONALD W. PARRY • JAY A. PARRY

DESERET BOOK COMPANY

SALT LAKE CITY, UTAH

Library of Congress Cataloging-in-Publication Data

Parry, Donald W.
    Understanding the signs of the times / Donald W. Parry and Jay A. Parry.
    p. cm.
    Includes bibliographical references.
    ISBN 1-57345-588-1
    1. Second Advent. 2. Mormon Church—Sacred books. 3. Church of Jesus Christ of Latter-day Saints—Doctrines. I. Title. II. Parry, Jay A.

    BX8643.S43 P37 1999
    236'.9 21—dc21
                                                                    99-043431

Printed in the United States of America   72082-6559

10 9   8   7   6   5   4   3   2   1

The lesson which the signs of the times should teach us is one of patience, endurance, and calm reliance on the Lord. The result will be that we shall be stronger, wiser, purer, happier, for the experience gained, and the work of the Lord . . . will yet triumph gloriously over all its foes, and the infinite atonement of the Redeemer will accomplish its perfect work. The final victory of the Saints is certain; after the trial comes the reward.

JOHN TAYLOR, GEORGE Q. CANNON, AND JOSEPH F. SMITH
"Epistle of the First Presidency," 301

CONTENTS

PREFACE

In preparing this work, we have based our understandings and commentary primarily on scripture, both ancient and modern, rather than on interpretations found elsewhere. We first systematically searched the four standard works of The Church of Jesus Christ of Latter-day Saints and identified hundreds of passages dealing with the last days, the Second Coming, and the Millennium (these passages are all listed in Appendix 4). We then closely studied these scriptures, scores of which, followed by discussion and notes, are presented in this volume. We also studied the words of our latter-day prophets, who have provided much revelation for our day on these important topics, and include many quotations from them in our discussion.

The primary reason we have gone to the standard, the scriptures, for our understanding of the signs of the times is that our prophets themselves have cautioned us to refer to the scriptures for our understanding of Church doctrine and principle. Elder Harold B. Lee explained the pattern this way: "All that we teach in this Church ought to be couched in the Scriptures. We ought to choose our texts from the Scriptures, and wherever you have an illustration in the Scriptures or a revelation in the Book of Mormon, use it, and do not draw from other sources where you can find it here in these books. Now we call these the Standard Church Works because they are standard. If you want to measure truth, measure it by the four Standard Church Works."[1]

President Gordon B. Hinckley added: "There are many books among us and many preachers, and I find virtue in the words of all. But the truest source of divine wisdom is the word of the Lord in these sacred volumes, the standard works of the Church. Here is

---

[1] Regional representatives' seminar, 28 Sept. 1967.

[ix]

found the doctrine to which we must hold fast if this work is to roll forth to its divinely charted destiny."[2]

President Wilford Woodruff specifically pointed us to the standard works when studying the signs of the times: "If you want to know what is coming to pass, read the revelations of God in the Bible, in the Book of Mormon and in the book of Doctrine and Covenants."[3]

In an effort to be true to these principles, we have drawn our understandings of passages of scripture from other scriptures whenever possible. We have sought to follow the guideline given by Elder Harold B. Lee to let our teaching be "couched in the scriptures" and to "choose our texts from the scriptures."[4] Of particular value in such a study are the scriptures of the Restoration. President Marion G. Romney gave us this valuable truth: "In each dispensation, from the days of Adam to the days of the Prophet Joseph Smith, the Lord has revealed anew the principles of the gospel. So that while the records of past dispensations, insofar as they are uncorrupted, testify to the truths of the gospel, still each dispensation has had revealed in its day sufficient truth to guide the people of the new dispensation, independent of the records of the past.

"I do not wish to discredit in any manner the records we have of the truths revealed by the Lord in past dispensations. What I now desire is to impress upon our minds that the gospel, as revealed to the Prophet Joseph Smith, is complete and is the word direct from heaven to this dispensation. It alone is sufficient to teach us the principles of eternal life. It is the truth revealed, the commandments given in this dispensation through modern prophets by which we are to be governed."[5]

We believe in the words of Isaiah, Zechariah, and John the Revelator, and we are grateful for them. They provide us with invaluable insight, understanding, and detail about the events of the last days, and in this volume we look at those prophetic words through the lens of latter-day revelation. This effort, we hope, will bring together the

---

[2] *Ensign,* May 1982, 45.
[3] "Discourse by President Wilford Woodruff," 227.
[4] "Using the Scriptures in Our Church Assignments," 13.
[5] "Glorious Promise," 2.

vision of former dispensations with the revelation that has been given specifically for our day.

We would like to thank all those who have helped us to bring this volume together. We express gratitude to Suzanne Brady of Deseret Book for her excellent editorial contributions, to Ronald O. Stucki for the cover and interior design, to Patricia J. Parkinson and Tonya-Rae Facemyer for the typography, and to their colleagues at Deseret Book Company for their assistance in turning a manuscript into a finished book. We thank Vicki Parry for her searching review of the manuscript and Marian H. Brady, Celeste Howard, and Ruth B. Howard for their painstaking proofreading of sources and galleys. We extend appreciation to Mindy J. Anderson and Erin F. Stamper for assisting us in researching and creating Appendix 4 and to Leslie Stitt for writing the subject index. Thanks goes to Kent J. Hunter and J. Max Young, instructors at the Orem Utah Institute of Religion at Utah Valley State College, for their review of parts of the manuscript for doctrinal accuracy.

Despite the helpful support others have given, this work represents our own thinking and our own understanding of what the Lord has said about the signs of the times. We have not been able to say all we would like to have said, for the last days, the signs of the times, and the second coming of Christ are subjects too broad to cover adequately in one volume. Nor is this study to be viewed as the last word on any of the topics we consider. The restoration of the gospel is a continuing process, both for the Church and for us as individuals, and further light will help us to see more clearly things that before were less clear. Further light also gives us deeper understanding of things we earlier thought we thoroughly understood.

This book, then, represents our understandings as of the day they were written. Our hope is that the reader will find truth here to increase his or her spiritual enlightenment, thus heightening a desire to be prepared for the great day of the Lord's coming. We hope further that this book will serve as a beginning point for continuing prayerful study and meditation on the significant and wonderful truths of the Lord's plan for us in these last days.

LIST OF ABBREVIATIONS

GNB	Good News Bible
JB	Jerusalem Bible
JST	Joseph Smith Translation of the Bible
KJV	Holy Bible, Authorized King James Version
NEB	New English Bible
NIV	New International Version of the Holy Bible
NJB	New Jerusalem Bible
RSV	Holy Bible, Revised Standard Version

"BEHOLD, I COME QUICKLY"

"Tell us . . . what shall be the sign of thy coming?" the disciples asked Jesus (Matt. 24:3). The pivotal occasions when Christ has come to the earth, meaning both his first and his second comings, have been preceded by signs, so that the faithful may know and be blessed. Signs help the Lord's people to be prepared and, because they know what to watch for, to avoid deception.

"Behold, this will I give unto you for a sign at the time of his coming," said Samuel, speaking to the Nephites before the first coming of Christ. "There shall be great lights in heaven, insomuch that . . . there shall be one day and a night and a day, as if it were one day and there were no night; and this shall be unto you for a sign; for ye shall know of the rising of the sun and also of its setting; . . . nevertheless the night shall not be darkened; and it shall be the night before he is born. And behold, there shall a new star arise, such an one as ye never have beheld; and this also shall be a sign unto you. And behold this is not all, there shall be many signs and wonders in heaven. And it shall come to pass that ye shall all be amazed, and wonder, insomuch that ye shall fall to the earth" (Hel. 14:3–7).

The writers of the four Gospels also spoke of many signs the Old Testament prophets had given, marking the circumstances of Christ's first sojourn on the earth. By these signs, those with eyes to see might recognize him:

He would be born of a virgin (Isa. 7:14; Matt. 1:22–23).

He would be born in Bethlehem (Micah 5:2; Matt. 2:4–6).

He would come forth out of Egypt (Hosea 11:1; Matt. 2:13–15).

In his childhood, the children in Bethlehem "and in all the coasts thereof" would be slain (Matt. 2:16–18; Jer. 31:15).

He would be called a Nazarene (Matt. 2:23).

He would be preceded by another who would come out of the wilderness to prepare the way of the Lord (Isa. 40:3; Matt. 3:1–3).

He would proclaim the gospel to the people of Zabulon and Nephthalim (Matt. 4:13–16; Isa. 9:1–2).

He would preach the gospel to the poor (Isa. 61:1–2; Luke 4:17–18).

He would heal the sick (Matt. 8:16–17).

He would speak in parables (Ps. 78:2; Matt. 13:34–35).

He would come unto the people riding on an ass (Zech. 9:9; Matt. 21:1–11).

The people would hate him (Ps. 69:4; John 15:24–25).

He would be betrayed by one who broke bread with him (Ps. 41:9; John 13:18).

He would be sold for thirty pieces of silver (Zech. 11:12; Matt. 27:3–5).

The thirty pieces of silver would be used to purchase a potter's field (Zech. 11:13; Matt. 27:6–10).

Enemies would cast lots for his clothing (Ps. 22:18; Matt. 27:35).

He would be numbered with the transgressors (Isa. 53:12; Mark 15:27–28).

He would thirst and be given vinegar to drink (Ps. 69:21; John 19:28–29).

None of his bones would be broken, though he would be pierced (Ps. 34:20; Zech. 12:10; John 19:33–37).

All of these events came to pass just as the prophets had foreseen: a new star appeared; the people in the Americas experienced a day, a night, and a day without any darkness; and every one of the prophecies about the mortal Jesus were fulfilled. Those who studied the prophecies in advance may have been confused by the seeming contradiction involving his beginnings: he would be born in Bethlehem, he would come out of Egypt, and he would be called a Nazarene. Only after the prophecies were fulfilled did their meaning become clear. The same can be said about some of the prophecies of our time: we will certainly understand them much better with hindsight.

A PATTERN OF PROPHECY

Just as prophets saw in advance many of the details of Christ's life, so too did they see and record in prophecy many details of the last days and his second coming. The record begins with Adam, the first prophet on the earth. Toward the end of his life, Adam met with the righteous people of his posterity and "predicted whatsoever should befall [them] unto the latest generation" (D&C 107:53, 56). Surely such a prediction included the first coming of Christ to the earth and his return in glory. The end of the earth and its return to an Edenic state were seen from the beginning.

Many prophets in the millennia that followed were given visions and truths about the second coming of Christ and the signs that would mark the years before his return. Enoch, Moses, Isaiah, Jeremiah, Ezekiel, Daniel, Hosea, Joel, Zechariah, John, Nephi, Mormon, and others saw our day, the last days of the earth before Jesus returns, and made a record of the signs that will be shown forth for those who have eyes to see that his coming is nigh.

Jesus Christ himself prophesied of his second coming and the signs that would precede it. During his last week on the earth, he taught his disciples the things that would befall the earth before he came again—the signs of his coming, "and of the end of the world, or the destruction of the wicked, which is the end of the world" (JS–M 1:4). He named those things we have become familiar with: false Christs and false prophets, wars and rumors of war, famines, pestilences, earthquakes, "the love of men shall wax cold," the gospel "shall be preached in all the world," "the sun shall be darkened, and the moon shall not give her light, and the stars shall fall from heaven. . . . Verily, I say unto you, this generation, in which these things shall be shown forth, shall not pass away until all I have told you shall be fulfilled" (JS–M 1:22–23, 28–34).

Weeks after uttering these prophecies, having ministered among his people for forty days, the risen Christ was lifted up into heaven while the disciples watched him ascend. "And while they looked stedfastly toward heaven as he went up, behold, two men stood by them in white apparel; which also said, Ye men of Galilee, why stand ye gazing up into heaven? this same Jesus, which is taken up from you into heaven, shall so come in like manner as ye have seen him go into heaven" (Acts 1:10–11).

Perhaps only a week then passed before the day of Pentecost,[1] when the apostles were "all filled with the Holy Ghost, and began to speak with other tongues" (Acts 2:3–4). On that historic day, Peter stood and bore testimony of Christ, saying that He would come again after showing "wonders in heaven above, and signs in the earth beneath; blood, and fire, and vapour of smoke: The sun shall be turned into darkness, and the moon into blood, before that great and notable day of the Lord come" (Acts. 2:19–20; see also Joel 2:30–31). Other testimonies followed, sprinkled throughout the New Testament, culminating in John's remarkable vision, wherein he saw "things which must shortly come to pass" (Rev. 1:1), including the Great Apostasy, earthquakes, plagues, wars, and the triumphal return of the Lord Jesus Christ.

One sign of the Lord's return would be the restoration of the gospel. When Moroni appeared to Joseph Smith in 1823, he was thus part of the fulfillment of prophecy, and at the same time he reaffirmed other prophecies to Joseph Smith and to all who have since accepted Joseph as a prophet. After telling young Joseph of the Book of Mormon, Moroni "commenced quoting the prophecies of the Old Testament," including Malachi's prophecy that "the day cometh that shall burn as an oven," referring to the second coming of Christ (JS–H 1:36–37). He also quoted Joel 2:28–32, the same prophecy Peter had quoted on the day of Pentecost. When Moroni returned later that night, he repeated all that he had previously said and also told Joseph "of great judgments which were coming upon the earth, with great desolations by famine, sword, and pestilence" (JS–H 1:45).

To make certain that this generation fully received the message of the signs of the last days, the Lord declared in his preface to the Doctrine and Covenants that all mankind must hearken to his voice, "and the voice of warning shall be unto all people." The Lord said he

---

[1] Christ was crucified the day after the Passover feast (during which feast he had performed the Last Supper for his apostles), on a Friday. He rose from the dead on Sunday. Thereafter, he walked and talked with his disciples for forty days (Acts 1:3). The day of Pentecost was fifty days after the Passover feast (LDS Bible Dictionary, s.v. "Feasts"), or approximately a week after Christ ascended into heaven.

would send forth messengers "to seal them [the wicked] up unto the day when the wrath of God shall be poured out upon the wicked without measure. . . . Wherefore the voice of the Lord is unto the ends of the earth, that all that will hear may hear: Prepare ye, prepare ye for that which is to come, for the Lord is nigh" (D&C 1:2, 4, 9, 11–12).

Knowing that his judgments were falling upon the earth, the Lord in his mercy revealed himself to a latter-day prophet, Joseph Smith, and gave him commandments whereby the gospel could go forth in its fulness to bless the people of the world (D&C 1:17–23): "The hour is not yet, but is nigh at hand, when peace shall be taken from the earth, and the devil shall have power over his own dominion. And also the Lord shall have power over his saints, and shall reign in their midst, and shall come down in judgment upon . . . the world" (D&C 1:35–36).

Further signs were given in subsequent revelations. In the "appendix" to the Doctrine and Covenants, the Lord revisited this theme: "Hearken, O ye people of my church," he said, "and hear the word of the Lord concerning you—The Lord who shall suddenly come to his temple; the Lord who shall come down upon the world with a curse to judgment; yea, upon all the nations that forget God, and upon all the ungodly among you. For he shall make bare his holy arm in the eyes of all the nations, and all the ends of the earth shall see the salvation of their God" (D&C 133:1–3).

The signs that will precede the second coming of Jesus Christ are a recurring theme in the scriptures in all dispensations. The Lord has felt it needful to tell his people in all generations about these great events to come. But ours is the generation that is seeing many of these things come to pass, and we, along with our children, and perhaps our children's children, will live through the days in which the Lord increasingly stretches forth his arm over the world, both in blessing and in cursing.

After telling his disciples of the signs of the times, the Lord spoke comfort to them, saying, "Be not troubled, for, when all these things shall come to pass, ye may know that the promises which have been made unto you shall be fulfilled." Then he gave them a parable. You see the fig trees, he said, and know that "when they begin to shoot forth, and their leaves are yet tender, that summer is now nigh at hand." In the same way, by watching the signs we have been given, we can know that the hour of his coming is nigh. "He that feareth me shall be looking forth for the great day of the Lord to come, even for the signs of the coming of the Son of Man" (D&C 45:35–39). "Wherefore, go forth, crying with a loud voice, saying: The kingdom of heaven is at hand. . . . Go forth baptizing with water, preparing the way before my face for the time of my coming; for the time is at hand; the day or the hour no man knoweth; but it surely shall come." Those who receive the gospel covenant "shall be looking forth for the signs of my coming, and shall know me. Behold, I come quickly" (D&C 39:19–21, 23–24).

THE LORD WILL NOT COME AS A THIEF TO THE "CHILDREN OF LIGHT"

"Of that day, and hour, no one knoweth," the Lord said concerning his coming, "no, not the angels of God in heaven, but my Father only" (JS–M 1:40). Many have supposed from this statement that the Lord has not given us any understanding about the time of his coming. After all, won't he come "as a thief in the night"? (1 Thes. 5:2). And don't thieves come when we least expect them?

The answer, clearly, is that we are to "watch" and "be ready" (D&C 50:46). Even though the Lord's coming may be "as a thief in the night," "if the good man of the house had known in what watch the thief would come, he would have watched, and would not have suffered his house to have been broken up, but would have been ready. Therefore be ye also ready, for in such an hour as ye think not, the Son of Man cometh" (JS–M 1:47–48). "And again, verily I say unto you, the coming of the Lord draweth nigh, and it overtaketh the world as a thief in the night—Therefore, gird up your loins, that you may be the children of light, and that day shall not overtake you as a thief" (D&C 106:4–5).

Here we have the key: we need to be "the children of light."

Paul wrote plainly: "Of the times and the seasons, brethren, ye have no need that I write unto you. For yourselves know perfectly that the day of the Lord so cometh as a thief in the night. . . . But ye, brethren, are not in darkness, that that day should overtake you as a thief.

Ye are all the children of light, and the children of the day: we are not of the night, nor of darkness. Therefore let us not sleep, as do others; but let us watch and be sober" (1 Thes. 5:1–6). Unto the children of light, the Lord says, "It shall be given to know the signs of the times, and the signs of the coming of the Son of Man" (D&C 68:11). It is for us that the signs have been given. We have both a duty and a privilege to watch, so that we may know the "times" during which the Lord will come; by watching in soberness, we can have our lives, our hearts, our families, and our overall circumstances in readiness for his coming. On the other hand, "he that watches not for me shall be cut off," the Lord has said (D&C 45:44).

And so we watch and pray, seeking his coming to cleanse a wicked world, to bring millennial peace and glory, and to deliver his people from the tyranny of the latter-day Babylon, the symbol for a world of sin. And when he comes, perhaps we will sing in triumph and rejoicing a song that is much more than a Christmas carol:

> Joy to the world, the Lord is come;
> Let earth receive her King!
> Let ev'ry heart prepare him room,
> And Saints and angels sing. . . .
>
> No more will sin and sorrow grow,
> Nor thorns infest the ground;
> He'll come and make the blessings flow
> Far as the curse was found.[2]

THESE ARE THE LAST DAYS

"Come, O thou King of Kings!" we sing. "We've waited long for thee, / With healing in thy wings / To set thy people free."[3] We have indeed waited long for the second coming of the Lord. And we have longer still to wait as the promised signs gradually (or perhaps quickly) are shown forth for those who have the wisdom to watch.

Latter-day prophets and apostles have repeatedly warned us that these are the last days of the world as we know it, and that the coming

---

[2] Isaac Watts, alt. by William W. Phelps, "Joy to the World," *Hymns,* no. 201.
[3] Parley P. Pratt, "Come, O Thou King of Kings," *Hymns,* no. 59.

of the Lord is nigh. As this dispensation opened, Joseph Smith said, "The scripture is ready to be fulfilled when great wars, famines, pestilence, great distress, judgments, &c., are ready to be poured out on the inhabitants of the earth."[4] Nearly eighty years later, Elder Orson F. Whitney of the Council of the Twelve Apostles wrote: "We stand at the present moment in the Saturday Evening of Time. . . . Morning will break upon the Millennium, the thousand years of peace, the Sabbath of the World!"[5]

Obviously, the ensuing decades have only brought us closer to the foreordained time of the Lord's coming, as our leaders have taught.[6] Using the same imagery that Elder Whitney used, Elder Bruce R. McConkie wrote: "We are now living during the final years of the sixth seal, that thousand year period which began in A.D. 1000 and will continue through the Saturday night of time and until just before the Sabbatical era when Christ shall reign personally on earth, when all of the blessings of the Great Millennium shall be poured out upon this planet. This, accordingly, is the era when the signs of the times shall be shown forth, and they are in fact everywhere to be seen."[7]

In recognizing the times, Elder Neal A. Maxwell advised that we be careful to become neither complacent nor out of balance in our lives: "I have no hesitancy in saying that there are some signs—but certainly not all—suggesting that 'summer is nigh' (Matt. 24:32). We would do well to notice and to ponder, but without either becoming preoccupied or ignoring any sprouting leaves because of being 'overcharged' with the 'cares of this life' (Luke 21:34)."[8]

THE LAST DAYS: A TIME OF FEAR AND BLESSING

Often when we think of prophecies of the last days, we focus on the challenging and the frightening. The Lord and his prophets have told us to watch for wars and rumors of wars, plagues and pestilences, devastating earthquakes. We have been warned of the spreading evil

---

[4] *History of the Church,* 6:364.
[5] *Saturday Night Thoughts,* 12.
[6] Elder Bruce R. McConkie taught that the time of Christ's return is predetermined, or "fixed"; see *Millennial Messiah,* 26–27, 649–50.
[7] *Doctrinal New Testament Commentary,* 3:485–86.
[8] *Ensign,* May 1988, 7; see also Maxwell, *Time to Choose,* 10.

in the world and the growing power of Babylon. But the last days are also times of joy and triumph. They bring the restoration of the gospel with its prophets, powers, gifts, and spiritual blessings. They bring the gathering of Israel, the establishment of Zion, the building of the New Jerusalem. They bring the Lord himself, as he returns in brightness and glory.

Satan rages in the world, but the Lord will conquer in the end. To focus on the frightening judgments to come, to the exclusion of the positive events that have been promised, is to have a distorted view of the future. It is to fail to see as God sees. With his eternal perspective, the Lord knows that the judgments are designed to bring the wicked to repentance and then to cleanse the earth of those who will not repent. He tells us further that Satan will be conquered and cast out, whereas the righteous who "have taken the Holy Spirit for their guide, and have not been deceived . . . shall abide the day" (D&C 45:57). Elder Neal A. Maxwell declared: "Yes, there will be wrenching polarization on this planet, but also the remarkable reunion with our colleagues in Christ from the City of Enoch. Yes, nation after nation will become a house divided, but more and more unifying Houses of the Lord will grace this planet. Yes, Armageddon lies ahead. But so does Adam-ondi-Ahman!"[9]

The Lord's work in the world is to bring to pass righteousness and holiness and to bring us to eternal life. Satan's work is to bring increasing darkness and evil into the world. The last days are marked by the monumental efforts of these two opposing forces: the destroyer seeking to tear down, to ruin, to waste; the Creator seeking to build, establish, bless, and prosper. Even in the trials, however, we can see the hand of the Lord. In his love and mercy, he will use judgments to seek to bring his children to repentance. If they will let their hearts be softened, if they will hearken and repent, they will have an opportunity to receive a fulness of the blessings of the Atonement. They will hear the words, "Well done, thou good and faithful servant: . . . enter thou into the joy of thy lord" (Matt. 25:21, 23).

If they choose not to repent, they will continue to suffer until, in the end, the judgments of God sweep them from the face of the earth.

---

[9] *Ensign,* Nov. 1981, 10.

As in Noah's day, the great judgments that cleanse the earth serve three purposes:

1. To bring people to repentance, if they will.

2. To remove them from mortality if they refuse to repent, cutting short their wickedness so that they sin no more in this sphere—and so that they will no longer inflict their wickedness on others.

3. To eventually cleanse the earth for the blessing of the righteous.

Thus, even though Satan rages, in the end he will be defeated, as the Lord our God emerges victorious over the devil and all his degraded forces of evil.

THE SAINTS WILL ESCAPE SOME OF THE JUDGMENTS

The scriptures make it plain that the current generation will see many dire events, so it is comforting to know that the Lord will care for his Saints. They are not promised immunity from the judgments to come, but those in Zion will receive a significant degree of protection. "Fear not, little children," the Lord has said, "for you are mine, and I have overcome the world, and you are of them that my Father hath given me; and none of them that my Father hath given me shall be lost. . . . Wherefore, I am in your midst, and I am the good shepherd, and the stone of Israel. He that buildeth upon this rock shall never fall. And the day cometh that you shall hear my voice and see me, and know that I am. Watch, therefore, that ye may be ready" (D&C 50:41–42, 44–46).

In 1894, President Wilford Woodruff spoke of his visions of calamities that would be poured out on the earth and offered hope of protection to the righteous: "I want to ask this congregation a question: When I have the vision of the night opened continually before my eyes, and can see the mighty judgments that are about to be poured out upon this world, when I know these things are true, and are at the door of Jew and Gentile; while I know they are true and while I am holding this position before God and this world, can I withhold my voice from lifting up a warning to this people and to the nations of the earth? . . . While I live and see these things continually before my eyes I shall raise my warning voice.

"Now, the question I wanted to ask you is this: We have fourteen [hundred] million people on this earth, and over them all there hangs a cloud of darkness almost entirely upon their shoulders. Can you tell me where the people are who will be shielded and protected from these great calamities and judgments which are even now at our doors?

"I'll tell you. The priesthood of God who honor their priesthood, and who are worthy of their blessings are the only ones who shall have this safety and protection. They are the only mortal beings. No other people have a right to be shielded from these judgments. They are at our very doors; not even this people will escape them entirely. They will come down like the judgments of Sodom and Gomorrah. And none but the priesthood will be safe from their fury.

"God has held the angels of destruction for many years, lest they should reap down the wheat with the tares. But I want to tell you now, that those angels have left the portals of heaven, and they stand over this people and this nation now, and are hovering over the earth waiting to pour out the judgments. And from this very day they shall be poured out. Calamities and troubles are increasing in the earth, and there is a meaning to these things.

"Remember this, and reflect upon these matters. If you do your duty, and I do my duty, we'll have protection, and shall pass through the afflictions in peace and in safety. Read the scriptures and the revelations. They will tell you about all these things. Great changes are at our doors. . . .

"I have felt oppressed with the weight of these matters, and I felt I must speak of them here. It's by the power of the Gospel that we shall escape."[10]

Other prophets and apostles have given us like reassurances of divine protection for the Lord's people, particularly when, as President Woodruff said, they are doing their duty:

"I promise you in the name of the Lord whose servant I am," President Howard W. Hunter said, "that God will always protect and care for his people. We will have our difficulties the way every

---

[10] In Gates, "Temple Workers' Excursion," 512–13; paragraphing has been modernized for readability.

generation and people have had difficulties. But with the gospel of Jesus Christ, you have every hope and promise and reassurance. The Lord has power over his Saints and will always prepare places of peace, defense, and safety for his people."[11]

In a 1981 message, President Marion G. Romney recalled the days of his childhood in war-torn Mexico. He told of living through days and nights of terror and uncertainty, fearful for his life and safety. His mother would sing at night to her children, seeking to comfort them. For example, she sang these words from "Guide Us, O Thou Great Jehovah":

> When the earth begins to tremble,
> Bid our fearful thoughts be still;
> When thy judgments spread destruction,
> Keep us safe on Zion's hill.[12]

She also sang these words from W. W. Phelps's hymn "Now Let Us Rejoice":

> In faith we'll rely on the arm of Jehovah
> To guide through these last days of trouble and gloom,
> And after the scourges and harvest are over,
> We'll rise with the just when the Savior doth come.[13]

As President Romney grew older, he learned from the scriptures that the Lord has promised to "care for his Saints through the calamities which he foresaw and foretold. . . . I think we are not safe because we say we intend to do what's right. I think the people who are safe are those who have taken the Holy Spirit for their guide and have not been deceived. . . . If I receive the Holy Ghost and follow his guidance, I will be among those who are protected and carried through these troubled times. And so will you, and so will every other soul who lives under his direction. If ye are prepared, ye need not fear."[14]

---

[11] *Ensign,* Oct. 1993, 72.

[12] William Williams, "Guide Us, O Thou Great Jehovah," *Hymns,* no. 83.

[13] "Now Let Us Rejoice," *Hymns,* no. 3.

[14] "'If Ye Are Prepared Ye Shall Not Fear,'" 3–5. For other such apostolic promises, see Stapley, Conference Report, Oct. 1971, 101; McConkie, Conference Report, Apr. 1979, 133.

FEAR OR OPTIMISM?

One need not be an alarmist to see the reality of the trials ahead. But when we put our lives in the hands of a loving and powerful God, we know that we will come forth in triumph through the fiery trials of the last days. The attitude of Elder Gordon B. Hinckley is a blessing to us:

"I stand here today as an optimist concerning the work of the Lord. I cannot believe that God has established his work in the earth to have it fail. I cannot believe that it is getting weaker. I know that it is getting stronger. I realize, of course, that we are beset with many tragic problems. I am a newspaper reader, and I have seen a good deal of this earth. I have seen its rot and smelled its filth. I have been in areas where war rages and hate smolders in the hearts of people. I have seen the appalling poverty that hovers over many lands. I have seen the oppression of those in bondage and the brutality of their overlords. . . . I have watched with alarm the crumbling morals of our society.

"And yet I am an optimist. I have a simple and solemn faith that right will triumph and that truth will prevail."[15]

This attitude is a common theme among the general Church leaders of our day. As we consider the challenge of the coming events, we can remember the encouragement of our prophets. The Lord will be with his Saints; he is ultimately in control of the events of the world; and in the end, he will order all things to the fulfillment of his purposes. Thus, as we have faith and as we obey, we will belong to the "winning team" and will emerge victorious with our Lord.

Here are just four of the many messages of hope from our leaders:

President Joseph Fielding Smith: "Trouble in the earth will continue; there will be distress, calamity, and perplexity among the nations. . . .

" . . . Nevertheless, we may look forward with rejoicing; we need not be downcast, but in the spirit of faith and hope, and in the fear of the Lord, we should look to the future with feelings of joy, of

---

[15] Conference Report, Oct. 1969, 113; see also Hinckley, "'We Need Not Fear His Coming,'" 83.

humility, and of worship, with the desire in our hearts, stronger if possible than ever, of serving the Lord and keeping his commandments, for the day of his coming draws near."[16]

Elder Marion G. Romney: "Naturally, . . . even those who have a mature faith in the gospel . . . are concerned and disturbed by the lowering clouds on the horizon. But they need not be surprised or frantic about their portent, for . . . the Lord [has] made it abundantly clear that through the tribulations and calamity . . . there would be a people who, through acceptance and obedience to the gospel, would be able to recognize and resist the powers of evil, build up the promised Zion, and prepare to meet the Christ and be with him in the blessed millennium. And we know further that it is possible for every one of us, who will, to have a place among those people. It is this assurance and this expectation that gives us understanding of the Lord's admonition, 'be not troubled.'"[17]

President Howard W. Hunter: "Despair, doom, and discouragement are not acceptable views of life for a Latter-day Saint. . . .

"The scriptures . . . indicate that there will be seasons of time when the whole world will have some difficulty. . . . But our task is to live fully and faithfully and not worry ourselves sick about the woes of the world or when it will end. . . .

"In this last dispensation there will be great tribulation. (See Matt. 24:21.) . . . All dispensations have had their perilous times, but our day will include genuine peril. (See 2 Tim. 3:1.) . . .

"Inevitably the natural result of some of these kinds of prophecies is fear. . . . But I want to stress that these feelings are not necessary for faithful Latter-day Saints, and they do not come from God. . . .

"For Latter-day Saints this is a time of great hope and excitement. . . . We need to have faith and hope, two of the great fundamental virtues of any discipleship of Christ. We must continue to exercise confidence in God, inasmuch as that is the first principle in our code of belief. We must believe that God has all power, that he loves us, and that his work will not be stopped or frustrated in our individual lives or in the world generally. He will bless us as a people because he

---

[16] *Doctrines of Salvation,* 3:51–52.
[17] Conference Report, Oct. 1966, 53–54.

always has blessed us as a people. He will bless us as individuals because he always has blessed us as individuals."[18]

Elder M. Russell Ballard: "Living in these difficult times . . . requires each one of us to maintain a positive, hopeful perspective about the future. . . .

"The Lord is in control. He knows the end from the beginning. He has given us adequate instruction that, if followed, will see us safely through any crisis. . . . We must be careful to not overreact, nor should we be caught up in extreme preparations, but what we must do is keep the commandments of God and never lose hope!

"But where do we find hope in the midst of such turmoil and catastrophe? Quite simply, our one hope for spiritual safety during these turbulent times is to turn our minds and our hearts to Jesus Christ."[19]

In deciding what attitude we should have toward the troubles of the last days, we can follow the lead of our prophets. We can know that the Lord will see us through the fiery trial; that if we stand with him, he will stand with us, just as he did Shadrach, Meshach, and Abednego in the furnace (Dan. 3:19–28); or that if we are killed in the fire, we can cry out as did Abinadi, "O God, receive my soul" (Mosiah 17:19).

The Lord warned Joseph Smith and his associates in words that apply also to us: "The enemy in the secret chambers seeketh your lives. Ye hear of wars in far countries, and you say that there will soon be great wars in far countries, but ye know not the hearts of men in your own land. . . . But if ye are prepared ye shall not fear" (D&C 38:28–30). If we are prepared temporally, spiritually, and with a good understanding of that which is to come, and if we are built upon that rock which is Christ, we shall not fear, but surely shall "abide the day" (Hel. 5:12; Mal. 3:2; D&C 35:21; 38:8; 45:57; 61:39).

INTERPRETING PROPHECY

As we look at the signs of the times and try to understand scripture, we need to be cautious. Even when we know prophecy, it is not

---

[18] *Ensign,* Oct. 1993, 70–72.
[19] *Ensign,* Nov. 1992, 31–32; see also Ballard, "When Shall These Things Be?" 192.

possible to predict precisely how the future will unfold, for the Lord seldom gives us all the details of a future event. He may say, for example, in reference to the return of the ten tribes, "an highway shall be cast up in the midst of the great deep" (D&C 133:27), but he may not tell us whether the highway is literal or symbolic, or where this highway will be found, or who will cast it up, or how. The Lord's purpose often seems to be to give us impressions and general understandings rather than specific details. It is more important to know that the Lord will bring the ten tribes safely back from their long dispersion than it is to know exactly what and where the highway is.

Our understanding of prophecy is also limited by what we now understand. Our understanding of the future is greatly affected by our perceptions in the present. Events in the world at large can change our anticipations of the future and can change how we understand prophecy. For example, before this century, no one had even conceived of a nuclear bomb. Although Albert Einstein and others began to develop theories about what was possible, before World War II few people were even aware of the possibility. In the years following that war, however, a nuclear holocaust came to be universally feared. The reality of nuclear warfare in our time may make one wonder if some of the wars and plagues seen by John the Revelator might be connected to the nuclear bomb.[20] A hundred years ago, such an interpretation was not even a possibility, because the atomic bomb was unknown and was not part of people's perceptions.

As another example, before the mid-1980s anyone who predicted the collapse of the Soviet Union was laughed at as extreme. But the social and political changes in Eastern Europe came virtually overnight, radically changing the face of the world. Those changes have opened nations to the prophesied missionary work in unexpected ways.

What unforeseen developments await us in future years? What will happen in the year 2010, or 2015, or 2025 that will suddenly cast new light on prophecies that at present we do not fully understand? What exactly are we to understand by "the moon shall be turned into

---

[20] Elder Bruce R. McConkie envisioned nuclear warfare in our future; see McConkie, Conference Report, Apr. 1979, 133; *Millennial Messiah,* 382–86.

blood" (D&C 29:14), by "every mountain and island [shall be] moved out of their places" (Rev. 6:14), by "a great mountain burning with fire was cast into the sea" (Rev. 8:8)? These picturesque expressions stand for future events. Precisely how will those events come to pass? Without prophetic vision of our own, we can only guess. Sometimes our understandings are deepened by explanations that appear elsewhere in the scriptures. Sometimes a living prophet gives insight. Sometimes the Lord simply has not clarified what a given prophecy means.

Our latter-day leaders are likewise concerned about interpreting prophecy. President Harold B. Lee warned against "loose writings predicting the calamities which are about to overtake us." He added wryly, "Most of such writers are not handicapped by having any authentic information on their writings."[21]

Elder John A. Widtsoe observed: "Much effort has been expended to reduce . . . general prophecies to exact dates, times, and persons. This has been a waste of time and energy, as prophecy uttered under divine inspiration usually contains all that the divine will desires to reveal. It behooves those to whom the prophecy is made to prepare for coming events, to watch for them, and to recognize them when they do appear. If more is needed, the power that gave the prophecy will no doubt furnish the interpretation. . . .

"The futility of reducing general prophecy to exact times or places is well illustrated by the famous visions of Daniel. It is conceded that the stone that broke the image to pieces is the Kingdom of God; but there has been and is interminable debate as to the historical kingdoms and meaning represented by the gold, silver, iron, and clay portions of the image; the horns of the beasts; the thousand, three hundred and five and thirty days; and the several other statements of Daniel. . . . Hundreds, perhaps thousands, of books have been published and tens of thousands of sermons have been preached in the attempt to interpret Daniel's prophecies. It has been a fruitless effort, at best a doubtful conjecture. There remains only the general meaning of these glorious visions: that righteousness will triumph in its battle with evil."[22]

---

[21] Conference Report, Oct. 1972, 128.
[22] *Evidences and Reconciliations,* 93–95.

Elder Neal A. Maxwell has taught how challenging it can be to foresee or understand specific future events, even when the general events are known: "Even as believers, . . . when we are a part of encapsulating events, we can scarcely savor all that swirls about us. It is unlikely, for instance, on that night so long ago in Bethlehem, that Joseph and Mary looked at the newly born Christ child's feet with the realization that those feet would, one day, walk the length and breadth of the Holy Land. And, further, that, later on, spikes would pierce those feet.

"As a loving Mary grasped those tiny hands, and, as in the months ahead those tiny hands clasped her, did she know that those hands, when grown, would ordain the original Twelve or, still later, carry the rough-hewn cross?

"As she heard her Baby cry, did she hear intimations of Jesus' later weeping at the death of Lazarus or after blessing the Nephite children? (See John 11:35; 3 Ne. 17:21–22.) Did she foresee that those baby-soft knees would later be hardened by so much prayer, including those glorious but awful hours in Gethsemane? (See Matt. 26:36–56.)

"As she bathed that Babe so many times to cleanse His pores, could she have been expected to foresee that one day, years later, drops of blood would come from His every pore? (See Mosiah 3:7.)

"There is such a thing as cheerful, believing participation—even without full understanding—when you and I keep certain things in our hearts and are nourished as we ponder them! (See Luke 2:19.)"[23]

Even though we know the general outline of what is to come, it is difficult to say just how it will come to pass. That challenge is increased when things come about naturally, as President George Q. Cannon taught they would: "Even Latter-day Saints have doubtless, in many instances, entertained erroneous views respecting the fulfillment of revelation and prophecies of the Bible. . . .

" . . . The Lord works in the midst of this people by natural means, and the greatest events that have been spoken of by the holy prophets will come along so naturally as the consequence of certain causes, that unless our eyes are enlightened by the Spirit of God, and

---

[23] Conference Report, Oct. 1982, 97–98.

the spirit of revelation rests on us, we will fail to see that these are the events predicted by the holy prophets.

" . . . They will come along in so natural a manner, the Lord will bring them to pass in such a way that they will not be accepted by the people, except by those who can comprehend the truth, as the fulfillment of the predictions of the prophets. It requires the Spirit of God to enable men and women to understand the things of God; it requires the Spirit of God to enable the people to comprehend the work of God and to perceive his movements and providences among the children of men. The man who is destitute of the Spirit of God cannot comprehend the work of God."[24]

Because of these and other dangers, we have generally avoided interpreting current events. The specific meaning of the Lord's word will be made manifest in the Lord's time. On the other hand, some events seem plainly to fit a pattern shown in the scriptures (an example is the increase of devastating wars on the earth since the American Civil War); in many such cases we have pointed out that pattern. In presenting these latter-day events, we have also avoided establishing any sequence in which they might come to pass. It does not seem to be the Lord's desire that we have such a sequence, for he has not given us one through either scriptural or latter-day prophets. Further complicating such an effort is that many events surely overlap with each other, and some events may occur more than once.

More important than sequence or multiple fulfillments is knowing what to watch for, so that we can continue to prepare ourselves. The Lord never intended that we know of the signs of the times simply to satisfy our curiosity. "Watch" the signs, he says—but why? So we can "be ready." We watch the signs of the times so we can be prepared. And the best way to be ready is to be the kind of person the Lord would have us be, a man or woman who has the Holy Ghost as a companion, as President Cannon said. Only then can we "comprehend the work of God."

---

[24] *Journal of Discourses,* 21:266–67.

WATCH AND BE READY

What is our duty, then? As the Lord said, we must "watch" and "be ready" (D&C 50:46). We "watch" by knowing the signs of the times and being aware of what is transpiring in the world. We stand "ready" by continuing in worthiness, by keeping all the covenants we have made before God, and by following the counsel of our living prophets. Elder Gordon B. Hinckley gave this vital counsel on being ready: "Let us . . . live each day so that if the Lord does come while we are yet upon the earth we shall be worthy of that change which will occur as in the twinkling of an eye and under which we shall be changed from mortal to immortal beings. And if we should die before he comes, then—if our lives have conformed to his teachings—we shall arise in that resurrection morning and be partakers of the marvelous experiences designed for those who shall live and work with the Savior in that promised Millennium. We need not fear the day of [Christ's] coming; the very purpose of the Church is to provide the incentive and the opportunity for us to conduct our lives in such a way that those who are members of the kingdom of God will become members of the kingdom of heaven when he establishes that kingdom on the earth."[25]

Concerning that readiness, the Lord said: "Prepare ye the way of the Lord, prepare ye the supper of the Lamb, make ready for the Bridegroom. . . . Call upon the Lord, that his kingdom may go forth upon the earth, that the inhabitants thereof may receive it, and be prepared for the days to come, in the which the Son of Man shall come down in heaven, clothed in the brightness of his glory, to meet the kingdom of God which is set up on the earth" (D&C 65:3, 5).

"And I heard as it were the voice of a great multitude, and as the voice of many waters, and as the voice of mighty thunderings, saying, Alleluia: for the Lord God omnipotent reigneth. Let us be glad and rejoice, and give honour to him: for the marriage of the Lamb is come, and his wife hath made herself ready. And to her was granted that she should be arrayed in fine linen, clean and white: for the fine linen is the righteousness of saints" (Rev. 19:6–8).

---

[25] "'We Need Not Fear His Coming,'" 83.

"Wherefore, be faithful, praying always, having your lamps trimmed and burning, and oil with you, that you may be ready at the coming of the Bridegroom—For behold, verily, verily, I say unto you, that I come quickly. Even so. Amen" (D&C 33:17).

THE LORD'S WORK
PROSPERS IN
THE LAST DAYS

CHAPTER 1

THE CHURCH PREPARES FOR THE SECOND COMING

SIGNS OF THE TIMES

1. A mighty prophet comes forth.

2. The gospel is restored.

3. The priesthood keys are restored.

4. The Book of Mormon comes forth.

5. Angelic visitations assist in the restoration of the gospel.

6. Spiritual gifts are restored.

7. The latter-day kingdom is established.

Without a doubt, the greatest sign to herald the second coming of Christ is the restoration of the gospel.[1] Paradoxically, the Restoration began quietly and unobserved, with one mortal boy kneeling in a grove in upstate New York, and it continues quietly to this day, through the Lord's whisperings to his living prophet. Other signs of the times are manifestly more obvious and more outwardly dramatic. Plagues and wars and earthquakes, with their attendant devastation and loss of life, attract much attention; such signs are sensational and may arouse fears in those who read and believe such scriptural prophecies. But plagues and wars and earthquakes have happened almost from the beginning of the world. In the last days, these events will likely be unequaled in their intensity and effect, yet we have seen such things before.

---

[1] Elder Bruce R. McConkie wrote: "This latter-day restoration of the same gospel taught by Jesus and his apostles is the most important of all the signs of the times. It is the greatest of all the events destined to occur before the end of the world" (*Doctrinal New Testament Commentary*, 1:650).

But when in the world's history has the gospel been sent forth from the heavens, restored after a long period of dark apostasy, with a promise that it will never again be taken from the earth? (Dan. 2:44). Such a promise is reserved for our time, the last days of the world before Christ returns. The restoration of the true gospel will reach much further with its divine blessings than any judgments will, both around the globe and also into the spirit world and the celestial world to come.

What a precious gift a loving God has promised to his children on the earth! For the restoration of the gospel not only must precede the second coming of Christ but also is an essential preparation for his return. Without the restoration of the gospel, there would be no priesthood, no keys, no worldwide missionary effort, no gathering of a people with knowledge of the truth, no gift of the Holy Ghost, no spiritual gifts, no true ordinances, no temples, no people of Zion, no building of the New Jerusalem—all of which are essential elements that help prepare the world for the Lord's return. No wonder the Lord designed that his gospel would precede his coming. And no wonder the restoration of the gospel may be considered the greatest of all the signs of the times. That this prophecy has largely been fulfilled makes it no less exciting, for the restoration of the gospel also sets the stage for other essential events of the last days, such as the calling of the 144,000, the gathering at Adam-ondi-Ahman, and the establishment and growth of temple work.[2]

THE COMING OF THE MIGHTY PROPHET
Isaiah 11:10

10 And in that day there shall be a root of Jesse, which shall stand for an ensign of the people; to it shall the Gentiles seek: and his rest shall be glorious.

"In that day," meaning the last days, the Lord will send a prophet who is called the "root of Jesse." That prophet will be "an ensign of the people" (Isa. 11:10). Lehi also taught that the Lord would send forth a latter-day prophet, one who is called "mighty . . . , both in

---

[2] For a detailed discussion of the restoration of the gospel, see Jackson, *From Apostasy to Restoration.*

word and in deed, being an instrument in the hands of God, with exceeding faith," who will "work mighty wonders, and do that thing which is great in the sight of God" (2 Ne. 3:24).

The root of Jesse and the mighty prophet of Lehi's prophecy likely are one and the same person, Joseph Smith, the prophet called to bring to pass "much restoration unto the house of Israel" (2 Ne. 3:24). How great was Joseph Smith? John Taylor wrote of him, "Joseph Smith, the Prophet and Seer of the Lord, has done more, save Jesus only, for the salvation of men in this world, than any other man that ever lived in it" (D&C 135:3). Wilford Woodruff, who also knew the Prophet personally, testified, "No greater prophet than Joseph Smith ever lived on the face of the earth save Jesus Christ."[3] The coming of this mighty prophet is one of the signs of the times, indicating that the Lord is preparing all things on the earth for his return.

NOTES AND COMMENTARY

Isa. 11:10 *root of Jesse.* "What is the root of Jesse?" we read in the Doctrine and Covenants. "Behold, thus saith the Lord, it is a descendant of Jesse, as well as of Joseph, unto whom rightly belongs the priesthood, and the keys of the kingdom, for an ensign, and for the gathering of my people in the last days" (D&C 113:5–6; Rom. 15:12). Latter-day Saint scholars generally agree that the *root of Jesse* refers to the Prophet Joseph Smith.[4] He is a descendant of both Jesse and Joseph; he held the priesthood; he possessed the keys of the kingdom; he played a primary role in the lifting of the ensign upon the tops of the mountains; and the keys of the gathering of Israel were committed into his hands (D&C 110:11).

an ensign of the people; to it shall the Gentiles seek. Elsewhere in scripture, we read that the ensign is God's everlasting covenant (D&C 45:9) or Zion (D&C 64:41–42), to which the peoples of the earth would come. Here we learn that the Lord's promised prophet is himself an ensign and would have an essential role in the gathering of Israel.

---

[3] *Journal of Discourses,* 21:317.
[4] See, for example, Sperry, *Voice of Israel's Prophets,* 34–38; Ludlow, *Isaiah,* 170–74; and McConkie, "Joseph Smith As Found in Ancient Manuscripts," 17–18.

his rest shall be glorious. The prophet's reward in God's kingdom would be rich and wonderful (Alma 40:12; D&C 84:23–24; 132:49).

THE RESTORATION OF THE GOSPEL
Acts 3:20–21

20 . . . [God] shall send Jesus Christ, which before was preached unto you:

21 Whom the heaven must receive until the times of restitution of all things, which God hath spoken by the mouth of all his holy prophets since the world began.

Beginning with Adam, the gospel was given from God to man through prophets. Unfortunately, however, the blessing of the gospel was periodically and inevitably interrupted by times of apostasy. After the crucifixion of Christ, the earth suffered a falling away from the truth, called the Great Apostasy; this apostasy began within decades of Christ's ascension into heaven and continued until all true believers of that dispensation had either died or were martyred. This same scene eventually played out in every locality that had the gospel, such as among the Nephites and Lamanites: the believers either fell away, died, or were persecuted unto death.[5] The world slipped into the dark ages, a period of time when the gospel and its light were no longer on the earth among any people.

These things were foreseen by ancient prophets, as well as by Christ's apostles in the meridian of time (see chap. 5 for a discussion of the Apostasy): they saw a day when the gospel and its powers and blessings were no longer found on the earth. "The Lord hath poured out upon you the spirit of deep sleep," Isaiah prophesied, "and hath closed your eyes: the prophets and your rulers, the seers hath he covered. Wherefore the Lord said, . . . this people draw near me with their mouth, and with their lips do honour me, but have removed their heart far from me, and their fear toward me is taught by the precept of men." Then, speaking of the Restoration, the Lord said through Isaiah, "Therefore, behold, I will proceed to do a marvellous work

---

[5] Four righteous men we know of from ancient times were not killed: John the Revelator and three Nephite disciples, all of whom were translated (3 Ne. 28:6–7; D&C 7:1–6). But, as translated beings, they apparently were no longer considered fully part of the mortal earth.

among this people, even a marvellous work and a wonder: for the wisdom of their wise men shall perish, and the understanding of their prudent men shall be hid" (Isa. 29:10, 12–14).

In 1820 the promised restoration began, when God began to send forth anew his keys and powers and covenants, his scriptures and spiritual gifts, his revelations, his authority to organize a church according to the ancient pattern.[6] As Parley P. Pratt wrote:

> The morning breaks, the shadows flee;
> Lo, Zion's standard is unfurled!
> The dawning of a brighter day
> Majestic rises on the world.[7]

The dark night of apostasy was breached by the bright and shining light of the gospel revealed anew.

The Apostasy cannot be viewed as one of the signs that the Lord's return is imminent, but the Restoration is a preeminent sign of that return, because the Lord has stated that he will not come again until his people have performed certain labors, such as taking the gospel to all the world and building the city of New Jerusalem (JS–M 1:31; D&C 45:65–66; 84:4). The Restoration was clearly and repeatedly prophesied, with Jesus Christ saying that Elias[8] would come to "restore all things," with Peter testifying that heaven would "receive" Christ until "the times of restitution of all things," and with John adding his witness that he saw an angel coming from heaven with the "everlasting gospel," implying that the gospel was not on the earth before the angel came (Matt. 17:11; Acts 3:21; Rev. 14:6; see also

---

[6] The Restoration did not spring forth upon the earth without preparation. The Lord brought the earth from darkness to light through the age of the Renaissance and the Reformation and then prepared a land of freedom where the gospel seed could be planted and could grow (Smith, "What the Century Has Brought," 6–8; Kimball, "Absolute Truth," 141; and Hales, "Freedom and Personal Liberty," 413).

[7] "The Morning Breaks," Hymns, no. 1.

[8] In this context, "Elias is . . . a title for one who is a forerunner, for example, John the Baptist. . . . The title Elias has also been applied to many others for specific missions or restorative functions that they are to fulfill, for example, John the Revelator (D&C 77:14); and Noah or Gabriel (D&C 27:6–7, cf. Luke 1:11–20)" (LDS Bible Dictionary, s.v. "Elias"). Apparently, many bearing the title Elias were appointed by God to jointly restore all things in the last dispensation (D&C 128:20–21).

1 Ne. 13:34–36; 15:13; D&C 77:9). We have an equally clear record of the fulfillment of those prophecies in the writings and revelations of Joseph Smith: "I am the Lord thy God," the Lord said through Joseph Smith, "and I gave unto thee, my servant Joseph, an appointment, and restore all things. . . . For I have conferred upon you the keys and power of the priesthood, wherein I restore all things, and make known unto you all things in due time" (D&C 132:40, 45; see also 86:10).

NOTES AND COMMENTARY

Acts 3:20 *[God] shall send Jesus Christ.* This apparently refers to the second coming of Christ, which occurs under the direction of his Father. According to the next verse, Jesus would not return "until the times of restitution of all things."

Acts 3:21 *restitution of all things.* The word *restitution* is a synonym for *restoration.* Joseph Smith described the fulfillment of this prophecy in these words: "Truly this is a day long to be remembered by the Saints of the last days,—a day in which the God of heaven has begun to restore the ancient order of His kingdom unto His servants and His people,—a day in which all things are concurring together to bring about the completion of the fullness of the Gospel, a fullness of the dispensation of dispensations, even the fullness of times; a day in which God has begun to make manifest and set in order in His Church those things which have been, and those things which the ancient prophets and wise men desired to see but died without beholding them; a day in which those things begin to be made manifest, which have been hid from before the foundations of the world, and which Jehovah has promised should be made known in His own due time unto His servants, to prepare the earth for the return of His glory, . . . which is to come to pass in the restitution of all things."[9]

all things, which God hath spoken by the mouth of all his holy prophets. The double use of the word *all* in this phrase indicates how all-inclusive the Restoration would be. None of the Lord's words or works would be exempted. The inclusiveness of this promise is also a witness to the breadth and depth of the Great Apostasy. It would not

---

[9] *History of the Church,* 4:492–93.

be necessary to restore all things unless all things had been lost from the earth.

THE RESTORATION OF PRIESTHOOD KEYS
Malachi 4:5–6

> *5 Behold, I will send you Elijah the prophet before the coming of the great and dreadful day of the Lord:*
>
> *6 And he shall turn the heart of the fathers to the children, and the heart of the children to their fathers, lest I come and smite the earth with a curse.*

An essential part of the restoration of the gospel was the restoration of priesthood keys. Without the keys of the priesthood, the gospel truth could be restored in its fulness, but there would be no authorized administrators of its ordinances, nor would there be anyone to pass the priesthood from generation to generation. Thus, we would have the truth without having the true kingdom of God. We would have saving knowledge without the power of salvation that the full gospel brings.

The priesthood is commonly defined as the power and authority to act in the name of God. The keys of the priesthood are the right and authority to preside over and direct the work of the priesthood—to call and release, to give permission to perform ordinances, and to perpetuate the priesthood on the earth by passing it from generation to generation. "While the majority of the male members hold the priesthood and are called to officiate in a general way in the ordinances of the gospel," President Joseph Fielding Smith taught, "yet we, one and all, should realize that it is the power vested in the President of the Church by virtue of the keys he holds, which come from Elijah in particular and from the other prophets of old in general, which makes valid the authority which we possess. Without that central authority with its commanding keys and the privilege extended to the men holding the priesthood by this one person who presides, the acts of those who are ordained to the priesthood could not be administered in righteousness."[10]

---

[10] *Doctrines of Salvation*, 3:139.

It should come as no surprise, then, that the Lord promised that the restoration of the gospel would be accompanied by the restoration of the keys of the priesthood. One of the most prominent of these promises was made through the prophet Malachi, through whom the Lord announced his intention to send Elijah back to earth sometime before the second coming of Christ. Elijah would restore a power to turn the hearts of the fathers and the children to one another. This power is known as the sealing power, but it is much more than simply the power to seal families together in the temple. Joseph Smith explained: "The spirit, power, and calling of Elijah is, that ye have power to hold the key of the revelations, ordinances, oracles, powers and endowments of the fulness of the Melchizedek Priesthood and of the kingdom of God on the earth; and to receive, obtain, and perform all the ordinances belonging to the kingdom of God. . . .

" . . . What you seal on earth, by the keys of Elijah, is sealed in heaven; and this is the power of Elijah."[11]

The keys of the priesthood were restored, in fulfillment of prophecy, at the beginning of the dispensation of the fulness of times. First, John the Baptist restored the keys of the Aaronic Priesthood, conferring them upon Joseph Smith and Oliver Cowdery on 15 May 1829 (D&C 13). Next, Peter, James, and John came with the keys of the Melchizedek Priesthood (D&C 27:12). Then, on 3 April 1836, Joseph Smith and Oliver Cowdery received a marvelous visitation in the Kirtland Temple. After seeing the Lord himself, in transcendent glory, they received a bestowal of keys from some of the Lord's great prophets:

First, Moses appeared and "committed unto us the keys of the gathering of Israel from the four parts of the earth, and the leading of the ten tribes from the land of the north."

Next, Elias came and "committed the dispensation of the gospel of Abraham," and pronounced upon Joseph and Oliver the promise God gave to Abraham, "saying that in us and our seed all generations after us should be blessed.

"After this vision had closed, another great and glorious vision burst upon us; for Elijah the prophet, who was taken to heaven

---

[11] *Teachings of the Prophet Joseph Smith,* 337–38.

without tasting death, stood before us, and said: Behold, the time has fully come, which was spoken of by the mouth of Malachi—testifying that he [Elijah] should be sent, before the great and dreadful day of the Lord come—To turn the hearts of the fathers to the children, and the children to the fathers, lest the whole earth be smitten with a curse—Therefore, the keys of this dispensation are committed into your hands; and by this ye may know that the great and dreadful day of the Lord is near, even at the doors" (D&C 110:11–16).

NOTES AND COMMENTARY

Mal. 4:5 *I will send you Elijah the prophet.* Elijah would come because God had sent him. But why Elijah? Why not Noah or Abraham or Moses?

Joseph Smith answered that question in one of his sermons: "Elijah was the last prophet that held the keys of this priesthood, and who will, before the last dispensation, restore the authority and deliver the keys of this priesthood in order that all the ordinances may be attended to in righteousness. . . . Why send Elijah? Because he holds the keys of the authority to administer in all the ordinances of the priesthood. And without the authority is given, the ordinances could not be administered in righteousness."[12]

great and dreadful day of the Lord. The "day of the Lord" is the day of his return to earth in power and glory. It is great in its scope and magnificence, and it is a great day of rejoicing for the righteous. It is dreadful to the wicked, because on that day they will be destroyed by fire, receiving a just punishment for the evil they have done in the world.

Mal. 4:6 *turn the heart of the fathers.* The restoration of the priesthood keys held by Elijah provides the power to bind the living and the dead into one great family. When that power was restored to the earth, the knowledge of the sealing blessings was also restored, and the hearts of the living (the children) began to be turned to their ancestors (the fathers), who in turn now look with fresh hope to their living children for the blessings of the gospel.

---

[12] *Words of Joseph Smith,* 43.

Joseph Smith clarified the meaning of *turn:* "Now the word turn here should be translated bind or seal."[13] He further explained that "without us, they could not be made perfect, nor we without them; the fathers without the children, nor the children without the fathers.

"I wish you to understand this subject, for it is important; and if you receive it, this is the spirit of Elijah, that we redeem our dead, and connect ourselves with our fathers which are in heaven, and seal up our dead to come forth in the first resurrection; and here we want the power of Elijah to seal those who dwell on earth to those who dwell in heaven. This is the power of Elijah and the keys of the kingdom of Jehovah."[14]

smite the earth with a curse. The Lord's purpose in creating the earth is given in Moses 1:39: "to bring to pass the immortality and eternal life of man."[15] Our immortality is assured, as a free gift of grace through the atonement of Jesus Christ. But to receive eternal life we must turn to God with all our hearts, becoming, as individuals, all that he requires of us. Then, having brought ourselves to Christ, we need to reach out to others, beginning with our families, including both the living and the dead. Should we fail to bring ourselves and others, being sealed up as one great family before the Lord, through the keys restored by Elijah, the earth would fail of its purpose. And we, the inhabitants of the earth, would fall short of God's promise of eternal life—certainly a curse of the highest magnitude.

THE COMING FORTH OF THE BOOK OF MORMON
Isaiah 29:11–12, 18–19, 24

> *11 And the vision of all is become unto you as the words of a book that is sealed, which men deliver to one that is learned, saying, Read this, I pray thee: and he saith, I cannot; for it is sealed:*
>
> *12 And the book is delivered to him that is not learned, saying,*

---

[13] *Words of Joseph Smith,* 318.

[14] *Teachings of the Prophet Joseph Smith,* 337–38.

[15] Immortality is the blessing of living forever in a resurrected body. Eternal life is the greater blessing of living forever in a resurrected body in God's presence, enjoying the kind of life he lives.

Read this, I pray thee: and he saith, I am not learned. . . .

18 And in that day shall the deaf hear the words of the book, and the eyes of the blind shall see out of obscurity, and out of darkness.

19 The meek also shall increase their joy in the Lord, and the poor among men shall rejoice in the Holy One of Israel. . . .

24 They also that erred in spirit shall come to understanding, and they that murmured shall learn doctrine.

As part of the restoration of the gospel, the Lord, through his prophets, promised the restoration of the record we know as the Book of Mormon. These prophecies are found not only in the Old Testament but also in the Book of Mormon itself: "For, behold, saith the Lamb: I will manifest myself unto thy seed, that they shall write many things which I shall minister unto them, which shall be plain and precious; and after thy seed shall be destroyed, and dwindle in unbelief, and also the seed of thy brethren, behold, these things shall be hid up, to come forth unto the Gentiles, by the gift and power of the Lamb. And in them shall be written my gospel, saith the Lamb, and my rock and my salvation" (1 Ne. 13:35–36).

The Book of Mormon was an essential part of the Restoration. In fact, as Elder Bruce R. McConkie wrote, "The Book of Mormon is the foundation upon which the house of the restoration is built. Take it away and there is no restoration, no true church and kingdom of God on earth, no plan of salvation, no power and authority whereby man may be saved and exalted."[16] As promised, the Book of Mormon has the power to help the spiritually deaf hear the word of the Lord and the spiritually blind to see the things of God. Its truths bring rejoicing to the meek and humble. Its doctrines correct many false understandings of those who adhere to the Bible alone.

The Book of Mormon would be viewed as "plain and precious" to those who read and believe it. It would contain the gospel of the Lamb, "and my rock and my salvation" (1 Ne. 13:35–36). Other

---

[16] *New Witness*, 450.

scriptures give additional understanding about the purposes of the restoration of the Book of Mormon:

It "shall make known to all kindreds, tongues, and people, that the Lamb of God is the Son of the Eternal Father, and the Savior of the world; and that all men must come unto him, or they cannot be saved" (1 Ne. 13:40).

It was given "that the Lamanites [and everyone else] . . . may believe the gospel and rely upon the merits of Jesus Christ, and be glorified through faith in his name, and that through their repentance they might be saved" (D&C 3:20).

It contains "the fulness of the gospel of Jesus Christ to the Gentiles and to the Jews also; . . . proving to the world that the holy scriptures are true, and that God does inspire men and call them to his holy work in this age and generation, as well as in generations of old; thereby showing that he is the same God yesterday, today, and forever" (D&C 20:9–12).

Nephi recorded the words of an angel who taught that the Bible and the Book of Mormon would work together in establishing their testimony of Christ (1 Ne. 13:40–41). This joining of testimonies is likewise a fulfillment of a prophecy Ezekiel received, whereon he performed the inspired action of bringing together into one hand two "sticks" (scrolls or wooden tablets), one representing Judah (the Bible) and the other representing Joseph (the Book of Mormon). "Thus saith the Lord God," the Lord announced through Ezekiel, "Behold, I will take the stick of Joseph, which is in the hand of Ephraim, and the tribes of Israel his fellows, and will put them with him, even with the stick of Judah, and make them one stick, and they shall be one in mine hand" (Ezek. 37:19; see also vv. 15–20). For other prophecies that foretell the coming forth of the Book of Mormon, see 1 Ne. 13:40; 2 Ne. 29:8; Enos 1:16.

"Let us take the Book of Mormon," Joseph Smith said, "which a man took and hid in his field, securing it by his faith, to spring up in the last days, or in due time; let us behold it coming forth out of the ground, which is indeed accounted the least of all seeds, but behold it branching forth, yea, even towering, with lofty branches, and God-like majesty, until it, like the mustard seed, becomes the greatest of all herbs. And it is truth, and it has sprouted and come forth out of the earth, and righteousness begins to look down from heaven, and God is sending down His powers, gifts and angels, to lodge in the branches thereof."[17]

Later he recorded, "I told the brethren that the Book of Mormon was the most correct of any book on earth, and the keystone of our religion, and a man would get nearer to God by abiding by its precepts, than by any other book."[18]

For its role in the restoration of the gospel, truly the Book of Mormon is a treasure. It also is a tangible and specific sign of the last days, since the gospel and the Book of Mormon had to be restored to the earth before the Lord would return.

NOTES AND COMMENTARY

Isa. 29:11 *a book that is sealed, which men deliver to one that is learned.* This prophecy was fulfilled in a remarkable and literal way, as recorded in Joseph Smith's historical account: "Sometime in this month of February, the aforementioned Mr. Martin Harris came to our place, got the characters which I had drawn off the plates, and started with them to the city of New York. For what took place relative to him and the characters, I refer to his own account of the circumstances, as he related them to me after his return, which was as follows:

"'I went to the city of New York, and presented the characters which had been translated, with the translation thereof, to Professor Charles Anthon, a gentleman celebrated for his literary attainments. Professor Anthon stated that the translation was correct, more so than any he had before seen translated from the Egyptian. I then showed him those which were not yet translated, and he said that they were Egyptian, Chaldaic, Assyriac, and Arabic; and he said they were true characters. He gave me a certificate, certifying to the people of Palmyra that they were true characters, and that the translation of such of them as had been translated was also correct. I took the certificate and put it into my pocket, and was just leaving the house, when

---

[17] *History of the Church,* 2:268.
[18] *History of the Church,* 4:461.

Mr. Anthon called me back, and asked me how the young man found out that there were gold plates in the place where he found them. I answered that an angel of God had revealed it unto him.

"'He then said to me, "Let me see that certificate." I accordingly took it out of my pocket and gave it to him, when he took it and tore it to pieces, saying that there was no such thing now as ministering of angels, and that if I would bring the plates to him he would translate them. I informed him that part of the plates were sealed, and that I was forbidden to bring them. He replied, "I cannot read a sealed book." I left him and went to Dr. Mitchell, who sanctioned what Professor Anthon had said respecting both the characters and the translation'" (JS–H 1:63–65).

Isa. 29:18 *in that day.* This phrase has reference to the day of the restoration of the gospel.

deaf hear the words of the book. The Book of Mormon will empower the spiritually deaf to hear the word of God, if they so choose.

blind shall see out of obscurity. The Book of Mormon removes darkness from our minds and hearts, permitting us to draw closer to God. President Ezra Taft Benson said, "There is a power in the book which will begin to flow into your lives the moment you begin serious study of the book. You will find greater power to resist temptation. You will find the power to avoid deception. You will find the power to stay on the strait and narrow path."[19]

Isa. 29:19 *The meek also shall increase their joy/the poor among men shall rejoice.* The terms *meek* and *poor* seem to refer to disciples of Christ (Matt. 5:3, "poor in spirit"; 5:5, "meek"). True disciples of Christ (the *meek* and the *poor*) will increase in their joy and rejoicing in Christ and his atonement, as they study the Book of Mormon, Another Testament of Jesus Christ.

Isa. 29:24 *They also that erred in spirit shall come to understanding/shall learn doctrine.* By making "known the plain and precious things which have been taken away" (1 Ne. 13:40) and by the "confounding of false doctrines and laying down of contentions, and

---

[19] *Ensign,* Nov. 1986, 7.

establishing peace" (2 Ne. 3:12), the Book of Mormon will teach true doctrine to those who have *erred in spirit.*

Elder Orson Pratt taught: "Oh, how precious must be the contents of a book which shall deliver us from all the errors taught by the precepts of uninspired men! Oh, how gratifying to poor, ignorant, erring mortals who have murmured because of the multiplicity of contradictory doctrines that have perplexed and distracted their minds, to read the plain, pure and most precious word of God, revealed in the Book of Mormon!"[20]

THE RESTORATION WILL BE ASSISTED BY ANGELIC VISITORS
Revelation 14:6–7

6 And I saw another angel fly in the midst of heaven, having the everlasting gospel to preach unto them that dwell on the earth, and to every nation, and kindred, and tongue, and people,

7 Saying with a loud voice, Fear God, and give glory to him; for the hour of his judgment is come.

The work of restoration is primarily a work involving angels and prophets. Joseph Smith spoke of "having received many visits from the angels of God unfolding the majesty and glory of the events that should transpire in the last days."[21] Elder Dallin H. Oaks has said: "The Prophet Joseph had no role models from whom he could learn how to be a prophet and leader of the Lord's people. He learned from heavenly messengers and from the harvest of his unique spiritual gifts."[22]

In a passage of inspired rejoicing, Joseph Smith wrote about those angels and their role in the gospel's restoration: "Now, what do we hear in the gospel which we have received? A voice of gladness! A voice of mercy from heaven; and a voice of truth out of the earth; glad

---

[20] *Orson Pratt's Works,* 278–79.
[21] *History of the Church,* 4:537. One researcher listed twenty-four angels or groups of angels who visited Joseph Smith; see Parry and Morris, *Mormon Book of Lists,* 18–19.
[22] *Ensign,* May 1996, 72.

tidings for the dead; a voice of gladness for the living and the dead; glad tidings of great joy. . . .

"And again, what do we hear? Glad tidings from Cumorah! Moroni, an angel from heaven, declaring the fulfilment of the prophets—the book to be revealed. A voice of the Lord in the wilderness of Fayette, Seneca county, declaring the three witnesses to bear record of the book! . . . The voice of Peter, James, and John in the wilderness . . . on the Susquehanna river, declaring themselves as possessing the keys of the kingdom, and of the dispensation of the fulness of times!

"And again, the voice of God . . . at sundry times, and in divers places through all the travels and tribulations of this Church of Jesus Christ of Latter-day Saints! And the voice of Michael, the archangel; the voice of Gabriel, and of Raphael, and of divers angels, from Michael or Adam down to the present time, all declaring their dispensation, their rights, their keys, their honors, their majesty and glory, and the power of their priesthood; giving line upon line, precept upon precept; here a little, and there a little; giving us consolation by holding forth that which is to come, confirming our hope!

"Brethren, shall we not go on in so great a cause? Go forward and not backward. Courage, brethren; and on, on to the victory! Let your hearts rejoice, and be exceedingly glad. Let the earth break forth into singing. Let the dead speak forth anthems of eternal praise to the King Immanuel, who hath ordained, before the world was, that which would enable us to redeem them out of their prison; for the prisoners shall go free.

"Let the mountains shout for joy, and all ye valleys cry aloud; and all ye seas and dry lands tell the wonders of your Eternal King! And ye rivers, and brooks, and rills, flow down with gladness. Let the woods and all the trees of the field praise the Lord; and ye solid rocks weep for joy! And let the sun, moon, and the morning stars sing together, and let all the sons of God shout for joy! And let the eternal creations declare his name forever and ever! And again I say, how glorious is the voice we hear from heaven, proclaiming in our ears, glory, and salvation, and honor, and immortality, and eternal life; kingdoms, principalities, and powers!" (D&C 128:19–23).

NOTES AND COMMENTARY

Rev. 14:6 *another angel.* After seeing many angels perform many functions pertaining to the last days, John the Revelator saw another angel, who was assigned to bring the everlasting gospel to the earth. This angel was Moroni, who brought the plates from which the Book of Mormon was translated, which book has the fulness of the gospel.[23] In latter-day revelation, the Lord confirmed that this angel has already come to earth: "And now, verily saith the Lord, that these things might be known among you, O inhabitants of the earth, I have sent forth mine angel flying through the midst of heaven, having the everlasting gospel, who hath appeared unto some and hath committed it unto man, who shall appear unto many that dwell on the earth" (D&C 133:36).

everlasting gospel. This is the gospel of Jesus Christ, which is the same from generation to generation.

every nation, and kindred, and tongue, and people. The Lord's plan is for the gospel to be heard in every part of the globe. As the resurrected Jesus said to his disciples immediately before he ascended into heaven, "Go ye therefore, and teach all nations, baptizing them in the name of the Father, and of the Son, and of the Holy Ghost" (Matt. 28:19).

Rev. 14:7 *the hour of his judgment.* The restoration of the gospel is to precede the judgments of God. The Lord will not execute his final judgments against the wicked until after he has restored the gospel and sent its word around the earth.

THE RESTORATION OF SPIRITUAL GIFTS
Joel 2:28–29

> *28 And it shall come to pass afterward that I will pour out my spirit upon all flesh; and your sons and your daughters shall prophesy, your old men shall dream dreams, your young men shall see visions:*
>
> *29 And also upon the servants and upon the handmaids in those days will I pour out my spirit.*

---

[23] Hinckley, Conference Report, Oct. 1995, 93.

In the days of Joseph Smith, many said that God had removed his gifts from the earth. When young Joseph tried to tell others of his First Vision, they rejected it out of hand because they did not believe that such a manifestation was possible. When Joseph told a Methodist minister of his vision, for example, "he treated my communication not only lightly, but with great contempt, saying it was all of the devil, that there were no such things as visions or revelations in these days; that all such things had ceased with the apostles, and that there would never be any more of them" (JS–H 1:21). Such an attitude was a denial of the power of the Spirit and also a denial of prophecy, as given by the prophet Joel (Joel 2:28–29).[24]

In January 1833, Joseph Smith recorded that that prophecy was beginning to be fulfilled: "The gifts which follow them that believe and obey the Gospel, as tokens that the Lord is ever the same in His dealings with the humble lovers and followers of truth, began to be poured out among us, as in ancient days."[25] The restoration of these spiritual gifts is not reserved only for the first prophet of the Restoration or only for his successor prophets. These gifts are promised to all who will seek the Lord with diligence and turn their hearts to him in sacrifice and desire (Alma 26:22; D&C 46:10–33), including both young and old ("sons," "daughters," "young men," "old men") and male and female ("sons," "daughters," "servants," "handmaids").

With Peter, with Joel, with Joseph Smith, we, in these last days, can sing with great rejoicing the words written by William W. Phelps:

> The Spirit of God like a fire is burning!
> The latter-day glory begins to come forth;
> The visions and blessings of old are returning,
> And angels are coming to visit the earth.
>
> The Lord is extending the Saints' understanding,
> Restoring their judges and all as at first.

---

[24] It may be that the minister misunderstood Peter's application of this prophecy (Acts 2:17–18) as being the last and final time when the gifts of the Spirit would be manifest. Of course, the many scriptural promises of spiritual gifts have no limit as to time or place.

[25] *History of the Church,* 1:322.

The knowledge and power of God are expanding;
The veil o'er the earth is beginning to burst.

We'll call in our solemn assemblies in spirit,
To spread forth the kingdom of heaven abroad,
That we through our faith may begin to inherit
The visions and blessings and glories of God.

We'll sing and we'll shout with the armies of heaven,
Hosanna, hosanna to God and the Lamb!
Let glory to them in the highest be given,
Henceforth and forever, Amen and amen![26]

NOTES AND COMMENTARY

Joel 2:28 *And it shall come to pass afterward.* Peter changed this phrase to "it shall come to pass in the last days," and he saw one fulfillment of it on the marvelous day of Pentecost, when the apostles "were all filled with the Holy Ghost, and began to speak with other tongues, as the Spirit gave them utterance" (Acts 2:17, 4). The fulfillment continues in our day among those who receive these gifts of the Spirit.

I will pour out my spirit upon all flesh. There are at least two possible ways to read this promise, both of which have been used by leaders of the Church, thus suggesting that we may appropriately look for a dual fulfillment of the prophecy.

As mankind began to emerge from the Dark Ages, the Lord poured out his Spirit, the light of Christ, upon all, to enlighten their minds and bless their lives. That blessing has continued to this day. "Whatsoever is light is Spirit, even the Spirit of Jesus Christ," the Lord said to Joseph Smith. "And the Spirit giveth light to every man that cometh into the world; and the Spirit enlighteneth every man through the world, that hearkeneth to the voice of the Spirit. And every one that hearkeneth to the voice of the Spirit cometh unto God, even the Father" (D&C 84:45–47). Thus, as we receive the Lord's Spirit (meaning the light of Christ) and let it magnify within us, it will bring us closer to God and bring us closer as well to the eventual

---

[26] "The Spirit of God," *Hymns*, no. 2.

blessing of receiving the gift of the Holy Ghost, which, in turn, brings such gifts as dreams, visions, and prophesying.

Another fulfillment of this prophecy may actually be millennial, when "all flesh" may eventually come to the rich and varied gifts of the Spirit. In 1833 the Lord seemed to suggest that this prophecy had not yet come to pass; he spoke of yet bringing "to pass my strange act, that I may pour out my Spirit upon all flesh" (D&C 95:4). Also, the context of the prophecy in Joel seems to have overtones of the millennial day (Joel 2:21–29).

Whatever the case may be, we know that the restoration of the gospel includes the gifts of the Spirit—prophesying, dreams, visions from God, and others.

your sons and your daughters shall prophesy, your old men shall dream dreams, your young men shall see visions. This prophecy was renewed to Joseph Smith when the angel Moroni visited him in September 1823. Moroni "said that this was not yet fulfilled, but was soon to be" (JS–H 1:41). The fulfillment likely began after the Melchizedek Priesthood was restored in 1829. With the higher priesthood on the earth, people could receive the laying on of hands for the gift of the Holy Ghost, who then could bring such gifts as these to those who sought them in righteousness.

One great truth shown in these verses is the universal availability of the Lord's gifts to those who will pay the necessary price. He desires to give the blessings of his Spirit to all who will qualify through obedience and a broken heart. Age, gender, worldly experience, social position, or wealth—none of these matter to the Lord. Instead, he desires that we love him and seek to serve him, and then he will grant to us all we are able to receive.

Joel 2:29 *upon the servants and upon the handmaids in those days will I pour out my spirit.* In quoting this prophecy on the day of Pentecost, Peter changed it to say, "On my servants and on my handmaidens I will pour out in those days of my Spirit; and they shall prophesy" (Acts 2:18). His change clarified that the recipients of this gift were not simply servants and handmaids but servants and handmaidens to the Lord. He also specified the result of their receiving the Spirit: "They shall prophesy."

THE ESTABLISHMENT OF THE LATTER-DAY KINGDOM
Daniel 2:44–45

44 And in the days of these kings shall the God of heaven set up a kingdom, which shall never be destroyed: and the kingdom shall not be left to other people, but it shall break in pieces and consume all these kingdoms, and it shall stand for ever.

45 Forasmuch as thou sawest that the stone was cut out of the mountain without hands, and that it brake in pieces the iron, the brass, the clay, the silver, and the gold; the great God hath made known to the king what shall come to pass hereafter: and the dream is certain, and the interpretation thereof sure.

The Lord promised to establish a kingdom as well as a Church in the latter days.[27] The Lord will return as king, and a king must have a kingdom to rule over. Especially would that be true of the King of kings. This kingdom of God will eventually destroy all other kingdoms on the earth.

In a dream given to the Babylonian king Nebuchadnezzar, as interpreted by Daniel, the Lord compared the kingdom of God to a stone that was cut out of a mountain. That stone apparently rolled down the mountainside to break the kingdoms of the earth "in pieces." In our dispensation, the Lord declared, "The keys of the kingdom of God are committed unto man on the earth, and from thence shall the gospel roll forth unto the ends of the earth, as the stone which is cut out of the mountain without hands shall roll forth, until it has filled the whole earth" (D&C 65:2).

That kingdom has now been established and is growing strong. Speaking in testimony of the restoration of the kingdom and its accompanying gifts and powers, President Ezra Taft Benson wrote: "I solemnly declare that the God of heaven has established his latter-day kingdom upon the earth in fulfillment of prophecies uttered by his ancient prophets and apostles. Holy angels have again communed

---

[27] For a discussion of the differences between the kingdom and the Church, as well as the ways in which they are the same, see Smith, *Answers to Gospel Questions*, 2:20–25.

with men on the earth. God has again revealed himself from heaven and restored to the earth his holy priesthood with power to administer in all the sacred ordinances necessary for the exaltation of his children. His Church has been reestablished among men with all the spiritual gifts enjoyed anciently.

"All this is done in preparation for Christ's second coming."[28]

NOTES AND COMMENTARY

Dan. 2:44 *And in the days of these kings/set up a kingdom.* In his dream, Nebuchadnezzar saw an image representing a series of kingdoms of the earth, each symbolized by a metal: gold (head), silver (breast and arms), brass (belly and thighs), iron (legs), and a mixture of iron and clay (feet). The kingdoms represented by the feet, which were made of the mixture of iron and clay, suggest a combination of strength and weakness and also may indicate that the great kingdoms of antiquity would be divided into smaller kingdoms. In the days of the weaker kingdoms, the Lord would begin to establish his own kingdom. We know by revelation that the fulfillment of this prophecy began in the 1820s and 1830s under the inspired direction of Joseph Smith, the founding prophet of our dispensation (D&C 65:2).

never be destroyed/shall stand for ever. In other dispensations, the Lord's kingdom was established only to be lost from the earth by persecution and apostasy. But the latter-day kingdom will stand until the Lord returns, ushering in the Millennium, and it will continue to stand "for ever."

the kingdom shall not be left to other people. The Lord's authorized administrators (those holding the keys of the kingdom), with the Lord's covenant people (who have joined the kingdom through legal ordinances), will possess his kingdom; those who do not receive the covenant ("other people") will not have part of the kingdom.

break in pieces and consume all these kingdoms. How will the kingdoms of man on the earth be destroyed? By the power of God, as it is manifest through his own kingdom on the earth. When Jesus, the king of that kingdom, returns in glory, he will put down all his

---

[28] *Labor of Love,* 243.

enemies, including the kingdoms of mankind (1 Cor. 15:24; for further discussion of the final destruction of all nations, see chap. 6).

Dan. 2:45 *the stone.* The stone represents the kingdom of God. The symbol is one of power and durability. In other scriptures, Christ himself is referred to as a stone (Ps. 78:35; Moses 7:53). The imagery suggests that the kingdom of God will share those characteristics of power and durability with its maker, Jesus Christ.

cut out of the mountain without hands. The mountain may represent the earth: the stone is cut out of the earth and later supersedes it, becoming itself a new mountain (Dan. 2:34–35). The hands are likely human hands, for the kingdom of God is established by God and not by the hands of man.

it brake in pieces the iron, the brass, the clay, the silver, and the gold. In the last days, the Lord will make an end to all earthly nations (Jer. 30:11; D&C 87:6) as he prepares the way for his own kingdom.

CHAPTER 2

THE GATHERING OF ISRAEL

SIGNS OF THE TIMES

1. The Lord remembers his covenant to gather Israel.

2. The Lord restores the keys of the gathering.

3. The gathering involves missionary work and conversion.

4. Ephraim will be gathered first.

5. A voice of warning goes forth to all people; after the Lord's warnings come his judgments.

6. Israel is gathered from many lands.

7. The gathered include the elect.

8. The Lamanites will blossom as a rose.

9. The coming forth of the Book of Mormon is a sign that the gathering is proceeding.

10. The Lord calls 144,000 high priests to help in the gathering.

11. The Saints are commanded to flee Babylon.

12. The Saints gather at the temples.

13. The times of the Gentiles are fulfilled.

14. The Jews gather to the land of Palestine.

15. The ten tribes are brought in from their long dispersion and are blessed to return to the lands of their inheritance.

16. The Saints gather to Zion, where the New Jerusalem is built.

"We believe in the literal gathering of Israel and in the restoration of the Ten Tribes" (A of F 10). Probably no event of the last days has been prophesied more often than the gathering of Israel. Because of their wickedness, the Lord allowed the children of Israel to be scattered among the nations in the millennium before the birth of Christ as well as afterward, by the hand of Rome. But though they were lost to history, the Lord knows where he placed them, and he ever remembers his promises to restore them to their inheritance.

The scattering had two phases. First, the people of Israel turned from God and his gospel and the covenant he had made with them, and their hearts became lost from him. Next, the people of Israel were removed from their land of promise, a symbol of the covenant, and were dispersed among the nations. These phases were prophesied by Moses many centuries before they actually took place. "If thou wilt not hearken unto the voice of the Lord thy God," he said, "to observe to do all his commandments and his statutes which I command thee this day . . . [you will be] removed into all the kindoms of the earth. . . . And the Lord shall scatter thee among all people, from the one end of the earth even unto the other; and there thou shalt serve other gods, which neither thou nor thy fathers have known" (Deut. 28:15, 25, 64; see also Jer. 16:11–13). First came the apostasy of heart—"if thou wilt not hearken unto the voice of the Lord thy God"—the spiritual removal from God's presence. Then came the scattering, the physical removal from the promised land.[1]

The gathering will have the same two phases, restoring that which was lost. First, the people of Israel (and Gentiles who are adopted into the family of Abraham) will receive the opportunity to come unto Christ and his Church. Their hearts will be restored to their true Redeemer. This gathering is a gathering of souls to Zion in the broad sense, to the wards and branches and stakes of the Church in all places throughout the world. Then, in due time, a representative part of those who come unto Christ and his Church will have the opportunity to go to the place called Zion (centered in the New Jerusalem on the American continent, specifically in Missouri);[2] also, in time, those of blood Israel will be restored to their lands of promise. This might be termed a gathering by migration.

---

[1] See McConkie, *New Witness*, 515; Millet and McConkie, *Our Destiny*, 66–67. There are, however, exceptions to the rule that Israel was scattered because of Israel's wickedness: Sometimes branches of Israel were dispersed to other locations to protect them from the wickedness of others (1 Ne. 17:36–38; 21:1; 2 Ne. 10:20–22); sometimes branches were scattered in order to bless other parts of the Lord's vineyard (Smith, "Mission of Ephraim," 2.)

[2] For a discussion of the gathering to New Jerusalem, see McConkie, *Millennial Messiah*, 294–96; and McConkie, *New Witness*, 519.

Some might say that for Jews the gathering has the same two phases but in reverse: First, they return to the land of their inheritance, the place called Zion (also known as Jerusalem). Then, in time, many will accept the returning Jesus Christ as their Messiah.

In truth, though, the gathering of the Jews will follow the same pattern as that of everyone else who comes (or returns) to the covenant. Jacob taught that the Lord "has spoken unto the Jews, by the mouth of his holy prophets, even from the beginning down, from generation to generation, until the time comes that they [the Jews, and by extension, all the house of Israel; see 2 Ne. 9:1] shall be restored to the true church and fold of God; when they shall be gathered home to the lands of their inheritance, and shall be established in all their lands of promise" (2 Ne. 9:2). First, Israel (including the Jews) would be "restored to the true church," after which they would be "gathered home to the lands of their inheritance." The spiritual gathering precedes and leads to the temporal gathering.

Jacob gave the entire pattern of scattering and gathering, in sequence: "Because of their iniquities, destructions, famines, pestilences, and bloodshed shall come upon them [the Jews]; and they who shall not be destroyed shall be scattered among all nations.

"But behold, thus saith the Lord God: When the day cometh that they shall believe in me, that I am Christ, then have I covenanted with their fathers that they shall be restored in the flesh, upon the earth, unto the lands of their inheritance. And it shall come to pass that they shall be gathered in from their long dispersion, from the isles of the sea, and from the four parts of the earth; and the nations of the Gentiles shall be great in the eyes of me, saith God, in carrying them forth to the lands of their inheritance" (2 Ne. 10:6–8).

First came the iniquity, and then the scattering, followed in some by a return to faith in Christ, which brings them to the true Church, culminating in a restoration to "the lands of their inheritance."

These promises of gathering, both spiritual and temporal, all flow from covenants the Lord made with his people anciently. The people of Israel have always been a covenant people. The covenant stems from the promises made to Abraham that his descendants would be very great in number, that his name would be great on the earth, that "in thee shall all families of the earth be blessed" (Gen. 12:2–3; 13:16). These promises were granted as well to Abraham's son, Isaac (Gen. 26:4), and to Isaac's son Jacob after him (Gen. 28:14). Jacob is the man who became known as Israel (Gen. 32:28). The covenant could be fulfilled only as Abraham's descendants received the priesthood and the gospel.

But even though this covenant was a promise to Abraham and his descendants, it was conditioned on righteousness. When Jesus was teaching the unbelieving Jews, he said, "Bring forth . . . fruits meet for repentance: and think not to say within yourselves, We have Abraham to our father: for I say unto you, that God is able of these stones to raise up children unto Abraham" (Matt. 3:8–9). With the Lord, righteousness is of greater significance than lineage. It follows, then, that those who join Abraham in righteousness will be privileged to join in his covenant. Nephi taught this truth: "As many of the Gentiles as will repent are the covenant people of the Lord; and as many of the Jews as will not repent shall be cast off; for the Lord covenanteth with none save it be with them that repent and believe in his Son, who is the Holy One of Israel" (2 Ne. 30:2). (In this context, Gentiles seems to refer to all who are not Jews.)

The gathering is clearly a last days event, one of the signs of the times. Jesus declared that the coming forth of the Book of Mormon was a sign that the gathering was about to begin (3 Ne. 20–21). In 1836, seven years after the publication of the Book of Mormon, the keys for gathering all of Israel were restored to Joseph Smith; the gathering thus occurs under the direction of those who have succeeded the Prophet in his presidency. The Prophet recorded, "Moses appeared before us, and committed unto us the keys of the gathering of Israel from the four parts of the earth, and the leading of the ten tribes from the land of the north" (D&C 110:11). Once the keys were restored to the earth, the gathering could begin.

Joseph Smith explained an overriding purpose of the gathering: to tap into the great blessings of combined righteousness. He said: "The greatest temporal and spiritual blessings which always come from faithfulness and concerted effort, never attended individual exertion or enterprise. The history of all past ages abundantly attests this fact.

In addition to all temporal blessings, there is no other way for the Saints to be saved in these last days [than by the gathering] as the concurrent testimony of all the holy prophets clearly proves. . . .

"It is also the concurrent testimony of all the prophets, that this gathering together of all the Saints, must take place before the Lord comes to 'take vengeance upon the ungodly,' and 'to be glorified and admired by all those who obey the Gospel.'"[3]

In another sermon Joseph Smith connected the gathering to the blessing of temples: "What was the object of gathering the Jews, or the people of God in any age of the world? . . .

"The main object was to build unto the Lord a house whereby He could reveal unto His people the ordinances of His house and the glories of His kingdom, and teach the people the way of salvation; for there are certain ordinances and principles that, when they are taught and practiced, must be done in a place or house built for that purpose."[4]

Providing protection for the Saints is another purpose of the gathering. As the Lord said in the early days of the Church, "Verily I say unto you all: Arise and shine forth, that thy light may be a standard for the nations; and that the gathering together upon the land of Zion, and upon her stakes, may be for a defense, and for a refuge from the storm, and from wrath when it shall be poured out without mixture upon the whole earth" (D&C 115:5–6).

THE LORD REMEMBERS HIS COVENANT
Isaiah 49:13–19

13 Sing, O heavens; and be joyful, O earth; and break forth into singing, O mountains: for the Lord hath comforted his people, and will have mercy upon his afflicted.

14 But Zion said, The Lord hath forsaken me, and my Lord hath forgotten me.

15 Can a woman forget her sucking child, that she should not have compassion on the son of her womb? yea, they may forget, yet will I not forget thee.

---

[3] *Teachings of the Prophet Joseph Smith*, 183.
[4] *History of the Church*, 5:423.

16 Behold, I have graven thee upon the palms of my hands; thy walls are continually before me.

17 Thy children shall make haste [against] thy destroyers[;] and they that made thee waste shall go forth [of] thee.[5]

18 Lift up thine eyes round about, and behold: all these gather themselves together, and come to thee. As I live, saith the Lord, thou shalt surely clothe thee with them all, as with an ornament, and bind them on thee, as a bride doeth.

19 For thy waste and thy desolate places, and the land of thy destruction, shall even now be too narrow by reason of the inhabitants, and they that swallowed thee up shall be far away.

In the last days, the Lord promises, "I [will] remember my covenant which I have made unto my people, O house of Israel, and I will bring my gospel unto them. And I will show unto thee, O house of Israel, that the Gentiles shall not have power over you; but I will remember my covenant unto you, O house of Israel, and ye shall come unto the knowledge of the fulness of my gospel" (3 Ne. 16:11–12).

In a broad sense, God's covenant with Israel is the Abrahamic covenant, where the Lord promised priesthood blessings and a land of promise to Abraham and his posterity. Specifically here, the covenant seems to be that the Lord will gather Israel, both to the gospel of Jesus Christ and to her promised lands.

As Isaiah saw, the Lord's people would come to feel that the Lord had forgotten them, and they would be fearful that the covenant would not be fulfilled (Isa. 49:14). But the Lord answers with compassion, saying that though a mother might forget her infant child, he would never forget (Isa. 49:15). He reminds them of his suffering in the Atonement ("I have graven thee upon the palms of my hands"). Having paid such a price for them, how can he ever forget? (Isa. 49:16).

---

[5] The changes in this verse are from 1 Ne. 21:17.

In time, the Lord says, many will "gather themselves together, and come to thee [Zion]" (Isa. 49:18). So many will gather that the land will actually become crowded (Isa. 49:19–20). "Therefore ye need not suppose that ye can turn the right hand of the Lord unto the left, that he may not execute judgment unto the fulfilling of the covenant which he hath made unto the house of Israel" (3 Ne. 29:9).

NOTES AND COMMENTARY

Isa. 49:13 *Sing, O heavens/be joyful, O earth/singing, O mountains.* This passage suggests that the very creations of God will rejoice at the fulfillment of his promises to gather Israel to the true gospel (see also Isa. 44:23; 52:9–10; 55:12; D&C 128:22). Or *heavens* may refer to God and those with him (in Moses 7:28 the weeping of God is described as the weeping of the heavens; perhaps the rejoicing of the heavens here represents the rejoicing of God); *earth* may refer to the righteous people on earth; *mountains* may refer to the Zion of God, established in the land of the everlasting hills.

his people/his afflicted. The Lord's people are afflicted because of their dispersion and long exile. They also are afflicted spiritually as a consequence for sin; but through the Atonement, the Lord will comfort and be merciful to the repentant, who are truly the Lord's people.

Isa. 49:14 *Zion.* Zion can be the Lord's people or a geographical location. In this context it seems to refer to scattered Israel, who felt that God had forgotten them.

The Lord hath forsaken me. So many millennia have passed since the Lord made his promises that the people of the covenant feel that the Lord has turned his back on them (compare Gideon's expression in Judg. 6:13).

Isa. 49:15 *woman forget her sucking child/son of her womb.* A loving mother would never forget her precious baby, "the son of her womb." But the Lord loves us even more than that (see also Isa. 43:4; 44:21; 46:3–4).

Isa. 49:16 *graven thee/palms of my hands.* This imagery refers to the crucifixion of Christ, in which nails pierced his hands and left scars that the Father caused to remain in the Resurrection (3 Ne. 11:13–14; Luke 24:39–40). These nail marks are a sign to Israel and to the world that Christ has indeed fulfilled his mission as Savior

(Isa. 22:23, 25; John 20:25; 3 Ne. 11:14–15; D&C 6:37; 45:48–53). The marks in his palms are also a constant reminder to him of the cost and the depth of his love for us.

walls/before me. The walls of Jerusalem are ever-present to those who dwell in the city. In the same way, an awareness of Israel is ever-present with the Lord (see also Isa. 60:18). Walls may also be a barrier or hindrance. The Lord is ever aware of our concerns, worries, problems, barriers—all those things that hinder us from being what he would have us be.

Isa. 49:17 *Thy children shall make haste [against] thy destroyers.* The *children* are the descendants of ancient Israel. The *destroyers* are the nations that attacked and captured ancient Israel. In the days when Israel shall be restored to her former blessings, the descendants of ancient Israel will quickly turn against their ancient enemies, who continue to oppress. This may also refer to the success the faithful of Israel will have against those who would destroy them spiritually, including Satan and his followers.

made thee waste/go forth. Those who conquered and wasted Israel will depart.

Isa. 49:18 *clothe/ornament.* As additional souls are gathered unto Zion, they will add to the glory of those already there. As fine clothing or expensive jewelry add beauty to a bride, so will the souls of those gathered add beauty to the Church.

bind/bride. In various scriptures, the bride is depicted as being the Saints (Isa. 61:10), the Church (D&C 109:73–74), and the New Jerusalem (Rev. 21:2). In this verse, the bride represents Zion. In Zion, we bind others to ourselves with a bond of charity. This binding, which brings us to union and oneness, is the very essence of Zion. Binding might also refer to the sealing ordinance.

Isa. 49:19 *waste/desolate places/narrow.* Israel's promised land has been laid waste and made empty, but when the gathering occurs, the available land will be too small for the great influx of those who are gathered (Isa. 54:1–3). The waste places of Zion are symbolic of Israel's loss, both spiritual and physical, that shall be restored (Isa. 58:12; D&C 101:75; 103:11–12). The restoration of the waste places thus brings joy and comfort (Isa. 48:13, 19; 51:3; 52:9; D&C 101:18).

they that swallowed thee shall be far away. Israel's enemies, or our spiritual enemies, will be far from us.

THE GATHERING WILL BE DIRECTED BY PRIESTHOOD KEYS
Doctrine and Covenants 110:11

11 . . . the heavens were . . . opened unto us; and Moses appeared before us, and committed unto us the keys of the gathering of Israel from the four parts of the earth, and the leading of the ten tribes from the land of the north.

The Lord directs his Church to function by proper authority in all it does. "Mine house is a house of order," he said to Joseph Smith, "and not a house of confusion" (D&C 132:8). To ensure that order, the Lord has delegated keys of authority to his servants who preside over the Church.[6] "I have appointed unto my servant Joseph to hold this power in the last days, and there is never but one on the earth at a time on whom this power and the keys of this priesthood are conferred" (D&C 132:7). The keys have been passed from Joseph Smith in proper succession to the current president of the Church. The work of the kingdom, in matters both great and small, is directed by the keys of authority that the Lord has given to his servants, the prophets.

The gathering of Israel is an example of a work that is directed by these keys. The president of the Church, assisted by the Twelve and others to whom he has delegated authority, determines where missions are established and where individual missionaries serve. The president of the Church decides where temples, which are focal points of gathering, will be built, and where stakes will be established. And should the divine direction for gathering ever change, that change will come through the president of the Church.

Elder Harold B. Lee taught this principle when he said: "Clearly, the Lord has placed the responsibility for directing the work of gathering in the hands of the leaders of the Church to whom he will reveal his will where and when such gatherings would take place in the future. It would be well . . . before the frightening events concerning

---

[6] See the commentary on the restoration of priesthood keys, page 31.

the fulfillment of all God's promises and predictions are upon us, that the Saints in every land prepare themselves and look forward to the instruction that shall come to them from the First Presidency of this Church as to where they shall be gathered and not be disturbed in their feelings until such instruction is given to them as it is revealed by the Lord to the proper authority."[7]

Elder Boyd K. Packer taught similarly, warning against those who might seek to take the Church in the wrong direction: "Those deceivers say that the Brethren do not know what is going on in the world or that the Brethren approve of their teaching but do not wish to speak of it over the pulpit. Neither is true. The Brethren, by virtue of traveling constantly everywhere on earth, certainly know what is going on and by virtue of prophetic insight are able to read the signs of the times.

"Do not be deceived by them—those deceivers. If there is to be any gathering, it will be announced by those who have been regularly ordained and who are known to the Church to have authority.

"Come away from any others. Follow your leaders, who have been duly ordained and have been publicly sustained, and you will not be led astray."[8]

The restoration of the keys of gathering is one of the signs of the times. According to the plan and purpose of God, the gathering will proceed as directed by the man who holds those keys, the living prophet of The Church of Jesus Christ of Latter-day Saints.

NOTES AND COMMENTARY

D&C 110:11 *The heavens were . . . opened unto us.* As part of a remarkable series of visions in the newly dedicated Kirtland Temple, Joseph Smith and Oliver Cowdery saw first the Lord, then Moses, then Elias, then Elijah, with each of the prophets bestowing sacred priesthood keys upon them.

Moses appeared before us. In rather matter-of-fact language, Joseph Smith informs us that the great ancient prophet who led Israel from its bondage in Egypt returned in 1836 to give him the "keys of

---

[7] Conference Report, Apr. 1948, 55.
[8] Conference Report, Oct. 1992, 102.

the gathering of Israel." Why Moses? Perhaps because he once led Israel forth from Egypt in mighty power, taking them to their promised land. Likewise, when our prophets lead Israel forth from spiritual Egypt, or Babylon, in the last days, they will do so with mighty power, like unto Moses.

keys. "Keys are the right of presidency; they are divine authorization to use the priesthood for a specified purpose; they empower those who hold them to use the power of God to do the work of Him whose power it is."[9]

keys of the gathering of Israel. Elder Bruce R. McConkie wrote: "How was Israel gathered the first time? In what way came they out of Egypt, free from bondage, carrying the riches of the land with them? Truly it was by the power of God. With a mighty hand and a stretched-out arm and with fury poured out, Jehovah led his ancient people. And he did it by the hand of Moses, his servant, who held the keys of the gathering, the keys and power to use the priesthood to part the Red Sea and do all else that must needs be.

"When 'the Lord shall set his hand again the second time to recover the remnant of his people' (Isa. 11:11) from all the countries whither he hath driven them, how shall the work be done? It shall be again as it was before. His prophets, holding again the keys and powers possessed by Moses, shall lead Israel out of the bondage of a modern Egypt. . . .

"Thus Israel returns at the direction of the president of The Church of Jesus Christ of Latter-day Saints. Thus when the Ten Tribes come forth from the lands of the north to receive their blessings in the temples of God, they will come at the command of the presiding officer in the true Church. . . . He alone is empowered to use all of the keys in their eternal fulness. There is never but one on earth at a time who can preside over and direct all of the affairs of the Lord among mortals, and this includes the gathering of all Israel as well as all else involved in the heaven-directed work."[10]

four parts of the earth. See the commentary on the gathering of Israel from many lands, page 71.

---

[9] McConkie, *Millennial Messiah,* 202.
[10] Ibid., 202–3.

leading of the ten tribes from the land of the north. See the commentary on the restoration of the ten tribes, page 103.

THE GATHERING OF ISRAEL THROUGH MISSIONARY WORK AND CONVERSION
Doctrine and Covenants 39:11

> *11 . . . Thou shalt preach the fulness of my gospel, which I have sent forth in these last days, the covenant which I have sent forth to recover my people, which are of the house of Israel.*

The gathering will occur not only through the migration of peoples but also by the bringing of people to the true gospel of Jesus Christ. As the Lord said to Joseph Smith, by preaching the gospel we also carry to the house of Israel the covenant "to recover my people." In other words, the very act of preaching the gospel to the house of Israel causes the covenant to be renewed to them, if they will repent and turn to the Lord.

Through Jeremiah the Lord described this same gathering process, that of the missionaries going forth diligently to find the honest in heart among those of the earth. The Lord called his missionaries fishers and hunters, who would "hunt them from every mountain, and from every hill, and out of the holes of the rocks" (Jer. 16:16).

The Lord used a different image when he spoke through Zechariah: "I will hiss for them, and gather them; for I have redeemed them" (Zech. 10:8; see also Isa. 5:26). The Lord "hisses" or calls to his people through the missionaries, and if they will hearken, they will be gathered, "one by one," as Isaiah prophesied (Isa. 27:12), or "one of a city, and two of a family," as Jeremiah foresaw (Jer. 3:14). The Savior taught the Nephites that through the Gentiles, the scattered Jews would be brought to a knowledge of Christ and would be gathered in from all parts of the earth. This same promise, he said, applied to "all the people of the house of Israel" (3 Ne. 16:4–5).

"The gathering of Israel is now in progress," President Spencer W. Kimball taught. "Hundreds of thousands of people have been baptized into the Church. Millions more will join the Church. And this is the way that we will gather Israel. . . .

"It is to be done by missionary work."[11]

As a snapshot of one point in time, in 1989 Elder M. Russell Ballard gave us a progress report of the growth of the Church missionary effort around the world: "In recent years the Lord's servants have unlocked the door and opened the work in the German Democratic Republic, Poland, Hungary, and Yugoslavia. They have opened many nations of Africa, including Nigeria, Ghana, Zaire, Liberia, Sierra Leone, Swaziland, Ivory Coast, and Namibia; they have also opened Papua New Guinea. Thirteen nations and territories have been opened for missionary work in just the past four years. Many others will be opened to the preaching of the gospel. Truly, no unhallowed hand can stop the sacred work of proclaiming life and salvation to all nations and peoples, but this work will not continue without challenges and risks."[12]

Six and a half years later, Elder Ballard said: "In the past six years we have carried the gospel to thirty-nine new countries. . . . This work is moving; it is beginning to cover the earth. While it is true that many of our Heavenly Father's children have never had the opportunity to hear the message of the Restoration, it's also true that the circumstances preventing them from receiving the gospel could quickly change—just as it did in eastern Europe. Who would have dreamed a decade ago that the Iron Curtain would be gone, almost overnight? It was remarkable—even miraculous—and today our missionaries are teaching the gospel where for fifty years we were prohibited from establishing a gospel presence. So it is happening, my brothers and sisters. Christ's gospel is going to all the world."[13]

NOTES AND COMMENTARY

D&C 39:11 *fulness of my gospel.* The Book of Mormon contains the "fulness of the everlasting Gospel" (JS–H 1:34; see also D&C 20:9; 42:12). President Ezra Taft Benson wrote: "That does not mean it contains every teaching, every doctrine ever revealed. Rather, it

---

[11] São Paulo Brazil Area Conference Report, Feb.–Mar. 1975, 73.
[12] Conference Report, Oct. 1989, 44.
[13] "When Shall These Things Be?" 190.

means that in the Book of Mormon we will find the fulness of those doctrines required for our salvation."[14]

the covenant. The covenant the Lord has sent forth in our day is a renewal of the Abrahamic covenant, in which the ordinances of the priesthood are given to those who come unto the Lord. Through the priesthood and its ordinances the world is blessed by the power of the atonement of Christ. As the gathering proceeds, the descendants of Abraham, whether through blood or by adoption, are brought unto Christ and his gospel. At the same time, Abraham's descendants are instruments in bringing the gathering to pass, in accordance to the promise of God to Abraham many millennia ago. All this, Nephi explained, will "be fulfilled in the latter days" (1 Ne. 15:18).

A fuller text of God's promises to Abraham, as restored in our day, explains how Abraham and his seed would bless "all the families of the earth"—and gives the relationship of that blessing to the gathering of Israel: "I will make of thee a great nation, and I will bless thee above measure, and make thy name great among all nations, and thou shalt be a blessing unto thy seed after thee, that in their hands they shall bear this ministry and Priesthood unto all nations; and I will bless them through thy name; for as many as receive this Gospel shall be called after thy name, and shall be accounted thy seed, and shall rise up and bless thee, as their father; And I will bless them that bless thee, and curse them that curse thee; and in thee (that is, in thy Priesthood) and in thy seed (that is, thy Priesthood), for I give unto thee a promise that this right shall continue in thee, and in thy seed after thee (that is to say, the literal seed, or the seed of the body) shall all the families of the earth be blessed, even with the blessings of the Gospel, which are the blessings of salvation, even of life eternal" (Abr. 2:9–11).

As we follow Abraham, seeking to emulate his life and live according to the covenant blessings he received, we participate in the first step of the gathering: coming unto Christ and his Church. Then, filled with desire to bless others through the priesthood and the gospel, we reach out to help them be gathered as well.

---

[14] *Witness and a Warning,* 18.

recover my people. This is a scriptural expression that means "gather my people," meaning the covenant people of the Lord (see also Isa.11:11; 2 Ne. 29:1, 5; Jacob 6:2; 3 Ne. 3:10).

EPHRAIM SHALL BE GATHERED FIRST
Isaiah 49:22–23

22 Thus saith the Lord God, Behold, I will lift up mine hand to the Gentiles, and set up my standard to the people: and they shall bring thy sons in their arms, and thy daughters shall be carried upon their shoulders.

23 And kings shall be thy nursing fathers, and their queens thy nursing mothers: they shall bow down to thee with their face toward the earth, and lick up the dust of thy feet; and thou shalt know that I am the Lord: for they shall not be ashamed that wait for me.

As the Lord begins the gathering, he will follow a prophesied sequence. First, he will bring the gospel forth to the Gentiles (those who received the gospel first, of course, were Joseph Smith and those who followed him). The Gentiles then have a responsibility to take it to all the nations of the world. Finally, the testimony of Christ will go to the Jews. As Isaiah saw, through the Gentiles the Lord would "set up my standard to the people." The Gentiles would gently and lovingly receive those of Israel who would come to the gospel of Jesus Christ, treating them with great respect. It would be through the ministrations of the Gentiles that the generality of the house of Israel would come to the gospel.

The Gentiles are sometimes defined as any people who are not Jews. But the Gentiles are also the many nations that received the dispersed people of Israel. They are the nations in which the blood of Israel was freely intermingled, making those nations also of Israel. In one important sense, then, the Gentile nations are the present home to the tribes of Israel. Elder Mark E. Petersen gave this valuable explanation, after citing 1 Nephi 22:7–9 and 3 Nephi 21:2–4: "Since Israel was scattered among all nations, the gospel would have to be taken to all those nations in order to reach the house of Israel living among them. That is why we send our missionaries to all parts of the world.

"And it is made clear that the gospel was destined to come to Israel from believing Gentiles in this land to whom the gospel would be revealed in latter days, and by them to be taken abroad. This is now being done. Note the clear statement that the gospel would be given first to the Gentiles in these latter days—and by act of the Father!

"Note also that it would be the mission of these same Gentiles to become the ministers of God, seeking out the house of Israel, even 'out of the holes of the rocks,' as one prophet said, that they might believe the gospel and be gathered home. (Jeremiah 16:16.)

"And who are these modern Gentiles? *We are!*

"We are they to whom the gospel was restored, and we have the keys of gathering as brought back by Moses and committed to the Prophet Joseph Smith to be used for this very purpose. (See D&C 110.) And we are they who have been commanded to preach the gospel to all the world. (See D&C 68:8; 112:28; 133:37.)

"We are also of Israel, however—mostly of Ephraim—but we are Gentiles too, inasmuch as Ephraim was widely scattered among the Gentiles in ancient times and intermarried with them.

"Ephraim now is the first of the scattered tribes to be gathered, since Ephraim holds the birthright in Israel."[15]

As the Gentiles who first received the gospel, who were also of Ephraim, go forth to the Gentile nations to share the good news they have received, they hunt for and find those members of the house of Israel who are willing to come unto Christ and his true Church. Those who are being converted through their missionary efforts, for the most part, are descendants of Ephraim, who are also Gentiles. Thus, in one sense the Gentile nations are Israelite nations, though they know it not.

Elder Joseph Fielding Smith bore testimony of the role of Ephraim in the gathering process: "It is essential in this dispensation that Ephraim stand in his place at the head, exercising the birthright in Israel which was given to him by direct revelation. Therefore Ephraim must be gathered first to prepare the way, through the Gospel and the Priesthood, for the rest of the tribes of Israel when the time comes for them to be gathered to Zion. The great majority of

---

[15] *Great Prologue,* 5.

those who have come into the Church are Ephraimites. It is the exception to find one of any other tribe, unless it is of Manasseh. . . .

"It is Ephraim, today, who holds the Priesthood. It is with Ephraim that the Lord has made covenant and has revealed the fulness of the Everlasting Gospel. It is Ephraim who is building Temples and performing the ordinances in them for both the living and for the dead. When the 'lost tribes' come . . . , they will have to receive the crowning blessings from their brother Ephraim, the 'firstborn' in Israel."[16]

NOTES AND COMMENTARY

Isa. 49:22 *lift up mine hand.* This phrase may signify the Lord's lifting his right arm in covenant, stretching forth his hand to accomplish his work, or perhaps reaching out to invite the Gentiles to come unto him (Gen. 14:22; Deut. 32:39–40; Isa. 5:26; 13:2).

standard. A *standard* is a flag or ensign that serves as a rallying point around which people may gather. The scriptures define the *standard* as God's words (specifically, the Book of Mormon; 2 Ne. 29:2), the everlasting covenant (D&C 45:9), the great Zion of the last days (D&C 64:41–43), and the light of the righteous or the Church and its faithful members (D&C 115:3–5). Overall, the *standard* is the true gospel and church of Jesus Christ (Isa. 5:26; 11:10–12; 62:10; Zech. 9:16).

Isa. 49:22–23 *thy sons/thy daughters/kings/queens.* Nephi comments on these verses in 1 Nephi 22:6–9, explaining that the Gentiles will bless his seed both temporally (meaning with physical nourishment) and spiritually (with spiritual nourishment, the gospel). Jacob casts further light on this prophecy of Isaiah. In 2 Nephi 10:5–9 he explains that when the Jews come to believe in Christ, they will be "gathered in from their long dispersion, . . . and the nations of the Gentiles shall be great in the eyes of me, saith God, in carrying them forth to the lands of their inheritance. Yea, the kings of the Gentiles

---

[16] "Mission of Ephraim," 2–3. For a brief explanation of how Ephraim came to be called the firstborn of Jacob, even though he was a grandson and was descended from Joseph, the eleventh son, see 1 Chr. 5:1–2 and Jer. 31:9.

shall be nursing fathers unto them, and their queens shall become nursing mothers" (see also Isa. 45:14; 49:7; 60:4).

One interpretation of these words was given by Elder Spencer W. Kimball: "The brighter day has dawned. The scattering has been accomplished; the gathering is in process. May the Lord bless us all as we become nursing fathers and mothers (see Isa. 49:23 and 1 Ne. 21:23) unto our Lamanite brethren and hasten the fulfillment of the great promises made to them."[17] The kings and queens may well be the righteous men and women who have entered into the covenants of the fulness of the priesthood in the temple of God.

Isa. 49:23 *bow down/face toward the earth/lick up the dust.* In the ancient Near East, bowing and other such actions were signs of submission to a king or ruler (Gen. 42:6; 1 Sam. 24:8; Ps. 72:8–11). In times past, Israel was repeatedly conquered and forced to submit to the kings of the earth. But in the last days, kings and queens will bow in obeisance and submission to the children of Israel (2 Ne. 6:13). If the kings and queens are the righteous people of covenant, however, this phrase would likely have a different meaning, which at present remains obscure.

not be ashamed that wait for me. Those who wait for the Lord are those who trust patiently in his plan. Their faith will be vindicated; they will not be ashamed that they believed, because all God's promises are fulfilled. The psalmist said, "O my God, I trust in thee: . . . let none that wait on thee be ashamed" (Ps. 25:2–3).

THE VOICE OF WARNING PRECEDES THE VOICE OF JUDGMENTS
Doctrine and Covenants 88:81, 88–92

81 Behold, I sent you out to testify and warn the people, and it becometh every man who hath been warned to warn his neighbor. . . .

88 And after your testimony cometh wrath and indignation upon the people.

---

[17] Conference Report, Oct. 1965, 72.

89 For after your testimony cometh the testimony of earthquakes, that shall cause groanings in the midst of her, and men shall fall upon the ground and shall not be able to stand.

90 And also cometh the testimony of the voice of thunderings, and the voice of lightnings, and the voice of tempests, and the voice of the waves of the sea heaving themselves beyond their bounds.

91 And all things shall be in commotion; and surely, men's hearts shall fail them; for fear shall come upon all people.

92 And angels shall fly through the midst of heaven, crying with a loud voice, sounding the trump of God, saying: Prepare ye, prepare ye, O inhabitants of the earth; for the judgment of our God is come.

The Lord calls on his servants to carry the word of the gospel unto the world "to testify and warn the people." Further, not only are we to warn those in distant lands but everyone who hears the gospel has an obligation to tell those around him, to "warn his neighbor." This essential part of the gathering is part of the great missionary effort the Lord requires of his people in the last days. Our broad missionary endeavor began in the days of Joseph Smith, and it has continued with power and effectiveness from his day to ours, causing the Church to grow from 6 members in 1830, to 600 the following year, to 6,000 in 1835, to 60,000 in 1853, to 600,000 in 1925, to 6 million in 1986. By 1999, the Church had more than 10 million members.[18]

What is the warning? That if people don't repent, they will suffer the judgments of God. They will be subject to his deep and righteous anger. And if they escape the judgments here in mortality, they certainly will not escape the eternal consequences for their actions in the world to come. They will receive a lesser glory, with lessened opportunities, "worlds without end" (D&C 76:112).

Of course, much of the missionaries' message is a testimony of joy and rejoicing for the great gifts our Savior has given us through his love and his atonement: repentance and forgiveness, the blessing

---

[18] Statistics for years before 1999 are from *Deseret News 1993–1994 Church Almanac*, 396–99; statistics for 1999 are from "Statistical Report, 1998," *Ensign*, May 1999, 22.

of covenants with God, gifts of the Spirit, the opportunity of eternal glory, fellowship with the Saints, and much, much more.

Unfortunately, the testimony of the servants of the Lord will be rejected by many. After the world has had its opportunity to receive and embrace the word, the Lord will send his judgments upon the unrepentant—judgments of wrath and indignation, earthquakes, great storms with thunder and lightning, tempests and dangerous ocean waves (which suggests *tsunamis,* or seismic sea waves that sometimes follow earthquakes at sea). These judgments will be so pervasive that truly it will be felt that "all things shall be in commotion." "Men's hearts shall fail them" because of their fright, and "all people" will be filled with terror at what they see and hear and experience in the natural world around them.[19]

After the voice of the missionaries goes forth, and after the voice of judgments is sent, then the Lord himself "shall utter his voice out of heaven, saying: Hearken, O ye nations of the earth, and hear the words of that God who made you. O, ye nations of the earth, how often would I have gathered you together as a hen gathereth her chickens under her wings, but ye would not! How oft have I called upon you by the mouth of my servants, and by the ministering of angels, and by mine own voice, and by the voice of thunderings, and by the voice of lightnings, and by the voice of tempests, and by the voice of earthquakes, and great hailstorms, and by the voice of famines and pestilences of every kind, and by the great sound of a trump, and by the voice of judgment, and by the voice of mercy all the day long, and by the voice of glory and honor and the riches of eternal life, and would have saved you with an everlasting salvation, but ye would not! Behold, the day has come, when the cup of the wrath of mine indignation is full" (D&C 43:23–26).[20]

NOTES AND COMMENTARY

D&C 88:81 *warn his neighbor.* Warning is a key element of missionary work: the missionary warns the listener that he must repent or suffer the consequences of lost opportunities, lost blessings, and

---

[19] See the commentary on God's judgments upon Satan's followers, page 321.

[20] See also *History of the Church,* 2:309, 418–19.

eventual deep sorrow for sin. The concept of warning one's neighbor suggests the principle of member-missionary work. Not only are the full-time missionaries to warn others but each person who has received the warning is to share it with others.

D&C 88:88 *wrath and indignation.* The deep and righteous anger of God.

D&C 88:89 *testimony of earthquakes.* The prophesied earthquakes will underscore and support the judgments as pronounced by God. They will help to accomplish the judgments as well as give an object lesson that the wicked are indeed punished.

not be able to stand. The earthquakes will be so powerful that people will be unable to keep their footing on the ground.

D&C 88:91 *all things shall be in commotion.* This passage suggests that "all things" particularly refers to the elements of nature, with specific examples of earthquakes, thunderstorms, and tempests.

men's hearts shall fail them. Although some have suggested that this passage refers to an increase in heart disease among mankind, the context of this phrase implies that the hearts of men and women will fail because of their fear as they see the judgments of God. "Hearts shall fail them," then, probably means that they will lose courage (see also 1 Sam. 17:32; D&C 124:75).

D&C 88:92 *trump of God.* The trump of God is a trumpet blown by an angel, as in ancient times a herald would blow a trumpet before making an announcement or introducing the arrival of a king. In the last days, the Lord will have his angels sound a number of trumpets to herald the coming of judgments and other important events. Whether these trumpets will be heard by those on earth or whether they are literal or symbolic is not yet clear.

THE VOICE OF WARNING IS EXTENDED TO ALL PEOPLE

Doctrine and Covenants 1:4–5, 11–14

4 And the voice of warning shall be unto all people, by the mouths of my disciples, whom I have chosen in these last days.

5 And they shall go forth and none shall stay them, for I the Lord have commanded them. . . .

11 Wherefore the voice of the Lord is unto the ends of the earth, that all that will hear may hear:

12 Prepare ye, prepare ye for that which is to come, for the Lord is nigh;

13 And the anger of the Lord is kindled, and his sword is bathed in heaven, and it shall fall upon the inhabitants of the earth.

14 And the arm of the Lord shall be revealed; and the day cometh that they who will not hear the voice of the Lord, neither the voice of his servants, neither give heed to the words of the prophets and apostles, shall be cut off from among the people.

In his preface to the Doctrine and Covenants, the Lord emphasizes that his gospel shall go to all people through his servants. They shall go to the "ends of the earth" with their message, giving all the opportunity to hear the true gospel of Jesus Christ. No one will have power to stop the onward course of the gospel as it moves across the world, for the Lord has so decreed ("none shall stay them"; D&C 1:5; see also 133:37).

Latter-day prophets and apostles have acknowledged the greatness of our commission. For example, President Spencer W. Kimball said: "It seems to me that the Lord chose his words when he said 'every nation,' 'every land,' 'uttermost bounds of the earth,' 'every tongue,' 'every people,' 'every soul,' 'all the world,' 'many lands.'

"Surely there is significance in these words!"[21] "We accept the responsibility to preach the gospel to every person on earth," Elder Boyd K. Packer has said. "And if the question is asked, 'You mean you are out to convert the entire world?' the answer is, 'Yes. We will try to reach every living soul.'"[22] And Elder M. Russell Ballard declared: "At the present time, more people are born in one day than

---

[21] *Ensign*, Oct. 1974, 4–5.
[22] Conference Report, Oct. 1975, 145.

are baptized into the Church in one year. The magnitude of our missionary task can appear to be overwhelming. Yet the assignment to the members of the Church is very clear. We are to take the gospel of Jesus Christ to every human soul."[23]

Receiving or rejecting the gospel message and the voice of warning is a matter of agency—"all that will hear may hear"—but the time will come when those who refuse to hear the message will be cut off from among the people. Spiritually, those who refuse the gospel will not be counted among the Lord's people. Temporally, those who continue in sin will be cut off from mortal life by the judgments of the last days and the fire at the coming of the Lord. As the Lord put it elsewhere, "This Gospel of the Kingdom shall be preached in all the world, for a witness unto all nations, and then shall the end come, or the destruction of the wicked" (JS–M 1:31).

NOTES AND COMMENTARY

D&C 1:4 *voice of warning.* The voice of warning is to go to "all people" through the Lord's chosen ministers—including his prophets and the missionaries. The warning is that the day of the Lord is near, and all must prepare by repenting of their sins and adhering to the commandments of God.

D&C 1:5 *none shall stay them.* Though some may attempt to hinder the Lord's missionaries in their work, they will not be able to do so, for the Lord's power and blessing are with his disciples (Dan. 4:35; Morm. 8:26). Further, the Lord has commanded his disciples to go forth with the warning voice, and no one—whether on earth, in heaven, or in hell—has power to countermand that which the Lord has decreed (D&C 1:38).

D&C 1:12 *Prepare ye, prepare ye.* This command is emphasized by the repetition. We are to prepare for that which is to come: the Lord's judgments on the earth.

the Lord is nigh. The time of the Lord's second coming is near (Joel 2:1; Jacob 5:71; D&C 1:12; 29:9; 43:17; 133:17).

D&C 1:13 *his sword is bathed in heaven, and it shall fall.* The sword is symbolic of the Lord's terrible judgments; it will fall from

---

[23] Conference Report, Oct. 1984, 17.

heaven upon the inhabitants of the earth to punish them for their wickedness (Isa. 34:5).

D&C 1:14 *arm of the Lord shall be revealed.* The Lord will make his power manifest for the people of the world to see (D&C 1:14; 90:10).

cut off from among the people. Those who refuse to listen to the Lord, his prophets, or his other servants will be cut off from fellowship among the Saints. Perhaps this means they will be excommunicated, or perhaps they will be physically cut off by death, so that they no longer have opportunity to mingle with the righteous on the earth (Acts 3:22–23; D&C 50:8; 56:3).

ISRAEL SHALL BE GATHERED FROM MANY LANDS
3 Nephi 5:24–26

> *24 And as surely as the Lord liveth, will he gather in from the four quarters of the earth all the remnant of the seed of Jacob, who are scattered abroad upon all the face of the earth.*
>
> *25 And as he hath covenanted with all the house of Jacob, even so shall the covenant wherewith he hath covenanted with the house of Jacob be fulfilled in his own due time, unto the restoring all the house of Jacob unto the knowledge of the covenant that he hath covenanted with them.*
>
> *26 And then shall they know their Redeemer, who is Jesus Christ, the Son of God; and then shall they be gathered in from the four quarters of the earth unto their own lands, from whence they have been dispersed; yea, as the Lord liveth so shall it be. Amen.*

The voice of warning is to all the people on the earth. By premortal covenant, the Lord has promised that all will have the opportunity to hear and accept the gospel sometime between their birth and their resurrection.[24] But the Lord has also specifically made covenant to gather in the descendants of Jacob from the "four quarters of the earth," because they are "scattered abroad upon all the face of the

---

[24] See Ballard, *Our Search for Happiness,* 72–73; Smith, *Doctrines of Salvation,* 2:134–35.

earth." Once those who belong to the tribes of Israel (or Jacob) are found and accept the gospel, they will first be gathered to the Church through baptism, and then later they will be gathered to the lands of their inheritance through migration.[25] The gathering to lands seems to be secondary to the gathering to the Church and the gospel. The promised restoration to lands is symbolic of the greater restoration to Christ and the way he cares for his children.

The gathering of Israel from many lands will be seen as a great miracle, surpassing even the impressive events that led to the deliverance of Israel from Egypt (Ex. 7–14): "Therefore, behold, the days come, saith the Lord, that it shall no more be said, The Lord liveth, that brought up the children of Israel out of the land of Egypt; but, The Lord liveth, that brought up the children of Israel from the land of the north, and from all the lands whither he had driven them: and I will bring them again into their land that I gave unto their fathers" (Jer. 16:14–15).

Many prophets have added their testimony that the Lord would gather Israel from their scattered condition throughout the world. In fact, this miracle of gathering Israel has been prophesied more frequently than most other latter-day events. The combined testimonies of these prophets is impressive. What follows is but a sampling:

Moses: "The Lord thy God will turn thy captivity, and have compassion upon thee, and will return and gather thee from all the nations, whither the Lord thy God hath scattered thee" (Deut. 30:3).

David: "And [the Lord] gathered them out of the lands, from the east, and from the west, from the north, and from the south" (Ps. 107:3).

Isaiah: "And it shall come to pass in that day, that the Lord shall set his hand again the second time to recover the remnant of his people, which shall be left, from Assyria, and from Egypt, and from Pathros, and from Cush, and from Elam, and from Shinar, and from Hamath, and from the islands of the sea" (Isa. 11:11).

Jeremiah: "And I will be found of you, saith the Lord: and I will turn away your captivity, and I will gather you from all the nations,

---

[25] See the commentary on the gathering of Israel through missionary work, page 59, and the commentary on Israel being gathered to their lands of inheritance, page 113.

and from all the places whither I have driven you, saith the Lord; and I will bring you again into the place whence I caused you to be carried away captive" (Jer. 29:14; see also 32:37).

Ezekiel: "Therefore say, Thus saith the Lord God; I will even gather you from the people, and assemble you out of the countries where ye have been scattered, and I will give you the land of Israel. . . . For I will take you from among the heathen, and gather you out of all countries, and will bring you into your own land" (Ezek. 11:17; 36:24).

Nephi: "Then will he remember the isles of the sea; yea, and all the people who are of the house of Israel, will I gather in, saith the Lord, according to the words of the prophet Zenos, from the four quarters of the earth" (1 Ne. 19:16).

Jacob: "And it shall come to pass that they shall be gathered in from their long dispersion, from the isles of the sea, and from the four parts of the earth; and the nations of the Gentiles shall be great in the eyes of me, saith God, in carrying them forth to the lands of their inheritance" (2 Ne. 10:8).

To these prophecies must be added that of the resurrected Lord himself, as he spoke to the Nephites at the temple: "The remnants, which shall be scattered abroad upon the face of the earth, [shall] be gathered in from the east and from the west, and from the south and from the north; and they shall be brought to the knowledge of the Lord their God, who hath redeemed them" (3 Ne. 20:13).

NOTES AND COMMENTARY

3 Ne. 5:24 *as surely as the Lord liveth.* By this statement of comparison and testimony, the Lord indicates how certain the gathering is—as certain as the truth of his existence. He repeats this expression at both the beginning and ending of this passage.

the four quarters of the earth. This common scriptural expression (1 Ne. 19:16; 3 Ne. 16:5; D&C 33:6; Moses 7:62) simply means "all parts of the earth." This phrase is repeated in verse 26.

remnant of the seed of Jacob. Jacob is another name for Israel, the son of Isaac and grandson of Abraham. The seed of Jacob are his descendants. The remnant of that seed are those who remain unto our day. In the last days, the Lord will gather that remnant from all parts of the earth. Captain Moroni said, "Let us remember the words of Jacob, before his death, for behold, he saw that a part of the remnant of the coat of Joseph was preserved and had not decayed. And he said—Even as this remnant of garment of my son hath been preserved, so shall a remnant of the seed of my son be preserved by the hand of God, and be taken unto himself, while the remainder of the seed of Joseph shall perish, even as the remnant of his garment" (Alma 46:24). In fulfillment of this prophecy, the Lord will gather his people from throughout the world.

3 Ne. 5:25 *he hath covenanted with all the house of Jacob.* The Lord has covenanted to remember the descendants of Jacob, bring them to the blessings of the gospel (if they will), renew in them the Abrahamic covenant, and restore them to their lands of promise. "The testimony of these verses [3 Ne. 5:23–25] is that the tribe of Joseph, which along with all the tribes of Jacob has been scattered among all people throughout the earth, will in the last days be restored to that covenant relationship known to their ancient fathers. That is, they shall come to 'know their Redeemer, who is Jesus Christ, the Son of God.'"[26] As we learn from this verse, not only will Jacob be restored to the covenant but he will also be restored to a knowledge of the covenant.

in his own due time. The Lord will bring Israel back from their long dispersal according to his own timetable, not that of anyone else.

THE LORD WILL GATHER HIS ELECT
Doctrine and Covenants 33:6

> 6 *And even so will I gather mine elect from the four quarters of the earth, even as many as will believe in me, and hearken unto my voice.*

The Lord will remember all of Israel, according to his promises, but he will specifically gather those who are called his "elect." He defines the elect as those who "believe in me, and hearken unto my voice." Elsewhere the Lord says to the elders of his Church, "Ye are called to bring to pass the gathering of mine elect; for mine elect hear

---

[26] McConkie, Millet, and Top, *Doctrinal Commentary on the Book of Mormon,* 4:25.

my voice and harden not their hearts" (D&C 29:7). All will hear the voice of the missionaries (either here or in the spirit world), but relatively few will accept their message and receive the ordinance of baptism (Matt. 7:13–14; D&C 132:22). Of those, fewer still will be valiant, fitting the definitions of the elect: first believing in Christ, then hearkening to his voice, and then continuing faithful without hardening their hearts (D&C 95:5; 121:34–40).[27]

Jesus' true disciples are those who recognize his voice and follow him: "My sheep hear my voice, and I know them, and they follow me" (John 10:27). These are the elect; and these are they who will be gathered to the Church. "And now I show unto you a parable. Behold, wheresoever the carcass is, there will the eagles be gathered together; so likewise shall mine elect be gathered from the four quarters of the earth" (JS–M 1:27). Just as eagles are drawn to the life-giving meat (the carcass), and just as their hunger is not satisfied until they come to that meat, so will the Lord's elect in all parts of the world find Christ, come unto his Church, and be satisfied.

NOTES AND COMMENTARY

D&C 33:6 *gather mine elect.* As with many other aspects of the gathering, the Lord's elect are gathered through the efforts of the missionaries of The Church of Jesus Christ of Latter-day Saints.

four quarters of the earth. See the discussion of this phrase on page 73.

believe in me. Some teach that all one must do to demonstrate belief in Christ is to confess him as their Savior. True belief, however, brings submission and obedience to that which Jesus Christ requires of us.

hearken unto my voice. To hearken is to listen and obey. How does the voice of the Lord come to us? We can hear his voice as we read scriptures, listen to living prophets, hear inspired talks and lessons, and receive inspired counsel given in many settings. But the most important ingredient in all these sources of the word of God is the Holy Ghost. When he is present with us, whatever the setting, we

---

[27] For further reference on the concept that "few" are chosen, see Smith, *History of the Church,* 6:185; McConkie, *Mortal Messiah,* 3:310.

will hear the voice of the Savior. That voice will generally come as the still small voice of the Spirit, giving us feelings, impressions, and understandings.

THE GATHERING OF ISRAEL IS LIKE A HARVEST OF WHEAT

Doctrine and Covenants 101:64–67

> *64 That the work of the gathering together of my saints may continue, that I may build them up unto my name upon holy places; for the time of harvest is come, and my word must needs be fulfilled.*
>
> *65 Therefore, I must gather together my people, according to the parable of the wheat and the tares, that the wheat may be secured in the garners to possess eternal life, and be crowned with celestial glory, when I shall come in the kingdom of my Father to reward every man according as his work shall be;*
>
> *66 While the tares shall be bound in bundles, and their bands made strong, that they may be burned with unquenchable fire.*
>
> *67 Therefore, a commandment I give unto all the churches, that they shall continue to gather together unto the places which I have appointed.*

Here the Lord compares the gathering of Israel to the process of harvesting wheat. First, a farmer scatters the seed across the field. Then, when the wheat has grown to maturity, he gathers the grain and puts it into a safe place to keep until his time of need. He also gathers the tares—essentially weeds that look like wheat—binds them into bundles, and burns them.

In Doctrine and Covenants 86 the Lord explains the symbolism of the wheat and the tares (referring to the parable of the wheat and the tares found in Matthew 13:24–30). "The field was the world," he said, "and the apostles were the sowers of the seed." After the apostles died, Satan sowed the tares, which began to "choke the wheat and drive the church into the wilderness." In the last days, the angels are "ready and waiting to be sent forth to reap down the fields." But the Lord tells them to wait until the wheat is more fully matured. "Then ye shall first gather out the wheat from among the tares, and after the gathering of the wheat, behold and lo, the tares are bound in bundles, and the field remaineth to be burned" (D&C 86:1–7).

The imagery of the gathering as a wheat harvest is used often in scripture, with the wheat representing the souls of men and women. For example, in speaking to potential missionaries, the Lord says, "Behold the field is white already to harvest; and lo, he that thrusteth in his sickle with his might, the same layeth up in store that he perisheth not, but bringeth salvation to his soul" (D&C 4:4; see also 3 Ne. 20:18; D&C 33:2–11).

NOTES AND COMMENTARY

D&C 101:64 *build them up unto my name.* Other scriptures speak of building "an house unto the name of the Lord" (1 Kgs. 5:3; D&C 124:22) and building "cities unto my name" (D&C 125:2–3). When we build up a temple or a city or a people unto the name of God, we do it according to his will, for his purposes, and for his glory.

upon holy places. One of the Lord's names is "the Holy One of Israel" (Isa. 47:4; 54:5; 2 Ne. 9:41), and the place where he dwells is "holy" (Isa. 57:15; see also Moses 6:57). Thus we see that holiness is one of the attributes of God. When we gather unto holy places, we come to places that are dedicated to God and that are blessed by the presence of God (Ex. 3:5). In the coming days of trial, holy places can be a safe haven for the Saints (D&C 45:32). President Ezra Taft Benson wrote, "Holy men and women stand in holy places, and these holy places consist of our temples, our chapels, our homes, and the stakes of Zion."[28]

for the time of harvest is come. A farmer harvests his crop when it is sufficiently ripe and ready to be eaten or stored. Likewise, the Lord "harvests" his people when the world is ripe in sin and the Zion of his Saints is fully ripe in righteousness.

D&C 101:65 *according to the parable of the wheat and the tares.* Jesus taught his disciples the parable of the wheat and the tares, in which a man sowed good seed in his field, but an enemy sowed tares in the same field. In time, the man harvested both the wheat and the

---

[28] *Come unto Christ,* 115; see also Lee, *Stand Ye in Holy Places,* 22.

tares. He stored the wheat in his barn, but he bound the tares in bundles to be burned. This parable is given and explained in Matthew 13:24–30, 36–43, and Doctrine and Covenants 86:1–7.

secured in the garners. A garner is a storehouse or granary. The righteous (the wheat) will be securely gathered into the safety provided by God in his love and his power, where they will be crowned with eternal life. The garner into which the Lord brings us may be the temple, the ultimate gathering place of the Saints.

D&C 101:66 *the tares shall be bound in bundles, and their bands made strong.* Just as the righteous will be securely brought into the Lord's storehouse, so will the wicked be securely bound by the bands of justice, prepared to be punished for their sins.

burned with unquenchable fire. This passage seems to refer to the fervent, hot fire with which the Lord will burn the wicked when he comes.[29]

THE LORD WILL GATHER HIS PEOPLE AS A SHEPHERD DOES HIS FLOCK
Ezekiel 34:11–16

11 For thus saith the Lord God; Behold, I, even I, will both search my sheep, and seek them out.

12 As a shepherd seeketh out his flock in the day that he is among his sheep that are scattered; so will I seek out my sheep, and will deliver them out of all places where they have been scattered in the cloudy and dark day.

13 And I will bring them out from the people, and gather them from the countries, and will bring them to their own land, and feed them upon the mountains of Israel by the rivers, and in all the inhabited places of the country.

14 I will feed them in a good pasture, and upon the high mountains of Israel shall their fold be: there shall they lie in a good fold, and in a fat pasture shall they feed upon the mountains of Israel.

---

[29] See the commentary on Jesus' second coming in power and glory, page 381.

15 I will feed my flock, and I will cause them to lie down, saith the Lord God.

16 I will seek that which was lost, and bring again that which was driven away, and will bind up that which was broken, and will strengthen that which was sick: but I will destroy the fat and the strong; I will feed them with judgment.

The Lord is the Good Shepherd, who cares for his sheep. As he said during his mortal ministry, "What man of you having a hundred sheep, if he lose one of them, doth not leave the ninety and nine, and go into the wilderness after that which is lost, until he find it? And when he hath found it, he layeth it on his shoulders, rejoicing. And when he cometh home, he calleth together his friends and neighbors, and saith unto them, Rejoice with me; for I found my sheep which was lost" (JST Luke 15:4–6; KJV Luke 15:5).

The gathering is like this shepherd, who leaves safely in the fold those sheep that have already been found and then goes forth to find those that are lost. The language of this passage tells us of the commitment and loving care the Lord has for his sheep. He will *search* for them and *seek them out;* he will *seek* them and *deliver them;* he will *bring them out from the people* and will *gather them* and will *bring them to their own land* and will *feed them.* Their pasture will be *good;* their fold will be *good;* they will *lie down* in safety (see also Jer. 23:3; 31:10). Through Nephi we have this wonderful promise: "He gathereth his children from the four quarters of the earth; and he numbereth his sheep, and they know him; and there shall be one fold and one shepherd; and he shall feed his sheep, and in him they shall find pasture" (1 Ne. 22:25).

NOTES AND COMMENTARY

Ezek. 34:12 *in the cloudy and dark day.* This phrase seems to refer to days of trouble and affliction (see also D&C 109:61).

Ezek. 34:13 *I will bring them out from the people.* The Lord will find his people wherever they have been scattered and will separate them from the people of the world.

Ezek. 34:13–15 *feed them upon the mountains/in a good pasture/in a good fold/in a fat pasture/cause them to lie down.* These expressions combine to reinforce the concept that we are sheep and that the Lord is our Shepherd: he will care for us as a good shepherd cares for his flock. These descriptions of the Lord as the Shepherd who gathers his sheep are reminiscent of the Lord's care of his people as described in the Twenty-third Psalm.

Ezek. 34:16 *I will seek that which was lost/that which was driven away.* As a good shepherd would do, the Lord as Shepherd will find his lost sheep. Israel is not lost to the Lord: he knows where they have been taken, but many have been lost from the gospel. This prophecy applies to the peoples of Israel who have been lost among the nations of the world but also to those who are lost from activity in the Church.

bind up that which was broken/strengthen that which was sick. The Lord not only will find his sheep but will heal them (see also 3 Ne. 9:13). The most significant injury the repentant have received is a broken heart, which the Lord stands ready to bind up in the bandages of his atonement and thereby bring healing (D&C 138:42).

destroy the fat and the strong. This passage likely refers to the wicked rich and the proud, who will be destroyed by the Lord at his coming (Mal. 4:1).

I will feed them with judgment. The New International Version of the Bible renders this phrase as "I will shepherd the flock with justice"—meaning, he will bring judgment upon the wicked, but will bless the repentant among his people according to his mercies.

THE LORD WILL GATHER HIS PEOPLE AS A HEN GATHERS HER CHICKENS
Doctrine and Covenants 29:1–2

1 Listen to the voice of Jesus Christ, your Redeemer . . .

2 Who will gather his people even as a hen gathereth her chickens under her wings, even as many as will hearken to my voice and humble themselves before me, and call upon me in mighty prayer.

The symbol of a hen and her chicks suggests tenderness, safety, and watchful care. As a hen is attentive to all her little ones, drawing them safely to her, so will the Lord gather his people to him. His people are those who hearken, who hear and obey, who are humble before the Lord, and who seek his blessings with all their hearts. As we do these things, we will be gathered to the true Church, to the latter-day Zion, and to the bosom of the Lord (see also D&C 10:65; 43:24).

In the meridian day, after the great destructions that followed the crucifixion, the Lord cried out to the Nephites and Lamanites: "O ye people of these great cities which have fallen, who are descendants of Jacob, yea, who are of the house of Israel, how oft have I gathered you as a hen gathereth her chickens under her wings, and have nourished you. And again, how oft would I have gathered you as a hen gathereth her chickens under her wings, yea, O ye people of the house of Israel, who have fallen; yea, O ye people of the house of Israel, ye that dwell at Jerusalem, as ye that have fallen; yea, how oft would I have gathered you as a hen gathereth her chickens, and ye would not. O ye house of Israel whom I have spared, how oft will I gather you as a hen gathereth her chickens under her wings, if ye will repent and return unto me with full purpose of heart" (3 Ne. 10:4–6).

NOTES AND COMMENTARY

D&C 29:2 *as a hen gathereth her chickens.* This figure of speech appears often in the scriptures, suggesting the Lord's tenderness and continuing, watchful love for his children (Matt. 23:37; D&C 10:65; 43:24).

under her wings. This image describes a place of safety and peace (Ps. 17:8). It is a place of nourishment (3 Ne. 10:4), a place where we can feel the loving kindness of the Lord (Ps. 36:7). It is a place of intimacy, where one is brought close to the Lord's heart (Ps. 17:8; 91:4).

hearken to my voice and humble themselves. This passage defines the elect, the souls who will be gathered to the bosom of Christ. We see essentially the same concept a few verses later: "Mine elect hear my voice and harden not their hearts" (D&C 29:7).

mighty prayer. One of the best examples of mighty prayer in the scriptures is found in the story of Enos: "My soul hungered; and I kneeled down before my Maker, and I cried unto him in mighty prayer and supplication for mine own soul; and all the day long did I cry unto him; yea, and when the night came I did still raise my voice high that it reached the heavens" (Enos 1:4; see also 2 Ne. 4:24; Alma 6:6; 8:10; 3 Ne. 27:1; Moro. 2:2; D&C 5:24). Mighty prayer seems to involve deep faith and a whole-souled, true-hearted pleading before God.

Those who call upon the Lord in this kind of prayer will be gathered to his bosom—under his wings.

THE GATHERING OF LEHI'S DESCENDANTS IS A TYPE OF THE GATHERING OF ISRAEL
1 Nephi 15:12–18

12 Behold, I say unto you, that the house of Israel was compared unto an olive-tree, by the Spirit of the Lord which was in our father; and behold are we not broken off from the house of Israel, and are we not a branch of the house of Israel?

13 And now, the thing which our father meaneth concerning the grafting in of the natural branches through the fulness of the Gentiles, is, that in the latter days, when our seed shall have dwindled in unbelief, yea, for the space of many years, and many generations after the Messiah shall be manifested in body unto the children of men, then shall the fulness of the gospel of the Messiah come unto the Gentiles, and from the Gentiles unto the remnant of our seed—

14 And at that day shall the remnant of our seed know that they are of the house of Israel, and that they are the covenant people of the Lord; and then shall they know and come to the knowledge of their forefathers, and also to the knowledge of the gospel of their Redeemer, which was ministered unto their fathers by him; wherefore, they shall come to the knowledge of their Redeemer and the very points of his doctrine, that they may know how to come unto him and be saved.

15 And then at that day will they not rejoice and give praise unto their everlasting God, their rock and their salvation? Yea, at that day, will they not receive the strength and nourishment from the true vine? Yea, will they not come unto the true fold of God?

16 Behold, I say unto you, Yea; they shall be remembered again among the house of Israel; they shall be grafted in, being a natural branch of the olive-tree, into the true olive-tree.

17 And this is what our father meaneth; and he meaneth that it will not come to pass until after they are scattered by the Gentiles; and he meaneth that it shall come by way of the Gentiles, that the Lord may show his power unto the Gentiles, for the very cause that he shall be rejected of the Jews, or of the house of Israel.

18 Wherefore, our father hath not spoken of our seed alone, but also of all the house of Israel, pointing to the covenant which should be fulfilled in the latter days; which covenant the Lord made to our father Abraham, saying: In thy seed shall all the kindreds of the earth be blessed.

This scripture teaches a number of truths about the gathering of Israel:

As we learn in verse 18, the prophecies about the descendants of Lehi apply as well to "all the house of Israel." These promises to the descendants of Lehi and to the house of Israel both fulfill the "covenant the Lord made to our father Abraham."

Lehi compares the house of Israel to an olive tree. Over time, Israel "shall have dwindled in unbelief" for "many years." In the "latter days," which will occur "many generations" after the mortal ministry of Christ, the fulness of the gospel will be given to the Gentiles, who in turn will give it to the house of Israel.

These events will occur after Israel has been "scattered by the Gentiles."

"At that day" the descendants of Lehi will "know that they are of the house of Israel, and that they are the covenant people of the Lord." They will come to a knowledge of Jesus Christ and his gospel, and will come unto him and "receive the strength and nourishment from the true vine." Again, the Lehites are a type of all Israel in this passage.

Because of apostasy, Israel has been cut off from the tree that represented them. But when they repent and return to Christ, they will be restored to the tree, as a branch is reunited with its tree by the grafting process.

This prophecy tells us the Gentiles will be divine instruments in both the scattering and gathering of Israel. It tells us that the gathering by conversion will occur in the latter days, when the fulness of the gospel has been placed in the hands of the Gentiles. It tells us that even though apostasy has cut Israel off, faith and repentance will restore them to their place.

NOTES AND COMMENTARY

1 Ne. 15:12 *the house of Israel was compared unto an olive-tree.* See Jacob 5.

1 Ne. 15:13 *grafting in of the natural branches.* The natural branches of Israel have been cut off and planted in various parts of the world. In time, they will be brought back, or gathered in, to the "true olive-tree" (v. 16), which seems to be a symbol for Christ himself.[30]

fulness of the Gentiles. This appears to mean that the Gentiles receive the fulness of the gospel; it should not be confused with the "times of the Gentiles [being] fulfilled" (Luke 21:24; D&C 45:25, 28, 30).[31] Elsewhere Nephi taught as he did here: "After the Gentiles had received the fulness of the Gospel, the natural branches of the olive-tree, or the remnants of the house of Israel, should be grafted in, or come to the knowledge of the true Messiah, their Lord and their Redeemer" (1 Ne. 10:14).

from the Gentiles unto the remnant of our seed. The Gentiles will receive the restored gospel first; they then will take it to the surviving descendants of Lehi, the Lamanites (as well as the Nephites who had intermingled with them).

1 Ne. 15:14 *they are of the house of Israel/the covenant people of the Lord.* Through centuries of apostasy, the descendants of Lehi lost

---

[30] See Thomas, "Jacob's Allegory," 13.
[31] See the commentary on the times of the Gentiles, page 99.

the understanding that they are members of the house of Israel, descendants of Abraham of old, and heirs of Abraham's covenant. When the gospel is taken to them, they are renewed in their understanding of who they are, of their heritage and their destiny.

they may know how to come unto him and be saved. We do not come to Christ and receive the blessings of his atonement merely by knowing of him and having a desire to be saved. There is a proper process that must be followed, involving priesthood authority, ordinances, covenants, service in the Lord's kingdom, and a change of one's heart and nature. Nephi prophesies that the descendants of Lehi will come to this saving knowledge when the Gentiles bring it to them "in the latter days" (v. 13).

1 Ne. 15:15 *will they not rejoice and give praise?* This response is typical among those who truly come to a knowledge of Jesus Christ, their redeemer, and his true gospel on the earth (Mosiah 4:3; 5:4). The descendants of Lehi will respond in this way when they learn of Christ and learn "how to come unto him and be saved."

the strength and nourishment from the true vine. Spiritual strength and nourishment come from Jesus Christ, who is the true vine (John 15:1). The descendants of Lehi will receive this spiritual strength and nourishment when they are gathered.

come unto the true fold of God. The true fold is The Church of Jesus Christ of Latter-day Saints, which keeps us safely in Christ (John 10:7–16; Alma 5:38–39, 60). Nephi prophesies that in the latter days the descendants of Lehi will come to the true vine and the true fold of God.

1 Ne. 15:16 *they shall be grafted in, being a natural branch.* The descendants of Lehi are a natural branch of the true olive tree, meaning they are lineal descendants of Abraham, heirs according to the flesh. But through the wickedness of the people, they lost their way and became separated from the rest of the house of Israel. By returning to the fold through faith and repentance, they are brought back to the tree and are grafted in by participating in ordinances and receiving covenants.

1 Ne. 15:18 *the covenant which should be fulfilled in the latter days.* This is the same covenant the Lord made with Abraham, that

"in thy seed shall all the kindreds of the earth be blessed." The blessing will come as the gospel, with its covenants and power, goes forth
from Abraham's descendants to the entire world.

THE LAMANITES SHALL BLOSSOM AS THE ROSE
Doctrine and Covenants 49:24

*24 But before the great day of the Lord shall come, Jacob
shall flourish in the wilderness, and the Lamanites shall blossom as the rose.*

Nephi prophesied that in the last days the Lamanites would
accept the gospel and become a "pure and a delightsome people"
(2 Ne. 30:6), perhaps meaning that through the power of the Atonement they would be changed in their very natures (Mosiah 3:19). In
the Doctrine and Covenants we are told that the Lamanites will
"come to the knowledge of their fathers, and that they might know the
promises of the Lord, and that they may believe the gospel and rely
upon the merits of Jesus Christ, and be glorified through faith in his
name, and that through their repentance they might be saved" (D&C
3:20).

These prophecies seem to combine in the Lord's statement that
the Lamanites would "blossom as the rose," that they will be converted to the gospel, receive the blessings of the Atonement, and
thereby become "pure" and "delightsome" before the Lord. These
things must occur before the Lord comes. An eye to the incredible
missionary success in Mexico and Central and South America suggests that this prophecy is even now being fulfilled.

Elder Marion G. Romney offered an enlightening commentary:
"It is concerning the covenants the Lord made with their fathers
which run in favor of the Lamanites and culminate in their blossom-
ing as the rose that I wish to speak. . . .

"Other covenants which the Lord made with their fathers were to
the effect that the remnant would accept the gospel, regain their inheritance and former blessings and take part in the latter-day redemption
of Zion. . . .

" . . . The Lord is pouring out his spirit upon the Lamanites.
They are accepting the record of their fathers and are coming to a

knowledge of the 'things' referred to by Jesus. . . . And they will continue to accept it in ever-increasing numbers. As they receive and live it, they are certain to regain their favored status in the house of Israel and participate in the redemption of Zion and the building of the New Jerusalem here in America. Jacob, even now, flourishes in the wilderness, and shortly the 'Lamanites shall blossom as the rose,' heralding 'the great day of the Lord.'"[32]

NOTES AND COMMENTARY

D&C 49:24 *the great day of the Lord.* This expression refers to the day of the Lord's second coming (D&C 128:24; 133:10).

Jacob shall flourish in the wilderness. This statement is parallel to "the Lamanites shall blossom as the rose" (D&C 49:24). Just as the Lamanites will blossom spiritually, so will Jacob flourish spiritually. *Jacob* refers to the descendants of Jacob of old, or Israel. *To flourish* is to thrive, to prosper. The wilderness may be the actual wilderness, or desert, of Israel or Utah or Mexico; more important, the thriving will be in the spiritual wilderness of the world, where the people of Jacob will return to the covenant once made with their father Abraham (see also Ps. 72:7; D&C 35:24).

THE BOOK OF MORMON IS A SIGN OF THE PROMISED BLESSINGS
3 Nephi 21:1–7

> *1 And verily I say unto you, I give unto you a sign, that ye may know the time when these things shall be about to take place—that I shall gather in, from their long dispersion, my people, O house of Israel, and shall establish again among them my Zion;*

> *2 And behold, this is the thing which I will give unto you for a sign—for verily I say unto you that when these things which I declare unto you, and which I shall declare unto you hereafter of myself, and by the power of the Holy Ghost which shall be given unto you of the Father, shall be made known*

---

[32] Conference Report, Apr. 1963, 75–78.

unto the Gentiles that they may know concerning this people who are a remnant of the house of Jacob, and concerning this my people who shall be scattered by them;

3 Verily, verily, I say unto you, when these things shall be made known unto them of the Father, and shall come forth of the Father, from them unto you;

4 For it is wisdom in the Father that they should be established in this land, and be set up as a free people by the power of the Father, that these things might come forth from them unto a remnant of your seed, that the covenant of the Father may be fulfilled which he hath covenanted with his people, O house of Israel;

5 Therefore, when these works and the works which shall be wrought among you hereafter shall come forth from the Gentiles, unto your seed which shall dwindle in unbelief because of iniquity;

6 For thus it behooveth the Father that it should come forth from the Gentiles, that he may show forth his power unto the Gentiles, for this cause that the Gentiles, if they will not harden their hearts, that they may repent and come unto me and be baptized in my name and know of the true points of my doctrine, that they may be numbered among my people, O house of Israel;

7 And when these things come to pass that thy seed shall begin to know these things—it shall be a sign unto them, that they may know that the work of the Father hath already commenced unto the fulfilling of the covenant which he hath made unto the people who are of the house of Israel.

The coming forth of the Book of Mormon is a sign the Lord has given us to show that the prophecies of the gathering are in the process of being fulfilled. Specifically, this passage tells us that the knowledge of the Lord's visit to the descendants of Lehi will come forth to the Gentiles, and at the same time the Gentiles will come to know "concerning this people" (v. 2), meaning the descendants of Lehi. In turn, Lehi's descendants themselves will receive the Book of

Mormon from the Gentiles (vv. 3, 5). This blessing will be given to the people of Lehi to fulfill the covenant the Lord has made with them (v. 4). Therefore, when the descendants of Lehi begin to know about the Book of Mormon and the true gospel, they can receive it as a sign that the Lord has already begun to fulfill his covenant with Israel that he would remember them, that he would gather them, and that he would send his true gospel unto them (v. 7).

Not only is the Book of Mormon a sign that the events preliminary to the gathering have "already commenced" but it is also an essential instrument of the gathering. President Ezra Taft Benson asked, "What is the instrument that God has designed for this gathering?" and then gave this answer: "It is the same instrument that is designed to convince the world that Jesus is the Christ, that Joseph Smith is His prophet, and that The Church of Jesus Christ of Latter-day Saints is true. It is that scripture which is the keystone of our religion.

"It is that most correct book which, if men will abide by its precepts, will get them closer to God than any other book. It is the Book of Mormon."[33]

THE CALLING OF THE 144,000
Revelation 14:1–5

1 And I looked, and, lo, a Lamb stood on the mount Sion, and with him an hundred forty and four thousand, having his Father's name written in their foreheads.

2 And I heard a voice from heaven, as the voice of many waters, and as the voice of a great thunder: and I heard the voice of harpers harping with their harps:

3 And they sung as it were a new song before the throne, and before the four beasts, and the elders: and no man could learn that song but the hundred and forty and four thousand, which were redeemed from the earth.

4 These are they which were not defiled with women; for they are virgins. These are they which follow the Lamb whithersoever

---

[33] Conference Report, Apr. 1987, 107–8.

he goeth. These were redeemed from among men, being the first-fruits unto God and to the Lamb.

5 And in their mouth was found no guile: for they are without fault before the throne of God.

Concerning this scripture, Joseph Smith wrote: "Q. What are we to understand by sealing the one hundred and forty-four thousand, out of all the tribes of Israel—twelve thousand out of every tribe?

"A. We are to understand that those who are sealed are high priests, ordained unto the holy order of God, to administer the ever-lasting gospel; for they are they who are ordained out of every nation, kindred, tongue, and people, by the angels to whom is given power over the nations of the earth, to bring as many as will come to the church of the Firstborn" (D&C 77:11). The purpose and mission of the 144,000, then, is focused on the gathering: they are called "to administer the everlasting gospel," and their specific assignment is "to bring as many as will come to the church of the Firstborn." They are missionaries and ministers of the gospel of Jesus Christ.

Joseph Smith taught that the sealing mentioned here "signifies sealing the blessing upon their heads, meaning the everlasting cove-nant, thereby making their calling and election sure."[34] God figura-tively marks and seals the righteous with his seal, making them his and placing them under his protection.

In the last days, those who possess God's seal on their foreheads will be protected from at least some of the judgments that come upon the earth (Rev. 7:1–3). The Prophet explained: "Having this promise [of one's calling and election made sure] sealed unto them, it was an anchor to the soul, sure and steadfast. Though the thunders might roll and lightnings flash, and earthquakes bellow, and war gather thick around, yet this hope and knowledge would support the soul in every hour of trial, trouble and tribulation."[35]

The calling of the 144,000, which is noted in Revelation 7:4–8, will occur during our dispensation. We read in Doctrine and Covenants 77:

---

[34] *Teachings of the Prophet Joseph Smith,* 321.
[35] *Teachings of the Prophet Joseph Smith,* 298.

"Q. What time are the things spoken of in this chapter [Revelation 7] to be accomplished?

"A. They are to be accomplished in the sixth thousand years, or the opening of the sixth seal" (v. 10). On 4 February 1844, Joseph Smith commented regarding the 144,000: "I attended prayer-meeting with the quorum in the assembly room, and made some remarks respecting the hundred and forty-four thousand mentioned by John the Revelator, showing that the selection of persons to form that number had already commenced."[36] He explained: "There will be 144,000 saviors on Mount Zion, and with them an innumerable host that no man can number. Oh! I beseech you to go forward, go forward and make your calling and your election sure."[37] Some commentators believe that the number 144,000 is not to be taken literally but that it signifies all the redeemed of the Lord.[38]

NOTES AND COMMENTARY

Rev. 14:1 *a Lamb.* The Lamb is Jesus Christ (Rev. 5:5–6).

mount Sion. This place appears to be the Mount Zion called New Jerusalem (D&C 84:2; 133:18, 56), which will be centered in Jackson County, Missouri. Mount Zion also sometimes refers to the temple;[39] thus, the Lord likely is standing on the temple mount or in the temple itself.

having his Father's name written in their foreheads. In Revelation 13:16–17, we see that the people of the world had the name of the beast written on their foreheads. Here the righteous have the Father's name written on their foreheads. We are marked by the name of him to whom we give our true loyalty. The Father's name is written on the righteous in a figurative rather than a literal way.

There is another way in which we may receive the name of the Father and the Son in our foreheads. A name stands for the person it belongs to. When Alma asked, "Can ye look up to God at that day [the day of judgment] . . . having the image of God engraven upon

---

[36] *History of the Church,* 6:196.

[37] *Teachings of the Prophet Joseph Smith,* 366.

[38] Draper, *Opening the Seven Seals,* 83; Metzger, *Breaking the Code,* 61.

[39] D&C 84:32; *Anchor Bible Dictionary,* 6:1096.

your countenances?" (Alma 5:19), he may have been referring to the same idea John is speaking of here.

Rev. 14:2 *a voice from heaven, as the voice of many waters, and . . . great thunder.* The voice may be that of the Lord (Rev. 1:15; D&C 110:3) or of the multitude of angels in heaven (Rev. 19:6). It is likely to be the latter, for the angels join in the song in the next verse. The sound is so loud it is like the roar of the ocean or of a rushing river; it is like the clapping of mighty thunder (see also Ezek. 1:24; 43:2).

the voice of harpers harping with their harps. John also hears the sound of harps accompanying the multitude in the song. Harps appear to be the musical instrument most often used by those in God's heavenly kingdom (see also Rev. 5:8; 15:2). The harps symbolize the praise and joy in the hearts of those in this scene.

Rev. 14:3 *they sung as it were a new song.* The harpers are singing a song before the throne of God. The song and its setting are likely those described in Doctrine and Covenants 84:96–102.

before the throne, and before the four beasts, and the elders. John reminds us that he is seeing a vision of the heavenly temple with God's throne (Rev. 4:2), before which are twenty-four exalted elders and four beasts (Rev. 4:4, 6–11). The singers proclaim their song in the heavenly temple.

no man could learn that song but the hundred and forty and four thousand. The song is sung by heavenly beings before the throne of God. But there are also some on earth who can learn the song: the 144,000 who stand on Mount Zion with Christ. Why are these the only ones who can learn the song? Perhaps it can be known only by revelation. Or perhaps such knowledge requires a certain relationship with God and his Spirit.

Rev. 14:4 *they are virgins.* The descriptions in Revelation 14:4–5 may apply to all who are exalted, although in this case they refer particularly to the 144,000. They are virgins in having refrained from any unlawful sexual intercourse, and they are also virgins in having remained true to Christ as their Bridegroom (Rev. 19:7; 21:9; see also Jer. 2:1–4)—in other words, having refrained from spiritual adultery (Ezek. 16; Hosea 1–3). The Lord has often referred to his true people as a virgin (2 Kgs. 19:21; Jer. 18:13; Lam. 2:13; Amos 5:2;

2 Cor. 11:2). The virgins in John's revelation are contrasted with the wicked who worship the beast in Revelation 13 and who join in consort with the "mother of harlots" that is Babylon (Rev. 17:5).

follow the Lamb. Those who are chosen of Christ are those who follow him in all circumstances. They have the attitude expressed in Luke, "Lord, I will follow thee whithersoever thou goest" (Luke 9:57).

redeemed. Christ, the Redeemer, has paid the price for the sins of the 144,000: they are redeemed from the demands of justice and the bonds of the devil (Mosiah 15:9; Alma 12:32–34; 34:15–16).

the firstfruits unto God. Under the law of Moses, the firstfruits of the harvest were offered to God in sacrifice (Ex. 34:22, 26). Because Jesus is the firstfruits of all the dead, being the first to be resurrected (1 Cor. 15:20), so are these 144,000 "the first fruits of the harvest of salvation"[40] (see also Jer. 2:2–3).

Rev. 14:5 *in their mouth was found no guile.* The 144,000 speak no deceit, being honest and true like their Master (Isa. 53:9). This characteristic is in contrast to the wicked, who include the liars (Rev. 21:8).

without fault before the throne of God. A proper sacrifice had to be without blemish (Lev. 1:3, 10; 22:21). These 144,000 are like the Lamb, "without blemish and without spot" (1 Pet. 1:19; Heb. 9:14). This purity and perfection, of course, are made possible through the sacrifice of that Lamb (Heb. 13:20–21; Moro. 10:33).

THE SAINTS ARE COMMANDED TO FLEE BABYLON
Doctrine and Covenants 133:1–2, 4–5, 7

1 Hearken, O ye people of my church, saith the Lord your God, and hear the word of the Lord concerning you—

2 The Lord who shall . . . come down upon the world with a curse to judgment; yea, upon all the nations that forget God, and upon all the ungodly among you. . . .

---

[40] Harrington, *Revelation,* 147.

4 Wherefore, prepare ye, prepare ye, O my people; sanctify yourselves; gather ye together, O ye people of my church, upon the land of Zion, all you that have not been commanded to tarry.

5 Go ye out from Babylon. Be ye clean that bear the vessels of the Lord. . . .

7 Yea, verily I say unto you again, the time has come when the voice of the Lord is unto you: Go ye out of Babylon; gather ye out from among the nations, from the four winds, from one end of heaven to the other.[41]

This scripture is directed to members of the Church (D&C 133:1, 4). The Lord is coming with judgments upon the earth. The Saints must therefore be prepared: they must sanctify themselves, and for safety, they must gather to Zion. For people to gather to Zion, the place of righteousness, they must of necessity leave Babylon, or wickedness. This instruction to "go ye out from Babylon" is so important that the Lord repeats it twice (D&C 133:5, 7; see also Isa. 48:10; Jer. 51:6). In addition, the Church is to send missionaries to the nations of the world, giving them similar counsel: go to Zion, prepare yourselves to meet the coming Lord, and leave Babylon, which is explicitly defined as "wickedness" (D&C 133:8–14).

How does one flee Babylon? Spiritually, it is done by turning from sin and turning to Christ, repenting, receiving sacred ordinances, and living the life of a Saint. It is done by gathering to the wards and stakes of Zion and joining with the Saints in a true unity of heart and mind.[42]

NOTES AND COMMENTARY

D&C 133:2 *come down . . . with a curse to judgment.* When the Lord comes again, he will bring judgment upon the wicked. To put it another way, the wicked have brought a curse upon themselves through their sins, which curse the Lord will fulfill with his

---

[41] Some of these verses, with additional commentary, are also discussed in chap. 7, which treats Babylon in detail; see page 296.

[42] See the commentary on Babylon, page 283.

judgments when he returns in glory. (For the curses pronounced on those who choose not to obey the Lord, see Deut. 28:15–68.)

upon all the nations that forget God, and upon all the ungodly among you. The Lord here names two groups that will be subject to his judgments: the ungodly nations and the ungodly individuals among the Saints.

D&C 133:4 *sanctify yourselves.* Make yourselves pure and clean and holy, set apart for the Lord.

the land of Zion. See the commentary on Zion and the New Jerusalem, page 152.

all you that have not been commanded to tarry. In the days of Joseph Smith, the Saints were generally commanded to hasten to the central gathering place of the Church, unless they were specifically told to do otherwise (exceptions may have been those called to serve in missions or to assist the Saints in other ways). This commandment was modified in 1911, when the First Presidency under Joseph F. Smith wrote, "The establishment of the latter-day Zion on the American continent occasions the gathering of the Saints from all nations. This is not compulsory, and particularly under present conditions, is not urged, because it is desirable that our people shall remain in their native lands and form congregations of a permanent character to aid in the work of proselyting."[43]

D&C 133:5 *Be ye clean that bear the vessels of the Lord.* This passage refers to the sacred *vessels* of the temple (Ezra 1:7–11), which could be borne only by those who held the priesthood. Here the vessels probably represent the ordinances of the priesthood. Thus the Lord is commanding priesthood holders to be clean, that they may be worthy to officiate in their office (Isa. 52:11; D&C 38:42).

D&C 133:7 *from the four winds, from one end of heaven to the other.* This symbolic language indicates that the righteous are to gather from all parts of the world as they flee Babylon.

---

[43] Clark, *Messages of the First Presidency,* 4:222.

THE SAINTS WILL GATHER AT THE TEMPLES
Isaiah 2:2–3

2 And it shall come to pass in the last days, that the mountain of the Lord's house shall be established in the top of the mountains, and shall be exalted above the hills; and all nations shall flow unto it.

3 And many people shall go and say, Come ye, and let us go up to the mountain of the Lord, to the house of the God of Jacob; and he will teach us of his ways, and we will walk in his paths: for out of Zion shall go forth the law, and the word of the Lord from Jerusalem.

To understand this prophecy, we must first understand the expression "the mountain of the Lord's house." Among the people of God, a mountain can be a temple. As Elder Joseph Fielding Smith explained, "No man can get the fullness of the priesthood outside of the temple of the Lord. There was a time when that could be done, for the Lord could give these things on the mountain tops—no doubt that is where Moses got it, that is no doubt where Elijah got it—and the Lord said that in the days of poverty, when there was no house prepared in which to receive these things, that they can be received on the mountain tops. But now we have got temples, and you cannot get these blessings on the mountain tops, you will have to go into the house of the Lord, and you cannot get the fullness of the priesthood unless you go there."[44] Isaiah recorded, "Them will I bring to my holy mountain, and make them joyful in my house of prayer: their burnt offerings and their sacrifices shall be accepted upon mine altar" (Isa. 56:7; see also Ezek. 20:40).

The holy mountain of the Lord is the house of the Lord, the Lord's temple. In the last days, the Lord said he would establish his temple in the top of the mountains. Members of the Church from all nations would be drawn to that temple, saying, "Let us go up to the mountain of the Lord, to the house of the God of Jacob; and he will teach us of his ways, and we will walk in his paths" (Isa. 2:3).

---

[44] *Elijah the Prophet*, 28–29.

We have seen the partial fulfillment of this prophecy. In the temple we do indeed learn the ways of the Lord, and we do make promises to walk in his paths. It appears, however, that the prophecy will not be completely fulfilled until a temple of the Lord is built in Jerusalem (see Isa. 2:1; see also the commentary on Isa. 2:1–3, page 125).

The building of temples is directly related to the gathering of Israel. As noted earlier, Joseph Smith wrote, "The object of gathering the Jews, or the people of God in any age of the world . . . was to build unto the Lord a house whereby He could reveal unto His people the ordinances of His house and the glories of His kingdom, and teach the people the way of salvation."[45]

NOTES AND COMMENTARY

Isa. 2:2 *mountain of the Lord's house.* This term represents the temple of God (Isa. 56:7; Ex. 15:17). "The whole of America is Zion itself from north to south, and is described by the Prophets, who declare that it is the Zion where the mountain of the Lord should be, and that it should be in the center of the land."[46] Jerusalem is also "Zion." The principal features of both Zions will be the temple that will be established in each, and the Lord who will sit as king in the throne rooms of the temples (D&C 133:12–13).

mountains/hills. Isaiah 2:2 is a prophecy with multiple applications; it refers to the Salt Lake Temple, nestled in the hills and mountains: to the future temple of Jerusalem, established in the mountains of Judea; and to other temples. Joseph Smith learned through revelation that "Zion shall flourish upon the hills and rejoice upon the mountains, and shall be assembled together unto the place which I [God] have appointed" (D&C 49:25).

shall be exalted. Spiritually, the temple represents the highest point on earth, which symbolically connects heaven and earth; it is where God's word is revealed to his prophet.

all nations shall flow. Joseph Smith taught that "there should be a place where all nations shall come up from time to time to receive

---

[45] *History of the Church,* 5:423.
[46] *Teachings of the Prophet Joseph Smith,* 362.

their endowments."[47] *All nations* (which means some people from all nations) shall come to obey the God of all nations and to build the kingdom of God. For something to "flow," like a river, up a mountain, a power greater than gravity must be at work; this power is the power of God.

Isa. 2:3 *house.* The temple is the Lord's house. As with a family home, the temple is a home where individuals can enjoy the family of God, can delight in peace and quiet away from the world's troubles and concerns, and can offer up their personal prayers to Heavenly Father.

he will teach us of his ways. The Lord will teach us through revelation given through his prophets and apostles, through the scriptures, and by way of personal revelation (Isa. 54:13). Specifically, we will learn of God's ways in his temple.

walk in his paths. The "path of the just" (Prov. 4:18) or the "strait and narrow path" (2 Ne. 31:18) leads first through the gates of baptism and then past the portals of the Lord's holy temple. Before being able to walk in God's paths, though, we must first let the Lord teach us his laws and his ways. Jesus Christ, of course, is the path or the way in which we must walk (John 14:6).

out of Zion/from Jerusalem. These will be the two religious "capitals for the kingdom of God during the millennium."[48] One will be in Independence, Missouri (D&C 57:3; 84:2–4); the other will be in old Jerusalem (Ether 13:2–11). Both centers will be called Zion and Jerusalem, and both will possess great temples.

shall go forth the law. President Harold B. Lee wrote: "I have often wondered what the expression meant, that out of Zion shall go forth the law. Years ago I went with the brethren to the Idaho Falls Temple, and I heard in that inspired prayer of the First Presidency a definition of the meaning of that term 'out of Zion shall go forth the law.' Note what they said: 'We thank thee that thou hast revealed to us that those who gave us our constitutional form of government were men wise in thy sight and that thou didst raise them up for the

---

[47] *Teachings of the Prophet Joseph Smith,* 367; see also 27.
[48] Smith, *Doctrines of Salvation,* 3:71.

very purpose of putting forth that sacred document [as revealed in Doctrine and Covenants section 101]. . . .

"'We pray that kings and rulers and the peoples of all nations under heaven may be persuaded of the blessings enjoyed by the people of this land by reason of their freedom and under thy guidance and be constrained to adopt similar governmental systems, thus to fulfill the ancient prophecy of Isaiah and Micah that " . . . out of Zion shall go forth the law and the word of the Lord from Jerusalem."' (*Improvement Era,* October 1945, p. 564.)"[49]

This prophecy could also mean that the laws of the millennial kingdom will originate in the millennial Zion.

word of the Lord. Joseph Smith taught the manner in which the Lord's word would proceed forth: "Moses received the word of the Lord from God Himself; he was the mouth of God to Aaron, and Aaron taught the people, in both civil and ecclesiastical affairs; . . . so will it be when the purposes of God shall be accomplished: when 'the Lord shall be King over the whole earth' and 'Jerusalem His throne.' 'The law shall go forth from Zion, and the word of the Lord from Jerusalem.'"[50]

THE TIMES OF THE GENTILES SHALL BE FULFILLED
Doctrine and Covenants 45:25, 28–30

> 25 [The Jews] shall be gathered again; but they shall remain until the times of the Gentiles be fulfilled. . . .
>
> 28 And when the times of the Gentiles is come in, a light shall break forth among them that sit in darkness, and it shall be the fulness of my gospel;
>
> 29 But they receive it not; for they perceive not the light, and they turn their hearts from me because of the precepts of men.
>
> 30 And in that generation shall the times of the Gentiles be fulfilled.

The "times of the Gentiles" is the time period during which the Gentiles will have an opportunity to hear the fulness of the gospel of

---

[49] *Ensign,* Nov. 1971, 15.
[50] *Teachings of the Prophet Joseph Smith,* 252.

Jesus Christ. The gospel will be as a light that suddenly shines on those who are in darkness, but instead of receiving the light with rejoicing, many will not even perceive its shining. They will cling to the understandings they already had ("the precepts of men") and thus will turn their hearts from God. In the generation that the Gentiles turn from God, their opportunity will be ended, for "the times of the Gentiles [will] be fulfilled." After the Gentiles have had a chance to hear the gospel, the gathering of the Jews will commence. When Moroni visited Joseph Smith, he "stated that the fulness of the Gentiles was soon to come in" (JS–H 1:41), meaning, the times of the Gentiles was about to begin.

Jesus said that the Jews would "fall by the edge of the sword, and shall be led away captive into all nations: and Jerusalem shall be trodden down of the Gentiles, until the times of the Gentiles be fulfilled" (Luke 21:24). This prophecy seems to coincide with what John saw in his vision. An angel declared to him that the Gentiles would tread the holy city "under foot forty and two months" (Rev. 11:2). Probably during that same period, two prophets will prophesy in great power, "clothed in sackcloth" (Rev. 11:3), a symbol of humility. After these witnesses have completed their mission, they will be killed by their enemies (Rev. 11:7), the Lord will begin his winding-up scenes (Rev. 11:7–18), and the times of the Gentiles will be completed.

Elder Bruce R. McConkie wrote: "This present era, which is named, *the times of the Gentiles,* shall come to an end before our Lord returns in power and glory. Then, with his return, *the times of the Jews* shall begin; that is the era will commence in which the Jews shall accept the gospel and be blessed spiritually in an abundant way.

"Within the meaning of these terms, all men are either Jews or Gentiles. The Jews are that portion of the house of Israel who inhabited Jerusalem and who were the remnant of the kingdom of Judah. (2 Ne. 30:4; 33:8.) All others were Gentiles, including the portion of Israel scattered among the Gentiles proper."[51]

Recognizing the times of the Gentiles gives us a clue as to where we are in the sequence of time. Elder Wilford Woodruff said: "No man knows the day or the hour when Christ will come, yet the

---

[51] McConkie, *Doctrinal New Testament Commentary,* 1:656.

generation has been pointed out by Jesus himself. . . . The Savior, when speaking to his disciples of his second coming and the establishment of his kingdom on the earth, said the Jews should be scattered and trodden under foot until the times of the Gentiles were fulfilled. But, said he, when you see light breaking forth among the Gentiles, referring to the preaching of his Gospel amongst them; when you see salvation offered to the Gentiles, and the Jews—the seed of Israel—passed by, the last first and the first last; when you see this you may know that the time of my second coming is at hand as surely as you know that summer is nigh when the fig tree puts forth its leaves; and when these things commence that generation shall not pass away until all are fulfilled. We are living in the dispensation and generation to which Jesus referred."[52]

NOTES AND COMMENTARY

D&C 45:25 *they shall remain.* The Jews will remain in their scattered condition until the times of the Gentiles is fulfilled, though there appears to be a transition period during which the Jews begin to return to their homeland.

D&C 45:28 *them that sit in darkness.* These are the people of the world in general, who are subject to the general state of apostasy on the earth.

D&C 45:29 *they perceive not the light.* How can people sitting in darkness not perceive it when a light is turned on? The Lord gives us the key elsewhere, telling us that their eyes are blind (Isa. 42:6–7). Such blindness is caused through the agency of man, which chooses to regard "the precepts of men" more than the "fulness of [the] gospel" sent by the Lord.

D&C 45:30 *in that generation.* "There have been various interpretations of the meaning of a generation. It is held by some that a generation is one hundred years; by others that it is one hundred and twenty years; by others that a generation as expressed in this and other scriptures has reference to a period of time which is indefinite. The Savior said: 'An evil and adulterous generation seeketh after a sign.' This did not have reference to a period of years, but to a period

---

[52] *Journal of Discourses,* 14:5.

of wickedness. A generation may mean the time of this present dispensation."[53]

THE GATHERING OF THE JEWS TO PALESTINE
Zechariah 2:1–5, 12

> *1 I lifted up mine eyes again, and looked, and behold a man with a measuring line in his hand.*
>
> *2 Then said I, Whither goest thou? And he said unto me, To measure Jerusalem, to see what is the breadth thereof, and what is the length thereof.*
>
> *3 And, behold, the angel that talked with me went forth, and another angel went out to meet him,*
>
> *4 And said unto him, Run, speak to this young man, saying, Jerusalem shall be inhabited as towns without walls for the multitude of men and cattle therein:*
>
> *5 For I, saith the Lord, will be unto her a wall of fire round about, and will be the glory in the midst of her. . . .*
>
> *12 And the Lord shall inherit Judah his portion in the holy land, and shall choose Jerusalem again.*

The return of the Jews is one of the best known aspects of the gathering, and it clearly will occur, at least to a degree, before the coming of Christ. As Zechariah learned, Jerusalem, which once was utterly laid waste, will be rebuilt and inhabited by a "multitude." The Lord also will be there (that seems to be millennial), providing protection and blessing the people with his glory.

More important than this gathering, however, is the spiritual gathering of the Jews that precedes it. As Elder Bruce R. McConkie wrote: "Judah will gather to old Jerusalem in due course; of this, there is no doubt. But this gathering will consist of accepting Christ, joining the Church, and receiving anew the Abrahamic covenant as it is administered in holy places. The present assembling of people of Jewish ancestry into the Palestinian nation of Israel is not the scriptural gathering of Israel or of Judah. It may be prelude thereto, and

---

[53] Smith, *Church History and Modern Revelation*, 2:102.

some of the people so assembled may in due course be gathered into the true church and kingdom of God on earth, and they may then assist in building the temple that is destined to grace Jerusalem's soil. But a political gathering is not a spiritual gathering, and the Lord's kingdom is not of this world."[54]

NOTES AND COMMENTARY

Zech. 2:4 *towns without walls.* This expression suggests that the inhabitants of Jerusalem will be so numerous that the walls of the city cannot contain them. It also indicates that the people there will be safe from enemies; they therefore will not need to have walls around their city to protect them.

Zech. 2:5 *a wall of fire round about.* Fire is often an indication of the presence of the Lord, as it is here. (See, for example, Ex. 3:2; 13:21; 19:18; 24:17.)

THE RESTORATION OF THE TEN TRIBES
Doctrine and Covenants 133:26–34

26 And they who are in the north countries shall come in remembrance before the Lord; and their prophets shall hear his voice, and shall no longer stay themselves; and they shall smite the rocks, and the ice shall flow down at their presence.

27 And an highway shall be cast up in the midst of the great deep.

28 Their enemies shall become a prey unto them,

29 And in the barren deserts there shall come forth pools of living water; and the parched ground shall no longer be a thirsty land.

30 And they shall bring forth their rich treasures unto the children of Ephraim, my servants.

31 And the boundaries of the everlasting hills shall tremble at their presence.

---

[54] *New Witness,* 519–20. For a more detailed view of the gathering of the Jews, see the commentary on the gathering of Israel, page 71. See the commentary on the conversion of the Jews to Christ, page 144.

32 And there shall they fall down and be crowned with glory,
even in Zion, by the hands of the servants of the Lord, even
the children of Ephraim.

33 And they shall be filled with songs of everlasting joy.

34 Behold, this is the blessing of the everlasting God upon
the tribes of Israel, and the richer blessing upon the head of
Ephraim and his fellows.[55]

This passage gives an impressive description of the miraculous
return of the lost ten tribes of Israel. Just as Israel was led from Egypt
by great miracles (Ex. 7–14), so will the ten tribes return through miracles: prophets will smite the rocks with power, ice will flow down as
they pass through, a highway will emerge from the ocean, the enemies of Israel will fall victim to them, deserts will flourish with water,
and the hills will tremble at their presence. Such a display of power is
also reminiscent of that exercised by Enoch: he successfully led his
people against their enemies; when he spake the earth trembled; and
rivers were turned out of their courses (Moses 7:13).

The miracles that brought the children of Israel forth from Egypt
were literal, but they were also symbolic in that they represented the
great power of God over the Egyptians and their pharaoh-gods. Will
the latter-day miracles that bring the ten tribes from their lost condition be literal or symbolic? Whatever the answer may be, we know
that those with eyes to see will greatly marvel at the wonderful work
the Lord has done in the return of the ten tribes (Jer. 16:14–15).

In the return of the ten tribes, those with priesthood authority
("their prophets") will receive revelation ("hear his voice") commanding the people to go forth, and they will do so in power ("smite
the rocks," "ice flow down"). A highway of righteousness (perhaps
this is the strait and narrow path)[56] will be established on which the
lost tribes may return. Those who might hinder them ("their enemies," or the servants of unrighteousness) will instead become their
prey (the scriptures do not explain how this will occur). Hearts and

---

[55] For more on the restoration of the ten tribes, see McConkie, *Millennial Messiah,* 215–17, 319–
29; Millet and McConkie, *Our Destiny,* 103–17.

[56] See the commentary on D&C 133:27, page 108.

souls that once were symbolically as barren as deserts will now be full of the knowledge and testimony of Jesus Christ, turned to him who is the living water. Where once there was drought ("parched ground"), there now will be abundance. In their return, the ten tribes will bring to Ephraim (the Church) "their rich treasures," perhaps referring to their scriptures, which likely includes a record of the visit of Christ to the ten tribes (2 Ne. 29:13; 3 Ne. 17:4), their genealogies, their righteous families—or all of these. They will be crowned with glory, perhaps through temple blessings, and will rejoice with singing.

Where are the ten tribes? The scriptures tell us that the ten tribes are in the lands of the north, the south, the west, "the ends of the earth," "all countries whither I had driven them," "the coasts of the earth," "all nations," "spread . . . abroad as the four winds of the heaven," "scattered . . . with a whirlwind among all the nations whom they knew not," "far countries," and "the four quarters of the earth" (Isa. 43:6; 49:12; Jer. 3:12, 18; 16:15; 23:8; 31:8; Amos 9:9; Zech. 2:6; 7:14; 10:9; Ether 13:11; D&C 110:11; see also 1 Ne. 22:3–5; D&C 77:11; 109:67). In other words, the ten tribes have been dispersed among nations throughout the world.

Over the years, a number of theories have been presented about who and where the ten tribes are, but far more important than any such ideas is the truth that the Lord will keep his promise to bring them to the gospel covenant and to unity and fellowship with the rest of covenant Israel in the last days.

Are the ten tribes all in one group? It has traditionally been thought by many in the Church that the ten tribes continued as one discrete and independent group of people from the time they were deported by Assyria until today, some twenty-seven hundred years later. They point to Doctrine and Covenants 133:26–34 to suggest that the ten tribes are together, having their own "prophets" (v. 26) and seeming to return as a group. But to others these verses in Doctrine and Covenants 133 seem metaphorical rather than literal ("ice shall flow down," "highway shall be cast up in the midst of the great deep," "pools of living water," "everlasting hills shall tremble at their presence," "crowned with glory," and so forth). It may therefore be appropriate to understand at least parts of this passage symbolically. Further, it is an important principle of scriptural interpretation that scripture must always be read in the light of other scripture.

The combined witnesses of many prophets in the scriptures clearly indicate that the ten tribes were dispersed to the four corners of the earth. More important than physical location, however, is spiritual placement. To be scattered is to be separated from Christ and the keys, power, and blessings of his gospel. To be gathered ultimately means to be gathered to Christ. When the ten tribes come unto Christ and his true Church, they will then be united as one group, regardless of their geographical location.

Who are the prophets of the ten tribes? The prophets of the ten tribes are men with divinely appointed stewardship over the people who also have the gift of the Spirit that enables them to lead by revelation. Because the Lord's house is a house of order, these leaders will not teach anything contrary to that which is being taught elsewhere in the Lord's kingdom, nor will they have ascendancy over the president of The Church of Jesus Christ of Latter-day Saints, who holds all the keys of the kingdom of God on the earth. Because there is only one at a time who holds all those keys (D&C 132:7), including the keys of the gathering (D&C 110:11), they will be subject to him. In fact, given the nature of the gathering, it seems very likely that the "prophets" of the ten tribes will either be one and the same as the prophets and apostles we sustain as leaders of The Church of Jesus Christ of Latter-day Saints, or they will be called by those leaders and given their authority in the same way any area authority, stake president, or bishop receives his authority.[57]

How will the ten tribes be gathered? Those who are dispersed among the nations will be found through missionary work, which is the primary means of the gathering of Israel in general, and thus they will be brought to the true fold of God. In time, many will also be gathered by migration, when the Lord so commands through his prophet, the president of The Church of Jesus Christ of Latter-day Saints.

---

[57] Elder Bruce R. McConkie addressed this question in *New Witness*, 520–21, and *Millennial Messiah*, 325–26.

One of the primary instruments of their gathering, in addition to the testimony of missionaries, is the Book of Mormon. Mormon pointed out that he was writing to the Gentiles and the house of Israel: "Yea, behold, I write unto all the ends of the earth; yea, unto you, twelve tribes of Israel" (Morm. 3:17–18). It is the design of the Lord that they receive the Book of Mormon and, with its help, come unto Christ.

Where shall the ten tribes go in their return? Initially, the ten tribes will likely be gathered into the stakes and wards and branches of the Church around the world, which is the established pattern for the gathering in our generation.[58] In time, many of them will migrate to the place where Ephraim dwells, which is a symbolic reference to the location of the headquarters of the Church (D&C 133:30–34).[59] Eventually, many of them will be restored to the original lands of their inheritance, in the region of Palestine (Jer. 3:18; 16:15; 23:8).

When will the ten tribes return? Joseph Smith taught that the return of the ten tribes would occur after the earth had experienced great judgments: "Not many years shall pass away before the United States shall present such a scene of *bloodshed* as has not a parallel in the history of our nation; pestilence, hail, famine, and earthquake will sweep the wicked of this generation from off the face of the land, to open and prepare the way for the return of the lost tribes of Israel from the north country."[60] Not only will these judgments help to cleanse the earth, but perhaps they will help to soften the hearts of the ten tribes, making them more open to receiving the word of the gospel.

This statement by Joseph Smith suggests that the return of the ten tribes is yet in the future. Yet we also know from revelation that a substantial part of this gathering will occur before the Lord returns. Doctrine and Covenants 77 tells us that during the sixth seal of time, or

---

[58] Kimball, Seoul Korea Area Conference Report, Aug. 1975, 60–61; McConkie, Mexico City Mexico Area Conference Report, Aug. 1972, 45.

[59] Joseph Smith wrote: "The land of America is a promised land unto [the Lamanites], and unto it all the tribes of Israel will come, with as many of the Gentiles as shall comply with the requisitions of the new covenant. But the tribe of Judah will return to old Jerusalem" (*History of the Church*, 1:315).

[60] *History of the Church*, 1:315–16.

"in the sixth thousand years" of the earth's "temporal existence," twelve thousand men from each tribe of Israel will be faithful high priests in the Church (vv. 10–11, 6).

The most important thing to know is that the ten tribes are in the hands of the Lord and that he will fully keep all his promises to them.[61]

NOTES AND COMMENTARY

D&C 133:26 *they who are in the north countries.* Those in the north countries are the lost tribes of Israel (Jer. 23:8; Ether 13:11), who were last seen traveling northward from the area of the Middle East.[62] Of course, as we have already said, the lost tribes are not only in the north but scattered all over the earth.

come in remembrance before the Lord. The Lord will "remember" his covenant to restore Israel to the gospel and to the lands of their inheritance (3 Ne. 29:1–3; Morm. 5:20).

their prophets. See the commentary on prophets of the ten tribes, page 106.

shall no longer stay themselves. Guided by the Lord, the leaders of the ten tribes will no longer hold back but will help their people to come forth from their place or places of dispersal.

they shall smite the rocks/ice shall flow down. When Moses led the tribes of Israel from captivity in Egypt, he followed the instructions of the Lord to smite a rock to provide water for the people (Ex. 17:6). When the Lord's prophets lead the ten tribes of Israel from their long dispersal, they will likewise exercise God's power to "smite the rocks." Moses' action was both literal (providing water to thirsty people) and symbolic (showing that Jehovah, or Jesus Christ, was the source of living water). The meaning of the action of the prophets among the ten tribes is not clear.

D&C 133:27 *an highway shall be cast up in the midst of the great deep.* This highway may be a literal passageway through or across the water, as was the highway Moses created through the deep

---

[61] Elder Bruce R. McConkie held the view that the return of the ten tribes was primarily a millennial event; see *Millennial Messiah*, 323–29.
[62] 2 Esdras 13.

of the Red Sea when he led the tribes of Israel from Egypt (Ex. 14:26–30). Or it may refer to the "highway of holiness," the strait and narrow path that leads through the "great deep" of the trials and temptations of mortality to the tree of life (Isa. 11:16; 35:8–10; 40:3; 42:16; 49:11; 51:10–11; 57:14; 62:10; 1 Ne. 11:8).

D&C 133:28 *Their enemies shall become a prey unto them.* Those who once sought to conquer or injure the ten tribes will instead be subject to them. In other words, no enemy will be able to permanently hinder the progress of Israel as she returns to God and to those promises which the Lord has made to her.

D&C 133:29 *in the barren deserts there shall come forth pools of living water.* This prophecy may have literal fulfillment as the deserts of both Utah and Israel are renewed and revitalized by the refreshment of water. And in the change of the earth that shall accompany the millennial day, all the barren deserts of the earth will "be renewed and receive [their] paradisiacal glory" (A of F 10).

But the use of the term *living water* also tells us that this passage has a symbolic meaning (Jer. 2:13; John 4:10–14). When in the deserts of our lives we partake of the living water, which provides us with truth and hope beyond price, we never thirst again. That is the promise to each of the Lord's people in all ages, and it is given as a promise to the ten tribes in the last days.

D&C 133:30 *they shall bring forth their rich treasures.* The rich treasures of the ten tribes may be the money and goods they bring with them, prepared to consecrate all they own to the Church and kingdom of God, or they may be their genealogies and family histories, their scriptures, or their righteous posterity—or all of these together.

the children of Ephraim, my servants. The children of Ephraim who are also the servants of the Lord are the established Church in the latter day, The Church of Jesus Christ of Latter-day Saints. The ten tribes will submit themselves to the authority of "the children of Ephraim."

D&C 133:31 *the boundaries of the everlasting hills shall tremble at their presence.* The lost tribes shall come to the place where Ephraim is, to the headquarters of the Church, to the place where the everlasting hills are. That place seems to be the Rocky Mountains or perhaps America in general.[63] The land will tremble when they come, perhaps metaphorically with joy or literally with an earthquake. Eventually, however, the ten tribes will return to the land of their inheritance, the land of Palestine; and perhaps the hills of Judea will tremble when they return.

D&C 133:32 *crowned with glory.* When the ten tribes return to the true gospel of Christ, they will be crowned with glory. This expression likely refers to the blessings of the temple endowment and sealing and ultimately to the blessings of celestial glory.

D&C 133:33 *filled with songs of everlasting joy.* When Israel returns to the covenant and the gospel, she will indeed be filled with great joy, as is any person who finds the riches of the gospel of Jesus Christ (Isa. 35:10; D&C 128:23).

D&C 133:34 *the richer blessing upon the head of Ephraim and his fellows.* What is the richer blessing that Ephraim shall receive? What can be a greater blessing than to receive the gospel and be crowned with glory? Perhaps it is to add to those blessings the great privilege of bringing others to Christ, of assisting the Savior in his work of bringing others to exaltation: "And if it so be that you should labor all your days in crying repentance unto this people, and bring, save it be one soul unto me, how great shall be your joy with him in the kingdom of my Father! And now, if your joy will be great with one soul that you have brought unto me into the kingdom of my Father, how great will be your joy if you should bring many souls unto me!" (D&C 18:15–16). Thus there are levels of joy: the joy of receiving the gospel, the greater joy of bringing another soul unto Christ, and the still greater joy in bringing many souls unto him. Perhaps this highest level of joy constitutes the "richer blessing" that Ephraim will receive as he brings many others to the true Church and gospel in the last days.

---

[63] Smith, *Gospel Doctrine,* 137–38; Smith, *Restoration of All Things,* 93; Whitney, *Saturday Night Thoughts,* 69–70.

THE GATHERING TO ZION, THE NEW JERUSALEM
Doctrine and Covenants 45:66–71

66 And it shall be called the New Jerusalem, a land of peace, a city of refuge, a place of safety for the saints of the Most High God;

67 And the glory of the Lord shall be there, and the terror of the Lord also shall be there, insomuch that the wicked will not come unto it, and it shall be called Zion.

68 And it shall come to pass among the wicked, that every man that will not take his sword against his neighbor must needs flee unto Zion for safety.

69 And there shall be gathered unto it out of every nation under heaven; and it shall be the only people that shall not be at war one with another.

70 And it shall be said among the wicked: Let us not go up to battle against Zion, for the inhabitants of Zion are terrible; wherefore we cannot stand.

71 And it shall come to pass that the righteous shall be gathered out from among all nations, and shall come to Zion, singing with songs of everlasting joy.

The scriptures give us the following characteristics of the establishment of New Jerusalem, as well as of those who are privileged to enter and dwell there:

New Jerusalem will be "prepared" "when it shall be revealed unto you from on high" (D&C 42:9).

"The city New Jerusalem shall be built by the gathering of the saints" (D&C 84:4).

New Jerusalem will be built by the Gentiles who "repent and hearken unto my words, and harden not their hearts," by the Lamanites, and by "as many of the house of Israel as shall come" (3 Ne. 21:22–23).

New Jerusalem will be centered in the land of Missouri (D&C 57:1).

The Lord will cleanse the land of Zion of his enemies (D&C 105:15).

Those in New Jerusalem will be "my people and I will be your God" (D&C 42:9).

Those who dwell in New Jerusalem are "they whose garments are white through the blood of the Lamb" (Ether 13:10).

Those who come to New Jerusalem are those who will later come to a celestial glory (D&C 76:66).

Those who are gathered to the New Jerusalem are "mine elect" (D&C 29:7–8).

Those who "call on the name of the Lord" are those who will be delivered in "mount Zion and in Jerusalem" (Joel 2:32).

People will be gathered "one of a city, and two of a family" (Jer. 3:14).

The elect will be gathered as "righteousness and truth" sweeps the earth "as with a flood" (Moses 7:62).

Those among the Gentiles who will hearken are invited to "flee unto Zion" (D&C 133:12).

Those who gather to Zion will find refuge from the storms of judgment and trouble that come upon the earth (D&C 115:6).

The gathering to New Jerusalem will occur before the second coming of Christ (Moses 7:62).

The temple of God will be found in New Jerusalem (Moses 7:62).

Joseph Smith wrote of the gathering to Zion: "In speaking of the gathering, we mean to be understood as speaking of it according to scripture, the gathering of the elect of the Lord out of every nation on earth, and bringing them to the place of the Lord of Hosts, when the city of righteousness shall be built, and where the people shall be of one heart and one mind, when the Savior comes: yea, where the people shall walk with God like Enoch, and be free from sin. The word of the Lord is precious; and when we read that the veil spread over all nations will be destroyed, and the pure in heart see God, and reign with Him a thousand years on earth, we want all honest men to have a chance to gather and build up a city of righteousness, where even upon the bells of the horses shall be written '*Holiness to the Lord.*'"[64]

---

[64] *Teachings of the Prophet Joseph Smith,* 93.

Prophets in this generation have explained that the gathering to the New Jerusalem remains in the future. For now, Saints are to gather to branches and wards and stakes in their own countries. President Spencer W. Kimball said: "In the early days of the Church we used to preach for the people to come to Utah as the gathering process, largely because that was the only place in the whole world where there was a temple. Now we have [many] temples, and . . . more that have been approved, scattered throughout the world. So it is no longer necessary that we bring the people all to Salt Lake City. Our missionaries preach baptism and confirmation. And then we come to you with conferences and to organize stakes. So we say again, stay in Korea. This is a beautiful land. In this land you can teach your children just as well as you could in Salt Lake City. Stay in Korea where you can teach the gospel to millions of people.

"And so the gathering is taking place. Korea is the gathering place for Koreans, Australia for Australians, Brazil for Brazilians, England for the English. And so we move forward toward the confirmation of this great program the Lord has established for us."[65]

ISRAEL WILL BE GATHERED TO THEIR LANDS OF INHERITANCE
Ezekiel 37:21–22, 25

> *21 . . . Thus saith the Lord God; Behold, I will take the children of Israel from among the heathen, whither they be gone, and will gather them on every side, and bring them into their own land:*
>
> *22 And I will make them one nation in the land upon the mountains of Israel; and one king shall be king to them all: and they shall be no more two nations, neither shall they be divided into two kingdoms any more at all. . . .*
>
> *25 And they shall dwell in the land that I have given unto Jacob my servant, wherein your fathers have dwelt; and they*

---

[65] Seoul Korea Area Conference Report, Aug. 1975, 60–61; see also Kimball, São Paulo Brazil Area Conference Report, Feb.–Mar. 1975, 73; McConkie, Mexico City Mexico Area Conference Report, Aug. 1972, 45. See the commentary on Zion and the New Jerusalem, page 152.

shall dwell therein, even they, and their children, and their children's children for ever: and my servant David shall be their prince for ever.

Before Israel was scattered among all nations, the children of Israel were divided into two kingdoms: the kingdom to the south comprised the tribe of Judah, most of Benjamin, and much of Levi; the northern kingdom held the remaining tribes. Eventually, of course, all the tribes were dispersed around the world. In the last days, perhaps during the Millennium, all of Israel will be restored to the lands God promised to their fathers (see also 2 Ne. 9:2; 3 Ne. 20:29; 29:1). They will no longer dwell in two nations but will live together in one united kingdom.

The land seems to be a symbol of the Abrahamic covenant; it also symbolizes spiritual blessings, temporal security, unity, the presence of God (with the temple), wealth, abundance, and a child's inheritance from its parent.

NOTES AND COMMENTARY

Ezek. 37:21 *gather them on every side.* The New International Version gives a clearer reading: "gather them from all around."

bring them into their own land. When Israel returns, they will return to their own land, meaning the land from whence they were dispersed, the land of Israel. Verse 25 reemphasizes this truth: "They shall dwell in the land that I have given unto Jacob my servant, wherein your fathers have dwelt." They and their posterity will receive that land as an inheritance forever.

Ezek. 37:22 *one nation.* As Israel was one nation under Moses, Joshua, and David, so will they be one under Christ.

one king shall be king to them all. The king, of course, is the King of kings, Jesus Christ (A of F 10).

Ezek. 37:25 *my servant David shall be their prince for ever.* The scriptures indicate that when the tribes of Israel are reunited as Ezekiel saw, their king will be like David of old, who reigned over a united Israel. Jeremiah prophesied that Israel would "serve the Lord their God, and David their king, whom I will raise up unto them" (Jer. 30:9; see also Ezek. 34:23–24; Hosea 3:5). This king is almost certainly Jesus Christ himself, of whom it was prophesied that God would give him "the throne of his father David: and he shall reign over the house of Jacob for ever; and of his kingdom there shall be no end" (Luke 1:32–33; see also Acts 2:30).[66]

---

[66] Most Latter-day Saint scholars agree that the millennial David is none other than Jesus Christ. See, for example, McConkie, *Millennial Messiah*, 602–11; *New Witness*, 518; Millet, "Life in the Millennium," 182; Jackson, "The Lord Is There," 306–7.

CHAPTER 3

JUDAH, JERUSALEM, AND THE HOLY LAND

SIGNS OF THE TIMES

1. The Jews return to the Holy Land.

2. A temple is built in Jerusalem.

3. All nations visit the temple of Jerusalem.

4. Water flows from the temple and heals the waters of the Dead Sea.

5. Voices of joy are heard in Jerusalem.

6. Two prophets work miracles and prophesy in Jerusalem.

7. The Messiah battles against the Jews' enemies and stands on the Mount of Olives.

8. Some ask Christ, "What are these wounds in thine hands?"

9. Judah and Jerusalem are redeemed.

Many prophets, ancient and modern, have identified Jerusalem and Israel to be the scene of great events that will take place in the last days. Ether, for instance, prophesied that the time would come when Jerusalem would once again become "a holy city unto the Lord." He spoke "concerning the house of Israel, and the Jerusalem from whence Lehi should come—after it should be destroyed it should be built up again, a holy city unto the Lord; wherefore, it could not be a new Jerusalem for it had been in a time of old; but it should be built up again, and become a holy city of the Lord; and it should be built unto the house of Israel" (Ether 13:5). This and other marvelous prophecies concerning Jerusalem, the Jews, and the land of Israel will be fulfilled during the last days, at Christ's coming, or in the

Millennium. A summary of several such prophecies follows (not in chronological order):

The wealth of many will be used for the gathering of Israel (Isa. 60:9, 13–14; Jer. 32:41–44; Zech. 14:14).

All nations will battle against Jerusalem (Ezek. 38–39; Joel 3:1–17; Zech. 12:6–9; 14:1–2).

Judah will again inhabit Jerusalem and the "land of Jerusalem," the Lord will again choose Jerusalem, and he will defend its inhabitants (Zech. 2:11–12; 12:6–8; 3 Ne. 20:29, 33–34, 46).

Judah will be saved and made holy (Jer. 23:5–6; D&C 133:35).

The Jews will someday believe in Jesus Christ, and they will not look for another Messiah (Deut. 4:29–31; Jer. 31:31–34; 1 Ne. 10:11–14; 2 Ne. 6:11; 9:2; 10:7–8; 25:16; 30:7; 3 Ne. 20:29–31; Morm. 5:12–14).

A temple will be built in Jerusalem (Isa. 2:1–3; Ezek. 37:26–28; chs. 40–46; D&C 124:36–37; 133:13).

Water will flow from the temple and heal the Dead Sea (Ezek. 47:1–12; Joel 3:18; Zech. 14:8).

Jerusalem and the New Jerusalem will be the two world capitals during the Millennium (Isa. 2:3; Ether 13:4–11; D&C 133:20–25).

Jerusalem will again become a holy city (Ether 13:5, 8).

Two prophets in Jerusalem will work miracles, prophesy, and be martyred (JST Isa. 51:18–20; Zech. 4:11–14; Rev. 11:3–12; D&C 77:15).

Christ will appear on the Mount of Olives (Zech. 14:3–5; D&C 45:48; 133:20).

Judah will return to the lands of their inheritance (Isa. 11:12; 14:1; 1 Ne. 19:13–16; 2 Ne. 6:11; 9:2; 10:7–8; Ether 13:11–12).

Jerusalem and its environs will become fruitful (Ezek. 36:33–36; Amos 9:14–15; cf. Isa. 35:1–2, 6–7).

THE JEWS RETURN TO THE HOLY LAND
Zechariah 8:1–8

1 Again the word of the Lord of hosts came to me, saying,

2 Thus saith the Lord of hosts; I was jealous for Zion with great jealousy, and I was jealous for her with great fury.

3 Thus saith the Lord; I am returned unto Zion, and will dwell in the midst of Jerusalem: and Jerusalem shall be called a city of truth; and the mountain of the Lord of hosts the holy mountain.

4 Thus saith the Lord of hosts; There shall yet old men and old women dwell in the streets of Jerusalem, and every man with his staff in his hand for very age.

5 And the streets of the city shall be full of boys and girls playing in the streets thereof.

6 Thus saith the Lord of hosts; If it be marvellous in the eyes of the remnant of this people in these days, should it also be marvellous in mine eyes? saith the Lord of hosts.

7 Thus saith the Lord of hosts; Behold, I will save my people from the east country, and from the west country;

8 And I will bring them, and they shall dwell in the midst of Jerusalem: and they shall be my people, and I will be their God, in truth and in righteousness.

The headnote to Zechariah 8 reads, "In the last days, Jerusalem shall be restored, Judah shall be gathered, and the Lord will bless his people beyond anything of the past." One prominent sign of the times is the return of the Jews to the Holy Land and its chief city, Jerusalem. Isaiah (Isa. 11:12), Jeremiah (Jer. 3:18; 32:37–44; 33:7–26), Ezekiel (Ezek. 11:17–21; 20:34–44; 37:21–25), Hosea (Hosea 1:11), Zechariah (Zech. 2; 10:6–12), Nephi (2 Ne. 25:11) and other ancient prophets prophesied of their return.

Many of our modern-day Church leaders also have spoken regarding the gathering of the Jews. Joseph Smith prayed concerning the redemption of Jerusalem and the return of the Jews: "We therefore ask thee to have mercy upon the children of Jacob, that Jerusalem, from this hour, may begin to be redeemed; . . . and the children of Judah may begin to return to the lands which thou didst give to Abraham, their father" (D&C 109:62, 64). Elder Ezra Taft Benson explained in 1950 that the gathering of the Jews "is one of the signs of the times, and is very important. . . .

"This miracle of the return of the Jews was to be one of the events to precede Christ's second coming, and the scriptures are very clear with reference to this fact."[1]

Approximately a quarter of a century later, Elder Benson stated: "Since 1948, the people of the world have witnessed a marvelous drama taking place before their eyes; and yet it is a miracle that has gone unnoticed and unappreciated. One of the greatest events in history is the literal gathering of the Jews to their homeland from the 'four corners of the earth.' It is, as Isaiah prophesied, 'a marvelous work and a wonder.' (See Isa. 29:14.)"[2]

Elder Orson Hyde (in 1841), and President George A. Smith (in 1872) dedicated the Holy Land for the "return of the Jews and the rebuilding of Jerusalem." Elder Orson F. Whitney recorded: "In the year 1872 a mission went from Salt Lake City to the Holy Land. President George A. Smith headed the party, which also included Lorenzo Snow, one of the Twelve Apostles, and his gifted sister, the poet, Eliza R. Snow. Upon reaching Palestine, President Smith duplicated the work done by Orson Hyde in 1841, dedicating the land for the return of the Jews and the rebuilding of Jerusalem. Other elders of the Church have since visited that once favored and yet to be glorified region. President Anthon H. Lund was there in 1898; and he likewise offered up an earnest prayer for the great consummation. All this because Moses restored the keys for the gathering of Israel in this dispensation."[3]

The present gathering of the Jews to the Holy Land is called by Elder Bruce R. McConkie a "political gathering" or a "preliminary gathering," an "Elias going before Messias; it is a preparatory work; it is the setting of the stage for the grand drama soon to be played on Olivet." The spiritual gathering of the Jews, Elder McConkie explained, will take place when they "believe the Book of Mormon

---

[1] Conference Report, Apr. 1950, 72–75.

[2] *Ensign,* Dec. 1976, 71. President Joseph Fielding Smith similarly called the gathering of the Jews "a miracle being performed before our eyes" which is "in fulfillment of the prophecies" ("Prophecy and the Scriptures," 14). See also the statements of Wilford Woodruff (*Journal of Discourses,* 15:278–79), Heber J. Grant ("Dedicatory Prayer," 285), George Albert Smith ("New Year's Greeting," 2), and Mark E. Petersen ("Homecoming to Palestine," 16).

[3] Conference Report, Oct. 1920, 34.

and when they accept the gospel. . . . They shall come again to the Holy One of Israel, . . . accept Christ as their Savior and plead with the Father in the name of the Son for the cleansing power of his blood. They shall return when they join the true Church, The Church of Jesus Christ of Latter-day Saints."[4]

NOTES AND COMMENTARY

Zech. 8:2 *Thus saith the Lord of hosts.* We are reminded in Zechariah 8 that it is the Lord who speaks, because "thus saith the Lord of hosts" appears nine times (vv. 2, 4, 6, 7, 9, 14, 19, 20, 23) in addition to "thus saith the Lord" (v. 3).

I was jealous for Zion with great jealousy. In scripture the Lord is depicted as a husband (Isa. 54:5; Jer. 31:32), and his people collectively are portrayed as his wife (Isa. 54:1–6). In Zechariah 8:2, God declares that in the past he has been jealous because his wife, who is here called Zion (speaking of members of the house of Judah), had committed spiritual adultery by worshipping the gods of the world (Jer. 3:8–9; Hosea 3:1) while shunning her true Lord (Hosea 1:2).

Zech. 8:3 *I am returned unto Zion, and will dwell in the midst of Jerusalem.* These two phrases, separated by the comma, produce a parallelism, with the names *Zion* and *Jerusalem* forming a synonymous word pair. During the Millennium the Lord will once again come unto Zion and will dwell in her midst.

Jerusalem shall be called a city of truth. Perhaps Jerusalem will be named *city of truth* because God, who is "the truth of the world" (Ether 4:12) and a "God of truth" (Deut. 32:4), will dwell there. In a future day, people from many nations will seek the Lord and his truth in the city of truth (Zech. 2:11; 8:20–23).

the mountain of the Lord of hosts the holy mountain. The temple of the Lord is called "the mountain of the Lord" (Isa. 2:2–3); it is called "holy" because it is his dwelling place. This verse brings together the concepts of Zion, Jerusalem, and temple in a way similar to that of Joel 3:17 and Isaiah 2:2–3. The Lord spoke through his servant Joel "so shall ye know that I am the Lord your God dwelling in Zion, my holy mountain: then shall Jerusalem be holy" (Joel 3:17);

---

[4] *Millennial Messiah,* 225, 229.

and Isaiah prophesied, "Let us go up to the mountain of the Lord, to the house of the God of Jacob; . . . for out of Zion shall go forth the law, and the word of the Lord from Jerusalem" (Isa. 2:3).

Zech. 8:4–5 *old men and old women/boys and girls.* Two generations are represented in these verses: "old men and old women," and "boys and girls." The city's inhabitants will dwell there long enough to become old, while a rising generation of boys and girls are seen playing in the streets. The elderly are pictured as leaning on their canes in comfort and peace. Children playing in the streets indicate a safe and carefree society. That the elderly are not working suggests a healthy economy; they are not required to produce goods but leave such labors for those who are younger. This scene of peace, comfort, and safety, which may come to fruition in the Millennium, is far different from the one in Lamentations, which portrays a depopulated Jerusalem and an exiled and downtrodden people shortly after the city was destroyed at the time of Jeremiah and Lehi. Lamentations 2:21 reads, "The young and the old lie on the ground in the streets: my virgins and my young men are fallen by the sword; thou hast slain them in the day of thine anger."

Zech. 8:7 *I will save my people from the east country, and from the west country.* East and west express totality. The Lord will gather Judah from the rising of the sun (east) to its setting (west), or from all parts of the earth. Isaiah used similar language when he prophesied that the Lord would gather his people from "the islands of the sea" and from "the four corners of the earth" (Isa. 11:11–12).

Zech. 8:8 *I will bring them.* The Lord takes an active role and uses his "mighty hand" and "stretched out arm" (Ezek. 20:34) in the gathering of the Jews. He promises: "Thus saith the Lord God; I will even gather you from the people, and assemble you out of the countries where ye have been scattered, and I will give you the land of Israel" (Ezek. 11:17). President Wilford Woodruff added: "The Lord has decreed that the Jews should be gathered from all the Gentile nations where they have been driven, into their own land, in fulfillment of the words of Moses their law-giver."[5]

---

[5] "Epistle of Elder Woodruff," 244.

they shall dwell in the midst of Jerusalem. Zechariah's prophecy is very specific: he provides the exact name *Jerusalem* as one of the cities to which the Jews will gather in the last days. In fact, in Zechariah 8:1–8, the prophet identifies Jerusalem by name on four occasions. Certainly, without the spirit of prophecy, Zechariah could not have known in 520–518 B.C. that Jerusalem would continue to exist for approximately twenty-five hundred years and would have the same name after that long period of time. Few cities exist so long, and those that do have often had their names changed one or more times. For example, the city of Beijing, China, has been in existence for three millennia; but it has been variously named Ch'i, Yen, Yu-chow, Nan-ching, Yenching, Chung-tu, Khanbaliq, Peiping, and Peking.[6]

Nephi also prophesied of the return of the Jews to their land and city: "Notwithstanding they have been carried away they shall return again, and possess the land of Jerusalem; wherefore, they shall be restored again to the land of their inheritance" (2 Ne. 25:11).

they shall be my people, and I will be their God. This statement speaks of the covenant relationship that will exist between God and his people after their gathering. The Lord through Jeremiah explains: "But this shall be the covenant that I will make with the house of Israel; after those days [after their return], saith the Lord, I will put my law in their inward parts, and write it in their hearts; and will be their God, and they shall be my people" (Jer. 31:33).

THE TEMPLE IN THE MIDST OF ISRAEL
Ezekiel 37:26–28

> 26 Moreover I will make a covenant of peace with them; it shall be an everlasting covenant with them: and I will place them, and multiply them, and will set my sanctuary in the midst of them for evermore.
>
> 27 My tabernacle also shall be with them: yea, I will be their God, and they shall be my people.

---

[6] See *Encyclopaedia Britannica*, s. v. "Peking."

28 And the heathen shall know that I the Lord do sanctify Israel, when my sanctuary shall be in the midst of them for evermore.

Twice in these three verses the Lord promises that he will set his sanctuary in the midst of Israel forever, and he declares once that his tabernacle will also be with them. Ezekiel received this remarkable prophecy during his exile in the land of Babylon. It pertains to the last days, when we, as members of the house of Israel, will again choose Jehovah to be our God, and he will elect us to be his people. Such is the "covenant of peace" spoken of here and more fully in Ezekiel 34:24–31. Part of this covenant includes the promise of peace and protection for the Saints who follow their great Shepherd.

NOTES AND COMMENTARY

Ezek. 37:26 *I will make a covenant of peace with them.* This covenant, or two-way promise, as explained in Ezekiel 34:24–31, is between God and the house of Israel in the last days. On the one hand, God promises Israel that he will be "their God" (Ezek. 34:24), and as such he will bless them with safety (Ezek. 34:25, 27), temporal blessings (Ezek. 34:26–27), and protection from wicked peoples and ravenous beasts, so that his people "shall dwell safely, and none shall make them afraid" (Ezek. 34:28). Further, God will break the bands of their bondage—speaking perhaps of both their physical bondage as well as their bonds of sin (Ezek. 34:27)—and he also promises that they will no longer suffer hunger (Ezek. 34:29). In short, God promises conditions of safety to his people, or a "covenant of peace."

In return for these great blessings, God's people promise him that he will be their God and they will be his people and his flock (Ezek. 34:30–31). As Ezekiel writes, "Thus shall they know that I the Lord their God am with them, and that they, even the house of Israel, are my people, saith the Lord God. And ye my flock, the flock of my pasture, are men, and I am your God" (Ezek. 34:30–31).

it shall be an everlasting covenant with them. The covenant of peace will last beyond our days of mortality and continue throughout eternity.

I will place them. God will establish us, his people, upon our lands of promise (America and the Holy Land), just as he set ancient Israel on their land after their forty years of wandering in the wilderness.

multiply them. He will also multiply us until we are great in numbers. The Lord spoke of this through Isaiah: "For thy waste and thy desolate places, and the land of thy destruction, shall even now be too narrow by reason of the inhabitants. . . . The children which thou shalt have, after thou hast lost the other, shall say again in thine ears, The place is too strait for me: give place to me that I may dwell" (Isa. 49:19–20; see also D&C 105:26, 31).

[I] will set my sanctuary in the midst of them for evermore. The meaning of the passage, which is repeated in verse 28 for emphasis, is not clear. It may refer to the temple in Jerusalem, which will be built in the last days before the Second Coming; or it may refer to any of the temples that now dot the earth; or it may refer to the temple as a blessing restored to the Lord's people; thus, any and all true temples serve as fulfillment of the Lord's promise.

Ezek. 37:27 *My tabernacle also shall be with them.* Ezekiel uses language that recalls to mind the Mosaic tabernacle, or the portable temple that Israel carried with them through their wilderness wanderings (Num. 9:15–22). This same tabernacle will not exist with Israel in the last days, however, for we now have temples in many countries of the world; instead, Ezekiel may be referring to the spiritual protection that God will provide for his people. As a tent offers protection from the elements, including the wind, sun, and hail, so also God's tabernacle will protect his people from spiritual harm and physical danger. Such is also the picture provided in Isaiah 4:6, wherein the prophet states that "there shall be a tabernacle for a shadow in the daytime from the heat, and for a place of refuge, and for a covert from storm and from rain." The underlying idea is that Christ himself will dwell with his people in the last days.

I will be their God, and they shall be my people. This phrase summarizes the "covenant of peace" identified in Ezekiel 37:26, wherein God promises to be Israel's God and provide them with countless blessings if they will but promise to be his people (see also Ezek. 34:24–31).

Ezek. 37:28 *the heathen shall know that I the Lord do sanctify Israel.* When the Lord establishes his sanctuary again in the midst of his people, the heathen or the nations of the world will know that God sanctifies (or cleanses, through the Atonement and the sanctifying power of the Holy Ghost) Israel. Complete fulfillment of this prophecy may not come to pass until the Millennium.

ALL NATIONS SHALL FLOW TO THE TEMPLE OF JERUSALEM
Isaiah 2:1–3

1 The word that Isaiah the son of Amoz saw concerning Judah and Jerusalem.

2 And it shall come to pass in the last days, that the mountain of the Lord's house shall be established in the top of the mountains, and shall be exalted above the hills; and all nations shall flow unto it.

3 And many people shall go and say, Come ye, and let us go up to the mountain of the Lord, to the house of the God of Jacob; and he will teach us of his ways, and we will walk in his paths: for out of Zion shall go forth the law, and the word of the Lord from Jerusalem.

Quite familiar to Latter-day Saints, these verses are often quoted with reference to the Salt Lake Temple, the first temple to be commenced in Utah, "in the top of the mountains."[7] Isaiah's prophecy also refers to the temple in Jerusalem, for verse 1, which introduces this section of Isaiah, states that it is about "Judah and Jerusalem,"[8] and Jerusalem is also mentioned in verse 3. These verses identify the temple explicitly. It is called "the Lord's house," "the mountain of the

---

[7] Latter-day prophets have applied this prophecy to the Salt Lake Temple. Elder Bruce R. McConkie applied the prophecy to the temple in Jerusalem, to the Salt Lake Temple, and to "all of the temples now built or that may be built in the high mountains of America" (*Millennial Messiah,* 276). This prophecy will have a dual fulfillment, including the latter-day temple in Jerusalem.

[8] See also McConkie, *Millennial Messiah,* 276.

Lord," and "the house of the God of Jacob." The time frame for the establishment of the temple is the "last days."[9]

We can also read about the latter-day Jerusalem temple in the Doctrine and Covenants. In one passage, the Lord commands the Gentiles to flee to Zion, where temples have been built, and the people of Judah to flee to "Jerusalem, unto the mountains of the Lord's house" (D&C 133:12–13). A second passage identifies Zion and Jerusalem as places of refuge where the Saints will conduct sacred ordinances in the temple: "For it is ordained that in Zion and in her stakes, and in Jerusalem, those places which I have appointed for refuge, shall be the places for your baptisms for your dead. And again, verily I say unto you, how shall your washings be acceptable unto me, except ye perform them in a house which you have built to my name?" (D&C 124:36–37).

NOTES AND COMMENTARY

Isa. 2:1 *The word that Isaiah the son of Amoz saw.* The word translated as *saw* means, literally, "to see in a vision" (Hebrew *haza*); Isaiah saw in a vision the temple that would be established in Jerusalem in the last days.

concerning Judah and Jerusalem. The words that follow verse 1 speak particularly about the people of Judah and the city of Jerusalem.

Isa. 2:2 *it shall come to pass in the last days.* Isaiah provides the general calendar for the establishment of the Lord's house when he writes that it will "come to pass in the last days."

mountain. In Isaiah 2:2–3, Isaiah emphasizes through repetition the words *mountains, hills,* and *mountain.* It sounds as though the temple in Jerusalem will be built in the Judean hills of modern Israel, for this temple will "be established in the top of the mountains," "be exalted above the hills," and worshippers will "go up" to the temple. In the ancient world, *mountain* also refers symbolically to temples and temple worship. When the followers of Jehovah were unable to

---

[9]McConkie, *Millennial Messiah,* 277, places the building of temples in both the old and the new Jerusalem before the Second Coming. See also *Teachings of the Prophet Joseph Smith,* 286.

build a temple, they often worshipped on mountaintops. Such was the case with Moses, Nephi, Jared, and others.

Lord's house. In the Bible, the temple is called "the house of the Lord," because it was there that God's people sought peace and spiritual refreshment from their Father, even as children seek peace and refreshment in their earthly homes. In our day, too, the temple is called a *house;* for instance, a single verse of Joseph Smith's prayer dedicating the Kirtland Temple calls the temple *house* eight times (D&C 109:8).

all nations shall flow unto it. Like a vast river that flows to the sea, peoples from all nations will journey to the temple. Unlike a river that flows downward, however, the river of people will flow upward to reach the temple.

Isa. 2:3 *many people.* Through the decades since its dedication, the Salt Lake Temple has attracted hundreds of thousands of worshippers to its sacred halls and even more thousands of visitors to Temple Square. Similarly, a vast number of visitors, or "many people," will travel to the temple in Jerusalem, some to worship there and others to gaze upon its imposing structure.

he will teach us of his ways. Worshippers will receive a great endowment of knowledge in the temple, for it is "a house of learning" (D&C 109:8). Joseph Smith prayed concerning the Kirtland Temple: "And do thou grant, Holy Father, that all those who shall worship in this house may be taught words of wisdom out of the best books, and that they may seek learning even by study, and also by faith, as thou hast said" (D&C 109:14).

we will walk in his paths. There is a cause-and-effect relationship in this verse: God teaches us of his ways and we then walk in his paths. Jesus Christ is the Way (John 14:6), or the path, that we must walk. When we learn to know the Way, we will want to follow him.

for out of Zion shall go forth the law, and the word of the Lord from Jerusalem. Zion and Jerusalem are the two religious capitals that will exist during the Millennium. One will be in Independence, Missouri (D&C 57:3; 84:2–4); the other, in old Jerusalem (Ether 13:2–11). Both centers will be called Zion and Jerusalem, and both will have great temples.

WATERS FLOW FROM THE TEMPLE AND HEAL THE DEAD SEA
Ezekiel 47:1–10

1 Afterward he brought me again unto the door of the house; and, behold, waters issued out from under the threshold of the house eastward: for the forefront of the house stood toward the east, and the waters came down from under from the right side of the house, at the south side of the altar.

2 Then brought he me out of the way of the gate northward, and led me about the way without unto the utter gate by the way that looketh eastward; and, behold, there ran out waters on the right side.

3 And when the man that had the line in his hand went forth eastward, he measured a thousand cubits, and he brought me through the waters; the waters were to the ankles.

4 Again he measured a thousand, and brought me through the waters; the waters were to the knees. Again he measured a thousand, and brought me through; the waters were to the loins.

5 Afterward he measured a thousand; and it was a river that I could not pass over: for the waters were risen, waters to swim in, a river that could not be passed over.

6 And he said unto me, Son of man, hast thou seen this? Then he brought me, and caused me to return to the brink of the river.

7 Now when I had returned, behold, at the bank of the river were very many trees on the one side and on the other.

8 Then said he unto me, These waters issue out toward the east country, and go down into the desert, and go into the sea: which being brought forth into the sea, the waters shall be healed.

9 And it shall come to pass, that every thing that liveth, which moveth, whithersoever the rivers shall come, shall live: and there shall be a very great multitude of fish, because these waters shall come thither: for they shall be healed; and every thing shall live whither the river cometh.

10 And it shall come to pass, that the fishers shall stand upon it from En-gedi even unto En-eglaim; they shall be a place to spread forth nets; their fish shall be according to their kinds, as the fish of the great sea, exceeding many.

These verses follow Ezekiel's lengthy prophecy regarding the future temple of Jerusalem (Ezek. 40–46). This section divides neatly into two parts: verses 1 through 7 pertain to waters that will flow from the temple; the result, described in verses 8 through 12, is the healing of the Dead Sea (so named because its high concentration of salt and minerals prevents it from sustaining life). Joseph Smith seemed to view these events as literal: "Judah must return, Jerusalem must be rebuilt, and the temple, and water come out from under the temple, and the waters of the Dead Sea be healed. It will take some time to rebuild the walls of the city and the temple, &c.; and all this must be done before the Son of Man will make His appearance."[10]

The prophecy regarding the waters flowing from the temple and the healing of the Dead Sea may speak of literal waters and an actual healing of the Dead Sea, or it may be figurative, or both. Unfortunately, Ezekiel's words remain somewhat veiled to us. In any case, the symbolic elements of Ezekiel's passage are important. The waters that flow from God's temple (cf. Rev. 22:1, "a pure river of water of life, clear as crystal, proceeding out of the throne of God and of the Lamb"; see also Joel 3:18; Zech. 14:8) refer to Jesus Christ and the blessings he extends to those who worship in his temples. Jeremiah referred to the Lord as the "fountain of living waters" (Jer. 2:13; 17:13), meaning the Lord provides eternal life to all who drink from his fountain. The Dead Sea seems to represent all who are dead spiritually, or in whom there is little or no spiritual life. The living waters of Christ flow through us, changing our individual "Dead Sea," and we are cleansed and renewed as we attend the temple and keep the covenants we make there.

---

[10] *Teachings of the Prophet Joseph Smith*, 286.

NOTES AND COMMENTARY

Ezek. 47:1 *Afterward he brought me again unto the door of the house.* The heavenly messenger (Ezek. 40:3–4) who guides Ezekiel through the future temple now takes him to one of the doors of the temple.

waters issued out from under the threshold of the house eastward. Ezekiel sees water flow from under the threshold of the temple eastward, or in the direction of the Dead Sea, which is just a few miles from Jerusalem. Whether actual waters will flow from the temple remains to be seen.

Ezek. 47:3–5 *he measured.* On four occasions the heavenly messenger measures the depth of the flowing water, and Ezekiel observes that the water grows deeper as it moves away from the temple: first it is ankle deep, then it reaches the knees, next it reaches the waist, and finally it is deep enough "to swim in, a river that could not be passed over."

Ezek. 47:6–7 *brink of the river/bank of the river.* The river brings life to its banks. Vegetation grows as the waters flow through the desert, and Ezekiel notes that trees grow on each side of the river.

Ezek. 47:8–9 *the waters shall be healed/they shall be healed.* The messenger explains to the prophet the route of the waters, which flow eastward from the temple through the desert to the sea. These waters freshen the Dead Sea, so that the sea can now sustain life. The messenger's words are clearly set forth: "And it shall come to pass, that every thing that liveth, which moveth, whithersoever the rivers shall come, shall live: and there shall be a very great multitude of fish, because these waters shall come thither: for they shall be healed; and every thing shall live whither the river cometh."

Ezek. 47:10 *fishers shall stand upon it.* At present, no one fishes the Dead Sea, for this great body of water does not sustain life. When the waters flow from the threshold of the temple eastward to the Dead Sea, healing its waters, fishermen will stand on its shore or cast their nets into the waters to catch fish of many kinds—"exceeding many." These verses may be symbolic only.

THE VOICE OF JOY WILL BE HEARD IN JERUSALEM
Jeremiah 33:7–11

7 And I will cause the captivity of Judah and the captivity of Israel to return, and will build them, as at the first.

8 And I will cleanse them from all their iniquity, whereby they have sinned against me; and I will pardon all their iniquities, whereby they have sinned, and whereby they have transgressed against me.

9 And it shall be to me a name of joy, a praise and an honour before all the nations of the earth, which shall hear all the good that I do unto them: and they shall fear and tremble for all the goodness and for all the prosperity that I procure unto it.

10 Thus saith the Lord; Again there shall be heard in this place, which ye say shall be desolate without man and without beast, even in the cities of Judah, and in the streets of Jerusalem, that are desolate, without man, and without inhabitant, and without beast,

11 The voice of joy, and the voice of gladness, the voice of the bridegroom, and the voice of the bride, the voice of them that shall say, Praise the Lord of hosts: for the Lord is good; for his mercy endureth for ever: and of them that shall bring the sacrifice of praise into the house of the Lord. For I will cause to return the captivity of the land, as at the first, saith the Lord.

Jerusalem, which has been destroyed numerous times during the past three thousand years, will once again be built up, along with other cities in modern-day Israel. Jeremiah proclaims that activities of great joy will take place in these cities, and the voices of brides, grooms, and those who worship the true and living God will be heard.

The Lord takes an active and personal role in the gathering of Judah and Israel in the last days. Note his firsthand activities in the lives of his people; the pronoun *I* is repeated seven times in the following phrases:

I will cause the captivity . . . to return.

I will build them.

I will cleanse them.

I will pardon all their iniquities.

all the good that *I* do unto them.

all the prosperity that *I* procure unto it.

I will cause to return the captivity.

NOTES AND COMMENTARY

Jer. 33:7 *I will cause the captivity of Judah and the captivity of Israel to return.* A better translation of this sentence reads, "I will bring about the restoration of Judah and the restoration of Israel."[11]

[I] will build them. The phrase hearkens back to Jeremiah 30:18, where the Lord explains that he will restore "Jacob's tents, and have mercy on his dwellingplaces; and the city shall be builded upon her own heap" (see also Jer. 31:4).

as at the first. Jerusalem and other cities of Israel will be built "as at the first," or as in former times.

Jer. 33:8 *their iniquity.* This verse emphasizes the wickedness of Israel and Judah: "all their iniquity"; "they have sinned against me"; "all their iniquities"; "they have sinned"; "they have transgressed against me." Such emphasis on wickedness makes God's forgiveness even more remarkable, for he promises to "cleanse" and "pardon" despite the great and numerous sins.

Jer. 33:9 *a name of joy, a praise and an honour.* Through Moses (Deut. 26:19) God aimed to make *Israel* three things in the sight of the peoples of the earth: a *name*, a *praise*, and an *honour*. Here Jeremiah prophesies that in the last days Israel and Judah will be unto God "a *name* of joy, a *praise* and an *honour* before all the nations of the earth," because the nations will hear of "all the good" and "all the prosperity" that the Lord will give unto his people. As a result, the nations will fear and tremble (see also D&C 45:74; 64:43).

Jer. 33:10–11 *Thus saith the Lord.* God is the author of this prophecy.

---

[11] Keown, Scalise, Smothers, *Jeremiah 26–52,* 164.

Again there shall be heard in this place. Inasmuch as Jerusalem and the cities of Judah on a number of occasions have been destroyed by various world powers, people say that these cities "shall be desolate without man and without beast . . . and without inhabitant." In spite of this, Jeremiah prophesies that there will yet be heard "the voice of joy, and the voice of gladness, the voice of the bridegroom, and the voice of the bride." This prophecy is now being partially fulfilled in Jerusalem and the cities of Judah (the cities of modern Israel): they are filled with joyful sounds, including the voices of brides and bridegrooms. Unfortunately, these joyful sounds are at present mingled with the sounds of war and trouble and will be so until Christ's second coming.

the voice of them that shall say, Praise the Lord of hosts. In addition to the voices of joy already described, those who worship the Lord make joyful sounds. These will sing, "Praise the Lord of hosts: for the Lord is good; for his mercy endureth for ever." These words may be partially fulfilled in a number of our Church hymns, which contain the words "praise the Lord" (Hebrew *halleluya*).

bring the sacrifice of praise into the house of the Lord. The New Jerusalem Bible renders this passage as "those who bring thanksgiving sacrifices to the Temple of Yahweh."

For I will cause to return the captivity of the land. This phrase, used in Jeremiah 33:7, is repeated here for emphasis.

TWO PROPHETS WORK MIRACLES, PROPHESY, AND ARE MARTYRED
Revelation 11:3–12

> *3 And I will give power unto my two witnesses, and they shall prophesy a thousand two hundred and threescore days, clothed in sackcloth.*

> *4 These are the two olive trees, and the two candlesticks standing before the God of the earth.*

> *5 And if any man will hurt them, fire proceedeth out of their mouth, and devoureth their enemies: and if any man will hurt them, he must in this manner be killed.*

6 These have power to shut heaven, that it rain not in the days of their prophecy: and have power over waters to turn them to blood, and to smite the earth with all plagues, as often as they will.

7 And when they shall have finished their testimony, the beast that ascendeth out of the bottomless pit shall make war against them, and shall overcome them, and kill them.

8 And their dead bodies shall lie in the street of the great city, which spiritually is called Sodom and Egypt, where also our Lord was crucified.

9 And they of the people and kindreds and tongues and nations shall see their dead bodies three days and an half, and shall not suffer their dead bodies to be put in graves.

10 And they that dwell upon the earth shall rejoice over them, and make merry, and shall send gifts one to another; because these two prophets tormented them that dwelt on the earth.

11 And after three days and an half the Spirit of life from God entered into them, and they stood upon their feet; and great fear fell upon them which saw them.

12 And they heard a great voice from heaven saying unto them, Come up hither. And they ascended up to heaven in a cloud; and their enemies beheld them.

In the last days, two prophets will serve in Jerusalem. These two are called "prophets" and "witnesses," and as such they will prophesy, preach repentance, warn the nations regarding coming judgments, work mighty miracles, bear testimony of Jesus Christ and his great atonement, and invite souls to come unto Christ. The length of this ministry will be approximately three and one-half years (Rev. 11:3). Elder Bruce R. McConkie wrote that "it is reasonable to suppose, knowing how the Lord has always dealt with his people in all ages, that they [the two prophets] will be two members of the Council of the Twelve or of the First Presidency of the Church."[12]

---

[12] *Millennial Messiah*, 390.

The scriptures give several clues to when the two prophets will prophesy: after the Jews "are gathered and have built the city of Jerusalem" (D&C 77:15), "at the time of the restoration" (D&C 77:15), and after the opening of the seventh seal but before the Second Coming (D&C 77:12–13); in the timetable of John the Revelator, the two prophets will prophesy during the events of the second "woe" (Rev. 11:14). They will possess great power from God to devour "their enemies" with fire, "shut heaven, that it rain not," turn waters to blood, and smite the earth with plagues according to their will (Rev. 11:5–6). The sackcloth mentioned in Revelation 11:3 may be symbolic, recalling Old Testament prophets who actually wore sackcloth during their ministry and suggesting a spirit and attitude of humility.

NOTES AND COMMENTARY

Rev. 11:3 *I will give power unto my two witnesses.* The word *power* does not belong in the text; it is not found in the original Greek (see note *a* to this verse in the LDS edition of the KJV); nevertheless, the verses that follow establish that the two witnesses will have great power indeed. With the number *two,* the law of witnesses is in effect: there are two witnesses so that God's word will be established (2 Cor. 13:1). The law of witnesses continues in our dispensation (D&C 6:28; 42:80–81). In Isaiah 51:20 the two prophets are called "sons," perhaps suggesting that they are sons of Abraham, either literally or by covenant; Zechariah 4:3 calls them "two olive trees," indicating that they possess oil and light. The two will bear witness to the people that Jesus is their Messiah, Savior, and God.

they shall prophesy a thousand two hundred and threescore days. The period of the two prophets' ministry in Jerusalem will be the same as that of Jesus Christ, three and one-half years. Perhaps significantly, the length of their ministry corresponds to the length of time that the Gentiles will "tread [Jerusalem] under foot" (Rev. 11:2). The number three and one-half, forty-two months, or 1,260 days (three and one-half years) occurs several times in Daniel and Revelation (Dan. 7:25; 9:27; 12:7; Rev. 11:2, 3, 11; 12:14; 13:5).[13]

---

[13] For the significance of these numbers, see Parry and Parry, *Understanding the Book of Revelation,* 137–38.

clothed in sackcloth. Sackcloth was a coarse, rough fabric used in making sacks (Gen. 42:25; Lev. 11:32; Josh. 9:4). Its use as clothing symbolized humility and sorrow (1 Kgs. 21:27; 2 Kgs. 6:30; Job 16:15; Isa. 22:11). The two prophets may not actually wear sackcloth, as did Isaiah and others (Isa. 20:2–4), but the phrase "clothed in sackcloth" does suggest a similarity between the two witnesses and the ancient prophets of Israel who were so attired. The two witnesses possess the same prophetic powers held by ancient prophets of Israel: the power to heal, shut the heavens, cause miracles, preach, teach, and bless lives in remarkable ways.

Rev. 11:4 *These are the two olive trees, and the two candlesticks.* The two witnesses are the same ones the prophet Zechariah envisioned (Zech. 4:11–14). He twice called them "two olive trees" (Zech. 4:3, 11), a symbolic expression that indicates they are "anointed ones" (Zech. 4:14), because olive trees produced the olive oil used in temple ritual. The two prophets as "anointed ones" perhaps means that they will have received the blessings of the holy temple, or perhaps it signifies that they have been anointed to their holy calling, as Christ, the Anointed One, was.

Rev. 11:5 *fire proceedeth out of their mouth.* The two witnesses will speak the word of God and thereby have power to destroy their enemies. They will possess immense God-given powers, as did Elijah, who caused fire to come down from heaven to consume his enemies by uttering the words, "If I be a man of God, then let fire come down from heaven, and consume thee and thy fifty" (2 Kgs. 1:10–14).

Rev. 11:6 *These have power to shut heaven, that it rain not.* The two prophets have threefold power: to shut heaven, to turn waters to blood, and to smite the earth with plagues. But these three are only representative of their powers; they will likely also have power to "put at defiance the armies of nations, to divide the earth, to break every band, to stand in the presence of God; to do all things according to his will, according to his command, to subdue principalities and powers; and this by the will of the Son of God" (JST Gen. 14:31).

Rev. 11:7 *when they shall have finished their testimony.* The two witnesses will not be destroyed by evil forces until after they have completed their appointed work on the earth. God will not permit his faithful servants to be killed before their time. The "testimony" they will bear is that Jesus Christ is the Messiah, the Son of God, the Savior of the world.

beast. John does not provide the identity of the beast, although it may be the same beast spoken of in Revelation 13:1–8.[14]

the bottomless pit. The pit, also called the abyss, or hell, is identified in Joseph Smith Translation Isaiah 14:15, 19. Although Satan is now the king of those in the pit (Rev. 9:11), God has total power over the pit (Rev. 20:1–3).

shall make war against them, and shall overcome them, and kill them. God will permit the "beast" to kill the two witnesses; evil forces do not have power over the righteous to harm or kill them, only insofar as it is part of God's plan. Later the beast and its allies will make war against Christ, but he will "overcome them, for he is Lord of lords, and King of kings" (Rev. 17:14; see also Rev. 19:11, 19).

Rev. 11:8 *their dead bodies shall lie in the street of the great city.* The "great city" identified here is Jerusalem, "where also our Lord was crucified."

Rev. 11:9 *they of the people and kindreds and tongues and nations shall see their dead bodies.* The Jerusalem Bible renders this passage as "men out of every people, race, language and nation will stare at their corpses." This event will be known internationally, perhaps through any number of modern communications systems (see also Rev. 11:10).

three days and an half. Similarly, Christ's body rested in the tomb three days ("after three days rise again"; Mark 8:31; 9:31; 10:34). For more on the number three and a half, see the commentary on Revelation 11:3, page 135.

shall not suffer their dead bodies to be put in graves. Great disrespect will be shown to the two prophets, for their enemies will not permit their bodies to receive a proper burial (Ps. 79:3; 2 Macc. 5:10). Joseph Smith explained, "It has always been considered a great calamity not to obtain an honorable burial: and one of the greatest

---

[14] For a discussion of the beasts in Rev. 13, see Parry and Parry, *Understanding the Book of Revelation,* 162–77.

curses the ancient prophets could put on any man, was that he should go without a burial."[15]

Rev. 11:10 *they that dwell upon the earth shall rejoice over them.* The pronoun *they* refers to "people and kindreds and tongues and nations" spoken of in the previous verse. The phrases "upon the earth" and "on the earth" emphasize that all people will be aware of the death of the two witnesses. That they will "make merry," exchange gifts, and not permit anyone to give the two prophets a proper burial indicates the wickedness of the people at this time. John explains that the wicked are making merry and exchanging gifts "because these two prophets tormented them." The torment may consist of the prophets' testimony against the world's wickedness, or it may be the plagues the prophets bring, or both.

Rev. 11:11–12 *the Spirit of life from God entered into them, and they stood upon their feet.* These words parallel Ezekiel's prophecy of the future resurrection of the house of Israel, suggesting that the two witnesses will not just come back to mortal life but will be resurrected at this time. Ezekiel's prophecy reads, "And the breath came into them, and they lived, and stood up upon their feet" (Ezek. 37:10).

great fear fell upon them which saw them. Many will witness the ascension of the two prophets: "their enemies beheld them" as "they ascended up to heaven."

Come up hither. And they ascended up to heaven in a cloud. A heavenly being directs the two prophets to "come up hither." Their ascension into a cloud recalls the ascension into heaven of Elijah (2 Kgs. 2:11) and of Christ (Acts 1:9).

THE MESSIAH BATTLES AGAINST THE JEWS' ENEMIES AND STANDS ON THE MOUNT OF OLIVES
Zechariah 14:1–5

1 Behold, the day of the Lord cometh, and thy spoil shall be divided in the midst of thee.

2 For I will gather all nations against Jerusalem to battle; and the city shall be taken, and the houses rifled, and the

---

[15] *History of the Church,* 5:361.

women ravished; and half of the city shall go forth into captivity, and the residue of the people shall not be cut off from the city.

3 Then shall the Lord go forth, and fight against those nations, as when he fought in the day of battle.

4 And his feet shall stand in that day upon the mount of Olives, which is before Jerusalem on the east, and the mount of Olives shall cleave in the midst thereof toward the east and toward the west, and there shall be a very great valley; and half of the mountain shall remove toward the north, and half of it toward the south.

5 And ye shall flee to the valley of the mountains; for the valley of the mountains shall reach unto Azal: yea, ye shall flee, like as ye fled from before the earthquake in the days of Uzziah king of Judah: and the Lord my God shall come, and all the saints with thee.

The Old Testament prophet Zechariah prophesied during the reign of Darius, king of Persia (Zech. 1:1). Zechariah described many of the signs of the times in his writings, especially regarding Jerusalem, the Jews, and Christ's appearance to them. Many of these signs will be fulfilled during the last of the last days, shortly before the Second Coming.

Zechariah 14 pertains directly to Judah and Jerusalem: Judah is mentioned explicitly in verses 14 and 21, and Jerusalem in verses 2, 4, 8, 10, 11, 12, 14, 16, 17, and 21. The five verses cited above (Zech. 14:1–5) speak of a great war in the last days, in which all nations will battle against Jerusalem. Jerusalem will fall in that battle, and many of her inhabitants will be captured.[16] During the heat of the battle, or perhaps at the time when total defeat appears imminent to the Jews, Jesus Christ will descend, set his feet on the Mount of Olives, and save the Jews.

Our modern prophets have spoken about these events as well. President Ezra Taft Benson said: "To these beleaguered sons of

---

[16] See the commentary on Armageddon, page 264.

Judah, surrounded by hostile Gentile armies, who again threaten to overrun Jerusalem, the Savior—their Messiah—will set His feet on the Mount of Olives, 'and it shall cleave in twain, and the earth shall tremble, and reel to and fro, and the heavens also shall shake' (Doctrine and Covenants 45:48).

"The Lord Himself will then rout the Gentile armies, decimating their forces. (See Ezekiel 38:39.) Judah will be spared, no longer to be persecuted and scattered. The Jews will then approach their Deliverer and ask, 'What are these wounds in thine hands and in thy feet?' He will say to them: 'These wounds are the wounds with which I was wounded in the house of my friends. I am he who was lifted up. I am Jesus that was crucified. I am the Son of God. And then shall they weep because of their iniquities; then shall they lament because they persecuted their king.' (Doctrine and Covenants 45:51–53.)

"What a touching drama this will be! Jesus—Prophet, Messiah, King—will be welcomed in His own country!"[17]

NOTES AND COMMENTARY

Zech. 14:1 *the day of the Lord cometh.* "The day of the Lord" is the time when the Lord will destroy Israel's enemies and then make his glorious appearance at his second coming. Other prophets give the same meaning to this expression (Isa. 2:12; Joel 1:15; 2:1, 11; Mal. 4:5). The "day of the Lord" theme continues throughout Zechariah 14 with the phrase "in that day" (vv. 4, 6, 8, 9, 13, 20, and 21); each time, the phrase hearkens back to the opening phrase in verse 1.

thy spoil shall be divided in the midst of thee. The verb *spoil* (Hebrew *salal*) is used seventy-five times in the Bible, most frequently with reference to booty or plunder taken by a conquering army (for example, see Deut. 20:14; Josh. 7:21). Zechariah explains that the nations identified in the following verse will battle against Jerusalem, take spoil from her, and divide it.

Zech. 14:2 *For I will gather all nations against Jerusalem to battle.* Shortly before Christ's coming, all nations will gather to battle against Jerusalem and Israel. Many prophets have prophesied of this

---

[17] Benson, *Come unto Christ,* 113–14; see also Smith, *Signs of the Times,* 61; McConkie, *New Witness,* 637.

event, including Joel (Joel 1–3, especially 2:2–4 and 3:2–14), Ezekiel (Ezek. 38–39, esp. 38:15–18), and John (Rev. 16:14–21). Joel describes these nations as "a great people and a strong; there hath not been ever the like, neither shall be any more after it" (Joel 2:2); he quotes the Lord, "I will also gather all nations. . . . Assemble your-selves, and come, all ye heathen, and gather yourselves together round about" (Joel 3:2, 11). The Lord said to Gog through Ezekiel, "Thou shalt come up against my people of Israel, as a cloud to cover the land; it shall be in the latter days, and I will bring thee against my land" (Ezek. 38:16). Apparently the nations will battle against Jerusa-lem at the same time the two prophets minister and prophesy in Jeru-salem (Rev. 11:1–13).

Why do the prophecies say that the Lord, the Prince of Peace, will gather nations to war? (This question takes on added significance when we read in Revelation 16:14 that "spirits of devils" gather the nations to battle.) Perhaps these prophecies mean that God is in con-trol of human history and that he ultimately orders all events for his purposes, to bring to pass his plan of happiness on the earth.

the city shall be taken, and the houses rifled, and the women rav-ished. These three actions describe the horrors that will accompany this war, when earth's nations fight against Jerusalem: the city will be captured, the houses looted, and the women forcibly abused (Isa. 13:16). Similar horrors are common in the wars throughout history.

half of the city shall go forth into captivity, and the residue of the people shall not be cut off from the city. During this war, approxi-mately half of Jerusalem's population will be captured, but the remaining half will survive capture. Compare Zechariah's prophecy (Zech. 13:8–9) that in the land of Israel two-thirds will be destroyed and one-third will remain.

Zech. 14:3 *Then shall the Lord go forth, and fight against those nations. Then* is a chronological term; it suggests that the Lord will fight against Israel's enemies *after* the city has been taken. Anciently, the Lord won every battle that he fought against the nations that sur-rounded Palestine (see, for example, Josh. 6:1–16; Judg. 7:9–15); in the last days, he will again fight on behalf of Jerusalem and Judah and prevail against the nations. Isaiah prophesied, "The Lord shall go forth as a mighty man, he shall stir up jealousy like a man of war: he shall cry, yea, roar; he shall prevail against his enemies" (Isa. 42:13; see also 26:21).

The text here is not immediately clear on how the Lord will fight against the nations, although verses 12 and 13 of the same chapter (Zech. 14) give two clues: he will smite these nations with a *plague,* and he will cause a *great tumult* to arise among them. These verses read: "And this shall be the plague wherewith the Lord will smite all the people that have fought against Jerusalem; their flesh shall consume away while they stand upon their feet, and their eyes shall consume away in their holes, and their tongue shall consume away in their mouth. And it shall come to pass in that day, that a great tumult from the Lord shall be among them; and they shall lay hold every one on the hand of his neighbour, and his hand shall rise up against the hand of his neighbour."

Perhaps the important thing for us to know is that the Lord will prevail in his battle against the nations. Elder Joseph Fielding Smith testified: "The Lord will come, according to His promise, unto His people in the hour of their distress, and will deliver them from their enemies. . . . And the nations that seek to destroy Jerusalem in that day will the Lord destroy, for he shall be King over all the earth and righteousness shall prevail among the people."[18]

Zech. 14:4 *his feet shall stand in that day upon the mount of Olives.* This prophecy is very specific regarding when, where, and how Jesus Christ will appear and rescue the remaining Jews from destruction during this great war (see also D&C 45:48). This event will also fulfill the prophecy uttered by two heavenly messengers when Christ ascended from the same Mount of Olives soon after his resurrection: "Ye men of Galilee, why stand ye gazing up into heaven? this same Jesus, which is taken up from you into heaven, shall so come in like manner as ye have seen him go into heaven" (Acts 1:11).

On one side of the Mount of Olives is the garden of Gethsemane, where Christ was "sorrowful and very heavy," prayed to the Father to let the cup pass from him, bled from every pore, and was betrayed by

---

[18] Conference Report, Apr. 1911, 125.

a kiss from Judas (Matt. 26:30–50). On Jesus' mortal visit to this mount, he submitted himself to wicked men; on his future visit he will destroy the wicked.

The phrase "in that day" hearkens back to "the day of the Lord" in Revelation 14:1.

which is before Jerusalem on the east. The Mount of Olives is immediately east of Jerusalem, a few minutes' walk through the narrow valley Kidron, which separates Jerusalem from the Mount of Olives.

the mount of Olives shall cleave in the midst thereof toward the east and toward the west. Having complete power over the elements of the earth, Christ will cause the mount to be split in half. And as the cleft will run through the mountain from east to west, then "half of the mountain shall remove toward the north, and half of it toward the south." As a result, "a very great valley" will be created, through which the Jews will flee to safety.

Zech. 14:5 *ye shall flee to the valley of the mountains.* When Christ causes the Mount of Olives to divide in half, the beleaguered Jews will escape to safety through this newly created rift. The verb *flee* is used three times in this verse (*flee* twice and *fled* once), emphasizing that the Jews will find safety at the feet of their Messiah.

for the valley of the mountains shall reach unto Azal. The newly created rift will extend fully to Azal, but the location of Azal is at present unknown.

like as ye fled from before the earthquake in the days of Uzziah king of Judah. Little is known about the earthquake in Uzziah's days, but it was of such importance that Amos mentions it in the opening words of his book (Amos 1:1).

the Lord my God shall come, and all the saints with thee. Many will accompany Christ at his coming. Matthew's testimony promises that "the Son of man shall come in the glory of his Father with his angels" (Matt. 16:27). Paul speaks of "the coming of our Lord Jesus Christ with all his saints" (1 Thes. 3:13; see also D&C 76:63; 1 Thes. 4:13–17).

"WHAT ARE THESE WOUNDS IN THINE HANDS?"
Doctrine and Covenants 45:47–53

47 Then shall the arm of the Lord fall upon the nations.

48 And then shall the Lord set his foot upon this mount, and it shall cleave in twain, and the earth shall tremble, and reel to and fro, and the heavens also shall shake.

49 And the Lord shall utter his voice, and all the ends of the earth shall hear it; and the nations of the earth shall mourn, and they that have laughed shall see their folly.

50 And calamity shall cover the mocker, and the scorner shall be consumed; and they that have watched for iniquity shall be hewn down and cast into the fire.

51 And then shall the Jews look upon me and say: What are these wounds in thine hands and in thy feet?

52 Then shall they know that I am the Lord; for I will say unto them: These wounds are the wounds with which I was wounded in the house of my friends. I am he who was lifted up. I am Jesus that was crucified. I am the Son of God.

53 And then shall they weep because of their iniquities; then shall they lament because they persecuted their king.

These verses from the Doctrine and Covenants cite several passages from the book of Zechariah, including 12:10–11, 13:6 and 14:3–4. Zechariah detailed many events regarding the last days and Jerusalem in chapters 12 through 14 but did not set the events in chronological order. The verses cited above (D&C 45:48–53) seem to set the chronology for many of Zechariah's prophecies by using the chronological term *then* six times (vv. 47, 48, 51–53).

The main actors in these verses are the Lord, the nations, and the Jews. The Lord's actions include destroying the nations (vv. 47, 50), standing on the Mount of Olives (v. 48), uttering his voice (v. 49), and testifying of his divinity (v. 52). The nations will hear the Lord's voice and mourn, and many individuals will be destroyed (vv. 49–50). The Jews will view the Savior's wounds from the crucifixion, hear his testimony of his divinity, recognize him to be their king, and weep and lament their folly.

NOTES AND COMMENTARY

D&C 45:48 *then shall the Lord set his foot upon this mount.* Zechariah 14:4 reads, "And his feet shall stand in that day upon the mount of Olives, which is before Jerusalem on the east."[19] A latter-day revelation sets forth many of the Lord's divine activities during this period of time: "For behold, he shall stand upon the mount of Olivet [another name for the mount of Olives], and upon the mighty ocean, even the great deep, and upon the islands of the sea, and upon the land of Zion" (D&C 133:20).

it shall cleave in twain. Zechariah 14:4 reads, "The mount of Olives shall cleave in the midst thereof toward the east and toward the west, and there shall be a very great valley."[20]

and the earth shall tremble, and reel to and fro, and the heavens also shall shake. Do these words speak of an earthquake that will occur when the mount splits in two? Interestingly, Zechariah 14:5 also refers to an earthquake, one that took place during the reign of Uzziah, king of Judah.

D&C 45:49 *the Lord shall utter his voice, and all the ends of the earth shall hear it.* A parallel revelation adds further light to this event: "And he shall utter his voice out of Zion, and he shall speak from Jerusalem, and his voice shall be heard among all people; and it shall be a voice as the voice of many waters, and as the voice of a great thunder, which shall break down the mountains, and the valleys shall not be found" (D&C 133:21–22).

The words which the Lord shall communicate are at present unknown. Perhaps his words will be similar to those he uttered when he descended from heaven and then "stood in the midst" of the Nephites at Bountiful: "Behold, I am Jesus Christ, whom the prophets testified shall come into the world" (3 Ne. 11:8, 10).

---

[19] See the commentary on Zech. 14:4, page 142.
[20] See the commentary on Zech. 14:4, page 142.

and the nations of the earth shall mourn, and they that have laughed shall see their folly. These words reveal that earth's nations will mourn after the events described in Doctrine and Covenants 45:47–49. Revelation 1:7 speaks similarly: "Behold, he cometh with clouds; and every eye shall see him, and they also which pierced him: and all kindreds of the earth shall wail because of him" (see also Matt. 24:30).

Zechariah 12:10–14 describes the mourning not of the nations but of the Jews. After they look upon Christ and recognize his wounds, they will "mourn for him, as one mourneth for his only son, and shall be in bitterness for him, as one that is in bitterness for his firstborn. In that day shall there be a great mourning in Jerusalem" (Zech. 12:10–11; see also vv. 12–14). The nations and Jews will mourn because they rejected Christ as their Savior, Messiah, and King.

D&C 45:50 *And calamity shall cover the mocker, and the scorner shall be consumed; and they that have watched for iniquity shall be hewn down and cast into the fire.* The three types of wicked people identified in this verse—*mocker, scorner,* and *they that have watched for iniquity*—represent unrepentant sinners of every kind. The four types of destruction set forth in this verse—*calamity, consumed, hewn down,* and *cast into the fire*—depict the manner in which sinners will be destroyed at Christ's second coming. The phrase *watched for iniquity* probably means that wicked people look for opportunities to commit, participate in, or take part in iniquity. They actively seek chances to be iniquitous, rather than just committing sins of omission.

D&C 45:51 *then shall the Jews look upon me and say.* Zechariah prophesied of this event with these words: "And they shall look upon me whom they have pierced" (Zech. 12:10). After Christ sets his foot on the Mount of Olives, and after the other events described in Doctrine and Covenants 45:47–50, then the Jews will look upon Christ and ask about the wounds they see on his body.

What are these wounds in thine hands and in thy feet? The Jews will look upon Christ and ask, "What are these wounds in thine hands and in thy feet?" Zechariah prophesied of this event with, "And one shall say unto him, What are these wounds in thine hands?" (Zech.

13:6). In the poignant event depicted here, the Jews will begin to see that they have been deceived about the identity of their Lord.

D&C 45:52 *Then shall they know that I am the Lord; for I will say unto them: These wounds are the wounds with which I was wounded in the house of my friends. I am he who was lifted up. I am Jesus that was crucified. I am the Son of God.* Zechariah's version of these events is abbreviated: "Then he shall answer, Those with which I was wounded in the house of my friends" (Zech. 13:6). The latter-day revelation just cited (D&C 45:52) identifies the speaker explicitly as Jesus, the Son of God. In addition, the latter-day revelation identifies Christ as one who was "lifted up" and "crucified." Note Christ's four statements, his testimony that he is the Crucified One, each beginning with the personal pronoun *I:*

"I was wounded in the house of my friends."

"I am he who was lifted up."

"I am Jesus that was crucified."

"I am the Son of God."

After Christ provides this testimony, and after viewing the marks in his hands and feet, then the Jews will at last understand and "know" that he is "the Lord."

The phrase "the house of my friends," found in both Zechariah 13:6 and Doctrine and Covenants 45:52, may indicate that perhaps some of Jesus' friends, acquired during his mortal ministry, betrayed him to some extent and favored the crucifixion. More likely, the phrase seems to speak of his own people, the Jewish nation, which sought his crucifixion.

After citing Doctrine and Covenants 45:51–52, Elder Bruce R. McConkie wrote: "And thus cometh the day of the conversion of the Jews. It is a millennial day, a day after the destruction of the wicked, a day when those who remain shall seek the Lord and find his gospel."[21]

D&C 45:53 *then shall they weep because of their iniquities; then shall they lament because they persecuted their king.* On this heartrending occasion, the Jews will be filled with profound grief. They will see that they rejected their very Savior, that they have lived for millennia in a degree of spiritual darkness, that they have lost rich

---

[21] *Millennial Messiah*, 231.

opportunities to know and love and be blessed by their Lord. The evocative words *weep* and *lament* suggest heartfelt sorrow and mourning that goes to the deepest core of their being.

THE REDEMPTION OF JUDAH AND JERUSALEM
Doctrine and Covenants 109:61–64, 67

> *61 But thou knowest that thou hast a great love for the children of Jacob, who have been scattered upon the mountains for a long time, in a cloudy and dark day.*
>
> *62 We therefore ask thee to have mercy upon the children of Jacob, that Jerusalem, from this hour, may begin to be redeemed;*
>
> *63 And the yoke of bondage may begin to be broken off from the house of David;*
>
> *64 And the children of Judah may begin to return to the lands which thou didst give to Abraham, their father. . . .*
>
> *67 And may all the scattered remnants of Israel, who have been driven to the ends of the earth, come to a knowledge of the truth, believe in the Messiah, and be redeemed from oppression, and rejoice before thee.*

This passage from the dedicatory prayer of the Kirtland Temple, offered on 27 March 1836, provides details regarding the redemption of the Jews and their city, Jerusalem. There is a reciprocal relationship in these verses between God and the Jews, a remnant of the house of Israel. God, on the one hand, will redeem the Jews because of his "great love" for them in his "mercy"; the Jews, on the other hand, will be redeemed as they "come to a knowledge of the truth" and "believe in the Messiah." The word *redeemed,* then, is used here first in connection with God's mercy upon the Jews and Jerusalem (v. 62), and again with the Jews' (and all the remnants of Israel) coming to the truth and accepting Jesus Christ (v. 67).

NOTES AND COMMENTARY

D&C 109:61 *great love for the children of Jacob.* God's perfect love for his children is the reason he keeps his covenants with us and remembers to restore Israel to their homelands and to the truth of the gospel.

scattered upon the mountains for a long time. The phrase "scattered upon the mountains" probably means "scattered throughout the nations." Members of the house of Israel, including Judah, have been scattered throughout the lands of the world for millennia. Perhaps the first great scattering occurred in 722–721 B.C., when the ten tribes were deported from their homeland and taken northward from ancient Palestine by the Assyrians. More than a century later the kingdom of Judah was destroyed by the Babylonians and many of Judah's people were scattered. Subsequent scatterings have occurred, so that Nephi prophesied, "Wherefore, the Jews shall be scattered among all nations; . . . wherefore, the Jews shall be scattered by other nations" (2 Ne. 25:15). Nephi also predicted concerning the Jews that they would be "scattered, and the Lord God [would scourge] them by other nations for the space of many generations, yea, even down from generation to generation until they shall be persuaded to believe in Christ, the Son of God, and the atonement" (2 Ne. 25:16).

a cloudy and dark day. This figure of speech may symbolize a time when the light of the gospel does not shine upon certain groups, or it may symbolize a time of trouble and tribulation.

D&C 109:62 *We therefore ask thee to have mercy upon the children of Jacob.* The Prophet Joseph Smith spoke for all of us when he used the plural pronoun *we* in "We therefore ask thee . . ." All of us should plead for God to extend mercy upon other members of the house of Jacob.

Jerusalem, from this hour, may begin to be redeemed. Since this dedicatory prayer, the city of Jerusalem has received tens of thousands of Jews, who have built homes, schools, parks, and businesses in the earliest stages of the redemption of her inhabitants.

D&C 109:63 *the yoke of bondage may begin to be broken off.* The yoke of bondage may refer to the nations who captured, scattered, persecuted, or enslaved the Jews through the ages to the present time; or it may speak of the great burden of sin or ignorance that accompanies all of us until we are taught and we repent and receive forgiveness (cf. Isa. 58:6).

the house of David. This expression is another name for the Jews, or those descended through the lineage of Judah, of which group King David was a prominent member.

D&C 109:64 *the children of Judah may begin to return to the lands.* After the time of this dedicatory prayer, history records that great numbers of Jews sought and returned to their homeland, beginning the fulfillment of many prophecies of their return (see, for example, Isa. 11:11–16; Isa. 14:1–3; Jer. 3:14–20; Jer. 50:19–20; Ezek. 11:17–21; Amos 9:11–15; 2 Ne. 25:9–11).

which thou didst give to Abraham, their father. This passage refers to the Abrahamic covenant, in which the Lord promised Abraham that his posterity would receive lands of promise. Abraham recorded: "The Lord appeared unto me, and said unto me: Arise, and take Lot with thee; for I have purposed to take thee away out of Haran, and to make of thee a minister to bear my name in a strange land which I will give unto thy seed after thee for an everlasting possession, when they hearken to my voice" (Abr. 2:6). Also, "I will give unto thee, and to thy seed after thee, the land wherein thou art a stranger, all the land of Canaan" (Gen. 17:8; see also Gen. 12:7; 13:15; 15:18).

D&C 109:67 *all the scattered remnants of Israel.* The prayer speaks of all the remnants of Israel, including the ten tribes, the Lamanites, and the Jews.

who have been driven to the ends of the earth. All of the remnants or branches of Israel have been scattered throughout the world, as many prophets have explained in plain terms (Jer. 29:18; Ezek. 12:15; 34:6; Amos 9:9; Zech. 7:14; 1 Ne. 10:12). Nephi's words are clear: "The house of Israel, sooner or later, will be scattered upon all the face of the earth, and also among all nations. . . . Yea, the more part of all the tribes have been led away; and they are scattered to and fro upon the isles of the sea; and whither they are none of us knoweth, save that we know that they have been led away. . . . Wherefore, they shall be scattered among all nations" (1 Ne. 22:3–5).

come to a knowledge of the truth, believe in the Messiah, and be redeemed from oppression, and rejoice before thee. Note the apparent cause-and-effect relationship that exists in these four clauses (which are separated by the three commas): the scattered remnants of Israel who seek and receive the truth and believe that Jesus Christ is the Messiah (the cause) will receive the blessings of redemption and joy (the effect). Note also the chronological order of the four clauses; they represent sequential acts of the investigator of religious truth: one must first receive the truth, which brings one to faith or a belief in Jesus Christ, which is followed by redemption, and after redemption comes true joy in knowing that one has come unto Christ.

CHAPTER 4

ZION AND THE NEW JERUSALEM

SIGNS OF THE TIMES

1. The New Jerusalem is built in Independence, Missouri.

2. Zion is redeemed after she fulfills certain conditions.

3. Zion flourishes and blossoms like a beautiful flower before Christ's coming.

4. Zion is a place of safety for the Saints.

5. Zion and her stakes serve as a refuge from the world's wickedness and God's judgments on sinners.

6. God blesses Zion with great blessings; she shall never be destroyed.

7. The Lord blesses Zion with his glory and light.

8. Zion, or the New Jerusalem, prepares the Saints for Christ's coming.

9. A great temple is built in Independence, Missouri.

10. The Lord appears in glory to Zion.

11. The Lord loves Zion and its inhabitants: it is his city, and its inhabitants are his people.

Joseph Smith declared that the building of Zion in the latter days "is a cause that has interested the people of God in every age; it is a theme upon which prophets, priests and kings have dwelt with peculiar delight; they have looked forward with joyful anticipation to the day in which we live; and fired with heavenly and joyful anticipations they have sung and written and prophesied of this our day; but they died without the sight; we are the favored people that God has made choice of to bring about the Latter-day glory."[1]

---

[1] *History of the Church,* 4:609–10.

The prophets have used numerous expressions to characterize Zion that are both prophetic and descriptive: *peace, refuge, safety, rejoice, flourish, glory, ensign, Mount Zion, beauty, holiness, prosper, glorious, very great, very terrible, honor, the pure in heart, multiplicity of blessings, songs of everlasting joy, kingdom of our God and his Christ, strength, power, light, standard for the nations, defense, Holy City,* and *New Jerusalem* (D&C 45:66; 49:25; 64:41–42; 82:14; 84:2; 97:18–19, 21, 28; 101:18; 105:32; 113:8; 115:5–6; Moses 7:62). These and other expressions create feelings of wonderment, joy, and great anticipation in the hearts of the Saints.

The nations of the world will in a future day also stand in awe because of Zion. They shall say, "Surely Zion is the city of our God" and "surely Zion cannot fall" (D&C 97:19); they "shall tremble because of her, and shall fear because of her terrible ones" (D&C 64:43); they will hold in high esteem those who are privileged to have been born in her (Ps. 87:5). The time will come when Zion will be called "the perfection of beauty" (Ps. 50:2) and "the joy of the whole earth" (Ps. 48:2); she will be known as the "city of God" (87:3), the "city of the great King" (Ps. 48:2), and the "city of our God" (D&C 97:19).

Joseph Smith, who saw in vision "the armies of heaven protecting the Saints in their return to Zion,"[2] summarized that the building of Zion is a "work that God and angels have contemplated with delight for generations past; that fired the souls of the ancient patriarchs and prophets."[3]

Other prophets and apostles have also defined *Zion.* Elder Harold B. Lee explained that "there are several meanings of the word Zion.

"It may have reference to the hill named Mt. Zion or by extension in the land of Jerusalem. [See Micah 4:2.]

"It has sometimes been used, as by the prophet Micah, to refer to the location of 'the mountain of the house of the Lord'—as some place apart from Jerusalem.

"Zion was so called by Enoch in reference to the 'City of Holiness,' or the 'City of Enoch.' [See Moses 7:18–19.] The Land of Zion

---

[2] *History of the Church,* 2:381.
[3] *History of the Church,* 4:610.

has been used to refer, in some connotations, to the Western Hemisphere.

"But there is another most significant use of the term by which the Church of God is called Zion, comprising, according to the Lord's own definition, 'the pure in heart.' (D&C 97:21.)"[4]

Elder Robert D. Hales provided many specific statements that explain what Zion means to each of us. "Zion is characterized in scripture as a city in which the people 'were of one heart and one mind, and dwelt in righteousness; and there was no poor among them.' (Moses 7:18.) Zion is 'every man seeking the interest of his neighbor, and doing all things with an eye single to the glory of God.' (D&C 82:19.) This promised Zion always seems to be a little beyond our reach. We need to understand that as much virtue can be gained in progressing toward Zion as in dwelling there. It is a process as well as a destination. We approach or withdraw from Zion through the manner in which we conduct our daily dealings, live within our families, whether we pay an honest tithe and generous fast offering, how we seize opportunities to serve and do so diligently. Many are perfected upon the road to Zion who will never see the city in mortality."[5]

INDEPENDENCE, THE CENTER PLACE
Doctrine and Covenants 57:1–3

> *1 Hearken, O ye elders of my church, saith the Lord your God, who have assembled yourselves together, according to my commandments, in this land, which is the land of Missouri, which is the land which I have appointed and consecrated for the gathering of saints.*

> *2 Wherefore, this is the land of promise, and the place for the city of Zion.*

> *3 And thus saith the Lord your God, if you will receive wisdom here is wisdom. Behold, the place which is now called Independence is the center place; and a spot for the temple is*

---

[4] Conference Report, Oct. 1968, 61–62.

[5] *Ensign,* May 1986, 30. Elder Bruce R. McConkie also defined Zion in *Millennial Messiah,* 282–84.

lying westward, upon a lot which is not far from the court-house.

Truths regarding the New Jerusalem have been revealed line upon line through Joseph Smith. In 1829 the Prophet learned as he translated the Book of Mormon that America is the place for the New Jerusalem (Ether 13:2–10), which would be built by the house of Israel (3 Ne. 21:23). In September 1830, the Lord promised to reveal the location of the city Zion (D&C 28:9); on 9 February 1831 he promised, "Thou shalt ask, and it shall be revealed unto you in mine own due time where the New Jerusalem shall be built" (D&C 42:62). Doctrine and Covenants 45:66–75 defines the New Jerusalem as a place of refuge, peace, and safety; Doctrine and Covenants 57 sets forth Independence as the place of the New Jerusalem and its temple (D&C 57:1–3). This section was revealed after the Prophet inquired, "When will the wilderness blossom as the rose? When will Zion be built up in her glory, and where will Thy temple stand, unto which all nations shall come in the last days?"[6] The same revelation explains that the land should be purchased for "an everlasting inheritance" (D&C 57:4–6) and provides instructions for settling the land (D&C 57:7–16).

Doctrine and Covenants 57:1–3 speaks of an actual physical gathering of Saints, for geographical terms are used: *land* is mentioned four times, *place* three times, *city* once, and the proper names *Missouri* and *Independence* are identified. The revelation specifically identifies the location of the temple: a *lot* not far from the *courthouse*. The ground where the temple will be built in Independence, Missouri, is sacred space and consecrated land (D&C 57:1): "The Garden of Eden was in Jackson County—the Center Place of Zion where a great temple will be reared."[7]

Many Saints will someday return to Jackson County to build the temple. The Lord comforted his people by revealing, "Zion shall not be moved out of her place, notwithstanding her children are scattered" (D&C 101:17). Elder Orson F. Whitney wrote: "Will our mission end here [in Utah]? Is the State of Utah the proper monument

---

[6] *History of the Church,* 1:189.
[7] See Dahl and Cannon, *Teachings of Joseph Smith,* 277; Dyer, *Refiner's Fire,* 17–18.

to the 'Mormon' people? No. . . . The monument to 'Mormonism' will stand in Jackson County, [Missouri]. There the great City will be built: There Zion will arise and shine, 'the joy of the whole Earth,' and there the Lord will come to His temple in His own time, when His people shall have made the required preparation."[8] President Joseph Fielding Smith declared that "the center place, where the City New Jerusalem is to be built, is in Jackson County, Missouri. It was never the intention to substitute Utah or any other place for Jackson County."[9] Elder Bruce R. McConkie commented in 1982: "There is no present call for the saints to purchase land or to live in Jackson Couny or in any place connected therewith. The revealed word relative to the gathering to Independence and its environs will come through the prophet of God on earth. When it does come . . . that call will not be for the saints in general to assemble there. The return to Jackson County will be by delegates, as it were. Those whose services are needed there will assemble as appointed. The rest of Israel will remain in their appointed places."[10]

NOTES AND COMMENTARY

D&C 57:1 *Hearken.* Pay strict heed.

D&C 57:1–2 *land of Missouri.* Four expressions here define Missouri's important future role in the building of Zion and its temple: Missouri is the *appointed* land, the *consecrated* land, the *land of promise,* and the *place for the city of Zion.* Other revelations explain that the land of Zion is God's "goodly land" (D&C 103:24), the land of inheritance for the faithful (D&C 52:42), "a choice land above all other lands, a chosen land of the Lord" (Ether 13:2), the place for the Lord's "holy sanctuary" (Ether 13:3). Article of Faith 10 affirms that "Zion (the New Jerusalem) will be built upon the American continent."

the land which I have appointed. The land of Missouri was appointed for the Saints' gathering long ago, and that appointment has not changed. Many Saints will yet gather there. Doctrine and

---

[8] In Smith and Sjodahl, *Commentary,* 147.
[9] *Doctrines of Salvation,* 3:72.
[10] *Millennial Messiah,* 294.

Covenants 101:20 states, "There is none other place appointed than that which I have appointed; neither shall there be any other place appointed than that which I have appointed, for the work of the gathering of my saints."

consecrated. To be consecrated is to be hallowed and set apart. The Lord himself consecrated the land of Zion (D&C 52:2; 103:24).

land of promise. The Jaredites (Ether 2:7–15), Nephites (1 Ne. 2:20; 5:5), Jews (2 Ne. 9:2), and others possessed or will yet possess lands of promise. The land of promise for the Latter-day Saints is "a land flowing with milk and honey," a land "upon which there shall be no curse when the Lord cometh," a land of "inheritance" both "while the earth shall stand" and "again in eternity, no more to pass away" (D&C 38:18–20).

D&C 57:3 *here is wisdom.* The Lord explains that what follows is his will.

Independence is the center place. Elsewhere Joseph Smith spoke regarding Zion and the "center" with these words: "You know there has been great discussion in relation to Zion—where it is, and where the gathering of the dispensation is, and which I am now going to tell you. The prophets have spoken and written upon it; but I will make a proclamation that will cover a broader ground. *The whole of America is Zion itself from north to south, and is described by the Prophets, who declare that it is the Zion where the mountain of the Lord should be, and that it should be in the center of the land.* When Elders shall take up and examine the old prophecies in the Bible, they will see it."[11]

the temple. The temple is again mentioned in Doctrine and Covenants 84:3–5, where the Lord explains that it will "be built unto the Lord, and a cloud shall rest upon it, which cloud shall be even the glory of the Lord, which shall fill the house" (see also D&C 84:31; 97:10).

a lot which is not far from the courthouse. According to Elder Alvin R. Dyer, "the courthouse [in Independence] was built in 1827. . . . It was first erected at Lexington Avenue and Lynn Street, just a little northeast of its present location. It remained there until 1916,

---

[11] *History of the Church,* 6:318–19.

when it was moved and restored at its present location, on West Kansas just west of Main Street.

"In its former location it was almost directly east of the spot of ground (River Street, just south of Lexington Avenue), where the Prophet Joseph Smith stood, on August 3, 1831, and pronounced a dedication for the erection of a temple on this consecrated land."[12]

WHEN WILL ZION BE REDEEMED?
Doctrine and Covenants 105:9–19, 23, 27–41

9 Therefore, in consequence of the transgressions of my people, it is expedient in me that mine elders should wait for a little season for the redemption of Zion—

10 That they themselves may be prepared, and that my people may be taught more perfectly, and have experience, and know more perfectly concerning their duty, and the things which I require at their hands.

11 And this cannot be brought to pass until mine elders are endowed with power from on high.

12 For behold, I have prepared a great endowment and blessing to be poured out upon them, inasmuch as they are faithful and continue in humility before me.

13 Therefore it is expedient in me that mine elders should wait for a little season, for the redemption of Zion.

14 For behold, I do not require at their hands to fight the battles of Zion; for, as I said in a former commandment, even so will I fulfil—I will fight your battles.

15 Behold, the destroyer I have sent forth to destroy and lay waste mine enemies; and not many years hence they shall not be left to pollute mine heritage, and to blaspheme my name upon the lands which I have consecrated for the gathering together of my saints.

16 Behold, I have commanded my servant Joseph Smith, Jun., to say unto the strength of my house, even my warriors, my

---

[12] *Refiner's Fire*, 22.

young men, and middle-aged, to gather together for the redemption of my people, and throw down the towers of mine enemies, and scatter their watchmen;

17 But the strength of mine house have not hearkened unto my words.

18 But inasmuch as there are those who have hearkened unto my words, I have prepared a blessing and an endowment for them, if they continue faithful.

19 I have heard their prayers, and will accept their offering; and it is expedient in me that they should be brought thus far for a trial of their faith. . . .

23 And let all my people who dwell in the regions round about be very faithful, and prayerful, and humble before me, and reveal not the things which I have revealed unto them, until it is wisdom in me that they should be revealed. . . .

27 And I will soften the hearts of the people, as I did the heart of Pharaoh, from time to time, until my servant Joseph Smith, Jun., and mine elders, whom I have appointed, shall have time to gather up the strength of my house,

28 And to have sent wise men, to fulfil that which I have commanded concerning the purchasing of all the lands in Jackson county that can be purchased, and in the adjoining counties round about.

29 For it is my will that these lands should be purchased; and after they are purchased that my saints should possess them according to the laws of consecration which I have given.

30 And after these lands are purchased, I will hold the armies of Israel guiltless in taking possession of their own lands, which they have previously purchased with their moneys, and of throwing down the towers of mine enemies that may be upon them, and scattering their watchmen, and avenging me of mine enemies unto the third and fourth generation of them that hate me.

31 But first let my army become very great, and let it be sanctified before me, that it may become fair as the sun, and clear as the moon, and that her banners may be terrible unto all nations;

32 That the kingdoms of this world may be constrained to acknowledge that the kingdom of Zion is in very deed the kingdom of our God and his Christ; therefore, let us become subject unto her laws.

33 Verily I say unto you, it is expedient in me that the first elders of my church should receive their endowment from on high in my house, which I have commanded to be built unto my name in the land of Kirtland.

34 And let those commandments which I have given concerning Zion and her law be executed and fulfilled, after her redemption.

35 There has been a day of calling, but the time has come for a day of choosing; and let those be chosen that are worthy.

36 And it shall be manifest unto my servant, by the voice of the Spirit, those that are chosen; and they shall be sanctified;

37 And inasmuch as they follow the counsel which they receive, they shall have power after many days to accomplish all things pertaining to Zion.

38 And again I say unto you, sue for peace, not only to the people that have smitten you, but also to all people;

39 And lift up an ensign of peace, and make a proclamation of peace unto the ends of the earth;

40 And make proposals for peace unto those who have smitten you, according to the voice of the Spirit which is in you, and all things shall work together for your good.

41 Therefore, be faithful; and behold, and lo, I am with you even unto the end. Even so. Amen.

On 16 December 1833 the Lord revealed why Zion would not be redeemed at that time by explaining that among Church members "there were jarrings, and contentions, and envyings, and strifes, and lustful and covetous desires." Also, they "were slow to hearken unto the voice of the Lord their God," and "they esteemed lightly [his] counsel." It was "in consequence of their transgressions" that the Saints were "afflicted, and persecuted, and cast out from the land of their inheritance" (D&C 101:6–8, 1–2). In the same revelation the Lord provided hope and comfort to his people by promising a future redemption of Zion (especially vv. 9–19, 43–62). Seven months later, on 22 June 1834, the Lord told his Church to "wait for a little season for the redemption of Zion" (D&C 105:9, 13). He also set forth specific events that must take place or circumstances that must occur before Zion would be established, thus providing a general time frame for Zion's redemption. Some events and circumstances are explicitly named, and others are implicitly referenced in this revelation, now known as Doctrine and Covenants 105, including the following duties of Church members:

Become "prepared" (v. 10).

"Be taught more perfectly" (v. 10).

"Have experience" (v. 10).

"Know more perfectly concerning their duty" (v. 10).

Receive the ordinances of the temple (vv. 11–12, 33).

Be faithful, prayerful, and humble (v. 23).

In addition, the Lord's servants are required to "gather up the strength of my house" (v. 27) and to purchase certain "lands in Jackson county" (vv. 28–30).

God's army must "become very great" and sanctified (v. 31).

Zion must "sue for peace," "lift up an ensign of peace, and make a proclamation of peace unto the ends of the earth; and make proposals for peace" (vv. 38–40).

President Spencer W. Kimball explained "three fundamental things we must do if we are to 'bring again Zion,' three things for which we who labor in Zion must commit ourselves.

"First, we must eliminate the individual tendency to selfishness that snares the soul, shrinks the heart, and darkens the mind. . . .

"Second, we must cooperate completely and work in harmony one with the other. There must be unanimity in our decisions and unity in our actions. . . .

"Third, we must lay on the altar and sacrifice whatever is required by the Lord. We begin by offering a 'broken heart and a contrite spirit.'"[13]

In the last days, a great battle will take place between the Saints of God and the powers of evil. Doctrine and Covenants 105 contains many terms concerning this battle: *Zion, power, fight, battles, warriors, army, banners, enemies, towers, watchmen, armies, strength, destroyer, destroy, peace.*

NOTES AND COMMENTARY

D&C 105:9 *in consequence of the transgressions of my people.* This passage repeats what was stated in an earlier revelation: "I, the Lord, have suffered the affliction to come upon them, wherewith they have been afflicted, in consequence of their transgressions" (D&C 101:2; see also 103:4). President Lorenzo Snow taught that the specific transgression of the Saints was a failure to obey the law of consecration.[14]

wait for a little season for the redemption of Zion. Perhaps for emphasis, this phrase is repeated in Doctrine and Covenants 105:13. *A little season* is a period of time that began in the Prophet's lifetime and will continue until the Church fulfills the conditions listed in Doctrine and Covenants 105.

D&C 105:10 *be prepared.* In 1834, the Church was a young organization, and its members were inexperienced in many aspects of building Zion in the last days. For example, Church members had not received the full temple ordinances as they exist in our temples today. Nor did the Saints at this time fully understand the role, power, and organization of the Quorum of the Twelve Apostles; in fact, this quorum was not established until the following year. This verse sets forth four specific requirements that must be met before the redemption of Zion: the Saints need to become "prepared"; they need to "be taught more perfectly"; they need to "have experience"; and they need to "know more perfectly concerning their duty."

---

[13] *Ensign,* May 1978, 81.
[14] *Journal of Discourses,* 16:276.

D&C 105:11 *endowed with power from on high.* This phrase, used elsewhere in the scriptures (D&C 38:32; 95:8), speaks about the temple endowment. Perhaps one cannot overemphasize the import of temples and temple ordinances in the building of Zion in the last days, for the temple serves as the very "foundation of Zion" (D&C 124:39), and the Lord's people gather for the purpose of enjoying the great blessings that come from the temple.[15] Before the full and glorious redemption of Zion, Church members must receive the power, gifts, and blessings of the temple. Such endowments and blessings will be "poured out" in great abundance upon the heads of "thousands and tens of thousands" of souls (D&C 110:9).

D&C 105:14 *I will fight your battles.* On occasion the Lord assisted ancient Israel in defeating its enemies by fighting its battles. "The Lord shall fight for you" (Ex. 14:14; Deut. 1:30; Josh. 10:14, 42; 23:10; Judg. 20:35) was the promise; Jehovah himself marched ahead of the army (Judg. 4:14; Deut. 20:4; 2 Sam. 5:24); and many battles were called "the Lord's battles" (1 Sam. 18:17; 25:28; Num. 21:14). Perhaps God's involvement in battles of ancient Israel serves as a type of Zion in the last days, when he will again fight Israel's battles. In an earlier revelation, the Lord promised, "And their arm shall be my arm, and I will be their shield and their buckler; and I will gird up their loins, and they shall fight manfully for me; and their enemies shall be under their feet; and I will let fall the sword in their behalf, and by the fire of mine indignation will I preserve them" (D&C 35:14). Again, in Doctrine and Covenants 98:37, the Lord pledged, "And I, the Lord, would fight their battles, and their children's battles, and their children's children's, until they had avenged themselves on all their enemies, to the third and fourth generation." These two passages fulfill words revealed to Isaiah: "For I [the Lord] will contend with him that contendeth with thee, and I will save thy children" (Isa. 49:25).

D&C 105:16 *my warriors.* These are the Lord's faithful servants, called here the "strength of [the Lord's] house" (see also D&C 101:55; 103:22, 30). Elsewhere we learn that the Lord's warriors wear the armor of God (Eph. 6); they battle against evil and the

---

[15] *History of the Church,* 5:423.

enemies of Zion through the power of the Atonement and by bearing pure testimony (Rev. 12:7–11). They may also go to battle in a more literal sense, wielding the power of God as Enoch did (Moses 7:13).

D&C 105:17 *But the strength of mine house have not hearkened unto my words.* This sentence summarizes the reason why Zion was not "redeemed" during the first decades after the restoration of the gospel: Only a few of the Lord's servants had responded to the call to join Zion's Camp, the "army" of brethren the Lord commanded to rescue the Saints in Missouri.[16]

D&C 105:18 *I have prepared a blessing and an endowment for them.* This phrase was stated in Doctrine and Covenants 105:12 and is repeated here for emphasis. The blessing and the endowment may be that which is bestowed on us in the temple and which we receive more fully as we keep our temple covenants and apply the principles of godliness in our lives.

D&C 105:23 *faithful/prayerful/humble.* These attributes are essential ones to Saints; those who embody these characteristics are thereby prepared to become a part of the Lord's people in Zion.

D&C 105:27 *as I did the heart of Pharaoh.* This reference likely refers to the time in history when Pharaoh of Egypt finally permitted Moses and the Israelites to depart from the land (Ex. 12:30–33). The scriptures cite numerous times when Pharaoh hardened his heart against Moses and his people, but finally Pharaoh permitted Israel to depart.

the strength of my house. This expression may refer to those the Lord calls "my warriors." See the commentary on Doctrine and Covenants 105:16, page 163.

D&C 105:28 *purchasing of all the lands in Jackson county.* See the commentary on Doctrine and Covenants 57:1–3, page 155.

D&C 105:29 *laws of consecration.* Elder Delbert L. Stapley taught in 1955: "The welfare program in operation since 1936 is a continuing plan for the people of the Church until a more perfect and higher plan is revealed. When we demonstrate our faith, worthiness, willingness, and unity to live fully the principles of the welfare plan,

---

[16] For a discussion of Zion's Camp, which marched in 1834, see Roberts, *Missouri Persecutions,* 128–51.

it will lead and prepare us for the higher law of the celestial kingdom. The Lord has affirmed in this dispensation: 'And Zion cannot be built up unless it is by the principles of the law of the celestial kingdom; otherwise I cannot receive her unto myself' (D&C 105:5)."[17] President Gordon B. Hinckley taught another aspect of this law when he said, "If we are to build that Zion of which the prophets have spoken and of which the Lord has given mighty promise, we must set aside our consuming selfishness."[18]

D&C 105:31 *let my army become very great, . . . that it may become fair as the sun, and clear as the moon, and that her banners may be terrible unto all nations.* The original scriptural source for this phrase is at present unknown, but the phrase is ancient, for King Solomon cited it when he wrote the Song of Solomon (Song. 6:10). The phrase here speaks of the Church after it comes out of the "wilderness of darkness" and "shine[s] forth" with greatness and power in the last days, even as the sun shines in its greatness and as the full moon lights up the night (D&C 109:73; 5:14). One can almost imagine mighty men gathered around a standard, bearing weapons, prepared for war, waiting for the command to battle. Such is the Church in the last days, prepared for battle against Satan and his troops of evil.

The army of the Lord in Zion appears also to be powerful in a mortal sense, as was Enoch's army, "the people of God" (Moses 7:13; see also D&C 45:20).

D&C 105:32 *kingdoms of this world may be constrained to acknowledge that the kingdom of Zion is in very deed the kingdom of our God and his Christ.* The day will come when earth's inhabitants will acknowledge that Zion is God's kingdom, established upon the earth. This event may find fulfillment in John's words, "And the seventh angel sounded; and there were great voices in heaven, saying, The kingdoms of this world are become the kingdoms of our Lord, and of his Christ; and he shall reign for ever and ever" (Rev. 11:15).

---

[17] Conference Report, Oct. 1955, 14–15.
[18] *Ensign,* Nov. 1991, 59.

D&C 105:33 *receive their endowment from on high in my house.*
The heightened temple building program of the Church seems to indicate, at least in part, an urgency to prepare Zion for the last days.

D&C 105:34 *her law be executed and fulfilled, after her redemption.* The law of consecration will be in full effect after the redemption of Zion.

D&C 105:37 *they shall have power . . . to accomplish all things pertaining to Zion.* God has always given his people power to fulfill his commandments, as Nephi taught so beautifully (1 Ne. 3:7).

D&C 105:38–40 *sue for peace.* The leading Church elders formally sued for peace in July 1834 when they created and delivered a document that read, in part: "We, the undersigned, do make this solemn appeal to the people and constitutional authorities of this nation, and to the ends of the earth, for peace."[19] The four imperatives in verses 38–40—*sue for peace, lift up an ensign of peace, make a proclamation of peace,* and *make proposals for peace*—also pertain to the preaching of Christ's gospel, which is the gospel of peace and which brings inner peace unto all who accept it.

D&C 105:41 *I am with you even unto the end.* Christ's Spirit will accompany the righteous even until the "end of the world" (Matt. 28:20), which signifies the end of wickedness. This is a promise of protection, of support, of guidance, and of comfort.

ZION WILL FLOURISH BEFORE CHRIST COMES
Doctrine and Covenants 49:24–28

24 But before the great day of the Lord shall come, Jacob shall flourish in the wilderness, and the Lamanites shall blossom as the rose.

25 Zion shall flourish upon the hills and rejoice upon the mountains, and shall be assembled together unto the place which I have appointed.

26 Behold, I say unto you, go forth as I have commanded you; repent of all your sins; ask and ye shall receive; knock and it shall be opened unto you.

---

[19] *History of the Church,* 2:128.

27 Behold, I will go before you and be your rearward; and I will be in your midst, and you shall not be confounded.

28 Behold, I am Jesus Christ, and I come quickly. Even so. Amen.

These verses may speak of a restoration of deserts, as Latter-day Saint communities cultivate and irrigate acres of land in Utah and elsewhere, bringing forth great crops and forests. More significantly, however, the verses refer metaphorically to the way that Jacob and the Lamanites will flourish spiritually, as they "repent of all [their] sins" and communicate with God in prayer by "asking" and "knocking" (D&C 49:26). The verbs *flourish* (used twice) and *blossom* liken Jacob and the Lamanites to plants. As they receive the light of Christ and the gifts of the Spirit, they will flourish spiritually, as plants flower after receiving water and sunlight. *Zion shall rejoice upon the hills and flourish* is found three times in the Doctrine and Covenants, underscoring its import (see D&C 35:24; 39:13; 49:25).

Isaiah used similar imagery:

The wilderness and the solitary place shall be glad for them;
and the desert shall rejoice, and blossom as the rose.

It shall blossom abundantly,
and rejoice even with joy and singing:

the glory of Lebanon shall be given unto it,
the excellency of Carmel and Sharon. (Isa. 35:1–2)

Israel shall "blossom and bud, and fill the face of the world with fruit" (Isa. 27:6). For Isaiah's prophetic world, the words *desert* and *wilderness* relate not only to a barren and desolate land but to a people or a nation (Isa. 1:30) who lack the living waters of Jesus Christ. When Isaiah prophesies that the desert shall blossom as the rose, he refers to the restoration of the gospel. At the time of the Great Apostasy the Church was driven "into the wilderness" (D&C 86:3), but when the gospel was restored through Joseph Smith, the Church came forth from the wilderness (D&C 5:14).

NOTES AND COMMENTARY

D&C 49:24 *the great day of the Lord.* This phrase refers to the Second Coming (cf. Isa. 2:10–22).

Jacob shall flourish in the wilderness. This passage speaks of *Jacob, Lamanites,* and *Zion,* which shall *flourish* (repeated twice) in the *wilderness* and on the *hills.* Other scriptures use similar metaphors (Isa. 27:6; 35:1–2; D&C 35:24; 39:13). Of note is the word *rejoice,* also used in these passages: "and the desert shall *rejoice,* and blossom as the rose" (Isa. 35:1); "it shall blossom abundantly, and *rejoice* even with joy and singing" (Isa. 35:2); "Zion shall *rejoice* upon the hills and flourish" (D&C 35:24); "bring forth Zion, that it may *rejoice* upon the hills and flourish" (D&C 39:13); "Zion shall flourish upon the hills and *rejoice* upon the mountains" (D&C 49:25). As soon as the gospel was restored to the earth in this dispensation, Jacob or the house of Israel began to flourish as a flower in the wilderness germinates and grows. This rejoicing and flourishing come to Israel from Christ and his power to bring light, nourishment, and living water to all who draw unto him.

the Lamanites shall blossom as the rose. The Lamanites, a remnant of the house of Israel, shall flourish and blossom (see also 2 Ne. 30:6; 3 Ne. 5:22; D&C 3:20; 28:8; 30:6) as a rose blossoms when receiving light and water.[20]

D&C 49:25 *the place which I have appointed.* See the commentary on Doctrine and Covenants 57:1–3, page 154.

D&C 49:26 *Behold.* The word means "pay attention." It is repeated three times in the final three verses of Doctrine and Covenants 49.

repent of all your sins. Zion flourishes when she repents of her sins, individually and collectively.

ask and ye shall receive; knock and it shall be opened unto you. Note the two parties involved in prayer; one asks and knocks; the other, God, answers and opens (see also D&C 88:63).

D&C 49:27 *I will go before you and be your rearward.* The Lord's promise parallels the words of Isaiah: "The Lord will go

---

[20] See the commentary on this phrase, page 86.

before you; and the God of Israel will be your rereward" (Isa. 52:12). Like the captain of an army, God will go before his people, leading them and protecting them; and similar to a military rear guard, the Lord will safeguard his people from behind. In this, as in all things, he is "the first and the last," our "Alpha and Omega." (Rev. 1:11; D&C 19:1).

I will be in your midst. This phrase, also found in 3 Nephi 21:24–25 with a discussion of the New Jerusalem, may speak of the Lord's Spirit that is ever-present among the righteous who are building Zion. The phrase may also refer to the Second Comforter, or Jesus Christ, who visits select souls.[21]

you shall not be confounded. Other revelations promise that those who trust in the Lord "shall not be confounded" (D&C 84:116; Ps. 22:5; cf. 1 Peter 2:6), meaning disgraced, confused, or destroyed (see also Ether 13:8).

D&C 49:28 *I am Jesus Christ.* The Lord identifies himself as the source of this revelation.

I come quickly. Later the Lord revealed, "And again, be patient in tribulation until I come; and, behold, I come quickly, and my reward is with me, and they who have sought me early shall find rest to their souls" (D&C 54:10).[22]

ZION, A PLACE OF REFUGE FOR THE SAINTS
Doctrine and Covenants 45:62–71

62 . . . verily I say unto you, that great things await you;

63 Ye hear of wars in foreign lands; but, behold, I say unto you, they are nigh, even at your doors, and not many years hence ye shall hear of wars in your own lands.

64 Wherefore I, the Lord, have said, gather ye out from the eastern lands, assemble ye yourselves together ye elders of my church; go ye forth into the western countries, call upon the inhabitants to repent, and inasmuch as they do repent, build up churches unto me.

---

[21] See *Teachings of the Prophet Joseph Smith,* 149–51.
[22] See the commentary on this concept, page 239.

65 And with one heart and with one mind, gather up your riches that ye may purchase an inheritance which shall here-after be appointed unto you.

66 And it shall be called the New Jerusalem, a land of peace, a city of refuge, a place of safety for the saints of the Most High God;

67 And the glory of the Lord shall be there, and the terror of the Lord also shall be there, insomuch that the wicked will not come unto it, and it shall be called Zion.

68 And it shall come to pass among the wicked, that every man that will not take his sword against his neighbor must needs flee unto Zion for safety.

69 And there shall be gathered unto it out of every nation under heaven; and it shall be the only people that shall not be at war one with another.

70 And it shall be said among the wicked: Let us not go up to battle against Zion, for the inhabitants of Zion are terrible; wherefore we cannot stand.

71 And it shall come to pass that the righteous shall be gath-ered out from among all nations, and shall come to Zion, singing with songs of everlasting joy.

Two reasons for Zion's existence are to prepare a people for the Lord's coming and to protect the Saints during the wars and desola-tions of the last days. Doctrine and Covenants 45:62–71 promises shelter for those who gather to Zion, or the New Jerusalem, while wars rage among peoples far and near. The revelation describes geo-graphical aspects of the New Jerusalem with the terms *land, city,* and *place,* while the words *peace, refuge, safety,* and *Zion* set forth her protective nature. The New Jerusalem will be a place of great safety for the following reasons:

"The glory of the Lord shall be there" (D&C 45:67).

"The terror of the Lord also shall be there" (D&C 45:67; see also vv. 74–75).

"The wicked will not come unto it" (D&C 45:67).

Zion's inhabitants will lack the desire to battle (D&C 45:68).

Zion "shall be the only people that shall not be at war one with another" (D&C 45:69).

The wicked will say, "Let us not go up to battle against Zion, for the inhabitants of Zion are terrible; wherefore we cannot stand" (D&C 45:70).

Joseph Smith explained the importance of Zion as a place of safety: "Without Zion, and a place of deliverance, we must fall; because the time is near when the sun will be darkened, and the moon turn to blood, and the stars fall from heaven, and the earth reel to and fro. . . . God will gather out his Saints from the Gentiles, and then comes desolation and destruction, and none can escape except the pure in heart who are gathered."[23] On another occasion he remarked, "We ought to have the building up of Zion as our greatest object. When wars come, we shall have to flee to Zion. The cry is to make haste."[24]

NOTES AND COMMENTARY

D&C 45:62 *great things await you.* "Great things" may refer to the wars mentioned in Doctrine and Covenants 45:63, 68–70; or more likely the expression speaks of the blessing of the New Jerusalem, a wonderful place of peace, refuge, and safety for the Lord's Saints, where both the glory and the terror of the Lord will be found.

D&C 45:63 *Ye hear of wars.* Many wars will occur before Christ's second coming, both in "foreign lands" and on the American continent ("your own lands"). The phrase "not many years hence ye shall hear of wars in your own lands" may speak particularly of the American Civil War (see also D&C 38:29; 87:1–5; 130:12).

D&C 45:64–65 *gather/assemble/go ye forth/call upon the inhabitants/build up churches/purchase an inheritance.* These imperatives summarize the work of building Zion.

D&C 45:65 *with one heart and with one mind.* The building of Zion must be accomplished with unity of purpose; the people of Enoch's Zion similarly were of a single heart and mind: "And the

---

[23] *Teachings of the Prophet Joseph Smith,* 71.
[24] *Teachings of the Prophet Joseph Smith,* 160.

Lord called his people ZION, because they were of one heart and one mind, and dwelt in righteousness; and there was no poor among them" (Moses 7:18). In direct connection with these words is the inspired instruction of Elder Henry B. Eyring, who related: "Not long ago a man asked me, 'Does your church still believe that when Christ comes you will be living as one, the way they did in the city of Enoch?' He put a spin on the word *still*, as if we might not believe such a thing anymore. I said, 'Yes, we do.' And then he said, 'You are the people who could do it.'"[25]

D&C 45:66–67 *it shall be called Zion.* These verses define Zion. It is a place where God's Saints shall be. It has many names, including *New Jerusalem* and *Zion*. Geographically, it is a *land,* a *city,* and a *place.* And five nouns emphasize it as a place of protection: *Jerusalem* (Hebrew, "city of peace"), *peace, refuge, safety,* and *Zion* (in the Hebrew, *Zion* denotes a stronghold, as in "citadel," "castle," or "crest of a hill").[26] Verse 67 declares that Zion will be a place of peace and safety for the following three reasons: "the glory of the Lord shall be there," "the terror of the Lord also shall be there," and "the wicked will not come into it."

D&C 45:67 *glory of the Lord shall be there.* Isaiah prophesied that "the glory of the Lord" would come upon the New Jerusalem: "Arise, shine; for thy light is come, and the glory of the Lord is risen upon thee. . . . The Lord shall arise upon thee, and his glory shall be seen upon thee" (Isa. 60:1–2; D&C 64:41).

terror of the Lord also shall be there. The phrase *terror of the Lord* is repeated in Doctrine and Covenants 45:75. The wicked will not come into Zion because both the glory and the terror of the Lord will be there. Webster's 1828 *American Dictionary of the English Language* (the edition contemporaneous with this revelation) defines *terror* as "that which may excite dread; the cause of extreme fear" or "awful majesty." The Lord's awful majesty will excite dread in the hearts of the wicked, causing them to "stand afar off and tremble" (D&C 45:74).

---

[25] *Ensign,* Nov. 1989, 13.
[26] Koehler and Baumgartner, *Hebrew and Aramaic Lexicon of the Old Testament,* 3:1022.

the wicked will not come unto it. It is difficult (but wonderful) to imagine a place where there is no wickedness—no immorality, no criminals, liars, robbers, perjurers, adulterers, murderers, rapists, and so forth—but such is the description of Zion.

D&C 45:68 *every man that will not take his sword against his neighbor.* Those who do not wish to conduct war or be a part of the wars of the world will "flee unto Zion for safety" (D&C 45:68). Doctrine and Covenants 45:68–71 contrasts the *wicked* with the *righteous.* The wicked are associated with the "sword," "war," and "battle"; the words "songs of everlasting joy" characterize the righteous.

D&C 45:69 *there shall be gathered unto it out of every nation under heaven.* This phrase is repeated twice (D&C 45:69, 71). The gathering in the last days will be universal, for people from all nations shall gather to Zion. The gathering is finding partial fulfillment now as missionaries labor in many countries of the world. In due time the gospel will be preached to all the world (Matt. 28:19–20), and converts "out of every nation" will become part of Zion.[27]

the only people that shall not be at war one with another. While the nations contend and war against one another, Zion will be a fortress of peace for her inhabitants (D&C 45:66–67).

D&C 45:70 *And it shall be said among the wicked: Let us not go up to battle against Zion, for the inhabitants of Zion are terrible; wherefore we cannot stand.* Other scriptural statements testify that Zion and her inhabitants will be terrible because the power of the Lord will be there. Doctrine and Covenants 64:43 promises that "the day shall come when the nations of the earth shall tremble because of her, and shall fear because of her terrible ones." Isaiah wrote that people will "be afraid of the ensign" that belongs to Zion because the Lord's "fire is in Zion, and his furnace in Jerusalem" (Isa. 31:9). Doctrine and Covenants 97:18–19 predicts that Zion "shall prosper, and spread herself and become very glorious, very great, and very terrible. And the nations of the earth shall honor her, and shall say: Surely Zion is the city of our God, and surely Zion cannot fall, neither be moved out of her place, for God is there, and the hand of the Lord is

---

[27] See the commentary on the different forms of the gathering, page 48.

there." Zion and her inhabitants will require such respect and honor because God himself has "sworn by the power of his might to be her salvation and her high tower" (D&C 97:20). The phrase uttered by the wicked, "we cannot stand," corresponds to an earlier prophecy that "the nations of the earth shall bow to it; and, if not of themselves, they shall come down, for that which is now exalted of itself shall be laid low of power" (D&C 49:10; see also Isa. 60:14).

D&C 45:71 *songs of everlasting joy.* This expression (see also D&C 66:11) characterizes Zion and her people. It speaks of the Saints singing in worship, reverence, and devotion to their God and in joy at the many transcendent blessings God has poured out upon them. Isaiah foresaw the day when "the ransomed of the Lord shall return, and come to Zion with songs and everlasting joy upon their heads: they shall obtain joy and gladness, and sorrow and sighing shall flee away" (Isa. 35:10).

ZION AND HER STAKES ARE A REFUGE FROM THE STORM
Doctrine and Covenants 115:4–6

> 4 For thus shall my church be called in the last days, even The Church of Jesus Christ of Latter-day Saints.
>
> 5 Verily I say unto you all: Arise and shine forth, that thy light may be a standard for the nations;
>
> 6 And that the gathering together upon the land of Zion, and upon her stakes, may be for a defense, and for a refuge from the storm, and from wrath when it shall be poured out without mixture upon the whole earth.

The revealed name of the Lord's Church (D&C 115:4) is set in context with the following terms, each of which bears on the Church in one way or another: *light, standard for the nations, Zion, stakes, defense,* and *refuge.* The last four terms pertain to the security that Church members will find against the great trials and tribulations of the last days. *Zion,* which speaks of a stronghold or citadel,[28] together with her *stakes,* will serve as a temporal and spiritual *defense* and

---

[28] Koehler and Baumgartner, *Hebrew and Aramaic Lexicon of the Old Testament,* 3:1022.

refuge to those who gather there (see also D&C 45:62–71). That meaning accords with two statements of Joseph Smith, uttered on different occasions: "The time is soon coming, when no man will have any peace but in Zion and her stakes";[29] "Without Zion, and a place of deliverance, we must fall."[30]

NOTES AND COMMENTARY

D&C 115:4 *For thus shall my church be called.* The Church, which bears the name of the Savior, was named by him. The Church's name accentuates the last days with the term *Latter-day* Saints.

D&C 115:5 *Verily I say unto you all.* Christ's revelation is directed to all, not just to the Church's prophet or the leading elders.

Arise and shine forth. These two commands are directed to all Church members. The command to *arise* encourages us to become spiritually active or to get to work and recalls similar words recorded in Isaiah, where Zion is commanded to "awake, awake . . . arise" (Isa. 52:1–2). The second command instructs us to let our light shine forth (*forth* denotes "outward" or "forward," that is, letting our light shine actively for all to see). A similar command was uttered in the Sermon on the Mount (Matt. 5:14–16) and in the Sermon at the Temple (3 Ne. 12:14–16). Our light, when it shines forth, is like a lighthouse that guides ships to safety, or as a banner set on a hill for all nations to see, fulfilling the Lord's injunction in this verse "that thy light may be a standard for the nations."

Isaiah, in beautiful chiastic poetry, similarly spoke of Zion in the last days when she would "arise, shine, for thy light is come":

A Arise,
  B shine;
    C for thy light is come,
      D and the glory
        E of the Lord is risen upon thee.
          F For, behold, the darkness shall cover the earth,
          F and gross darkness the people:

---

[29] *Teachings of the Prophet Joseph Smith,* 161.
[30] *Teachings of the Prophet Joseph Smith,* 71.

E but the Lord shall arise upon thee,
D and his glory shall be seen upon thee.
C And the Gentiles shall come to thy light,
B and kings to the brightness
A of thy rising. (Isa. 60:1–3)

D&C 115:6 *land of Zion, and upon her stakes.* The city of Independence is the center place in Missouri, which was called the "land of Zion" in an earlier revelation (D&C 57:1–3). Zion has expanded its borders, according to subsequent revelations, so that now its stakes are found in numerous countries of the world. Doctrine and Covenants 82:14 reads, "For Zion must increase in beauty, and in holiness; her borders must be enlarged; her stakes must be strengthened." President Harold B. Lee referred to this verse when he taught: "The borders of Zion, where the righteous and pure in heart may dwell, must now begin to be enlarged. The stakes of Zion must be strengthened. All this so that Zion may arise and shine by becoming increasingly diligent in carrying out the plan of salvation throughout the world."[31]

Doctrine and Covenants 101:21 also speaks of Zion's stakes: "Until the day cometh when there is found no more room for them; and then I have other places which I will appoint unto them, and they shall be called stakes, for the curtains or the strength of Zion" (see also D&C 115:18).

for a defense, and for a refuge from the storm (see also D&C 124:36). Two words serve to define Zion: *defense* and *refuge.* A defense is a fortification or protective covering designed to protect an individual or an entire community. The defense in this verse seems to pertain to physical protection as well as to spiritual fortification against the forces of evil. A refuge, quite different from a defense, denotes a haven, shelter, or sanctuary. The *storm* here refers not to blizzards or hurricanes but to spiritual tempests that now rage upon the earth in many forms and of various kinds.

from wrath when it shall be poured out without mixture upon the whole earth. This phrase recalls Revelation 14:10, which says of

---

[31] *Ensign,* July 1973, 3.

those who worship the beast, "The same shall drink of the wine of the wrath of God, which is poured out without mixture into the cup of his indignation; and he shall be tormented with fire and brimstone in the presence of the holy angels, and in the presence of the Lamb." While the righteous in Zion are enjoying the sweet blessings associated with the sacrament, the wicked will be experiencing God's judgments, drinking "the wine of the wrath of God."

GOD WILL MULTIPLY BLESSINGS ON ZION
Doctrine and Covenants 97:18–28

18 And, now, behold, if Zion do these things she shall prosper, and spread herself and become very glorious, very great, and very terrible.

19 And the nations of the earth shall honor her, and shall say: Surely Zion is the city of our God, and surely Zion cannot fall, neither be moved out of her place, for God is there, and the hand of the Lord is there;

20 And he hath sworn by the power of his might to be her salvation and her high tower.

21 Therefore, verily, thus saith the Lord, let Zion rejoice, for this is Zion—THE PURE IN HEART; therefore, let Zion rejoice, while all the wicked shall mourn.

22 For behold, and lo, vengeance cometh speedily upon the ungodly as the whirlwind; and who shall escape it?

23 The Lord's scourge shall pass over by night and by day, and the report thereof shall vex all people; yea, it shall not be stayed until the Lord come;

24 For the indignation of the Lord is kindled against their abominations and all their wicked works.

25 Nevertheless, Zion shall escape if she observe to do all things whatsoever I have commanded her.

26 But if she observe not to do whatsoever I have commanded her, I will visit her according to all her works, with sore

*affliction, with pestilence, with plague, with sword, with ven-
geance, with devouring fire.*

*27 Nevertheless, let it be read this once to her ears, that I, the
Lord, have accepted of her offering; and if she sin no more
none of these things shall come upon her;*

*28 And I will bless her with blessings, and multiply a multi-
plicity of blessings upon her, and upon her generations forever and ever, saith the Lord your God. Amen.*

These few verses set forth the wonderful blessings that await
Zion in the last days. The terms *prosper, glorious, great, terrible,
honor, salvation, pure in heart, rejoice,* and *blessings* all describe that
which the Lord will make of Zion. The Lord promises us that Zion
will "spread herself and become very glorious, very great, and very
terrible" (D&C 97:18). This promise is being fulfilled as individuals
throughout the world become part of Zion and become purified
through the ordinances and Christ's atonement. The day is approaching when the nations will honor Zion, and they will say, "Surely Zion
is the city of our God, and surely Zion cannot fall . . . for God is there,
and the hand of the Lord is there" (v. 19).

Twice God tells Zion to rejoice ("let Zion rejoice"). She is to
rejoice because she is in the hand of the Lord and because God himself "is there" (vv. 19–20), is "pure in heart" (v. 21), and her purity
will protect her from the Lord's judgments (v. 25). If she is not pure
and does not obey God's commands, however, Zion will suffer God's
vengeance (vv. 25–26). At the same time that Zion (if obedient)
rejoices and escapes God's judgments, "the wicked shall mourn" and
experience the whirlwind and the scourge of the Lord (vv. 21–24).

Zion is God's city. By his power God will make certain that she
will not fall or be moved, for he is her salvation and high tower: he
will watch over Zion and defend her as a faithful watchman stands in
his high tower to protect a city.

In verse 28 God emphasizes the numerous blessings that will be
Zion's with the words *bless* and *blessings.* In fact, the revelation says
that he will "multiply a multiplicity of blessings upon her."

NOTES AND COMMENTARY

D&C 97:18 *if Zion do these things.* The previous verses of Doctrine and Covenants 97 tell Zion what she must do to prosper: build a house unto the Lord "in the land of Zion" (v. 10); "let it be built speedily, by the tithing of my people" (v. 11); "do not suffer any unclean thing to come into it, that it be not defiled" (v. 15); and so on.

she shall prosper. Prosper, in this context, speaks of the spiritual prosperity that is found in Zion, including the gifts of the Spirit (healing, tongues, interpretation of tongues, knowledge, working of miracles, prophecy, discerning of spirits; 1 Cor. 12:9–10) and the fruits of the Spirit ("love, joy, peace, longsuffering, gentleness, goodness, faith, meekness, self-control"; Gal. 5:22–23).

spread herself. Zion will become great in numbers and will "spread herself" throughout the world. The spreading of Zion is an important way to prepare people to receive Jesus Christ, as Elder Ezra Taft Benson taught: "Only a Zion people can bring in a Zion society. And as the Zion people increase, so we will be able to incorporate more of the principles of Zion until we have a people prepared to receive the Lord."[32]

become very glorious, very great, and very terrible. Each of the three nouns—*glorious, great,* and *terrible*—is preceded by the term *very,* which accentuates Zion's prominence in the last days.[33]

D&C 97:19 *the nations of the earth shall honor her.* An earlier revelation confirms that "the nations of the earth shall bow to it; and if not of themselves, they shall come down, for that which is now exalted of itself shall be laid low of power" (D&C 49:10). Isaiah prophesied similarly: "The sons also of them that afflicted thee shall come bending unto thee; and all they that despised thee shall bow themselves down at the soles of thy feet; and they shall call thee, The city of the Lord, The Zion of the Holy One of Israel" (Isa. 60:14).

Surely Zion is the city of our God. Note the emphatic beginning to this statement. The word *surely* means "certainly" or "assuredly." Zion is God's city because his power and presence are there and because the pure in heart dwell within her walls.

---

[32] "Jesus Christ—Gifts and Expectations," 305.
[33] On Zion as "terrible," see the commentary on D&C 45:70, page 173.

surely Zion cannot fall, neither be moved out of her place, for God is there, and the hand of the Lord is there. Zion cannot fall or be moved out of her place because God himself is there with his power and might (symbolized in the word *hand*).

D&C 97:20 *he hath sworn by the power of his might to be her salvation and her high tower.* God himself promises Zion's inhabitants that he will be as a great protective tower for this fortified city; the city of Zion represents the Saints' fortress, and their God is the watchtower of that fortress. 2 Samuel 22:3 speaks similarly: "The God of my rock; in him will I trust: he is my shield, and the horn of my salvation, my high tower, and my refuge, my saviour; thou savest me from violence."

D&C 97:21 *thus saith the Lord.* The Lord is the speaker in this revelation.

let Zion rejoice. This command form is stated and then repeated for emphasis. The Lord explains why Zion will rejoice: because he is with her, protecting and blessing her.

for this is Zion—THE PURE IN HEART. This expression defines Zion. The pure in heart are those who have repented of their sins and made the Atonement effective in their lives.

"What do we mean when we use the word 'Zion'?" Elder Harold B. Lee asked. His response is important to our understanding of the meaning of Zion. "In some Biblical references, and in modern scripture, Zion is referred to as a place—a city. In other places it is referred to as a continent; but in another sense, the Lord has spoken of Zion in these words:

"'Therefore, verily, thus saith the Lord, let Zion rejoice, for this is Zion—THE PURE IN HEART; therefore, let Zion rejoice, while all the wicked shall mourn.' (D&C 97:21.)

"In other words, he is saying again what the Master said: 'The kingdom of God is within you.' Here, within the righteous heart of every member of the Church might be said to be the seed-corn of the growth of the Church. The pure in heart is the beginning of the growth of Zion. When the Lord therefore said: 'Zion must increase in beauty, and in holiness'[D&C 82:14], he was saying in effect, every individual member of the Church must strive to improve himself therein, within his own station, becoming greater in order to strengthen the place where he lives."[34]

President Spencer W. Kimball also spoke of "purity of heart" with regard to Zion: "Zion is a name given by the Lord to his covenant people, who are characterized by purity of heart and faithfulness in caring for the poor, the needy, and the distressed."[35]

while all the wicked shall mourn. As the pure in heart experience joy and the presence of God, the wicked mourn because of vengeance and the whirlwind of judgments they will experience.

D&C 97:22 *vengeance cometh speedily upon the ungodly as the whirlwind.* In the last days, the wicked will be destroyed by God's judgments as easily as the mighty whirlwind destroys all things in its path. Proverbs 10:25 declares, "As the whirlwind passeth, so is the wicked no more: but the righteous is an everlasting foundation" (Prov. 10:25). Similarly, Jeremiah wrote, "Behold, a whirlwind of the Lord is gone forth in fury, even a grievous whirlwind: it shall fall grievously upon the head of the wicked" (Jer. 23:19).

D&C 97:23 *The Lord's scourge shall pass over by night and by day.* This scourge may be the same "overflowing scourge" or "desolating sickness" identified in Doctrine and Covenants 45:31 (cf. Isa. 28:15). The scourge is one of God's judgments upon the wicked. It will be of such magnitude that "all people" will hear of it and will be vexed or tormented by it. Apparently the scourge will continue until the Lord's second coming: the revelation states that "it shall not be stayed until the Lord come."

D&C 97:24 *For the indignation of the Lord is kindled against their abominations.* The Lord will send forth his scourge because of the great evils that are committed by earth's inhabitants.

D&C 97:25–26 *Zion shall escape if she observe to do all things whatsoever I have commanded her.* If Zion obeys God's commandments, she will escape his vengeance and judgments, which are described as a *scourge, sore affliction, pestilence, plague, sword,* and *devouring fire* (see also D&C 84:58). President Joseph F. Smith referred to this verse with these words: "We firmly believe that

---

[34] "Stake Is Born," 189–90.
[35] *Ensign,* Nov. 1977, 78.

Zion—which is the pure in heart—shall escape, if she observe to do all things whatsoever God has commanded; but, in the opposite event, even Zion shall be visited 'with sore affliction, with pestilence, with plague, with sword, with vengeance, and with devouring fire.' (Doctrine and Covenants 97:26.) All this that her people may be taught to walk in the light of truth, and in the way of the God of their salvation."[36]

D&C 97:28 *And I will bless her with blessings.* God promises that Zion will receive great blessings, multiplied many times. Note the emphatic pledge, "I will . . . multiply a multiplicity of blessings upon her."

THE GLORY OF THE LORD WILL BE UPON ZION IN THE LAST DAYS
Doctrine and Covenants 64:41–43

> *41 For, behold, I say unto you that Zion shall flourish, and the glory of the Lord shall be upon her;*
>
> *42 And she shall be an ensign unto the people, and there shall come unto her out of every nation under heaven.*
>
> *43 And the day shall come when the nations of the earth shall tremble because of her, and shall fear because of her terrible ones. The Lord hath spoken it. Amen.*

These three verses refer to Zion as a woman, using the pronouns *her* four times and *she* once. Elsewhere the scriptures speak of Zion as the bride (Isa. 54:1–6; D&C 109:73–74) and the Lord as the bridegroom (Matt. 9:15; Rev. 21:9; D&C 33:17–18; 65:3). This metaphor between the Lord and his Church indicates the special and unique relationship that exists between them: the Lord is ever faithful and honorable to his bride, and the bride or the Church must remain pure and holy before the Lord.

The revelation teaches the following concepts about Zion:

She shall flourish (D&C 64:41).

The Lord's glory shall be upon her (D&C 64:41).

She shall be an ensign to the world (D&C 64:42).

---

[36] "Lesson in Natural Calamities," 653.

People from all nations shall join her (D&C 64:42).

Nations shall tremble and fear because of her and her inhabitants (D&C 64:43).

NOTES AND COMMENTARY

D&C 64:41 *Zion shall flourish.* Zion will prosper and grow like a flowering rose in the desert.[37]

glory of the Lord shall be upon her. The glory of the Lord will also rest upon his holy temple, if those who worship therein are clean (D&C 97:15–17).[38]

D&C 64:42 *she shall be an ensign unto the people.* Earth's inhabitants will notice Zion's light and glory; Zion will be like a flag or banner on the hill, and people will gather around the banner.

come unto her out of every nation. Zion will consist of people from all lands, nations, and tongues, who are united in their love of God and his truths and who desire to obey his commands.

D&C 64:43 *nations of the earth shall tremble because of her.* The Lord spoke similarly to ancient Israel through Moses: "This day will I begin to put the dread of thee and the fear of thee upon the nations that are under the whole heaven, who shall hear report of thee, and shall tremble, and be in anguish because of thee" (Deut. 2:25).

Latter-day scripture contains many great promises concerning Zion and the nations: earth's nations "shall honor [Zion]," in part because of their knowledge that "Zion cannot fall" and because "God is there" (D&C 97:19). Isaiah promised that the children of those who afflicted and despised Zion will someday call her "The city of the Lord, The Zion of the Holy One of Israel" (Isa. 60:14); and Jeremiah prophesied that nations will hear of the goodness and prosperity that the Lord imparts to Zion and will tremble and fear: "And it shall be to me a name of joy, a praise and an honour before all the nations of the earth, which shall hear all the good that I do unto them: and they shall fear and tremble for all the goodness and for all the prosperity that I procure unto it" (Jer. 33:9).

---

[37] See the commentary on D&C 49:24, page 168.
[38] See the commentary on D&C 45:67, page 172.

ZION, THE NEW JERUSALEM
Moses 7:62–64

62 And righteousness will I send down out of heaven; and truth will I send forth out of the earth, to bear testimony of mine Only Begotten; his resurrection from the dead; yea, and also the resurrection of all men; and righteousness and truth will I cause to sweep the earth as with a flood, to gather out mine elect from the four quarters of the earth, unto a place which I shall prepare, an Holy City, that my people may gird up their loins, and be looking forth for the time of my coming; for there shall be my tabernacle, and it shall be called Zion, a New Jerusalem.

63 And the Lord said unto Enoch: Then shalt thou and all thy city meet them there, and we will receive them into our bosom, and they shall see us; and we will fall upon their necks, and they shall fall upon our necks, and we will kiss each other;

64 And there shall be mine abode, and it shall be Zion, which shall come forth out of all the creations which I have made; and for the space of a thousand years the earth shall rest.

In this remarkable revelation to Enoch, the Lord reveals much regarding the latter-day Zion. He designates this city by four names: *Zion, New Jerusalem, Holy City,* and *mine abode.* The first name attests that the city will be a place of safety: the Hebrew word *Zion* means "stronghold" or "citadel."[39] *New Jerusalem,* the second name, relates Zion to Jerusalem of ancient Palestine but is marked *New* to differentiate it from *Old* Jerusalem; the third name, *Holy City,* shows Zion to be consecrated and set apart from other places; and the fourth, *mine abode,* indicates that Zion will be the Lord's home, where he will reign for a thousand years.

The Lord refers to Zion's inhabitants as "mine elect" and "my people," referring to his Saints. He affirms that his holy temple will be

---

[39] Koehler and Baumgartner, *Hebrew and Aramaic Lexicon of the Old Testament,* 3:1022, reads "citadel," "castle," or "crest of a hill."

a part of the city. He provides a central purpose for Zion's existence: to prepare the people ("gird up their loins") for the Second Coming ("and be looking forth for the time of my coming"). The Lord informs Enoch that Enoch's own ancient city of Zion will one day join with the latter-day Zion; then "we [the Lord, Enoch, and the inhabitants of his ancient city] will receive them [the inhabitants of the New Jerusalem] into our bosom" (Moses 7:63).

NOTES AND COMMENTARY

Moses 7:62 *righteousness will I send down out of heaven; and truth will I send forth out of the earth.* President Ezra Taft Benson gave this interpretation for these words: "The Lord promised, therefore, that righteousness would come from heaven and truth out of the earth. We have seen the marvelous fulfillment of that prophecy in our generation. The Book of Mormon has come forth out of the earth, filled with truth, serving as the very 'keystone of our religion' (see Introduction to the Book of Mormon). God has also sent down righteousness from heaven. The Father Himself appeared with His Son to the Prophet Joseph Smith. The angel Moroni, John the Baptist, Peter, James, and numerous other angels were directed by heaven to restore the necessary powers to the kingdom. Further, the Prophet Joseph Smith received revelation after revelation from the heavens during those first critical years of the Church's growth."[40]

to bear testimony of mine Only Begotten. The chief purpose of all scripture is to bear record of Jesus Christ; hence the Book of Mormon came forth out of the earth to convince "Jew and Gentile that Jesus is the Christ, the Eternal God, manifesting himself unto all nations" (Book of Mormon title page).

his resurrection from the dead. Scripture bears testimony that the Only Begotten was resurrected from the dead. Luke testified that the resurrected Jesus appeared unto many, declaring, "Behold my hands and my feet, that it is I myself: handle me, and see; for a spirit hath not flesh and bones, as ye see me have. And when he had thus spoken, he shewed them his hands and his feet" (Luke 24:39–40). Other scriptures also so testify (for example, 3 Ne. 11).

---

[40] *Ensign,* Nov. 1986, 79–80.

the resurrection of all men. Scripture bears record that all human-kind will be resurrected.

righteousness and truth will I cause to sweep the earth as with a flood. The Prophet Joseph Smith spoke of angels and men as being "co-workers" in bringing righteousness and truth to the earth in the last days. "Righteousness and truth are to sweep the earth as with a flood. And now, I ask, how righteousness and truth are going to sweep the earth as with a flood? I will answer. Men and angels are to be co-workers in bringing to pass this great work, and Zion is to be pre-pared, even a new Jerusalem, for the elect that are to be gathered from the four quarters of the earth, and to be established an holy city, for the tabernacle of the Lord shall be with them."[41]

to gather out mine elect. Over and over, the Book of Mormon teaches that it will help gather the Saints by bringing them to Christ.

unto a place which I shall prepare, an Holy City. Psalm 102:16 teaches a similar truth: "The Lord shall build up Zion." The holy city of New Jerusalem will be the center point, or capital city, of Zion.

that my people may gird up their loins, and be looking forth for the time of my coming. This passage sets forth a fundamental purpose of the Holy City of Zion: Zion will assist the Saints in preparing for Christ's coming. The phrase "gird up their loins" indicates that they will become prepared, probably for spiritual battle. In a revelation set forth in the Doctrine and Covenants the Lord promises that he will protect and preserve the people by girding up their loins: "And their arm shall be my arm, and I will be their shield and their buckler; and I will gird up their loins, and they shall fight manfully for me; and their enemies shall be under their feet; and I will let fall the sword in their behalf, and by the fire of mine indignation will I preserve them" (D&C 35:14).

for there shall be my tabernacle. The term *tabernacle* in this verse refers to the holy temple, which protects the Saints physically and spiritually. Isaiah taught, "There shall be a tabernacle for a shadow in the daytime from the heat, and for a place of refuge, and for a covert from storm and from rain" (Isa. 4:6).

---

[41] *History of the Church,* 2:260.

Moses 7:63 *Then shalt thou and all thy city meet them there.* Enoch and his people will descend from their heavenly abode to meet the mortal Saints who are citizens of the New Jerusalem.

we will receive them into our bosom, . . . and we will fall upon their necks. We will rejoice to be united with these noble fellow-citizens in the kingdom. To "fall on one's neck" suggests an eager greeting and enthusiastic embrace (Gen. 33:4; Luke 15:20). President John Taylor taught that eventually many from Zion would be translated: "And then when the time comes that these calamities we read of, shall overtake the earth, those that are prepared will have the power of translation, as they had in former times, and the city will be translated. And Zion that is on the earth will rise, and the Zion above will descend, as we are told, and we will meet and fall on each other's necks and embrace and kiss each other."[42] (JST Gen. 9:17–25 provides additional details regarding Enoch and his city.)

Moses 7:64 *there shall be mine abode.* Zion is the Lord's home because it is a city of the pure in heart. Zion is commanded to "sing and rejoice" because the Lord will "dwell in the midst of [her]" (Zech. 2:10; see also Moses 7:21).

for the space of a thousand years the earth shall rest. Moses 7:48 records that Enoch heard a voice from the earth's bowels, saying: "Wo, wo is me, the mother of men; I am pained, I am weary, because of the wickedness of my children. When shall I rest, and be cleansed from the filthiness which is gone forth out of me? When will my Creator sanctify me, that I may rest, and righteousness for a season abide upon my face?" The earth will finally rest during the Millennium.

NEW JERUSALEM AND ITS TEMPLE
Doctrine and Covenants 84:2–5

2 Yea, the word of the Lord concerning his church, established in the last days for the restoration of his people, as he has spoken by the mouth of his prophets, and for the gathering of his saints to stand upon Mount Zion, which shall be the city of New Jerusalem.

---

[42] *Journal of Discourses,* 21:253.

3 Which city shall be built, beginning at the temple lot, which is appointed by the finger of the Lord, in the western boundaries of the State of Missouri, and dedicated by the hand of Joseph Smith, Jun., and others with whom the Lord was well pleased.

4 Verily this is the word of the Lord, that the city New Jerusalem shall be built by the gathering of the saints, beginning at this place, even the place of the temple, which temple shall be reared in this generation.

5 For verily this generation shall not all pass away until an house shall be built unto the Lord, and a cloud shall rest upon it, which cloud shall be even the glory of the Lord, which shall fill the house.

Before the Second Coming, the great temple in the New Jerusalem will be built "unto the Lord," and, like the tabernacle of Moses, "a cloud shall rest upon it, which cloud shall be even the glory of the Lord, which shall fill the house" (D&C 84:5). The Prophet spoke of the glories and beauties of the temple: "The glory of Lebanon is to come upon her; the fir tree, the pine tree, and the box tree together, to beautify the place of His sanctuary, that He may make the place of His feet glorious. Where for brass, He will bring gold; and for iron, He will bring silver; and for wood, brass; and for stones, iron; and where the feast of fat things will be given to the just; yea, when the splendor of the Lord is brought to our consideration for the good of His people, the calculations of men and the vain glory of the world vanish, and we exclaim, 'Out of Zion the perfection of beauty, God hath shined.'"[43]

NOTES AND COMMENTARY

D&C 84:2 *his church, established in the last days.* This revelation explains that The Church of Jesus Christ of Latter-day Saints was established for two reasons: "for the restoration of his people" and "for the gathering of his saints to stand upon Mount Zion, which shall be the city of New Jerusalem." Of course, these two purposes lead to

---

[43] *History of the Church,* 1:198.

other reasons for the establishment of the Church, including bringing to the covenant the pure in heart among the dead and "the perfecting of the saints" (Eph. 4:12) once they have been restored to the covenant and gathered to the temple.

as he has spoken by the mouth of his prophets. Many of the ancient prophets have spoken concerning the establishment of the Church and the restoration of the people in the last days. President Gordon B. Hinckley explained: "I need not remind you that this cause in which we are engaged is not an ordinary cause. It is the cause of Christ. It is the kingdom of God our Eternal Father. It is the building of Zion on the earth, the fulfillment of prophecy given of old and of a vision revealed in this dispensation."[44]

to stand upon Mount Zion. "To stand" here denotes victory and conquest—victory over the powers of evil and over God's enemies. The Saints of the last days (D&C 84:2) will stand on Mount Zion; so will resurrected Saints, who will "stand on the right hand of the Lamb, when he shall stand upon Mount Zion" (D&C 133:56); and God's word attests that 144,000 will also stand with the Lamb on Mount Zion (Rev. 14:1; D&C 133:18). The timing of these wonderful events has not yet been revealed.

Here Mount Zion is equated with the New Jerusalem. Why *Mount?* Because the gospel banner, or ensign,[45] must be erected upon a high mountain for all nations to see. Mountains signify temples, and the temple in New Jerusalem will be one of the great religious symbols of the holy city.

Many prophets of old envisioned and prophesied of Mount Zion, or the New Jerusalem. They foresaw that it would be a place of deliverance for those who call upon God (Joel 2:32). It would be the place where the Lord would reign, whose reign would be so glorious and full of light and truth that even the moon will be confounded and the sun ashamed (Isa. 24:23). It would be the place where the very "powers of heaven" or Christ himself will be found in the midst of the Saints of the New Jerusalem (3 Ne. 20:22).

---

[44] *Ensign,* Nov. 1989, 53.
[45] The ensign symbolizes the gospel of Jesus Christ (D&C 45:9; 105:39) and its accompanying light (D&C 115:4–5); also, the Book of Mormon is an ensign (2 Ne. 29:2–3; Moro. 10:27–28).

the city of New Jerusalem. For a description of the New Jerusa-lem, see the commentary on Doctrine and Covenants 45:62–71, page 169.

D&C 84:3 *Which city shall be built.* Although the early Saints experienced much tribulation and were eventually prevented from building the city of New Jerusalem, the Lord comforted his Saints with a revelation, dated 16 December 1833, in which he promised that this city would yet be built: "Therefore, let your hearts be com-forted concerning Zion; for all flesh is in mine hands; be still and know that I am God. Zion shall not be moved out of her place, not-withstanding her children are scattered. They that remain, and are pure in heart, shall return, and come to their inheritances, they and their children, with songs of everlasting joy, to build up the waste places of Zion—and all these things that the prophets might be ful-filled" (D&C 101:16–19). After the Saints' expulsion from Jackson County, Missouri, Joseph Smith wrote to Edward Partridge, "We have nothing to fear if we are faithful, God will strike through kings, in the days of His wrath but what He will deliver His people where ere long in Jackson County He will set His feet, when earth and heaven shall tremble."[46]

in the western boundaries of the State of Missouri. An earlier rev-elation, Doctrine and Covenants 57:1–3, revealed that the city would be built in what is now called Independence, Missouri.[47]

D&C 84:4 *which temple shall be reared in this generation.* The temple lot was dedicated 3 August 1831 by Joseph Smith, in the presence of Joseph Coe, Oliver Cowdery, Martin Harris, Edward Partridge, W. W. Phelps, and Sidney Rigdon. The scene was described as "solemn and impressive."[48]

The enemies of the Church hindered the Saints from building the New Jerusalem and its temple, and the Saints were temporarily excused from these sacred assignments. The Lord explained: "Verily, verily, I say unto you, that when I give a commandment to any of the sons of men to do a work unto my name, and those sons of men go

---

[46] In Dyer, *Refiner's Fire,* 5.
[47] See the commentary on D&C 57:1–3, page 156.
[48] *History of the Church,* 1:199.

with all their might and with all they have to perform that work, and cease not their diligence, and their enemies come upon them and hinder them from performing that work, behold, it behooveth me to require that work no more at the hands of those sons of men, but to accept of their offerings. . . . Therefore, for this cause have I accepted the offerings of those whom I commanded to build up a city and a house unto my name, in Jackson county, Missouri, and were hindered by their enemies, saith the Lord your God" (D&C 124:49, 51). The Lord, notwithstanding that the New Jerusalem was not built, accepted the Saints' righteous intent and offerings and promised to "save all those . . . who have been pure of heart, and have been slain in the land of Missouri" (D&C 124:54). In due time the city of New Jerusalem and its temple will be built by the Saints (3 Ne. 20:22; 21:23–25; Ether 13:3–4, 6–8).

D&C 84:5 *a cloud shall rest upon it, . . . which shall fill the house.* During the era of the Israelite wanderings, a cloud oftimes covered the Mosaic tabernacle (Ex. 33:9) or accompanied it as it was transported through the wilderness (Num. 14:14). Later, a "cloud filled the house of the Lord" when Solomon dedicated it unto God (1 Kgs. 8:10; 2 Chron. 5:13–14; 7:1–3). Such a cloud, which represents "the glory of the Lord" (D&C 84:5; cf. Ex. 40:34; 2 Chron. 5:14), accompanied Christ's glorious ascension after his ministry in the Old World (Acts 1:9–11) and in the New World (3 Ne. 18:38). Clouds will yet again accompany Christ at his second coming (Mark 13:26; Rev. 1:7; cf. Acts 1:9–11).

THE LORD BUILDS ZION AND APPEARS IN GLORY
Psalm 102:13–22

13 Thou shalt arise, and have mercy upon Zion: for the time to favour her, yea, the set time, is come.

14 For thy servants take pleasure in her stones, and favour the dust thereof.

15 So the heathen shall fear the name of the Lord, and all the kings of the earth thy glory.

16 When the Lord shall build up Zion, he shall appear in his glory.

17 He will regard the prayer of the destitute, and not despise their prayer.

18 This shall be written for the generation to come: and the people which shall be created shall praise the Lord.

19 For he hath looked down from the height of his sanctuary; from heaven did the Lord behold the earth;

20 To hear the groaning of the prisoner; to loose those that are appointed to death;

21 To declare the name of the Lord in Zion, and his praise in Jerusalem;

22 When the people are gathered together, and the kingdoms, to serve the Lord.

Psalm 102 speaks of the latter-day Zion, which will be built upon the American continent. Joseph Smith taught, "The city of Zion spoken of by David, in the one hundred and second Psalm, will be built upon the land of America, 'And the ransomed of the Lord shall return, and come to Zion with songs and everlasting joy upon their heads' (Isaiah xxxv:10); and then they will be delivered from the overflowing scourge that shall pass through the land."[49] Many specific signs of the last days given in this Psalm include the following: the Lord will have great mercy and favor on Zion and her inhabitants (v. 13); the heathen and kings will fear the Lord because of the glory that will attend Zion (v. 15); Zion will be built under the direction of the Lord (v. 16); the Saints will declare and praise Jehovah's name in Zion and in Jerusalem (v. 21); and peoples and kingdoms will gather together "to serve the Lord" (v. 22).

NOTES AND COMMENTARY

Ps. 102:13 *arise, and have mercy.* This verse is prophetic; it anticipates the last days when the Lord will take action ("arise") and once again "have mercy upon Zion." Isaiah also prophesied

---

[49] *History of the Church,* 1:315.

concerning the Lord's mercy on Israel at the time when he will gather them to their land of promise: "For the Lord will have mercy on Jacob, and will yet choose Israel, and set them in their own land" (Isa. 14:1).

the set time, is come. The time of Zion's "favour," her "set time," may be the time of the restoration of the gospel, with all of its glories, blessings, and privileges.

Ps. 102:14 *stones/dust.* Zion is so remarkable to the servants of God that they cherish even the stones scattered throughout her fields and the dust of her streets.

Ps. 102:15 *heathen/kings.* The "heathen" (unbelievers) and "kings" (those who rule the earth) will fear the Lord because of the favor, mercy, and glory he extends to Zion and her inhabitants. This same "fear of the Lord was upon all nations" at the time of Enoch's Zion because "so great was the glory of the Lord, which was upon his people" (Moses 7:17). A modern revelation foretells that "the glory of the Lord shall be [upon Zion], and the terror of the Lord also shall be there, insomuch that the wicked will not come unto it" (D&C 45:67; see also vv. 74–75).

Ps. 102:16 *he shall appear in his glory.* This verse has at least three possible meanings, all of which may be correct. One is that the Lord will appear in glory to his servants at the establishment of Zion; such occurred when the Lord's glory was upon Enoch, who recorded, "I beheld the heavens open, and I was clothed upon with glory; and I saw the Lord; and he talked with me, even as a man talketh one with another, face to face" (Moses 7:3–4). Joseph Smith wrote: "I saw a pillar of light exactly over my head, above the brightness of the sun. . . . When the light rested upon me I saw two Personages, whose brightness and glory defy all description" (JS–H 1:16–17). Another meaning is that the Lord will appear in glory at his second coming, after Zion is built and her inhabitants are ready to receive him. Still another meaning is that the Lord will appear in glory in his temple in New Jerusalem.

Ps. 102:17 *prayer of the destitute.* The spiritually impoverished, as well as those destitute of temporal things and blessings, will receive answer to their prayers.

Ps. 102:18 *written for the generation to come.* The rising generations, those yet to be born to parents in Zion, will praise the Lord and
read the "written" account of the Lord's mighty acts on behalf of
Zion. These mighty acts include the following: He answers the
prayers of the destitute (v. 17); from heaven he beholds and acknowledges his children (v. 19); and he hearkens to the prisoner's cry of distress (v. 20). Further, these rising generations will testify of the Lord,
or "declare the name of the Lord in Zion" and sing songs of him in
"Jerusalem" (v. 21).

Ps. 102:19 *he hath looked down from the height of his sanctuary.*
From heaven, the Lord constantly watches over his children who
dwell on the earth; he knows their deeds and hears their cries. The
expression "the height of his sanctuary" refers to the temple in
heaven, or the celestial kingdom.[50]

Ps. 102:20 *hear the groaning of the prisoner.* The Hebrew word
for *hear* denotes action. God does not simply "hear" the prisoner's
groaning; he acknowledges his childrens' needs and then sends divine
help in the form of caring Church members, priesthood leaders, and
the Holy Ghost. On occasion heavenly attendants are sent to assist
those in need. *Prisoner* may refer to those who are in the bondage of
sin, to those in the spirit prison, or both.

Ps. 102:21 *To declare the name of the Lord in Zion.* To bear testimony or witness of the Lord; to preach the gospel to the heathen and
to kings, identified in verse 15, and to the people and kingdoms mentioned in verse 22.

THE LORD LOVES ZION
Psalm 87:1–7

1 His foundation is in the holy mountains.

*2 The Lord loveth the [cities][51] of Zion more than all the
dwellings of Jacob.*

*3 Glorious things are spoken of thee, O city of God. . . .
Selah.*

---

[50] See Parry and Parry, "Temple in Heaven," in *Temples of the Ancient World,* 515–32.

[51] This change is made in note *a* to Ps. 87:2 in the LDS edition of the KJV.

4 I will make mention of Rahab and Babylon to them that know me: behold Philistia, and Tyre, with Ethiopia; this man was born there.

5 And of Zion it shall be said, This and that man was born in her: and the highest himself shall establish her.

6 The Lord shall count, when he writeth up the people, that this man was born there. . . . Selah.

7 As well the singers as the players on instruments shall be there: all my springs are in thee.

This beautiful psalm was read at the dedication of the site of the future temple in New Jerusalem. Joseph Smith recorded: "On the third day of August [1831], I proceeded to dedicate the spot for the Temple, a little west of Independence, and there was also present Sidney Rigdon, Edward Partridge, W. W. Phelps, Oliver Cowdery, Martin Harris and Joseph Coe.

"The 87th Psalm was read. . . ."

"The scene was solemn and impressive."[52]

Perhaps this psalm was read on that historic occasion because its central message pertains to Zion and the Lord's love of her.

NOTES AND COMMENTARY

Ps. 87:1 *holy mountains.* This expression refers to the Lord's temples (Isa. 2:1–4), which are an essential part of the building of Zion.

Ps. 87:2 *The Lord loveth the [cities] of Zion.* This verse seems to be contrasting true Zion with those who are only nominally part of the covenant. The Lord loves Zion, the place of the pure in heart, more than all the other dwellings of those who may be of the covenant but who are not valiant therein.

Ps. 87:3–4 *Glorious things/born there.* Certainly many "glorious things" will be spoken of Zion, such as that she is a "a land of peace," "a city of refuge," and "a place of safety for the saints of the Most High God" (D&C 45:66). This psalm adds another glorious thing that will be said of Zion: This man or woman was privileged to have been

---

[52] *History of the Church,* 1:199.

born in Zion. This idea is repeated three times in the psalm, emphasizing its import: "this man was born there" (v. 4); "this and that man was born in her" (v. 5); and "this man was born there" (v. 6). In fact, the Lord himself will announce this to the nations outside of the city of God, including Babylon, Philistia, and Ethiopia, that "this and that man was born" there (v. 5). Further, the Lord himself will take a census of the number of people in Zion and will then write the individual names of those who were "born there" (v. 6). This reference may be to the privilege of being born physically in Zion; but it may also refer to those souls who attained to a spiritual rebirth, being born again, in Zion.

city of God. Zion is God's city; it belongs to him.

Ps. 87:5 *the highest himself shall establish her.* God takes a personal role in the creation of his city. Psalm 102:16 accords with this expression: "The Lord shall build up Zion."

Ps. 87:6 *The Lord shall count, when he writeth up the people.* The Lord "registers" the people, indicating their right to be citizens of God's city. This phrase also alludes to the Lord's Book of Life, wherein are recorded the names of the righteous. Zion is composed of righteous souls who long to be in his presence.

Ps. 87:7 *singers as the players on instruments.* This expression brings to mind Church hymns sung by individuals, congregations, and choirs. Zion's chapels and temples are filled with sacred music. "Singers" are accompanied by those who play musical "instruments." When the Saints gather it is commonly said that they will "come to Zion, singing with songs of everlasting joy" (D&C 45:71; Isa. 35:10).

all my springs are in thee. This passage may refer to springs of living waters, which are centered in Zion. Or, as the footnote to this passage in the LDS edition of the Bible suggests, the springs may be "sources . . . of joy, happiness, etc."

SATAN'S WORK PROSPERS IN THE LAST DAYS

CONDITIONS ON THE EARTH BEFORE CHRIST'S COMING

SIGNS OF THE TIMES

1. The last days are a time of apostasy.

2. It is a time of false churches, false prophets, and false Christs.

3. It is a time of the antichrist.

4. Iniquity abounds.

5. The love of many waxes cold.

6. The Saints are persecuted.

7. Secret combinations are built up.

8. The United States Constitution hangs by a thread.

9. Men's hearts fail them.

10. Despite God's judgments, men refuse to repent.

11. Scoffers mock at the signs of the times.

12. Eventually, the Lord's Spirit ceases to strive with mankind.

In what must have been a searing vision, Moroni saw our day, the day when the Book of Mormon would come forth, and saw that it was a time when the adversary would rule the world. "I speak unto you as if ye were present," Moroni wrote, "and yet ye are not. But behold, Jesus Christ hath shown you unto me, and I know your doing."

Moroni saw the following:

a day of "secret combinations and the works of darkness";

a day "when the power of God shall be denied";

a day when churches would "become defiled and be lifted up in the pride of their hearts";

a day when "there shall be murders, and robbing, and lying, and deceivings, and whoredoms, and all manner of abominations";

a day when people would "walk in the pride of [their] hearts";

a day of "envying, and strifes, and malice, and persecutions, and all manner of iniquities";

a day when people would "love money, and . . . substance";

a day when people would "build up . . . secret abominations to get gain" (see also Morm. 8:27–41).

"For behold," Nephi wrote, "at that day shall he [Satan] rage in the hearts of the children of men, and stir them up to anger against that which is good. And others will he pacify, and lull them away into carnal security, . . . and thus the devil cheateth their souls, and leadeth them away carefully down to hell. And behold, others he flattereth away, . . . and thus he whispereth in their ears, until he grasps them with his awful chains, from whence there is no deliverance" (2 Ne. 28:20–22).

Surely these are troublesome times. These are days of sin and evil, as was prophesied by the Lord and his servants. "Considering conditions in the world generally," President Hugh B. Brown said, "there never was a time more cut off from Christ than ours, or one that needed him more."[1] Satan, the "prince of this world" (John 12:31; 14:30; 16:11), the "god of this world" (2 Cor. 4:4), the "prince of the power of the air" (Eph. 2:2), is in the great day of his power—and he is doing all he can to conquer as many souls as will hearken to him.

"We are meeting the adversary every day," President Ezra Taft Benson said. "The challenges of this era will rival any of the past, and these challenges will increase both spiritually and temporally."[2]

Yet through it all the Lord ever reaches out in mercy and blessing to help the people of the world turn from Satan and his works to Christ and his righteousness.

"Wo be unto the Gentiles, saith the Lord God of Hosts!" Nephi recorded. "For notwithstanding I shall lengthen out mine arm unto them from day to day, they will deny me; nevertheless, I will be merciful unto them, saith the Lord God, if they will repent and come unto

---

[1] Conference Report, Apr. 1965, 43.
[2] Conference Report, Oct. 1987, 104.

me; for mine arm is lengthened out all the day long, saith the Lord God of Hosts" (2 Ne. 28:32).

A TIME OF APOSTASY

Isaiah 24:5–6

5 The earth also is defiled under the inhabitants thereof; because they have transgressed the laws, changed the ordinance, broken the everlasting covenant.

6 Therefore hath the curse devoured the earth, and they that dwell therein are desolate: therefore the inhabitants of the earth are burned, and few men left.

Isaiah saw a day when the people of the earth would violate God's laws, change his divinely given ordinances to a form that was more pleasing to the carnal mind, and break the covenant God had given them. This condition of apostasy would be universal, for it would devour the earth and leave desolate earth's inhabitants. He described the depths of this apostasy in another way: "Darkness shall cover the earth," he said, "and gross darkness the people" (Isa. 60:2). This is not a partial or limited apostasy: it would cover the earth. And it is not an insignificant departure from truth: Isaiah calls it "gross darkness." Enoch heard the voice of the Lord proclaim the same truth. Before the millennial day, the Lord said, "the heavens shall be darkened, and a veil of darkness shall cover the earth" (Moses 7:61). In 1837, the Lord declared that this prophecy had come to pass: "Verily, verily, I say unto you, darkness covereth the earth, and gross darkness the minds of the people, and all flesh has become corrupt before my face" (D&C 112:23; see also 1:15–16; 33:4; 38:11; JS–H 1:19). Other prophets also foresaw a great apostasy:

"Behold, the days come, saith the Lord God, that I will send a famine in the land, not a famine of bread, nor a thirst for water, but of hearing the words of the Lord: And they shall wander from sea to sea, and from the north even to the east, they shall run to and fro to seek the word of the Lord, and shall not find it" (Amos 8:11–12).

"Now the Spirit speaketh expressly, that in the latter times some shall depart from the faith, giving heed to seducing spirits, and doctrines of devils; speaking lies in hypocrisy; having their conscience seared with a hot iron" (1 Tim. 4:1–2).

"For the time will come when they will not endure sound doctrine; but after their own lusts shall they heap to themselves teachers, having itching ears" (2 Tim. 4:3).

"Because of the many plain and precious things which have been taken out of the book [the Bible], which were plain unto the understanding of the children of men, according to the plainness which is in the Lamb of God—because of these things which are taken away out of the gospel of the Lamb, an exceedingly great many do stumble, yea, insomuch that Satan hath great power over them" (1 Ne. 13:29).

This apostasy is one of the signs of the times, one of the conditions that will prevail on the earth before the Lord returns in his glory: "Let no man deceive you by any means: for that day shall not come, except there come a falling away first, and that man of sin be revealed, the son of perdition" (2 Thes. 2:3).[3]

NOTES AND COMMENTARY

Isa. 24:5 *earth also is defiled under the inhabitants.* To *defile* (Hebrew *chanap*) means "to pollute, profane or make godless."[4] Earth's inhabitants have polluted her by transgressing laws, changing ordinances, and breaking the everlasting covenant.

transgressed the laws. People have disregarded the revealed word of God by transgressing the laws given to them by the prophets. *Law* (Hebrew *torah*), used here in a rare plural form (Gen. 26:5; Ex. 16:28; Ps. 105:45), indicates that all God's laws have been transgressed; that by itself is enough to bring a curse upon the people (Dan. 9:10–11).

changed the ordinance. Ordinance (Hebrew *choq*)[5] comes from the root word *chaqaq*, which means "to carve or engrave." God's ordinances were essentially "carved" in stone and were not meant to be changed; rather, they were to be engraved on the hearts of the

---

[3] For details on the circumstances of the Great Apostasy, see Talmage, *Great Apostasy;* Roberts, *Outlines of Ecclesiastical History,* part 2, "The Apostasy"; and Jackson, *From Apostasy to Restoration.*

[4] Brown, Driver, and Briggs, *Hebrew and English Lexicon,* 337–38.

[5] Brown, Driver, and Briggs, *Hebrew and English Lexicon,* 349.

children of God. When the ordinances, such as baptism (JST Gen. 17:3–6; Moro. 8:14, 16), are changed, their power to save is lost.

broken the everlasting covenant. The everlasting covenant is the gospel with its covenants and ordinances. Because the ordinances had been perverted or lost, the Lord revealed for the last time through the Prophet Joseph Smith the everlasting covenant for the earth (D&C 1:12–16, 22; 29:8–10), "lest the whole earth be smitten with a curse" (D&C 138:48).

24:6 *curse devoured the earth.* The Lord pronounces blessings for faithfulness (Mosiah 2:41) and cursings for rebellion (Deut. 28:15–68). War, slavery, pestilence, plague, disease, famine, poverty, and death are all curses sent from God for failing to keep the commandments (Deut. 27–30). All these curses will be poured out on the earth in the last days (D&C 112:23–24).

they that dwell therein are desolate. The word *desolate* here comes from the Hebrew *'asham,*[6] which could more correctly be translated *guilty.* The term *guilty* refers to the guilt that requires restitution and cleansing ordinances before it can be removed. Those who continue to be *held guilty* (do not repent) must bear the punishment of their sins.

the inhabitants of the earth are burned. See the commentary on the burning of the earth, page 427.

THE ESTABLISHMENT OF FALSE CHURCHES
2 Nephi 28:11–14

> *11 [Their churches] have all gone out of the way; they have become corrupted.*
>
> *12 Because of pride, and because of false teachers, and false doctrine, their churches have become corrupted, and their churches are lifted up; because of pride they are puffed up.*
>
> *13 They rob the poor because of their fine sanctuaries; they rob the poor because of their fine clothing; and they persecute the meek and the poor in heart, because in their pride they are puffed up.*

---

[6] Brown, Driver, and Briggs, *Hebrew and English Lexicon,* 79.

14 They wear stiff necks and high heads; yea, and because of pride, and wickedness, and abominations, and whoredoms, they have all gone astray save it be a few, who are the humble followers of Christ; nevertheless, they are led, that in many instances they do err because they are taught by the precepts of men.

Nephi minces no words in his description of the false churches in the last days: they *all* are following the wrong path, he says. They are corrupt, prideful, oppressive to the poor, wicked (see also 2 Ne. 26:20). Only a few on the earth truly follow Christ, and even they are often misled by the precepts of men.

Moroni was equally condemning of the churches in the last days. The Book of Mormon would come forth "in a day when the power of God shall be denied, and churches become defiled and be lifted up in the pride of their hearts," he wrote. These churches would be corrupt, established to get gain for their leaders. "Come unto me," these leaders would say, "and for your money you shall be forgiven of your sins." Moroni also accused the false latter-day churches of pride: "I know that ye do walk in the pride of your hearts; . . . and your churches, yea, even every one, have become polluted because of the pride of your hearts. For behold, ye do love money, and your substance, and your fine apparel, and the adorning of your churches, more than ye love the poor and the needy, the sick and the afflicted." Then he pleaded with them from the depths of his heart: "O ye pollutions, ye hypocrites, ye teachers, who sell yourselves for that which will canker, why have ye polluted the holy church of God? Why are ye ashamed to take upon you the name of Christ? Why do ye not think that greater is the value of an endless happiness than that misery which never dies—because of the praise of the world? Why do ye adorn yourselves with that which hath no life, and yet suffer the hungry, and the needy, and the naked, and the sick and the afflicted to pass by you, and notice them not? . . . Behold, the sword of vengeance hangeth over you" (Morm. 8:28, 32, 36–39, 41).

NOTES AND COMMENTARY

2 Ne. 28:11 *gone out of the way.* Surely this *way* refers to the strait and narrow way of the true gospel of Jesus Christ (Hel. 6:31; 3 Ne. 27:32). "The anger of God kindleth against the inhabitants of the earth; and none doeth good, for all have gone out of the way" (D&C 82:6). Paul uttered the same lament about those who were typical of his day: "There is none righteous, no, not one: There is none that understandeth, there is none that seeketh after God. They are all gone out of the way, they are together become unprofitable; there is none that doeth good, no, not one" (Rom. 3:10–12). Jesus said the same thing of the scribes, Pharisees, priests, and Levites of his day: "They teach in their synagogues, but do not observe the law, nor the commandments; and all have gone out of the way, and are under sin" (JST Matt. 7:6).

corrupted. When something becomes corrupted, it loses its purity. In the days of Noah, "God looked upon the earth, and, behold, it was corrupt; for all flesh had corrupted his way upon the earth" (Gen. 6:12). When Moses was on the mount for forty days and nights receiving the stone tables, the Lord said to him, "Arise, get thee down quickly from hence; for thy people which thou hast brought forth out of Egypt have corrupted themselves; they are quickly turned aside out of the way which I commanded them; they have made them a molten image" (Deut. 9:12). So will it be in the last days: the people of the earth will turn from the right way of God unto corruption.

2 Ne. 28:12 *churches are lifted up.* This expression is a metaphor for pride, in which someone feels lifted up in status or importance above another. When a church begins to be lifted up, it can lead its members to abandon all that is good and turn to increasing iniquity (Alma 5:37, 53; Hel. 4:11–12). Earlier in this same discourse, Nephi prophesied of the last days: "The Gentiles are lifted up in the pride of their eyes, and have stumbled, . . . that they have built up many churches; nevertheless, they put down the power and miracles of God, and preach up unto themselves their own wisdom and their own learning, that they may get gain and grind upon the face of the poor" (2 Ne. 26:20).

2 Ne. 28:14 *stiff necks and high heads*. These expressions also are metaphors for pride. A stiff neck suggests stubbornness, and a neck stretched to hold a "high head" suggests a person trying to elevate himself above his fellows (Jacob 2:13).

precepts of men. The precepts of men are the philosophies and doctrines they teach when they are not inspired by the Holy Ghost. "Wo be unto him that hearkeneth unto the precepts of men, and denieth the power of God, and the gift of the Holy Ghost! . . . Cursed is he that putteth his trust in man, or maketh flesh his arm, or shall hearken unto the precepts of men, save their precepts shall be given by the power of the Holy Ghost" (2 Ne. 28:26, 31).

A TIME OF FALSE CHRISTS AND FALSE PROPHETS
Joseph Smith–Matthew 1:21–26

> *21 If any man shall say unto you, Lo, here is Christ, or there, believe him not;*

> *22 For in those days there shall also arise false Christs, and false prophets, and shall show great signs and wonders, insomuch, that, if possible, they shall deceive the very elect, who are the elect according to the covenant.*

> *23 Behold, I speak these things unto you for the elect's sake; . . .*

> *24 Behold, I have told you before;*

> *25 Wherefore, if they shall say unto you: Behold, he is in the desert; go not forth: Behold, he is in the secret chambers; believe it not;*

> *26 For as the light of the morning cometh out of the east, and shineth even unto the west, and covereth the whole earth, so shall also the coming of the Son of Man be.*

This prophecy began to be fulfilled in the generation of Christ's original apostles. Both Peter and John noted that there were false prophets in their day—John even said there were "many" such (2 Pet. 2:1–2; 1 Jn. 4:1). Paul added a warning against "false apostles, deceitful workers, transforming themselves into the apostles of Christ" (2

Cor. 11:13). As we learn from Christ's prophecy above, false prophets are one of the signs of the times (see also Rev. 16:13; D&C 50:2).

False prophets can make themselves appear to be true. "And no marvel; for Satan himself is transformed into an angel of light. Therefore it is no great thing if his ministers also be transformed as the ministers of righteousness" (2 Cor. 11:14–15). "Beware of false prophets," the Lord said, "which come to you in sheep's clothing, but inwardly they are ravening wolves." He then gave us the way to judge false prophets from true: "Ye shall know them by their fruits. Do men gather grapes of thorns, or figs of thistles? Even so every good tree bringeth forth good fruit; but a corrupt tree bringeth forth evil fruit. A good tree cannot bring forth evil fruit, neither can a corrupt tree bring forth good fruit. Every tree that bringeth not forth good fruit is hewn down, and cast into the fire. Wherefore by their fruits ye shall know them" (Matt. 7:15–20).

False prophets and false Christs can come not only as individuals but as doctrines, philosophies, and false views of who Jesus Christ is. Elder Bruce R. McConkie shared this valuable insight: "[With few exceptions] a false Christ is not a person. It is a false system of worship, a false church, a false cult that says: 'Lo, here is salvation; here is the doctrine of Christ. Come and believe thus and so, and ye shall be saved.' It is any concept or philosophy that says that redemption, salvation, sanctification, justification, and all of the promised rewards can be gained in any way except that set forth by the apostles and prophets."[7]

Joseph Fielding McConkie added: "Clearly the prophetic warnings against false Christs embrace more than the strange assortment of souls who periodically come on the scene professing to be the hope of the world. In most instances the false Christs we face will take the form of false systems of salvation which inevitably embrace false notions about the true nature of the Son of God. The preface to the Doctrine and Covenants, given in 1831, describes an apostate world in which people walk after the image of gods of their own making. The authors of these gods, we are told, do not seek the Lord nor do they care to establish his righteousness (D&C 1:16). They have their

---

[7] *Millennial Messiah*, 48; see also McConkie, *Doctrinal New Testament Commentary*, 1:647.

own agendas. . . . Everybody, it appears, wants to assimilate Jesus into the spirit of one's own ambitions."[8]

NOTES AND COMMENTARY

JS–M 1:22 *great signs and wonders.* When Moses and Aaron went before Pharaoh to seek the deliverance of the Israelite people, they performed great miracles by the power of God: they turned a rod into a serpent, changed water to blood, and caused countless frogs to come up out of the river to torment the Egyptians. In each case, acting by the power of the devil,[9] Pharaoh's false prophets, his priests, dupli- cated these first few miracles (Ex. 7:10–8:7). In the latter days, Satan's false prophets and false Christs will again "show great signs and wonders" to deceive the people. For instance, in the book of Rev- elation we read of one who "doeth great wonders, so that he maketh fire come down from heaven on the earth in the sight of men, and deceiveth them that dwell on the earth by the means of those miracles which he had power to do" (Rev. 13:13–14). Later we read of "the spirits of devils, working miracles," by which they cause the people of earth to be gathered "to the battle of that great day of God Almighty" (Rev. 16:14).

if possible . . . deceive the very elect. The "signs and wonders" displayed by certain false Christs, false prophets, and false churches will be so impressive that even the "elect according to the cove- nant"—meaning those who have received the gospel covenant and have truly lived according to its precepts—must take care not to be deceived. "There is a possibility that man may fall from grace and depart from the living God" (D&C 20:32). To avoid deception, Latter-day Saints must be faithful in following the living prophet, and they must live worthy of and follow the directions of the Holy Ghost as they are spoken to their hearts. The elect are those who "hear my voice and harden not their hearts" (D&C 29:7).

A time of apostasy, false churches, false prophets, and false Christs is a time of deception indeed. In fact, Satan's ongoing efforts to deceive are among the signs of the times. Our Church leaders have

---

[8] "False Christs," 47–48.
[9] Smith, *Answers to Gospel Questions,* 1:176–78; McConkie, *Millennial Messiah,* 83.

repeatedly and emphatically warned us to be on our guard against deception. Elder Harold B. Lee said: "This is a day of deception of which the Master warned. He said one of the signs of His second coming would be that we would be in danger of being deceived. And then He said to His disciples, 'Take heed that no man deceive you, for in those days, if it were possible, the very elect according to the covenant would be deceived' (see Joseph Smith–Matthew 1:5, 22). And, of course, 'according to the covenant' means members of the Church of Jesus Christ."[10]

A few years later, as president of the Church, President Lee issued a strong and lengthy warning in the priesthood session of general conference: "There are some as wolves among us. . . . Among our own membership, men are arising speaking perverse things. Now *perverse* means diverting from the right or correct, and being obstinate in the wrong, willfully, in order to draw the weak and unwary members of the Church away after them. . . . [I]t never ceases to amaze me how gullible some of our Church members are in broadcasting these sensational stories, or dreams, or visions, some alleged to have been given to Church leaders, past or present, supposedly from some person's private diary, without first verifying the report with proper Church authorities."[11]

Then President Lee gave us the keys to avoiding deception: "If our people want to be safely guided during these troublous times of deceit and false rumors, they must follow their leaders and seek for the guidance of the Spirit of the Lord in order to avoid falling prey to clever manipulators who, with cunning sophistry, seek to draw attention and gain a following to serve their own notions and sometimes sinister motives.

"The Lord has very plainly set forth a test by which anyone may challenge any and all who may come claiming, clandestinely, to have received some kind of priesthood authority. Now this is what the Lord said in the 42nd section of the Doctrine and Covenants, verse 11:

"'Again, I say unto you, that it shall not be given to any one to go forth to preach my gospel, or to build up my church, except he be

---

[10] *Teachings of Harold B. Lee,* 401.
[11] Conference Report, Oct. 1972, 125–26.

ordained by someone who has authority, and it is known to the church that he has authority and has been regularly ordained by the heads of the church.'

"Now, if one comes claiming that he has authority, ask him, 'Where do you get your authority? Have you been ordained by someone who has authority, who is known to the Church, that you have authority and have been regularly ordained by the heads of the Church?' If the answer is no, you may know that he is an imposter. This is the test that our people should always apply when some imposter comes trying to lead them astray."[12]

Twenty years later, Elder Boyd K. Packer warned: "There are some among us now who have *not* been regularly ordained by the heads of the Church and who tell of impending political and economic chaos, the end of the world—something of the 'sky is falling, chicken licken' of the fables. They are misleading members to gather to colonies or cults."[13]

"You may not be aware of it," Elder M. Russell Ballard said, "but there are 'false prophets' rising within and without the Church. They believe they have had revelations, that they know something the First Presidency and the Twelve Apostles don't know. You need to be very careful of such people. If you are ever approached by anyone who claims special authority or revelation from God outside the sustained priesthood authority, turn and run from them as fast as you can. The Savior said that in the last days even the very elect could be pulled away from the truth by such false prophets."[14]

JS–M 1:25 *in the desert/in the secret chambers.* Whether the Lord is purported to be out in the wilderness or hiding in some secret place, do not believe it. Jesus will not return in that manner. As the next verse explains, he will come in a way that will be obvious to all.

JS–M 1:26 *as the light of the morning cometh out of the east.* After Joseph Smith saw the Father and the Son, he said their "brightness and glory defy all description" (JS–H 1:17). In the Kirtland

---

[12] Conference Report, Oct. 1972, 126–27; see also the statement of Joseph F. Smith and his counselors in Clark, *Messages of the First Presidency,* 4:285–86.
[13] Conference Report, Oct. 1992, 102.
[14] "When Shall These Things Be?" 187.

Temple, Joseph Smith and Oliver Cowdery saw the Lord and said that "his countenance shone above the brightness of the sun" (D&C 110:3). Thus, when the Lord comes in his glory, he will shine with a brightness that cannot be missed. It will be as bright and as noticeable as the rising of the sun.

THE COMING OF THE ANTICHRIST

1 John 2:18–22

18 Little children, it is the last time: and as ye have heard that antichrist shall come, even now are there many antichrists; whereby we know that it is the last time.

19 They went out from us, but they were not of us; for if they had been of us, they would no doubt have continued with us: but they went out, that they might be made manifest that they were not all of us.

20 But ye have an unction from the Holy One, and ye know all things.

21 I have not written unto you because ye know not the truth, but because ye know it, and that no lie is of the truth.

22 Who is a liar but he that denieth that Jesus is the Christ? He is antichrist, that denieth the Father and the Son.

Antichrist is "a word used by John to describe one who would assume the guise of Christ, but in reality would be opposed to Christ. . . . In a broader sense it is anyone or anything that counterfeits the true gospel or plan of salvation and that openly or secretly is set up in opposition to Christ. The great antichrist is Lucifer, but he has many assistants both as spirit beings and as mortals."[15] Thus, there appear to be three kinds of antichrist: those who are opposed to and deny Christ; those who are counterfeit Christs; and any organization or philosophy that seeks to supplant the true gospel and its author, Jesus Christ.

There are many antichrists in every age, as John noted there were in his day. Antichrists are people who deny the Father and the Son or

---

[15] LDS Bible Dictionary, 609.

who deny that Jesus has come in the flesh (1 John 4:3–6; 2 John 1:7). The Book of Mormon gives us several examples of men who were antichrists, each of which stands as a warning for our day:

Sherem taught the people "that there should be no Christ . . . and this he did that he might overthrow the doctrine of Christ" (Jac. 7:1–2). Later, Sherem admitted that "he had been deceived by the power of the devil" (Jacob 7:18).

Nehor "testified unto the people that all mankind should be saved at the last day, and that they need not fear nor tremble, . . . and, in the end, all men should have eternal life" (Alma 1:4), thus effectively denying the need for Christ as our Savior. Before he died he "did acknowledge, between the heavens and the earth, that what he had taught to the people was contrary to the word of God" (Alma 1:15).

Korihor "was antichrist, for he began to preach unto the people against the prophecies which had been spoken by the prophets, concerning the coming of Christ. . . . And this antichrist . . . began to preach unto the people that there should be no Christ" (Alma 30:6, 12). Korihor confessed in the end that "the devil hath deceived me; . . . and he taught me that which I should say" (Alma 30:53).

Zoram taught his people to cry aloud in prayer, "Holy God, we believe that . . . thou hast made it known unto us that there shall be no Christ" (Alma 31:16).

All these are different but very similar manifestations of the spirit of antichrist, and we have seen (and shall see) all these and many more in our lifetimes. Also partaking of that same spirit are false prophets and false Christs.[16] But the scriptures warn in particular of latter-day antichrists. Paul wrote: "Let no man deceive you by any means: for that day [the Second Coming] shall not come, except there come a falling away first, and that man of sin be revealed, the son of perdition; who opposeth and exalteth himself above all that is called God, or that is worshipped; so that he as God sitteth in the temple of God, shewing himself that he is God. . . .

"For the mystery of iniquity doth already work: only he who now letteth will let, until he be taken out of the way. And then shall that Wicked be revealed, whom the Lord shall consume with the spirit of

---

[16] See the commentary on false Christs and false prophets, page 206.

his mouth, and shall destroy with the brightness of his coming: Even him, whose coming is after the working of Satan with all power and signs and lying wonders, and with all deceivableness of unrighteousness in them that perish; because they received not the love of the truth, that they might be saved" (2 Thes. 2:3).

Who is the "man of sin" that shall be revealed, who is also called "the son of perdition"? He is none other than Satan himself.[17] He opposes God; he seeks to elevate himself above all that is of God; he is worshipped by others; he sits "in the temple of God," pretending to be God himself. He is "Wicked"; he uses his power to display "signs and lying wonders." Those who do not love the truth will be deceived. Those who follow Satan in opposing Christ are themselves antichrists. Paul called this frightful circumstance "the mystery of iniquity," which brings to mind a description of Babylon as "MYSTERY, . . . THE MOTHER OF HARLOTS AND ABOMINATIONS OF THE EARTH" (Rev. 17:5). Certainly Satan, as the ultimate antichrist, and the Babylon of the last days are closely connected.

John the Revelator gave us another description of a latter-day antichrist, calling him a beast. He has an appearance "like a lamb," a counterfeit of the true Lamb. He exercises great power and perpetuates a false worship of his mentor, another beast. "And he doeth great wonders, so that he maketh fire come down from heaven on the earth in the sight of men, and deceiveth them that dwell on the earth by the means of those miracles which he had power to do" (Rev. 13:11–14). Joseph Smith, in his translation of the Bible, noted that the first beast was "in the likeness of the kingdoms of the earth" (JST Rev. 13:1), and the second beast probably also is in such a likeness. Thus, in this sense, the beasts are not individuals but earthly kingdoms, cultures, or philosophies that follow Satan, that stand opposed to Christ, and that seek to supplant Him in the hearts and minds of the people of the earth (Rev. 13). Thus, both the beasts and the antichrist are individuals, nations, and philosophies. And thus we understand that Satan has set up his kingdoms and has raised up his followers to oppose Christ, and the followers of our great enemy will not slacken in their efforts

---

[17] McConkie, *Millennial Messiah,* 40–41, 50–51.

to establish the cause of their master until they are conquered and cast out in the end (Rev. 19:19–21).

NOTES AND COMMENTARY

1 Jn. 2:18 *even now are there many antichrists.* Even in John's day there were many antichrists, meaning those who denied the reality or divinity of Christ.

1 Jn. 2:19 *They went out from us, but they were not of us.* The antichrists in John's day apparently had been members of the Church, but they were not truly converted in their hearts. Perhaps some of those who will rise up as antichrists in our day will likewise be apostates from the true Church.

1 Jn. 2:20 *ye have an unction from the Holy One, and ye know all things.* The Holy One is the Holy One of Israel, or Jehovah (Isa. 60:9; 2 Ne. 9:15, 26; Omni 1:25). The word *unction* means anointing, perhaps referring to an anointing received in the temple. Because the Saints have received this anointing from God, they "know all things," including how to discern the true followers of Christ. As Moroni taught concerning those who received the Holy Ghost, "by the power of the Holy Ghost ye may know the truth of all things" (Moro. 10:5).

INIQUITY WILL ABOUND
2 Timothy 3:1–7

1 This know also, that in the last days perilous times shall come.

2 For men shall be lovers of their own selves, covetous, boasters, proud, blasphemers, disobedient to parents, unthankful, unholy,

3 Without natural affection, trucebreakers, false accusers, incontinent, fierce, despisers of those that are good,

4 Traitors, heady, highminded, lovers of pleasures more than lovers of God;

5 Having a form of godliness, but denying the power thereof: from such turn away.

6 For of this sort are they which creep into houses, and lead captive silly women laden with sins, led away with divers lusts,

7 Ever learning, and never able to come to the knowledge of the truth.

When the apostles asked Jesus about his second coming, he detailed many signs of the times. Included in his list: "iniquity shall abound" (Matt. 24:12).

Moroni wrote that the Book of Mormon would come forth "in a day when there shall be great pollutions upon the face of the earth; . . . and all manner of abominations. . . . But wo unto such, for they are in the gall of bitterness and in the bonds of iniquity" (Morm. 8:31). The pollutions Moroni saw may well be spiritual pollutions, things that defile and canker the spirit. These conditions will continue, and even worsen, until the Lord returns. So wicked are the people of the last days that Moroni called them "wicked and perverse and stiffnecked" (Morm. 8:33). When the Lord comes, Jude declared, he will "execute judgment upon all, and . . . convince all that are ungodly among them of all their ungodly deeds which they have ungodly committed, and of all their hard speeches which ungodly sinners have spoken against him. These are murmurers, complainers, walking after their own lusts" (Jude 1:15–16). "All flesh is corrupted before me," the Lord said in 1831, "and the powers of darkness prevail upon the earth, among the children of men, in the presence of all the hosts of heaven—which causeth silence to reign, and all eternity is pained, and the angels are waiting the great command to reap down the earth, to gather the tares that they may be burned; and, behold, the enemy is combined" (D&C 38:11–12).

In our time, Elder Spencer W. Kimball compiled a "lengthy list" of "modern transgressions," each of which is all too prevalent in our society: "Murder, adultery, theft, cursing, unholiness in masters, disobedience in servants, unfaithfulness, improvidence, hatred of God, disobedience to husbands, lack of natural affection, high-mindedness, flattery, lustfulness, infidelity, indiscretion, backbiting, whispering, lack of truth, striking, brawling, quarrelsomeness, unthankfulness, inhospitality, deceitfulness, irreverence, boasting, arrogance, pride, double-tongued talk, profanity, slander, corruptness, thievery, embezzlement, despoiling, covenant breaking, incontinence, filthiness, ignobleness, filthy communications, impurity, foolishness, slothfulness, impatience, lack of understanding, unmercifulness, idolatry, blasphemy, denial of the Holy Ghost, Sabbath breaking, envy, jealousy, malice, maligning, vengefulness, implacability, bitterness, clamor, spite, defiling, reviling, evil speaking, provoking, greediness for filthy lucre, disobedience to parents, anger, hate, covetousness, bearing false witness, inventing evil things, fleshliness, heresy, presumptuousness, abomination, insatiable appetite, instability, ignorance, self-will, speaking evil of dignitaries, becoming a stumbling block; and in our modern language, masturbation, petting, fornication, adultery, homosexuality; and every sex perversion, every hidden and secret sin and all unholy and impure practices.

"These are transgressions the Lord has condemned through his servants. Let no one rationalize his sins on the excuse that a particular sin of his is not mentioned nor forbidden in scripture."[18]

On another occasion President Kimball lamented, "Perhaps never before has the world accepted sin so completely as a way of life."[19]

Other latter-day prophets have spoken plainly concerning the sins of our day. Their combined voices are stunning in their clarity and sobering in their message. Following is a sampling:

Joseph Smith: "We behold that darkness covers the earth, and gross darkness the minds of the inhabitants thereof—that crimes of every description are increasing among men—vices of great enormity are practiced—the rising generation growing up in the fullness of pride and arrogance—the aged losing every sense of conviction, and seemingly banishing every thought of a day of retribution—intemperance, immorality, extravagance, pride, blindness of heart, idolatry, the loss of natural affection; the love of this world, and indifference toward the things of eternity increasing among those who profess a belief in the religion of heaven, and infidelity spreading itself in consequence of the same—men giving themselves up to commit acts of the foulest kind, and deeds of the blackest dye, blaspheming, defrauding, blasting the reputation of neighbors, stealing, robbing,

---

[18] *Miracle of Forgiveness*, 25.
[19] Conference Report, Apr. 1972, 29.

murdering; advocating error and opposing the truth, forsaking the covenant of heaven, and denying the faith of Jesus—and in the midst of all this, the day of the Lord fast approaching when none except those who have won the wedding garment will be permitted to eat and drink in the presence of the Bridegroom, the Prince of Peace!"[20]

Marion G. Romney: "The world in which we live today is sick nigh to death. The disease of which it suffers is not a new one. It is as old as history. Its name is unrighteousness. The cure for it is repentance."[21]

Gordon B. Hinckley: "One need not . . . read statistics to recognize a moral decay that seems to be going on all about us. It is evident in the easy breakup of marriages, in widespread infidelity, in the growth of youth gangs, in the increased use of drugs and the epidemic spread of AIDS, and in a growing disregard for the lives and property of others. It is seen in the defacement of private and public property with graffiti, which destroys beauty and is an insult to art. It is expressed in the language of the gutter, which is brought into our homes.

"The endless sex and violence on network TV, the trash of so many motion pictures, the magnified sensuality found in much of modern literature, the emphasis on sex education, a widespread breakdown of law and order—all are manifestations of this decay."[22]

Thomas S. Monson: "We observe business without morality; science without humanity; knowledge without character; worship without sacrifice; pleasure without conscience; politics without principle; and wealth without works."[23]

Bruce R. McConkie: "Even now the generality of men love Satan more than God; even now sodomic practices—immorality, homosexuality, and all manner of perversions—are found among great segments of our society; even now the righteous are leaving the world and finding place in the stakes of Zion. And as the residue of men go forward in their normal activities, reveling in their wickedness as did

---

[20] *History of the Church,* 2:5.
[21] Conference Report, Apr. 1950, 86.
[22] *Ensign,* Nov. 1993, 59.
[23] "In Quest of the Abundant Life," 2.

they of old, the day of burning, coming, as it were, from the midst of eternity, shall come upon them. And should any of the saints look back as did Lot's wife, they will be burned with the wicked."[24]

David B. Haight: "In [a] brief period . . . , this country and most of the free world have been converted into a space-age Sodom and Gomorrah, aided by some publishers, movie producers, and even some so-called educators. Moral principles have been eclipsed by the blind, ungodly pursuit of pleasure—pleasure at any price."[25]

Even without such prophetic testimony, one does not have to look far to see that ours is a day when iniquity does indeed abound. Those with just a moderate awareness of our world can readily see the iniquity of our age in the high incidence of divorce, sexual relations outside the sacred bonds of marriage, the high crime rate, the continuing proliferation of wars around the world, pornography on the Internet and elsewhere, profanity and the emphasis on sexual situations on television and in movies, the lamented loss of civility in our discourse and our dealings with others, drug abuse, abortion, assisted suicide, and on and on.[26]

NOTES AND COMMENTARY

2 Tim. 3:1 *perilous times.* Certainly the last days will be perilous in terms of judgments and disasters, for there will be unprecedented famines, pestilences, and earthquakes.[27] But Paul is referring here to perilous times spiritually; when men turn themselves over to the kinds of sin mentioned in this passage, both society and individuals are imperiled.

2 Tim. 3:2 *lovers of their own selves.* Men will be so selfish that they will care first and foremost for themselves, making their own pleasure and desires and goals their highest priority.

unholy. That which is holy is that which is worthy to receive God's presence, such as a temple or a pure and righteous person

---

[24] *Millennial Messiah,* 362.

[25] Conference Report, Apr. 1973, 84.

[26] This is a phenomenon both Latter-day Saints and others notice. For a perceptive discussion of the moral perils of our time, see Bork, *Slouching towards Gomorrah,* and Bennett, *Death of Outrage.*

[27] See the commentary on God's judgments, page 321.

(Ps. 11:4; 1 Cor. 3:16–17). When a person becomes unholy, he or she becomes separated from God and his Spirit, and is no longer able to receive that divine presence (Mosiah 2:37; Alma 7:21).

2 Tim. 3:3 *without natural affection.* Paul here implies that it is in our nature to have affection or regard for others, but in the last days, that natural affection will be lost as people turn themselves over to sin. In the book of Moses the Lord said, "Unto thy brethren have I said, and also given commandment, that they should love one another, and that they should choose me, their Father; but behold, they are without affection, and they hate their own blood" (Moses 7:33; see also Rom. 1:31). There may be a second meaning to this phrase: perhaps it also refers to affection that is not natural, such as homosexuality.

incontinent. This word in the original Greek may be translated as "without self-control."[28]

2 Tim. 3:4 *heady.* The original Greek word used by Paul may also be translated as "rash."[29]

highminded. The original Greek word used by Paul may also be translated as "lifted up with pride."[30]

2 Tim. 3:5 *Having a form of godliness.* "A form of godliness" may refer to having the ordinances of the priesthood or the outward trappings of the gospel. It may also refer to hypocrisy, in which people have the appearance of godliness without really being godly. During the First Vision, the Lord indicated that this prophecy had come to pass and seemed to suggest that this phrase referred to both of these concepts: "The Personage who addressed me said that all their creeds were an abomination in his sight; that those professors were all corrupt; that: 'they draw near to me with their lips, but their hearts are far from me, they teach for doctrines the commandments of men, having a form of godliness, but they deny the power thereof'" (JS–H 1:19).

but denying the power thereof. Even though the people being described here have a form of godliness, they are not able to

---

[28] *Dictionary of the Greek New Testament,* in *Strong's Exhaustive Concordance of the Bible,* 9.
[29] Ibid., 61.
[30] Ibid., 73.

appreciate or even give place to the true power of godliness. In fact, they go beyond lack of recognition of that power to the point of denial (3 Ne. 29:6; Morm. 9:26).

2 Tim. 3:6 *silly women laden with sins.* The New International Version of the Bible refers to these women as "weak-willed women, who are loaded down with sins and are swayed by all kinds of evil desires."

2 Tim. 3:7 *ever learning, and never able to come to the knowledge of the truth.* Such people increase in worldly knowledge but never come to the richer knowledge of the gospel of Jesus Christ. Those who hope to learn the things of eternal significance must cast away "their learning, and their wisdom, and their riches . . . and consider themselves fools before God, and come down in the depths of humility" (2 Ne. 9:42; see also Alma 17:2–3).

THE LOVE OF MANY SHALL WAX COLD
Matthew 24:12

> 12 And because iniquity shall abound, the love of many shall wax cold.

Latter-day scripture changes this passage to "the love of men shall wax cold" (D&C 45:27; see also JS–M 1:30). The cause of the lack of love is the iniquity. "Because iniquity shall abound," the Lord said, love will "wax cold." The New International Version of the Bible renders it this way: "Because of the increase of wickedness, the love of most will grow cold."

Iniquity and loss of love are intimately and inextricably connected; each leads to the other in an unhappy cycle. Love grows cold when people love their sins more than goodness or the Lord; when they are selfish, caring more about themselves than about others; when other people become tools or objects to be used, rather than souls to care about; when they are filled with pride. Manifestations in our time of love growing cold are crime rates, divorce rates, desertions, abuse, pornography, abortion, and sin in general. Elder Neal A. Maxwell wrote: "Indifference, insensitivity, and cruelty will extend beyond obvious manifestations, such as abortion, to other things as well. Previous societies in deep decay and deterioration were characterized by the words *past feeling, without order,* and *without mercy.* (See Moroni 9:18.)"[31]

To illustrate how love has waxed cold in our day, Elder M. Russell Ballard quoted the following statistics: "During the . . . 30-year period [1960–1990] there has been more than a 500 percent increase in violent crime; more than a 400 percent increase in illegitimate births; a tripling of the percentage of children living in single-parent homes; a tripling in the teenage suicide rate; a doubling in the divorce rate. . . . By 2000, according to some projections, 40 percent of all American births . . . will occur out of wedlock." Elder Ballard further noted that "in the United States the birthrate of children to unwed mothers is at an all-time high, as is the divorce rate."[32]

The prophet Mormon has given us a disturbing view of the depths to which man can sink when his love waxes cold. Speaking of the Nephites, whose story is given to provide lessons for our day, he said: "So exceedingly do they anger that it seemeth me that they have no fear of death; and they have lost their love, one towards another; and they thirst after blood and revenge continually.

"And notwithstanding [the] great abomination of the Lamanites, it doth not exceed that of our people in Moriantum. For behold, many of the daughters of the Lamanites have they taken prisoners; and after depriving them of that which was most dear and precious above all things, which is chastity and virtue—and after they had done this thing, they did murder them in a most cruel manner, torturing their bodies even unto death. . . .

"Behold, my heart cries: Wo unto this people. Come out in judgment, O God, and hide their sins, and wickedness, and abominations from before thy face!

"O the depravity of my people! They are without order and without mercy. . . . And they have become strong in their perversion; and they are alike brutal, sparing none, neither old nor young; and they delight in everything save that which is good; and the suffering of our

---

[31] *Wherefore, Ye Must Press Forward,* 79.
[32] "When Shall These Things Be?" 187; the statistics were quoted from William J. Bennett, *The Index of Leading Cultural Indicators* (New York: Simon and Schuster, 1994), 8, 47.

women and our children upon all the face of this land doth exceed everything; yea, tongue cannot tell, neither can it be written.

"And now, my son, I dwell no longer upon this horrible scene. Behold, thou knowest the wickedness of this people; thou knowest that they are without principle, and past feeling; and their wickedness doth exceed that of the Lamanites. . . . And if they perish it will be like unto the Jaredites, because of the wilfulness of their hearts, seeking for blood and revenge" (Moro. 9:5, 9–10, 15, 18–20, 23).

Notes and Commentary

Matt. 24:12 *wax cold.* Love can grow warm or cold. In the last days, because of sin, many men and women will lose their natural love for others. This loss of love will be marked enough that those who are watching can see it as one of the signs of the times.

The Persecution of the Saints
1 Nephi 14:13

> *13 And it came to pass that I beheld that the great mother of abominations did gather together multitudes upon the face of all the earth, among all the nations of the Gentiles, to fight against the Lamb of God.*

Persecution is the lot of the Saints in all ages, and the last days are no exception. Sometimes persecution stems from simple prejudice in the minds of individuals; sometimes it is orchestrated, as stated in this verse: "the great mother of abominations did gather together multitudes . . . to fight against the Lamb of God" (1 Ne.14:13). But, the Lord said, "Blessed are they which are persecuted for righteousness' sake, for theirs is the kingdom of heaven. Blessed are ye, when men shall revile you, and persecute you, and shall say all manner of evil against you falsely, for my sake. Rejoice, and be exceeding glad: for great is your reward in heaven: for so persecuted they the prophets which were before you" (Matt. 5:10–12). Again, he said, "They shall put you out of the synagogues: yea, the time cometh, that whosoever killeth you will think that he doeth God service" (John 16:2; see also Dan. 7:21; Rev. 13:6–8; D&C 88:94). Paul added this sobering observation: "All that will live godly in Christ Jesus shall suffer persecution" (2 Tim. 3:12).

The persecution of the latter-day church of Christ is a dominant element of our history, beginning with Joseph Smith ("I was hated and persecuted"; JS–H 1:25) and continuing in some geographical areas to the present. Our latter-day prophets give us some idea of what we may expect:

Joseph Smith said, "This one thing is sure, that they who will live godly in Christ Jesus, shall suffer persecution; . . . they will pass through great tribulation."[33] "The enemies of this people will never get weary of their persecution against the Church, until they are over-come. . . . He that will war the true Christian warfare against the cor-ruptions of these last days will have wicked men and angels of devils, and all the infernal powers of darkness continually arrayed against him. . . . But it will be but a little season, and all these afflictions will be turned away from us, inasmuch as we are faithful, and are not overcome by these evils."[34]

And Elder Gordon B. Hinckley taught: "Our history is one of being driven, of being winnowed and peeled, of being persecuted and hounded. . . . I go back to these words of Paul: 'We are troubled on every side, yet not distressed; we are perplexed, but not in despair; persecuted, but not forsaken; cast down, but not destroyed' (2 Corin-thians 4:8–9)."[35]

NOTES AND COMMENTARY

1 Ne. 14:13 *great mother of abominations.* This expression is a reference to the great and abominable church of the devil.[36]

multitudes upon the face of all the earth, among all the nations of the Gentiles. The persecution of the Saints of God will be found in all nations.

fight against the Lamb of God. When the people of the earth fight against the Lamb of God, who is Christ, they of course will do so by fighting against his Church, his people, and the truth of his gospel.

---

[33] *History of the Church,* 1:449.
[34] *History of the Church,* 5:141.
[35] *Loneliness of Leadership,* 4.
[36] See the commentary on the great and abominable church, page 285.

SECRET COMBINATIONS WILL BE BUILT UP
Mormon 8:27

27 And it shall come in a day when the blood of saints shall cry unto the Lord, because of secret combinations and the works of darkness.

The Book of Mormon will come in a day when there are secret combinations and works of darkness on the earth. That day, or time in the earth's history, continues to our present generation—only it grows worse. In the time of Joseph Smith, the Lord warned those who "shall be converted to flee to the west, and this in consequence of that which is coming on the earth, and of secret combinations" (D&C 42:64). When he served as president of the Church, Ezra Taft Benson repeatedly warned us against secret combinations. For example, he taught: "Pride results in secret combinations which are built up to get power, gain, and glory of the world (see Helaman 7:5; Ether 8:9, 16, 22–23; Moses 5:31). This fruit of the sin of pride, namely secret combinations, brought down both the Jaredite and the Nephite civilizations and has been and will yet be the cause of the fall of many nations (see Ether 8:18–25)."[37] On another occasion he said: "I testify that wickedness is rapidly expanding in every segment of our society (see D&C 1:14–16; 84:49–53). It is more highly organized, more cleverly disguised, and more powerfully promoted than ever before. Secret combinations lusting for power, gain, and glory are flourishing."[38]

What are the characteristics of secret combinations?

1. They are inspired by the devil (2 Ne. 9:9; 26:22; Ether 8:16, 25).

2. They date back to Cain (Ether 8:15; Moses 5:29–31, 49–51).

3. They are "combinations" or "bands" of people who agree to do "works of darkness" in "secret" (2 Ne. 9:9; 26:22; Hel. 2:8; 3 Ne. 7:10; 9:9; Moses 5:51).

4. They join together in oaths to keep their works secret (Hel. 6:30; Ether 8:15; Moses 5:29–30).

---

[37] Conference Report, Apr. 1989, 5.
[38] Conference Report, Oct. 1988, 103.

5. Their "great secret" is to "murder and get gain" (Moses 5:31). Therefore, murder is one of their recurring characteristics (2 Ne. 9:9; Hel. 2:8; 6:38; 3 Ne. 5:6; 9:9; Ether 8:16, 25).

6. Their goal is to "get power and gain" (Ether 8:15–16, 22–23; 11:15; see also Hel. 2:8; Morm. 8:40).

7. In addition to murder, they engage in robbery, plunder, lying, and "all manner of wickedness and whoredoms." These combinations are "most abominable and wicked above all, in the sight of God" (Alma 37:21; Hel. 2:9; 10:3; Ether 8:16, 18).

8. They murder the prophets and the Saints (3 Ne. 7:6; 9:9; Morm. 8:41; Ether 8:22, 25).

9. They seek to destroy governments and "the freedom of all lands, nations, and countries"; they caused the destruction of both the Jaredites and Nephites (3 Ne. 7:6; 9:9; Ether 8:21, 25; 11:15).

10. "They are had among all people" (Ether 8:20).

"What are these secret combinations which have such powers that whole civilizations are destroyed by them? They wear many guises and appear in many forms. They were the Gadianton robbers among the Nephites, and the perpetrators of the Spanish inquisition in the dark ages. Among us they include some secret and oath-bound societies and such Mafia-like groups as engage in organized crime. They include some political parties, some revolutionists who rise up against their governments, and those evil and anarchist groups which steal and kidnap and murder in the name of this or that political objective. They are always groups that seek money and power and freedom from the penalties that should attend their crimes. . . .

"Next Moroni turns the key so that all who have ears to hear can understand what the secret combination is and can identify those who build it up. 'For it cometh to pass,' he says, 'that whoso buildeth it up seeketh to overthrow the freedom of all lands, nations, and countries.' This is a worldwide conspiracy. It is now entrenched in many nations, and it seeks dominion over all nations. It is Godless, atheistic, and operates by compulsion. It is communism."[39]

---

[39] McConkie, *Millennial Messiah*, 64, 66.

Related to secret combinations is Babylon, the mother of abominations on the earth.[40]

NOTES AND COMMENTARY

Morm. 8:27 *blood of saints.* This expression indicates that those who were martyred require justice against those who killed them; it is as though their very blood cries unto the Lord for vengeance against those who, as part of secret combinations, have slain them. Killing the Saints and prophets is also a key characteristic of Babylon, the whore of all the earth (Rev. 16:6; 17:6; 18:24; Ether 8:22; D&C 87:7).

works of darkness. It is characteristic of Satan to seek to do his evil works in darkness, and he teaches his followers to do the same. Thus, "works of darkness" refers to works inspired by the devil.

THE CONSTITUTION OF THE UNITED STATES WILL HANG BY A THREAD
Joseph Smith

> *Even this Nation will be on the very verge of crumbling to pieces and tumbling to the ground and when the constitution is upon the brink of ruin this people will be the Staff up[on] which the Nation shall lean and they shall bear the constitution away from the very verge of destruction. . . . I know these things by the visions of the Almighty.[41]*

One of the conditions of the last days is that the Constitution of the United States will be in jeopardy and will seem to hang as though upon a single thread. Our source of this prophecy is not the scriptures but Joseph Smith. Brigham Young recalled the prophecy in this way: "Will the Constitution be destroyed? No; it will be held inviolate by this people; and, as Joseph Smith said, 'The time will come when the destiny of the nation will hang upon a single thread. At this critical

---

[40] See the commentary on Babylon, page 283.

[41] *Words of Joseph Smith,* 416. President J. Reuben Clark Jr. warned that if we continued on the course that allowed "one man, or . . . a small group of men, . . . [to] amend the Constitution,"—referring perhaps to amendment by interpretation of presidents or government regulators or inappropriate judicial decree—"then we shall lose the Constitution." He continued, "I say unto you with all the soberness I can, that we stand in danger of losing our liberties, and that once lost, only blood will bring them back; and once lost, we of this Church will, in order to keep the Church going forward, have more sacrifices to make and more persecutions to endure than we have yet known, heavy as our sacrifices and grievous as our persecutions of the past have been" (Conference Report, Apr. 1944, 116).

juncture, this people will step forth and save it from the threatened destruction.' It will be so."[42]

Joseph Smith said we would see the time when the nation was on the "verge of crumbling to pieces" and "the constitution is upon the brink of ruin." President Wilford Woodruff said "the time will come when the country will be distracted and general lawlessness prevail. Then the Mormon people will step forward and take an active part in rescuing the nation from ruin."[43] Speaking of this prophecy, Elder Ezra Taft Benson said: "I have heard our present Prophet leader [President David O. McKay] say we are very near to that time. It is my solemn conviction we are near the time which the Prophet saw. What are we going to do about it? Will we, as Latter-day Saints, favored of the Lord, 'arise and shine forth,' as the Lord has commanded, 'that thy light may be a standard for the nations' (D&C 115:5)?"[44]

How will "this people step forward" to save the Constitution? Elder Benson suggested that "it is entirely possible that that may come about in a rather natural way. Our young people—as they mature and develop and take their positions in industry, in the professions, and in agriculture clear across this land—might represent the balance of power in a time of crisis, when they will stand up and defend those eternal principles upon which this Constitution has been established."[45] On another occasion he said: "I have faith that the Constitution will be saved as prophesied by Joseph Smith. But it will not be saved in Washington. It will be saved by the citizens of this nation who love and cherish freedom. It will be saved by enlightened members of this Church—men and women who will subscribe to and abide by the principles of the Constitution."[46] Elder Mark E. Petersen offered another possibility of how this prophecy would come to pass: "You will remember that there have been prophecies made that the Constitution sometime will hang by a thread and that the elders of Israel will save it. I don't believe that that is through some political means particularly. I believe that the way this Church may save our

[42] *Discourses of Brigham Young,* 469.
[43] "Discourse by President Wilford Woodruff," 788.
[44] *Vietnam—Victory or Surrender,* 12.
[45] *Four-Fold Hope,* 7.
[46] "Constitution, a Heavenly Banner," 43–44.

country is by being the leaven in the lump which will be so recognized by the Almighty that he will spare the country for the Church. The country, our nation, was made by act of God to bring about the purposes related to the restoration of the gospel and to the final fulfillment of his work which will lead to the second coming of Jesus Christ."[47]

MEN'S HEARTS SHALL FAIL THEM
Doctrine and Covenants 88:91

91 And all things shall be in commotion; and surely, men's hearts shall fail them; for fear shall come upon all people.

The commotion on the earth in the last days will be so great that it will bring a terrifying fear into the hearts of all people, a fear that causes men's hearts to fail them. Doctrine and Covenants 88:90–91 say: "And also cometh the testimony of the voice of thunderings, and the voice of lightnings, and the voice of tempests, and the voice of the waves of the sea heaving themselves beyond their bounds. And all things shall be in commotion; and surely, men's hearts shall fail them; for fear shall come upon all people."

Wars are a corollary source of terrible fear: "I have sworn in my wrath, and decreed wars upon the face of the earth," the Lord said, "and the wicked shall slay the wicked, and fear shall come upon every man" (D&C 63:33).

Enoch, in seeing our day, saw another source of great fear. He "saw great tribulations among the wicked; and he also saw the sea, that it was troubled, and men's hearts failing them, looking forth with fear for the judgments of the Almighty God, which should come upon the wicked" (Moses 7:66).

Fear from the unprecedented commotion on the earth, fear from wars and death, fear from the judgments of God—surely these will be great indeed to cause men's hearts to fail. The fear, of course, stems from lack of faith coupled with wickedness. As the people of the world turn from God, they lose confidence before him, resulting in a fear of him and his judgments. A loss of love is a related cause of fear,

---

[47] *Our Divine Destiny,* 2–3.

for "perfect love casteth out fear" (1 Jn. 4:18; Moro. 8:16), and those who lack that love are filled with fear. This prophecy seems to tell us that people's courage will fail, they will lose hope, they will be more utterly terrified than they have ever before been in their lives.

NOTES AND COMMENTARY

D&C 88:91 *all things shall be in commotion.* The elements will be in commotion (D&C 88:90); the nations will be in commotion (D&C 63:33); the wicked will be engaged in the commotion of great tribulations (Moses 7:66)—all of these will likely reach unprecedented levels in the last days.

MEN WILL REFUSE TO BELIEVE AND REPENT
Revelation 9:20–21

20 And the rest of the men which were not killed by these plagues yet repented not of the works of their hands, that they should not worship devils, and idols of gold, and silver, and brass, and stone, and of wood: which neither can see, nor hear, nor walk:

21 Neither repented they of their murders, nor of their sorceries, nor of their fornication, nor of their thefts.

This is an astounding prophecy. John has just seen a vision of many frightening plagues and other judgments:

1. A third of the plants on earth were burned (Rev. 8:7; the use of "third" here is likely symbolic, perhaps meaning a large portion, but less than half).

2. A third of all sea creatures were killed (Rev. 8:9).

3. A third of the earth's fresh water was poisoned, killing many people (Rev. 8:11).

4. A third of the sun, moon, and stars were darkened (Rev. 8:12).

5. A torment symbolized by locusts afflicted the earth for five months, torturing men but not killing them, although the pain was so great that "in those days shall men seek death, and shall not find it" (Rev. 9:5–6, 10).

6. A third of the earth's population is killed in a gigantic battle involving an army of "two hundred thousand thousand" horsemen (Rev. 9:15–18).

After all these judgments, the surviving wicked "yet repented not" (Rev. 9:20; see also 16:11, 21).

This prophecy calls to mind the Jaredites and Nephites, who were so deep in iniquity that they refused to repent even when facing the extinction of their people. Mormon recorded his frustrating and heartrending experience:

"And it came to pass that the Lord did say unto me: Cry unto this people—Repent ye, and come unto me, and be ye baptized, and build up again my church, and ye shall be spared. And I did cry unto this people, but it was in vain; and . . . they did harden their hearts against the Lord their God.

"And when they had sworn by all that had been forbidden them by our Lord and Savior Jesus Christ, that they would go up unto their enemies to battle, and avenge themselves of the blood of their brethren, behold the voice of the Lord came unto me, saying: Vengeance is mine, and I will repay; and because this people repented not after I had delivered them, behold, they shall be cut off from the face of the earth.

"And it came to pass that the three hundred and sixty and sixth year had passed away, and the Lamanites came again upon the Nephites to battle; and yet the Nephites repented not of the evil they had done, but persisted in their wickedness continually. And it is impossible for the tongue to describe, or for man to write a perfect description of the horrible scene of the blood and carnage which was among the people, both of the Nephites and of the Lamanites; and every heart was hardened, so that they delighted in the shedding of blood continually. And there never had been so great wickedness among all the children of Lehi, nor even among all the house of Israel, according to the words of the Lord, as was among this people.

"And now behold, this I speak unto their seed, and also to the Gentiles who have care for the house of Israel, that realize and know from whence their blessings come. For I know that such will sorrow for the calamity of the house of Israel; yea, they will sorrow for the destruction of this people; they will sorrow that this people had not repented that they might have been clasped in the arms of Jesus" (Morm. 3:2–3, 14–15; 4:10–12; 5:10–11; see also Ether 15:2, 6, 15–19; Moro. 9:3).

After the Nephites were destroyed, Mormon wrote in deep grief: "My soul was rent with anguish, because of the slain of my people, and I cried:

"O ye fair ones, how could ye have departed from the ways of the Lord! O ye fair ones, how could ye have rejected that Jesus, who stood with open arms to receive you! Behold, if ye had not done this, ye would not have fallen. But behold, ye are fallen, and I mourn your loss.

"O ye fair sons and daughters, ye fathers and mothers, ye husbands and wives, ye fair ones, how is it that ye could have fallen! But behold, ye are gone, and my sorrows cannot bring your return.

"O that ye had repented before this great destruction had come upon you. But behold, ye are gone, and the Father, yea, the Eternal Father of heaven, knoweth your state; and he doeth with you according to his justice and mercy" (Morm. 6:16–20, 22).

The righteous may yet experience such sorrow themselves, as the world ripens in iniquity and refuses to repent. As those days approach, the Lord gives us the prophecy: "My disciples shall stand in holy places, and shall not be moved; but among the wicked, men shall lift up their voices and curse God and die" (D&C 45:32).

NOTES AND COMMENTARY

Rev. 9:20 *works of their hands.* In the scriptures, this expression often refers to idols, which people created to worship (Jer. 1:16; Acts 7:41). The context of this passage seems to carry the same meaning.

worship devils, and idols. We worship devils or idols when we turn from the true God and let other things replace him in our hearts. Arthur Henry King has spoken of "the idols of prosperity: the car, the camper, the boat (bane of bishops), the color TV, the football game, two weeks of hunting." He added, "These become idols when more enthusiasm and time are given to them than to the worship of God."[48]

---

[48] *Abundance of Heart,* 48.

Elder Spencer W. Kimball had a similar view. "Today we worship the gods of wood and stone and metal. Not always are they in the form of a golden calf, but equally real as objects of protection and worship. They are houses, lands, bank accounts, leisure. They are boats, cars, and luxuries. They are bombs and ships and armaments. We bow down to the god of mammon, the god of luxuries, the god of dissipation."[49] Years later, as president of the Church, he said, "Whatever thing a man sets his heart and his trust in most is his god; and if his god doesn't also happen to be the true and living God of Israel, that man is laboring in idolatry."[50]

In 1930, Elder James E. Talmage gave a conference address in which he identified idolatry as one of the signs of the times: "This is an idolatrous generation. . . . Do you wonder that wickedness and crime have increased to terrifying proportions under those conditions? The prophets of old foresaw it. They spoke of the days of wickedness and vengeance immediately precedent to the second coming of the Lord. . . .

"Where do we stand . . . ? Are we worshipping the true and living God, or are we going idolatrously after the gods of gold and silver, of iron and wood, and brass, diamonds and other idols of wealth? Are we worshipping our farms, our cattle and sheep? Who is our God? To whom are we yielding homage, allegiance and worship? Not worship by means of words only, in ritualistic form, but worship in action, devotion, and sacrificial service?"[51]

SCOFFERS WILL MOCK AT THE SIGNS OF THE TIMES
2 Peter 3:3–4

> 3 Knowing this first, that there shall come in the last days scoffers, walking after their own lusts,
>
> 4 And saying, Where is the promise of his coming? for since the fathers fell asleep, all things continue as they were from the beginning of the creation.

---

[49] Conference Report, Oct. 1961, 33.
[50] Ensign, June 1976, 3.
[51] Conference Report, Oct. 1930, 71–73.

Even though the signs of the times may be obvious to those who are watching for them and who have faith in the prophecies in the scriptures, there will be many who will scoff at them and deny them. "What you claim as signs are natural events," they will say. "What do they have to do with a return of Jesus Christ?" Or: "There have always been earthquakes and wars. We just know about more of them now because of modern means of communication." Or: "What do you mean Christ is coming again? There is no Second Coming, and there are no signs." As Jude put it, echoing Peter's words, "The apostles . . . told you there should be mockers in the last time, who should walk after their own ungodly lusts" (Jude 1:18). Rather than believe and repent, they will deny, mock, sneer, scoff, and rationalize, thereby justifying themselves in their sinfulness and their "ungodly lusts."

A corollary to these attitudes is that there is still time to "eat, drink, and be merry" before the Lord comes. "As it was in the days of Noah, so it shall be also at the coming of the Son of Man," the Lord said. "For it shall be with them, as it was in the days which were before the flood; for until the day that Noah entered into the ark they were eating and drinking, marrying and giving in marriage; and knew not until the flood came, and took them all away; so shall also the coming of the Son of Man be" (JS–M 1:41–43).

We know that the last days will be fully ripened in iniquity, as were the days of Noah, but this prophecy is not necessarily referring to sinfulness. Instead, the Lord speaks of the people participating in the normal activities of life—eating, drinking, getting married—simply unmindful and unbelieving that the Flood would really come. So it will be in the last days. The people will continue with their normal lives, despite the signs of the times, not believing what the signs portend. The result will be that they will be unprepared for the Lord's return. They will not have put their houses in order. They will not have repented of their sins, whether gross or minor; they will not have turned their hearts and their minds and their lives to Christ.

The first group, then, consists of those who do not believe in the signs. The second group consists of those who "shall say that Christ delayeth his coming" (D&C 45:26). They believe in Christ, but they do not think he's going to come in the immediate future, giving them time to continue in sin or their self-centered activities.

To illustrate this truth, the Lord gave us a parable, comparing the people of the world to two kinds of servants: "Be . . . ready, for in such an hour as ye think not, the Son of Man cometh. Who, then, is a faithful and wise servant, whom his lord hath made ruler over his household, to give them meat in due season? Blessed is that servant whom his lord, when he cometh, shall find so doing; and verily I say unto you, he shall make him ruler over all his goods. But if that evil servant shall say in his heart: My lord delayeth his coming, and shall begin to smite his fellow-servants, and to eat and drink with the drunken, the lord of that servant shall come in a day when he looketh not for him, and in an hour that he is not aware of, and shall cut him asunder, and shall appoint him his portion with the hypocrites; there shall be weeping and gnashing of teeth" (JS–M 1:48–54).

NOTES AND COMMENTARY

2 Pet. 3:3 *walking after their own lusts.* Rather than walking along the strait and narrow path, being guided by the iron rod, these people walk according to their own base desires, letting their lusts be their guide.

2 Pet. 3:4 *since the fathers fell asleep. The fathers* seems to be the ancient patriarchal fathers of the covenant people: Adam, Noah, Abraham, and so forth (see John 7:22 and Rom. 15:8, where "the fathers" has reference to Abraham, Isaac, and Jacob). Or this expression may have the more general meaning of "previous generations" (Mal. 4:6). "Fell asleep" refers to the death of those fathers (Deut. 31:16; 2 Sam. 7:12; Acts 7:60).

all things continue as they were. Those who reject the signs of the times will say in essence, "The prophecies have not come to pass; nothing has changed. Everything is the same as it was from the beginning."

THE LORD'S SPIRIT WILL CEASE STRIVING WITH MAN
Doctrine and Covenants 1:32–35

32 Nevertheless, he that repents and does the commandments of the Lord shall be forgiven;

33 And he that repents not, from him shall be taken even the light which he has received; for my Spirit shall not always strive with man, saith the Lord of Hosts.

34 And again, verily I say unto you, O inhabitants of the earth: I the Lord am willing to make these things known unto all flesh;

35 For I am no respecter of persons, and will that all men shall know that the day speedily cometh; the hour is not yet, but is nigh at hand, when peace shall be taken from the earth, and the devil shall have power over his own dominion.

This is not a prophecy that deals only with the last days; it is true in any age that the Lord's Spirit will not always strive with the unrepentant. But we also know that because of the iniquity of earth's inhabitants in the last days, combined with their unwillingness to repent, the time will come when they are "ripened in iniquity" (Ether 2:9; 9:20) and the Spirit will no longer strive to bring them to repentance. The final result will be a world war that will destroy a third of mankind (Rev. 9:16–18), followed by a number of devastating plagues (Rev. 16), and culminating in the destruction of the wicked at the Lord's coming (Mal. 4:1; Rev. 18:8).

"I prophesy, in the name of the Lord God of Israel," said Joseph Smith, "anguish and wrath and tribulation and the withdrawing of the Spirit of God from the earth await this generation, until they are visited with utter desolation. This generation is as corrupt as the generation of the Jews that crucified Christ; and if He were here to-day, and should preach the same doctrine He did then, they would put Him to death."[52]

The scriptural history of the world gives a number of sad precedents for the loss of the Spirit and the destruction that eventually results. In Noah's time, "God saw that the wickedness of man was great in the earth, and that every imagination of the thoughts of his heart was only evil continually" (Gen. 6:5). "And the Lord said unto Noah: My Spirit shall not always strive with man, for he shall know that all flesh shall die; yet his days shall be an hundred and twenty

---

[52] *History of the Church,* 6:58.

years; and if men do not repent, I will send in the floods upon them" (Moses 8:17). We know, of course, that men did not repent, and the floods of mass destruction were sent forth.

The Jews in the time of Lehi were warned that Jerusalem would be destroyed because of their wickedness. "For behold, the Spirit of the Lord ceaseth soon to strive with them," Nephi testified, "for behold, they have rejected the prophets, and Jeremiah have they cast into prison. And they have sought to take away the life of my father, insomuch that they have driven him out of the land" (1 Ne. 7:14).

Later, looking into the future, Nephi said that four generations after the Lord's ministry among the Nephites, "a speedy destruction cometh unto my people; for, notwithstanding the pains of my soul, I have seen it; wherefore, I know that it shall come to pass; and they sell themselves for naught; for, for the reward of their pride and their foolishness they shall reap destruction; for because they yield unto the devil and choose works of darkness rather than light, therefore they must go down to hell. For the Spirit of the Lord will not always strive with man. And when the Spirit ceaseth to strive with man then cometh speedy destruction, and this grieveth my soul" (2 Ne. 26:10–11).

That vision was fulfilled even as Nephi foresaw. Mormon wrote: "Behold, my son, . . . the pride of this nation, or the people of the Nephites, hath proven their destruction except they should repent. Pray for them, my son, that repentance may come unto them. But behold, I fear lest the Spirit hath ceased striving with them; and in this part of the land they are also seeking to put down all power and authority which cometh from God; and they are denying the Holy Ghost. And after rejecting so great a knowledge, my son, they must perish soon, unto the fulfilling of the prophecies which were spoken by the prophets, as well as the words of our Savior himself.

"And now behold, my son, I fear lest the Lamanites shall destroy this people; for they do not repent, and Satan stirreth them up continually to anger one with another. Behold, I am laboring with them continually; and when I speak the word of God with sharpness they tremble and anger against me; and when I use no sharpness they harden their hearts against it; wherefore, I fear lest the Spirit of the Lord hath ceased striving with them. For so exceedingly do they anger that it seemeth me that they have no fear of death; and they have lost their love, one towards another; and they thirst after blood and revenge continually" (Moro. 8:27–29; 9:3–6).

The Jaredites suffered a similar fate, as recorded by the prophet Ether: "The Spirit of the Lord had ceased striving with them," he wrote, "and Satan had full power over the hearts of the people; for they were given up unto the hardness of their hearts, and the blindness of their minds that they might be destroyed" (Ether 15:19).

Mormon taught us the awful consequences of this loss of the Lord's Spirit: "This people shall be scattered, and shall become a dark, a filthy, and a loathsome people, beyond the description of that which ever hath been amongst us, . . . and this because of their unbelief and idolatry. For behold, the Spirit of the Lord hath already ceased to strive with their fathers; and they are without Christ and God in the world; and they are driven about as chaff before the wind.

"They were once a delightsome people, and they had Christ for their shepherd; yea, they were led even by God the Father. But now, behold, they are led about by Satan, even as chaff is driven before the wind, or as a vessel is tossed about upon the waves, without sail or anchor, or without anything wherewith to steer her; and even as she is, so are they" (Morm. 5:15–18; see also Ether 2:14–15).

This dreadful condition has now returned to the earth, only this time it has become worldwide. "I, the Lord, am angry with the wicked," the Lord proclaimed in Joseph Smith's day. "I am holding my Spirit from the inhabitants of the earth" (D&C 63:32).

President Joseph Fielding Smith has given an interpretation of that scripture: "The present turmoil and contentions in the world are due to the fact that the leaders of nations are getting their inspiration from Satan, not from the Lord. His Spirit is withdrawn from them, according to his promise, in spiritual things. The Lord would be glad to direct them, but they seek not his counsel. The spirit of the evil one is placing in their minds vain and fantastic notions and leading mankind farther away from the truth as they boast in their own strength. . . .

"The Spirit of the Lord has not been taken away from those who are willing to keep his commandments."[53]

Even though it appears that the die is cast, that mankind will continue in increasing iniquity until the end, we must not give in to fatalism, comfortable in the knowledge that we have the gospel and will be ready to meet the Lord. As long as time lasts and as long as the Lord allows it, we are to continue to share the gospel message, seeking to build up our neighbors, our communities, and our nations, seeking to somehow stem the tide of evil that surges around us. The perspective of Mormon is valuable for each of us: "And now, my beloved son, notwithstanding their hardness, let us labor diligently; for if we should cease to labor, we should be brought under condemnation; for we have a labor to perform whilst in this tabernacle of clay, that we may conquer the enemy of all righteousness, and rest our souls in the kingdom of God" (Moro. 9:6).

NOTES AND COMMENTARY

D&C 1:33 *from him shall be taken even the light which he has received.* This passage appears to be a description of an eternal principle, as expressed in the parable of the talents. After the owner of the talents received an accounting from his stewards, he said regarding the one who had buried his talent, "Take . . . the talent from him, and give it unto him which hath ten talents. For unto every one that hath shall be given, and he shall have abundance: but from him that hath not shall be taken away even that which he hath" (Matt. 25:28–29; see also D&C 60:2–3). Alma applied this principle directly to spiritual things: "It is given unto many to know the mysteries of God. . . . And . . . he that will harden his heart, the same receiveth the lesser portion of the word; and he that will not harden his heart, to him is given the greater portion of the word, until it is given unto him to know the mysteries of God until he know them in full. And they that will harden their hearts, to them is given the lesser portion of the word until they know nothing concerning his mysteries; and then they are taken captive by the devil, and led by his will down to destruction" (Alma 12:9–11).

---

[53] *Answers to Gospel Questions,* 2:156.

D&C 1:34 *I the Lord am willing to make these things known unto all flesh.* The Lord repeats this idea in the next verse: "I . . . will that all men shall know." The Lord does not do his work "in a corner" (Acts 26:25), hidden from the view of the people. He is willing for us to know "the calamity which should come upon the inhabitants of the earth" (v. 17) and the way in which repentance can deliver us (vv. 31–32). To accomplish that, "the voice of the Lord is unto all men, and there is none to escape; . . . the voice of warning shall be unto all people" (v. 2, 4).

D&C 1:35 *I am no respecter of persons.* "The Lord is no respecter of persons," wrote Elder Joseph Fielding Smith. "However, let us not misinterpret this saying. It does not mean that the Lord does not respect those who obey him in all things more than he does the ungodly. Without question the Lord does respect those who love him and keep his commandments more than he does those who rebel against him. The proper interpretation of this passage is that the Lord is not partial and grants to each man, if he will repent, the same privileges and opportunities of salvation and exaltation. He is just to every man, both the righteous and the wicked. He will receive any soul who will turn from iniquity to righteousness, and will love him with a just love and bless him with all that the Father has to give; but let it not be thought that he will grant the same blessings to those who will not obey him and keep his law. If the Lord did bless the rebellious as he does the righteous, without their repentance, then he would be a respecter of persons. His justice and his mercy are perfect."[54] (See also Deut. 10:17–18; Acts 10:9–35; 2 Ne. 26:33; Alma 1:29–30; 16:13–14; D&C 38:16.)

the day speedily cometh. In 1831, the Lord told us that the time had not then arrived ("the hour is not yet") but it would soon come ("is nigh at hand"), when peace would be taken from the earth (D&C 1:35). In scriptural terminology, *speedily* does not necessarily mean soon. For instance, Nephi quotes Isaiah as teaching that "the time cometh speedily that Satan shall have no more power over the hearts of the children of men; for the day soon cometh that all the proud and they who do wickedly shall be as stubble" (1 Ne. 22:15). Nephi lived

---

[54] *Church History and Modern Revelation,* 2:27.

and taught about six hundred years before Christ, and Isaiah ministered more than a hundred years before that. Yet those things that they said would come "speedily" have not yet occurred (for other examples of the scriptural use of "speedily," see Moro. 10:27; D&C 112:24–26; 124:10).

If *speedily* does not mean in the scriptures what we commonly suppose, what does it mean? Latter-day Saint scholar Daniel Ludlow gives this helpful perspective about a similar expression: "The term *'I come quickly'* refers to the nearness of the second coming of Jesus Christ and is found in at least 13 sections of the Doctrine and Covenants. Although nearly 150 years have passed since some of these revelations were given, yet that is a relatively short period of time when compared to the nearly 6,000 years that the earth has existed in a telestial condition. The recent fulfillment of many of the prophecies pertaining to the second coming indicate that event is indeed near."[55]

Elder Joseph Fielding Smith cast further light on this phrase: "'I come quickly.' This is a scriptural expression that occurs frequently, especially in the book of Revelation. This is 'speaking after the manner of the Lord.' (D&C 63:53.) This does not mean that immediately the Lord will make his appearance, but when he does come he will come suddenly, when he is least expected. . . . For this reason we should watch and pray. . . . There is no excuse for any of us, then, not to be prepared, for we have been fully and frequently warned."[56]

Elder Neal A. Maxwell said: "The Lord's 'soon' may be our century. If I were to say to you at 11:35 P.M., 'When will it be midnight?' you would say 'soon' or 'right away.'"[57]

peace shall be taken from the earth. See the commentary on wars, page 242.

the devil shall have power over his own dominion. The devil's dominion is the wicked world, where those who have yielded their hearts to him yield also their obedience. The Lord said to Moses that Satan, "even the devil, the father of all lies," sought "to deceive and to

---

[55] *Companion to Your Study of the Doctrine and Covenants,* 2:223.
[56] *Church History and Modern Revelation,* 1:145.
[57] *Deposition of a Disciple,* 61.

blind men, and to lead them captive at his will, even as many as would not hearken unto my voice" (Moses 4:4). But the Lord gives us the comfort to know that at the same time Satan would increase in power in his dominion, "the Lord shall have power over his saints, and shall reign in their midst" (D&C 1:35–36).

CHAPTER 6

WARS AND RUMORS OF WARS

SIGNS OF THE TIMES

1. War is poured out on all nations.

2. Slaves rise up against their masters.

3. The "remnants of the land" vex the Gentiles.

4. A five-month war torments mankind.

5. A war with two hundred million soldiers kills one-third of mankind (may be the same war as Armageddon).

6. All nations gather to battle against Israel in the valley of Armageddon.

7. The Saints receive a degree of protection.

8. All nations come to an end.

The Lord warned his disciples that the last days would be a time of "wars and rumors of wars . . . for nation shall rise against nation, and kingdom against kingdom" (Matt. 24:6–7). Doctrine and Covenants 45, which gives us a more complete account of the Lord's words to his disciples, says: "And in that day shall be heard of wars and rumors of wars, and the whole earth shall be in commotion, and men's hearts shall fail them. . . . And there shall be earthquakes also in divers places, and many desolations; yet men will harden their hearts against me, and they will take up the sword, one against another, and they will kill one another." The Lord added for our dispensation, "Ye hear of wars in foreign lands; but, behold, I say unto you, they are nigh, even at your doors, and not many years hence ye shall hear of wars in your own lands" (D&C 45:26, 33, 63; see also 38:29).

With vision that saw our day clearly, Jeremiah proclaimed, "The Lord hath a controversy with the nations, he will plead with all flesh; he will give them that are wicked to the sword" (Jer. 25:31). "I have sworn in my wrath," the Lord said to Joseph Smith, "and decreed wars upon the face of the earth, and the wicked shall slay the wicked, and fear shall come upon every man" (D&C 63:33).

The unfolding fulfillment of these prophecies is clear for all to see. During this century, advances in transportation, communications, and weapons technology have given nations of the world an ever-greater capacity for mass destruction of an enemy. While man has developed newer and more effective ways of destroying an enemy, there has not been corresponding progress in character, love of God, or love of one's neighbor—in fact, love in many men has dwindled. Thus, World War I was so deadly it was called "The Great War" and "The War to End All Wars": it claimed the lives of more than ten million soldiers. Less than a generation later, World War II erupted, involving far larger armies and killing far more people than World War I had done—a total of forty-five million.[1]

A commission investigating violence in society declared: "The twentieth century proved to be the most violent and destructive in all human history, with armed conflict taking the lives of over 100 million people and political violence responsible for 170 million more deaths. . . . At the time of this writing, there is conflict in over two dozen locations around the world in which, over the years, tens of thousands have been killed and millions of persons displaced.

"For many governments and their publics, the mounting losses from war have ceased to shock, as the rhythm of daily existence has settled into a routine of attack and counterattack. Yet wars have become ever more brutal. In some wars today, 90 percent of those killed in conflict are noncombatants, compared with less than 15 percent when the century began. In Rwanda alone, approximately 40 percent of the population has been killed or displaced since 1994. . . .

"Since the fall of the Berlin Wall [Nov. 1989], over four million people have been killed in violent conflicts. In January 1997, there were over 35 million refugees and internally displaced persons around the

---

[1] *World Almanac and Book of Facts,* 509, 512.

world. The violence that generated this trauma has been in some cases chronic. In others, there have been tremendous spasms of destruction. For example, the 1990s have witnessed protracted violent confrontation in Bosnia and Chechnya and a massive genocide in Rwanda. . . . With well over one-half million people killed in three months, this has been one of the most horrifying chapters in human history."[2]

Tragically, wars have become so prevalent that the Lord's prophecy has now come to pass: "the hour is not yet, but is nigh at hand, when peace shall be taken from the earth, and the devil shall have power over his own dominion" (D&C 1:35).[3] These wars are not a new tool of the devil. He has used warfare as a means of accomplishing his ends—and of corrupting the souls of men—since the beginning, when he instigated the war in heaven. When he tempted Cain to kill Abel for jealousy and to get gain, Satan brought this technique to the earth, where it has remained ever since. As men increase in wickedness on the earth, it only stands to reason that they will also be more inclined to use organized methods of causing death and destruction (which is what war is) to obtain their goals.

Truly, then, this is a day of "wars and rumors of wars," giving us a sign of the times that is clearly discernible. As the wars of our time proceed, the Saints feel to cry out with President Gordon B. Hinckley: "War I hate with all its mocking panoply. It is a grim and living testimony that Satan, the father of lies, the enemy of God, lives. War is earth's greatest cause of human misery. It is the destroyer of life, the promoter of hate, the waster of treasure. It is man's costliest folly, his most tragic misadventure."[4]

WAR WILL BE POURED OUT ON ALL NATIONS
Doctrine and Covenants 87:1–3

1 Verily, thus saith the Lord concerning the wars that will shortly come to pass, beginning at the rebellion of South

---

[2] "Preventing Deadly Conflict: Final Report," 1, prologue.
[3] Our latter-day prophets have repeatedly testified that the prophesied day "when peace shall be taken from the earth" has come. See, for example, Brigham Young and his counselors in the First Presidency, "Ninth General Epistle," 437; Smith, *Progress of Man,* 398, 478; Lee, *Decisions for Successful Living,* 221–22; and Benson, *So Shall Ye Reap,* 98.
[4] *Lest We Forget,* 3.

Carolina, which will eventually terminate in the death and misery of many souls;

2 And the time will come that war will be poured out upon all nations, beginning at this place.

3 For behold, the Southern States shall be divided against the Northern States, and the Southern States will call on other nations, even the nation of Great Britain, as it is called, and they shall also call upon other nations, in order to defend themselves against other nations; and then war shall be poured out upon all nations.

Most Latter-day Saints are familiar with Joseph Smith's prophecy of the American Civil War, but all may not have noticed that Joseph Smith gave the Civil War as a sign that marks the beginning of the latter-day wars. This concept is repeated twice: "thus saith the Lord concerning the wars that will shortly come to pass, beginning at the rebellion of South Carolina" (D&C 87:1), and "war will be poured out upon all nations, beginning at this place" (v. 2).

Elsewhere Joseph Smith gave the prophecy in a slightly different way but with the same meaning: "I prophesy, in the name of the Lord God, that the commencement of the difficulties which will cause much bloodshed previous to the coming of the Son of Man will be in South Carolina. It may probably arise through the slave question. This a voice declared to me, while I was praying earnestly on the subject, December 25, 1832" (D&C 130:12–13).

Beginning in South Carolina, then, the world will move into an era of war that "will eventually terminate in the death and misery of many souls" (D&C 87:1) because of "much bloodshed" (D&C 130:12). "Nation shall rise against nation, and kingdom against kingdom" (Matt. 24:6). "The whole earth shall be in commotion" (D&C 45:26). "War will be poured out upon all nations" (D&C 87:2, 3). "And it shall come to pass among the wicked, that every man that will not take his sword against his neighbor must needs flee unto Zion for safety. And there shall be gathered unto it out of every nation under heaven; and it shall be the only people that shall not be at war one with another" (D&C 45:68–69).

World War I was essentially a European war, with Turkey and the United States of America joining in. Japan had only limited participation. World War II clearly was much more of a world war. It involved most of the nations that fought in World War I, plus Australia, Brazil (limited involvement), Canada, China, India, Japan, New Zealand, and South Africa. Still, neither war involved most of Asia, Africa, South America, or Central America.

When the Lord tells us, therefore, that the time will come when *all nations* will be at war, he is foretelling a time of horror such as we have never seen. This will come not because the Lord has decreed it but because the wicked people of the world will choose it. We can, however, take some comfort in knowing that the Saints will receive a degree of protection. Following is the sequence the Lord has given us:

1. South Carolina will enter into rebellion, as one of the southern states against the northern states. This event happened in 1861, beginning the American Civil War.

2. The southern states will call on Great Britain for help. The southern states made formal overtures to Great Britain as early as 1861.[5]

3. Great Britain, in turn, will call on other nations to defend itself in war. This prophecy may have begun to be fulfilled in 1909, when Great Britain instigated a defensive alliance called the Allied and Associated Powers, which was formed in opposition to the Central Powers, an alliance including Germany, Austria, Hungary, Bulgaria, and Turkey.[6] Historian Sidney Bradshaw Fay calls the formation of these alliances "the greatest single underlying cause" of World War I.[7]

4. "Then war shall be poured out upon all nations."

It appears that we have seen the first three conditions occur in the recent past, and the fourth condition has seen a deeply sobering and partial fulfillment in the two world wars of this century with an even greater fulfillment yet to come. The way in which these prophecies have come to pass indicates that the Lord views these wars as

---

[5] Roberts, *Comprehensive History of the Church,* 1:297–98.
[6] Andrus, *Doctrinal Themes of the Doctrine and Covenants,* 96.
[7] *Origins of the World War,* 34–35.

different phases of one great, continuing struggle: the battle between good and evil, God and Satan, on the earth.

NOTES AND COMMENTARY

D&C 87:1 *will eventually terminate in the death and misery of many souls.* It is not possible to tell from the context whether this phrase refers to death and misery from "the rebellion at South Carolina" or from "the wars that will shortly come to pass." Certainly the expression applies to both.

One historian wrote of the American Civil War: "The Federal records show that they had, from first to last, 2,600,000 men in the service; while the Confederates all told, and in like manner, had but little over 600,000. . . . Of Federal prisoners during the war, the Confederates took in round numbers 270,000; while the whole number of Confederates captured and held in prisons by the Federals was in like round numbers 220,000. . . . Of these 270,000 Federal prisoners taken, 22,576 died in Confederate hands; and of the 220,000 Confederates taken by Federals, 26,436 died in their hands. . . . The entire loss on both sides, including those who were permanently disabled, as well as those killed in battle, and who died from wounds received and diseases contracted in the service, amounted, upon a reasonable estimate, to the stupendous aggregate of 1,000,000 of men!

" . . . Both sides during the struggle relied for means to support it upon the issue of paper money, and upon loans secured by bonds. An enormous public debt was thus created by each, and the aggregate of money thus expended on both sides, including the loss and sacrifice of property, could not have been less than 8,000,000,000 of dollars— a sum fully equal to three-fourths of the assessed valuation of the taxable property of all the states together when it commenced."[8]

Of course, the cost in dead and wounded, monies, and other property for the many succeeding wars worldwide has been astronomically greater. And what B. H. Roberts said of the American Civil War could be said of all wars: "To the terrible loss of life and property let there be added the consideration of the suffering of the wounded and

---

[8] Alexander H. Stephens, *History of the United States,* as cited in Roberts, *Comprehensive History of the Church,* 1:299–300.

the sick who languished in loathsome prisons; the sorrow of widows and orphans who looked in vain for the return of husbands and fathers, who marched in the fulness of manly strength to the war; the anguish of parents, whose dim eyes looked in vain for sons thrown into unknown graves; and the gentler yet equally tender sorrows of sisters which in the fierce war lost the companions of their childhood. Let all this, I say, be taken into account, as resulting from this war and the 'misery of many souls,' no less than the death of many others will be apparent."[9]

SLAVES SHALL RISE UP AGAINST THEIR MASTERS
Doctrine and Covenants 87:4

> *4 And it shall come to pass, after many days, slaves shall rise up against their masters, who shall be marshaled and disciplined for war.*

This prophecy may have had a partial fulfillment during the American Civil War, even though the Civil War was primarily a war not of slaves against masters but of free men from the South fighting free men from the North. It is true, however, that African-American slaves had at least some involvement in the war; in fact, some two hundred thousand African-Americans fought in the Civil War.[10]

But a number of Church authorities and scholars suggest that the American Civil War was not the final fulfillment of this part of the prophecy. For example, in discussing Joseph Smith's prophecy on war, Elder Hyrum M. Smith of the Council of the Twelve wrote: "We have lived to see war poured out upon every continent and every ocean. And it is a great question whether this war will not be followed by a race war, still more destructive."[11] Later he said, "There are other parts [of the prophecy on war] which yet remain unfulfilled, but they,

---

[9] *Comprehensive History of the Church,* 1:299.

[10] When compared to the total war effort, the involvement of blacks in the war was quite limited. In 1861, there were 4 million blacks in the United States. The 200,000 of these who fought in the Civil War represented only 5 percent of the total. To look at it another way, 2.2 million soldiers fought on the Union side during the Civil War; 9 percent of those were blacks. A number of them, of course, were free men before the war (*Time Almanac 1999,* 393, 795–96).

[11] *Doctrine and Covenants Commentary,* 536.

too, will come to pass, in time." His first example: "Slaves shall rise up against their masters" (v. 4).[12]

Elder B. H. Roberts, in speaking of parts of the prophecy on war that "are still in the future," wrote of "a great race war in America—slaves are to rise up against their masters."[13]

Doctrine and Covenants scholar Roy Doxey commented: "Some Latter-day Saints have considered that this part of the prophecy pertains to the Civil War because nearly 200,000 [blacks] were marshalled by the North against the South. . . . The future fulfillment concerning slaves may arise out of the agitation of the civil rights movement in the United States, but if a person thinks of a world-wide fulfillment it might be the struggle of people in communist nations seeking their freedom."[14] Elsewhere Brother Doxey wrote: "In preserving the order of events given in the remainder of this prophecy, one might well believe that the events are yet future. This would, however, allow for the partial fulfillment of some of these events in the past, as for example, 'slaves shall rise up against their masters who shall be marshaled and disciplined for war,' as [black] soldiers were during the Civil War. But are there not slaves in the world today (people in bondage without the freedom to act because of unrighteous leaders) who may yet rise up against their masters?"[15]

Latter-day Saint scholar Hyrum Andrus gives this interesting commentary: "Let me go back in history and show you a background picture that I feel helps to explain the true meaning of this statement about slaves. . . . In the latter part of the nineteenth century we had a movement on the international scene to carve up the various unenlightened areas of the world and bring them under the subjection of one industrialized nation or another. . . . So it was that the whole African continent was divided off into areas that came under the direct influence of one European nation or another.

---

[12] Ibid., 537.

[13] *New Witnesses for God*, 1:332.

[14] *Prophecies and Prophetic Promises*, 197.

[15] *Doctrine and Covenants and the Future*, 40. Others who have thought that this part of the prophecy about the slaves may have seen only partial fulfillment include Smith (*Church History and Modern Revelation*, 2:127), Whitney (*Saturday Night Thoughts*, 50), and Otten and Caldwell (*Sacred Truths of the Doctrine and Covenants*, 2:95).

"This was also true with Asia to a large extent. Thus, there was a period of time when the dominant nations of the earth exerted a tyrannical force over the unenlightened peoples of the world. Since that day we have had a revolt against it. The whole nation of India, for example, revolted against British rule. We now have a revolt in the Middle East and Africa where slaves are arising against their masters. What is going on in Algeria today with regard to France? Slaves are rising against their masters. What is going on throughout the whole of Africa? Has not the British Commonwealth greatly diminished in its influence throughout the world? Why has it? Because of the revolt against the British rule of one group of unenlightened people after another to the point that they have revolted against their masters who, during this era of international conflict, are marshaled and disciplined for war. This type of revolt has been one of the greatest causes of conflict on the international scene today. It gives strength to the communist attack against the West and causes disunion among western countries themselves."[16]

Another possible fulfillment of this prophecy has to do with the countries held captive by communism. In a sense, the people of these countries have been slaves: their freedom of expression, of movement, of worship, of speech, of economic choice were all strictly circumscribed by the government. But in the late 1980s and the 1990s, the people of several of these nations rose up against their masters. Other such peoples may yet rise up.

THE "REMNANTS OF THE LAND" WILL VEX THE GENTILES
Doctrine and Covenants 87:5

5 And it shall come to pass also that the remnants who are left of the land will marshal themselves, and shall become exceedingly angry, and shall vex the Gentiles with a sore vexation.

As with the previous verse, this passage in the Doctrine and Covenants may have been misunderstood, as some readers may suppose it

---

[16] *Doctrinal Themes of the Doctrine and Covenants,* 97–98.

refers only to the Indian wars in the United States in the last half of the nineteenth century. The native American peoples do indeed seem to be "the remnants" referred to here,[17] and the Indian wars may have been a partial fulfillment of the prophecy, but there may be a greater fulfillment yet to come. Elder Joseph Fielding Smith taught: "The history of this American continent . . . gives evidence that the Lamanites have risen up in their anger and vexed the Gentiles. This warfare may not be over. It has been the fault of people in the United States to think that this prophetic saying has reference to the Indians in the United States, but we must remember that there are millions of the 'remnant' in Mexico, Central and South America. . . . The independence of Mexico and other nations to the south has been accomplished by the uprising of the 'remnant' upon the land. However, let us not think that this prophecy has completely been fulfilled."[18]

On three different occasions the resurrected Lord prophesied of these things to the righteous descendants of Lehi. Speaking to the Israelite people in America he said: "If the Gentiles do not repent after the blessing which they shall receive [the Book of Mormon and the gospel], after they have scattered my people—then shall ye, who are a remnant of the house of Jacob, go forth among them; and ye shall be in the midst of them who shall be many; and ye shall be among them as a lion among the beasts of the forest, and as a young lion among the flocks of sheep, who, if he goeth through both treadeth down and teareth in pieces, and none can deliver. Thy hand shall be lifted up upon thine adversaries, and all thine enemies shall be cut off. For I will make my people with whom the Father hath covenanted, yea, I will make thy horn iron, and I will make thy hoofs brass. And thou shalt beat in pieces many people; and I will consecrate their gain unto the Lord, and their substance unto the Lord of the whole earth. And behold, I am he who doeth it. And it shall come to pass, saith the Father, that the sword of my justice shall

---

[17] A number of authorities have identified the "remnants" as the American Indians. See, for example, Richards, *Compendium of the Doctrines of the Gospel,* 116; Roberts, *Comprehensive History of the Church,* 1:293, 303; Whitney, *Saturday Night Thoughts,* 49–50; and Wells, "Editorial," 186–87. Some, including Joseph Fielding Smith, have been careful to expand the concept to include the Indians of both North and South America.

[18] *Church History and Modern Revelation,* 2:127.

hang over them at that day; and except they repent it shall fall upon them, saith the Father, yea, even upon all the nations of the Gentiles" (3 Ne. 20:15–17, 19–20; see also 3 Ne. 16:12–15; 21:12–15, 18, 21–22).

JOHN THE REVELATOR'S VISION OF A FIVE-MONTH WAR
Revelation 9:1–11

1 And the fifth angel sounded, and I saw a star fall from heaven unto the earth: and to him was given the key of the bottomless pit.

2 And he opened the bottomless pit; and there arose a smoke out of the pit, as the smoke of a great furnace; and the sun and the air were darkened by reason of the smoke of the pit.

3 And there came out of the smoke locusts upon the earth: and unto them was given power, as the scorpions of the earth have power.

4 And it was commanded them that they should not hurt the grass of the earth, neither any green thing, neither any tree; but only those men which have not the seal of God in their foreheads.

5 And to them it was given that they should not kill them, but that they should be tormented five months: and their torment was as the torment of a scorpion, when he striketh a man.

6 And in those days shall men seek death, and shall not find it; and shall desire to die, and death shall flee from them.

7 And the shapes of the locusts were like unto horses prepared unto battle; and on their heads were as it were crowns like gold, and their faces were as the faces of men.

8 And they had hair as the hair of women, and their teeth were as the teeth of lions.

9 And they had breastplates, as it were breastplates of iron; and the sound of their wings was as the sound of chariots of many horses running to battle.

10 And they had tails like unto scorpions, and there were stings in their tails: and their power was to hurt men five months.

11 And they had a king over them, which is the angel of the bottomless pit, whose name in the Hebrew tongue is Abaddon, but in the Greek tongue hath his name Apollyon.

The events described in this passage will "be accomplished after the opening of the seventh seal, before the coming of Christ" (D&C 77:13). When the fifth angel[19] blows his trumpet, John sees the complete unleashing of hell upon the earth, as the great abyss is opened and smoke billows forth onto the earth, darkening the world with great evil. This certainly is part of the fulfillment of the prophecy that "peace shall be taken from the earth, and the devil shall have power over his own dominion" (D&C 1:35). Armies, perhaps unknowingly, will be influenced and led by the devil into battle. As locusts ravage green plants and trees, the armies will scourge the men and women of the earth, save those who are citizens of Zion and who possess the seal of the living God on their foreheads (Rev. 7:3–4; 9:4). The Saints, we are told in a modern-day revelation, will dwell safely in Zion (D&C 45:66–70). These events are designed to encourage people to repent of their sins and to acknowledge God as their Lord and King (Rev. 9:20–21).

NOTES AND COMMENTARY

Rev. 9:1 *star fall from heaven.* This metaphor refers to Lucifer, who is "fallen from heaven" (Isa. 14:12). Jesus said, "I beheld Satan as lightning fall from heaven" (Luke 10:18; Rev. 12:9).

key of the bottomless pit. According to his divine schedule, God permits the inhabitants of hell to come forth with Satan as their king (Rev. 9:11) and unleash their torment on earth's inhabitants. Later, an angel will come out of heaven with a key and a chain which he will use to bind Satan for a thousand years (Rev. 20:1–3).

---

[19] In his vision, John sees a series of seven angels blow their trumpets; with the sounding of each trumpet, a new plague begins.

bottomless pit. The pit is the abyss, or the "place of imprisonment for disobedient spirits."[20] This pit is identified in Joseph Smith's translation of Isaiah 14:15, 19. The king of the abyss is Lucifer, who is also called Abaddon and Apollyon (Rev. 9:11). God, of course, has complete control over this prison (Rev. 20:1–3).

Rev. 9:2 *he opened the bottomless pit.* The angel uses the key to open the pit so that wicked spirits will unleash, perhaps as never before, their evil forces upon humanity. Joseph Smith taught: "Some may have cried peace, but the Saints and the world will have little peace from henceforth. . . . The time is soon coming, when no man will have any peace but in Zion and her stakes."[21]

there arose a smoke out of the pit . . . the sun and the air were darkened. Hell is opened and evil arises "as the smoke of a great furnace," blackening the air and hiding the sun's light. John seems to be describing darkness that "pertains to Satan, his kingdom, his disciples, and their works. The devil is the perpetuator of dark and evil things (2 Ne. 9:9; Hel. 6:28–29)."[22] The darkening of the air with evil is the result of Satan's work, for he is called "the prince of the power of the air" (Eph. 2:2).

New Testament scholar Richard Draper has written: "As the pit is opened, smoke billows forth and obscures the light of the sun. Darkness reigns. Through this powerful symbol, John reveals the nature of the first thrust against mankind: a blow against the light."[23] The smoke, like the "mists of darkness" in Lehi's dream, represents evil, darkness, and "the temptations of the devil, which blindeth the eyes, and hardeneth the hearts of the children of men, and leadeth them away into broad roads, that they perish and are lost" (1 Ne. 12:17).

Rev. 9:3 *there came out of the smoke locusts upon the earth.* These creatures are not actual insects (grasshoppers; see Prov. 30:27), for they sting like scorpions, strike out at mankind, have a king, and are commanded not to eat vegetation (Rev. 9:3–5, 11). These are actually wicked men and armies with power to torment all of humanity

[20] *Theological Dictionary of the New Testament,* 1:9, s.v. "abyss."
[21] *History of the Church,* 3:390–91.
[22] McConkie and Parry, *Guide to Scriptural Symbols,* 36.
[23] *Opening the Seven Seals,* 101.

except those who have God's seal in their foreheads (Rev. 9:4). John's imagery of locusts is similar to Joel's description of the locust-like armies that will "come up upon my land, strong, and without number. . . . He hath laid my vine waste, and barked my fig tree: he hath made it clean bare, and cast it away; the branches thereof are made white" (Joel 1:4–7; 2:25). The locusts that plagued ancient Egypt and "covered the face of the whole earth, so that the land was darkened" (Ex. 10:15) are types of this great army of wicked people.

unto them was given power. God gives agency to humankind, and he permits the wicked to destroy one another, but he sets boundaries for them. Compare Revelation 6:4, 8, in which power is given through the red and pale horses.

as the scorpions of the earth. Here and in Revelation 9:5 the locusts are likened to scorpions, which torment humans, often without killing them.

Rev. 9:4 *it was commanded them.* God controls the destiny of this army of locusts and commands them to harm only those who do not have God's seal on their foreheads. This seal was first mentioned in Revelation 7:3. It is a figurative mark placed by God and indicates those who have had their calling and election made sure. Joseph Smith explained: "Four destroying angels holding power over the four quarters of the earth until the servants of God are sealed in their foreheads, which signifies sealing the blessing upon their heads, meaning the everlasting covenant, thereby making their calling and election sure. When a seal is put upon the father and mother, it secures their posterity, so that they cannot be lost, but will be saved by virtue of the covenant of their father and mother."[24]

not hurt the grass/green thing/tree. These objects are those locusts feed on in their developmental stages (cankerworm, palmerworm, caterpillar, locust; see Joel 1:4). The creatures of Revelation 9 are not like the locusts that plagued the Egyptians and "did eat every herb of the land, and all the fruit of the trees which the hail had left: and there remained not any green thing in the trees, or in the herbs of the field, through all the land of Egypt" (Ex. 10:15). These creatures are soldiers who seek to destroy humans.

---

[24] *History of the Church,* 5:530.

men which have not the seal of God in their foreheads. Only the inhabitants of Zion, many of whom will have the seal of God (Rev. 9:4) can have confidence that they will be preserved during this time. Many of them will dwell in the New Jerusalem, which is called "a land of peace, a city of refuge, a place of safety for the saints of the Most High God. And there shall be gathered unto it out of every nation under heaven; and it shall be the only people that shall not be at war one with another. And it shall be said among the wicked: Let us not go up to battle against Zion, for the inhabitants of Zion are terrible; wherefore we cannot stand" (D&C 45:66, 69–70). The righteous in the stakes of Zion will also have safety (D&C 115:5–6; 124:36).

Rev. 9:5 *to them it was given that they should not kill them.* The armies of locusts will not kill humans; instead they will harm and torment them. Elder Bruce R. McConkie suggested that "perhaps John is seeing such things as the effects of poisonous gas, or bacteriological warfare, or atomic fallout, which disable but do not kill."[25]

tormented five months. Five months is the life cycle of the locust. Five months may represent a short period and not exactly five months.

torment of a scorpion. The scorpion's sting rarely results in death, but it causes great pain and discomfort. Torment in this context pertains to more than war and warfare. Torment is also associated with "guilt and abominations, which doth cause [the wicked] to shrink from the presence of the Lord into a state of misery and endless torment" (Mosiah 3:25). Alma spoke of both the abyss and torment when he declared: "My soul hath been redeemed from the gall of bitterness and bonds of iniquity. I was in the darkest abyss. . . . My soul was racked with eternal torment" (Mosiah 27:29).

Rev. 9:6 *shall men seek death.* It seems that the torment brought about by the locusts will cause such pain that people will want to die to end their pain. In another context the Lord said, "And death shall be chosen rather than life by all the residue of them that remain of this evil family" (Jer. 8:3). Also, Job spoke of the wicked "which long for

---

[25] *Doctrinal New Testament Commentary,* 3:502.

death, but it cometh not; and dig for it more than for hid treasures" (Job 3:21).

Rev. 9:7 *shapes of the locusts.* John seems to be describing soldiers that are trained and equipped to fight on land, sea, or in the air, with their various types of uniforms and protective gear, including helmets, body armor, and protective masks; their war vehicles, including aircraft, helicopters, tanks, and dozens of other military machines; and their weaponry and artillery of many types and kinds, each designed to harm, maim, or kill humans. He may be describing that which belongs to military units of our era, or he may be seeing that which belongs to our own future.

President Joseph Fielding Smith, citing Isaiah 5:26–30, Nahum 2:2–5, and Revelation 9:6–10, suggested that the ancient prophets saw "our automobiles, our railroad trains; . . . the airplanes flying in the midst of the heavens, because we can read in the prophecies of these ancient scriptures many things that indicate that these things were revealed unto those ancient prophets."[26]

John described the things that he envisioned by using objects or creatures that were known to him in the first century after Christ: locusts, horses, crowns, hair, lions, breastplates, chariots, and scorpions. These images create a symbolic picture for his audience.

like unto horses prepared unto battle. This phrase recalls Joel 2:4, which reads, "The appearance of them is as the appearance of horses; and as horsemen, so shall they run." The image of locusts depicts an army of tens of thousands of warriors, an army so great that its soldiers darken the land and cannot be numbered. The phrase "horses prepared unto battle" portrays warriors wearing body armor similar to the protective body and headgear worn by warhorses of John's day.

on their heads were as it were crowns like gold. This expression may refer to the soldier's helmet, in all of its shapes and varieties; or it may be symbolic of kings' headgear ("crowns of gold"). If the passage does pertain to kings' headgear, it may mean that governments are banding together for war.

---

[26] *Doctrines of Salvation,* 1:146.

their faces were as the faces of men. This expression seems to indicate that the locusts represent men.

Rev. 9:8 *they had hair as the hair of women.* We don't know what this expression means, but there is precedent in scripture for long hair on men being seen as a sign of strength (Judg. 16:17).

their teeth were as the teeth of lions. This expression describes the warriors' ability to ravage and destroy. It also recalls Joel's description of warriors: "For a nation is come up upon my land, strong, and without number, whose teeth are the teeth of a lion, and he hath the cheek teeth of a great lion" (Joel 1:6). Satan himself has been called a "roaring lion, [who] walketh about, seeking whom he may devour" (1 Pet. 5:8).

Rev. 9:9 *they had breastplates.* Modern soldiers' armor and protective gear covers vital organs. It may also refer to the armor of war vehicles.

sound of chariots of many horses. Natural locusts in flight make a fearful noise, and the reference here may be to the mingled sound of chariot wheels and the hooves of the horses (Joel 2:5). Anciently the chariot and its horses were used for war, and in prophetic language they may be a metaphor for modern war vehicles (Ezek. 39:20; Dan. 11:40; Joel 2:5).

Rev. 9:10 *they had tails like unto scorpions.* This expression could refer to any of a variety of weapons.

power was to hurt men five months. This particular battle, or war, will have a limited duration. It may serve as a precursor to the great war that will accompany the blasting of the sixth trumpet, when two hundred million soldiers will fight and kill one-third of humanity.[27]

Rev. 9:11 *they had a king over them.* Actual locusts have no king; the locusts described in Revelation 9:6–10 are warriors, and they and their leaders hearken unto Satan, who is their king.

angel of the bottomless pit. Satan.

Abaddon/Apollyon. John gives a Hebrew name followed by the Greek equivalent, as was his custom (John 1:38, 42; 4:25; 9:7; 11:16), perhaps so that his audience would understand his words. The angel is named *Abaddon,* meaning "destruction" or "ruin"; he is also called

---

[27] See the commentary on Revelation 9:13–19, page 260.

Apollyon, meaning "destruction" or "destroyer." Such names relate to Satan's evil mission and goals.

JOHN THE REVELATOR'S VISION OF THE ARMY OF HORSEMEN
Revelation 9:13–21

13 And the sixth angel sounded, and I heard a voice from the four horns of the golden altar which is before God,

14 Saying to the sixth angel which had the trumpet, Loose the four angels which are bound in the [bottomless pit].[28]

15 And the four angels were loosed, which were prepared for an hour, and a day, and a month, and a year, for to slay the third part of men.

16 And the number of the army of the horsemen were two hundred thousand thousand: and I heard the number of them.

17 And thus I saw the horses in the vision, and them that sat on them, having breastplates of fire, and of jacinth, and brimstone: and the heads of the horses were as the heads of lions; and out of their mouths issued fire and smoke and brimstone.

18 By these three was the third part of men killed, by the fire, and by the smoke, and by the brimstone, which issued out of their mouths.

19 For their power is in their mouth, and in their tails: for their tails were like unto serpents, and had heads, and with them they do hurt.

20 And the rest of the men which were not killed by these plagues yet repented not of the works of their hands, that they should not worship devils, and idols of gold, and silver, and brass, and stone, and of wood: which neither can see, nor hear, nor walk:

21 Neither repented they of their murders, nor of their sorceries, nor of their fornication, nor of their thefts.

---

[28] This change is from JST Rev. 9:14.

Some scriptural scholars believe that this passage is a description of the war of Armageddon,[29] and they may well be correct: the army described here is so huge and the number of dead so astounding that one wonders how it could be anything other than Armageddon. Their reasoning is based in part on the belief that the seven trumpets of judgment in Revelation 8, 9, and 11 (which includes the war) and the seven vials of judgment poured out in Revelation 16 (which includes Armageddon) are different descriptions of the same events.[30] The similarities are indeed striking. Yet the differences seem to argue that the war described in Revelation 9:13–21 is not the same as that described in Revelation 16:12–16. The following outlines both the similarities and the differences:

Trumpet	*Judgment*
1	hail, fire mixed with blood burn one-third of trees and all grass
2	one-third of sea turns to blood, one-third of all sea creatures die, one-third of ships sink
3	one-third of rivers turn poisonous, killing many
4	one-third of sun, moon, stars darkened
5	five-month war in which men will suffer much pain but not death; plants not harmed
6	army of 200 million kills one-third of mankind
7	voices proclaim the reign of Christ; voices, lightnings, thunderings, great earthquake, great hail; one-tenth of city falls

Vial	*Judgment*
1	a grievous sore on those who worship beast
2	sea becomes as blood, all sea creatures die
3	rivers become blood
4	sun scorches men with great heat

---

[29] See, for example, Lund, "Things Which Must Shortly Come to Pass," 274.

[30] See, for example, Draper, *Opening the Seven Seals,* 172–73, 251; Mounce, *Book of Revelation,* 291–92.

5   kingdom of the beast is darkened; men filled
        with pain
6   spirits of devils gather kings to Armageddon
7   voice proclaims: "It is done"; voices, thunders,
        lightnings, great earthquake, great hail; city divided
        into three parts; cities of nations fall

The similarities in these two lists are impressive. So also are the differences. In most cases the two lists differ only in the degree of their effect. In fact, in every case except two (numbers 1 and 4), the judgment accompanying the vial simply seems to complete that which was begun with the trumpet, but the degree of difference seems important. Nevertheless, despite our attempts at reasoning through this question, the ultimate truth will remain obscure until the Lord's prophet speaks clearly on the matter or until the actual events make the truth known. Whether there are two great wars or whether the two are one, the fact remains that all nations will be engaged in terrible warfare, killing many millions of people, until the Lord returns and ushers in the millennium of peace.

The events identified in this section, called the "second woe" (Rev. 9:12; 11:14), will "be accomplished after the opening of the seventh seal, before the coming of Christ" (D&C 77:13). This second woe brings great anguish upon humankind, for two hundred million warriors battle in war and bring great destruction, ultimately causing the death of one-third of humanity. John uses descriptive and symbolic terms in describing this great conflagration, including *fire* (three times), *brimstone* (three times), *smoke* (twice), *lions,* and *serpents.* The sixth trump announces these events, but Satan and his angels set them in motion through their evil influence and guidance. The events recall numerous other historical time periods when "Satan had great dominion among men, and raged in their hearts; and from thenceforth came wars and bloodshed" (JST Gen. 6:13).

The Lord's purpose during these events is to encourage humankind to repent of their many grievous sins, which John lists as idolatry, murders, sorceries, fornication, and thefts. Sadly, they do not repent of their wickedness.

NOTES AND COMMENTARY

Rev. 9:14 *Loose the four angels which are bound in the [bottomless pit].* The "bound" angels may belong to that group of "angels that sinned" and thus who God "cast . . . down to hell, and delivered them into chains of darkness" (2 Pet. 2:4; see also Jude 1:6). They will be set loose to prompt and persuade the wicked to kill one-third of humankind during the great war described in Revelation 9:15–19.

Rev. 9:15 *prepared for an hour/day/month/year.* The time mentioned here does not indicate how long the four angels will be loosed, but it does say they will be loosed at a specific, divinely appointed time. The Jerusalem Bible reads, "These four angels had been put there ready for this hour of this day of this month of this year."

slay the third part of men. The army of two hundred million individuals with their modern weapons of destruction will kill one-third of the earth's inhabitants. It is unclear whether the figure "one-third" is to be taken as literal or symbolic.

Rev. 9:16 *number of the army . . . were two hundred thousand thousand.* The number of fighting men that John "saw" was two hundred million, twice the number of the angels who were worshipping God in the celestial kingdom (Rev. 5:11). The numerical figure is likely symbolic, intended to represent great hosts of warriors. Latter-day Saint scholar Victor Ludlow wrote: "The sixth woe also separates the righteous from the wicked, as a great army of 'two legions of legions' of cavalry gather for battle while bringing much destruction and death to the world. (See Rev. 9:13–21; 16:14–16.) Since a full Roman legion contained ten thousand soldiers, the King James translators interpreted the phrase as 'two ten-thousand ten thousand,' or, keeping the same total number, 'two hundred thousand thousand.' Since actual numbers are not a part of John's record, the phrase 'two legions of legions' should probably be translated as 'two armies of armies' instead of being seen as representing a specific number, such as two hundred million soldiers."[31]

Rev. 9:17 *I saw the horses in the vision, and them that sat on them.* John describes this scene of horses using various images and

---

[31] *Principles and Practices,* 615.

symbols; he makes threefold repetition of *fire* and *brimstone* (the Jerusalem Bible says *fire* and *sulfur*) and twofold repetition of *smoke* and *horses* in Revelation 9:17–18. Fire, smoke, and brimstone may describe the bombs and destructive devices associated with present-day or future warfare. Horses often represent war vehicles.

Rev. 9:18 *by these three was the third part of men killed.* Fire, smoke, and brimstone are the weapons of this mighty army that will destroy one-third of humanity. *The third part* is probably symbolic, indicating a huge number of people but fewer than half.

Rev. 9:19 *power is in their mouth, and in their tails.* The fire-breathing capacity of these lion-headed horses symbolizes "the torment of hell and [underscores their] diabolical nature."[32] Like the scorpions in Revelation 9:10, there is destructive power in the horses' tails. In fact, the tails are snakes with heads, another evidence that they are sent from the devil.[33]

Rev. 9:20 *rest of the men . . . repented not.* The "rest of the men" speaks of those who are not sealed (Rev. 9:4) and who survive the warfare. The purpose for the blowing of the sixth trumpet is manifest here: to encourage the wicked to repent, for they are idolaters, devil worshippers, murderers, fornicators, thieves, and sorcerers (Rev. 9:21). The great war, however, during which one-third of humankind is destroyed, does not succeed in bringing the wicked to repentance: they "repented not of the works of their hands, that they should not worship devils, and idols," wrote John.

works of their hands. This expression seems to refer to idol worship (Ps. 115:4–7; Isa. 2:8; Jer. 1:16), which consists both of images and statues created by human hands, and of all the evil deeds and actions of humanity that replace one's righteous desire to serve the true and living God.

that they should not worship devils. Humanity continues to worship devils, even after the great war that destroys so many. Devil worship has long been a gross evil conducted upon the earth (Deut. 32:17; Ps. 106:37; 1 Cor. 10:20–21).

---

[32] Draper, *Opening the Seven Seals,* 108.
[33] Mounce, *Book of Revelation,* 197.

idols of gold. Nephi warned, "Yea, wo unto those that worship idols, for the devil of all devils delighteth in them" (2 Ne. 9:37). In our dispensation we are told of those who "have strayed from [God's] ordinances, and have broken [God's] everlasting covenant; they seek not the Lord to establish his righteousness, but every man walketh in his own way, and after the image of his own god, whose image is in the likeness of the world, and whose substance is that of an idol, which waxeth old and shall perish in Babylon, even Babylon the great, which shall fall" (D&C 1:15–16).

Rev. 9:21 *neither repented they of their murders/sorceries/fornication/ thefts.* In Revelation 9:20 John identified idolatry as a chief sin belonging to humanity in the last days; now he lists other iniquities—murder, sorcery, fornication, and thievery—that represent all of the wickedness that will prevail upon the earth during this time.

THE BATTLE OF ARMAGEDDON
Revelation 16:13–14, 16

> *13 And I saw three unclean spirits like frogs come out of the mouth of the dragon, and out of the mouth of the beast, and out of the mouth of the false prophet.*
>
> *14 For they are the spirits of devils, working miracles, which go forth unto the kings of the earth and of the whole world, to gather them to the battle of that great day of God Almighty.*
>
> . . .
>
> *16 And he gathered them together into a place called in the Hebrew tongue Armageddon.*

With his characteristic mixture of boldness and eloquence, Elder Bruce R. McConkie described the final great war at Armageddon: It is "the greatest war of the ages," he said, " . . . the final great war that will usher in the Millennium, . . . the war of wars. . . . Armageddon is the final great battle in a war that covers the earth and involves all nations. . . . It will exceed in horror, intensity, and scope all prior wars. . . . The final war will be long and perilous, with many battles and much bloodshed and continuing horrors. . . .

"The battles will be fought by the warriors of earth, but the Lord's hand will be in it. . . . The Lord will fight for Israel as he fought times without number for them during the long years of their sorrow and travail. . . .

"This war will be a religious war, a war in which the servants of Satan assail the servants of the Lord and those allied with them. . . . It is a holy war. . . . Clearly the great issues at Armageddon are God and religion and a way of worship. Satan will have done his work well; by then billions of earth's inhabitants (even more so then than now) will be in open rebellion against the gospel and every principle of truth and virtue found therein. . . .

"There are three great things that will grow out of and come because of Armageddon. They are:

"1. In the course of this final great conflict the Lord himself shall return, the vineyard shall be burned, and the millennial day will dawn.

"2. Out of the defeat of Gog and Magog comes the end of all the nations of the earth and the final triumph of Israel as a people and as a nation.

"3. Out of Armageddon comes the destruction of the political kingdom on earth of Lucifer and the fall of the great and abominable church."[34]

The scriptures cover the great battle of Armageddon in surprising detail. The multitude of prophetic witnesses tells us that this event must have special importance in the last days. Particularly enlightening are Isaiah 13, Ezekiel 38 and 39, Jeremiah 25 and 51, Joel 1 through 3, and Zechariah 12 through 14. From the various sources that deal with Armageddon, we gain the following insights:[35]

---

[34] *Millennial Messiah,* 448, 449, 458–59, 468, 476, 477, 479, 490.

[35] As we have noted, some prophecies that seem to apply to the last days may have been long since fulfilled, whereas others may have more than one fulfillment. The specific application of a particular prophecy can be challenging, especially where modern prophets have not given an interpretation. In this case, Elder Bruce R. McConkie of the Quorum of the Twelve Apostles applied to Armageddon virtually all of the scriptures we use in this section (see *Millennial Messiah,* 448–94). If we have erred, and if in any specific instance an ancient prophet may have been speaking exclusively of ancient battles rather than the last great battle of the world, it is nevertheless true that the descriptions given here may legitimately be said to serve as types and shadows of the battle of Armageddon, revealed to heighten our understanding.

1. Armageddon will occur in the latter days (Ezek. 38:8), during the seventh seal, or the seventh thousand-year period of the earth's history (Rev. 8:1; 16:16).

2. Satan will move among men to bring them to the destruction of Armageddon: "For they are the spirits of devils, working miracles, which go forth unto the kings of the earth and of the whole world, to gather them to the battle of that great day of God Almighty. . . . And he gathered them together into a place called in the Hebrew tongue Armageddon" (Rev. 16:14, 16).

3. Though Satan brings the war, the Lord will turn it to his purposes; he will exercise his power to bring the armies to the circumstances he requires: "Thus saith the Lord of hosts, the God of Israel; Drink ye, and be drunken, and spue, and fall, and rise no more, because of the sword which I will send among you. . . . For, lo, I begin to bring evil on the city which is called by my name. . . . I will call for a sword upon all the inhabitants of the earth, saith the Lord of hosts" (Jer. 25:27, 29; see also Isa. 13:4; Ezek. 38:16–17, 21; Jer. 51:20).

4. Armageddon is a great fulfillment of God's judgment against a world steeped in wickedness: "For the indignation of the Lord is upon all nations, and his fury upon all their armies: he hath utterly destroyed them, he hath delivered them to the slaughter. . . . For my sword shall be bathed in heaven: behold, it shall come down upon Idumea, and upon the people of my curse, to judgment. The sword of the Lord is filled with blood, it is made fat with fatness, and with the blood of lambs and goats, with the fat of the kidneys of rams: for the Lord hath a sacrifice in Bozrah, and a great slaughter in the land of Idumea. . . . For it is the day of the Lord's vengeance, and the year of recompences for the controversy of Zion" (Isa. 34:2, 5–6, 8; see also Lev. 26:25; Isa. 13:5–6, 9, 11; 66:14–16; Jer. 25:31, 37; Ezek. 38:18–19; Joel 3:13–14; Rev. 14:15, 19–20).

5. All nations will come to battle at Armageddon (Jer. 25:17–20, 22–23, 26; Joel 3:2; Zech. 12:3; 14:2; Rev. 16:14).

6. Nations will come from "a far country" to gather to the battle (Isa. 13:5).

7. The enemy will come speedily: "Behold, he shall come up as clouds, and his chariots shall be as a whirlwind: his horses are swifter than eagles" (Jer. 4:13).

8. The enemy army will come in great numbers and will be very powerful: "The noise of a multitude in the mountains, like as of a great people; a tumultuous noise of the kingdoms of nations gathered together: the Lord of hosts mustereth the host of the battle" (Isa. 13:4; see also Ezek. 38:9, 15; Joel 1:6; 2:2, 11; 3:9–11, 14).

9. The gathering of all nations is specifically directed against Israel: "Behold, in those days, and in that time, when I shall bring again the captivity of Judah and Jerusalem, I will also gather all nations, and will bring them down into the valley of Jehoshaphat, and will plead with them there for my people and for my heritage Israel, whom they have scattered among the nations, and parted my land" (Joel 3:1–2; see also Zech. 12:2–3).

10. Those in Israel will suffer great fear and consternation: "Howl ye; for the day of the Lord is at hand; it shall come as a destruction from the Almighty. Therefore shall all hands be faint, and every man's heart shall melt: And they shall be afraid: pangs and sorrows shall take hold of them; they shall be in pain as a woman that travaileth: they shall be amazed one at another; their faces shall be as flames" (Isa. 13:6, 8; see also Jer. 4:13; 25:34; Joel 2:6; Zech. 11:2; 12:11–12).

11. The righteous will respond with faith and many pleadings for protection: "Sanctify ye a fast, call a solemn assembly, gather the elders and all the inhabitants of the land into the house of the Lord your God, and cry unto the Lord. . . . Therefore also now, saith the Lord, turn ye even to me with all your heart, and with fasting, and with weeping, and with mourning: And rend your heart, and not your garments, and turn unto the Lord your God: for he is gracious and merciful, slow to anger, and of great kindness, and repenteth him of the evil" (Joel 1:14; 2:12–13; see also 1:13; 2:1, 15–17).

12. The war will last many years (Ezek. 38:17).

13. It may well be during this war that the Lord's two witnesses in Jerusalem will testify of Christ and help to protect the city for the allotted 1,260 days (JST Isa. 51:18–20; Rev. 11:2–3, 5–12).[36]

14. The land of Israel will be laid waste, and the city Jerusalem will be taken, bringing desolation and death: "For I will gather all nations against Jerusalem to battle; and the city shall be taken, and the houses rifled, and the women ravished; and half of the city shall go forth into captivity, and the residue of the people shall not be cut off from the city" (Zech. 14:2; see also Isa. 13:5, 9; Joel 2:3; Zech. 12:11–12; 13:8; Rev. 11:2).

15. When Jerusalem is taken, the city will be spoiled (Jer. 4:13; Zech. 14:1).

16. The taking of Jerusalem may fulfill the prophecies about the abomination of desolation. These prophecies refer, historically and prophetically, to the abominable desecration of the temple and the terrible desolation of the city. Joseph Smith–Matthew 1:12–21 records one example of the abomination of desolation that happened when the Romans destroyed Jerusalem in about A.D. 70. The events on that occasion are types of that which will happen in the future, when the abomination of desolation occurs again (see JS–M 1:32–35). These things may occur as part of the battle of Armageddon.[37]

17. The hostility among the combatants who are attacking Jerusalem will degenerate into a civil war: "It shall come to pass in that day, that a great tumult from the Lord shall be among them; and they shall lay hold every one on the hand of his neighbour, and his hand shall rise up against the hand of his neighbour" (Zech. 14:13; see also Isa. 9:19; Ezek. 38:21; Zech. 11:6).

18. The enemy of Israel (and of God) will suffer many desolations and much death to the extent that only one-sixth of them will survive the battle (Ezek. 39:2): "Behold, the day of the Lord cometh, cruel both with wrath and fierce anger, to lay the land desolate: and he shall destroy the sinners thereof out of it. . . . Every one that is found

---

[36] See the commentary on the two witnesses in Jerusalem, page 135. See also Parry, Parry, and Peterson, *Understanding Isaiah,* 456–60; Parry and Parry, *Understanding the Book of Revelation,* 132–43.

[37] For a discussion of the relationship of the abomination of desolation to Armageddon, as well as the possible destruction of the temple, see McConkie, *Millennial Messiah,* 471–74.

shall be thrust through; and every one that is joined unto them shall fall by the sword. Their children also shall be dashed to pieces before their eyes; their houses shall be spoiled, and their wives ravished. . . . Their bows also shall dash the young men to pieces; and they shall have no pity on the fruit of the womb; their eye shall not spare children. . . . Their slain also shall be cast out, and their stink shall come up out of their carcases, and the mountains shall be melted with their blood" (Isa. 13:9, 15–18; 34:3; see also Isa. 9:19; 34:6–7; 66:16–17, 24; Jer. 51:21–26, 29, 37, 43, 47, 49, 54, 58, 62; Ezek. 39:2–5; Joel 3:19; Rev. 14:15–20).

19. When the tide turns against them, there will be fear among those who attack Israel: "The mighty men of Babylon have forborn to fight, they have remained in their holds: their might hath failed; they became as women: they have burned her dwellingplaces; her bars are broken. . . . The men of war are affrighted" (Jer. 51:30, 32).

20. When Israel's enemy is conquered, they shall be spoiled (Jer. 51:48, 53, 55–56; Ezek. 39:10).

21. Associated with Armageddon are such plagues as hailstones, fire, and brimstone.[38] These may be scriptural descriptions of atomic warfare,[39] or they may have a meaning we do not yet understand. "I will plead against him with pestilence and with blood; and I will rain upon him, and upon his bands, and upon the many people that are with him, an overflowing rain, and great hailstones, fire, and brimstone. And I will send a fire on Magog, and among them that dwell carelessly in the isles: and they shall know that I am the Lord" (Ezek. 38:22; 39:6; see also Isa. 34:9; Joel 1:19; 2:3–5, 30; Zech. 12:6; Rev. 11:5; 16:21; D&C 29:14, 16–17, 21).

22. A great earthquake is associated with Armageddon: "It shall come to pass at the same time when Gog shall come against the land of Israel, saith the Lord God, that my fury shall come up in my face. For in my jealousy and in the fire of my wrath have I spoken, Surely in that day there shall be a great shaking in the land of Israel; so that the fishes of the sea, and the fowls of the heaven, and the beasts of the

---

[38] See the commentary on natural phenomena serving as judgments in the last days, page 229.

[39] See McConkie, *Millennial Messiah,* 63, 382.

field, and all creeping things that creep upon the earth, and all the men that are upon the face of the earth, shall shake at my presence, and the mountains shall be thrown down, and the steep places shall fall, and every wall shall fall to the ground" (Ezek. 38:18–20; see also Isa. 13:4–5, 13–14; Joel 2:2–5, 10; Rev. 16:16–18).

23. The darkening of the sun, moon, and stars is associated with Armageddon. These events may be related to tremendous dust in the atmosphere caused by the great earthquake, smoke, and other effects of atomic warfare, or some other cause entirely.[40] "The noise of a multitude in the mountains, like as of a great people; a tumultuous noise of the kingdoms of nations gathered together: the Lord of hosts mustereth the host of the battle. They come from a far country, from the end of heaven, even the Lord, and the weapons of his indignation, to destroy the whole land. For the stars of heaven and the constellations thereof shall not give their light: the sun shall be darkened in his going forth, and the moon shall not cause her light to shine" (Isa. 13:4–5, 10; see also Joel 2:2, 5, 10, 31; 3:15–16; D&C 29:14).

24. God will provide deliverance for his people, Israel: "In that day shall the Lord defend the inhabitants of Jerusalem; and he that is feeble among them at that day shall be as David; and the house of David shall be as God, as the angel of the Lord before them. And it shall come to pass in that day, that I will seek to destroy all the nations that come against Jerusalem. Then shall the Lord go forth, and fight against those nations, as when he fought in the day of battle" (Zech. 12:8–9; 14:3; see also Isa. 13:19–20; Jer. 51:40–41; Joel 2:20–21, 32; Zech. 13:8–9).

25. The Lord will make his power manifest through the outcome of Armageddon: "I will plead against him with pestilence and with blood; and I will rain upon him, and upon his bands, and upon the many people that are with him, an overflowing rain, and great hailstones, fire, and brimstone. Thus will I magnify myself, and sanctify myself; and I will be known in the eyes of many nations, and they shall know that I am the Lord. So will I make my holy name known in the midst of my people Israel; and I will not let them pollute my holy name any more: and the heathen shall know that I am the Lord, the

---

[40] See the commentary on earthquakes in the last days, page 344.

Holy One in Israel" (Ezek. 38:22–23; 39:7; see also 38:18, 21; 39:6, 21–22).

26. The battle of Armageddon is associated with plagues of flies, maggots, and decaying flesh. These things could be connected to the decay of dead bodies after the battles, or to the quicker destruction of bodies through atomic warfare or other means:[41] "This shall be the plague wherewith the Lord will smite all the people that have fought against Jerusalem; their flesh shall consume away while they stand upon their feet, and their eyes shall consume away in their holes, and their tongue shall consume away in their mouth" (Zech. 14:12; see also D&C 29:18–19).

27. After the battle of Armageddon, the Lord will invite birds of carrion and ravenous beasts to feast on the bodies of the dead. This is called "the supper of the great God": "Thus saith the Lord God; Speak unto every feathered fowl, and to every beast of the field, Assemble yourselves, and come; gather yourselves on every side to my sacrifice that I do sacrifice for you, even a great sacrifice upon the mountains of Israel, that ye may eat flesh, and drink blood. Ye shall eat the flesh of the mighty, and drink the blood of the princes of the earth. . . . And ye shall eat fat till ye be full, and drink blood till ye be drunken, of my sacrifice which I have sacrificed for you. Thus ye shall be filled at my table with horses and chariots, with mighty men, and with all men of war, saith the Lord God" (Ezek. 39:17–20; see also Rev. 19:17–21; D&C 29:20).

28. After the war is over it will take Israel seven years to burn the weapons of war: "They that dwell in the cities of Israel shall go forth, and shall set on fire and burn the weapons, both the shields and the bucklers, the bows and the arrows, and the handstaves, and the spears, and they shall burn them with fire seven years: So that they shall take no wood out of the field, neither cut down any out of the forests; for they shall burn the weapons with fire: and they shall spoil those that spoiled them, and rob those that robbed them, saith the Lord God" (Ezek. 39:9–10). This passage is probably symbolic because it does not seem likely that the armies attacking Israel will use bows and arrows and bucklers and spears instead of guns and tanks. Perhaps the

---

[41] See the commentary on these plagues, page 347.

point here is that the battle is so enormous, with the enemy so vast, it will take many years to clean up the weapons they leave behind.

29. After the war is over, it will take Israel seven months to bury the dead of their enemy. The number seven here and in the previous passage may be symbolic. In the scriptures, seven often symbolizes perfection or completion. Perhaps by using the number seven the Lord is underscoring the fact that the destruction of the wicked is complete: The last vestiges of their weapons and their dead bodies are now gone. "It shall come to pass in that day, that I will give unto Gog a place there of graves in Israel, the valley of the passengers on the east of the sea: and it shall stop the noses of the passengers: and there shall they bury Gog and all his multitude. . . . And seven months shall the house of Israel be burying of them, that they may cleanse the land. Yea, all the people of the land shall bury them. . . . And they shall sever out men of continual employment, passing through the land to bury with the passengers those that remain upon the face of the earth, to cleanse it: after the end of seven months shall they search. And the passengers that pass through the land, when any seeth a man's bone, then shall he set up a sign by it, till the buriers have buried it in the valley of Hamon-gog. . . . Thus shall they cleanse the land" (Ezek. 39:11–16).

The horror of this war or series of wars, which culminates in the battle at Armageddon, is reminiscent of the final great conflicts among the Jaredites and Nephites. In fact, Mormon and Moroni may have included those wars for the express purpose of warning us of things to come. In the final Book of Mormon wars we see that which will come in the last days: wars with astounding levels of bloodshed, wars in which hearts are hard and emotions are cold, wars conducted under the motivating whisperings of Satan and his evil followers, wars that persist to the point of the utter destruction of a people (Morm. 2–6; Ether 14–15).

Nephi witnessed in vision a great war that may well have been the battle of Armageddon, seen from a spiritual perspective. He saw the "whore of all the earth" (the devil's church) and saw that "she had dominion over all the earth, among all nations, kindreds, tongues, and people." In contrast, when he saw "the church of the Lamb of God, . . .

its numbers were few," but it also had a presence "upon all the face of the earth."

"And it came to pass that I beheld that the great mother of abominations did gather together multitudes upon the face of all the earth, among all the nations of the Gentiles, to fight against the Lamb of God. And . . . I, Nephi, beheld the power of the Lamb of God, that it descended upon the saints of the church of the Lamb, and upon the covenant people of the Lord, who were scattered upon all the face of the earth; and they were armed with righteousness and with the power of God in great glory.

"And . . . I beheld that the wrath of God was poured out upon that great and abominable church, insomuch that there were wars and rumors of wars among all the nations and kindreds of the earth."

Nephi then saw John the Revelator, and was told by his angel guide, "Behold, he shall see and write the remainder of these things; yea, and also many things which have been. And he shall also write concerning the end of the world" (1 Ne. 14:11–15, 21–22).

We learn from Nephi's vision that there will be a world war instigated by the great and abominable church of the devil; that it will be a holy war, because the devil's church will be fighting against "the church of the Lamb"; that the Lord will pour out his wrath upon the great and abominable church; and that the Lord will arm his Saints "with the power of God in great glory" to assist them in their battles. It appears from the angel's comments that this war is related in time to the end of the world, as seen by John the Revelator.

If this passage does indeed describe the final great battles of earth, culminating in the battle of Armageddon, we learn that this war truly is a continuation of the battle in heaven, which is a battle between light and darkness, good and evil, God and Satan. We learn that Satan will rage in his continuing attempts to destroy "the covenant people of the Lord." And we learn that God will protect them by his power and help them to come to the last and lasting victory. Joseph Smith said, speaking perhaps of these same events, "In the former days God sent His servants to fight; but in the last days, He has promised to fight the battle Himself."[42]

---

[42] *History of the Church,* 5:356.

In his classic work *A Voice of Warning,* Elder Parley P. Pratt gave us a helpful summary of the events of the battle of Armageddon: "Chapters 38 and 39 [of Ezekiel] present us with a view of many nations united under one great head, whom the Lord is pleased to call Gog; and being mounted on horseback, and armed with all sorts of armor, they come up against the mountains of Israel, as a cloud to cover the land; their object is to take a prey, to take away silver and gold, and cattle, and goods in great abundance.

"This is an event which is to transpire after the return of the Jews and the rebuilding of Jerusalem; while the towns and the land of Judea are without walls, having neither bars nor gates. But while they are at the point to swallow up the Jews, and lay waste their country, behold, the Lord's fury comes up in His face, a mighty earthquake is the result, insomuch that the fishes of the sea, and the fowls of the air, and all the creeping things, and all men upon the face of the earth shall shake at His presence, and every wall shall fall to the ground, and every man's sword shall be turned against his neighbor in this army, and the Lord shall rain upon him, and upon his bands, and upon the many people that are with him an overflowing rain, great hailstones, fire and brimstone.

"And thus He will magnify Himself and sanctify Himself, in the eyes of many nations, and they shall know that He is the Lord; thus they shall fall upon the open field, upon the mountains of Israel, even Gog and all his army, horses and horsemen; and the Jews shall go forth and gather the weapons of war such as hand staves, spears, shields, bows and arrows; and these weapons shall last the cities of Israel seven years for fuel, so that they shall cut no wood out of the forest, for they shall burn the weapons with the fire; and they shall spoil those that spoiled them; and rob those that robbed them, and they shall gather gold and silver, and apparel, in great abundance.

"At this time the fowls of the air and the beasts of the field shall have a great feast; yea, they are to eat fat until they be full, and drink blood until they be drunken. They are to eat the flesh of captains, and kings, and mighty men, and all men of war.

"But the Jews will have a very serious duty to perform, which will take no less than seven months; namely, the burying of their enemies. They will select a place on the east side of the sea, called the Valley of the Passengers, and there shall they bury Gog and all his multitude, and they shall call it the valley of Hamon Gog. And the scent shall go forth, insomuch that it shall stop the noses of the passengers; thus shall they cleanse the land. . . .

"Zechariah in his 14th [chapter] has told us much concerning the great battle and overthrow of the nations who fight against Jerusalem, and he has said, in plain words, that the Lord shall come at the very time of the overthrow of that army, yes, in fact, even while they are in the act of taking Jerusalem, and have already succeeded in taking one-half the city, and spoiling their houses, and ravishing their women. Then, behold their long-expected Messiah, suddenly appearing, shall stand upon the Mount of Olives, a little east of Jerusalem, to fight against those nations and deliver the Jews. . . .

"John, in his 11th chapter of Revelation, gives us many more particulars concerning this same event. He informs us that, after the city and temple are rebuilt by the Jews, the Gentiles will tread it under foot forty and two months, during which time there will be two Prophets continually prophesying and working mighty miracles. And it seems that the Gentile army shall be hindered from utterly destroying and overthrowing the city, while these two Prophets continue. But, after a struggle of three years and a half, they at length succeed in destroying these two Prophets, and then overrunning much of the city; they send gifts to each other because of the death of the two Prophets; and in the meantime will not allow their dead bodies to be put in graves; but suffer them to lie in the streets of Jerusalem three days and a half, during which the armies of the Gentiles, consisting of many kindreds, tongues and nations, passing through the city, plundering the Jews see their dead bodies lying in the street. But, after three days and a half, on a sudden, the spirit of life from God enters them, and they will arise and stand upon their feet, and great fear will fall upon them that see them. And then they shall hear a voice from heaven saying, 'Come up hither,' and they will ascend up to heaven in a cloud, and their enemies beholding them. And having described all these things, then comes the shaking, spoken of by Ezekiel, and the rending of the Mount of Olives, spoken of by Zechariah. John says,

'The same hour was there a great earthquake, and the tenth part of the city fell, and in the earthquake were slain of men seven thousand.' And then one of the next scenes that follow is the sound of voices, saying, 'The kingdoms of this world are become the kingdom of our Lord, and of his Christ; and he shall reign forever and ever.'"[43]

NOTES AND COMMENTARY

Rev. 16:13 *I saw three unclean spirits like frogs come out of the mouth of the dragon/beast/false prophet.* The symbolic "satanic trinity"[44] of the dragon, the beast, and the false prophet send forth evil spirits, or devils, to do their work. Their emergence from the mouths of the devil and his helpers suggests that these evil spirits are symbolic of false communications, lies, and propaganda designed to deceive the people of the world. Similarly, in Revelation 12:15, a river that may represent lies comes from the mouth of the dragon; in Revelation 13:5, blasphemies come from the mouth of the beast; and in Revelation 13:14, the false prophet, or second beast, seems to speak threats and ungodly commands.

Frogs, to which the spirits are compared, are unclean animals under the law of Moses (Lev. 11:10). One of the plagues that Moses and Aaron brought on Egypt was a plague of frogs (Ex. 8:2–6). Interestingly, Pharaoh's magicians, using Satan's power, duplicated this plague (Ex. 8:7). In nearby Persia, which was east of the Euphrates (Rev. 16:12), frogs were "considered to be the instrument of Ahriman, the god of darkness."[45] Further, Ahriman had power to change his shape, and the animal form that fit him most naturally was that of a frog.[46]

The fact that three unclean spirits come forth from three different evil beings suggests that those beings (the dragon, the beast, and the false prophet) may each send forth one of the spirits. These evil spirits are the agents and representatives of those who send them forth. As righteous men on earth can stand for God by virtue of the priesthood

[43] *Voice of Warning,* 38–42.
[44] Harrington, *Revelation,* 166.
[45] Schick, *Revelation of St. John,* 2:51.
[46] *Interpreter's Bible,* 12:485.

they hold, so can these unclean spirits stand for Satan through the evil power he bestows on them.

Rev. 16:14 *For they are the spirits of devils.* Here we learn definitively that the three unclean spirits of Revelation 16:13 are the spirits of devils. Devils, of course, are not body and spirit combined but are only spirits. Perhaps a better translation would be "spirits that are devils." The Lord has told us: "Hearken, O ye elders of my church, and give ear to the voice of the living God; and attend to the words of wisdom which shall be given unto you, according as ye have asked and are agreed as touching the church, and the spirits which have gone abroad in the earth. Behold, verily I say unto you, that there are many spirits which are false spirits, which have gone forth in the earth, deceiving the world. And also Satan hath sought to deceive you, that he might overthrow you" (D&C 50:1–3).

working miracles. Jesus Christ prophesied that "there shall arise false Christs, and false prophets, and shall shew great signs and wonders; insomuch that, if it were possible, they shall deceive the very elect" (Matt. 24:24; see also Rev. 13:14). These evil spirits are part of the fulfillment of that prophecy. The miracles of Satan and the miracles of God may often be indistinguishable from one another to the outward senses. Only through the discernment given by the Spirit of God can we know the difference. Elder Orson Pratt wrote, "The reason the Lord will suffer the devil to work miracles to deceive 'the kings of the earth and of the whole world,' is because they will previously have rejected 'the everlasting gospel'; therefore the devil will deceive them, and lead them on to destruction, as he did the Egyptians."[47]

go forth unto the kings of the earth and of the whole world. The deceiving spirits sent forth by Satan will have worldwide influence, including with the rulers of the nations of the earth. The spirits will cause the gathering of the kings and their armies together to battle.

to gather them to the battle. This battle is the great final battle at Armageddon, which will be fought by the armies of the earth (Rev. 16:16). That battle, perhaps when it reaches its crisis point, will be

---

[47] *Divine Authenticity of the Book of Mormon,* no. 5, 66.

interrupted by the coming of the Lord (Zech. 14:1–4), "the great day of God Almighty."

Rev. 16:16 *he gathered them together . . . Armageddon.* Armageddon is the site of the last great battle before the coming of the Lord. The person gathering the armies together is not identified, but it is likely Satan, working through the evil spirits he sends to the earth (Rev. 16:14). Armageddon is the New Testament name for Megiddo, an ancient city some sixty miles north of Jerusalem. Megiddo lay "on the north side of the Carmel ridge and command[ed] the strategic pass between the coastal plain and the valley of Esdraelon." The area "is one of history's famous battlefields, having witnessed major conflicts all the way 'from one fought by Tuthmosis III in 1468 B.C. to that of Lord Allenby of Megiddo in 1917.' 'By the waters of Megiddo' Barak and Deborah defeated the chariots of Sisera (Judg. 4–5; cf. 5:19)."[48] In that same area, Gideon and his three hundred soldiers defeated the Midianites (Judg. 7), and Saul and Jonathan were killed in battle (1 Sam. 31:1–6), as was King Josiah (2 Kgs. 23:29–30). "The kings of the whole world will be destroyed in final conflict outside the city of Jerusalem. . . . Armageddon is symbolic of the final overthrow of all the forces of evil by the might and power of God."[49]

The great battle of Armageddon will be not a localized conflict but the center of a worldwide war. Elder Bruce R. McConkie explained, "The center of the battle will be on the mount and in the valley of Megiddo and on the plains of Esdraelon, though, since all nations are involved, it cannot be other than a worldwide conflict."[50] Ultimately, the objective of Satan and his armies is not merely the conquest of northern Israel or Jerusalem but the destruction of the Lord's temple and the Lord's work.[51]

THE SAINTS WILL RECEIVE A DEGREE OF PROTECTION
Doctrine and Covenants 63:32–34

> 32 I, the Lord, am angry with the wicked; I am holding my Spirit from the inhabitants of the earth.

---

[48] Mounce, *Book of Revelation*, 301.

[49] Mounce, *Book of Revelation*, 302.

[50] *Millennial Messiah*, 397.

[51] See McConkie, *Millennial Messiah*, 476–85.

33 I have sworn in my wrath, and decreed wars upon the face of the earth, and the wicked shall slay the wicked, and fear shall come upon every man;

34 And the saints also shall hardly escape; nevertheless, I, the Lord, am with them, and will come down in heaven from the presence of my Father and consume the wicked with unquenchable fire.

Because of the wickedness of the people of the world, the Lord has become angry and has "sworn in [his] wrath" that they will suffer wars. Through these wars, "the wicked shall slay the wicked" until the wars (along with other judgments) bring the end of this world. Unfortunately, the righteous have no guarantee that they will escape the wars of the latter days. Some will be killed, for death is the lot of all mankind, and even the righteous sometimes are killed when the wicked choose to exercise their agency in destructive ways.

But the Lord offers us a measure of comfort. Though the Saints will "hardly escape," as a body they will nevertheless escape (Matt. 24:22), and they can know that the Lord is with them. As we read in the Doctrine and Covenants: "The day speedily cometh . . . when peace shall be taken from the earth, and the devil shall have power over his own dominion. And also the Lord shall have power over his saints, and shall reign in their midst" (D&C 1:35–36). Before the final great judgments on the earth, including Armageddon, the Lord will "gather his wheat into the garner"—meaning that he will bring the Saints to a place of protection—and then "he will burn up the chaff with unquenchable fire" (Matt. 3:12).

Those who will receive the Lord's protection are the "wise virgins" who "have received the truth, and have taken the Holy Spirit for their guide, and have not been deceived." Of these wise virgins the Lord says, "Verily I say unto you, they shall not be hewn down and cast into the fire, but shall abide the day" (D&C 45:57). Those who follow the Holy Spirit will be gathered to the safety of Zion:[52] "And it shall come to pass among the wicked, that every man that will not take his sword against his neighbor must needs flee unto Zion for

---

[52] See the commentary on the safety of the latter-day Zion, page 357.

safety. And there shall be gathered unto it out of every nation under heaven; and it shall be the only people that shall not be at war one with another. And it shall be said among the wicked: Let us not go up to battle against Zion, for the inhabitants of Zion are terrible; wherefore we cannot stand" (D&C 45:68–70).

The key to the Lord's protection, then, is faithfulness. As the Lord said to his disciples, "Watch ye therefore, and pray always, that ye may be accounted worthy to escape all these things that shall come to pass, and to stand before the Son of Man when he shall come clothed in the glory of his Father" (JST Luke 21:36).

NOTES AND COMMENTARY

D&C 63:32 *I, the Lord, am angry with the wicked.* The Lord is not an unfeeling, impersonal God. He feels all things perfectly, and much more deeply than we do. Thus, he can feel anger at those who choose wickedness—anger at the pain it brings to others, as well as anger at the way it leads others into sin (Deut. 9:8; 1 Kgs. 11:9; 2 Kgs. 17:18; Alma 33:16; D&C 61:20; Moses 6:27).

I am holding my Spirit from the inhabitants of the earth. It is not a right but a privilege to receive the Spirit and its blessings. When people in general choose wickedness, then the people in general will not receive the Spirit, but those who qualify will, of course, still receive the blessing.

D&C 63:33 *I have sworn in my wrath.* Wrath is a deep-seated anger. When the Lord swears in his wrath, he does so to bring righteous ends from that which aroused the anger in the first place (Heb. 4:3; Ether 2:8).

decreed wars upon the face of the earth. The purpose for this decree may be explained in the next phrase: "The wicked shall slay the wicked"—through wars, the wicked will exercise their agency to kill others who are wicked, thus helping to cleanse the earth.

fear shall come upon every man. The cause of the fear is the wars themselves, as well as the other violent acts of the wicked upon the earth.

D&C 63:34 *the saints also shall hardly escape.* So great will be the unrest and violence on the earth that no one will be completely protected from it. Yet the Lord offers us hope when he implies here that the Saints (meaning many, or most, of the Saints) will escape, even if it is only barely so.

I, the Lord, am with them. This sweet promise is often repeated in the scriptures:

"Be not afraid of the king of Babylon, of whom ye are afraid; be not afraid of him, saith the Lord: for I am with you to save you, and to deliver you from his hand" (Jer. 42:11; see also Hag. 1:13; 2:4).

"Lo, I am with you alway, even unto the end of the world" (Matt. 28:20).

"Wherefore, be of good cheer, and do not fear, for I the Lord am with you, and will stand by you" (D&C 68:6; see also 30:11; 31:13; 105:41).

In this context, the Lord is saying that he will protect us in the times of great trouble, and in the end he will deliver us. "And should we die before our journey's through," nevertheless, "all is well,"[53] for the Lord will be with us in life or in death, to bless us and to keep us.

ALL NATIONS WILL COME TO AN END
Doctrine and Covenants 87:6

> *6 And thus, with the sword and by bloodshed the inhabitants of the earth shall mourn; and with famine, and plague, and earthquake, and the thunder of heaven, and the fierce and vivid lightning also, shall the inhabitants of the earth be made to feel the wrath, and indignation, and chastening hand of an Almighty God, until the consumption decreed hath made a full end of all nations.*

The Lord has decreed that when he reigns on the earth in the Millennium, the world will no longer have any nations that were created by man. "It shall come to pass in that day," the Lord announced, "that I will seek to destroy all the nations that come against Jerusalem" (Zech. 12:9). "The consumption decreed [shall make] a full end of all nations," he said (D&C 87:6).

If "all nations" have been destroyed, what remains is that which the Lord has established and created. As he said through Jeremiah,

---

[53] William Clayton, "Come, Come, Ye Saints," *Hymns,* no. 30.

speaking to Israel: "I am with thee, saith the Lord, to save thee: though I make a full end of all nations whither I have scattered thee, yet will I not make a full end of thee: but I will correct thee in measure, and will not leave thee altogether unpunished" (Jer. 30:11; see also Jer. 47). Thus, all the nations of man will come to a full and complete end through the judgments of the last days, including the wars that precede the Lord's coming. But the nation that is bound to the Lord by covenant will continue. This nation is repentant Israel and, perhaps, a constitutional America.[54] Thus, in the Millennium, the Lord will rule mankind from his two capital cities of Jerusalem and New Jerusalem: "Out of Zion shall go forth the law, and the word of the Lord from Jerusalem" (Isa. 2:3).

NOTES AND COMMENTARY

D&C 87:6 *the consumption decreed.* The Lord has decreed that all evil, all things temporal, all things of the earth shall be destroyed, or consumed, to make way for the new world of the Millennium. He said to Joseph Smith: "Everything that is in the world, whether it be ordained of men, by thrones, or principalities, or powers, or things of name, whatsoever they may be, that are not by me or by my word, saith the Lord, shall be thrown down, and shall not remain after men are dead, neither in nor after the resurrection, saith the Lord your God. For whatsoever things remain are by me; and whatsoever things are not by me shall be shaken and destroyed" (D&C 132:13–14).

---

[54] Elder Bruce R. McConkie wrote: "It is our firm conviction as a people that the stars and stripes will be waving triumphantly in the breeze, as a symbol of the greatness and stability of the United States of America, when the Lord comes" (*Millennial Messiah,* 491).

CHAPTER 7

THE BABYLON OF THE LAST DAYS

SIGNS OF THE TIMES

1. Babylon, the mother of harlots, or the wicked world, gains great power on earth.

2. The Saints must flee Babylon and go to Zion.

3. Babylon falls by the power of God; the wicked world is destroyed.

Babylon is the recurring scriptural symbol for Satan's kingdom on the earth. Babylon represents the wicked world, the world of sin, the world of immorality and idolatry. It is the world of false philosophy, false religion, coercive government. At various times the world of sin has been called the kingdom of the devil, the great and abominable church, the church of the devil, secret combinations—or Egypt, Sodom, Nineveh, wicked Jerusalem, or Rome. She is antichrist. She is the antithesis of Zion.

The symbol of Babylon as the great evil is drawn from the history of ancient Israel: Babylon was the epitome of wickedness in the ancient world. In addition, Babylon was a dire enemy of the Lord's covenant people. King Nebuchadnezzar of Babylon first attacked Judah in 597 B.C., eventually overrunning the nation and destroying the city of Jerusalem. He took the people captive and transported them to live in bondage in Babylon. In time, the Lord delivered the people of Judah and blessed them to return to their homeland. Later, the Lord utterly destroyed Babylon.

These ancient events all clearly parallel events that have been prophesied for the last days. Babylon, the wicked world, is taking "captive" many of the Lord's people. As they turn to the ways of

Babylon, they sell themselves into bondage to sin. But in time the Lord will gather back to his kingdom those who will hear him. And, in the end, the Lord will utterly destroy spiritual Babylon.

The Babylon presented by John (Rev. 17) seems disgusting, foreign, obviously undesirable. That is the way the prophets typically see her—she is all glitz and glitter; she is grossly overdressed; she has no refinement or sensitivity. She is not the type of person we want to associate with. That is Babylon with the deceptive veils ripped off; it is Babylon seen truly. But she is often painted in a different light by Satan and those who follow him. She is painted as attractive and beautiful and most desirable. Satan seeks to make the world of sin enticing. The evidence of his success is that so many people on earth follow him and join in his worldly ways. If Satan can appear as an angel of light, certainly Babylon can appear as a beautiful and desirable woman.

It is often difficult in reading the Old Testament to discern whether a prophet is speaking of the literal, ancient Babylon or the symbolic, latter-day Babylon. Ultimately, however, it usually does not matter. Such prophecies seem to have a dual fulfillment; and what was true of ancient Babylon seems also to be true of the Babylon of the last days, both in her characteristics and her ultimate destiny, for the Babylon of wickedness is not just a phenomenon of the last days. She is as old as Cain and continues to the end of the world. Thus, the existence of Babylon is not one of the signs of the times, but her growing power and dominion is one of those signs, and her great fall will occur even as the Lord comes in glory.

In the following discussions of Babylon, we must constantly look past the symbol to the reality: Babylon represents all the false beliefs, sinful actions, and ungodly associations found on the earth. By extension, Babylon also represents all the people who hold those beliefs, perform those actions, and join with those associations. The fall of Babylon is nothing less than the obliteration of those beliefs and sins and associations from the face of the earth—and the destruction of the people who cast their lot with such things.

BABYLON, THE MOTHER OF HARLOTS
Revelation 17:1–6

1 And there came one of the seven angels which had the seven vials, and talked with me, saying unto me, Come hither; I will shew unto thee the judgment of the great whore that sitteth upon many waters:

2 With whom the kings of the earth have committed fornication, and the inhabitants of the earth have been made drunk with the wine of her fornication.

3 So he carried me away in the spirit into the wilderness: and I saw a woman sit upon a scarlet coloured beast, full of names of blasphemy, having seven heads and ten horns.

4 And the woman was arrayed in purple and scarlet colour, and decked with gold and precious stones and pearls, having a golden cup in her hand full of abominations and filthiness of her fornication;

5 And upon her forehead was a name written, MYSTERY, BABYLON THE GREAT, THE MOTHER OF HARLOTS AND ABOMINATIONS OF THE EARTH.

6 And I saw the woman drunken with the blood of the saints, and with the blood of the martyrs of Jesus: and when I saw her, I wondered with great admiration.

As Revelation 17 begins, John is invited to see the "judgment" of "the whore," but first he sees her arrayed in her power. The angel bears witness that the whore has power over all the earth ("many waters") and that she has influence over the kings and people of the world. Through the power of the Spirit, John actually sees the whore, though he is seeing a symbol surrounded by other symbolic layers of meaning. He sees her excesses in her lust for wealth and pleasure, as shown by her clothing and jewelry. He sees her pride, as shown by the name on her forehead. He sees her wickedness by that name and by her murder of the righteous.

Centuries earlier, Nephi saw a similar vision, which helps us understand what John saw and recorded in Revelation. Nephi saw the "whore of all the earth" "many generations" after the time of peace that followed the coming of Christ to the Americas (1 Ne. 12:21; 13:4–6; 14:10). This part of his vision clearly concerns the time of the Great Apostasy and the last days. As 1 Nephi 13 opens, Nephi sees "the nations and kingdoms of the Gentiles" (v. 3). Among those nations, he sees "the formation of a church which is most abominable above all other churches, which slayeth the saints of God, yea, and tortureth them and bindeth them down, and yoketh them with a yoke of iron, and bringeth them down into captivity" (v. 5). The founder of "this great and abominable church" is the devil himself (v. 6). "And I also saw gold, and silver, and silks, and scarlets, and fine-twined linen, and all manner of precious clothing; and I saw many harlots," which, the scripture explains, "are the desires of this great and abominable church" (vv. 7–8).

Next, Nephi sees Columbus discovering America (v. 12), followed by the Revolutionary War (vv. 17–19), which further helps to place the prophecies in the time of the Great Apostasy. Nephi learns that the "great and abominable church, which is most abominable above all other churches" was formed after the Bible went forth "from the Jews unto the Gentiles" (v. 26). Further, he sees that the great and abominable church takes "away from the gospel of the Lamb many parts which are plain and most precious; and also many covenants of the Lord" (v. 26). Their motive is malicious: "And all this have they done that they might pervert the right ways of the Lord, that they might blind the eyes and harden the hearts of the children of men" (v. 27). "Because of these things which are taken away out of the gospel of the Lamb, an exceedingly great many do stumble, yea, insomuch that Satan hath great power over them" (v. 29).

In the verses that follow, Nephi learns that the "abominable church . . . is the mother of harlots" (v. 34), that that church had dug a "great pit . . . for the destruction of men" (1 Ne. 14:3), and that "that great and abominable church . . . is the mother of abominations" (v. 9). Nephi learns that there are finally only two churches on the earth: "The one is the church of the Lamb of God, and the other is the church of the devil; wherefore, whoso belongeth not to the church of the Lamb of God belongeth to that great church, which is the mother of abominations; and she is the whore of all the earth" (v. 10). This whore "sat upon many waters; and she had dominion over all the earth, among all nations, kindreds, tongues, and people" (v. 11). Because of that dominion, and "because of the wickedness and abominations of the whore," the numbers of the church of the Lamb of God "were few" (v. 12).

"And it came to pass," Nephi wrote, "that I beheld that the great mother of abominations did gather together multitudes upon the face of all the earth, among all the nations of the Gentiles, to fight against the Lamb of God. And it came to pass that I beheld that the wrath of God was poured out upon that great and abominable church, insomuch that there were wars and rumors of wars among all the nations and kindreds of the earth. And when the day cometh that the wrath of God is poured out upon the mother of harlots, which is the great and abominable church of all the earth, whose founder is the devil, then, at that day, the work of the Father shall commence, in preparing the way for the fulfilling of his covenants, which he hath made to his people who are of the house of Israel" (vv. 13, 15, 17). In sum, then, this great and abominable church is the church of the devil.[1] It is the "mother of abominations." It is the "whore of all the earth." It is Babylon.

Elder Bruce R. McConkie gave a powerful description of that church: "The church of the devil is every evil and worldly organization on earth. It is all of the systems, both Christian and non-Christian, that have perverted the pure and perfect gospel; it is all of the governments and powers that run counter to the divine will; it is the societies and political parties and labor unions that sow strife and reap contention. It is communism; it is Islam; it is Buddhism; it is modern Christianity in all its parts. It is Germany under Hitler, Russia under Stalin, and Italy under Mussolini. It is the man of sin speaking in churches, orating in legislative halls, and commanding the armies of men. And its headquarters are everywhere—in Rome and Moscow, in Paris and London, in Teheran and Washington—everywhere that

---

[1] For further commentary on the great and abominable church of the devil, see Robinson, "Early Christianity and 1 Nephi 13–14," 177–90; and Parsons, "Great and Abominable Church," 44–59.

evil forces, either of church or state or society, can be influenced. The immanent and all-pervading presence of evil in high places is one of the signs of the times."[2]

NOTES AND COMMENTARY

Rev. 17:1 *the judgment of the great whore.* The image of prostitution was commonly used in the Old Testament to depict extreme apostasy from all that is godly and good (Isa. 1:21; 23:16–17; Jer. 2:20–31; 13:27; Ezek. 16:15, 28–29; Hosea 2:5; Nahum 3:4). Nephi defines who the great whore is: "He that fighteth against Zion, both Jew and Gentile, both bond and free, both male and female, shall perish; for they are they who are the whore of all the earth; for they who are not for me are against me, saith our God" (2 Ne. 10:16). The "judgment of the great whore" means, simply, the punishment of the world of wickedness. The judgment is described in detail in Revelation 17 and 18.

sitteth upon many waters. The interpretation of the expression "many waters" is given in Revelation 17:15: "The waters which thou sawest, where the whore sitteth, are peoples, and multitudes, and nations, and tongues." Nephi saw that "[the whore] had dominion over all the earth, among all nations, kindreds, tongues, and people" (1 Ne. 14:11).

Rev. 17:2 *With whom the kings of the earth have committed fornication.* The rulers of the earth, who ought to lead in righteousness, instead lead the people into sin. They "commit fornication" with the whore by selling that which is good and right and true, even their very souls, for the pleasure and power the whore will give them. They commit fornication by turning from their true husband, or at least him to whom they are betrothed—God himself—to Babylon.

the inhabitants of the earth have been made drunk with the wine of her fornication. Drunkenness here is a symbol of apostasy, in which the people lose the power of good judgment because of their unwise choices. "They are drunken, but not with wine," Isaiah prophesied, "they stagger, but not with strong drink" (Isa. 29:9; see Jer.

---

[2] *Millennial Messiah,* 54–55.

51:6–9). The wine that makes them drunk is not the fornication of sexuality but that of unfaithfulness to God.

Rev. 17:3 *So he carried me away in the spirit.* Nephi (son of Lehi) received the same blessing when he experienced his vision of the last days (1 Ne. 14:30; 15:1; 2 Ne. 4:25), as did Jesus in the days of his temptation (JST Matt. 4:8). It appears that in these instances the Spirit, or the Holy Ghost, may carry a person to another location, while at the same time enabling him to transcend his physical limitations to rend the veil between mortality and the world of the Spirit. In the years before the coming of Christ to the Americas, the prophet Nephi (son of Helaman) was cast into prison, but by "the power of God . . . he was taken by the Spirit and conveyed away out of the midst of them" (Hel. 10:16). Others in the scriptures who received this blessing include Adam (Moses 6:64), Lehi (1 Ne. 1:8), Ezekiel (Ezek. 37:1), and Mary, the mother of Jesus (1 Ne. 11:19).

into the wilderness. In Revelation 12 we see the woman, who represented the church of God, the bride of Christ, go into the wilderness for safety. Here we see her counterfeit, the woman who represents the church of the devil, dwelling in the wilderness. In the first instance, the wilderness symbolized a place of refuge; here it symbolizes the dryness and desolation of sin.

I saw a woman sit upon a scarlet coloured beast. This beast is most likely the same as that found in Revelation 13:1, for both have seven heads and ten horns.[3] The woman is the whore spoken of in Revelation 17:1. The scarlet color of the beast is the same color as the ribbon that was tied around the neck of the scapegoat on the Day of Atonement; the ribbon represented the sins of Israel.[4] In the same way, the scarlet of the beast seems to represent sin (Isa. 1:18).

Rev. 17:4 *And the woman was arrayed in purple and scarlet colour.* Purple clothing symbolizes royalty (Judg. 8:26), and scarlet clothing symbolizes wealth and nobility (2 Sam. 1:24; Prov. 31:21; Lam. 4:5; Dan. 5:7; Matt. 27:28–29); the scarlet color, of course, also symbolizes sin. The woman's clothing indicates her position of

---

[3] For a discussion of the beasts in Revelation, see Parry and Parry, *Understanding the Book of Revelation,* 162–77.
[4] Edersheim, *Temple,* 312.

wealth and power in the world, but there is a deeper significance. In the Old Testament, purple and scarlet appear together only in Exodus (occurring twenty-six times), and in every instance the colors are used, together with blue and white linen, to describe the tabernacle of the Lord and the clothing of the high priest (see, for example, Ex. 26:1, 31, 36). Purple and scarlet were used in the curtains of the tabernacle, the hanging for the door, the hanging for the gate of the court, and the veil itself. They were used for the ephod (linen apron) of the high priest, as well as for his girdle, the hems of his robe, the breastplate, and the cloths used in the temple rituals.

Thus, the woman is standing as counterfeit for the most sacred elements of the true religion—the temple and the high priest who presided over all the people. She is trying to supplant the religion of God with a false religion, one that points the people to sin and excess and ultimately to a worship of Satan himself (Rev. 13:4). Thus, the woman who is Babylon is not only wickedness and political power, but also religious systems that entice all men to turn their hearts away from the true God. She seems to combine elements of the first and second beasts and the false prophet (described in Rev. 13).

Even with all her worldly trappings, the glory of this woman pales when compared to the "woman clothed with the sun" in Revelation 12:1 and the simple beauty of the bride of the Lamb in Revelation 19:7–8.

decked with gold and precious stones and pearls. These items are symbols of wealth. The word *decked* indicates that the woman wears an excessive amount of jewelry. In fact, everything about the woman speaks of pride, worldliness, and excess.

having a golden cup in her hand full of abominations and filthiness of her fornication. A golden cup indicates wealth, and a person seeing such a cup would expect to find in it something pleasurable to drink. Instead, the woman's cup is filled with "abominations and filthiness," which stem from the woman's "fornication" in turning her heart from God to Satan (Jer. 7–8; D&C 10:20–22). Abominations are offenses against God that are particularly vile and disgusting.

Rev. 17:5 *And upon her forehead was a name written.* The book of Revelation speaks of a mark on the forehead seven times. We read in Revelation 13:16, 14:9, and 20:4 of the mark of the beast on the forehead or in the hands of those who follow him. In Revelation 7:3, 9:4, 14:1, and 22:4 we read of the righteous receiving the name or seal of God on their foreheads. But here the woman has her own name written on her forehead. Some authorities believe it was common in ancient Rome for prostitutes to write their names on their foreheads, probably on a headband.[5]

MYSTERY. The righteous know the hidden things of God, called the "mysteries." The greatest mysteries are reserved for those who receive the keys to such mysteries in the temple, who keep their temple covenants, and who hunger and thirst after the things of godliness. The woman here is the embodiment of the mysteries of Satan, the counterfeit of the mysteries of God. These mysteries are found in false religious creeds, in "the secret works of darkness" (2 Ne. 10:15; 9:9; 26:22; 28:9), and in secret combinations, "which . . . is most abominable and wicked above all, in the sight of God" (Ether 8:18; Hel. 6:22–23; Moses 5:51).

BABYLON THE GREAT. "Babylon the great is the church of the devil; it is the world with all its evil and carnality; it is every organization of every kind, sort and form—whether religious, civic, political, fraternal, or otherwise—which espouses a philosophy or promotes a cause which leads men away from salvation and toward the kingdoms of lesser glory in the eternal world."[6] As the Lord says in latter-day revelation, Babylon is "the midst of wickedness" (D&C 133:14).

MOTHER OF HARLOTS AND ABOMINATIONS. Babylon not only is a prostitute herself but is the mother of other prostitutes, other harlots on the earth. Not only does the woman embody one form of great wickedness on the earth but she fosters organizations, religions, governments, philosophies, and attitudes that embrace the devil and his world. The abominations here include those spoken of in Daniel, where the temple and other sacred things are desecrated and corrupted (Dan. 11:31; Matt. 24:15). And they include the evil practice of combining harlotry with idolatry (Hosea 4:12–14). In the

---

[5] See, for example, Mounce, *Book of Revelation,* 311.
[6] McConkie, *Doctrinal New Testament Commentary,* 3:558.

scriptures the Lord calls the following things abominations—all are engendered by Babylon, the mother of abominations:

incest (Lev. 18:6–16, 26–27);

homosexuality (Lev. 18:22);

idolatry (Deut. 7:25; 12:29–31; Mal. 2:11);

impure sacrifices to God (Deut. 17:1);

human sacrifice (Deut. 18:10, 12);

using practitioners of divination, enchantments, witchcraft (Deut. 18:10, 12);

transvestism (Deut. 22:5);

dishonesty in financial dealings (Deut. 25:13–16; Prov. 11:1);

pride (Prov. 6:17; 16:5; Jacob 2:13, 16; Hel. 4:11–12);

lying (Prov. 6:17, 19; 12:22);

murder (Prov. 6:17);

contentiousness (Prov. 6:19);

justifying the wicked and condemning the just (Prov. 17:15);

adultery (Ezek. 18:11; 22:11);

oppressing the poor and needy (Ezek. 18:12; Hel. 4:11–12);

whoredoms (Jacob 2:28);

fornication (Alma 39:3–5);

secret combinations (Hel. 7:25);

rape (Moro. 9:9);

apostate creeds (JS–H 1:18–19).

Rev. 17:6 *drunken with the blood of the saints/martyrs.* Babylon is the name of the spirit that comes over those who kill the prophets. That spirit has infected much of the world (Rev. 16:6; 18:24; Matt. 23:34–35; Heb. 9:16). The word *drunken* suggests that through the ages the righteous have been victims of a great slaughter, a slaughter that was intoxicating to the perpetrators.

when I saw her, I wondered with great admiration. John does not feel "admiration" for this embodiment of great wickedness. A better translation of the Greek word here would be "astonishment."[7] John feels amazement, or astonishment, at the extreme level of Babylon's wickedness.

---

[7] See note *c* to Rev. 17:6 in the LDS edition of the KJV.

BABYLON HAS GREAT POWER IN THE WORLD
1 Nephi 14:11–14

11 And it came to pass that I looked and beheld the whore of all the earth, and she sat upon many waters; and she had dominion over all the earth, among all nations, kindreds, tongues, and people.

12 And it came to pass that I beheld the church of the Lamb of God, and its numbers were few, because of the wickedness and abominations of the whore who sat upon many waters; nevertheless, I beheld that the church of the Lamb, who were the saints of God, were also upon all the face of the earth; and their dominions upon the face of the earth were small, because of the wickedness of the great whore whom I saw.

13 And it came to pass that I beheld that the great mother of abominations did gather together multitudes upon the face of all the earth, among all the nations of the Gentiles, to fight against the Lamb of God.

14 And it came to pass that I, Nephi, beheld the power of the Lamb of God, that it descended upon the saints of the church of the Lamb, and upon the covenant people of the Lord, who were scattered upon all the face of the earth; and they were armed with righteousness and with the power of God in great glory.

Babylon, the "whore of all the earth," has "dominion over all the earth." She rules "all nations, kindreds, tongues, and people." Because of her deep and widespread wickedness, she is able to hinder the "church of the Lamb of God" in its growth. The whore has such strength and audacity, combined with an intrinsically evil nature, that she thinks to gather "multitudes upon the face of all the earth, among all the nations of the Gentiles, to fight against the Lamb of God" (see also D&C 88:94). This is a world war—but not one for temporal wealth or power. It is a war fought to destroy the people of the Lord, with their faith, their gospel, and their holy way of life. Despite the power of Babylon, though, despite the countless multitudes who gather to fight with and for her, the Saints will prevail. "The power of the Lamb of God" will descend upon the Saints, arming them "with righteousness and with the power of God in great glory."

Other passages confirm the power and dominion of wicked Babylon. John saw a beast with ten horns and ten crowns, symbolizing kings with great power (Rev. 13:1; 17:12). Many additional kings lend their power and strength to this beast (Rev. 17:13). The beast has power over "all kindreds, and tongues, and nations" (Rev. 13:7). This powerful beast, in turn, supports the whore. The kings of the earth, who have power over all, give power to the whore of all the earth. And the whore responds by ruling over the kings (Rev. 17:18). In other words, the kings promote the works of evil on the earth, and the works of evil control the lives and actions of the kings.

John also saw a second beast, another kind of kingdom on the earth (Rev. 13:11–18). This beast turns people's hearts to the first beast, and thus to the whore, by performing wondrous signs and miracles (Rev. 13:13). This beast (or kingdom) also controls the economy of the earth (buying and selling) and requires people to associate themselves with the beast if they wish to have part in that economy (Rev. 13:16–17). Thus, through the power of the second beast, the whore gains control of the world economy and rules over all those who wish to partake of her wealth and many comforts.

These two beasts do not represent specific political kingdoms on the earth but rather symbolize many kingdoms who serve Satan and support Babylon. And they go beyond political power to influence and have power over people's philosophies, religious beliefs and practices, economies, and so forth. In concert with the two beasts, the whore makes all nations "drink of the wine" of her wickedness (D&C 88:94). She leads them in "fornication," following passions that lead them away from God rather than righteous passions that guide them to him.

Thus, Babylon seems to control the political kingdoms of the world, all of which seem to use some form of coercion or violence to attain their ends. She controls the economy of the world, in which money is more important than love, mercy, compassion, service, or the things of God. She controls the hearts of men, causing them to follow her into the abyss of selfishness, lust, and all kinds of abominations.

Truly this Babylon is a symbol of power. She is so powerful in the world, following her master, Satan, that no power on earth can conquer her. But God's power from on high has no equal, and he will prevail mightily.

NOTES AND COMMENTARY

1 Ne. 14:11 *she sat upon many waters.* John used this same description of Babylon.[8]

1 Ne. 14:12 *the church of the Lamb . . . were also upon all the face of the earth.* Nephi sees a worldwide church. Nevertheless, even though Church members are to be found in all nations, they do not have broad or powerful dominions; the church of the devil prevented that through its wickedness.

1 Ne. 14:13 *great mother of abominations.* See the commentary on Revelation 17:5, page 290.

fight against the Lamb of God. The Lamb, of course, is Jesus Christ. The whore and all those who align themselves with her will not simply be fighting against Christ, but they will be fighting against the followers of Christ and his gospel. The war is part of the war that began in heaven (Rev. 12:7) and continues as the beast and his followers try to destroy the true believers in Christ (Rev. 13:7). This war will come to a bloody conclusion at Armageddon.[9] We also read about this war in Revelation 17:14, which says "the Lamb shall overcome them."

1 Ne. 14:14 *armed with righteousness and with the power of God in great glory.* This passage is reminiscent of the power held by Enoch as he built Zion in ancient days: "And so great was the faith of Enoch that he led the people of God, and their enemies came to battle against them; and he spake the word of the Lord, and the earth trembled, and the mountains fled, even according to his command; and the rivers of water were turned out of their course; and the roar of the lions was heard out of the wilderness; and all nations feared

---

[8] See the commentary on Rev. 17:1, page 288.
[9] See the commentary on Armageddon, page 264.

greatly, so powerful was the word of Enoch, and so great was the power of the language which God had given him. . . . And there went forth a curse upon all people that fought against God; and from that time forth there were wars and bloodshed among them; but the Lord came and dwelt with his people, and they dwelt in righteousness. The fear of the Lord was upon all nations, so great was the glory of the Lord, which was upon his people" (Moses 7:13, 15–17; see also D&C 45:63–70).

THE SAINTS ARE COMMANDED TO FLEE BABYLON
Doctrine and Covenants 133:1–7, 12–15

1 Hearken, O ye people of my church, saith the Lord your God, and hear the word of the Lord concerning you—

2 The Lord who shall suddenly come to his temple; the Lord who shall come down upon the world with a curse to judgment; yea, upon all the nations that forget God, and upon all the ungodly among you.

3 For he shall make bare his holy arm in the eyes of all nations, and all the ends of the earth shall see the salvation of their God.

4 Wherefore, prepare ye, prepare ye, O my people; sanctify yourselves; gather ye together, O ye people of my church, upon the land of Zion, all you that have not been commanded to tarry.

5 Go ye out from Babylon. Be ye clean that bear the vessels of the Lord.

6 Call your solemn assemblies, and speak often one to another. And let every man call upon the name of the Lord.

7 Yea, verily I say unto you again, the time has come when the voice of the Lord is unto you: Go ye out of Babylon; gather ye out from among the nations, from the four winds, from one end of heaven to the other. . . .

12 Let them, therefore, who are among the Gentiles flee unto Zion.

13 And let them who be of Judah flee unto Jerusalem, unto the mountains of the Lord's house.

14 Go ye out from among the nations, even from Babylon, from the midst of wickedness, which is spiritual Babylon.

15 But verily, thus saith the Lord, let not your flight be in haste, but let all things be prepared before you; and he that goeth, let him not look back lest sudden destruction shall come upon him.[10]

Because the Lord is coming, the revelation says, members of the Church are to leave Babylon and go to Zion. Nonmembers as well are invited to do the same, as are the Jews. But they are warned, "Do not leave so hastily that you leave unprepared, but do not hesitate, and once you begin, do not look back."

The call to flee from Babylon comes from ancient prophets as well. Isaiah said, "Go ye forth of Babylon" (Isa. 48:20), speaking both literally and symbolically. Jeremiah echoed the command: "Flee out of the midst of Babylon, and deliver every man his soul: be not cut off in her iniquity; for this is the time of the Lord's vengeance; he will render unto her a recompence. My people, go ye out of the midst of her, and deliver ye every man his soul from the fierce anger of the Lord" (Jer. 51:6, 45). John said, "Love not the world, neither the things that are in the world. If any man love the world, the love of the Father is not in him. For all that is in the world, the lust of the flesh, and the lust of the eyes, and the pride of life, is not of the Father, but is of the world. And the world passeth away, and the lust thereof: but he that doeth the will of God abideth for ever" (1 Jn. 2:15–17).

The Lord will bless us greatly in our flight from Babylon. As he did for Moses and the children of Israel as they fled the bondage of Egypt (Num. 20:7–11; Deut. 8:15; Ps. 78:15–20; 2 Ne. 25:20), so will he do for us as we flee the bondage of Babylon: "And they thirsted not when he led them through the deserts: he caused the waters to flow out of the rock for them: he clave the rock also, and the waters gushed out" (Isa. 48:21). Thus will he lead us through spiritual deserts and

---

[10] Parts of this passage are also discussed in relation to fleeing Babylon as part of the gathering of Israel, page 93.

give us living waters to drink (Isa. 41:18; 43:19; 44:3). The rock symbolizes Christ, the source of our living water (see also Isa. 51:1; John 4:10–11; 7:38).

We must leave Babylon, meaning the world of sin, with her philosophies, attitudes, desires, iniquities, and associations, for three reasons: so that we can become clean of her influence, so that we can build a Zion of holiness, and so that we will not be destroyed when she is destroyed. Said the Lord to Joseph Smith: "After today cometh the burning—this is speaking after the manner of the Lord—for verily I say, tomorrow all the proud and they that do wickedly shall be as stubble; and I will burn them up, for I am the Lord of Hosts; and I will not spare any that remain in Babylon" (D&C 64:24). To those who choose not to go, the Lord gives this warning through Isaiah: "There is no peace, saith the Lord, unto the wicked" (Isa. 48:22; see also Isa. 57:21; 1 Ne. 20:22; Alma 41:10).

NOTES AND COMMENTARY

D&C 133:1 *Hearken, O ye people of my church.* Even though Church members have made covenants to follow the Lord and have ostensibly left the world behind, many have not done so. Here the Lord invites them to listen to his plea to leave Babylon once and for all.

D&C 133:2 *The Lord shall come to his temple/come down upon the world.* See the commentary on the second coming of Christ, page 381.

D&C 133:3 *he shall make bare his holy arm.* In ancient times, men prepared for battle by throwing their cloak away from the shoulder of their fighting arm (Ps. 74:11). At the second coming of Christ, God will "make bare" his arm when he shows forth his power for all to see (D&C 133:2–3). This phrase and the remainder of the verse is a quotation from Isaiah 52:10.

eyes of all the nations. All the world will know of the deliverance of God (D&C 40:5).

ends of the earth shall see the salvation of their God. Every part of the earth will see and know the power of the Lord; all will see how he delivers those who turn to him. Joseph Smith promised the suffering Saints: "The days of tribulation are fast approaching, and the time to test the fidelity of the Saints has come. . . . [But] in these times of sore trial, let the Saints be patient and see the salvation of God. Those who cannot endure persecution, and stand in the day of affliction, cannot stand in the day when the Son of God shall burst the veil, and appear in all the glory of His Father, with all the holy angels."[11]

D&C 133:4 *prepare ye, prepare ye.* How do we prepare for the great and dreadful day of the Lord, when he shall return in power and great glory? We prepare, first, by listening to the prophets and to the voice of the Lord as he speaks directly to us to give us guidance in all aspects of our lives; and second, by obeying with all our hearts that which we are told to do. If we listen and obey in this manner, we will be fully prepared for his coming.

sanctify yourselves. Noah Webster's *An American Dictionary of the English Language* (1828) gives this definition of *sanctify* that fits with the command to flee Babylon: "To cleanse from corruption; to purify from sin; to make holy by detaching the affections from the world and its defilements, and exalting them to a supreme love of God."

gather ye together. The Saints gain strength against temptation (the inner enemy) and against attacks (the outer enemy) by gathering and forming a righteous union, even Zion.[12]

D&C 133:5 *Be ye clean that bear the vessels of the Lord.* Here the Lord is referring to the sacred *vessels* of the temple (Ezra 1:7–11), which could be borne only by those who held the priesthood. Thus the Lord here is commanding priesthood holders to be clean (D&C 38:41–42; 133:5). The sacred vessels directly contrast with "that which is unclean" (Isa. 52:11).

D&C 133:6 *Call your solemn assemblies.* Solemn assemblies are sacred meetings held to sustain a Church president, to dedicate a temple, or to give special instructions.

speak often one to another . . . call upon the name of the Lord. Only by strengthening one another and by relying on the Lord will we be able to escape Babylon and come to Zion.

---

[11] *Teachings of the Prophet Joseph Smith,* 42.
[12] See the commentary on the gathering of Israel, page 48.

D&C 133:12 *Gentiles flee unto Zion.* See the commentary on the gathering of the Gentiles, page 48.

D&C 133:13 *the mountains of the Lord's house.* This term refers to the temple of God (Isa. 2:2; 56:7; Ex. 15:17), one of the principal features of Zion.

D&C 133:14 *the midst of wickedness, which is spiritual Babylon.* The Lord makes very plain what he is talking about here, lest we make any mistake about it. He is speaking not only of cities and nations of sin but also of the sinful state that can be found anywhere, of wickedness without and within, a corruption of the spirit. Not only must we leave places where sin predominates but we must leave behind an inner state of sin in a "flight" to righteousness.

D&C 133:15 *let not your flight be in haste.* When Israel left Egypt, she did so in *haste* and in *flight* (Ex. 12:39; Deut. 16:3). When her people now go forth in the gathering to Zion, leaving Babylon, they are to do so with neither haste nor flight but with calm and confidence, knowing that the Lord is with them (Isa. 52:12).

let him not look back. One potential disciple said to Jesus, "Lord, I will follow thee; but let me first go bid them farewell, which are at home at my house. And Jesus said unto him, No man, having put his hand to the plough, and looking back, is fit for the kingdom of God" (Luke 9:61–62). If we look back, longing for the comforts of Babylon or thinking we will partake just one more time, we are not fit disciples, and we are at risk of "sudden destruction."

BABYLON SHALL FALL
Revelation 18:1–24

> *1 And after these things I saw another angel come down from heaven, having great power; and the earth was lightened with his glory.*
>
> *2 And he cried mightily with a strong voice, saying, Babylon the great is fallen, is fallen, and is become the habitation of devils, and the hold of every foul spirit, and a cage of every unclean and hateful bird.*
>
> *3 For all nations have drunk of the wine of the wrath of her fornication, and the kings of the earth have committed*

fornication with her, and the merchants of the earth are waxed rich through the abundance of her delicacies.

4 And I heard another voice from heaven, saying, Come out of her, my people, that ye be not partakers of her sins, and that ye receive not of her plagues.

5 For her sins have reached unto heaven, and God hath remembered her iniquities.

6 Reward her even as she rewarded you, and double unto her double according to her works: in the cup which she hath filled fill to her double.

7 How much she hath glorified herself, and lived deliciously, so much torment and sorrow give her: for she saith in her heart, I sit a queen, and am no widow, and shall see no sorrow.

8 Therefore shall her plagues come in one day, death, and mourning, and famine; and she shall be utterly burned with fire: for strong is the Lord God who judgeth her.

9 And the kings of the earth, who have committed fornication and lived deliciously with her, shall bewail her, and lament for her, when they shall see the smoke of her burning,

10 Standing afar off for the fear of her torment, saying, Alas, alas, that great city Babylon, that mighty city! for in one hour is thy judgment come.

11 And the merchants of the earth shall weep and mourn over her; for no man buyeth their merchandise any more;

12 The merchandise of gold, and silver, and precious stones, and of pearls, and fine linen, and purple, and silk, and scarlet, and all thyine wood, and all manner vessels of ivory, and all manner vessels of most precious wood, and of brass, and iron, and marble,

13 And cinnamon, and odours, and ointments, and frankincense, and wine, and oil, and fine flour, and wheat, and beasts, and sheep, and horses, and chariots, and slaves, and souls of men.

14 And the fruits that thy soul lusted after are departed from thee, and all things which were dainty and goodly are departed from thee, and thou shalt find them no more at all.

15 The merchants of these things, which were made rich by her, shall stand afar off for the fear of her torment, weeping and wailing,

16 And saying, Alas, alas, that great city, that was clothed in fine linen, and purple, and scarlet, and decked with gold, and precious stones, and pearls!

17 For in one hour so great riches is come to nought. And every shipmaster, and all the company in ships, and sailors, and as many as trade by sea, stood afar off,

18 And cried when they saw the smoke of her burning, saying, What city is like unto this great city!

19 And they cast dust on their heads, and cried, weeping and wailing, saying, Alas, alas, that great city, wherein were made rich all that had ships in the sea by reason of her costliness! for in one hour is she made desolate.

20 Rejoice over her, thou heaven, and ye holy apostles and prophets; for God hath avenged you on her.

21 And a mighty angel took up a stone like a great millstone, and cast it into the sea, saying, Thus with violence shall that great city Babylon be thrown down, and shall be found no more at all.

22 And the voice of harpers, and musicians, and of pipers, and trumpeters, shall be heard no more at all in thee; and no craftsman, of whatsoever craft he be, shall be found any more in thee; and the sound of a millstone shall be heard no more at all in thee;

23 And the light of a candle shall shine no more at all in thee; and the voice of the bridegroom and of the bride shall be heard no more at all in thee: for thy merchants were the great men of the earth; for by thy sorceries were all nations deceived.

24 And in her was found the blood of prophets, and of saints, and of all that were slain upon the earth.

The Babylonian captivity is perhaps the lowest point of Israel's history. Elder Bruce R. McConkie wrote: "Both Isaiah and Jeremiah spoke at length of the devastations of that day and of the cursings and destruction that would come upon Babylon as a result. (Isa. 13 and 21; Jer. 50 and 51.) Babylon was truly the great enemy of the Lord's people anciently, and her overthrow and the destruction of her worldliness and wickedness was one of the things of greatest interest and concern to them. What was more natural, then, than for John and all the prophets to use Babylon as the symbol of sin, and her destruction as the overthrow of wickedness on earth."[13]

The fall of Babylon was foreseen by John in Revelation 14:8: "And there followed another angel, saying, Babylon is fallen, is fallen, that great city, because she made all nations drink of the wine of the wrath of her fornication." That destruction is not actually described until Revelation 18, which is an extended lament, or a funeral dirge, over the loss of the great city of Babylon.

Babylon was convinced that in her strength she would never fall: "I sit a queen," she said, "and shall see no sorrow." But she will fall indeed and become a "habitation of devils." Her destruction shall be complete: "She shall be utterly burned with fire," the prophecy says. Because the world has given herself over to Babylon's enticements, the world will lament her demise. Joining in the lament are earth's kings, merchants, and shippers.[14] But the righteous will have cause to rejoice over her downfall (Isa. 14:7–8; Rev. 19:1–5).

Latter-day revelation tells us: "And the great and abominable church, which is the whore of all the earth, shall be cast down by devouring fire, according as it is spoken by the mouth of Ezekiel the prophet, who spoke of these things, which have not come to pass but surely must, as I live, for abominations shall not reign" (D&C 29:21; see also Ezek. 39:6). "For the time speedily shall come that all

---

[13] *Doctrinal New Testament Commentary,* 3:559.
[14] A paradox in this account is that the kings, merchants, and shippers lament the destruction of Babylon; but in reality, when Babylon is destroyed, all those who aligned themselves with her will also be destroyed: none of her adherents will remain to lament her loss.

churches which are built up to get gain, and all those who are built up to get power over the flesh, and those who are built up to become popular in the eyes of the world, and those who seek the lusts of the flesh and the things of the world, and to do all manner of iniquity; yea, in fine, all those who belong to the kingdom of the devil are they who need fear, and tremble, and quake; they are those who must be brought low in the dust; they are those who must be consumed as stubble; and this is according to the words of the prophet" (1 Ne. 22:23).

Elder Orson Pratt added his testimony: "John predicts another great event to take place immediately after the proclamation of the everlasting gospel, namely, the downfall of great Babylon. . . . [S]he must fall, after she has been warned with the sound of 'the everlasting gospel.' Her overthrow will be by a series of the most terrible judgments which will quickly succeed each other, and sweep over the nations where she has her dominion, and at last she will be utterly burned by fire, for thus hath the Lord spoken. Great, and fearful, and most terrible judgments are decreed upon these corrupt powers—the nations of modern Christendom; for strong is the Lord God who shall execute his fierce wrath upon them, and he will not cease until he has made a full end, and until their names be blotted out from under heaven."[15]

The fall of Babylon is also called the end of the world. It is the time when the world as we know it will be overthrown, utterly destroyed, along with its philosophies, false belief systems, governments of man, sinfulness, and everything else that is not of God. And when those things are destroyed, the people who clung to them will be destroyed as well (D&C 64:24). The fall of Babylon will be complete the moment the Lord comes in his glory. At the same moment, Satan will be deposed from his high position and cast down into the bottomless pit (Isa. 14:4–23; Rev. 20:1–3).

The prophet Jeremiah left a detailed record of his vision of the fall of Babylon the great. The vision emphasized five things:

1. The fall of Babylon comes as God stretches out his arm in wrath and judgment against Babylon's wickedness:

---

[15] *Divine Authenticity of the Book of Mormon*, no. 6, 84–85.

"I will punish the king of Babylon and his land" (Jer. 50:18).

"The Lord hath . . . brought forth the weapons of his indignation: for this is the work of the Lord of hosts" (Jer. 50:25).

"Recompense her according to her work" (Jer. 50:29).

"I will raise up against Babylon" (Jer. 51:1).

"His device is against Babylon, to destroy it; because it is the vengeance of the Lord" (Jer. 51:11).

"Behold, I am against thee, . . . and I will stretch out mine hand upon thee, and roll thee down from the rocks" (Jer. 51:25).

"The daughter of Babylon is like a threshingfloor, it is time to thresh her" (Jer. 51:33).

"The Lord hath spoiled Babylon" (Jer. 51:55).

2. Those in Babylon will experience intense fear and mourning as they see God's judgments coming forth:

"The land shall tremble and sorrow" (Jer. 51:29).

"The mighty men of Babylon . . . became as women. . . . The men of war are affrighted" (Jer. 51:30, 32).

3. Babylon will fall amidst much slaughter and bloodshed:

"All her men of war shall be cut off" (Jer. 50:30).

"Spare ye not her young men; destroy ye utterly all her host. Thus the slain shall fall in the land . . . , and they that are thrust through in her streets" (Jer. 51:4).

"With thee [Israel] also will I break in pieces man and woman; and with thee will I break in pieces old and young; and with thee will I break in pieces the young man and the maid; I will also break in pieces with thee the shepherd and his flock; and with thee will I break in pieces the husbandman and his yoke of oxen; and with thee will I break in pieces captains and rulers" (Jer. 51:22–23).

"I will bring them down like lambs to the slaughter" (Jer. 51:40).

"Through all her land the wounded shall groan" (Jer. 51:52).

4. Babylon's destruction will be total, resulting in complete desolation:

"The nation shall be a wilderness, a dry land, and a desert" (Jer. 50:12).

"Her foundations are fallen, her walls are thrown down" (Jer. 50:15).

"Waste and utterly destroy after them" (Jer. 50:21).

"A sound of battle is in the land, and of great destruction" (Jer. 50:22).

"Cast her up as heaps, and destroy her utterly: let nothing of her be left" (Jer. 50:26).

"Let none thereof escape" (Jer. 50:29).

"I will kindle a fire in his cities, and it shall devour all round about him" (Jer. 50:32).

"A sword is upon the Chaldeans,[16] saith the Lord, and upon the inhabitants of Babylon, and upon her princes, and upon her wise men. A sword is upon the liars; and they shall dote: a sword is upon her mighty men; and they shall be dismayed. A sword is upon their horses, and upon their chariots, and upon all the mingled people that are in the midst of her; and they shall become as women: a sword is upon her treasures; and they shall be robbed" (Jer. 50:35–37).

"He shall make their habitation desolate with them" (Jer. 50:45).

"Empty her land" (Jer. 51:2).

"Make the land of Babylon a desolation without an inhabitant" (Jer. 51:29).

"As Babylon hath caused the slain of Israel to fall, so at Babylon shall fall the slain of all the earth" (Jer. 51:49).

5. Babylon will remain desolate throughout all generations:

"Make her land desolate, and none shall dwell therein" (Jer. 50:3).

"It shall not be inhabited, but it shall be wholly desolate" (Jer. 50:13).

"The wild beasts of the desert . . . shall dwell there, and the owls shall dwell therein: and it shall be no more inhabited forever; never shall it be dwelt in from generation to generation. As God overthrew Sodom and Gomorrah and the neighbour cities thereof, saith the Lord; so shall no man abide there, neither shall any son of man dwell therein" (Jer. 50:39–40).

"Thou shalt be desolate forever, saith the Lord" (Jer. 51:26).

"Babylon shall become heaps, . . . without an inhabitant" (Jer. 51:37).

---

[16] Chaldea was a district, or province, in Babylon.

"Her cities are a desolation, a dry land, and a wilderness, a land wherein no man dwelleth, neither doth any son of man pass thereby" (Jer. 51:43).

"O, Lord, thou hast spoken against this place, to cut it off, that none shall remain in it, neither man nor beast, but that it shall be desolate forever" (Jer. 51:62).

Jeremiah's descriptions seem to have a threefold application: First, they apply to the fall of Babylon anciently. Second, they apply to the destruction of the physical world of sin at the last days, of which the fall of ancient Babylon is a type and symbol. Third, they apply to the destruction of the spiritual world of wickedness at the last day, of which the fall of ancient Babylon is also a symbol.[17]

As Babylon falls, the Saints can take heart that they will be in the hands of the Lord. If they live, they shall live in the Lord; and if they die, they will die in the Lord. "Blessed are the dead which die in the Lord from henceforth: Yea, saith the Spirit, that they may rest from their labours; and their works do follow them" (Rev. 14:13).

NOTES AND COMMENTARY

Rev. 18:1 *the earth was lightened with his glory.* This angel is so brilliant that the very earth is illuminated by his presence. In fact, this angel's glory is like that of Christ, who will yet return: "And, behold, the glory of the God of Israel came from the way of the east: and his voice was like a noise of many waters: and the earth shined with his glory" (Ezek. 43:2). "For as the light[e]ning [of the sun] cometh out of the east, and shineth even unto the west; so shall also the coming of the Son of man be" (Matt. 24:27).

Rev. 18:2 *Babylon the great is fallen, is fallen.* The angel's words are almost a direct quotation from a passage in Isaiah: "Babylon is fallen, is fallen; and all the graven images of her gods he hath broken unto the ground" (Isa. 21:9; Jer. 51:8). This same expression is found in latter-day scripture: "And again, another angel shall sound his trump, which is the sixth angel, saying: She is fallen who made all

---

[17] On the fall of Babylon, see Isa. 13; 14; 34; 47; Rev. 14:15–20; see also the commentary on Armageddon, page 264.

nations drink of the wine of the wrath of her fornication; she is fallen, is fallen!" (D&C 88:105).

the habitation of devils/foul spirit/hateful bird. Where once Babylon boasted of being the great and powerful city that controlled kings (Rev. 17:18) and was the site of opulence and wealth (Rev. 17:4), it now is not fit for human habitation. Rather than being a city or kingdom with a place of prominence and power in the world, it now is the home for devils, foul spirits, and unclean birds.

Old Testament prophets saw the fallen city of Babylon as a wasteland, good only for foul and unclean creatures: "From generation to generation it shall lie waste; none shall pass through it for ever and ever. But the cormorant and the bittern shall possess it; the owl also and the raven shall dwell in it: and he shall stretch out upon it the line of confusion, and the stones of emptiness. They shall call the nobles thereof to the kingdom, but none shall be there, and all her princes shall be nothing. And thorns shall come up in her palaces, nettles and brambles in the fortresses thereof: and it shall be an habitation of dragons, and a court for owls. The wild beasts of the desert shall also meet with the wild beasts of the island, and the satyr shall cry to his fellow; the screech owl also shall rest there, and find for herself a place of rest. There shall the great owl make her nest, and lay, and hatch, and gather under her shadow: there shall the vultures also be gathered, every one with her mate" (Isa. 34:10–16; see also Isa. 13:19–22; Jer. 50:35–36, 40; Zeph. 2:13–15).

This symbolic description emphasizes that the mighty Babylon will be brought to the lowest possible point. As it was with the ancient city of Babylon, so shall it be with the spiritual Babylon that spreads itself across the world in our time.

Rev. 18:3 *For all nations have drunk of the wine of the wrath of her fornication.* The expression *wine of the wrath of her fornication* combines two phrases that are found elsewhere in Revelation: "the wine of the wrath of God" (Rev. 14:10) and "the wine of her fornication" (Rev. 17:2). *Fornication* here refers to the evil practice of spiritual adultery—leaving the true Bridegroom and going after other gods—as both the world and the Lord's people too often do (Rev. 2:20). *Fornication* may also refer to sexual immorality, which often accompanies gross wickedness on the earth. The underlying meaning is that Babylon (the wicked element of the world) has enticed the nations to become intoxicated with sin and that both Babylon and the nations of the world will be punished by God in his wrath. In bringing others to this fornication, Babylon is nothing less than a harlot (Rev. 17:1–6).

Drunkenness here is a symbol of apostasy, in which the people lose the power of good judgment because of their unwise choices. "They are drunken, but not with wine," Isaiah prophesied, "they stagger, but not with strong drink" (Isa. 29:9; see Jer. 51:6–9). The wine that makes them drunk is not the fornication of sexuality but that of unfaithfulness to God.

the merchants of the earth are waxed rich through the abundance of her delicacies. The world's merchants have partaken of the wealth and luxury of Babylon, and they thereby have become part of her. This verse points out the worldwide power of Babylon (the wicked world, the church of the devil), as well as her involvement and influence in economic affairs.

Rev. 18:4 *Come out of her, my people.* This is the recurring cry of the prophets: Leave the world and its wickedness, and bind yourself to God (Isa. 52:11; Jer. 51:6; D&C 133:7, 14). This counsel has particular application to the Saints in our day. There is much in our world that partakes of the pride, the lust, the materialism, and the sins of Babylon. There is much that seeks to replace God in our hearts—the endless quest for wealth, the near-worship of sports and entertainment "stars," the deep desire of most people to seek and reach their own goals rather than God's. Babylon is alive and well in our times; nevertheless, as prophesied, Babylon will fall.

that ye be not partakers of her sins. The Saints are called to leave Babylon so that they can be fortified against the temptation to partake of her sins. What are those sins? Certainly the people of Babylon are guilty of all the typical sins of mankind at their worst: murder, adultery, abortion, theft, pornography, lying, and on and on. But in addition, as Revelation records, Babylon is also guilty of persecuting and killing the Saints (Rev. 17:6), leading the nations of the world into idolatry and gross wickedness (Rev. 17:2–4), and fostering all manner of abominations (Rev. 17:5).

that ye receive not of her plagues. By leaving Babylon and refusing to partake of her sins, the righteous are also protected from her plagues, enumerated in Revelation 8, 9, and 16.

Rev. 18:5 *For her sins have reached unto heaven/God hath remembered her iniquities.* God is fully aware of the grossness and the extent of the sins of Babylon: not one escapes his notice. Even if he does not act immediately to judge and to punish in a given instance, he will remember until the time of retribution.

Rev. 18:6 *Reward her even as she rewarded you.* Babylon will receive according to the law of the harvest: that which she has sown, so shall she reap. As she has given out, so shall it come back to her in punishment (Job 4:8; D&C 6:33). "Wherefore, fear and tremble, O ye people, for what I the Lord have decreed . . . shall be fulfilled. And verily I say unto you, that they who go forth, bearing these tidings unto the inhabitants of the earth, to them is power given to seal both on earth and in heaven, the unbelieving and rebellious; yea, verily, to seal them up unto the day when the wrath of God shall be poured out upon the wicked without measure—unto the day when the Lord shall come to recompense unto every man according to his work, and measure to every man according to the measure which he has measured to his fellow man" (D&C 1:7–10; see also Jer. 50:15, 29).

double unto her double according to her works. Babylon will receive not only a full portion of punishment for her iniquities but a double portion. Under the law of Moses, a thief was to pay double for that which he had taken (Ex. 22:4, 7). A double punishment is a common consequence in the scriptures (Isa. 40:2; Jer. 16:18).

the cup which she hath filled. Babylon has filled a cup of iniquity and caused the nations of the world to drink of it (Rev. 14:8). That same cup will now be filled with the wrath of God for Babylon to drink in double portions.

Rev. 18:7 *How much she hath glorified herself/lived deliciously.* Babylon, which is the wicked world, has exalted herself and lived in great pride and luxury. *Deliciously* can also be rendered *wantonly* or *riotously.*[18]

so much torment and sorrow give her. The Lord says that as Babylon has exalted herself in pride and given herself to riotous living, to that same degree Babylon will suffer torment and sorrow. This punishment will come immediately before the second coming of Christ.

I sit a queen, and am no widow. Babylon gives herself so thoroughly to pride and sin that she sees herself as invincible. She rules over the people of the world, a great queen over many kings. She fears nothing, not even death. This arrogant claim repeats a prophecy found in Isaiah: "And thou saidst, I shall be a lady for ever: so that thou didst not lay these things to thy heart, neither didst remember the latter end of it. Therefore hear now this, thou that art given to pleasures, that dwellest carelessly, that sayest in thine heart, I am, and none else beside me; I shall not sit as a widow, neither shall I know the loss of children" (Isa. 47:7–8). The prophecy in Isaiah continues, foreseeing that which John also saw next: "But these two things shall come to thee in a moment in one day, the loss of children, and widowhood: they shall come upon thee in their perfection for the multitude of thy sorceries, and for the great abundance of thine enchantments. For thou hast trusted in thy wickedness: thou hast said, None seeth me. Thy wisdom and thy knowledge, it hath perverted thee; and thou hast said in thine heart, I am, and none else beside me. Therefore . . . desolation shall come upon thee suddenly, which thou shalt not know" (Isa. 47:9–11).

Rev. 18:8 *Therefore shall her plagues come in one day, death, and mourning, and famine.* Some translations replace the word *death* with *disease* or *pestilence.*[19] *In one day* indicates that these things will come suddenly on the wicked.

In Deuteronomy Moses prophesied the horror of plagues and calamities to come upon the wicked: "The Lord shall send upon thee cursing, vexation, and rebuke, in all that thou settest thine hand unto for to do, until thou be destroyed, and until thou perish quickly;

---

[18] See note *a* to Rev. 18:7 in the LDS edition of the KJV.
[19] See RSV, GNB, JB, and NEB.

because of the wickedness of thy doings, whereby thou hast forsaken me. Then the Lord will make thy plagues wonderful, and the plagues of thy seed, even great plagues, and of long continuance, and sore sicknesses, and of long continuance. Moreover he will bring upon thee all the diseases of Egypt, which thou wast afraid of; and they shall cleave unto thee. Also every sickness, and every plague, which is not written in the book of this law, them will the Lord bring upon thee, until thou be destroyed" (Deut. 28:20, 59–61; see also 2 Ne. 6:15; 10:6).

she shall be utterly burned with fire: for strong is the Lord God who judgeth her. After the plagues comes the burning. When the Lord returns, the wicked will be destroyed by burning, and the earth itself will be cleansed by fire. "For after today cometh the burning—this is speaking after the manner of the Lord—for verily I say, tomorrow all the proud and they that do wickedly shall be as stubble; and I will burn them up, for I am the Lord of Hosts; and I will not spare any that remain in Babylon" (D&C 64:24; 3 Ne. 26:3). Certainly a God who has power to bring such a judgment is a strong and powerful God.

This scene is also depicted in latter-day scripture: "And another angel shall sound his trump, saying: That great church, the mother of abominations, that made all nations drink of the wine of the wrath of her fornication, that persecuteth the saints of God, that shed their blood—she who sitteth upon many waters, and upon the islands of the sea—behold, she is the tares of the earth; she is bound in bundles; her bands are made strong, no man can loose them; therefore, she is ready to be burned" (D&C 88:94).

Rev. 18:9 *the kings of the earth, who have committed fornication and lived deliciously with her.* The kings represent the people of the earth, who also have joined in the "fornication."[20] The kings and the people have joined together in celebrating the idolatry, immorality, and lust of the world. They have "lived deliciously" in luxury, excess, and wantonness, loving the pleasures of the world more than the treasures of God.

bewail her, and lament for her, when they shall see the smoke of her burning. When the kings of the earth see the utter destruction of

---

[20] See the commentary on spiritual fornication, page 308.

Babylon, meaning the lifestyle of lust and wealth to which they have given themselves, they will weep and mourn for her loss (Jer. 51:8).

Rev. 18:10 *Standing afar off for the fear of her torment.* Though they regret her loss, kings try to separate themselves from Babylon for fear that they will share in her fate.

Alas, alas, that great city Babylon, that mighty city! The cry of lament for the destruction of wicked Babylon is repeated three times in this chapter: once by the kings, once by the merchants, and once by the sea traders. "The city is Babylon; she is the similitude. The city is Rome; but she too is only a type and a figure. The city is all the cities of the world—San Francisco, Chicago, and New York City; London, Paris, and Berlin; Moscow, Tokyo, and São Paulo—all of which are subject to the rule and dominion of evil and carnality."[21]

for in one hour is thy judgment come. This expression suggests that the punishments and disasters that will overtake Babylon (symbolizing the wicked world) will come suddenly. Variations of this expression are repeated in Revelation 18:17, 19.

Rev. 18:11–13 *And the merchants of the earth shall weep and mourn over her.* The merchants, symbolizing all those who seek to increase their wealth by association and dealings with a godless culture, will mourn for the loss of that culture, that society, that way of life. Their mourning will be particularly poignant because of their personal loss: they will likely grieve for themselves more than for Babylon.

The long list of items bought and sold in Babylon is impressive, showing the broad variety that is available there. Most of the items listed fall into the category of luxuries. In Babylon, it is not enough to wear simple clothing: one must wear "fine linen, and purple, and silk, and scarlet." It is not enough to eat bread: one must have "wine, and oil, and fine flour."

Ezekiel received a vision similar to that depicted in this chapter: "The word of the Lord came again unto me, saying, Now, thou son of man, . . . say unto Tyrus, . . . [Many merchants] traded in thy fairs . . . with horses and horsemen and mules . . . ivory and ebony . . . emeralds, purple, and broidered work, and fine linen, and coral, and agate

---

[21] McConkie, *Millennial Messiah,* 445.

. . . and honey, and oil, and balm . . . [and] wine . . . and white wool . . . lambs, and rams, and goats . . . [and] all spices, and with all precious stones, and gold . . . [and] blue clothes, and broidered work, and in chests of rich apparel. . . . [T]hy merchandise, thy mariners, . . . and all thy men of war, that are in thee . . . shall fall into the midst of the seas in the day of thy ruin. . . . [They] shall come down from their ships, they shall stand upon the land; and shall cause their voice to be heard against thee, and shall cry bitterly, and shall cast up dust upon their heads, they shall wallow themselves in the ashes. . . . And in their wailing they shall take up a lamentation for thee, and lament over thee, saying, What city is like Tyrus, like the destroyed in the midst of the sea? . . . The merchants among the people shall hiss at thee; thou shalt be a terror, and never shalt be any more" (Ezek. 27:1–3, 12–24, 27, 29–32, 36).

Rev. 18:13 *slaves, and souls of men.* This passage represents the worst of the merchandising that takes place in Babylon: the merchants are trading in the souls and bodies of human beings. Throughout history, millions upon millions of men, women, and children have been kidnapped from their homes, during war or otherwise, and taken to distant places where they have been forced to labor for another.[22] In return for their labors, which were often excessive and accompanied by force and violence, the slave received, at best, only food, some clothing, shelter, and the opportunity to continue to live. Certainly such traffic in human beings is reprehensible to God.

Another form of trading and merchandising that occurs in Babylon is in what John calls the "souls of men." This expression may refer to false religions that buy and sell men's souls, as Moroni recorded: "There shall be churches built up that shall say: Come unto me, and for your money you shall be forgiven of your sins" (Morm. 8:32). Or John's vision may refer to what Hugh Nibley called the "Mahan Principle." Here is Nibley's description of how Babylon trades in the souls of men: "The story begins . . . with Satan seeking to promote himself even in the premortal existence, and being cast out of heaven in his pride, and dedicating himself upon his fall to the

---

[22] "It is estimated that there were as many as 60,000,000 slaves in the Roman Empire [alone]" (Mounce, *Book of Revelation,* 334).

destruction of this earth, 'for he knew not the mind of God' (Moses 4:6). [On earth] he . . . will control the world economy by claiming possession of the earth's resources; and by manipulation of its currency—gold and silver—he will buy up the political, military, and ecclesiastical complex and run . . . . . . He not only offers employment but a course of . . . the whole thing works, teaching the ultimate . . . et' (Moses 5:49–50) of converting life into . . . degree of Master Mahan, tried the system ou . . . ied in its brilliant success, declaring that at last he could be free, as only property makes free, and that Abel had been a loser in a free competition.

"The discipline was handed down through Lamech and finally became the pattern of the world's economy (Moses 5:55–56). . . . One may see Mahan at work all around, from the Mafia, whose adherence to the principle needs no argument, down to the drug pusher, the arms dealer, the manufacturer and seller of defective products, or those who poison the air and water as a shortcut to gain and thus shorten and sicken the lives of all their fellow creatures."[23]

Rev. 18:14 *the fruits that thy soul lusted after/all things . . . dainty and goodly . . . thou shalt find them no more at all.* The sweet and exotic foods that the world has enjoyed will be destroyed with Babylon itself. These foods may symbolize the excesses and extravagances of the world.

Rev. 18:15 *The merchants of these things . . . stand afar off . . . weeping and wailing.* Greed and luxury are powerful motivators. Those who have become rich by trafficking in the things of the world feel great grief at the loss of their source of wealth, but even in their mourning they remove themselves from Babylon at the end, standing "afar off" for fear of partaking of her torment.

Rev. 18:16 *Alas, alas, that great city.* The cry of the merchants, the sea traders, and the kings in mourning the loss of Babylon is one of self-interest: they feel deeply the loss of her wealth, symbolized by the linen, the royal clothing made of purple and scarlet, and the precious metals and gems.

---

[23] Nibley, *Approaching Zion,* 165–67.

Rev. 18:17 *For in one hour so great riches is come to nought/as many as trade by sea, stood afar off.* See the commentary on Revelation 18:10, page 313.

Rev. 18:18 *What city is like unto this great city!* When the sea traders see the destruction of Babylon, they are amazed. Babylon was so powerful and so rich—how could it be destroyed? In the same way, those who embrace the philosophies and lifestyle of a world without the true God, which world seems uniquely powerful and important, will be amazed at its destruction.

Rev. 18:19 *And they cast dust on their heads.* In Middle Eastern culture, this gesture is traditionally a sign of humiliation and deep mourning (Ezek. 27:30).

Rev. 18:20 *Rejoice over her, thou heaven/holy apostles and prophets.* While the wicked kings, merchants, and sea traders mourn the loss of Babylon, heaven and the righteous have cause to rejoice. Their great nemesis, the unholy antagonist of all that is good and right, has been destroyed.

God hath avenged you on her. Babylon orchestrated war against the righteous and has become "drunken with the blood of the saints" (Rev. 17:6). But God will come down in vengeance and bring judgments upon her according to all her wickedness. This vengeance fulfills a promise made in Revelation 6:9–11.

Rev. 18:21 *a mighty angel took up a stone like a great millstone, and cast it into the sea.* Of those who abuse or offend the Lord's "little ones," the Lord said, "It were better for him that a millstone were hanged about his neck, and that he were drowned in the depth of the sea" (Matt. 18:6). This is the very fate destined for Babylon, the wicked culture, philosophy, governments, religion, and lifestyle of the world. As an object lesson, "a mighty angel" will lift up a huge stone and throw it into the sea, illustrating how "with violence shall that great city Babylon be thrown down, and shall be found no more at all." This passage may also depict some otherwise undefined natural disaster.

The destruction of Babylon was foreseen by Jeremiah (Jer. 51:37), Nephi (1 Ne. 14:15–16; 22:14), and Joseph Smith (D&C

1:16), among others. We read in Jeremiah of this impressive prophecy: "So Jeremiah wrote in a book all the evil that should come upon Babylon. . . . And Jeremiah said to Seraiah, When . . . thou hast made an end of reading this book, . . . thou shalt bind a stone to it, and cast it into the midst of Euphrates: And thou shalt say, Thus shall Babylon sink, and shall not rise from the evil that I will bring upon her" (Jer. 51:60–64). Just as a weighty stone has no power to rise again from the depths of the sea, in the same way Babylon will have no power to rise again from the destruction a just God brings upon her.

Rev. 18:22 *harpers/musicians/pipers/trumpeters . . . heard no more at all in thee.* The sounds of people seeking worldly pleasure and entertainment will be lost when Babylon is destroyed (Isa. 24:8; Ezek. 26:13). Contrast that with the promise in Revelation 15:2, which says that those who resist the beast, gaining a personal victory over him, will have "the harps of God," making music of true joy and praise.

no craftsman . . . shall be found any more in thee. Daily labor for pay in the city will cease. The economy of Babylon will be destroyed along with the city.

the sound of a millstone shall be heard no more at all in thee. The grinding of wheat and other such daily tasks will no longer be heard in Babylon, because Babylon will be no more. This prophecy has an ominous undertone: when the millstone ceases to grind, food soon ceases to be available.

Rev. 18:23 *And the light of a candle shall shine no more at all in thee.* The city will be plunged into darkness. It will no longer have any light at all.

the voice of the bridegroom and of the bride shall be heard no more at all in thee. Of an earlier and parallel event the Lord said, "Then will I cause to cease from the cities of Judah, and from the streets of Jerusalem, the voice of mirth, and the voice of gladness, the voice of the bridegroom, and the voice of the bride: for the land shall be desolate" (Jer. 7:34). The loss of such sounds indicates that normal life has stopped, or that all life in that place has ceased to be.

This verse (Rev. 18:23) is also reminiscent of Jeremiah 25:9–12, a description of the long exile of Israel. In that passage, the Lord says he will allow Babylon to conquer his people, but Babylon will be destroyed in the end. During the exile, the Lord says, "I will take from them the voice of mirth, and the voice of gladness, the voice of the bridegroom, and the voice of the bride, the sound of the millstones, and the light of the candle" (Jer. 25:10).

thy merchants were the great men of the earth. Those who traded in and with Babylon were great, rich, and powerful, but they do not have power to save her.

by thy sorceries were all nations deceived. The Lord abhors sorcery, the use of witchcraft and evil powers to deceive others. We read in Revelation 13 of the miracles of the beast, which deceived the people of the earth and caused them to worship the beast rather than God (Rev. 13:12–15). Though the sorceries of Babylon enabled her to deceive the nations and thus to rule the world, those dark, satanic powers are unable to save her in the end: "Stand now with thine enchantments, and with the multitude of thy sorceries, wherein thou hast laboured from thy youth; if so be thou shalt be able to profit, if so be thou mayest prevail. . . . Let now the astrologers, the stargazers, the monthly prognosticators, stand up, and save thee from these things that shall come upon thee. Behold, they shall be as stubble; the fire shall burn them; they shall not deliver themselves from the power of the flame: there shall not be a coal to warm at, nor fire to sit before it" (Isa. 47:12–14).

Rev. 18:24 *in her was found the blood of prophets/saints/all that were slain upon the earth.* Ultimately, Babylon, or the wicked world, is responsible for the martyrdom of all the prophets and Saints who have ever been killed for their faith, as well as all who have been killed by murder and war. This persecution of the righteous is probably Babylon's greatest sin. That these things were "found" in Babylon at the end suggests that all her wickedness will be uncovered.

THE LORD
SENDS SIGNS
AND JUDGMENTS

CHAPTER 8

GOD'S JUDGMENTS UPON SATAN'S FOLLOWERS ON EARTH

SIGNS OF THE TIMES

1. The scriptures provide a guide to the judgments of God.

2. God sends plagues and other judgments to the earth to encourage the wicked to repent.

3. A scourge goes forth upon the earth to encourage the people to repent.

4. God sends his first judgments to Zion's hypocrites.

5. As Zion's inhabitants are faithful, they escape God's judgments.

6. The Lord's servants "seal up the law" after they have warned the world.

7. Those who escape God's judgments are purified.

8. The earth is harvested by angels.

Our God is a God of righteous judgment. He generously grants gifts and blessings to all who will seek them, obeying his laws. In fact, as King Benjamin explained, "If ye should serve him with all your whole souls yet ye would be unprofitable servants" (Mosiah 2:21), because he has given us so much to start with, and if we seek to repay him through praise and service and obedience, he gives us much, much more (Mosiah 2:20–24). On the other hand, those who turn from him, disobeying his word and his will, receive only what they truly deserve in punishment. No one can ever be correct in accusing God of being unfair.

Yet even God's punishments are designed to bless, as they help turn some of the wicked from their sins and as they cleanse the unrepentant from the earth for the sake of the righteous who remain. Elder John Taylor said of God's works in the last days, "Concerning events yet to transpire, we must trust them in the hands of God, and feel that 'whatever is is right,' and that God will control all things for our best good and the interest of his Church and kingdom on the earth. . . . By-and-by, when we come to gaze on the fitness of things that are now obscure to us, we shall find that . . . , although he has moved in a mysterious way to accomplish his purposes on the earth . . . , all things are governed by that wisdom which flows from God, and all things are right and calculated to promote every person's eternal welfare before God."[1] In the last days the Lord's judgments will be plainly manifest to all who have eyes to see. The righteous will receive a rich outpouring of blessings, and the wicked will receive a full portion of punishment according to that which they have earned through their evil deeds.

On 21 September 1823, the angel Moroni revealed himself to Joseph Smith and "informed [him] of great judgments which were coming upon the earth, with great desolations by famine, sword, and pestilence; and that these grievous judgments would come on the earth in this generation" (JS–H 1:45; see also D&C 1:36). Later, Joseph Smith declared that "the scripture is ready to be fulfilled when great wars, famines, pestilence, great distress, judgments, &c., are ready to be poured out on the inhabitants of the earth."[2] On yet another occasion, the Prophet taught that "the coming of the Son of Man never will be—never can be till the judgments spoken of for this hour are poured out: which judgments are commenced."[3]

These judgments will be of many forms, as the prophets have clearly and abundantly testified, and they will include earthquakes, famine, and pestilences (D&C 5:19–20; 29:16–21; 45:26–33). Significantly, Elder M. Russell Ballard spoke of the "ever-increasing regularity" and the "accelerating pattern" of many judgments upon the earth. After citing Matthew 24:5–7, which speaks of "wars and

---

[1] *Journal of Discourses*, 6:114.
[2] *History of the Church*, 6:363–64.
[3] *Teachings of the Prophet Joseph Smith*, 286.

rumours of wars," nations rising against nations, famines, pestilences, and earthquakes, Elder Ballard observed: "Some of these things seem to be occurring with ever-increasing regularity. If you measured the natural disasters that have occurred in the world during the last ten years and plotted that year by year, you would see an acceleration."[4]

There is a pattern set forth in the scriptures that pertains to God's sending judgments upon the ungodly, which pattern is summarized in Ether 11:20: "And in the days of Coriantor there also came many prophets, and prophesied of great and marvelous things, and cried repentance unto the people, and except they should repent the Lord God would execute judgment against them to their utter destruction." This pattern of warning and judgment consists of the following:

prophets come among the people;[5]

the prophets prophesy great things;

they cry repentance;

they warn the wicked that if they do not repent God will send his judgments (such as earthquakes, sword, famine);

many of the unrepentant are destroyed by God's judgments.[6]

This pattern is repeated scores of times in the scriptures. A celebrated example is recorded in Genesis 6–7, in which Noah is sent to declare repentance and prophesy many great things to his contemporaries. He warns them of a great flood that will destroy the iniquitous. Much of Genesis 6 describes the destruction caused by the Flood, showing that God fulfilled his promise to destroy the unrepentant.

First Nephi 1 provides another example of the pattern of warning and judgment. Nephi recorded that during the first year of King Zedekiah's reign, many prophets came among the people and prophesied, declared repentance, and warned the people that Jerusalem would be destroyed unless its inhabitants repented (1 Ne. 1:4, 13, 18). These prophets included Lehi, Micah, Urijah, and Jeremiah (Jer. 26:18–24; 1

---

[4] "When Shall These Things Be?" 186.

[5] Joseph Smith explained that "it is not the design of the Almighty to come upon the earth and crush it and grind it to powder, but he will reveal it to His servants the prophets" (*History of the Church,* 5:336–37).

[6] The Prophet revealed: "In consequence of rejecting the Gospel of Jesus Christ and the Prophets whom God hath sent, the judgments of God have rested upon people, cities, and nations, in various ages of the world, which was the case with the cities of Sodom and Gomorrah, that were destroyed for rejecting the Prophets" (*History of the Church,* 5:256–57).

Ne. 1:18). Later, Nephi testified to his family that he had seen in vision the destruction of Jerusalem and comforted them by saying, "Had we remained in Jerusalem we should also have perished" (2 Ne. 1:4).

Moses, Isaiah, Ezekiel, Joel, Amos, Nephi, Alma, Moroni, Joseph Smith, and perhaps all of God's prophets have followed this pattern by prophesying, crying repentance, and warning of great judgments that would afflict and destroy the ungodly. Recipients of God's judgments in history have included Sodom and Gomorrah, Nineveh, Moab, Edom, Egypt, Philistia, Assyria, Babylon, the Jaredite and Nephite nations, and the kingdoms of Israel and Judah. Each of these cities, kingdoms, and nations are types of the great judgments that will come upon the world, or modern-day Edom or Babylon (D&C 1:16, 36), in the last days.

God's judgments cleanse the earth of wickedness and corruptible things and render justice to Satan's followers on earth. God is called *Righteous* because of his judgments. After three of seven angels pour their bowls of God's wrath (representing God's judgments) upon the earth, an angel exclaims, "Thou art righteous, O Lord . . . because thou hast judged thus"; another angel declares, "Even so, Lord God Almighty, true and righteous are thy judgments" (Rev. 16:1–7).

God, because of his great mercy, will uphold his Saints of the last days during the judgments (D&C 109:38). In the past he offered a way for the obedient to escape. Noah and his family survived the Flood by finding refuge in an ark. Lot and his two daughters escaped from Sodom by following God's specific instructions: "Escape for thy life; look not behind thee, neither stay thou in all the plain; escape to the mountain, lest thou be consumed" (Gen. 19:17). Lehi and his family fled Jerusalem to safety, according to the Lord's word. And Jesus instructed the Saints of his generation to "flee into the mountains" (Matt. 24:16) to escape the abomination of desolation.

In our day, God will likewise protect us according to his will, although "it is a false idea that the Saints will escape all the judgments," taught Joseph Smith.[7] We may not be required to flee from

---

[7] Joseph Smith also taught that "all flesh is subject to suffer, and 'the righteous shall hardly escape;' still many of the Saints will escape, for the just shall live by faith; yet many of the righteous shall fall a prey to disease, to pestilence, etc., by reason of the weakness of the flesh, and yet be saved in the Kingdom of God" (*History of the Church,* 4:11).

our homes or cities, as some were in the past. Perhaps instead we may be required to shut ourselves in our homes, as did the Israelites the night of Passover, when the destroying angel moved through the community and smote the firstborn within those households that did not have the blood of the lamb marked on their doorposts. Or perhaps the Lord will provide a way of deliverance that has no precedent in scripture.

Whatever the case may be with regard to God's judgments, we should always remember, as Elder James E. Faust testified, that "our spirits are special spirits and were reserved until this generation to stand strong against the evil winds that blow, and to stand straight and upright with the heavy burdens that will be placed on us."[8]

A CATALOG OF JUDGMENTS
Doctrine and Covenants 88:87–92

87 For not many days hence and the earth shall tremble and reel to and fro as a drunken man; and the sun shall hide his face, and shall refuse to give light; and the moon shall be bathed in blood; and the stars shall become exceedingly angry, and shall cast themselves down as a fig that falleth from off a fig-tree.

88 And after your testimony cometh wrath and indignation upon the people.

89 For after your testimony cometh the testimony of earthquakes, that shall cause groanings in the midst of her, and men shall fall upon the ground and shall not be able to stand.

90 And also cometh the testimony of the voice of thunderings, and the voice of lightnings, and the voice of tempests, and the voice of the waves of the sea heaving themselves beyond their bounds.

91 And all things shall be in commotion; and surely, men's hearts shall fail them; for fear shall come upon all people.

92 And angels shall fly through the midst of heaven, crying

---

[8] *Ensign,* Apr. 1994, 10.

with a loud voice, sounding the trump of God, saying: Pre-
pare ye, prepare ye, O inhabitants of the earth; for the judg-
ment of our God is come. Behold, and lo, the Bridegroom
cometh; go ye out to meet him.

Four things—God's own voice, God's servants, God's angels, and earth's elements—work together to warn earth's inhabitants to repent and prepare for the coming of the Lord (D&C 43:25; 88:87–92). God's servants, or the elders of the Church (D&C 88:72, 85), are sent "to testify and warn the people" because "it becometh every man who hath been warned to warn his neighbor" (D&C 88:81). At present a great number of Church authorities, full-time missionaries, and other Church members are bearing testimony to the world, inviting individuals and families to come unto Christ. In a real sense, all of these servants of God are preparing the earth's inhabitants for the coming judgments and ultimately for Christ's coming.

But after their testimony, God explains (D&C 88:88–89), will come the testimony from the natural world in the form of earthquakes, thunderings, tempests, and others. God will send multiple judgments to prepare the world for his coming. Doctrine and Covenants 88 catalogs at least eight separate judgments: signs in the heavens, earthquakes, thunderings, lightnings, tempests, ocean waves moving beyond their normal bounds, commotions, and the failure of human hearts. Doctrine and Covenants 43:25 adds great hailstones, famines, and pestilences.

Perhaps concurrently with the testimony of God's servants and the natural world, heavenly messengers warn earth's inhabitants to prepare for God's judgments and the Bridegroom's coming. They proclaim: "Prepare ye, prepare ye, O inhabitants of the earth; for the judgment of our God is come. Behold, and lo, the Bridegroom cometh; go ye out to meet him" (D&C 88:92). Revelation 8 and 9 describes more fully the role of angels in the preparation of the world for the Second Coming.[9]

The Saints should find comfort in knowing that while God is sending judgments upon the earth, they can "look calmly" on them

---

[9] See Parry and Parry, *Understanding the Book of Revelation,* 102–23.

while waiting for Christ's coming. Brigham Young and his counselors in the First Presidency, Heber C. Kimball and Willard Richards, comforted us with these words: "While the wicked fear and tremble at surrounding judgments, the Saints will watch and pray; and waiting the final event in patience, will look calmly on the passing scenery of a corrupted world, and view transpiring events as confirmation of their faith in the holy gospel which they profess and rejoice more and more, as multiplied signs shall confirm the approach of the millennial day."[10]

In 1979, Elder Gordon B. Hinckley compared the reactions of the wicked and the righteous to God's judgments in the last days. He said that this period "will be a time of great and terrible fears, of cataclysmic upheavals of nature, of weeping and wailing, of repentance too late, and of crying out unto the Lord for mercy" to the wicked, but to the righteous this will "be a day for thanksgiving."[11]

NOTES AND COMMENTARY

D&C 88:87 *the earth shall tremble and reel to and fro as a drunken man.* This poetic expression seems to describe an earthquake or earthquakes (D&C 45:33). In an earlier revelation, the Lord associated this expression with the valleys being exalted, the mountains being made low, and the rough places becoming smooth, all of which also suggests one or more great earthquakes (D&C 49:23).

the sun shall hide his face, and shall refuse to give light; and the moon shall be bathed in blood. See the commentary on Revelation 6:12, page 370.

D&C 88:88 *after your testimony.* After the testimony of the elders of the Church.

cometh wrath and indignation upon the people. The *wrath* and *indignation* of God will come upon those who do not hearken to the testimony of the elders. Isaiah prophesied of the last days, using the terms *wrath* and *fierce anger:* "Behold, the day of the Lord cometh, cruel both with wrath and fierce anger, to lay the land desolate; and he shall destroy the sinners thereof out of it" (Isa. 13:9; see also v. 13).

---

[10] "Fifth General Epistle," 209, 216.
[11] "'We Need Not Fear His Coming,'" 82–83.

Similarly, because of the Lord's indignation and anger Noah's wicked contemporaries were destroyed by the Flood: "And the fire of mine indignation is kindled against them; . . . for my fierce anger is kindled against them" (Moses 7:34). The judgments listed in verses 89 through 91 are the result of God's wrath.

cometh the testimony of earthquakes. Although earthquakes have existed upon the earth for millennia, those of the latter days serve as one of the signs of the times. "There shall be earthquakes also in divers places" (D&C 45:33), the Lord promised his disciples during his mortality (D&C 45:16). Note especially the "great earthquake" associated with the opening of the sixth seal (Rev. 6:12) and the "great earthquake, such as was not since men were upon the earth, so mighty an earthquake, and so great," associated with the seventh seal (Rev. 16:18).

D&C 88:90 *also cometh the testimony.* Earthquakes, thunderings, lightnings, tempests, tidal waves, and other natural phenomena which cause anxiety and even hysteria in many are voices that warn the wicked to repent. These, along with the testimony of the Lord's servants, serve as a second witness for the ungodly to prepare for God's judgments. The Lord asks the wicked: "What will ye say when the day cometh when the thunders shall utter their voices from the ends of the earth, speaking to the ears of all that live, saying—Repent, and prepare for the great day of the Lord? Yea, and again, when the lightnings shall streak forth from the east unto the west, and shall utter forth their voices unto all that live, and make the ears of all tingle that hear, saying these words—Repent ye, for the great day of the Lord is come?" (D&C 43:21–22).

In the same context Jesus explains that he has called upon the nations to repent with four voices: the voice of his servants, the voice of the ministering of angels, his own voice, and the voice of nature— "by the voice of thunderings, and by the voice of lightnings, and by the voice of tempests, and by the voice of earthquakes, and great hailstorms, and by the voice of famines and pestilences of every kind" (D&C 43:25).

D&C 88:91 *all things shall be in commotion.* An earlier revelation also promises, "The whole earth shall be in commotion" (D&C

45:26). That commotion seems to refer to things mentioned in verses 87 through 90: signs in the heavens, earthquakes, tempests, lightnings, tidal waves, and so on. In a parallel passage, Luke summarized the commotion that would exist in the last days: "And there shall be signs in the sun, and in the moon, and in the stars; and upon the earth distress of nations, with perplexity; the sea and the waves roaring; men's hearts failing them for fear, and for looking after those things which are coming on the earth" (Luke 21:25–26).

Elder Marion G. Romney may have had the phrase *all things shall be in commotion* in mind when he said: "Our whole world is in confusion. The wisdom of our wise men has proved inadequate to stay the rising crisis. With the means to unleash universal destruction in the hands of evil men, fear and apprehension ride with every breeze. In the past, situations similar to ours have generally terminated in destruction. It would seem that the judgments of God are about to be once more poured out upon the nations."[12]

D&C 88:92 *angels shall fly through the midst of heaven.* Ministering angels serve God in preparing people for his coming (compare D&C 7:6).

sounding the trump of God. The angels of this verse who blow their trumpets are probably the seven angels who are identified in Revelation 8 and 9, of whom it is written that "the sounding of the trumpets of the seven angels are the preparing and finishing of his work, in the beginning of the seventh thousand years—the preparing of the way before the time of his coming" (D&C 77:12). In Revelation 8:1–5 the angels prepare to blow their trumps; then the angels blow their trumps, one after another (Rev. 8:6–9:21). The blast of the trumpets serves a twofold purpose: to herald the calamities identified in Doctrine and Covenants 88:89–90 and elsewhere, and to encourage earth's sinners to repent (Rev. 9:20–21; 16:9, 11). Both of these purposes serve to prepare the earth for Christ's coming.

Prepare ye, prepare ye. The phrase is repeated for emphasis. A parallel passage reads, "For behold, the Lord God hath sent forth the angel crying through the midst of heaven, saying: Prepare ye the way

---

[12] Conference Report, Apr. 1958, 128–29.

of the Lord, and make his paths straight, for the hour of his coming is nigh" (D&C 133:17).

O inhabitants of the earth. The angels' message is for all, not just select individuals or particular groups.

for the judgment of our God is come. The angels warn all to prepare because God's judgments are coming, including his great, last judgment.

the Bridegroom cometh; go ye out to meet him. In the parable of the ten virgins, the cry of these words is made at midnight (Matt. 25:6); correspondingly, a latter-day revelation adds the words "awake and arise," suggesting that the people are asleep when the cry goes out. "Yea, let the cry go forth among all people: Awake and arise and go forth to meet the Bridegroom; behold and lo, the Bridegroom cometh; go ye out to meet him. Prepare yourselves for the great day of the Lord" (D&C 133:10).

Go ye is a command, not a suggestion or exhortation. Doctrine and Covenants 133:19 includes the same command, repeated twice: "Wherefore, prepare ye for the coming of the Bridegroom; go ye, go ye out to meet him."

SEVEN ANGELS WITH THE SEVEN LAST PLAGUES
Revelation 15:1–8

> *1 And I saw another sign in heaven, great and marvellous, seven angels having the seven last plagues; for in them is filled up the wrath of God.*
>
> *2 And I saw as it were a sea of glass mingled with fire: and them that had gotten the victory over the beast, and over his image, and over his mark, and over the number of his name, stand on the sea of glass, having the harps of God.*
>
> *3 And they sing the song of Moses the servant of God, and the song of the Lamb, saying, Great and marvellous are thy works, Lord God Almighty; just and true are thy ways, thou King of saints.*

4 Who shall not fear thee, O Lord, and glorify thy name? for thou only art holy; for all nations shall come and worship before thee; for thy judgments are made manifest.

5 And after that I looked, and, behold, the temple of the tabernacle of the testimony in heaven was opened:

6 And the seven angels came out of the temple, having the seven plagues, clothed in pure and white linen, and having their breasts girded with golden girdles.

7 And one of the four beasts gave unto the seven angels seven golden [bowls]¹³ full of the wrath of God, who liveth for ever and ever.

8 And the temple was filled with smoke from the glory of God, and from his power; and no man was able to enter into the temple, till the seven plagues of the seven angels were fulfilled.

In this scene, John sees a vision of celestial glory. He sees those who have "gotten the victory over the beast" singing a song of praise to God. Paradoxically, many who gain victory over the beast were first slain by that beast (Rev. 13:7, 15); by standing firm in their testimonies, even unto death, they eventually emerge victorious. John also sees seven angels being prepared to pour out seven final judgments on the earth (Rev. 15:1, 7). We do not yet see what those judgments are (that is reserved for the next chapter in Revelation), but they appear to be terrible: "In them is filled up the wrath of God" (Rev. 15:1).

NOTES AND COMMENTARY

Rev. 15:1 *I saw another sign in heaven, great and marvellous.* The words *another sign* give us to understand that the scene in the vision has shifted. As with the other signs in John's vision, what he sees as a sign symbolizes a great truth. In this case, the truth is that God will indeed exact judgment against the wicked, a judgment that will be complete and terrible. The words *great and marvellous* suggest a sign that is truly impressive.

---

¹³ The KJV *vials* may more appropriately be translated *bowls*. See, for example, RSV, GNB, NIV, and JB.

seven angels having the seven last plagues. These seven last plagues are the Lord's final attempt to cause the hearts of the wicked to be softened and to turn to him. After these plagues will come the actual fall of Babylon and the second coming of Christ. Because seven is a number signifying perfection, seven angels with seven plagues indicates perfect and complete judgment against the wicked of the earth. This prophecy is reminiscent of the curse the Lord gave against the wicked in Leviticus 26:21: "If ye walk contrary unto me, and will not hearken unto me; I will bring seven times more plagues upon you according to your sins." These plagues are poured out in Revelation 16.

in them is filled up the wrath of God. The plagues bring a full measure of God's wrath to the world but not the final consummation. That consummation comes in the chapters that follow.

Rev. 15:2 *a sea of glass mingled with fire.* The sea of glass indicates a celestial sphere (D&C 130:6–7), and the presence of fire indicates the presence of God, who dwells amid everlasting burnings (Isa. 33:14–16).

them that had gotten the victory over the beast . . . stand on the sea of glass. Those who have refused to bow to the beast, either physically or spiritually, inherit a celestial glory. These may be the same Saints who were sealed in Revelation 7:1–8 and were named among the 144,000 in Revelation 14:1–5.

harps of God. The harps symbolize an attitude of worship and giving glory to God (2 Sam. 6:5; Neh. 12:27; Ps. 92:1–3; Rev. 14:2).

Rev. 15:3 *And they sing the song of Moses . . . and the song of the Lamb.* The song of Moses was sung by that great prophet and his followers after they were delivered from the great "beast" of ancient Egypt (Ex. 15:1–19). The lyrics to the song spoken of in this verse include the words, "Great and marvellous are thy works, Lord God Almighty; just and true are thy ways, thou King of saints."[14] These words are not found in the song of Moses in Exodus 15, but the common element is that the Lord's people were in bondage and the Lord delivered them from their enemy.

---

[14]This song contains phrases from many Old Testament sources, in this order: Ps. 111:2; 139:14; Amos 4:13; Ps. 145:17; Deut. 32:4; Jer. 10:7; Ps. 86:9; Mal. 1:11.

This song is also the song of the Lamb, because he is the great Deliverer. The song of the Lamb will ultimately be sung by all true Saints. On the day of resurrection, the scripture says, "The graves of the saints shall be opened; and they shall come forth and stand on the right hand of the Lamb, when he shall stand upon Mount Zion, and upon the holy city, the New Jerusalem; and they shall sing the song of the Lamb, day and night forever and ever" (D&C 133:56).

Rev. 15:4 *Who shall not fear thee/all nations shall come and worship before thee.* The Saints cry out their praise and admiration to the Lord. All nations will fear and honor him, for the time will come when "every knee shall bow, and every tongue confess" that the Lord is God (Mosiah 27:31; see also Rom. 14:11; D&C 88:104).

The Saints in our day sing a song that echoes these words:

> How wondrous and great
> Thy works, God of praise!
> How just, King of Saints,
> And true are thy ways!
> Oh, who shall not fear thee
> And honor thy name?
> Thou only art holy,
> Thou only supreme.[15]

thy judgments are made manifest. The nations will acknowledge the power and supremacy of God as they see them manifest through the judgments he brings on the wicked of the earth.

Rev. 15:5 *I looked.* Again the vision shifts to a new scene.

the temple of the tabernacle of the testimony in heaven was opened. The ancient tabernacle in the days of Moses was called the *tabernacle of the testimony,* or *tabernacle of witness* (Num. 17:7) because it contained the two stone "tables of the testimony" on which God had written (Deut. 10:5). The New International Version renders this idea as follows: "I looked and in heaven the temple, that is, the tabernacle of testimony, was opened." The tabernacle of Moses served as a temple until Solomon's day, when a more permanent

---

15 "How Wondrous and Great," *Hymns,* no. 267.

structure was built (1 Kgs. 8:18–20). When John looked into the heavens again, he saw the temple in heaven open and seven angels came out.

Rev. 15:6 *the seven angels came out of the temple, having the seven plagues.* Apparently the seven angels received their charge in heaven's temple and then emerged with the seven plagues. The number seven indicates that the judgments are perfect and complete. That the judgments come from the temple is a mark of their godly origin.

clothed in pure and white linen/their breasts girded with golden girdles. The linen dress of the angels, pure and white, indicates that they hold a sacred and holy office (Ezek. 9:2; Dan. 10:5). Linen also suggests the bride of Christ (Rev. 19:7–8) and the armies of heaven (Rev. 19:14). The high rank of the angels is deduced from the golden girdles (or sashes) they wear, which are like that worn by Christ himself (Rev. 1:13).

Rev. 15:7 *one of the four beasts.* In Revelation 4:6–9 John saw four beasts at the throne of God. In Revelation 5:8 the beasts worship the Lamb. In Revelation 6:1, 3, 5, and 7 the beasts invite John to see the events that occur when the seals on the book are opened. Now one of these same beasts, which are intelligent creatures, gives the angels the bowls that contain the judgments that are to be poured out on the earth.

seven golden [bowls] full of the wrath of God. The seven bowls contain the judgments that represent God's wrath (Rom. 1:18; Heb. 10:30–31) and will soon be poured out on mankind. Golden bowls, or vials, mentioned in Revelation 5:8, symbolize the prayers of the Saints. Perhaps the Saints' pleading for justice and deliverance is answered in the judgments in the seven golden bowls here.

who liveth for ever and ever. This interjection reaffirms the power and dominion of God (Rev. 4:9; 10:6). As one who lives forever, unlike the mortals on the earth, God has full power to accomplish all his will against the wicked of the world.

Rev. 15:8 *the temple was filled with smoke.* The source of the smoke is "the glory of God, and . . . his power." Smoke or a cloud is a typical sign of the presence of God. When the Lord descended on Mount Sinai "in fire," the mount "was altogether on a smoke, . . . and the smoke thereof ascended as the smoke of a furnace, and the whole mount quaked greatly" (Ex. 19:18; see also Isa. 6:4; Ezek. 10:4).

no man was able to enter into the temple. Because God is present in the heavenly temple, filling it with his glory, no one is able to go into it until the seven plagues are completed. This expression evidently indicates that God continues to actively exercise his power in judgment until the wicked are destroyed. No one can approach him, pleading mercy.

We read in the Old Testament of another circumstance in which God's power prevented man from entering his temple: "Then a cloud covered the tent of the congregation, and the glory of the Lord filled the tabernacle. And Moses was not able to enter into the tent of the congregation, because the cloud abode thereon, and the glory of the Lord filled the tabernacle" (Ex. 40:34–35; see also 1 Kgs. 8:10–11).

SEVEN ANGELS WITH THE BOWLS OF GOD'S WRATH
Revelation 16:1–21

1 And I heard a great voice out of the temple saying to the seven angels, Go your ways, and pour out the [bowls] of the wrath of God upon the earth.

2 And the first went, and poured out his [bowl] upon the earth; and there fell a noisome and grievous sore upon the men which had the mark of the beast, and upon them which worshipped his image.

3 And the second angel poured out his [bowl] upon the sea; and it became as the blood of a dead man: and every living soul died in the sea.

4 And the third angel poured out his [bowl] upon the rivers and fountains of waters; and they became blood.

5 And I heard the angel of the waters say, Thou art righteous, O Lord, which art, and wast, and shalt be, because thou hast judged thus.

6 For they have shed the blood of saints and prophets, and thou hast given them blood to drink; for they are [deserving].[16]

---

[16] From the Greek; see note *c* to Rev. 16:6 in the LDS edition of the KJV.

7 And I heard another [angel who came out from the altar saying],[17] Even so, Lord God Almighty, true and righteous are thy judgments.

8 And the fourth angel poured out his [bowl] upon the sun; and power was given unto him to scorch men with fire.

9 And men were scorched with great heat, and blasphemed the name of God, which hath power over these plagues: and they repented not to give him glory.

10 And the fifth angel poured out his [bowl] upon the seat of the beast; and his kingdom was full of darkness; and they gnawed their tongues for pain,

11 And blasphemed the God of heaven because of their pains and their sores, and repented not of their deeds.

12 And the sixth angel poured out his [bowl] upon the great river Euphrates; and the water thereof was dried up, that the way of the kings of the east might be prepared.

13 And I saw three unclean spirits like frogs come out of the mouth of the dragon, and out of the mouth of the beast, and out of the mouth of the false prophet.

14 For they are the spirits of devils, working miracles, which go forth unto the kings of the earth and of the whole world, to gather them to the battle of that great day of God Almighty.

15 Behold, I come as a thief. Blessed is he that watcheth, and keepeth his garments, lest he walk naked and they see his shame.

16 And he gathered them together into a place called in the Hebrew tongue Armageddon.

17 And the seventh angel poured out his [bowl] into the air; and there came a great voice out of the temple of heaven, from the throne, saying, It is done.

18 And there were voices, and thunders, and lightnings; and

---

[17] JST Rev. 16:7 amends this passage from the KJV, which reads, "And I heard another out of the altar say, . . ."

there was a great earthquake, such as was not since men were upon the earth, so mighty an earthquake, and so great.

19 And the great city was divided into three parts, and the cities of the nations fell: and great Babylon came in remembrance before God, to give unto her the cup of the wine of the fierceness of his wrath.

20 And every island fled away, and the mountains were not found.

21 And there fell upon men a great hail out of heaven, every stone about the weight of a talent: and men blasphemed God because of the plague of the hail; for the plague thereof was exceeding great.

The day of God's judgment is a day of God's wrath, and that day is fast approaching. "Vengeance cometh speedily," the Lord says, "as a whirlwind it shall come upon all the face of the earth" (D&C 112:24).

The righteous will be blessed with a degree of protection: "Zion shall escape if she observe to do all things whatsoever I have commanded her" (D&C 97:25). But those among the Saints who are hypocrites have no such promise; indeed, they will be the first to be judged: "Upon my house shall it [the day of vengeance] begin, and from my house shall it go forth, saith the Lord; first among those among you, saith the Lord, who have professed to know my name and have not known me, and have blasphemed against me in the midst of my house, saith the Lord" (D&C 112:25–26).

Revelation 16 details the scourges and plagues that will afflict mankind in the day of the final judgments, plagues that will smite the land, the sea, the rivers, the sun, and the kingdoms of spiritual darkness. Through the power of God, the very foundations of the earth are shaken, and Babylon is totally destroyed. These plagues may well fit the description the Lord gave us in modern revelation: "For behold, and lo, vengeance cometh speedily upon the ungodly as the whirlwind; and who shall escape it? The Lord's scourge shall pass over by night and by day, and the report thereof shall vex all people; yea, it shall not be stayed until the Lord come; for the indignation of the

Lord is kindled against their abominations and all their wicked works" (D&C 97:22–24). And again: "Their testimony [the elders] shall also go forth unto the condemnation of this generation if they harden their hearts against them; for a desolating scourge shall go forth among the inhabitants of the earth, and shall continue to be poured out from time to time, if they repent not, until the earth is empty, and the inhabitants thereof are consumed away and utterly destroyed by the brightness of my coming" (D&C 5:18–19).

Some commentators believe that the judgments in Revelation 16 are a repetition of the plagues seen in Revelation 8, 9, and 11.[18] That is one possible reading, and there are remarkable parallels between the two sections. But it seems more likely that Revelation 16 represents a later and more severe occurrence of plagues. In Revelation 8, for instance, a third of the sea becomes blood and a third of the creatures in the sea die (Rev. 8:8–9). But in Revelation 16, all of the sea becomes blood and all creatures therein die (Rev. 16:3). A comparison of the plagues in both sections shows a similar progression: as God continues to plead with and to punish the earth through his judgments, those judgments become more severe.

NOTES AND COMMENTARY

Rev. 16:1 *I heard a great voice out of the temple.* In Revelation 15:8 we read that no one could enter the temple until the next seven plagues were completed. This voice might, then, be the voice of God himself, commanding the seven angels to act.

Go your ways. The voice tells the angels to move ahead with their commission to administer plagues to the earth.

pour out the [bowls] of the wrath of God. Under the law of Moses, the priests used a sacred bowl to capture the blood of the sacrifice. As part of the ritual, the priest then sprinkled the blood around the altar (Lev. 1:5; 3:8). Perhaps in this part of the vision John is seeing a reversal of this ritual: rather than blood coming from the bowls to save the people, John sees something come from the bowls that

---

[18] See, for example, Draper, *Opening the Seven Seals,* 172–73; 251; Mounce, *Book of Revelation,* 291–92.

sheds blood and punishes the people. That which is poured from the bowls represents different manifestations of God's wrath.

Rev. 16:2 *the first . . . poured out his [bowl] upon the earth; and there fell a noisome and grievous sore.* The first plague, which is directed at the wicked, is of "disgusting and virulent sores," according to the Jerusalem Bible. This plague parallels the sixth plague that fell on the Egyptians in the time of Moses (Ex. 9:8–12). The contents of this bowl are poured out on the earth itself, and the affliction falls on those who dwell on the earth. The wicked have earlier worn the mark of the beast; now they will wear the mark of the wrath of God.[19]

Zechariah prophesies a plague that may be similar: "This shall be the plague wherewith the Lord will smite all the people that have fought against Jerusalem; their flesh shall consume away while they stand upon their feet, and their eyes shall consume away in their holes, and their tongue shall consume away in their mouth" (Zech. 14:12). And we read in latter-day revelation: "Their tongues shall be stayed that they shall not utter against me; and their flesh shall fall from off their bones, and their eyes from their sockets" (D&C 29:19). These descriptions sound very much like some of the effects of nuclear war.[20]

Rev. 16:3 *the second angel poured out his [bowl] upon the sea; and it became as . . . blood/every living soul died in the sea.* This plague and that which follows it parallel the first plague the Lord brought on the ancient Egyptians: the waters turned to blood (Ex. 7:19–21). In Revelation 8:8–9, a third of the waters were afflicted; here, the polluted water kills every creature. This may have connection with words of the Lord given in our dispensation: "Behold, there are many dangers upon the waters, and more especially hereafter; for I, the Lord, have decreed in mine anger many destructions upon the waters" (D&C 61:4–5). We can only speculate on the cause of this destruction; it may be related to fallout from nuclear war.

There may be another meaning to *sea* in this passage. In Revelation 17:15, the waters symbolize "peoples, and multitudes, and

---

[19] Mounce, *Book of Revelation,* 293.
[20] The horrific results of atomic warfare can be read in Hersey, *Hiroshima.* For a description of the effects on the skin and eyes, see pages 59 and 67 of that book.

nations, and tongues." Perhaps here, as well, the sea represents the wicked people of the world, all of whom are eventually destroyed.

as the blood of a dead man. A person's blood gives life to the body, as water gives life to the world and the creatures on it. But a dead man's blood is corrupted and coagulated, no longer able to help sustain life. So shall it be with the waters of the seas as a result of this plague.

Rev. 16:4 *the third angel poured out his [bowl] upon the rivers . . . they became blood.* This plague (like that of Revelation 16:3) parallels the one in Exodus 7:19–21 (see also Ps. 78:44). In Revelation 8:10–11, a burning star turned a third of the rivers and fountains of waters bitter. Here, all the rivers and fountains are polluted, though the result is not given.

Rev. 16:5 *the angel of the waters.* Anciently, the Jews believed that different angels had charge of different elements of nature. The vision of John seems to draw on this belief. In Revelation 7:1 we see four angels who have power over "the four winds of the earth." In Revelation 14:18 we read of an angel who has "power over fire." Here we have one or more angels who seem to have power over the fate of the waters. Or, if we read this verse more simply, we might understand that it refers only to the angel who, in Revelation 16:4, poured his bowl out upon the rivers.

Thou art righteous, O Lord, . . . because thou hast judged thus. Even though the judgments on the earth are terrible, the angel proclaims that the Lord is righteous and correct to have so judged (Ps. 119:137). Not only have the people chosen lives of sin but they have slain those who desired to follow the Lord. For such great sin, the Lord rightly punishes them with devastating judgments.

Rev. 16:6 *For they have shed the blood of saints and prophets/ given them blood to drink.* The motif of blood continues as we are reminded that the wicked have slain many of the righteous (Rev. 13:7, 15; 17:6; 18:24) and learn that, in a punishment that fits the crime, the wicked will themselves be forced to drink blood (Isa. 49:26). "To be drunk with blood . . . signifies slaughter by the sword."[21] The King

---

[21] Davidson, *New Bible Commentary,* 1187.

James Version says the wicked are "worthy" of this punishment; a more accurate translation may be "deserving."[22]

The scriptures tell of many specific instances of martyrdom (1 Kgs. 18:13; 2 Chr. 24:20–21; Mark 6:25–28; Acts 7:57–60; 12:1–2; Rev. 2:13; 11:7; Mosiah 17:20; Alma 25:7). They also record many general statements documenting the rejection and killing of the Lord's prophets (1 Thes. 2:15; Heb. 11:37; Rev. 6:9; 12:11; 16:6; Hel. 13:24; 3 Ne. 10:15). The mortal Jesus prophesied that martyrdom was precisely what many of his followers would suffer (Matt. 23:29–38; 24:9).

Rev. 16:7 *I heard another [angel who came out from the altar].* Almost without exception, the altar in Revelation is connected with the judgments of God (Rev. 8:3–5; 9:13–14; 14:18; the one exception is Rev. 11:1). The angel declares that God's judgments are indeed "true and righteous" (see also Rev. 15:3–5; Ps. 19:9), as is the case with all his works.

Rev. 16:8 *the fourth angel poured out his [bowl] upon the sun . . . scorch men with fire.* The righteous are promised in Revelation 7:16 that "neither shall the sun light on them, nor any heat," meaning that they will not suffer from the heat of the sun. But here the wicked suffer from intense heat, perhaps from the sun. That may result from a breakdown of the ozone layer of the atmosphere, which could be the result of a nuclear blast and which would remove much of our protection from the sun's potentially deadly rays, or it may have a cause that we cannot yet imagine.[23] The scriptures often connect fire with judgment (Deut. 28:22; 1 Cor. 3:13; 2 Pet. 3:7); this fire prefigures the scorching fire of the last judgment (Mal. 4:1). The fourth angel acts under the direction of God and by "power" that "was given unto him."

Rev. 16:9 *men were scorched with great heat . . . blasphemed the name of God . . . repented not to give him glory.* The heat of this plague is here described as *great,* and the idea of scorching is repeated, perhaps for emphasis. But rather than acknowledge their guilt, the wicked appear to blame God for their troubles, speaking evil

---

[22] See note *c* to Rev. 16:6 in the LDS edition of the KJV.

[23] For a discussion of the effects of nuclear war on the ozone layer, see Schell, *Fate of the Earth,* 20–21, 79–92.

of him and his righteousness. Blasphemy is a recurring accusation against the wicked in Revelation (Rev. 2:9; 16:11, 21). Even at this late hour in the world's history, men have an opportunity to repent, but still they refuse (Rev. 9:20–21; 16:11; see the contrast in Rev. 11:13). An angel in Revelation 14:7 admonishes the world to "fear God, and give glory to him," but the great body of people on earth choose their sin instead.

Rev. 16:10 *the fifth angel poured out his [bowl] upon the seat of the beast . . . his kingdom was full of darkness.* In the ninth plague that Moses proclaimed in Egypt, the whole kingdom was stricken with thick darkness (Ex. 10:21–23). Here, darkness fills the kingdom of the beast (Isa. 60:2; D&C 82:5; 84:49; 112:23). The darkness may be literal or spiritual or both. Because the darkness results from an action of an angel of God, who would not likely be the source of spiritual darkness, it is probably a literal darkness that reflects the spiritual darkness in the beast's kingdom. The "seat of the beast" may more accurately be translated the "throne of the beast" (RSV, NEB, JB, NIV). The idea is that the Lord will attack the beast at his very headquarters, striking at his power and authority.

This plague of darkness may be a fulfillment of a curse that the Lord pronounced on the wicked in the times of Moses: "The Lord shall smite thee with madness, and blindness, and astonishment of heart: and thou shalt grope at noonday, as the blind gropeth in darkness, and thou shalt not prosper in thy ways: and thou shalt be only oppressed and spoiled evermore, and no man shall save thee" (Deut. 28:28–29).

Rev. 16:10–11 *they gnawed their tongues for pain . . . blasphemed the God of heaven . . . repented not of their deeds.* The terrible pain that men suffer may be a result of the sores described in Revelation 16:2, combined with the lack of clean water spoken of in verse 4 and the scorching heat of the sun recorded in verse 9. The darkness into which they are plunged can only exacerbate their plight. Again they follow their leader, the beast, in blaspheming God (Rev. 13:1, 5–6; 17:3), blaming him for their pains and sores. And still they will not repent. It seems incredible that people will not turn to God with humble spirits after suffering so much, but they follow the pattern of a scriptural type of long ago: Despite all that he and his people suffered, the Egyptian pharaoh in the time of Moses only hardened his heart (JST Ex. 7–10). The plagues of this angel may also be connected with nuclear war.

Rev. 16:12 *the sixth angel poured out his [bowl] upon the great river Euphrates . . . the water thereof was dried up.* In the days of Moses and Joshua, the Lord divided and dried up a passage through two different bodies of water to enable his people to be delivered from bondage and then to inherit their land of promise (Ex. 14:21; Josh. 3:13–17). But in John's vision, the Lord through his angel will dry up the water of a river to clear the way for destruction and war. The Euphrates formed the eastern and northeastern boundary of the land the Lord gave to Abraham and his descendants (Gen. 15:18; Deut. 1:7–8; Josh. 1:3–4) and served as a natural barrier to the enemies of Israel. When that barrier is removed, the enemies of Israel can begin their march. The Old Testament speaks often of the Lord drying up waters to accomplish his purposes (Ex. 14:21; Josh. 3:13–17; Isa. 11:15–16; 44:27; Jer. 51:36; Zech. 10:11).

that the way of the kings of the east might be prepared. It is uncertain who the kings of the east may be. One commentator notes that there have been more than fifty different interpretations of this expression.[24] What most agree on is that the kings are enemies of the Lord's people and of the Lord himself and that they are prepared to go forth to war.

Rev. 16:13–16 For commentary on these verses, see page 276.

Rev. 16:17 *the seventh angel poured out his [bowl] into the air.* Other angels poured their bowls out upon the earth, the sea, the rivers, the sun, the seat of the beast, and the Euphrates. By pouring his bowl out into the air, the angel seems to be affecting all the earth through its all-encompassing atmosphere. The sounding of the last trumpet (Rev. 11:15–19) and the pouring forth of the last bowl are quite similar in their results, both signifying the end of earth's history.

great voice out of the temple of heaven, from the throne, saying, It is done. Because this voice comes from the throne in the temple of heaven, it must belong to God the Father, who is seated on that throne and rules over all. By saying "It is done," he announces that all things

---

[24] Walvoord, *Revelation of Jesus Christ,* 236.

have been accomplished and the time has come for the final destruction of Babylon and of the earth.

Rev. 16:18 *there were voices, and thunders, and lightnings.* The thunders and lightnings may indicate that all nature is in an uproar as a result of the judgments poured forth from the last bowl. The voices may be God's proclamations of judgment and command, as we see in the Doctrine and Covenants, in which he prepares the earth to return to its paradisiacal glory: "And he shall utter his voice out of Zion, and he shall speak from Jerusalem, and his voice shall be heard among all people; and it shall be a voice as the voice of many waters, and as the voice of a great thunder, which shall break down the mountains, and the valleys shall not be found. He shall command the great deep, and it shall be driven back into the north countries, and the islands shall become one land; and the land of Jerusalem and the land of Zion shall be turned back into their own place, and the earth shall be like as it was in the days before it was divided. And the Lord, even the Savior, shall stand in the midst of his people, and shall reign over all flesh" (D&C 133:21–25).

there was a great earthquake. This earthquake is different from the ones spoken of in Revelation 6:12 and 11:13–14. The earthquake in Revelation 6:12 is so great that the mountains and islands are "moved out of their places" (6:14), but that earthquake occurs in the period of the sixth thousand years (D&C 77:6–7). The earthquake in Revelation 11:13–14 is the first in the seventh thousand years and is of indeterminate size and intensity. The earthquake in Revelation 16:18 is described as the greatest in the history of the world. It is so great, as we read in Revelation 16:20, that it appears to be connected with the flattening of the mountains and the unifying of the continents: "One of the plainest and most-oft-repeated statements about the ushering in of the Millennium is the promise of a great shaking of the earth, of earthquakes that are everywhere at one and the same time, and of mountains and valleys and seas and landmasses that move. 'Yet once, it is a little while,' saith the Lord, 'and I will shake the heavens, and the earth, and the sea, and the dry land; and I will shake all nations, and the desire of all nations shall come.' (Hag. 2:6–7.) Christ, the Desire of all nations, shall come amid the greatest shaking of the earth and of all things that there has ever been or ever will be in the entire history of this planet. Everything on earth—the historical events then in progress, the beasts and all forms of life, and the inanimate objects that do not act for themselves—everything on earth will be affected by the great shaking."[25] (See also Ezek. 38:19–20; Joel 3:16; D&C 133:31.)

Rev. 16:19 *the great city was divided into three parts.* The great city seems to be Babylon, which in this verse is a figurative city, representative of all the wicked societies of the earth. The division into three parts suggests that the city is fully weakened and prepared for the final destructive blow.

the cities of the nations fell. The cities of the nations fall in the earthquake, but this passage also seems to refer to the destruction of governments. The events in these verses bring about the fulfillment of the latter-day prophecy made by Joseph Smith: "With the sword and by bloodshed the inhabitants of the earth shall mourn; and with famine, and plague, and earthquake, and the thunder of heaven, and the fierce and vivid lightning also, shall the inhabitants of the earth be made to feel the wrath, and indignation, and chastening hand of an Almighty God, until the consumption decreed hath made a full end of all nations" (D&C 87:6).

Rev. 16:20 *every island fled away/the mountains were not found.* This passage describes the great leveling of the earth as the Lord prepares it for the millennial era. This leveling will occur as a result of the tremendous earthquake in Revelation 16:18. As we read in the Doctrine and Covenants, we should "continue in steadfastness, looking forth for the heavens to be shaken, and the earth to tremble and to reel to and fro as a drunken man, and for the valleys to be exalted, and for the mountains to be made low, and for the rough places to become smooth—and all this when the angel shall sound his trumpet" (D&C 49:23; see also 109:74; 133:21–23).

Elder Parley P. Pratt wrote of this event: "From these verses [Isaiah 40:1–5] we learn, first, that the voice of one shall be heard in the wilderness, to prepare the way of the Lord, just at the time when Jerusalem has been trodden down of the Gentiles long enough to have received, at the Lord's hands, double for all her sins, yea, when the

---

[25] McConkie, *Millennial Messiah,* 620–21.

warfare of Jerusalem is accomplished, and her iniquities pardoned. Then shall this proclamation be made as it was before by John [the Baptist], yea, a second proclamation, to prepare the way of the Lord, for his second coming; and about that time every valley shall be exalted, and every mountain and hill shall be made low, and the crooked shall be made straight, and rough places plain, and then the glory of the Lord shall be revealed, and all flesh shall see it together, for the mouth of the Lord hath spoken it. . . .

"Having restored the earth to the same glorious state in which it first existed—leveling the mountains, exalting the valleys, smoothing the rough places, making the deserts fruitful, and bringing all the continents and islands together, causing the curse to be taken off, that noxious weeds, and thorns, and thistles shall no longer be produced; the next thing is to regulate and restore the brute creation to their former state of peace and glory, causing enmity to cease from off the earth. But this will never be done until there is a general destruction poured out upon man, which will entirely cleanse the earth, and sweep all wickedness from its face."[26]

Rev. 16:21 *there fell upon men a great hail out of heaven.* Deadly hailstones are an element of nature that God periodically uses to assist the righteous in their battles and to punish the wicked (Josh. 10:11; Mosiah 12:6), and hailstorms are often prophesied among the troubles to come (Ezek. 13:13; 38:22; Rev. 11:19; D&C 29:16). A "very grievous hail" was one of the plagues sent upon Egypt in the days of Moses (Ex. 9:18).

every stone about the weight of a talent. Each hailstone weighs between forty-five and ninety pounds (the exact weight of a talent is uncertain).[27] The point is that these hailstones are tremendous in size and catastrophic in their effect.

men blasphemed God because of the plague of the hail. Not only do the people of the world fail to repent but they speak evil of God for that which he does in perfect justice.

---

[26] *Voice of Warning,* 159–60, 162.
[27] *New Bible Dictionary,* 1324.

"A DESOLATING SCOURGE SHALL GO FORTH"
Doctrine and Covenants 5:19–20

19 For a desolating scourge shall go forth among the inhabitants of the earth, and shall continue to be poured out from time to time, if they repent not, until the earth is empty, and the inhabitants thereof are consumed away and utterly destroyed by the brightness of my coming.

20 Behold, I tell you these things, even as I also told the people of the destruction of Jerusalem; and my word shall be verified at this time as it hath hitherto been verified.

One definition of a *scourge* is a whip used to flog and inflict great pain upon individuals. From time to time the Lord uses a scourge (meaning, the Lord punishes or afflicts) to whip earth's inhabitants on account of their wickedness. Isaiah prophesied, for instance, that the Lord would send an "overflowing scourge" to the inhabitants of the southern kingdom of Judah because they had made a "covenant with death" and an "agreement with hell" (Isa. 28:18). Hence, Isaiah promised that "the overflowing scourge shall pass through, then ye shall be trodden down by it. From the time that it goeth forth it shall take you: for morning by morning shall it pass over, by day and by night: and it shall be a vexation only to understand the report" (Isa. 28:18–19).

The scourge that inflicted great pain upon ancient Judah was none other than the cruel Assyrians (see also Isa. 10:26), whom God engaged to scatter and destroy the people who once possessed his name and his religion. Judah's inhabitants were aware of the Assyrians but erroneously believed that their alliances would protect them (Isa. 30:1; 31:1); the "overflowing scourge . . . shall not come unto us," they said (Isa. 28:15).

The Lord has decreed one or more great scourges for the last days, scourges that will cleanse the world. Four separate passages from the Doctrine and Covenants speak of such latter-day scourges (D&C 5:19; 45:30–32; 84:96–98; 97:23–24), named "a desolating scourge" or "an overflowing scourge" (D&C 5:19; 45:31). These passages inform us that the scourge will come because of wicked works.

"For I, the Almighty, have laid my hands upon the nations, to scourge them for their wickedness" (D&C 84:96); also, "The Lord's scourge shall pass over by night and by day, and the report thereof shall vex all people; . . . For the indignation of the Lord is kindled against their abominations and all their wicked works" (D&C 97:23–24).

Zion's inhabitants, those who "stand in holy places," should be consoled in knowing that they will not fall on account of the scourge of the Lord. Although there will be a scourge that overflows, God instructs, "my disciples shall stand in holy places, and shall not be moved; but among the wicked, men shall lift up their voices and curse God and die" (D&C 45:31–32). Joseph Smith declared the same: "Repent ye, repent ye, and embrace the everlasting covenant, and flee to Zion, before the overflowing scourge overtake you."[28] Also, "'the ransomed of the Lord shall return, and come to Zion with songs and everlasting joy upon their heads' [Isa. 35:10]; and then they will be delivered from the overflowing scourge that shall pass through the land."[29] The Prophet also made this statement: "[In that] city of Zion . . . [the saints] will be delivered from the overflowing scourge that shall pass through the land."[30]

NOTES AND COMMENTARY

D&C 5:19 *For a desolating scourge shall go forth among the inhabitants of the earth.* Perhaps this scourge refers to "a desolating sickness" (D&C 45:31), plagues (D&C 84:96–97), armies causing destruction (Isa. 10:26; 28:18–19), or to other terrible events.

if they repent not. The prophecy regarding the desolating scourge is conditional and will receive fulfillment only if earth's inhabitants "repent not." But if they refuse to repent, they will be flogged with a desolating scourge as long as they refuse to repent (see also D&C 84:96–97) or "until the earth is empty," meaning empty of wicked people.

utterly destroyed by the brightness of my coming. Sinners who survive thrashings and other forms of punishments that are sent upon

---

[28] *Teachings of the Prophet Joseph Smith,* 18; cf. D&C 45:31.
[29] *Teachings of the Prophet Joseph Smith,* 17.
[30] *History of the Church,* 1:315.

the earth in the last days will be destroyed by Christ when he "shall come down in heaven, clothed in the brightness of his glory, to meet the kingdom of God which is set up on the earth" (D&C 65:5). Paul also warned, "The Lord shall consume [sinners] . . . with the brightness of his coming" (2 Thes. 2:8). One reason that the ungodly will be consumed at Christ's coming is that "no sinful man hath at any time, neither shall there be any sinful man at any time, that shall see my face and live" (JST Ex. 33:20; see also D&C 67:12).

D&C 5:20 *Behold, I tell you these things.* Jesus Christ is the source of the statements made in this revelation.

even as I also told the people of the destruction of Jerusalem. The prophet Lehi warned Jerusalem's inhabitants about their city's impending destruction, but they failed to repent, preferring rather to mock God's prophet (1 Ne. 1:18–19; cf. 2 Ne. 25:9). Nonetheless, the city was destroyed according to God's word. Similarly, God's desolating scourge will go forth in the last days, and God's "word shall be verified" regarding the scourge just "as it hath hitherto been verified" with regard to the destruction of Jerusalem.

GOD'S JUDGMENTS WILL BEGIN WITH THE HYPOCRITES OF ZION
Doctrine and Covenants 112:24–26

24 Behold, vengeance cometh speedily upon the inhabitants of the earth, a day of wrath, a day of burning, a day of desolation, of weeping, of mourning, and of lamentation; and as a whirlwind it shall come upon all the face of the earth, saith the Lord.

25 And upon my house shall it begin, and from my house shall it go forth, saith the Lord;

26 First among those among you, saith the Lord, who have professed to know my name and have not known me, and have blasphemed against me in the midst of my house, saith the Lord.

The Lord's day of vengeance will come as quickly upon earth's inhabitants as a whirlwind: with great speed and without forewarning.

Six words are used to describe this great day: *wrath, burning, desolation, weeping, mourning,* and *lamentation.* The prophet Zephaniah similarly describes this day:

The great day of the Lord is near . . .

That day is a day of wrath,

a day of trouble and distress,

a day of wasteness and desolation,

a day of darkness and gloominess,

a day of clouds and thick darkness,

a day of the trumpet and alarm (Zeph. 1:14, 15–16).

So fearsome will this day be to the wicked, says Zephaniah, that "the mighty man shall cry there bitterly" (Zeph. 1:14). Joel also describes the day of the Lord as "a day of darkness and of gloominess, a day of clouds and of thick darkness" (Joel 2:1–2).

The Lord's day of vengeance will not begin with those who are considered to be the darkest and most ungodly of individuals but with those who belong to the Church who are hypocrites and blasphemers. The Lord states: "Upon my house shall it begin," and then explains, "first among those among you . . . who have professed to know my name and have not known me, and have blasphemed against me" (D&C 112:26). Afterward, God's judgments will go forth from these to the sinners of the world: "from my house shall it go forth," says the Lord (v. 25).

NOTES AND COMMENTARY

D&C 112:24 *vengeance cometh speedily.* The term *speedily* and the corresponding expression *as a whirlwind* describe the swiftness with which God's judgments will come; *whirlwind* also expresses the idea that the judgments will be as destructive as a sudden burst of wind that destroys all that is in its path. The phrases *inhabitants of the earth* and *all the face of the earth* correspond and signify the universality of the destruction: none will escape it. Doctrine and Covenants 112:23 explains that vengeance is coming to the inhabitants of the earth because "darkness covereth the earth, and gross darkness the minds of the people, and all flesh has become corrupt before [God's] face."

a day of wrath, a day of burning, a day of desolation, of weeping, of mourning, and of lamentation. The first three expressions—wrath, burning, and desolation—describe the devastation that sinners will experience, while the second three—weeping, mourning, and lamentation—announce the reaction of sinners to God's vengeance.

D&C 112:25–26 *upon my house shall it begin, and from my house shall it go forth.* God's judgments, described in Doctrine and Covenants 112:24, will begin with those in the Church who profess to know God, but do not, and who blaspheme God's name. These judgments will serve to cleanse the Church and to purge her of her dross. Elder Ezra Taft Benson spoke of a cleansing that is coming: "It is well that our people . . . not be misled by those apostates within the Church who have not yet repented or been cut off. But there is a cleansing coming. The Lord says that his vengeance shall be poured out 'upon the inhabitants of the earth. . . . And upon my house shall it begin, and from my house shall it go forth, saith the Lord; First among those among you, saith the Lord, who have professed to know my name and have not known me. . . .' (D&C 112:24–26). I look forward to that cleansing."[31]

saith the Lord. This phrase, used in Doctrine and Covenants 112:25 and 26, declares that Jesus Christ is the source of this revelation.

ZION WILL ESCAPE, IF FAITHFUL
Doctrine and Covenants 97:22–28

> 22 For behold, and lo, vengeance cometh speedily upon the ungodly as the whirlwind; and who shall escape it?
>
> 23 The Lord's scourge shall pass over by night and by day, and the report thereof shall vex all people; yea, it shall not be stayed until the Lord come;
>
> 24 For the indignation of the Lord is kindled against their abominations and all their wicked works.
>
> 25 Nevertheless, Zion shall escape if she observe to do all things whatsoever I have commanded her.

---

[31] Conference Report, Apr. 1969, 10.

26 But if she observe not to do whatsoever I have commanded her, I will visit her according to all her works, with sore affliction, with pestilence, with plague, with sword, with vengeance, with devouring fire.

27 Nevertheless, let it be read this once to her ears, that I, the Lord, have accepted of her offering; and if she sin no more none of these things shall come upon her;

28 And I will bless her with blessings, and multiply a multiplicity of blessings upon her, and upon her generations forever and ever, saith the Lord your God. Amen.

Two contrasting themes compete for attention in these verses: *vengeance* and *blessings*. The theme of vengeance, or God's punishment of the wicked for their iniquity, controls the first five verses (vv. 22–26) and bears upon the ungodly, whether of the world or of Zion. The words *scourge, sore affliction, pestilence, plague, sword,* and *devouring fire* all help to define vengeance (vv. 23, 26).

Certainly one great blessing that will belong to Zion is mentioned in verse 25, which is "Zion shall escape" the Lord's scourge. But note the escape is conditional: she escapes "if she observe to do all things whatsoever I have commanded her." President Joseph F. Smith's remarks concerning Zion's escape are instructive: "We firmly believe that Zion—which is the pure in heart—shall escape, if she observe to do all things whatsoever God has commanded; but in the opposite event, even Zion shall be visited 'with sore affliction, with pestilence, with plague, with sword, with vengeance, and with devouring fire.' (Doctrine and Covenants 97:26.) All this that her people may be taught to walk in the light."[32]

In 1977 Elder Marion G. Romney spoke at general conference and proposed the *only way* that humans can escape the calamities of the last days: "All the acts of governments, all the armies of the nations, all the learning and the wisdom of man together cannot turn these calamities aside. The only way they can be averted is for men to accept and conform to the way of life revealed by God our Heavenly Father. Calamities will come as a matter of cause and effect."[33]

---

[32] "Lesson in Natural Calamities," 653.
[33] Conference Report, Apr. 1977, 76.

The theme of blessings is the subject of two verses (vv. 27–28). God accents the numerous blessings that will belong to those who are obedient in Zion with special language where the following terms are used in repetition: *bless, blessings, multiply, multiplicity, her, forever and ever.* Hence God promises, "I will bless her with blessings, and multiply a multiplicity of blessings upon her, and upon her generations forever and ever" (v. 28).[34]

"SEAL UP THE LAW, AND BIND UP THE TESTIMONY"
Doctrine and Covenants 109:38–46

38 Put upon thy servants the testimony of the covenant, that when they go out and proclaim thy word they may seal up the law, and prepare the hearts of thy saints for all those judgments thou art about to send, in thy wrath, upon the inhabitants of the earth, because of their transgressions, that thy people may not faint in the day of trouble.

39 And whatsoever city thy servants shall enter, and the people of that city receive their testimony, let thy peace and thy salvation be upon that city; that they may gather out of that city the righteous, that they may come forth to Zion, or to her stakes, the places of thine appointment, with songs of everlasting joy;

40 And until this be accomplished, let not thy judgments fall upon that city.

41 And whatsoever city thy servants shall enter, and the people of that city receive not the testimony of thy servants, and thy servants warn them to save themselves from this untoward generation, let it be upon that city according to that which thou hast spoken by the mouths of thy prophets.

42 But deliver thou, O Jehovah, we beseech thee, thy servants from their hands, and cleanse them from their blood.

43 O Lord, we delight not in the destruction of our fellow men; their souls are precious before thee;

---

[34] See the commentary on D&C 97, page 177.

44 But thy word must be fulfilled. Help thy servants to say, with thy grace assisting them: Thy will be done, O Lord, and not ours.

45 We know that thou hast spoken by the mouth of thy prophets terrible things concerning the wicked, in the last days— that thou wilt pour out thy judgments, without measure;

46 Therefore, O Lord, deliver thy people from the calamity of the wicked; enable thy servants to seal up the law, and bind up the testimony, that they may be prepared against the day of burning.

These verses are a passage from Joseph Smith's dedicatory prayer of the Kirtland Temple, given by revelation and offered 27 March 1836. The verses contain language consistent with prayer, such as "O Jehovah," "O Lord," "we beseech thee," "thy will be done," in addition to the third-person respectful imperatives where the term *let* is used, such as "let thy peace," "let not thy judgments," "let it be upon that city."

The phrases "seal up the law, and bind up the testimony" (D&C 109:46) are found in other scriptures. Isaiah used this phrase but in reverse order: "Bind up the testimony, seal the law" (Isa. 8:16). Two other revelations from the Doctrine and Covenants transpose the verbs *seal* and *bind* to read: "to bind up the law and seal up the testimony" (D&C 88:84; see also 133:72).

According to this passage of scripture, these actions of binding and sealing the testimony and the law fit into a divine sequence: the Saints must first receive their temple endowments, then they warn the world's inhabitants of God's coming judgments; this is followed by the binding up of the testimony and the sealing of the law; finally the judgments of God will come (D&C 88:84; 109:38, 46; 133:72). After the Lord's servants have testified to and warned the nations, they will figuratively "bind," "tie up," "shut up"[35] or close their testimonies and "affix [a] seal"[36] to the law of God (the prophetic

---

[35] The word *bind* used in Isa. 8:16 (Hebrew *tsor*) also means to "tie up" or "shut up"; see Brown, Driver, and Briggs, *Hebrew and English Lexicon*, 864.

[36] The word *seal* used in Isa. 8:16 (Hebrew *chatim*) also means to "affix [a] seal"; see Brown, Driver, and Briggs, *Hebrew and English Lexicon*, 864.

word).[37] Joseph Smith explained these things to the First Presidency and the Quorum of the Twelve Apostles on 12 November 1835: "But when you are endowed and prepared to preach the Gospel to all nations, kindreds, and tongues, in their own languages, you must faithfully warn all, and bind up the testimony, and seal up the law, and the destroying angel will follow . . . upon the children of disobedience; and destroy the workers of iniquity, while the Saints will be gathered out from among them, and stand in holy places ready to meet the Bridegroom when he comes."[38] In sum, then, God's judgments follow the Saints' warning voice to the world.

NOTES AND COMMENTARY

D&C 109:38 *Put upon thy servants the testimony of the covenant.* The Prophet prays that God's servants, or his Latter-day Saints (D&C 109:1–5), will have a testimony of the gospel.

when they go out and proclaim thy word. This passage pertains to missionary work and proclaiming the gospel to the world.

prepare the hearts of thy saints for all those judgments thou art about to send. Proclaiming the gospel benefits not only nonmembers who receive the truth and accept the gospel but also prepares the Saints themselves for God's judgments. This concept is explained beautifully in Doctrine and Covenants 88:81–85.

in thy wrath. Doctrine and Covenants 88:85 declares "the wrath of God" to be "the desolation of abomination which awaits the wicked, both in this world and in the world to come."

because of their transgressions. God's judgments, which constitute the "day of trouble" (D&C 109:38) for the ungodly, have always come because of transgression.

D&C 109:39 *the people of that city receive their testimony.* This verse identifies three things that accompany those who accept and act upon the testimony of the Lord's servants: peace, salvation, and songs of joy (Matt. 10:11–15).

D&C 109:40 *until this be accomplished, let not thy judgments fall upon that city.* The Lord will hold back his judgments until his

---

[37] See Parry, Parry, and Peterson, *Understanding Isaiah,* 88.
[38] *Teachings of the Prophet Joseph Smith,* 92.

servants preach the gospel, testify, and warn the people (compare 2 Ne. 25:9).

D&C 109:42 *deliver thou . . . thy servants from their hands, and cleanse them from their blood.* The Lord has declared: "I sent you out to testify and warn the people, and it becometh every man who hath been warned to warn his neighbor. Therefore, they are left without excuse, and their sins are upon their own heads" (D&C 88:81–82; see also Jacob 1:19).

D&C 109:45 *that thou wilt pour out thy judgments, without measure.* God will not weigh or measure his judgments when he pours them from the cup of his wrath upon the wicked; meaning, his judgments will be exceedingly great.

Do&C 109:46 *O Lord, deliver thy people from the calamity of the wicked.* The Prophet prays that the Saints will escape the judgments of God that are poured out upon sinners.

seal up the law, and bind up the testimony. Hugh Nibley wrote, "We seal and bind up things to keep them safe from fire and flood, or, in nautical terms, we 'batten down the hatches' for what is to come, in this case a burning. . . . The words *sealing* and *binding* are not vague theological jargon; they actually mean putting things in such a condition as to resist destructive forces."[39]

the day of burning. The day of burning refers to Christ's second coming, when all corruptible things will be burned.

THOSE WHO ESCAPE THE JUDGMENTS OF GOD WILL BE CLEANSED

Isaiah 4:2–6

2 *In that day shall the branch of the Lord be beautiful and glorious, and the fruit of the earth shall be excellent and comely for them that are escaped of Israel [and Judah].*[40]

3 *And it shall come to pass, [they that are]*[41] *left in Zion, and*

---

[39] "House of Glory," 44.

[40] The Great Isaiah Scroll from the Dead Sea Scrolls inserts the words *and Judah,* which is consistent with the theme of the section.

[41] The change is from 2 Ne. 14:3 and JST Isa. 4:2

[remain][42] *in Jerusalem, shall be called holy, even every one that is written among the living in Jerusalem:*

4 When the Lord shall have washed away the filth of the daughters of Zion, and shall have purged the blood of Jerusalem from the midst thereof by the spirit of judgment, and by the spirit of burning.

5 And the Lord will create upon every dwelling place of mount Zion, and upon her assemblies, a cloud and smoke by day, and the shining of a flaming fire by night: for upon all the glory [of Zion][43] *shall be a defence.*

6 And there shall be a [shelter][44] *for a shadow in the daytime from the heat, and for a place of refuge and for a covert from storm and from rain.*

This section of Isaiah 4 deals with those who have survived the judgments of God, as listed in Isaiah 3:14–26, perhaps in the dawning of the millennial day. The survivors are those who are the "escaped of Israel and Judah" and have been "left in Zion" (JST Isa. 4:2) to be "written among the living in Jerusalem" (Isa. 4:3). The survivors will love to participate in the ordinances of the Lord's temple, for they will be "called holy" (Isa. 4:3; the term *holy* is generally connected to the temple), their filth and iniquity will be removed, and the same elements (cloud, smoke, fire, glory) that attended and protected the ancient Israelite temples will exist among them in Zion.

The temple theme is also present in the four explicit references to *Zion* or *mount Zion*. The temple, always an integral part of Zion, is located at its center. Further, Zion's inhabitants are pure in heart and worthy to enter the temple and participate in its ordinances.[45] It is significant that the survivors of God's judgments will be a temple-oriented people, for it is their temple orientation that will help them escape his judgments. Isaiah 4:6 states that the Lord's true servants will find safety and refuge in Zion, an idea repeated in Doctrine and

---

[42] 2 Ne. 14:3 changes the KJV words *he that remaineth* to *remain*.
[43] JST Isa. 4:4 and 2 Ne. 14:5 add the words *of Zion*.
[44] From the Hebrew word *sukah*.
[45] *History of the Church*, 5:423–24.

Covenants 45:66–70. The command to us in this dispensation is, "Stand ye in holy places, and be not moved, until the day of the Lord come; for behold, it cometh quickly" (D&C 87:8; see also D&C 45:32).

NOTES AND COMMENTARY

Isa. 4:2 *In that day.* The same expression links earlier sections of Isaiah (Isa. 2:12, 17, 20; 3:7, 18; 4:1) and is a continuation of the theme of the "day of the Lord," meaning the time shortly before, during, or after the day of the coming of the Lord.

branch. This word may have a double meaning. First, the Lord is called *Branch* messianically (Jer. 23:5–6; 33:15–17; Zech. 3:8–10; 6:12–15). Second, an offshoot of the house of Israel is often called "a righteous branch" (Jacob 2:25) or "a branch of the house of Israel" (1 Ne. 15:12; see also 2 Ne. 3:5). The context of this section suggests that the *branch* represents a specific remnant, or *branch,* of Israel that remains in Israel after God's judgments (identified in Isa. 3).

fruit. Those who "are escaped of Israel and Judah" will be blessed with the bounties and blessings of the earth. The earth will be fruitful once again because of the presence of temples. "The temple," says John Lundquist, "is associated with abundance and prosperity, indeed is perceived as the giver of these."[46] We are reminded by the promise of Book of Mormon prophets that those who are obedient to God's commands will prosper in the land.

Isa. 4:2–3 *escaped of Israel/left in Zion/remain in Jerusalem.* These phrases refer to those who will survive the latter-day judgments of God that will destroy many of the people of the earth (Isa. 10:20). The *escaped of Israel* will consist of both Jews and other members of the house of Israel (D&C 133:11–13).

holy. God is called Holy One (Isa. 41:14; 1 Jn. 2:20). In the last days, those in Zion will be like God in holiness.

written among the living. The primary object of this phrase seems to be those who are counted among the mortal living. Temporally, those who survived the judgments identified in Isaiah 3 will be *among the living.* The phrase may also refer to the book of life, speaking

---

[46] "What Is a Temple?" 97.

spiritually of those who are written in the Lamb's book of life and who will go to God's kingdom of heaven (Dan. 12:1; Philip. 4:3; Rev. 20:15).

Isa. 4:4 *washed/purged.* The filth of the children of Israel, which includes us, will be washed away by the ordinance of baptism (1 Ne. 20:1; Alma 7:14) and cleansed by the blood of Jesus (Mal. 3:2–3; Heb. 9:22; Rev. 7:14), a process in which the Holy Ghost plays a prominent role. Joseph Smith taught that "as the Holy Ghost falls upon one of the literal seed of Abraham, it is calm and serene; and his whole soul and body are only exercised by the pure spirit of intelligence; while the effect of the Holy Ghost upon a Gentile, is to purge out the old blood, and make him actually of the seed of Abraham"[47] (see also 3 Ne. 27:20).

blood/filth. The blood of humanity can represent iniquity (Isa. 59:3; Micah 3:10). Paradoxically, Jesus' blood is able to purge and cleanse our souls from iniquity because of Jesus' innocence, sinlessness, and perfection (Lev. 17:11; John 6:53–54; Moses 6:59–60). In its root sense, the Hebrew word for *filth* refers to human excrement.[48] The term *filth* is used symbolically to emphasize the terrible nature of the sins of Israel and the impurities found in the daughters of Zion.

spirit of judgment/burning. Together, God's judgments and his cleansing fires (speaking symbolically of trials and tribulations) will purge Israel of her sins.

Isa. 4:5 *every dwelling place of mount Zion.* Isaiah compares the individual homes in Zion to the temple, thus emphasizing the sanctity of Zion and her people in this glorious day.

cloud and smoke/fire. These elements often accompany a theophany or God's presence in the temple. For instance, God appeared at the Sinai sanctuary (Ex. 15:17) and was accompanied by a cloud, smoke, and fire (Ex. 19:9, 18). Similar elements were associated with Solomon's Temple (1 Kgs. 8:10) and the temple in heaven (Isa. 6:4; Rev. 15:8). The cloud symbolizes the Lord's glory (D&C 84:2–5). The people of the latter-day (or perhaps millennial) Zion will be so righteous that they will all enjoy such blessings.

---

[47] *Teachings of the Prophet Joseph Smith,* 149–50.
[48] Brown, Driver, and Briggs, *Hebrew and English Lexicon,* 844.

shall be a defence. The word *defence* should read *canopy* or *protective covering.*[49] Hence Zion and her inhabitants will be protected by God from spiritual harm in the same way that individuals are protected from physical harm by seeking shelter during the heat of the day or in great storms (Isa. 4:6).

Isa. 4:6 *shelter/refuge/covert.* Similar language is used in a modern-day revelation, in which Zion is called "a city of refuge" and "a place of safety." It will be a "land of peace" and "the terror of the Lord also shall be there, insomuch that the wicked will not come unto it, . . . and it shall be the only people that shall not be at war one with another. And it shall be said among the wicked: Let us not go up to battle against Zion, for the inhabitants of Zion are terrible; wherefore we cannot stand" (D&C 45:66–70; see also 115:6). Jesus, of course, is our ultimate refuge and shelter from life's battles (Isa. 25:4). And he will be in Zion, sanctifying it and thus protecting it.

storm/rain. These weather events are symbols for God's judgments on the wicked (Ps. 83:15). The *storms* remove the wicked from their places as chaff is removed from the wheat (Job 21:18; 27:21), while the righteous, like wheat, are gathered into protected units and preserved in the Lord's temples and other holy places.

JOHN'S VISION OF EARTH'S HARVEST
Revelation 14:14–20

> *14 And I looked, and behold a white cloud, and upon the cloud one sat like unto the Son of man, having on his head a golden crown, and in his hand a sharp sickle.*
>
> *15 And another angel came out of the temple, crying with a loud voice to him that sat on the cloud, Thrust in thy sickle, and reap: for the time is come for thee to reap; for the harvest of the earth is ripe.*
>
> *16 And he that sat on the cloud thrust in his sickle on the earth; and the earth was reaped.*
>
> *17 And another angel came out of the temple which is in heaven, he also having a sharp sickle.*

---

[49] Brown, Driver, and Briggs, *Hebrew and English Lexicon,* 342.

18 And another angel came out from the altar, which had power over fire; and cried with a loud cry to him that had the sharp sickle, saying, Thrust in thy sharp sickle, and gather the clusters of the vine of the earth; for her grapes are fully ripe.

19 And the angel thrust in his sickle into the earth, and gathered the vine of the earth, and cast it into the great winepress of the wrath of God.

20 And the winepress was trodden without the city, and blood came out of the winepress, even unto the horse bridles, by the space of a thousand and six hundred furlongs.

This section of Revelation 14 gives us scenes of the two-phase harvest of the earth. First we see Christ with a sharp sickle, which he uses to select the righteous as if they were wheat to be harvested. This harvest is that which was described by Jesus in his parable of the wheat field (JST Matt. 13:24–30, 37–43; for a modern interpretation, see D&C 86:1–7.[50]

Next, we see an angel gathering the wicked as if they were clusters of grapes and then casting them into a winepress that represents God's wrath. We see the blood that comes from the winepress as juice flows from crushed grapes, blood so deep it reaches to a horse's bridle. Though this is a horrifying scene in John's vision, it is a scene not of injustice and wrong but of setting things right and fulfilling the law of justice. Whatever God in his wisdom and love decides to do is best for his children, both individually and as a group; whatever God chooses to do is just and merciful and right (Alma 42:15).

Joel saw a similar vision: "Let the heathen be wakened, and come up to the valley of Jehoshaphat: for there will I sit to judge all the heathen round about. Put ye in the sickle, for the harvest is ripe: come, get you down; for the press is full, the fats overflow; for their wickedness is great" (Joel 3:12–13).

---

[50] See the commentary on the latter-day gathering as a harvest, page 76.

NOTES AND COMMENTARY

Rev. 14:14 *a white cloud.* This scene is reminiscent of one beheld by Daniel long before: "I saw in the night visions, and, behold, one like the Son of man came with the clouds of heaven. . . . And there was given him dominion, and glory, and a kingdom" (Dan. 7:13–14). Elsewhere we read of Christ coming "in the clouds of heaven with power and great glory" (Matt. 24:30; see also D&C 45:16, 44), but this appearance does not seem to be the Second Coming, when Christ returns in great power with his angels. Instead, he sits as a judge and conqueror upon the clouds in heaven. The cloud probably symbolizes Christ's glory (D&C 84:5). The whiteness of the cloud may symbolize victory, purity, and grace.

upon the cloud one sat like unto the Son of man. The Son of man here is Christ (Rev. 1:12–20). After listing events of the last days, Jesus said, "And then shall they see the Son of man coming in the clouds with great power and glory. And then shall he send his angels, and shall gather together his elect from the four winds, from the uttermost part of the earth to the uttermost part of heaven" (Mark 13:26–27).

on his head a golden crown, and in his hand a sharp sickle. The Greek (the original language of the New Testament) tells us that the golden crown is instead a golden wreath (*stephanos*), such as victors would wear.[51] Christ comes victorious, with power to gather his Saints unto himself. The sharp sickle, the instrument of the gathering, may symbolize the missionaries, who go forth with his true gospel, bearing the priesthood and conveying ordinances, bringing the righteous, like sheaves, into the Lord's barn (Matt. 13:30).

Rev. 14:15 *another angel came out of the temple.* This angel comes forth from the place where God is (Rev. 7:15; 11:15–19), bearing the message that it is time for the final harvest of the righteous on the earth, preparatory to the burning of the wicked.

Thrust in thy sickle, and reap. The reaping in this verse refers to the gathering of the righteous out of the field that is the world (JST Matt. 13:24–30, 36–43; D&C 86:1–7). The time for that gathering has come; it is the last days, and "the harvest of the earth is ripe." *Ripe*

---

[51] Harrington, *Revelation*, 154.

means fully ready; the righteous have proved themselves and are ready to be gathered into the arms of their Lord.

"Behold, the field is white already to harvest," the latter-day revelation says, "therefore, whoso desireth to reap, let him thrust in his sickle with his might, and reap while the day lasts, that he may treasure up for his soul everlasting salvation in the kingdom of God" (D&C 6:3). Gathering the people of the world in harvest—whether for safety in the barn (or bosom) of the Lord, or for punishment and burning—has long been an image used by the Lord and his prophets (Jer. 51:33; Hosea 6:11; Matt. 9:37–38; 13:30, 40–42; Mark 4:29; Luke 10:2; John 4:35–38).

Rev. 14:16 *he that sat on the cloud thrust in his sickle on the earth; and the earth was reaped.* Through his sickle, the Lord reaches down and gathers his people from every part of the world. This gathering seems to be that of those who will come unto Christ; the gathering of the wicked is depicted in Revelation 14:19–20.

Through the Prophet Joseph Smith, the Lord described the two parts of the gathering that will occur before the Millennium: the gathering of the righteous unto blessing, and the gathering of the wicked unto burning: "But behold, in the last days, even now while the Lord is beginning to bring forth the word, and the blade is springing up and is yet tender—behold, verily I say unto you, the angels are crying unto the Lord day and night, who are ready and waiting to be sent forth to reap down the fields; but the Lord saith unto them, pluck not up the tares while the blade is yet tender (for verily your faith is weak), lest you destroy the wheat also. Therefore, let the wheat and the tares grow together until the harvest is fully ripe; then ye shall first gather out the wheat from among the tares, and after the gathering of the wheat, behold and lo, the tares are bound in bundles, and the field remaineth to be burned" (D&C 86:4–7).

Rev. 14:17 *another angel came out of the temple which is in heaven.* That the angel comes out of the temple in heaven, where God is, suggests that he has first received his commission or assignment from God and then goes forth to accomplish it.

he also having a sharp sickle. If the sickle of the Lord (Rev. 14:16) is the Saints going forth to do his work of gathering, this sickle, in the hands of an angel, may also be mortal beings doing the harvesting work of the Lord, but they are harvesting the wicked, preparing them to be crushed in the winepress of God or, as we read elsewhere, preparing them to be burned (Matt. 13:38–40; D&C 86:7). Perhaps this harvesting is done by bearing strong testimony to all people, and those who refuse to repent are then judged worthy to be destroyed.

Rev. 14:18 *another angel came out from the altar, which had power over fire.* This angel also comes from the temple and specifically from the altar. The passage may refer to the angel in Revelation 8:3–5, who stood at the altar of incense, which incense was offered with the prayers of the Saints: "And the angel took the censer, and filled it with fire of the altar, and cast it into the earth" (Rev. 8:5). This angel, who has authority over the fire of the altar, commands the angel with the sickle to gather the wicked to be destroyed. Ultimately, that destruction will come by fire (Rev. 18:8).

a loud cry to him that had the sharp sickle. The angel from the altar commands the angel with the sickle to thrust the sickle down to earth, to cut down and gather the wicked. The wicked are "the clusters of the vine of the earth"; they are "fully ripe" in their wickedness (contrast with the ripeness of the righteous in Rev. 14:15).

Rev. 14:19 *the angel thrust in his sickle into the earth, and gathered the vine of the earth.* The wheat that represents the righteous has been gathered and separated unto itself. The ripened grapes of the vine represent the wicked, those who bring forth evil fruit (Matt. 7:16–20), who are now ready to be harvested. The angel is the destroying angel, sent forth by God to perform his work of destruction and judgment. The gathering depicted here, however, is not the end of the world, for much must still transpire.

cast it into the great winepress of the wrath of God. As grapes were harvested, they were placed in a trough and trampled by foot; the juice then flowed through a duct into a lower basin. In symbolic terms, the winepress represents the great press of God's wrath (meaning the execution of his judgments), which, according to justice, exacts the full terrible payment for sin. The grapes, which represent the sinner, are trodden under foot until nothing is left but pulp and wine, the wine being a symbol of the blood of the sinner. In performing the Atonement, Christ suffered that wrath for us, so that we might escape both the wrath and the consequent suffering if we would repent. In the time of judgment, all those who have not truly repented and come unto Christ will suffer the wrath of God themselves; it will be for them as if they themselves were cast into the winepress and trampled. "I have trodden the winepress alone," the Lord said through Isaiah, "I will tread them in mine anger, . . . and their blood shall be sprinkled upon my garments" (Isa. 63:3).

Doctrine and Covenants 19:11–19 describes the suffering of Christ in performing the Atonement and the suffering of unrepentant souls who will be cast into the winepress themselves (see also D&C 133:46–51; Rev. 14:8–11).

Rev. 14:20 *the winepress was trodden without the city.* Jesus suffered for the sins of the world outside the city of Jerusalem, in the Garden of Gethsemane, and later at Golgotha (Heb. 13:12; Luke 22:39–44; John 19:20). In the same way, the nations will come to their judgment outside the city of Jerusalem, with the destruction centered in the valley of Jehoshaphat (probably the Kidron Valley, which runs between Jerusalem and the Mount of Olives; Joel 3:12–14; Zech. 14:1–4).[52] Because the wicked refused the blessings of the suffering of Christ, the benefits of the blood that was shed for them, they must now suffer for themselves.

blood came out of the winepress, even unto the horse bridles, . . . a thousand and six hundred furlongs. The language here is very plain: rather than using wine or red grape juice as a symbol for blood, John simply says, "blood came out of the winepress." The slaughter of the wicked in the day of their judgment creates a river of their blood. The depth of the flow of blood reaches up to the bridle of a horse. The length of the river of blood (sixteen hundred furlongs) is about 184 miles, or the approximate length of the land of Palestine. In this verse, the city seems to symbolize the holy places that are protected by God; the land outside the city may represent all the people of the world who are subjected to God's terrible but righteous judgments.[53]

---

[52] Mounce, *Book of Revelation,* 281.
[53] Mounce, *Book of Revelation,* 281.

CHAPTER 9

SIGNS AND WONDERS IN THE HEAVENS AND IN THE EARTH

SIGNS OF THE TIMES

1. God shows great signs and wonders in the skies.

2. The sun is darkened and the moon becomes "as blood."

3. The absence of the rainbow is a sign that the end is near.

4. The sign of the Son of Man appears in the sky shortly before Christ's second coming.

Since earth's creation God has used celestial objects and wonders as signs to earth's inhabitants. During the creation of the earth God "organized the lights in the expanse of the heaven" so that they would "be for signs and for seasons, and for days and for years" (Abr. 4:14; see also Gen. 1:14). Correspondingly, the prophet Samuel foretold of several signs that would indicate the time of Christ's birth, including the appearance of a new star, plus "many signs and wonders in heaven." These things produced amazement and wonderment, causing people to "fall to the earth" (Hel. 14:5–7; see also 3 Ne. 1:21; 2:1; Matt. 2:2).

Such signs at Christ's first coming typify the many signs in the sky that will appear in the last days. It is not a coincidence that the phrase "signs and wonders," used to describe the first coming of Christ, is used also to describe the signs that presage Christ's second coming (Hel. 14:5–7; D&C 45:40). In both Christ's first and second comings, celestial objects serve as signs. These signs are universal, and all will behold them regardless of where one is located upon the globe. All of earth's inhabitants will witness the darkening of the sun, all will see the moon turn blood red, and everyone will view the stars as they fall from heaven. These and other grand signs and wonders in the heavens will cause mortals to pause and to consider God's greatness and excellence. For those who are attuned to the Spirit, these signs will be grand revelations and will prepare them for Christ's coming.

SIGNS AND WONDERS WILL BE SHOWN IN THE LAST DAYS
Doctrine and Covenants 45:40–42

40 And they shall see signs and wonders, for they shall be shown forth in the heavens above, and in the earth beneath.

41 And they shall behold blood, and fire, and vapors of smoke.

42 And before the day of the Lord shall come, the sun shall be darkened, and the moon be turned to blood, and the stars fall from heaven.

These verses in Doctrine and Covenants 45 are nearly identical to a prophecy of Joel, recorded in Joel 2:30–31, but one important difference between the two texts is that the Lord speaks in the first person in Joel: "And I will shew wonders in the heavens and in the earth." The use of the personal pronoun *I* rather than the third person *they* (as in D&C 45:40) verifies that the *signs and wonders* of the heavens and earth, as well as the darkened sun, blood-red moon, and falling stars, are signs given of the Lord. They will not simply be atmospheric phenomena that indifferent observers may easily dismiss but are God's signs and wonders for the last days. The precise meaning of *signs and wonders* is at present unknown, although the spiritually alert will discern them to be signs of the times when they are revealed in the heavens and in the earth.

Joseph Smith enjoyed a view of God's signs in heaven the night of 13 November 1833, which he described as a "shower of fire" and "fireworks of eternity." He recorded in his journal that he was awakened at 4 A.M. by a "Brother Davis," who invited him to "arise and behold the signs in the heavens. I arose, and to my great joy, beheld

the stars fall from heaven like a shower of hailstones; a literal fulfilment of the word of God, as recorded in the holy Scriptures, and a
sure sign that the coming of Christ is close at hand. In the midst of
this shower of fire, I was led to exclaim, 'How marvelous are Thy
works, O Lord! I thank Thee for Thy mercy unto Thy servant; save
me in Thy kingdom for Christ's sake. Amen.'"

The Prophet's journal continues: "The appearance of these signs
varied in different sections of the country: in Zion, all heaven seemed
enwrapped in splendid fireworks, as if every star in the broad expanse
had been suddenly hurled from its course, and sent lawless through
the wilds of ether. Some at times appeared like bright shooting meteors, with long trains of light following in their course, and in numbers
resembled large drops of rain in sunshine. . . . The appearance was
beautiful, grand, and sublime beyond description; and it seemed as if
the artillery and fireworks of eternity were set in motion to enchant
and entertain the Saints, and terrify and awe the sinners of the earth.
Beautiful and terrific as was the scenery, it will not fully compare
with the time when the sun shall become black like sack-cloth of hair,
the moon like blood, and the stars fall to the earth—Rev. vi:13."[1] This
appearance in the sky, grand as it was, is but a preview of the signs
and wonders that will yet appear in the heavens.[2]

NOTES AND COMMENTARY

D&C 45:40 *they shall see signs and wonders.* Luke similarly
recorded: "And there shall be signs in the sun, and in the moon, and in
the stars" (Luke 21:25). *Signs and wonders* accompanied the first
coming of Christ (Hel. 14:5–7; 3 Ne. 1:21) and will be shown (or
heard; see 3 Ne. 2:1) in both the heavens and in the earth in the last
days. They will "enchant and entertain the Saints" but "terrify and
awe the sinners of the earth."[3] What the signs and wonders are and
when they shall appear have not been revealed.

D&C 45:41 *they shall behold blood, and fire, and vapors of
smoke.* The blood, fire, and smoke refer to wars and bloody battles,

---

[1] *History of the Church,* 1:439–40.
[2] Parley P. Pratt and others with him saw the same amazing scene on the same night; see *Autobi-
ography of Parley P. Pratt,* 110.
[3] *History of the Church,* 1:440.

but because this verse appears in the context of heavenly and earthly signs and wonders, perhaps the three refer to other events. For instance, earthquakes, volcanoes, and other natural catastrophes may cause injuries and death (hence blood), fire, and smoke; or the fire may come down from heaven as it did by the word of Elijah when two groups of fifty-one souls were destroyed (2 Kgs. 1:9–14). Yet another possibility is that the raining of brimstone and fire from heaven upon Sodom and Gomorrah, causing a great smoke to ascend "as the smoke of a furnace" (Gen. 19:24–28; see also 1 Ne. 19:11; 3 Ne. 10:13–14), may be a type of the destruction that will befall some in the last days. Moroni's prophecy of the conditions and events at the coming forth of the Book of Mormon included these words: "Yea, it shall come in a day when there shall be heard of fires, and tempests, and vapors of smoke in foreign lands" (Morm. 8:29).

D&C 45:42 *before the day of the Lord shall come.* Before the second coming of Jesus Christ.

sun shall be darkened, and the moon be turned to blood, and the stars fall from heaven. See the commentary on Revelation 6:12–17, below.

THE SUN WILL BECOME BLACK AS SACKCLOTH AND THE MOON AS BLOOD
Revelation 6:12–17

12 And I beheld when he had opened the sixth seal, and, lo, there was a great earthquake; and the sun became black as sackcloth of hair, and the moon became as blood;

13 And the stars of heaven fell unto the earth, even as a fig tree casteth her untimely figs, when she is shaken of a mighty wind.

14 And the heaven[s opened]⁴ as a scroll [is opened]⁵ when it is rolled together; and every mountain and island were moved out of their places.

15 And the kings of the earth, and the great men, and the rich

---

⁴ JST Rev. 6:14 changes *heaven departed* to *heavens opened*.
⁵ JST Rev. 6:14 adds *is opened*.

men, and the chief captains, and the mighty men, and every
bondman, and every free man, hid themselves in the dens and
in the rocks of the mountains;

16 And said to the mountains and rocks, Fall on us, and hide
us from the face of him that sitteth on the throne, and from the
wrath of the Lamb.

17 For the great day of his wrath is come; and who shall be
able to stand?

This section of Revelation 6 sets forth seven signs of the times
that will occur after the opening of the sixth seal but before the second coming of the Lord. The seven signs are the earthquake, the darkened sun, the blood-red moon, falling stars, the heavens opening as a
scroll, the movement of mountains and islands, and fear coming upon
humanity. Many other passages of scripture parallel John's vision
(Joel 3:15–16; D&C 29:14; JS–M 1:33).

These signs of the times warn the earth's inhabitants that the end
of the earth is near. They are designed, in part, to encourage the
wicked to repent of their sins. In fact, many will misinterpret these
signs, believing that the time of the Second Coming has actually
arrived. They will say, "The great day of his wrath is come; and who
shall be able to stand?" (Rev. 6:17). But the scriptures inform us that
Jesus will not make his great appearance until some time after the
opening of the seventh seal (D&C 77:12–13).

Yet these signs are imminent. On 27 December 1832, the Lord
revealed, "Not many days hence and the earth shall tremble and reel
to and fro as a drunken man; and the sun shall hide his face, and shall
refuse to give light; and the moon shall be bathed in blood; and the
stars shall become exceedingly angry, and shall cast themselves down
as a fig that falleth from off a fig-tree" (D&C 88:87).

NOTES AND COMMENTARY

Rev. 6:12 *he . . . opened the sixth seal.* Christ opens the sixth seal,
which "contains the revealed will, mysteries, and the works of God"
(D&C 77:6), for the sixth thousand years of the earth's temporal existence.

there was a great earthquake. The great earthquake identified in Revelation 6:12 will be a testimony and a warning voice to earth's people that the Lord is God. The earthquake (and possible accompanying phenomena) may cause the sun to become black and the moon to look like blood. Other earthquakes are identified in Revelation 11:13; 16:17–20.

sun became black as sackcloth. The sun will look as if it is covered with black sackcloth, which is made from the hair of black goats. Sackcloth often symbolizes mourning, and its connection with the darkened sun implies that all God's creations are in mourning over the wickedness of the world. As seen by the inhabitants of the earth, the sun may appear to be darkened on account of volcanic ash, dust, smoke, or other such things. This darkening may be a result of the "great earthquake," or some other cause. We must remember that "the events of that day shall be so unprecedented and so beyond human experience, that the prophets are and have been at an almost total loss for words to describe those realities pressed in upon them by the spirit of revelation."[6] Many prophecies have testified of this great event: "the sun shall be turned into darkness" (Joel 2:31); "shall the sun be darkened" (Matt. 24:29; JS–M 1:33); "the sun shall be darkened" (D&C 29:14; 34:9; 45:42); "the sun shall hide his face, and shall refuse to give light" (D&C 88:87).

moon became as blood. The moon does not become actual blood but becomes "as blood," probably meaning that it will look red to the inhabitants of the earth. This change in the appearance of the moon may be the result of the great earthquake spoken of in Revelation 6:12, which would send a great amount of dust and debris into the atmosphere. Such airborne particles could make the moon appear red "as blood." Many prophets have foretold this event, using such phrases as "the moon into blood" (Joel 2:31; Acts 2:20), "the moon shall be turned into blood" (D&C 29:14), "the moon be turned into blood" (D&C 34:9; 45:42), and "the moon shall be bathed in blood" (D&C 88:87). Though we may not know the actual cause in the change of the appearance of the moon—as well as any symbolism the

---

[6]McConkie, *Doctrinal New Testament Commentary,* 3:486.

Lord intended with this imagery—we can have confidence that this sign will somehow be given and that all the world will see it and fear.

Rev. 6:13 *stars of heaven fell unto the earth.* Many of the stars that we see in the sky are much larger than our sun, and their size alone, not to mention their extreme heat, would pulverize and melt the earth should they come in forceful contact with it. That will almost certainly not happen. Elder Bruce R. McConkie explained: "Such an earthquake [as the one prophesied in the sixth seal] has never before been known (Rev. 16:17–21), and it shall appear to man on earth as though the stars in the sidereal heavens are falling. And in addition, as here recorded, some heavenly meteors or other objects, appearing as stars, will fall 'unto the earth.'"[7]

Other prophets besides John have foreseen this event. They wrote: "the stars shall fall from heaven" (Matt. 24:29; JS–M 1:33; D&C 29:14); and "the stars shall refuse their shining, and some shall fall" (D&C 34:9); "the stars fall from heaven" (D&C 45:42); "and the stars shall become exceedingly angry, and shall cast themselves down as a fig that falleth from off a fig-tree" (D&C 88:87).

as a fig tree casteth her untimely figs. "Untimely figs" should read "unripe figs," meaning figs that, before they are ripe, fall off the tree during a great storm or a great gust of wind. Isaiah's words are similar: "And the heavens shall be rolled together as a scroll: and all their host shall fall down, as the leaf falleth off from the vine, and as a falling fig from the fig tree" (Isa. 34:4).

Rev. 6:14 *heaven[s opened] as a scroll.* This difficult expression parallels a similar one in Isaiah 34:4; there, however, the heavens are "rolled together as a scroll," whereas here they are "opened as a scroll." The expression "heavens opened as a scroll" may correspond to an experience described by Wilford Woodruff: "When the five men entered the camp there was not a cloud to be seen in the whole heavens, but as the men left the camp there was a small cloud like a black spot appeared in the north west, and it began to unroll itself like a scroll, and in a few minutes the whole heavens were covered with a pall as black as ink. This indicated a sudden storm which soon broke upon us."[8]

---

[7] *Doctrinal New Testament Commentary,* 3:486.
[8] *History of the Church,* 2:104.

every mountain and island [was] moved out of their places. This movement may be the result of the "great earthquake" spoken of in Revelation 6:12. In the following verse we learn that fearful individuals also hide in the "rocks of the mountains."

Rev. 6:15 *kings of the earth . . . and every free man, hid themselves.* John lists seven categories of individuals here, the number seven denoting completeness.[9] The list includes individuals belonging to the upper social class (kings; great, rich, and mighty men; and chief captains), middle class (free men), and lower class (bondmen). All will be affected by these cataclysmic events. Children are not included in this list, perhaps because of their innocence before God.

Why will people attempt to hide themselves from God? Three times Isaiah states that they will do so because of their "fear of the Lord" (Isa. 2:10, 19, 21), which fear is due to their wickedness and its consequences. According to Doctrine and Covenants 29:15, these signs of the times will cause "weeping and wailing among the hosts of men." Meanwhile, the righteous, or those who worship the Lord in his sacred temples, will receive deliverance. The prophet Joel stated, "Whosoever shall call on the name of the Lord shall be delivered: for in mount Zion and in Jerusalem shall be deliverance" (Joel 2:32). A modern revelation, speaking of the same events, commands us to "be not troubled" (D&C 45:35).

Rev. 6:16 *said to the mountains and rocks, Fall on us, and hide us.* Jesus Christ prophesied of these events to "a great company of people" who followed him as he walked to Calvary: "Then shall they begin to say to the mountains, Fall on us; and to the hills, Cover us" (Luke 23:27–30; see also Hosea 10:8).

face of him that sitteth on the throne. This expression is a reference to God the Father (Rev. 4:2).

wrath of the Lamb. This phrase speaks of Jesus' righteous indignation.

Rev. 6:17 *great day of his wrath is come.* The wicked, as they hide themselves in the rocks, make this statement out of their own fear. Because of the extraordinary events described in Revelation 6:12–14, the wicked will believe it is the end of the world. Though these events

---

[9] McConkie and Parry, *Guide to Scriptural Symbols,* 98–99.

are certainly signs of the times, they do not occur at the Second Coming, for the revelations state explicitly that Christ will not come until after the opening of the seventh seal (see, for example, D&C 77:12–13). In John's book of Revelation, Christ does not make his appearance in glory until Revelation 19. Further, the same writers who prophesied of the darkening of the sun, the moon becoming as blood, and stars falling from heaven (Rev. 6:12–14) record that those events would occur before the Second Coming, not at the Second Coming: "The sun shall be turned into darkness, and the moon into blood, *before* the great and the terrible day of the Lord come" (Joel 2:31; emphasis added; see also Acts 2:20); "but, behold, I say unto you that *before* this great day shall come the sun shall be darkened" (D&C 29:14; emphasis added); "but *before* that great day shall come, the sun shall be darkened (D&C 34:9; emphasis added); "and *before* the day of the Lord shall come, the sun shall be darkened" (D&C 45:42; emphasis added). Doctrine and Covenants 88:87 notes that these events will occur "not many days hence."

who shall be able to stand? The psalmist asked, "Thou, even thou, art to be feared: and who may stand in thy sight when once thou art angry?" (Ps. 76:7). When the judgments of God come, the wicked will fall to the earth in fear. Also, being unable to *stand* when God sends his judgments corresponds with *kneeling* "when the hour of his judgment is come." Doctrine and Covenants 88:104 states that "every knee shall bow, and every tongue shall confess, . . . for the hour of his judgment is come."

THE SIGN OF THE BOW

Joseph Smith

> The Lord hath set the bow in the cloud for a sign that while it shall be seen, seed time and harvest, summer and winter shall not fail; but when it shall disappear, woe to that generation, for behold the end cometh quickly.[10]

Twice Joseph Smith spoke concerning the sign of the rainbow, one of the signs of the times that is not identified in the scriptures (but compare Gen. 9:13–16; JST Gen. 9:21–25).[11] The Prophet made the

---

[10] *History of the Church,* 5:402.
[11] See McConkie, *Millennial Messiah,* 413–17.

statement cited above on 21 May 1843 and offered a second, more expansive statement less than a year later, on 10 March 1844: "I have asked of the Lord concerning His coming; and while asking the Lord, He gave a sign and said, 'In the days of Noah I set a bow in the heavens as a sign and token that in any year that the bow should be seen the Lord would not come; but there should be seed time and harvest during that year: but whenever you see the bow withdrawn, it shall be a token that there shall be famine, pestilence, and great distress among the nations, and that the coming of the Messiah is not far distant.'

"But I will take the responsibility upon myself to prophesy in the name of the Lord, that Christ will not come this year . . . for we have seen the bow."[12]

Both statements reveal specific aspects of this sign. Both speak of "seedtime and harvest," but the first adds "summer and winter." The first statement reads "woe to that generation" following the bow's disappearance, with no explanation as to why there will be "woe" or anguish and misfortune. The second, however, explains the meaning of the woe as being "famine, pestilence, and great distress among the nations." Both statements include the prediction that with the withdrawal of the bow, "behold the end cometh quickly," or "the coming of the Messiah is not far distant."

We may conjecture that the Lord will withhold rain from the earth for a period of time, preventing rainbows from forming in the sky. The lack of rain, in turn, may be the cause of "famines" mentioned in Joseph Smith's statement that "it shall be a token that there shall be famine, pestilence, and great distress among the nations."

THE SIGN OF THE SON OF MAN
Joseph Smith–Matthew 1:26, 36

26 For as the light of the morning cometh out of the east, and shineth even unto the west, and covereth the whole earth, so shall also the coming of the Son of Man be. . . .

36 And as I said before, after the tribulation of those days, and the powers of the heavens shall be shaken, then shall

[12] *History of the Church,* 6:254.

*appear the sign of the Son of Man in heaven, and then shall
all the tribes of the earth mourn; and they shall see the Son of
Man coming in the clouds of heaven, with power and great
glory.*

The principal statements regarding the "sign of the Son of Man"
may be found in Matthew's record or in Joseph Smith's teachings:[13]

The sign, which is some kind of heavenly manifestation, will
appear after the events and tribulations listed in Joseph Smith–
Matthew 1:28–32, for Christ prophesies that "after the tribulation of
those days . . . then shall appear the sign of the Son of Man" (JS–M
1:36).[14]

The sign will appear "in heaven" (JS–M 1:36), which presumably
means the sky.

After the sign appears, then shall the people of earth "see the Son
of Man coming in the clouds of heaven" (JS–M 1:36).

No man will see "the sign of the Son of Man, as foretold by Jesus
. . . until after the sun shall have been darkened and the moon bathed
in blood."[15]

Perhaps due to its sacredness or its significance, or perhaps to
preempt efforts at deception, God has withheld from the devil knowledge of this sign. Joseph Smith explained that "the devil knows many
signs, but does not know the sign of the Son of Man, or Jesus."[16] At
the same time, little has been revealed to the Saints or the world concerning the exact nature of this sign. But "when the sign is given, the
Lord's servants the prophets, including all the faithful saints, will
know it for what it is, and thus be made aware that the long-expected
day has arrived.[17]

The Prophet referred to the sign as "one grand sign of the Son of
Man in heaven,"[18] the word *grand* underscoring the sign's significance
and import. The sign will apparently have the appearance of a comet

---

[13] See also McConkie, *Millennial Messiah,* 418–20.

[14] Joseph Smith also placed the chronology of the sign of the Son of Man after several tribulations (*History of the Church,* 5:337).

[15] *Teachings of the Prophet Joseph Smith,* 280.

[16] *History of the Church,* 4:608.

[17] McConkie, *Millennial Messiah,* 419.

[18] *History of the Church,* 5:337.

or another heavenly sphere. The Prophet explained in a general conference address in Nauvoo, on 6 April 1843: "There will be wars and rumors of wars, signs in the heavens above and on the earth beneath, the sun turned into darkness and the moon to blood, earthquakes in divers places, the seas heaving beyond their bounds; then will appear one grand sign of the Son of Man in heaven. But what will the world do? They will say it is a planet, a comet, &c. But the Son of Man will come as the sign of the coming of the Son of Man, which will be as the light of the morning cometh out of the east."[19]

NOTES AND COMMENTARY

JS–M 1:26 *For as the light of the morning cometh out of the east.* "East is the sacred direction. Holy temples are oriented eastward, and the east wind (the 'wind of God') originates from this direction. Jesus Christ enters his temples from the east (Ezek. 43:1–2; see also Ezek. 10:19); and at the time of the Second Coming, the Lord will come from the east."[20] East is also the direction from which earth's inhabitants receive sunlight every morning, which serves as a constant reminder of Christ's glory and may be considered a type of his second coming; and at Christ's first coming in mortality, the wise men stated, "We have seen his star in the east" (Matt. 2:2).

shineth even unto the west, and covereth the whole earth, so shall also the coming of the Son of Man be. Jesus likens his coming to the rising of the sun, the light of which originates in the east, then shines to the west, until the entire land is covered with light. Joseph Smith explained, "The Son of Man will come as the sign of the coming of the Son of Man, which will be as the light of the morning cometh out of the east."[21] Thus, the sign of the coming of the Son of Man also appears to shine out of the east like the sun. Joseph Smith–Matthew 1:26 provides us with a description of Christ's second coming and assures us that on that occasion he will not come in any other way.

Such was clearly taught by President Harold B. Lee: "We are actually seeing [false Christs and false prophets] among us today,

---

[19] *History of the Church,* 5:337.
[20] McConkie and Parry, *Guide to Scriptural Symbols,* 44.
[21] *History of the Church,* 5:337.

where individuals are coming forward with claims of Deity for their leaders. These arch-deceivers are among us, and some have come in person claiming to be God. . . .

"The Master gave a sure way for the saints to herald the coming of our Lord again to the earth, as he promised. This is how the Savior said he would appear: 'Wherefore if they [meaning heralds of the false Christs] shall say unto you, Behold, he is in the desert; go not forth: behold, he is in the secret chambers; believe it not. For as the lightning cometh out of the east, and shineth even unto the west; so shall also the coming of the Son of man be.' (Matt. 24:26–27; see also JS–M 1:25–26.)

"If we could remember that, and put to flight all the foolish ideas about how the Savior will appear, we would be ready when he comes."[22]

JS–M 1:36 *as I said before, after the tribulation of those days.* Jesus refers to the tribulations that he listed in Joseph Smith–Matthew 1:28–32, which include wars, famines, pestilences, earthquakes, iniquity, lack of love, and the abomination of desolation.

then shall all the tribes of the earth mourn. The Revelator similarly prophesied that Jesus "cometh with clouds; and every eye shall see him, and they also which pierced him: and all kindreds of the earth shall wail because of him" (Rev. 1:7). Perhaps people will mourn or wail at this event because they realize that during their mortal probation they rejected their Savior and his redeeming grace and also because they know that suffering and destruction are imminent.

they shall see the Son of Man coming in the clouds of heaven. Earth's people will first see the sign of the Son of Man, and afterwards they will see the Son of Man appear with great glory in the clouds.

---

[22] *Ensign*, Dec. 1971, 31.

CHRIST COMES
IN GLORY

⸺◦⁄◦⁄◦⸺

CHAPTER 10

JESUS' SECOND COMING IN POWER AND GLORY

SIGNS OF THE TIMES

1. No one knows the exact time of the Second Coming.

2. Christ's coming is for the wicked like that of a thief in the night, but the righteous are prepared.

3. The Saints wait patiently for Christ's second coming.

4. Those who have the Holy Ghost as their guide are prepared for Christ's coming.

5. The great council at Adam-ondi-Ahman meets to prepare the Saints for Jesus' coming.

6. Jesus Christ comes "suddenly" to his temples and to the earth.

7. The Saints rejoice in knowing that the Lord will come again to the earth.

8. The Second Coming is a time of darkness and trouble for sinners.

9. Jesus Christ appears in glory, majesty, and power.

10. Righteous people from all ages of the earth will accompany Jesus Christ at his coming.

11. Sinners are burned with fire when Christ appears again.

12. Jesus joins the righteous in a joyous reunion at his coming.

Prophets from all ages and every dispensation have prophesied that Jesus Christ will make a great and glorious appearance to the earth; yet only once in the entire standard works does the expression *second coming* appear (D&C 34:6). In place of this expression, so

[3 8 1]

commonly used in our Church, the scriptures use the terms *coming, come,* and *cometh.* The following examples demonstrate this usage:

Asaph: "Our God shall come, . . . a fire shall devour before him, and it shall be very tempestuous round about him" (Ps. 50:3).

The psalmist: "Before the Lord: for he cometh, for he cometh to judge the earth" (Ps. 96:13).

Isaiah: "The Lord will come with fire, and with his chariots like a whirlwind, to render his anger with fury, and his rebuke with flames of fire" (Isa. 66:15).

Zechariah: "The Lord my God shall come" (Zech. 14:5).

Matthew: "The Son of man shall come in the glory of his Father with his angels" (Matt. 16:27).

Luke: "Blessed are those servants, whom the lord when he cometh shall find watching" (Luke 12:37).

John: "Behold, he cometh with clouds; and every eye shall see him" (Rev. 1:7).

Paul: "And then shall that Wicked be revealed, whom the Lord shall consume with the spirit of his mouth, and shall destroy with the brightness of his coming" (2 Thes. 2:8).

James: "Be patient therefore, brethren, unto the coming of the Lord" (James 5:7).

Peter: "There shall come in the last days scoffers, walking after their own lusts, and saying, Where is the promise of his coming?" (2 Pet. 3:3–4).

Jude (citing Enoch): "Behold, the Lord cometh with ten thousands of his saints" (Jude 1:14).

Joseph Smith: "O Lord, thou shalt come down . . . and all nations shall tremble at thy presence" (D&C 133:42).

The Doctrine and Covenants uses the verbs *coming, come,* and *cometh* extensively to express Christ's return to the earth. For instance, the Lord invites the faithful to pray for his coming: "Calling upon the name of the Lord day and night, saying: O that thou wouldst rend the heavens, that thou wouldst come down, that the mountains might flow down at thy presence" (D&C 133:40). He commands the Saints to "be faithful, praying always, having your lamps trimmed and burning, and oil with you, that you may be ready at the coming of the Bridegroom" (D&C 33:17). And he promises those who over-come the world that they will accompany Christ, "when he shall come in the clouds of heaven to reign on the earth over his people" (D&C 76:63).

Sinners receive a different message. The Lord warns that the unrepentant will be "utterly destroyed by the brightness of my com-ing" (D&C 5:19). The Lord's word to the children of darkness is, "The coming of the Lord draweth nigh, and it overtaketh the world as a thief in the night" (D&C 106:4).

Many from different spheres are preparing for Christ's coming, including God's angels, his mortal ministers, those who have passed on, and at least some of the 144,000 high priests.[1] Angels are also making preparations. The Revelator speaks of angels who are prepar-ing to sound their trumpets while there is "silence in heaven" (Rev. 8:1). Six angels then sound their trumpets in Revelation 8 and 9 and bring to the earth judgments that serve to cleanse the earth for Christ's coming. Three angels of judgment (Rev. 14:6–13) fulfill sacred duties, as do the angels of earth's harvest (Rev. 14:14–20). Seven angels also prepare and then pour out seven final judgments on the earth, encouraging people to repent (Rev. 15–16). Angels with their trumpets will herald the resurrection, destruction of the mother of abominations, the judgment, and other events (D&C 88:94–107).

In sum, "the sounding of the trumpets of the seven angels are the preparing and finishing of his work, in the beginning of the seventh thousand years—the preparing of the way before the time of his com-ing" (D&C 77:12). Further, angels cry out to the world: "Behold, and lo, the Bridegroom cometh; go ye out to meet him" (D&C 88:92). Paul taught that Michael the archangel would announce Christ's descent from heaven: "The Lord himself shall descend from heaven with a shout, with the voice of the archangel, and with the trump of

---

[1] On 4 February 1844, Joseph Smith commented regarding the 144,000: "I attended prayer-meeting with the quorum in the assembly room, and made some remarks respecting the hundred and forty-four thousand mentioned by John the Revelator, showing that the selection of persons to form that number had already commenced" (*History of the Church*, 6:196). The calling of the 144,000 is to "administer the everlasting gospel" and to help bring people to "the church of the Firstborn" (D&C 77:11)—tasks that do indeed help prepare the earth for the Second Coming.

God" (1 Thes. 4:16). The scriptures also attest that angels will accompany Christ at his coming (Matt. 25:31).

We as members of the Church are also preparing for Christ's coming. We are instructed to "go forth, crying with a loud voice, saying: The kingdom of heaven is at hand; crying: Hosanna! blessed be the name of the Most High God. Go forth baptizing with water, preparing the way before my face for the time of my coming. . . . And again, it shall come to pass that on as many as ye shall baptize with water, ye shall lay your hands, and they shall receive the gift of the Holy Ghost, and shall be looking forth for the signs of my coming, and shall know me" (D&C 39:19–20, 23).

On 3 November 1831, the Lord gave, through Joseph Smith, Doctrine and Covenants 133, addressed to "ye people of my church." It begins with a command to *hearken* and *hear* (D&C 133:1). In verses 8–10 the Lord commands the Church's elders to "call upon all nations, first upon the Gentiles, and then upon the Jews" and to "awake and arise and go forth to meet the Bridegroom; behold and lo, the Bridegroom cometh; go ye out to meet him. Prepare yourselves for the great day of the Lord."

Other revelations command the elders to declare repentance, to baptize, to make the Lord's paths straight, to harvest the field, and to gather people to Zion, all of which prepares souls for the coming of the Bridegroom (D&C 4; 11:1–4; 12:1–4; 14:1–4; 33:1–18). Although Doctrine and Covenants 34:6 was revealed to Orson Pratt, the verse is directed to all of the Church's elders: "Lift up your voice as with the sound of a trump, both long and loud, and cry repentance unto a crooked and perverse generation, preparing the way of the Lord for his second coming."

Many scriptures indicate that the righteous dead are making preparations for Christ's coming (D&C 61:38–39; 133:57–59; see also 1 Thes. 4:13–17).[2] And the 144,000 individuals fulfill a special function in the last days. They are "high priests, ordained unto the holy order of God, to administer the everlasting gospel" and "to whom is given power over the nations of the earth, to bring as many as will come to the church of the Firstborn" (D&C 77:11; see also Rev. 14:1–5).

---

[2] See also *History of the Church,* 3:390.

Christ, of course, promises to make many appearances to the earth before his coming in great power and glory. He will "suddenly come to his temple" (Mal. 3:1; see also D&C 36:8; 42:36); he will make an appearance at the great council of Adam-ondi-Ahman (Dan. 7:13–14);[3] he will stand on the Mount of Olives and save the Jews (Zech. 14:3–5); and he will make other appearances (D&C 133:18–25).[4]

President Ezra Taft Benson described the order of three of Jesus' appearances to the earth: "[At his second coming, the Savior's] first appearance will be to the righteous Saints who have gathered to the New Jerusalem. In this place of refuge they will be safe from the wrath of the Lord, which will be poured out without measure on all nations. . . .

"The second appearance of the Lord will be to the Jews. To these beleaguered sons of Judah, surrounded by hostile Gentile armies, who again threaten to overrun Jerusalem, the Savior—their Messiah—will appear and set His feet on the Mount of Olives. . . .

"The third appearance of Christ will be to the rest of the world. . . .

"All nations will see Him 'in the clouds of heaven, clothed with power and great glory; with all the holy angels.'"[5]

NO ONE KNOWS THE DAY OR THE HOUR
Joseph Smith–Matthew 1:40–46

40 But of that day, and hour, no one knoweth; no, not the angels of God in heaven, but my Father only.

41 But as it was in the days of Noah, so it shall be also at the coming of the Son of Man;

42 For it shall be with them, as it was in the days which were

---

[3] See the commentary on Christ's appearance at Adam-ondi-Ahman, page 399.

[4] Elder Bruce R. McConkie spoke of the multiple appearances of Jesus Christ when he wrote, "The second coming of the Son of Man consists not of one but of many appearances. Our blessed Lord will come—attended by all the hosts of heaven, and in all the glory of his Father's kingdom—not to one but to many places. He will stand on one continent after another, speak to one great assemblage after another, and work his will among succeeding groups of mortals" (*Millennial Messiah,* 575; see also 576–78).

[5] "Five Marks of the Divinity of Jesus Christ," 49–50.

before the flood; for until the day that Noah entered into the ark they were eating and drinking, marrying and giving in marriage;

43 And knew not until the flood came, and took them all away; so shall also the coming of the Son of Man be.

44 Then shall be fulfilled that which is written, that in the last days, two shall be in the field, the one shall be taken, and the other left;

45 Two shall be grinding at the mill, the one shall be taken, and the other left;

46 And what I say unto one, I say unto all men; watch, therefore, for you know not at what hour your Lord doth come.

Jesus Christ uttered these words to his disciples privately, while sitting on the Mount of Olives. They asked him, "Tell us when shall these things be which thou hast said concerning the destruction of the temple, and the Jews; and what is the sign of thy coming, and of the end of the world, or the destruction of the wicked, which is the end of the world?" (JS–M 1:4). Jesus responded by giving them signs by which they would know that Christ's coming was "near, even at the doors" (JS–M 1:39), and then he said, "But of that day, and hour, no one knoweth; no, not the angels of God in heaven, but my Father only."

The value of this statement should not be underestimated, for it has helped God's true followers in many generations discern false prophets who have attempted to declare the exact day or hour of Christ's coming. The statement also warns every generation to be constantly alert for his coming, because no one knows the day of his appearance.

Nevertheless, the Saints, as "children of light" (1 Thes. 5:5) are expected to know the season or the generation of his coming. This truth is taught clearly by Paul, who wrote, "But ye, brethren, are not in darkness, that that day should overtake you as a thief. Ye are all the children of light, and the children of the day: we are not of the night, nor of darkness" (1 Thes. 5:4–5).

Furthermore, although we do not know the exact time of Jesus' second coming, we should be ever mindful that the time draws ever closer. Elder N. Eldon Tanner taught during general conference of October 1968 that "the last days are here and now."[6] Elder Neal A. Maxwell concurred: "The Savior has told us that just as when the fig tree puts forth its leaves, we may know that summer is nigh, so it will be with his second coming (see Luke 21:28–30). The foreseen summer of circumstances is now upon us. Let us not, therefore, complain of the heat!"[7] And in 1951, President Joseph Fielding Smith told the Saints at general conference: "I believe that the coming of the Son of God is not far away, how far I do not know, but I do know that it is over one hundred years nearer than it was when Elijah the prophet came to the Prophet Joseph Smith and Oliver Cowdery in the Kirtland Temple on the third day of April, 1836. Elijah's words point to the fact that we are that much nearer. And this ancient prophet declared that by the restoration of those keys we should know that the great and dreadful day of the Lord is near, even at our doors. (D&C 110:13–16.)"[8]

NOTES AND COMMENTARY

JS–M 1:40 *But of that day, and hour, no one knoweth.* This saying is expressed again in the Doctrine and Covenants: "For the time is at hand; the day or the hour no man knoweth; but it surely shall come" (D&C 39:21); and again, "which time is nigh at hand—I, the Lord God, have spoken it; but the hour and the day no man knoweth, neither the angels in heaven, nor shall they know until he comes" (D&C 49:6–7). Elder M. Russell Ballard said: "I am called as one of the apostles to be a special witness of Christ in these exciting, trying times, and I do not know when He is going to come again. As far as I know, none of my brethren in the Council of the Twelve or even in the First Presidency know. And I would humbly suggest . . . that if we do not know, then nobody knows, no matter how compelling their arguments, or how reasonable their calculations. The Savior said that 'of

---

[6] Conference Report, Oct. 1968, 46.
[7] Conference Report, Oct. 1980, 19.
[8] Conference Report, Apr. 1951, 58.

that day and hour knoweth no man, no, not the angels of heaven, but my Father only' (Matthew 24:36)."[9]

no, not the angels of God in heaven, but my Father only. Jesus uses a triple negative ("no one knoweth; no, not") to stress that even the angels do not know the time of his coming.

JS–M 1:41–43 *as it was in the days of Noah.* Jesus likens the events connected with the great deluge to those preceding his second coming. Noah's contemporaries "were eating and drinking," an idiom that suggests riotous living (2 Ne. 28:7–8). They were involved in all types of sins. Moses listed some of these: "Behold, they are without affection, and they hate their own blood . . . and among all the workmanship of mine hands there has not been so great wickedness" (Moses 7:33, 36); "the earth was corrupt before God, and it was filled with violence. And God looked upon the earth, and, behold, it was corrupt, for all flesh had corrupted its way upon the earth. And God said unto Noah: The end of all flesh is come before me, for the earth is filled with violence, and behold I will destroy all flesh from off the earth" (Moses 8:28–30).

"As it was in the days of Noah," explained Jesus, "so it shall be also at the coming of the Son of man." Most of earth's inhabitants will either be involved in riotous living or will simply be walking heedlessly through life, unaware of impending disaster. Once again they will ignore the prophet's warning to repent and to come unto Christ, and once again they will be destroyed for their iniquities.[10]

Luke, as did his contemporary Matthew, recorded Jesus' comparison of the circumstances surrounding the deluge with those of the Second Coming (Luke 17:26–27); but Luke adds a teaching of Christ that underscores the idea that the world will not be mindfully watching for Christ's coming: "Likewise also as it was in the days of Lot; they did eat, they drank, they bought, they sold, they planted, they builded; but the same day that Lot went out of Sodom it rained fire and brimstone from heaven, and destroyed them all. Even thus shall it be in the day when the Son of man is revealed" (Luke 17: 28–30).

---

[9] "When Shall These Things Be?" 186.
[10] See the commentary on the flood of Noah, page 437.

JS–M 1:44–45 *grinding at the mill.* When Christ comes again, many people will be caught unaware: they will be "eating and drinking, marrying" (JS–M 1:42), working in their businesses and generally pursuing their occupations. Verse 44 specifically mentions farmers; verse 45 speaks of grinders, but farmers and grinders seem to represent people from all occupations. Elder Bruce R. McConkie explained the phrase "the one shall be taken, and the other left" as follows: "The one who is taken, of the two laboring side by side, is the righteous one, the one to be gathered with the saints. He is taken to the body of the Church."[11]

JS–M 1:46 *And what I say unto one, I say unto all men.* Although Christ speaks privately to his disciples on the Mount of Olives, his message is addressed to all people of all ages.

watch. This injunction means "be alert and ready." Doctrine and Covenants 61:38 states it this way: "Gird up your loins and be watchful and be sober, looking forth for the coming of the Son of Man, for he cometh in an hour you think not." Then the following verse explains how to watch for Christ's coming: "Pray always that you enter not into temptation, that you may abide the day of his coming, whether in life or in death" (D&C 61:39).

for you know not at what hour your Lord doth come. Christ returns to his statement of Joseph Smith–Matthew 1:40: "But of that day, and hour, no one knoweth; no, not the angels of God in heaven, but my Father only." It is spiritually healthy for us not to know the time of Jesus' coming. Elder Gordon B. Hinckley explained, "To know when [the Second Coming] will come would take from us much of the self-discipline needed to walk daily in obedience to the principles of the gospel."[12] "Deliberately and advisedly the actual time of [Jesus'] coming has been left uncertain and unspecified," taught Elder Bruce R. McConkie, "so that men of each succeeding age shall be led to prepare for it as though it would be in their mortal lives."[13]

---

[11] *Doctrinal New Testament Commentary,* 1:670.
[12] "'We Need Not Fear His Coming,'" 83.
[13] *Doctrinal New Testament Commentary,* 1:675.

CHRIST'S COMING IS LIKE THAT OF A THIEF FOR THE WICKED BUT NOT FOR THE RIGHTEOUS

1 Thessalonians 5:1–8

1 But of the times and the seasons, brethren, ye have no need that I write unto you.

2 For yourselves know perfectly that the day of the Lord so cometh as a thief in the night.

3 For when they shall say, Peace and safety; then sudden destruction cometh upon them, as travail upon a woman with child; and they shall not escape.

4 But ye, brethren, are not in darkness, that that day should overtake you as a thief.

5 Ye are all the children of light, and the children of the day: we are not of the night, nor of darkness.

6 Therefore let us not sleep, as do others; but let us watch and be sober.

7 For they that sleep in the night; and they that be drunken are drunken in the night.

8 But let us, who are of the day, be sober, putting on the breastplate of faith and love; and for an helmet, the hope of salvation.

Paul, the author of these verses in 1 Thessalonians 5, explained that the Second Coming will catch the wicked unprepared and unaware. To illustrate his point he used the images of a calendar, a thief, war, a pregnant woman, nighttime, sleep, a drunken person, and a warrior.

The calendar: The wicked can read "the times and the seasons" (v. 1) because of weather changes, leaves turning colors and falling to the ground, snow falling, new plant growth in the spring, fowls flying south, and so on, but they seem unable to detect the signs of the times.

A thief: To the wicked, the day of the Lord will come quickly and unexpectedly, as a thief breaks into one's home during the night. The righteous, or the children of light, will be alert and awake when Christ comes, fully expecting him.

War: Many say "peace and safety," but they are caught unaware when war breaks out and they experience "sudden destruction" (v. 3). Similarly, at the Second Coming many will believe they are secure, but suddenly "destruction cometh upon them" (v. 3). The theme of war continues in verse 8, in which a breastplate and a helmet are mentioned.

A pregnant woman: Although a pregnant woman knows the approximate time of her delivery and receives indications that she is about to give birth, still the beginning moment of her travail (labor) comes quickly and by surprise. In a like manner, the day of the Lord will surprise the wicked (v. 3).

Nighttime: Paul wrote of "darkness" and "night" (vv. 4–5) and hinted that the wicked, in their spiritual darkness, cannot be alert to Christ's coming. The righteous, on the other hand, are "children of light" and "children of the day" and are "not of the night, nor of darkness" (v. 5). This terminology suggests that the righteous, who have the light of the Holy Ghost, will know the season of Christ's coming.

Sleep: This image, set forth in verses 6–7, is connected to the previous two verses that speak of darkness and night. Paul suggests that the wicked will be caught "sleeping" when the Lord comes, while the righteous, "who are of the day" (v. 8), will be watching for Christ's coming.

A drunken person: A righteous person is like a "sober" (vv. 6, 8) person, who is alert and has a clear mind; an evil person is like one who is drunk (v. 7) and has a clouded mind and impaired judgment. The drunk will lie in his or her stupor when Christ comes, while the sober person welcomes him.

Warrior: Children of light are prepared for the Second Coming, for they have armed themselves with the "breastplate of faith and love" and they wear the "helmet, the hope of salvation" (v. 8). Paul implies that the evil are not so prepared.

NOTES AND COMMENTARY

1 Thes. 5:2 *the day of the Lord so cometh as a thief in the night.* Paul borrowed images and language from the teachings of Jesus Christ, who taught, "Watch therefore: for ye know not what hour your Lord doth come. But know this, that if the goodman of the house had known in what watch the thief would come, he would have watched, and would not have suffered his house to be broken up. Therefore be ye also ready: for in such an hour as ye think not the Son of man cometh" (Matt. 24:42–44). Peter also compared the day of the Lord to the coming of "a thief in the night" (2 Pet. 3:10). In our dispensation, the Lord has told us that "the coming of the Lord draweth nigh, and it overtaketh the world as a thief in the night—Therefore, gird up your loins, that you may be the children of light, and that day shall not overtake you as a thief" (D&C 106:4–5).

1 Thes. 5:3 *For when they shall say.* The pronoun *they* refers to those who are unprepared for the coming of the Lord, those who cry "peace and safety," failing to recognize that destruction is imminent. Paul warned that such people "shall not escape."

1 Thes. 5:4 *But ye . . . are not in darkness.* Those who obey God's commands are "children of light" (v. 5) and will be prepared for Christ's coming; it shall not overtake them as a thief in the night.

1 Thes. 5:5 *Ye are all the children of light, and the children of the day: we are not of the night, nor of darkness.* In four separate phrases, Paul instructed Church members that they are children of light. Those who await Christ's coming are of light and day, not of night and darkness. To the Ephesian Saints Paul wrote, "Now are ye light in the Lord: walk as children of light" (Eph. 5:8). A child of light is one who wears "the whole armour of God," also called the "armour of light" or the "armour of righteousness" (Eph. 6:11–16; Rom. 13:12; 2 Cor. 6:7). Such have learned to love and walk in God's light while shunning Satan's darkness.

1 Thes. 5:6 *let us not sleep . . . but let us watch and be sober.* Elder Delbert L. Stapley emphasized how we should "watch and be sober," or how to prepare for Christ's coming: "Let us be sure we thoroughly understand the most important things we can do to prepare ourselves for our Lord's second coming to earth and, by our obedience and faithfulness, escape his punishment. . . . We must set our lives and homes in order. This means a searching of our souls, an admittance of wrongdoing, and repentance where needed. It means keeping all of God's commandments. It means loving our neighbor. It means being good husbands and wives. It means teaching and training our children in the ways of righteousness. It means being honest in all our doings, in business and at home. It means spreading the gospel of Jesus Christ to all the peoples of the world."[14]

1 Thes. 5:7 *For they that sleep in the night.* Sleep is often a metaphor for physical death (Dan. 12:2; 1 Thes. 4:14; 1 Cor. 15:6), but here it stands for one who is spiritually dead, especially as it pertains to an awareness of the signs of the times.

1 Thes. 5:8 *breastplate of faith and love.* The breastplate and the helmet are two parts of the "whole armor of God" that assist the righteous in the spiritual war "against principalities, against powers, against the rulers of the darkness of this world, against spiritual wickedness in high places." Other parts of this spiritual armor include the "sword of the Spirit" and the "shield of faith" (Eph. 6:11–17; D&C 27:15–18). The armor of God is also called the "armor of righteousness" (2 Cor. 6:7; 2 Ne. 1:23) and the "armor of light" (Rom. 13:12). From 1 Thessalonians 5:8 we learn that those who wear God's armor will be prepared for Christ's coming.

THE SAINTS PATIENTLY AWAIT THE COMING OF JESUS
James 5:7–11

> *7 Be patient . . . therefore, brethren, unto the coming of the Lord. Behold, the husbandman waiteth for the precious fruit of the earth, and hath long patience for it, until he receive the early and latter rain.*
>
> *8 Be ye also patient; stablish your hearts: for the coming of the Lord draweth nigh.*
>
> *9 Grudge not one against another, brethren, lest ye be condemned: behold, the judge standeth before the door.*
>
> *10 Take, my brethren, the prophets, who have spoken in the name of the Lord, for an example of suffering affliction, and of patience.*

---

[14] Conference Report, Oct. 1975, 71.

*11 Behold, we count them happy which endure. Ye have heard
of the patience of Job, and have seen the end of the Lord; that
the Lord is very pitiful, and of tender mercy.*

James, who addressed his epistle "to the twelve tribes which are
scattered abroad" (James 1:1), counseled us to await patiently the
coming of Jesus Christ. He used several expressions to encourage our
patience, including *be patient, waiteth, hath long patience* (v. 7), *be
ye . . . patient* (v. 8), *patience* (v. 10), *endure,* and *patience of Job* (v.
11). James provided a primary reason for patiently waiting for the
Second Coming: "Behold, we count them happy which endure" (v.
11).

What should the Saints do to be patient? James gives us the
answer: "Stablish your hearts . . . grudge not one against another" and
follow the prophets "for an example of suffering affliction, and of
patience" (James 5:8–10). "Patience will see us through troubles,"
Elder Neal A. Maxwell taught, "because of the perspective that
patience brings. A patient Paul declared, 'We are troubled on every
side, yet not distressed; we are perplexed, but not in despair; persecuted, but not forsaken; cast down but not destroyed.' (2 Corinthians
4:8–9.)"[15] On another occasion Elder Maxwell stated, "While the virtue of *patience,* which was fully developed in Him, is never out of
season, patience in tribulation will surely be a premiere virtue in the
last days."[16]

As we patiently wait for Christ's coming, we should be obedient
and prepare. As Elder Joseph B. Wirthlin said: "We do not know the
precise time of the Second Coming of the Savior, but we do know that
we are living in the latter days and are closer to the Second Coming
than when the Savior lived his mortal life in the meridian of time. We
should resolve to begin a new era of personal obedience to prepare for
His return. Mortality is fleeting. We all have much to accomplish in
preparation to meet Him."[17]

---

[15] *Notwithstanding My Weakness,* 64.
[16] *Even As I Am,* 17.
[17] Conference Report, Oct. 1998, 31.

NOTES AND COMMENTARY

James 5:7 *Be patient . . . unto the coming of the Lord. Be patient* is an imperative found here and again in James 5:8. The *coming of the Lord* refers to Christ's second coming.

the husbandman waiteth . . . and hath long patience. James likened those who look for the Lord's coming to the farmer who patiently waits for his crops to grow. Both are required to be patient, and eventually both receive their reward. While the farmer is waiting for his crops to grow, he waters, fertilizes, weeds, and generally cares for his crops. We are required to do likewise while awaiting Christ's coming: attend to the Lord's work, provide spiritual nourishment for others, provide tender care, and show forth great love for others.

James 5:8 *stablish your hearts.* James instructs us not to lose heart, because "the coming of the Lord draweth nigh." Be firm.

the coming of the Lord draweth nigh. This phrase is revealed anew in our dispensation (D&C 106:4).

James 5:9 *Grudge not one against another.* Do not judge or complain against one another.

the judge standeth before the door. Jesus Christ is the Judge to whom James refers. James seems to say, in different terms, what he has already stated in verse 8: "for the coming of the Lord draweth nigh."

James 5:10 *Take . . . the prophets . . . for an example of suffering affliction.* Prophets of all ages have suffered afflictions, setting an example of patience, faith, and humility for us. Paul, for instance, summarized the afflictions he received while ministering on behalf of Christ. He wrote: "Of the Jews five times received I forty stripes save one. Thrice was I beaten with rods, once was I stoned, thrice I suffered shipwreck, a night and a day I have been in the deep; in journeyings often, in perils of waters, in perils of robbers, in perils by mine own countrymen, in perils by the heathen, in perils in the city, in perils in the wilderness, in perils in the sea, in perils among false brethren; in weariness and painfulness, in watchings often, in hunger and thirst, in fastings often, in cold and nakedness" (2 Cor. 11:24–27; see also Mosiah 17:23; Alma 14:26; JS–H 1:22). Yet through it all he remained faithful, praising God and saying, "The God and Father of our Lord Jesus Christ . . . is blessed for evermore" (2 Cor. 11:31).

an example . . . of patience. James held up the ancient prophets (only Job is explicitly mentioned; see v. 11) as an example of patience.

James 5:11 *we count them happy which endure.* This short phrase sums up the essence of the entire section. Those who remain patient in the face of the adversity of the last days, looking to the coming of the Lord, will be happy. They will receive the Spirit, the gifts of the Spirit, and the comfort and blessing of the atonement of Christ.

Ye have heard of the patience of Job. The prophet Job is well known for his patience in affliction. Though he lost his children, his flocks, and his worldly goods, and though he suffered in body, mind, and spirit, he still trusted in the Lord.

have seen the end of the Lord. We have seen the Lord's purpose with Job—and with us.

the Lord is very pitiful, and of tender mercy. The Lord is kind, compassionate, and full of loving gentleness.

THOSE WITH THE HOLY SPIRIT WILL BE PREPARED
Doctrine and Covenants 45:56–59

56 And at that day, when I shall come in my glory, shall the parable be fulfilled which I spake concerning the ten virgins.

57 For they that are wise and have received the truth, and have taken the Holy Spirit for their guide, and have not been deceived—verily I say unto you, they shall not be hewn down and cast into the fire, but shall abide the day.

58 And the earth shall be given unto them for an inheritance; and they shall multiply and wax strong, and their children shall grow up without sin unto salvation.

59 For the Lord shall be in their midst, and his glory shall be upon them, and he will be their king and their lawgiver.

The parable of the ten virgins (Matt. 25:1–13) describes five wise virgins who had oil for their lamps and five foolish virgins who did not. All ten took their lamps as they went out to meet the bridegroom (who represents Christ), but only those with oil were permitted to enter with him to the marriage (representing the union of Christ with his Saints); the others were shut out when the door was closed.

On 7 March 1831 the Lord revealed a partial interpretation of this parable when he explained that the wise virgins are they who "have received the truth, and have taken the Holy Spirit for their guide, and have not been deceived" (D&C 45:57). Elder Spencer W. Kimball explained that "the Ten Virgins represent the people of the Church of Jesus Christ and not the rank and file of the world."[18]

The parable's central message is set forth in verse 13: "Watch therefore, for ye know neither the day nor the hour wherein the Son of man cometh." We must do these three things—receive the truth, take the Holy Ghost as our guide, and be not deceived—if we hope to be prepared for the coming of the Bridegroom. All three focus on the Holy Ghost, who helps us to receive the truth, serves as our guide, and helps us to avoid deception.

NOTES AND COMMENTARY

D&C 45:56 *at that day. Day* hearkens back to Doctrine and Covenants 45:39, which speaks of "the great day of the Lord," or the time of "the coming of the Son of Man" (see also D&C 45:42).

when I shall come in my glory. This phrase refers to the Second Coming. Many prophets have described Jesus as coming "with power and great glory" (Matt. 24:30; D&C 29:11; 34:7; see also Isa. 2:10; D&C 65:5). The word *glory* means brightness, splendor, and magnificence.[19]

the parable be fulfilled which I spake concerning the ten virgins. This parable, recorded in the testimony of Matthew (Matt. 24:1–13), speaks of Church members. Elder Spencer W. Kimball taught: "There are even many members of the Church who are lax and careless and who continually procrastinate. They live the gospel casually but not devoutly. They have complied with some requirements but are not valiant. They do no major crimes but merely fail to do the things

---

[18] *Faith Precedes the Miracle,* 253.
[19] Webster, *American Dictionary,* s.v. "glory."

required—things like paying tithing, living the Word of Wisdom, having family prayers, fasting, attending meetings, serving. . . . The ten virgins belonged to the kingdom and had every right to the blessings—except that five were not valiant and were not ready when the great day came. They were unprepared through not living all the commandments. They were bitterly disappointed at being shut out from the marriage—as likewise their modern counterparts will be."[20]

D&C 45:57 *have taken the Holy Spirit for their guide, and have not been deceived.* The first statement, "have taken the Holy Spirit for their guide," implies the second, "and have not been deceived." Those who have learned how to hear and listen to the Holy Spirit will not be deceived, and will therefore not be "cast into the fire, but shall abide the day" of Christ's coming. The Holy Ghost is symbolized by oil (see, for example, 1 Sam. 10:1, 6, 9; 16:13–14; Isa. 61:1; Acts 10:38; 2 Cor. 1:21–22).[21] In the parable of the ten virgins, there is a connection between the lamp oil and the Holy Ghost: those who possess oil are guided by the Spirit, have received the truth, and are not deceived.

they shall not be hewn down and cast into the fire. The words *hewn down* imply that people are like trees that are cut down with an ax. Other scriptures are explicit in their symbolic identification of people as trees. Green trees often represent the righteous (Ps. 1:3; D&C 135:6; Rev. 11:4); dry trees symbolize the wicked (Luke 23:31; 3 Ne. 14:17–18). Alma 5:52, using language similar to that of Doctrine and Covenants 45:57, summarizes the eventual destination of the wicked, "Behold, the ax is laid at the root of the tree; therefore every tree that bringeth not forth good fruit shall be hewn down and cast into the fire, yea, a fire which cannot be consumed, even an unquenchable fire."

but shall abide the day. The green trees, or the righteous, may be scathed by fire (D&C 135:6), but they will not be destroyed, and will abide (meaning they will survive) the great day of the Lord.

D&C 45:58–59 *an inheritance.* These two verses set forth blessings that will belong to those who are guided by the Holy Spirit

---

[20] *Miracle of Forgiveness,* 7–8.
[21] For a discussion of this symbolism, see Parry, "Ritual Anointing with Olive Oil," in Ricks and Welch, *Allegory of the Olive Tree,* 279–81.

during mortality and who abide the day of Christ's coming. The specific blessings are that they will inherit the earth and have many, sinless children; moreover, Jesus Christ will dwell with them, place his glory upon them, and rule over them as their king and lawgiver.

the earth shall be given unto them. The Lord's people often possess a land of promise during mortality, and those who abide the day of the Lord's coming will inherit the earth "to possess . . . forever and ever" (D&C 103:7; see also Ps. 37:9; Matt. 5:5; D&C 63:20). The land of promise possessed by mortals is a type of the greater "land of promise" (D&C 38:18), speaking of the earth in its celestial state. This celestialized land of promise will be "a land flowing with milk and honey, upon which there shall be no curse when the Lord cometh; and I will give it unto you for the land of your inheritance, if you seek it with all your hearts. And this shall be my covenant with you, ye shall have it for the land of your inheritance, and for the inheritance of your children forever, while the earth shall stand, and ye shall possess it again in eternity, no more to pass away" (D&C 38:18–20).

ADAM-ONDI-AHMAN: PREPARING THE SAINTS FOR CHRIST'S COMING
Daniel 7:9–27

9 I beheld till the thrones were cast down, and the Ancient of days did sit, whose garment was white as snow, and the hair of his head like the pure wool: his throne was like the fiery flame, and his wheels as burning fire.

10 A fiery stream issued and came forth from before him: thousand thousands ministered unto him, and ten thousand times ten thousand stood before him: the judgment was set, and the books were opened.

11 I beheld then because of the voice of the great words which the horn spake: I beheld even till the beast was slain, and his body destroyed, and given to the burning flame.

12 As concerning the rest of the beasts, they had their dominion taken away: yet their lives were prolonged for a season and time.

13 I saw in the night visions, and, behold, one like the Son of man came with the clouds of heaven, and came to the Ancient of days, and they brought him near before him.

14 And there was given him dominion, and glory, and a kingdom, that all people, nations, and languages, should serve him: his dominion is an everlasting dominion, which shall not pass away, and his kingdom that which shall not be destroyed.

15 I Daniel was grieved in my spirit in the midst of my body, and the visions of my head troubled me.

16 I came near unto one of them that stood by, and asked him the truth of all this. So he told me, and made me know the interpretation of the things.

17 These great beasts, which are four, are four kings, which shall arise out of the earth.

18 But the saints of the most High shall take the kingdom, and possess the kingdom for ever, even for ever and ever.

19 Then I would know the truth of the fourth beast, which was diverse from all the others, exceeding dreadful, whose teeth were of iron, and his nails of brass; which devoured, brake in pieces, and stamped the residue with his feet;

20 And of the ten horns that were in his head, and of the other which came up, and before whom three fell; even of that horn that had eyes, and a mouth that spake very great things, whose look was more stout than his fellows.

21 I beheld, and the same horn made war with the saints, and prevailed against them;

22 Until the Ancient of days came, and judgment was given to the saints of the most High; and the time came that the saints possessed the kingdom.

23 Thus he said, The fourth beast shall be the fourth kingdom upon earth, which shall be diverse from all kingdoms, and shall devour the whole earth, and shall tread it down, and break it in pieces.

24 And the ten horns out of this kingdom are ten kings that shall arise: and another shall rise after them; and he shall be diverse from the first, and he shall subdue three kings.

25 And he shall speak great words against the most High, and shall wear out the saints of the most High, and think to change times and laws: and they shall be given into his hand until a time and times and the dividing of time.

26 But the judgment shall sit, and they shall take away his dominion, to consume and to destroy it unto the end.

27 And the kingdom and dominion, and the greatness of the kingdom under the whole heaven, shall be given to the people of the saints of the most High, whose kingdom is an everlasting kingdom, and all dominions shall serve and obey him.

At some point in the near future, before the Second Coming, a great meeting or grand council will be held at Adam-ondi-Ahman, located in Daviess County, Missouri (D&C 116:1). Elder Joseph Fielding Smith called this meeting "one of the greatest events this troubled earth has ever seen."[22] One purpose of this meeting, wrote Joseph Smith, is to prepare the Saints for Christ's coming: "Daniel in his seventh chapter speaks of the Ancient of Days; he means the oldest man, our Father Adam, Michael, he will call his children together and hold a council with them to prepare them for the coming of the Son of Man."[23] Part of this preparation, as explained by Elder Joseph Fielding Smith, will involve "all who have held keys [making] their reports and [delivering] their stewardships, as they shall be required. Adam will direct this judgment, and then he will make his report, as the one holding the keys for this earth, to his Superior Officer, Jesus Christ."[24]

In all of the standard works there is no greater or more complete description of the council to be held at Adam-ondi-Ahman than in Daniel 7. There the prophet Daniel details "a dream and visions of his

---

[22] *Progress of Man,* 481.

[23] *History of the Church,* 3:386–87. Joseph Fielding Smith stated that the council at Adam-ondi-Ahman will be a time of "preparation"; see *Way to Perfection,* 290.

[24] *Way to Perfection,* 291. Joseph Smith spoke also regarding this event: "He (Adam) is the father of the human family, and presides over the spirits of all men, and all that have had the keys must stand before him in this grand council" (*History of the Church,* 3:386–87).

head upon the bed: then he wrote the dream" (Dan. 7:1). Throughout this chapter we are reminded that he beheld a vision: "I saw in my vision" (v. 2), "I beheld" (v. 6, 9, 11, 21), "I saw in the night visions" (v. 7, 13), "the visions of my head troubled me" (v. 15). A revelation from God, this dream may be divided into three parts: the four beasts (Dan. 7:1–8); the council at Adam-ondi-Ahman (Dan. 7:9–14); and the interpretation of the dream (Dan. 7:15–28).

The four beasts (Dan. 7:1–8). Daniel's entire vision is full of symbolism. He sees four ferocious creatures: a lion, a bear, a leopard, and an unnamed beast, each representing a king or kingdom (or political system). All have great political power in the earth (see also Dan. 7:17–19, 23–25). The predatory nature of these four beasts represents power to rule with terror, to kill and destroy. Daniel described the fourth beast as "the fourth kingdom upon earth, which . . . shall devour the whole earth, and shall tread it down, and break it in pieces" (Dan. 7:23).

The council at Adam-ondi-Ahman (Dan. 7:9–14). This section of Daniel holds considerable significance for members of the Church because it provides much information regarding the great council, including the following:

Thrones for Adam and others will be set up (Dan. 7:9).

The four beasts, or kingdoms, will be stripped of their dominion and powers (Dan. 7:12) because of the events that will take place at Adam-ondi-Ahman (Dan. 7:17–18, 22–23, 25–27).

The fourth beast, the most ferocious of the four, will be "slain, and his body destroyed, and given to the burning flame" (Dan. 7:11) because of events that will occur at Adam-ondi-Ahman (Dan. 7:19–27).

A great spiritual court will be held, judgment will be given to the Saints, and they will take the kingdom (Dan. 7:10, 18, 22, 27).

Jesus Christ will appear, and upon him will be given "dominion, and glory, and a kingdom, that all people, nations, and languages, should serve him" (Dan. 7:13–14).

There is historical precedent for this council to be held at Adam-ondi-Ahman, "the land where Adam dwelt" (D&C 117:8). Doctrine and Covenants 107:53–57 describes a meeting that was held three years before Adam's death, at which Adam and his posterity gathered at Adam-ondi-Ahman. At least three major events occurred there: Adam bestowed a blessing upon his posterity, the premortal Christ appeared and made Adam a head and a prince, and Adam "predicted whatsoever should befall his posterity unto the latest generation" (D&C 107:56), perhaps also prophesying of the latter-day council at Adam-ondi-Ahman.

The interpretation of the dream (Dan. 7:15–28). Perhaps because of the strange symbolism or the graphic scenes in the dream, Daniel stated that "the visions of my head troubled me" (Dan. 7:15). He therefore asked for (Dan. 7:16) and received an interpretation, but only in the broadest terms. The meaning of the four beasts of verses 2–7 is touched on in verses 17, 19, 23–24; brief interpretative comments about the ten horns mentioned in verse 7 are provided in verses 20 and 24; the import of the small horn of verse 8 is presented in verses 20–21, 24–26; the divine judgment of verses 9–10 is further discussed in verses 22, 26; and mention of the great hosts in verse 10 is explained further in verses 18, 22, 27.

The text of Revelation 11:14–18 and Revelation 13 corresponds with Daniel 7; these passages should be studied together.

NOTES AND COMMENTARY

Dan. 7:9 *the thrones were cast down.* A more correct reading of this phrase is "the thrones were set in place," or "the thrones were set up" (see footnote to Dan. 7:9 in the LDS edition of the KJV). In his vision Daniel saw places of honor being set up in preparation for the great meeting to be held at Adam-ondi-Ahman. Thrones rather than chairs are set in place because exalted beings will be present (see also Rev. 20:4). For part of the council, at least, the "ten thousand times ten thousand" Saints are standing (see Dan. 7:10).

the Ancient of days did sit. "Daniel in his seventh chapter speaks of the Ancient of Days; he means the oldest man, our Father Adam"[25] (see also D&C 138:38). It is Adam who "will call his children [or posterity] together" to hold this council because he is the "father of

---

[25] *History of the Church,* 3:386.

the human family" and because he "presides over the spirits of all men."[26]

garment was white as snow, and the hair of his head like the pure wool. Daniel described Adam as a glorious, exalted being, using images (snow and wool) that characterize purity and glory.

his throne was like the fiery flame, and his wheels as burning fire. Adam's throne, like his garment and resurrected body, are shown to be glorious and heavenly, surrounded by great light. Daniel spoke in similes: actual fire may not be present on the throne and wheels, but the glory and brightness are real. This throne with its wheels recalls God's celestial throne described in Ezekiel 1:13–19, which, like a chariot, may symbolize God's power to move about through the heavens.

Dan. 7:10 *A fiery stream issued and came forth from before him.* The fiery stream is yet another symbol used by Daniel to describe the glory of Adam, who is a celestial being. Fire is often used to describe glorified beings or settings (see, for example, Ex. 3:2; 1 Ne. 1:6; 3 Ne. 17:24; and D&C 110:3).

ten thousand times ten thousand stood before him. This number is the same as that of the exalted beings who will worship God in the celestial kingdom as he sits upon his throne (Rev. 5:11). The numerical expression "ten thousand times ten thousand," or one hundred million, is probably a symbolic expression for a vast number of Saints who will be present at the council. Who are these ten thousand times ten thousand? Elder Bruce R. McConkie explained that Jesus Christ "will come in private to his prophet and to the apostles then living. Those who have held keys and powers and authorities in all ages from Adam to the present will also be present. And further, all the faithful members of the Church then living and all the faithful saints of all the ages past will be present. It will be the greatest congregation of faithful saints ever assembled on planet Earth. It will be a sacrament meeting. It will be a day of judgment for the faithful of all the ages. And it will take place in Daviess County, Missouri, at a place called Adam-ondi-Ahman."[27]

---

[26] *History of the Church,* 3:386.
[27] *Millennial Messiah,* 578–79.

the judgment was set. The term *judgment,* a legal term used numerous times in the Mosaic legal code (Deut. 17:8), also means *court,*[28] and some biblical translators prefer to translate this phrase as "a court was held" (NJB). Daniel used the term three times in this section: here, and again in verses 22 and 26. This court is not an earthly court of law but a spiritual forum or tribunal held by celestial beings together with righteous mortals. This court will be held by the Saints, and it is in this setting that "the saints of the most High shall take the kingdom, and possess the kingdom" (Dan. 7:18).

Daniel explained: "The Ancient of days came, and judgment was given to the saints of the most High; and the time came that the saints possessed the kingdom," concluding, "the kingdom and dominion, and the greatness of the kingdom under the whole heaven, shall be given to the people of the saints of the most High, whose kingdom is an everlasting kingdom, and all dominions shall serve and obey him" (Dan. 7:22, 27; see also Rev. 11:14–18).

The earthly kingdoms, then, will be succeeded by the heavenly kingdom, or God's kingdom, and Adam-ondi-Ahman will be the place where this will occur. Little is known regarding when this council will be held or how long earth's kingdoms will endure after the judgment is set.

Daniel 7:10 describes not the Last Judgment, in which wicked individuals will be judged by Jesus Christ, but the judgment of the time when the fourth kingdom (perhaps representing earth's kingdoms, dominions, governments, and political systems in the last days), spoken of in Daniel 7:23–25, will lose its power. Hence, Daniel 7:26 reads, "a court will be held and his [speaking of a king belonging to the fourth kingdom] power will be stripped from him, consumed and utterly destroyed" (NJB).

the books were opened. Revelation 13 parallels Daniel 7, and Revelation 13:8 speaks of "the book of life of the Lamb," wherein are written the names of the righteous. Perhaps the book of life is opened during the council at Adam-ondi-Ahman and judgment is directed against all those who worship the beast and whose names are not written in the Lamb's book of life (see also 1 Cor. 6:2).

---

[28] Brown, Driver, and Briggs, *Hebrew and English Lexicon of the Old Testament,* 1088.

Dan. 7:11 *I beheld even till the beast was slain . . . and given to the burning flame.* The same or a similar event is described in Revelation 19:20: "And the beast was taken, and with him the false prophet that wrought miracles before him, with which he deceived them that had received the mark of the beast, and them that worshipped his image. These both were cast alive into a lake of fire burning with brimstone" (see also Rev. 20:10).

Dan. 7:12 *they had their dominion taken away.* The other beasts, representing other earthly kingdoms, lost their "dominion," but they continued to exist for a period of time: "their lives were prolonged for a season."

Dan. 7:13 *one like the Son of man.* The divine title *Son of man,* revealed to Adam (Moses 6:57), is an abbreviated form of "Son of Man of Holiness." *Son of man* speaks of Jesus Christ, who will come with the clouds of heaven to the council of Adam-ondi-Ahman.

with the clouds of heaven. Christ will come down from heaven to attend the council. Clouds, located high in the skies and brilliantly white, represent the Lord's glory. For instance, after the New Jerusalem temple is built, "a cloud shall rest upon it, which cloud shall be even the glory of the Lord" (D&C 84:5; see also Ezek. 10:3–4). Perhaps these clouds of heaven that reveal Jesus Christ to those at Adam-ondi-Ahman will conceal his presence from outsiders (3 Ne. 18:38; Ether 2:4–5).

came to the Ancient of days. Although there is a great host in attendance at this meeting, Christ proceeds to the Ancient of Days (Adam), and then "the Son of Man stands before him, and there is given him glory and dominion. Adam delivers up his stewardship to Christ, that which was delivered to him as holding the keys of the universe."[29]

Dan. 7:14 *there was given him dominion, and glory, and a kingdom.* Jesus Christ will be invested as king at Adam-ondi-Ahman, and he will receive dominion, glory, and a kingdom. After the judgment is set (Dan. 7:10), and earth's kingdoms lose their power, "all people, nations, and languages" will serve Jesus Christ, and "his dominion is

---

[29] *History of the Church,* 3:387.

an everlasting dominion, which shall not pass away, and his kingdom that which shall not be destroyed."

Dan. 7:15–16 *I Daniel was grieved in my spirit.* The vision, perhaps especially the graphic scenes dealing with the four ferocious beasts, disturbs Daniel. He seeks understanding from one of the heavenly attendants who is standing nearby, and receives the interpretation, presented in Daniel 7:16–27. The attendant, perhaps one of the thousands mentioned in verse 10, remains unnamed, although it may have been Gabriel (Dan. 8:16).

Dan. 7:17 *These great beasts . . . are four kings.* The four beasts are kings or kingdoms (Dan. 7:23) that belong to this earth, our telestial world. These four kingdoms may be identified with actual kingdoms, as some scholars have argued, or they may signify all of this world's kingdoms and governments since its beginning.

Dan. 7:18 *the saints of the most High shall take the kingdom.* Although earth's kingdoms at present rule the world's inhabitants, eventually the Saints will inherit the earth and reign over it with their Lord, Jesus Christ (D&C 43:29; 103:7–8). As Jesus is granted his dominion at Adam-ondi-Ahman (Dan. 7:14), it appears the Saints may receive theirs at that time as well. The "Most High" is one of God's titles, perhaps used in this context as a contrast to the lowly and beastly kingdoms of this world.

possess the kingdom for ever, even for ever and ever. Note the triple use of *ever* in this phrase, emphasizing that the Saints will possess God's kingdom throughout eternity.

Dan. 7:19–20 *fourth beast.* These two verses elaborate on Daniel's vision of the fourth beast, described in Daniel 7:7–8.

Dan. 7:21–27 *the same horn.* The horn in these verses represents a great and mighty king who will war against the Saints and for a period of time prevail (see also Rev. 13:7); he will be powerful enough to conquer three other kings with their kingdoms; he will blaspheme God; and he will attempt to change seasons and laws (Dan. 7:21, 24–25; Rev. 13:5–6). But the rule of this king will be short-lived and his kingdom will be destroyed, along with all other kingdoms, because Adam will come and organize the great council at Adam-ondi-Ahman. At this meeting the Saints will counsel together as a spiritual court of law, judgment will be given to God's righteous (Dan. 7:22, 26; see also Rev. 11:14–18), "and the kingdom and dominion, and the greatness of the kingdom under the whole heaven, shall be given to the people of the saints of the most High, whose kingdom is an everlasting kingdom, and all dominions shall serve and obey him" (Dan. 7:27).

The Lord Shall Suddenly Come to His Temple
Malachi 3:1

1 Behold, I will send my messenger, and he shall prepare the way before me: and the Lord, whom ye seek, shall suddenly come to his temple, even the messenger of the covenant, whom ye delight in: behold, he shall come, saith the Lord of hosts.

When we read the context of this verse we readily see it pertains to the Second Coming. The passage continues: "Who may abide the day of his coming? and who shall stand when he appeareth? for he is like a refiner's fire." Also, "I will come near to you to judgment; and I will be a swift witness against the sorcerers, and against the adulterers, and against false swearers" (Mal. 3:2, 5). Malachi 4:1 continues the theme of Christ's coming: "For, behold, the day cometh, that shall burn as an oven; and all the proud, yea, and all that do wickedly, shall be stubble: and the day that cometh shall burn them up," and Malachi 4:5 speaks about the "coming of the great and dreadful day of the Lord."

Notes and Commentary

Mal. 3:1 *I will send my messenger . . . he shall prepare the way before me.* In the last days Sidney Rigdon was one of the Lord's messengers who was sent forth to prepare the way for his coming. The Lord revealed to him: "Behold thou wast sent forth, even as John, to prepare the way before me, and before Elijah which should come" (D&C 35:4). Many others have served as the Lord's special messengers to prepare the way for his coming, including John the Baptist (D&C 13), Moroni, Peter, James, John (D&C 128:20), and others. The Lord has revealed that the gospel of Jesus Christ also serves as a messenger to prepare the way. "And even so I have sent mine everlasting covenant into the world, to be a light to the world, and to be a standard for my people, and for the Gentiles to seek to it, and to be a messenger before my face to prepare the way before me" (D&C 45:9).

the Lord, whom ye seek, shall suddenly come to his temple. This prophecy was revealed anew in our dispensation: "I am Jesus Christ, the Son of God; wherefore, gird up your loins and I will suddenly come to my temple" (D&C 36:8). Doctrine and Covenants 42:35–36 suggests that the temple mentioned in this prophecy will be the temple in New Jerusalem, but the phrase "the Lord . . . shall suddenly come to his temple" likely has multiple fulfillments. Elder Bruce R. McConkie explained: "The Lord, whom we seek, shall suddenly come to his temple, meaning that he will come to the earth, which is his temple, and also that he will come to those holy houses which he has commanded us to build unto his blessed name. Indeed, he came suddenly to the Kirtland Temple on the 3rd day of April in 1836; he has also appeared in others of his holy houses; and he will come in due course to the temples in Jackson County and in Jerusalem."[30]

THE RIGHTEOUS SING AND REJOICE, FOR THE LORD COMETH

Psalm 96:1–13

*1 O sing unto the Lord a new song:
sing unto the Lord, all the earth.*

*2 Sing unto the Lord, bless his name;
shew forth his salvation from day to day.*

*3 Declare his glory among the heathen,
his wonders among all people.*

*4 For the Lord is great, and greatly to be praised:
he is to be feared above all gods.*

*5 For all the gods of the nations are idols:
but the Lord made the heavens.*

---

[30] *Millennial Messiah*, 577.

6 Honour and majesty are before him:
strength and beauty are in his sanctuary.

7 Give unto the Lord, O ye kindreds of the people,
give unto the Lord glory and strength.

8 Give unto the Lord the glory due unto his name:
bring an offering, and come into his courts.

9 O worship the Lord in the beauty of holiness:
fear before him, all the earth.

10 Say among the heathen that the Lord reigneth:
the world also shall be established that it shall not be moved:
he shall judge the people righteously.

11 Let the heavens rejoice,
and let the earth be glad;
let the sea roar,
and the fulness thereof.

12 Let the field be joyful,
and all that is therein:
then shall all the trees of the wood rejoice

13 Before the Lord:
for he cometh,
for he cometh to judge the earth:
he shall judge the world with righteousness,
and the people with his truth.

When Jesus Christ returns to the earth in great glory and power, those who have loved truth and righteousness will sing, worship, and be joyful. This psalm sets forth several such expressions of joy, as shown by the terms *sing* (three times), *rejoice* (twice), *glad,* and *joyful.* In fact, it appears we are not simply *invited* to sing and rejoice at the Second Coming; we are *commanded* to have joy, as indicated by the nineteen imperatives—*sing, sing, sing, bless, shew forth, declare, give, give, give, bring, come, worship, fear, say, rejoice, be glad, roar, be joyful*—all of which pertain to the expression of joy, particularly in context. The gladness and joy in this psalm emphasize the rejoicing at the second coming of Jesus Christ: "He cometh . . . he cometh to judge the earth" with righteousness and truth (Ps. 96:13).

Elder Russell M. Nelson taught that the wonderful spiritual experiences of our lives, "glorious as they are, become but prelude to that great day ahead, when the faithful will stand at the latter day upon the earth. They shall abide the Second Coming of the Lord and shall stand with him when he appears (see Malachi 3:2–12; 3 Nephi 24:2–12). On that joyous morning, . . . [the] faithful shall be crowned with glory, immortality, and eternal life (see D&C 75:5; 138:51).

"Once again 'morning stars [will] sing together, and . . . all the sons [and daughters] of God [will] shout for joy!' (D&C 128:23; see also Job 38:7). For on that morning, 'the glory of the Lord shall be revealed, and all flesh shall see it together' (Isaiah 40:5; see also Ezekiel 20:48; Luke 3:6; D&C 101:23).

"Then, 'there'll be peace and contentment evermore, ev'ry heart, ev'ry voice on that day will rejoice. . . . There'll be joy in the morning on that day' (Natalie Sleeth, "Joy in the Morning," Carol Stream, Ill.: Hope Publishing Co., 1977, pp. 4–5, 9–10)."[31]

NOTES AND COMMENTARY

Ps. 96:1 *sing unto the Lord.* This expression is repeated three times in verses 1 and 2. The song is directed to the Lord; it is a song of worship.

a new song. The psalmist may refer to a specific "new song" (see, for example, Isa. 42:10; Rev. 14:3; D&C 84:98); or he may be speaking generically of all hymns and inspired religious songs.

all the earth. The command to sing a new song is directed to all earth's inhabitants, not just Church members.

Ps. 96:2 *bless his name.* This expression speaks of formal prayer as well as the prayer of the heart, which belongs to the righteous, who continually consider God's greatness and mercy.

shew forth his salvation from day to day. This passage is one of four imperatives in which we are commanded to share with others our knowledge of God's goodness. The other three imperatives are to "declare his glory among the heathen" (v. 3), "[declare] his wonders

---

[31] Conference Report, Oct. 1986, 88.

among all people" (v. 3), and "say among the heathen that the Lord reigneth" (v. 10). We are to frequently ("from day to day") "shew forth" (or proclaim) God's salvation.

Ps. 96:3 *Declare his glory/his wonders among all people.* We are to declare God's glory and wonders to all of earth's people because "the Lord is great," because he is "greatly to be praised," and because "he is to be feared above all gods."

Ps. 96:5 *For all the gods of the nations are idols: but the Lord made the heavens.* The psalmist contrasts the Lord with the nations' idols. The colossal difference between the two is this: The Lord created the heavens. Not stated but certainly implied is that idols do not create the heavens but rather are created by the hands of mortals.

Ps. 96:6 *Honour and majesty are before him: strength and beauty are in his sanctuary.* Four terms describe the Lord in this verse: *honor, majesty, strength,* and *beauty.* The sanctuary mentioned here refers to his temple in heaven, or the celestial kingdom.

Ps. 96:7 *Give unto the Lord . . . glory and strength.* Of course, we can give neither glory nor strength to the Lord, but we can and must fully acknowledge these attributes in him.

O ye kindreds of the people. The psalm speaks of and to everyone: "all the earth" (vv. 1, 9), "heathen" (vv. 3, 10), "all people" (v. 3), "nations" (v. 5), "kindreds of the people" (v. 7), "people" (v. 10), "the earth" (v. 13), "the world" (v. 13).

Ps. 96:8 *the glory due unto his name.* God's name is hallowed (Matt. 6:9), Christ's name is "far above . . . every name that is named" (Eph. 1:21), and "there is no other name under heaven given among men, whereby we must be saved" (Acts 4:12).

bring an offering, and come into his courts. Psalm 96 may have been sung in the temple of Jerusalem as one of the hymns that existed during that period. The psalm may be one that is sung in worship during the Millennium, when the nations will worship the Lord in the temple of Jerusalem during the feast of tabernacles (Zech. 14:16–21).

Ps. 96:9 *O worship the Lord in the beauty of holiness.* The New Jerusalem Bible correctly renders "in the beauty of holiness" as "in his sacred court"; hence, the entire phrase reads, "O worship the Lord in his sacred court." *Court* refers to the court of the temple; we are to worship God in our temples.

fear before him. The word *fear* here means to reverence, meaning "show reverence before him."

Ps. 96:10 *he shall judge the people righteously.* The theme of judgment is introduced here, at the beginning of the psalm, and its significance is underscored at the end. Its final words read, "he cometh to judge the earth, he shall judge the world with righteousness, and the people with his truth." At his second coming Jesus Christ will judge the wicked with righteous judgment; Christ's original Old World twelve apostles will "judge the whole house of Israel, even as many as have loved me and kept my commandments, and none else" (D&C 29:12).

Ps. 96:11–12 *heavens rejoice.* These verses use a poetic figure of speech, called personification, through which inanimate objects or things acquire qualities or perform the actions of humans. Here the heavens, earth, sea, field, and trees are commanded to perform human actions: to rejoice, be glad, roar, and be joyful, because the Lord comes to judge the earth and to establish a new order wherein there will be peace and righteousness. The heavens, earth, sea, field, and trees may refer symbolically to groups or individuals. *Heavens* may refer to those in heaven who will rejoice when Christ comes again upon the earth, and *earth, sea, field,* and *trees* may refer to earth's inhabitants who look for his coming in power and glory.

Ps. 96:13 *Before the Lord.* These words belong to verses 11 and 12, which should read, "Let the heavens rejoice, . . . all the trees of the wood rejoice before the Lord."

for he cometh, for he cometh to judge the earth. One common technique used in ancient Hebrew poetry was the placement of the poem's most significant words at the poem's conclusion or end. Such is the case in Psalm 96, in which the words "he cometh" close the poem and represent the psalm's central point. Note that these words are repeated for emphasis: "for he cometh, for he cometh."

THE LORD'S DAY IS DARKNESS TO THE UNREPENTANT

Amos 5:18–20

18 Woe unto you that desire the day of the Lord! to what end is it for you? the day of the Lord is darkness, and not light.

19 As if a man did flee from a lion, and a bear met him; or went into the house, and leaned his hand on the wall, and a serpent bit him.

20 Shall not the day of the Lord be darkness, and not light? even very dark, and no brightness in it?

In Amos 5 the Lord speaks through his prophet, who warns his contemporaries, especially those who belong to the house of Israel, to repent and to "seek" Jehovah (Amos 5:4, 6, 8). The chapter is introduced with "hear ye this word which I take up against you, even a lamentation, O house of Israel" (Amos 5:1). Amos speaks against Israel's corrupt temple practices, their social injustices and various iniquities, and promises destruction: "Wailing shall be in all streets; and they shall say in all the highways, Alas! alas!" (Amos 5:16). Verses 18 through 20 speak expressly about the "day of the Lord," a phrase repeated three times in these three verses. The day of the Lord is the time of the Second Coming and includes the period that immediately precedes this event, when the Lord's judgments are sent to earth's inhabitants. Although these verses were uttered to ancient Israel, they have direct application to every generation of earth's inhabitants, including our own.

NOTES AND COMMENTARY

Amos 5:18 *Woe unto you that desire the day of the Lord! to what end is it for you?* The Lord addresses unrepentant souls (Amos 5:4–17). Rhetorically he asks, "Why do you look forward to the day of the Lord, since to you it is a day of darkness and not light?"

the day of the Lord is darkness, and not light. This phrase has at least two meanings. First, the words *darkness* and *not light* refer to the spiritual darkness that attends the unrepentant, those who feel the guilt and pain associated with personal sin. When the Lord sends his fierce judgments on the world, the unrepentant will feel the weight of their sins. Second, the words may also describe the actual atmosphere in our skies in the last days. Joel similarly describes the day of the Lord as "a day of darkness and of gloominess, a day of clouds and of thick darkness" (Joel 2:2), and Zephaniah characterizes that day as "a day of wrath, a day of trouble and distress, a day of wasteness and desolation, a day of darkness and gloominess, a day of clouds and thick darkness" (Zeph. 1:15). Yet to the righteous who dwell in Zion, the day of the Lord is not darkness but a time when they will sing praises, worship the Lord, and be joyful.[32] They will experience "peace," "refuge," and the "glory of the Lord" (D&C 45:66–67).

Amos 5:19 *As if a man did flee from a lion, and a bear met him.* To the unrepentant the Second Coming is likened to a person who encounters a ferocious lion on the path. In great fear this person turns to flee, running for his life, but immediately encounters a great bear. Like the person who encounters the lion and the bear, the wicked will experience great fear when they face God's judgments but will be unable to escape them.

or went into the house, and leaned his hand on the wall, and a serpent bit him. To the unrepentant the Second Coming is like a person entering his home, thinking to find safety and finding instead a poisonous snake.

Amos 5:20 *Shall not the day of the Lord be darkness, and not light?* This phrase, introduced in Amos 5:18, is repeated here for emphasis. The final phrase of verse 20 expresses the same idea: "even very dark, and no brightness in it." Consequently Amos 5:18, 20, in defining the day of the Lord to the unrepentant, twice asserts that the day of the Lord is *darkness* and *not light,* and once uses the expressions *dark* and *no brightness.*

THE LORD COMES IN GLORY ON A WHITE HORSE
Revelation 19:11–16

11 And I saw heaven opened, and behold a white horse; and he that sat upon him was called Faithful and True, and in righteousness he doth judge and make war.

---

[32] See the commentary on Ps. 96, page 411.

12 His eyes were as a flame of fire, and on his head were many crowns; and he had a name written, that no man knew, but he himself.

13 And he was clothed with a vesture dipped in blood: and his name is called The Word of God.

14 And the armies which were in heaven followed him upon white horses, clothed in fine linen, white and clean.

15 And out of his mouth goeth a sharp sword, that with it he should smite the nations: and he shall rule them with a rod of iron: and he treadeth the winepress of the fierceness and wrath of Almighty God.

16 And he hath on his vesture and on his thigh a name written, KING OF KINGS, AND LORD OF LORDS.

John the Revelator saw a vision of the second coming of Jesus Christ, when he will return to the earth with great glory, power, and judgment. John saw Christ as a mighty warrior-king: as a warrior, Christ "make[s] war," his vesture is blood-red, he rides a white horse, he "smite[s] the nations," and his armies follow him, also riding white horses. As a king Jesus wears "many crowns," judges the nations, rules "with a rod of iron," wears a regal vesture, and possesses the royal name "King of kings and Lord of lords." Much of John's language describing Jesus Christ as a warrior-king is symbolic. Christ's names and titles are instructive and explain his character and divine mission. He is called "Faithful and True," "the Word of God," "King of kings," and "Lord of lords" (Rev. 19:11, 13, 16).

Elder Charles W. Penrose provided the following beautiful description of Jesus Christ's coming: "He comes! The earth shakes, and the tall mountains tremble; the mighty deep rolls back to the north as in fear, and the rent skies glow like molten brass. He comes! The dead Saints burst forth from their tombs, and 'those who are alive and remain' are 'caught up' with them to meet him. The ungodly rush to hide themselves from his presence, and call upon the quivering rocks to cover them. He comes! with all the hosts of the righteous glorified. The breath of his lips strikes death to the wicked. His glory is a consuming fire. The proud and rebellious are as stubble; they are burned and 'left neither root nor branch.' He sweeps the earth 'as with the besom of destruction.' He deluges the earth with the fiery floods of his wrath, and the filthiness and abominations of the world are consumed. Satan and his dark hosts are taken and bound—the prince of the power of the air has lost his dominion, for He whose right it is to reign has come, and 'the kingdoms of this world have become the kingdoms of our Lord and of his Christ.'"[33]

NOTES AND COMMENTARY

Rev. 19:11 *I saw heaven opened.* This expression may mean that John saw an opening in our atmospheric sky as Jesus descended, or perhaps more likely, that the veil was parted and the heavens were opened in a metaphoric sense. A latter-day revelation explains the power by which heaven was opened to John: "The power and authority of the higher, or Melchizedek Priesthood, is to hold the keys of all the spiritual blessings of the church—to have the privilege of receiving the mysteries of the kingdom of heaven, to have the heavens opened unto them" (D&C 107:18–19).

behold a white horse. As the horse in scripture is representative of warfare (Isa. 31:3; Jer. 4:13; 8:16), the white horses in this section (vv. 11, 14) are symbolic, presenting Christ and members of his armies as great warriors. Christ's white horse, as envisioned by John, may have looked as terrible, mighty, and fierce as the following warhorse, described in Job 39:19–24:

> Hast thou given the horse strength?
> hast thou clothed his neck with thunder?
> . . . the glory of his nostrils is terrible.
> He paweth in the valley,
> and rejoiceth in his strength:
> he goeth on to meet the armed men.
> He mocketh at fear, and is not affrighted;
> neither turneth he back from the sword.
> The quiver rattleth against him,
> the glittering spear and the shield.
> He swalloweth the ground with fierceness and rage.

---

[33] "Second Advent," 583.

Contrast Christ's two comings on two different kinds of animals: during his first coming he was "meek, and sitting upon an ass" (Matt. 21:5; cf. Zech. 9:9) as he entered into Jerusalem shortly before his death; at his second coming he will ride an indomitable warhorse, bringing judgment to the earth.

he that sat upon him was called Faithful and True. These two titles characterize Christ and recall earlier passages in Revelation in which he is called "faithful witness" (Rev. 1:5) and "he that is true" (Rev. 3:7). He is faithful in that he holds steadfastly to the right and keeps all his promises. He is true in that he acts always in accordance with true and righteous principles.

in righteousness he doth judge. The Father has "committed all judgment unto the Son" (John 5:22). As the God who is called "Faithful and True," Jesus Christ's judgments are "true and righteous altogether" (Ps. 19:9; cf. Isa. 11:4; 2 Ne. 9:46); he renders proper justice to both the righteous and the wicked.

and make war. Jesus Christ, the meek and gentle "Prince of Peace" (Isa. 9:6), will render judgment on the world. As a "man of war" (Ex. 15:3) he will destroy all corruptible things at his coming in power and glory to cleanse the earth for his millennial reign.

Rev. 19:12 *His eyes were as a flame of fire.* The phrase is found elsewhere in the scriptures where the glory of the resurrected Lord is described in symbolic language (Rev. 1:14; D&C 110:3). The eyes "as a flame of fire" suggest light and knowledge (D&C 77:4) as well as the resolute countenance of a warrior.

on his head were many crowns. The crown, along with the royal vesture (Rev. 19:13), is part of the regal attire belonging to the king. But Christ will have "many crowns" upon his head. This signifies that Christ, as the "King of kings" (Rev. 19:16), is ruler over all. Revelation 11:15 clarifies that "the kingdoms of this world are become the kingdoms of our Lord, and of his Christ; and he shall reign forever and ever." As Paul explained, Christ is "far above all principality, and power, and might, and dominion, and every name that is named, not only in this world, but also in that which is to come" (Eph. 1:21; see also Col. 1:16; 2:10). Satan attempts to deceive people when he imitates Jesus Christ by wearing seven crowns (Rev. 12:3), as does the beast who wears ten crowns (Rev. 13:1).

he had a name written, that no man knew, but he himself. Jesus Christ has a name that no man knows. Those who overcome the world will be identified with Christ and his new name. Revelation 3:12 explains, "Him that overcometh will I . . . write upon him the name of my God, and the name of the city of my God, . . . new Jerusalem, which cometh down out of heaven from my God: and I will write upon him my new name."[34] Those who overcome the world also will receive "a new name written, which no man knoweth saving he that receiveth it" (Rev. 2:17). By contrast, the great whore has a name on her forehead that identifies her as "Babylon the Great, the Mother of . . . Abominations" (Rev. 17:5). While Christ's name is one that no man knows, the name of the Mother of Abominations, because of her pride and arrogance, is prominently visible.

Rev. 19:13 *he was clothed with a vesture dipped in blood.* At his second coming Jesus will be clothed in red garments. A latter-day prophecy portrays Christ coming "down from God in heaven with dyed garments, . . . clothed in his glorious apparel, . . . red in his apparel, and his garments like him that treadeth in the wine-vat" (D&C 133:46, 48; see also Isa. 63:1–4). Jesus' red garments recall his atoning sacrifice, when he bled from every pore (D&C 19:18), thus staining his clothing with his own blood. Elder Neal A. Maxwell testified: "Soon, He who was once mockingly dressed in purple will come again, attired in red apparel, reminding us whose blood redeemed us."[35] And further, "having bled at every pore, how red His raiment must have been in Gethsemane, how crimson that cloak! No wonder, when Christ comes in power and glory, that He will come in reminding red attire (see D&C 133:48), signifying not only the winepress of wrath, but also to bring to our remembrance how He suffered for each of us in Gethsemane and on Calvary!"[36]

---

[34] For a discussion of Rev. 3:12, see Parry and Parry, *Understanding the Book of Revelation,* 49.

[35] *Even As I Am,* 120.

[36] *Ensign,* May 1987, 72.

Isaiah 63:2–3 provides a second reason for the red garments. The text is placed in a question-and-answer format. At the second coming the people will ask Christ why his garments are red:

> Why are your garments red,
> your clothes as if you had trodden the winepress?

His reply:

> I have trodden the winepress alone.
> Of the men of my people not one was with me.
> In my anger I trod them down,
> trampled them in my wrath.
> Their juice spattered my garments,
> and all my clothes stained.
> (New Jerusalem Bible)

This passage is describing a winepress not of atonement but of judgment. At Christ's second coming, he will trample to destruction the nations as if they were grapes, and their juice (that is, blood) will splatter his garments so that they become red (see also D&C 133:48–51).

his name is called The Word of God. In Joseph Smith's translation of John 1:14 and 16, Jesus Christ refers to himself as the Word.

Rev. 19:14 *the armies which were in heaven followed him.* Jesus Christ, as "captain" (2 Chr. 13:12), "commander" (Isa. 55:4), "leader" (Isa. 55:4), and "Lord of Sabaoth" (D&C 87:7; 98:2; *Sabaoth* is a Hebrew word which means "armies" or "hosts"), leads his armies to "make war" (Rev. 19:10) against the world. The armies that follow Jesus Christ are his Saints, those who wear the "whole armour of God" (Eph. 6:11–17; see also D&C 27:15). They, together with their Commander, will battle and overcome the evil in the world.

All the true Saints will accompany Christ at his coming (D&C 88:96–98). Matthew recorded that "the Son of man shall come in the glory of his Father with his angels" (Matt. 16:27); Paul spoke of "the coming of our Lord Jesus Christ with all his saints" (1 Thes. 3:13); and Doctrine and Covenants 76:63 says of those who "overcome all things": "These are they whom [Christ] shall bring with him, when he shall come in the clouds of heaven to reign on the earth over his people" (see also 1 Thes. 4:13–17; Col. 3:4).

upon white horses. See the commentary on Revelation 19:11, page 417.

clothed in fine linen, white and clean. Contrast the white garments of Christ's armies with his blood-red vesture, identified in Revelation 19:13, and note the paradox: the Saints' "white and clean" garments have become such because they have washed and "made them white in the blood of the Lamb" (Rev. 7:14; see also 1 Ne. 12:10–11; Alma 5:21), meaning they have become sanctified through Jesus' atonement. The linen symbolizes "the righteousness of saints" (Rev. 19:8).

Rev. 19:15 *out of his mouth goeth a sharp sword.* The Joseph Smith Translation makes an important change that clarifies this phrase, reading "out of his mouth proceedeth the word of God." God will use his word, which "is quick and powerful, and sharper than any two-edged sword, piercing even to the dividing asunder of soul and spirit" (Heb. 4:12), to "smite the nations" at his second coming. The smiting of the nations may have reference to the great burning that will accompany Christ's coming (D&C 64:23–25).

he shall rule them with a rod of iron. The Joseph Smith Translation renders this phrase as "he will rule them with the word of his mouth." God will first "smite the nations" with his word, and then he will rule them with that word.

he treadeth the winepress of the fierceness and wrath of Almighty God. As grapes were harvested, they were placed in a trough and trampled by foot to produce juice, or wine. The winepress represents God's terrible wrath (meaning the execution of his judgments), which, according to justice, exacts the full and terrible payment for sin. The grapes, which represent the sinner, are trodden under foot until nothing is left but pulp and wine, the wine being a symbol of the blood of the sinner.

In performing the Atonement, Christ suffered that wrath for us, so that we might escape both the wrath and the consequent suffering if we would repent. In the time of judgment, all those who did not truly repent and come unto Christ will suffer the wrath of God themselves;

it will be for them as if they themselves were cast into the winepress and trampled. "I have trodden the winepress alone," the Lord said through Isaiah, "I will tread them in mine anger, . . . and their blood shall be sprinkled upon my garments" (Isa. 63:3). Doctrine and Covenants 19:11–19 describes the suffering of Christ in performing the Atonement and the suffering of those unrepentant souls who will be cast into the winepress themselves.

Rev. 19:16 *he hath on his vesture and on his thigh a name written.* The name "King of kings and Lord of lords," shown prominently on the Lord's red clothing and on his thigh, communicates his supremacy to those who see him. The name written "on [the] thigh" may instead be written on the vesture that covers the thigh; or the thigh may be a symbol or figure of speech for the sword found at the warrior's side, meaning the name is written on the horseman's sword.

KING OF KINGS, AND LORD OF LORDS. Jesus Christ is the King and Lord over all of the heavenly hosts, including those who are "kings and priests of the Most High God"[37] (see also Rev. 1:6; 5:10; 20:6). President Ezra Taft Benson testified of the power that Jesus will possess at his coming: "Not many years hence Christ will come again. He will come in power and might as King of Kings and Lord of Lords. And ultimately every knee shall bow and every tongue confess that Jesus is the Christ." (See Romans 14:11; D&C 88:104; Mosiah 27:31.)[38]

THE RIGHTEOUS WILL APPEAR WITH CHRIST IN THE SKY
Doctrine and Covenants 29:11–13

11 For I will reveal myself from heaven with power and great glory, with all the hosts thereof, and dwell in righteousness with men on earth a thousand years, and the wicked shall not stand.

12 And again, verily, verily, I say unto you, and it hath gone forth in a firm decree, by the will of the Father, that mine apostles, the Twelve which were with me in my ministry at

---

[37] *History of the Church,* 5:555.
[38] *Ensign,* Mar. 1986, 5.

Jerusalem, shall stand at my right hand at the day of my com-
ing in a pillar of fire, being clothed with robes of righteous-
ness, with crowns upon their heads, in glory even as I am, to
judge the whole house of Israel, even as many as have loved
me and kept my commandments, and none else.

13 For a trump shall sound both long and loud, even as upon
Mount Sinai, and all the earth shall quake, and they shall
come forth—yea, even the dead which died in me, to receive a
crown of righteousness, and to be clothed upon, even as I am,
to be with me, that we may be one.

When Jesus Christ appears in the clouds of glory, he will be accompanied by a great number of righteous individuals. Matthew and Luke identified them as "angels" when they wrote, "For the Son of man shall come in the glory of his Father with his angels" (Matt. 16:27; see also Mark 8:38; Luke 9:26). Paul identified those who will accompany Christ as "saints" (1 Thes. 3:13), as does the Old Testament prophet Zechariah (Zech. 14:5). Paul wrote an epistle "to the saints and faithful brethren in Christ which are at Colosse" (Col. 1:2), prophesying, "When Christ, who is our life, shall appear, then shall ye also appear with him in glory" (Col. 3:4; see also 1 Thes. 2:19).

Doctrine and Covenants 76 is the clearest in its description of those who shall appear with Christ in the sky at his coming. It speaks of those who "received the testimony of Jesus," who kept "the commandments" and were "washed and cleansed from all their sins," who received "the Holy Spirit by the laying on of the hands," "who overcome by faith and are sealed by the Holy Spirit of promise," "who are the church of the Firstborn," and "who are priests and kings. . . . And are priests of the Most High, after the order of Melchizedek. . . . These are they whom he shall bring with him, when he shall come in the clouds of heaven to reign on the earth over his people" (D&C 76:51–63).

Paul's epistle to Church members of Thessalonica indicates that righteous souls who are on the earth when Jesus comes again will actually ascend into the clouds to meet him in the air as he descends. The apostle wrote: "For this we say unto you by the word of the Lord, that we which are alive and remain unto the coming of the Lord shall not [precede][39] them which are asleep. For the Lord himself shall descend from heaven with a shout, with the voice of the archangel, and with the trump of God: and the dead in Christ shall rise first: Then we which are alive and remain shall be caught up together with them in the clouds, to meet the Lord in the air: and so shall we ever be with the Lord" (1 Thes. 4:15–17).

NOTES AND COMMENTARY

D&C 29:11 *For I will reveal myself from heaven.* Christ's second coming will be a revelation of the greatest magnitude because "every eye shall see him" when "he cometh with clouds" (Rev. 1:7). He explains elsewhere, "Prepare for the revelation which is to come, when the veil of the covering of my temple, in my tabernacle, which hideth the earth, shall be taken off, and all flesh shall see me together" (D&C 101:23).

with power and great glory. Power and *glory* describe Christ himself (Isaiah uses the phrase "glory of his majesty" to describe Christ at his coming; Isa. 2:10, 19, 21), as well as his appearance at his coming (Matt. 24:30; D&C 34:7; 65:5). His power and glory, with the attending fire, will be of such great intensity that even the mountains of the earth will "flow down at [his] presence" (D&C 133:40, 44), and the hills will melt "like wax at the presence of the Lord" (Ps. 97:5).

with all the hosts thereof. A great company of Saints will accompany Christ in the air at his coming.

and dwell in righteousness with men on earth a thousand years. This phrase refers to the Millennium, when Christ will reign in peace and righteousness. Those who live during the reign of Christ will sing praises and clap their hands:

> O clap your hands, all ye people;
> shout unto God with the voice of triumph.
> For the Lord most high is terrible;
> he is a great King over all the earth.
> He shall subdue the people under us,
> and the nations under our feet.

---

[39] The word *precede* is found in note *c* to 1 Thes. 4:15 in the LDS edition of the KJV.

> He shall choose our inheritance for us,
> the excellency of Jacob whom he loved. Selah.
> God is gone up with a shout,
> the Lord with the sound of a trumpet.
> Sing praises to God, sing praises:
> sing praises unto our King, sing praises.
>
> For God is the King of all the earth:
> sing ye praises with understanding.
> God reigneth over the heathen:
> God sitteth upon the throne of his holiness.
> (Psalm 47:1–8)

the wicked shall not stand. These five words summarize the state of the wicked at the Second Coming. Isaiah uses similar words in his prophecy regarding the wicked at Jesus' coming. He wrote, "The lofty looks of man shall be humbled, and the haughtiness of men shall be bowed down, and the Lord alone shall be exalted in that day. For the day of the Lord of hosts shall be upon every one that is proud and lofty, and upon every one that is lifted up; and he shall be brought low" (Isa. 2:11–12).

D&C 29:12 *the Twelve which were with me in my ministry at Jerusalem.* It is Heavenly Father's clear desire that the Twelve Apostles who served with Christ in Jerusalem accompany him at his coming.[40]

stand at my right hand at the day of my coming. The right hand is a place of great honor and is associated with power (Ex. 15:3; Ps. 89:13). The exalted Jesus Christ himself stands at the Father's right hand (Acts 7:55–56); at the right hand of Christ will stand the Twelve Apostles.

in a pillar of fire. Speaking of Jesus at his coming, the psalmist testified that "a fire shall devour before him, and it shall be very tempestuous round about him" (Ps. 50:3). The pillar of fire recalls the fire that led ancient Israel through the wilderness. "And the Lord went

---

[40] We assume that Matthias, who replaced Judas Iscariot in the original Twelve (Acts 1:21–26), will also be the twelfth member of the group at the Second Coming.

before them by day in a pillar of a cloud to lead them the way; and by night in a pillar of fire" (Ex. 13:21).

being clothed with robes of righteousness, with crowns upon their heads, in glory even as I am. The apostles who will stand at Christ's right hand will be glorified beings, just as Christ is glorified. Like Jesus, who shall wear "many crowns" (Rev. 19:12), signifying that he is the King of kings, the Twelve will have crowns upon their heads; but unlike Jesus, who will wear a red vesture, the Twelve will wear robes that are "white and clean" (Rev. 19:13–14). The robes and crowns indicate that the Twelve are "priests and kings, who have received of his fulness, and of his glory" (D&C 76:56; see also D&C 76:63).

to judge the whole house of Israel, even as many as have loved me and kept my commandments, and none else. Christ's Twelve Apostles will judge those members of the house of Israel who have kept Jesus' commandments and loved him. Mormon declared, "I write unto all the ends of the earth; yea, unto you, twelve tribes of Israel, who shall be judged according to your works by the twelve whom Jesus chose to be his disciples in the land of Jerusalem" (Morm. 3:18; see also Matt. 19:28; 1 Ne. 12:9). Although Jesus will delegate authority to the Twelve to judge members of the house of Israel, he will judge the wicked himself (Matt. 25:31–46; Jude 1:14–16).

D&C 29:13 *For a trump shall sound both long and loud, even as upon Mount Sinai, and all the earth shall quake.* The Lord promised ancient Israel that he would meet with them on Mount Sinai, if they would first sanctify themselves and properly prepare for this event. The signal that would inform Israel to "come up to the mount" would be the long sound of a trumpet (Ex. 19:13; see also vv. 16, 19). At this great event, "the whole mount quaked greatly" (Ex. 19:18). The event at Sinai is a type and shadow of similar events that will occur when Christ comes. Again there will be a trumpet blast, an earthquake, and a sanctified people, and once again the Lord will descend to meet with his Saints.

they shall come forth—yea, even the dead which died in me. This particular resurrection will occur at the sound of a trumpet and at the time of an earthquake. Doctrine and Covenants 43:18 describes the events that will occur: "For the day cometh that the Lord shall utter his voice out of heaven; the heavens shall shake and the earth shall tremble, and the trump of God shall sound both long and loud, and shall say to the sleeping nations: Ye saints arise and live; ye sinners stay and sleep until I shall call again."

to receive a crown of righteousness, and to be clothed upon, even as I am. Jesus Christ, his apostles, and the Saints will possess a crown and regal vestments consistent with their royal nature.

that we may be one. God will make his Saints "equal in power, and in might, and in dominion" (D&C 76:95).

THE PROUD SHALL BE BURNED AT HIS COMING
Doctrine and Covenants 64:23–25

23 Behold, now it is called today until the coming of the Son of Man, and verily it is a day of sacrifice, and a day for the tithing of my people; for he that is tithed shall not be burned at his coming.

24 For after today cometh the burning—this is speaking after the manner of the Lord—for verily I say, tomorrow all the proud and they that do wickedly shall be as stubble; and I will burn them up, for I am the Lord of Hosts; and I will not spare any that remain in Babylon.

25 Wherefore, if ye believe me, ye will labor while it is called today.

Many prophets, including Isaiah, Micah, Nahum, Malachi, and Joseph Smith, have prophesied that a great burning will accompany Christ at his coming (Isa. 30:27–33; Micah 1:3–4; Nahum 1:1–10; Mal. 4:1; D&C 29:9). They have promised that all the proud and wicked, along with all corruptible things, will be destroyed by Christ's glory and brightness. For instance, Asaph, one of the authors of the Psalms, predicted, "Our God shall come . . . : a fire shall devour before him, and it shall be very tempestuous round about him" (Ps. 50:3). Using a poetic style, Isaiah explained that Jesus Christ himself is the source of the burning fire: "Behold, the name of the Lord cometh from far, burning with his anger, and the burden thereof is heavy: his lips are full of indignation, and his tongue as a devouring fire: and his breath, as an overflowing stream, shall reach to the midst of the neck" (Isa. 30:27–28). The prophet Nahum spelled out the magnitude of the Lord's destructive fire: "The mountains quake at him, and the hills melt, and the earth is burned at his presence, yea, the world, and all that dwell therein" (Nahum 1:5).

Elder Gordon B. Hinckley told us how to avoid the burning and destruction that will accompany Christ's second coming: "Some years ago one of our brethren spoke of the payment of tithing as 'fire insurance.' That statement evoked laughter. Nonetheless, the word of the Lord is clear that those who do not keep the commandments and observe the laws of God shall be burned at the time of his coming. For that shall be a day of judgment and a day of sifting, a day of separating the good from the evil. I would venture a personal opinion that no event has occurred in all the history of the earth as dreadful as will be the day of the Second Coming; no event as fraught with the destructive forces of nature, as consequential for the nations of the earth, as terrible for the wicked, or as wonderful for the righteous."[41]

In Doctrine and Covenants 64, the Lord revealed his divine calendar: The present era is called *today* until Christ's second coming. *Today* is the time to prepare, to pay tithing, and to sacrifice for the kingdom of God. *Tomorrow,* when Christ comes in power and glory, the wicked and the proud will burn as stubble.

NOTES AND COMMENTARY

D&C 64:23 *Behold.* Pay strict heed.

now it is called today until the coming of the Son of Man. God sets forth his divine calendar by explaining that the present era, which began 11 September 1831 (the date of this revelation) or even before that date, is called *today.* It will remain *today* until Jesus' second coming (see also D&C 45:6). The divine title *Son of Man,* first revealed to Adam (Moses 6:57), is an abbreviated form of "Son of

---

[41] "'We Need Not Fear His Coming,'" 82–83.

Man of Holiness." The title is also used six times in Matthew 24, an important chapter on the signs of the times.

it is a day of sacrifice. Today is the season to sacrifice, to give of our time, means, and talents for the sake of Zion. By sacrificing we prepare for Christ's coming.

a day for the tithing of my people. The payment of tithing is a commandment, or "standing law," to the Church; the money is used "for the building of [the Lord's] house and for the laying of the foundation of Zion" (D&C 119:1–5). Those who faithfully tithe are promised that they "shall not be burned at [Jesus'] coming."

D&C 64:24 *For after today cometh the burning.* The word *today* refers to the era or season belonging to the restoration of the gospel before the Second Coming. Christ will come *tomorrow,* and that will be the day when all sinners will burn.

this is speaking after the manner of the Lord. The Lord explains that he is not speaking in these verses of twenty-four-hour time periods when he names *today* and *tomorrow;* he is speaking of broader periods of history.

tomorrow all the proud and they that do wickedly shall be as stubble. Tomorrow signifies the time when the wicked and proud will burn with fire. The burning fire will be complete, not partial, for the wicked will "be as stubble." Nothing will be left except charred remnants.

I will burn them up. Jesus Christ himself will burn the wicked with the brightness of his glory and the great power of his judgments.

for I am the Lord of Hosts. Jesus reminds us that he is the Lord of hosts, perhaps because the hosts of heaven will accompany him in his second coming (Matt. 17:27; 1 Thes. 4:13–17; Rev. 19:14).

I will not spare any that remain in Babylon. None who belong to the world of wickedness will escape the Lord's burning. Although the proud and wicked will attempt to hide in holes, rocks, and caves at the Lord's appearance (Isa. 2:19–21; Rev. 6:15–16), they will not escape.

D&C 64:25 *if ye believe me, ye will labor while it is called today.* We who have faith in Jesus Christ are commanded to work and prepare now for his coming.

THE MARRIAGE SUPPER OF THE LAMB
Revelation 19:6–10

> *6 And I heard as it were the voice of a great multitude, and as the voice of many waters, and as the voice of mighty thunderings, saying, Alleluia: for the Lord God omnipotent reigneth.*
>
> *7 Let us be glad and rejoice, and give honour to him: for the marriage of the Lamb is come, and his wife hath made herself ready.*
>
> *8 And to her was granted that she should be arrayed in fine linen, clean and white; for the fine linen is the righteousness of saints.*
>
> *9 And he saith unto me, Write, Blessed are they which are called unto the marriage supper of the Lamb. And he saith unto me, These are the true sayings of God.*
>
> *10 And I fell at his feet to worship him. And he said unto me, See [that][42] thou do it not: I am thy fellow servant, and of thy brethren that have the testimony of Jesus: worship God: for the testimony of Jesus is the spirit of prophecy.*

The marriage of the Lamb, who is Christ (D&C 33:17–18), to his bride, who is the Church (D&C 109:73–74) and also the New Jerusalem (Rev. 21:2, 9–10), is a metaphor for the union between the Lord and his people, made possible through the atonement of Christ. In fact, the very name of Christ's sacrifice (*at-one-ment*) suggests the purpose of that sacrifice: to make us one with both the Father and the Son (John 17:11, 19–23). The Lord uses marriage as a symbol to underscore the sweetness and blessing of that union. There is no sweeter or more meaningful relationship on earth than that between a holy husband and a holy wife; that is the kind of relationship (in depth of feeling and completeness of union) that the Lord is inviting us to participate in. That marriage is between Christ and the Church, but the Church is not just an organization on the earth; it is also the individual souls who belong to that organization. Though we are to prepare for the marriage all our lives (Matt. 25:1–13; D&C 45:56–57), it will be brought to its

---

[42] This addition is found in JST Rev. 19:10.

culmination, with the body of the Church, when Christ returns in glory. Of course, as individuals, we are bound to Christ as soon as we are ready.

The marriage supper may refer to a time when the Saints sit with Jesus Christ and partake of the sacrament. He taught: "Behold, this is wisdom in me; wherefore, marvel not, for the hour cometh that I will drink of the fruit of the vine with you on the earth. . . . And also with all those whom my Father hath given me out of the world" (D&C 27:5, 14).

NOTES AND COMMENTARY

Rev. 19:6 *the voice of a great multitude.* This multitude is probably the "many angels round about the throne" spoken of in Revelation 5:11, "and the number of them was ten thousand times ten thousand, and thousands of thousands."

as the voice of many waters. The noisy sound of a huge rushing river or of the crashing breakers of the ocean is a very apt description of the sound of an immense crowd of people.

as the voice of mighty thunderings. This expression is another apt description of the sound of many people.

saying, Alleluia: for the Lord God omnipotent reigneth. To paraphrase this passage, "Praise Jehovah, for the Lord who has power over all kingdoms" (see Mosiah 3:5; A of F 1:10). This is the fourth cry of *Alleluia* recorded in Revelation 19; unlike the other cries, which praised him for his judgments against Babylon, this cry praises God for coming to bless and reign over his Saints. The establishment of Christ's reign is the fulfillment of the request made in the Lord's prayer, "Thy kingdom come" (Matt. 6:10).

Rev. 19:7 *Let us be glad and rejoice, and give honour to him.* We do indeed have cause to be glad, to rejoice, and to give honor to the Lord. He has offered the great mediating sacrifice for us, enabling us to repent and be cleansed from our sins, and to draw near to him to be joined in an eternal, holy union with him (John 17:11, 19–23). The specific reason for this present rejoicing is that union, "the marriage of the Lamb."

for the marriage of the Lamb is come. The marriage of the Lamb has been described in the scriptures (for example, Isa. 54:4–5; 62:5; Jer. 31:32; JST Matt. 22:1–14; Eph. 5:23, 32; D&C 58:6–11; 65:3; 88:92; 133:10, 19). In latter-day revelation the Lord speaks of "a feast of fat things . . . for the poor; yea, a feast of fat things, of wine on the lees well refined, that the earth may know that the mouths of the prophets shall not fail; yea, a supper of the house of the Lord, well prepared, unto which all nations shall be invited. First, the rich and the learned, the wise and the noble; and after that cometh the day of my power; then shall the poor, the lame, and the blind, and the deaf, come in unto the marriage of the Lamb, and partake of the supper of the Lord, prepared for the great day to come" (D&C 58:8–11; see also 65:3).

Joseph Smith wrote of this feast and our attendance: "Those who keep the commandments of the Lord and walk in His statutes to the end, are the only individuals permitted to sit at this glorious feast. . . . [Paul wrote:] 'I have fought a good fight, I have finished my course, I have kept the faith. . . .' His labors were unceasing to spread the glorious news: and like a faithful soldier, when called to give his life in the cause which he had espoused, he laid it down. . . . Follow the labors of this Apostle from the time of his conversion to the time of his death, and you will have a fair sample of industry and patience in promulgating the Gospel of Christ. Derided, whipped, and stoned, the moment he escaped the hands of his persecutors he as zealously as ever proclaimed the doctrine of the Savior. . . . Reflect for a moment, brethren, and enquire, whether you would consider yourselves worthy a seat at the marriage feast with Paul and others like him, if you had been unfaithful? Had you not fought the good fight, and kept the faith, could you expect to receive?"[43]

his wife hath made herself ready. Through repentance, sanctification, and a heart that is fully turned to God, the wife of Christ, which is the Church, has prepared herself to be joined with him.

Rev. 19:8 *to her was granted.* It was granted to the bride to wear fine linen, which represents the righteousness of the Saints. *To her was granted* is an expression that reveals an important truth. Though

---

[43] *History of the Church,* 2:19–20.

we may labor hard to be righteous, in the final event even our righteousness is possible only because of the grace and power and gifts granted to us by God (Deut. 30:20; John 1:12; 2 Cor. 4:7; Col. 1:10–11).

she should be arrayed in fine linen, clean and white. The bride of Christ wears simple clothing, which symbolizes "the righteousness of saints" (see also Rev. 15:6). The linen is white because it was "washed . . . in the blood of the Lamb" (Rev. 7:14), meaning that the Saints are sanctified through the atonement of Christ.

Rev. 19:9 *And he saith unto me, Write.* An angel tells John specific words to record.

Blessed are they which are called unto the marriage supper of the Lamb. This passage is one of the "beatitudes" of the book of Revelation.[44] Those who are invited guests at the Lamb's celebratory marriage feast are blessed indeed. There are three persons or groups at the marriage supper: the Bridegroom, Jesus Christ, who is the Lamb; the Bride, who is the Church (as an institution but also as a collection of many individuals); and the guests ("they which are called unto the marriage supper"), who also are likely the individual members, those who have qualified by righteousness for the grace of Christ.

he saith unto me, These are the true sayings of God. The angel bears witness that these words, which he has instructed John to write, come from God himself.

---

[44] For the beatitudes of the book of Revelation, see Parry and Parry, *Understanding the Book of Revelation,* 324–25.

CHAPTER 11

Scriptural Types of the Last Days and the Second Coming

Signs of the Times

1. The Second Coming is like the destruction at the time of the Flood.

2. The gifts of the Spirit exist in the latter-day Church as they did during Pentecost.

3. The Jews gather to Jerusalem, as they did during the days of Cyrus.

4. The Saints again gather at Adam-ondi-Ahman.

5. Many unbelievers deny the signs of the times.

6. Many cities are destroyed before Christ's coming, similar to the manner in which Sodom and Gomorrah were destroyed anciently.

7. The wars of the last days are in some respects similar to the Jaredite wars.

8. Sinners are destroyed when Christ comes again.

9. Those who are righteous at Christ's coming are spared.

10. Jesus Christ appears to the righteous at his temples.

11. Jesus Christ reigns in glory and splendor during the Millennium.

12. The events preliminary to the visit of the resurrected Christ to ancient America give a pattern for many events of the last days.

13. The Sabbath day, a day of rest, is a type of the Millennium.

The Lord has given us many tools to understand the last days and the second coming of Christ. For instance, he has spoken in parables,[1] in symbols,[2] and in plain language. He has also given us scriptural types to teach important truths about these things. When we understand the meaning of types he has given us, we better understand these great events to come. In the language of the Book of Mormon, a type is an event or image that encourages one to *look forward* to the future. The law of Moses, for instance, encouraged the Israelites to "*look forward* to the coming of Christ, considering that the law of Moses was a type of his coming" (Alma 25:15). The "ordinances were given after this manner, that thereby the people might *look forward* on the Son of God, it being a type of his order, or it being his order, and this that they might *look forward* to him for a remission of their sins" (Alma 13:16). King Benjamin declared that God had given to ancient Israel "many signs, and wonders, and types, and shadows" (Mosiah 3:15).[3] As with all types, these types encourage us to *look forward* to the signs of the times and Christ's glorious second coming. Types are a great blessing to us because they add to our understanding of the future and help to prepare us for what is to come.

EXAMPLES OF SCRIPTURAL TYPES

Abinadi's death by fire was "a type and a shadow of things which [were] to come" (Mosiah 13:10), speaking of the manner in which the descendants of the priests of Noah would be destroyed. The fulfillment of this prophecy is outlined in Alma 25:9–12: "Thus the words of Abinadi were brought to pass, which he said concerning the seed of the priests who caused that he should suffer death by fire. For he said unto them: What ye shall do unto me shall be a type of things to come. . . . And he said unto the priests of Noah that their seed should cause many to be put to death, in the like manner as he was, . . . and now behold, these words were verified."

The brazen serpent lifted up by Moses before the children of Israel, as recorded in Numbers 21:6–9, served as a type. It was lifted

---

[1] For parables concerning the last days and the Second Coming, see Appendix 3, page 483.
[2] See the commentary on Babylon, page 285.
[3] See also Bruce R. McConkie's discussion of similitudes of the Second Coming, *Millennial Messiah,* 361–65.

up in similitude of Jesus Christ, who would be raised up on the cross: "And as Moses lifted up the serpent in the wilderness, even so must the Son of man be lifted up" (John 3:14–15). Those who looked at the raised brazen serpent were healed of their physical wounds; this healing was a type of those who look to Jesus Christ for spiritual healing. "And as many as should look upon that serpent should live, even so as many as should look upon the Son of God with faith, having a contrite spirit, might live, even unto that life which is eternal" (Hel. 8:14–15; see also Alma 33:19).

The binding of Isaac on Mount Moriah was an event that looked forward to the sacrifice of Jesus Christ. Abraham and Isaac were types of the Father and the Son. As the Father would offer up Jesus, his Only Begotten Son, so Abraham was to "[offer] up Isaac, . . . his only begotten son" (Heb. 11:17). Jacob, the son of Lehi, wrote that "it was accounted unto Abraham in the wilderness to be obedient unto the commands of God in offering up his son Isaac, which is a similitude of God and his Only Begotten Son" (Jacob 4:5).

The law of Moses was "a law of performances and of ordinances, a law which they were to observe strictly from day to day, to keep them in remembrance of God and their duty towards him. But behold, I say unto you, that all these things were types of things to come" (Mosiah 13:30–31), meaning, the life, ministry, and sacrifice of Christ.

The three days and three nights that Jonah remained in the belly of the fish was an event that anticipated the death, burial, and resurrection of Jesus. Jesus prophesied, "For as Jonas was three days and three nights" in the belly of the great fish, "so shall the Son of man be three days and three nights in the heart of the earth" (Matt. 12:39–40).

Numerous types and shadows symbolize Christ's mission, ministry, and atonement. "All things bear record of me" (Moses 6:63), the Lord testified, as did Nephi: "All things which have been given of God from the beginning of the world, unto man, are the typifying of him" (2 Ne. 11:4). Baptism, for example, is a type of Christ's death, burial, and resurrection (Rom. 6; D&C 128:12–13). Elder Bruce R. McConkie explained, "If we had sufficient insight, we would see in every gospel ordinance, in every rite that is part of revealed religion, in every performance commanded of God, in all things Deity gives his people, something that typifies the eternal ministry of the Eternal Christ."[4] Both Melchizedek and Moses were types of the Son of God (Heb. 7:15; Moses 1:6). Their lives, ministries, teachings, sacrifices, prophecies, and priesthood looked forward to the life of Christ.

NOAH AND THE FLOOD

Matthew 24:37–39

> *37 But as the days of Noe were, so shall also the coming of the Son of man be.*
>
> *38 For as in the days that were before the flood they were eating and drinking, marrying and giving in marriage, until the day that Noe entered into the ark,*
>
> *39 And knew not until the flood came, and took them all away; so shall also the coming of the Son of man be.*

Noah and the Flood are clearly a type of the last days and the Second Coming. Perhaps for emphasis, twice in three verses in Matthew 24 the Lord compared the "days of Noah" to the "coming of the Son of man" (vv. 37, 39).[5] There are at least four great parallels between Noah's time and that of Christ's second coming:

The wickedness of the people. Great wickedness existed during Noah's lifetime: "Behold, they are without affection, and they hate their own blood, . . . and among all the workmanship of mine hands there has not been so great wickedness" (Moses 7:33, 36); "and God saw that the wickedness of men had become great in the earth; and every man was lifted up in the imagination of the thoughts of his heart, being only evil continually" (Moses 8:22). "The earth was corrupt before God, and it was filled with violence. And God looked upon the earth, and, behold, it was corrupt, for all flesh had corrupted its way upon the earth. And God said unto Noah: The end of all flesh is come before me, for the earth is filled with violence, and behold I will destroy all flesh from off the earth" (Moses 8:28–30). The

---

[4] *Promised Messiah*, 378.
[5] See also Elder McConkie's discussion of Noah and the Flood as a similitude of the Second Coming, *Millennial Messiah*, 357–61.

iniquity of the people during Noah's time was a prelude to the sinfulness of the world in our own dispensation, at the time when the Lord will destroy the wicked with his presence.

A significant difference, however, between the events connected with Noah and those of the last days is in the number of persons who accept or reject the principles of the gospel. Apparently, most of Noah's contemporaries rejected his preaching of faith, repentance, baptism, and the Holy Ghost (Moses 8:19–24), a sharp contrast to the great numbers of Church members who will accept the principles and ordinances of the gospel in the latter days, follow the modern prophet, and await Christ's coming.

The heedlessness of the people. Despite the warnings of Noah, most of the people paid him little attention, continuing with their normal lives without concern for the coming disasters.[6]

The destruction of the wicked. The prophet Enoch foresaw many events that would take place on the earth before the coming of Christ, including the destruction by flood of those who refused to repent and heed Noah's warnings: "Upon the residue of the wicked the floods came and swallowed them up" (Moses 7:43). This destruction of evil people by water looks forward to the end of days when wickedness will be destroyed by fire.

The righteous, who heeded the words of the prophet, were saved. Moses 7:43 records: "Noah built an ark; and . . . the Lord smiled upon it, and held it in his own hand" (Moses 7:43). Two expressions in this verse teach us about how God cares for and secures obedient souls during great tribulation: "the Lord smiled upon [the ark]," and the Lord "held [Noah's family] in his own hand." The first expression evokes the image of a caring mother who lovingly shelters her young child from danger; the second evokes that of a father who holds his beloved child in his arm in a protective manner. As God preserved Noah and his family "with a temporal salvation" (Moses 7:42), so will he smile upon those who obey him and who follow the prophets of our own dispensation.

---

[6] See the commentary on conditions in Noah's day, page 233.

THE DAY OF PENTECOST
Acts 2:1–4

> *1 And when the day of Pentecost was fully come, they were all with one accord in one place.*
>
> *2 And suddenly there came a sound from heaven as of a rushing mighty wind, and it filled all the house where they were sitting.*
>
> *3 And there appeared unto them cloven tongues like as of fire, and it sat upon each of them.*
>
> *4 And they were all filled with the Holy Ghost, and began to speak with other tongues, as the Spirit gave them utterance.*

This record gives us several significant details regarding the outpouring of the Spirit on the day of Pentecost, which occurred soon after the ascension of Christ into heaven (Acts 1:9–11). Luke writes of "a sound from heaven as of a rushing mighty wind," of "cloven tongues like as of fire" which "sat upon each" of the persons who were in the house, who "were all filled with the Holy Ghost, and began to speak with other tongues" (Acts 2:1–4). According to Peter, who spoke to an "amazed" audience who had witnessed the speaking in tongues (Acts 2:7, 12), the great blessings of the Holy Ghost on this occasion satisfied Joel's prophecy: "And it shall come to pass in the last days, saith God, I will pour out of my Spirit upon all flesh: and your sons and your daughters shall prophesy, and your young men shall see visions, and your old men shall dream dreams" (Acts 2:17–18; see also Joel 2:28–29).

That spiritual outpouring almost two millennia ago anticipates and serves as a type of similar blessings that have been and will yet be received by the Saints of this last dispensation. Moroni, during an appearance to Joseph Smith, quoted Joel 2:28–32 and promised that the words would soon be fulfilled (JS–H 1:41). One fulfillment of Joel's prophecy, a latter-day Pentecost, took place at the Kirtland Temple after Joseph Smith prayed: "Let the anointing of thy ministers be sealed upon them with power from on high. Let it be fulfilled upon them, as upon those on the day of Pentecost; let the gift of tongues be poured out upon thy people, even cloven tongues as of fire, and the interpretation thereof. And let thy house be filled, as with a rushing mighty wind, with thy glory" (D&C 109:35–37). Joel's prophecy will again find fulfillment "in the last days" many times as the Saints build Zion, worship the Lord in sacred places, and prepare for his coming. The promises of this prophecy will come to full fruition during the Millennium.

EXILED JEWS RETURN TO JUDAH AND REBUILD THE TEMPLE

Ezra 1:2–5

> *2 Thus saith Cyrus king of Persia, The Lord God of heaven hath given me all the kingdoms of the earth; and he hath charged me to build him an house at Jerusalem, which is in Judah.*
>
> *3 Who is there among you of all his people? his God be with him, and let him go up to Jerusalem, which is in Judah, and build the house of the Lord God of Israel, (he is the God,) which is in Jerusalem.*
>
> *4 And whosever remaineth in any place he sojourneth, let the men of his place help him with silver and with gold, and with goods, and with beasts, beside the freewill offering for the house of God is in Jerusalem.*
>
> *5 Then rose up the chief of the fathers of Judah and Benjamin, and the priests, and the Levites, with all them whose spirit God had raised, to go up to build the house of the Lord which is in Jerusalem.*

In the year 538 B.C., the Persian king Cyrus issued a decree to the inhabitants of his kingdom, inviting the exiled Jews to return to their homeland to rebuild the temple in Jerusalem, which had been destroyed decades earlier by Nebuchadnezzar, king of Babylon (2 Kgs. 24–25; 2 Chr. 36). Thousands returned to Judah to rebuild the temple's foundation, walls, and altar, under the direction of Zerubbabel, the representative of the royal house of Judah. Although the temple was considered inferior to Solomon's,[7] the Jews found great satisfaction when the builders laid its foundation, celebrating with music, song, thanksgiving, praise, and great shouts (Ezra 3:10–13).

This historic return of the Jews to their homeland and their rebuilding of the temple anticipates the Jewish return to Israel during our own day as well as the future rebuilding of the Jerusalem temple. Joseph Smith prophesied: "Judah must return, Jerusalem must be rebuilt, and the temple, and water come out from under the temple, and the waters of the Dead Sea be healed. It will take some time to rebuild the walls of the city and the temple, &c.; and all this must be done before the Son of Man will make his appearance."[8]

THE GATHERINGS AT ADAM-ONDI-AHMAN
Doctrine and Covenants 107:53–57

53 Three years previous to the death of Adam, he called Seth, Enos, Cainan, Mahalaleel, Jared, Enoch, and Methuselah, who were all high priests, with the residue of his posterity who were righteous, into the valley of Adam-ondi-Ahman, and there bestowed upon them his last blessing.

54 And the Lord appeared unto them, and they rose up and blessed Adam, and called him Michael, the prince, the archangel.

55 And the Lord administered comfort unto Adam, and said unto him: I have set thee to be at the head; a multitude of nations shall come of thee, and thou art a prince over them forever.

56 And Adam stood up in the midst of the congregation; and, notwithstanding he was bowed down with age, being full of the Holy Ghost, predicted whatsoever should befall his posterity unto the latest generation.

57 These things were all written in the book of Enoch, and are to be testified of in due time.

---

[7] LDS Bible Dictionary, 783, s.v. "Temple of Zerubbabel."
[8] *Teachings of the Prophet Joseph Smith,* 286.

These verses detail the great, ancient meeting at Adam-ondi-Ahman, in which Adam's righteous posterity gathered and received great blessings, including the following:

Adam "bestowed upon them his last blessing" (D&C 107:53).

"The Lord appeared unto them" (D&C 107:54).

The assemblage honored Adam, calling him "Michael, the prince, the archangel" (D&C 107:54).

The Lord "administered comfort unto Adam" and spoke great promises to him (D&C 107:55).

Adam prophesied "whatsoever should befall his posterity unto the latest generation" (D&C 107:56).

Joseph Smith testified: "I saw Adam in the valley of Adam-ondi-Ahman. He called together his children and blessed them with a patriarchal blessing. The Lord appeared in their midst, and he (Adam) blessed them all, and foretold what should befall them to the latest generation. This is why Adam blessed his posterity; he wanted to bring them into the presence of God."[9]

In the last days, before Christ's second coming, another great gathering will take place at Adam-ondi-Ahman. This second great gathering will parallel, in many respects, the earlier one. Again Adam will be present;[10] he, as a glorious being, will sit upon a throne, wearing brilliant white garments, and "ten thousand times ten thousand" will stand before him. During this gathering Jesus Christ will come, and there will be "given him dominion, and glory, and a kingdom, that all people, nations, and languages should serve him: his dominion is an everlasting dominion, which shall not pass away, and his kingdom that which shall not be destroyed" (Dan. 7:9–14). One purpose of this meeting is to prepare the Saints for the Second Coming;[11] this preparation will be accomplished in part when the "kingdom," "dominion" and "greatness of the kingdom . . . shall be given to the people of the saints of the most High" (Dan. 7:27; see also vv. 18, 21–22).[12]

---

[9] *Teachings of the Prophet Joseph Smith,* 158–59.

[10] *Teachings of the Prophet Joseph Smith,* 122.

[11] Dahl and Cannon, *Teachings of Joseph Smith,* 364.

[12] See the commentary on Adam-ondi-Ahman, page 399.

MANY DENY THE SIGNS OF CHRIST'S COMING
3 Nephi 1:4–10

4 And it came to pass that in the commencement of the ninety and second year, behold, the prophecies of the prophets began to be fulfilled more fully; for there began to be greater signs and greater miracles wrought among the people.

5 But there were some who began to say that the time was past for the words to be fulfilled, which were spoken by Samuel, the Lamanite.

6 And they began to rejoice over their brethren, saying: Behold the time is past, and the words of Samuel are not fulfilled; therefore, your joy and your faith concerning this thing hath been vain.

7 And it came to pass that they did make a great uproar throughout the land; and the people who believed began to be very sorrowful, lest by any means those things which had been spoken might not come to pass.

8 But behold, they did watch steadfastly for that day and that night and that day which should be as one day as if there were no night, that they might know that their faith had not been vain.

9 Now it came to pass that there was a day set apart by the unbelievers, that all those who believed in those traditions should be put to death except the sign should come to pass, which had been given by Samuel the prophet.

10 Now it came to pass that when Nephi, the son of Nephi, saw this wickedness of his people, his heart was exceedingly sorrowful.

Notwithstanding the "greater signs and greater miracles" (3 Ne. 1:4) that existed among the Nephites during the years shortly before Christ's birth, some of the people denied them, persecuting those who believed in the signs. An account of the denial and also the fulfillment of the signs is recorded in 3 Nephi 1:4–22, where Nephi, the author of the account, concludes, "And it had come to pass, yea, all things, every whit, according to the words of the prophets" (3 Ne. 1:20).

History will repeat itself during the last days, when many will deny the signs of the times. Peter taught that "there shall come in the last days scoffers, walking after their own lusts, and saying, Where is the promise of his coming? for since the fathers fell asleep, all things continue as they were from the beginning of the creation" (2 Pet. 3:3–9). A latter-day revelation adds that some "shall say that Christ delayeth his coming until the end of the earth" (D&C 45:26).

Even Church members are not exempt from claiming that Jesus delays his coming. President Joseph Fielding Smith taught: "I know that there are many, and even some among the Latter-day Saints, who are saying just as the Lord said they would say, 'The Lord delayeth his coming.' One man said: 'It is impossible for Jesus Christ to come inside of three or four hundred years.' But I say unto you, Watch."[13]

As the signs of the times continue to unfold in this dispensation, some will rationalize away the signs, arguing, "Some things they may have guessed right, among so many; but behold, we know that all these great and marvelous works cannot come to pass, of which has been spoken. And they began to reason and to contend among themselves, saying: That it is not reasonable that such a being as a Christ shall come. . . . And notwithstanding the signs and the wonders which were wrought among the people of the Lord, and the many miracles which they did, Satan did get great hold upon the hearts of the people upon all the face of the land" (Hel. 16:16–18, 23).

THE DESTRUCTION OF SODOM AND GOMORRAH
Genesis 19:24–28

24 Then the Lord rained . . . brimstone and fire from the Lord out of heaven;

25 And he overthrew those cities, and all the plain, and all the inhabitants of the cities, and that which grew upon the ground.

---

[13] *Doctrines of Salvation,* 3:52.

26 But [Lot's] wife looked back from behind him, and she became a pillar of salt.

27 And Abraham gat up early in the morning to the place where he stood before the Lord:

28 And he looked toward Sodom and Gomorrah, and toward all the land of the plain, and beheld, and, lo, the smoke of the country went up as the smoke of a furnace.

The destruction of Sodom and Gomorrah by God is well known. The sins of Sodom were enumerated by Ezekiel: "Behold, this was the iniquity of thy sister Sodom, pride, fulness of bread, and abundance of idleness was in her and in her daughters, neither did she strengthen the hand of the poor and needy. And they were haughty, and committed abomination before me: therefore I took them away as I saw good" (Ezek. 16:49–50). Jude added that Sodom and Gomorrah committed "fornication" and went "after strange flesh" (Jude 1:7).

These cities were destroyed because of the evil lives of their inhabitants. Their destruction was total and absolute, for they had become "the breeding of nettles, and saltpits, and a perpetual desolation" (Zeph. 2:9) wherein "no man shall abide" or "a son of man dwell" (Jer. 49:18). The very definition of the Hebrew names of these cities describes their final desolate condition, for *Sodom* is a "volcanic" or "bituminous" area, and *Gomorrah,* "a ruined heap."[14] Because of their enormous sins and the resultant destruction, these cities "are set forth for an example" (Jude 1:7; see also 2 Pet. 2:6) of the places that await desolation when the Lord returns in judgment and glory.

Luke made this comparison: "And as it was in the days of Noe, so shall it be also in the days of the Son of man. . . . Likewise also as it was in the days of Lot; they did eat, they drank, they bought, they sold, they planted, they builded; but the same day that Lot went out of Sodom it rained fire and brimstone from heaven, and destroyed them all. Even thus shall it be in the day when the Son of man is revealed" (Luke 17:26, 28–30).

---

[14] See McConkie and Parry, *Guide to Scriptural Symbols,* 61.

JAREDITE WARFARE
Ether 15:1–3

1 And it came to pass when Coriantumr had recovered of his wounds, he began to remember the words which Ether had spoken unto him.

2 He saw that there had been slain by the sword already nearly two millions of his people, and he began to sorrow in his heart; yea, there had been slain two millions of mighty men, and also their wives and their children.

3 He began to repent of the evil which he had done; he began to remember the words which had been spoken by the mouth of all the prophets, and he saw them that they were fulfilled thus far, every whit; and his soul mourned and refused to be comforted.

A preeminent sign of the last days pertains to "wars and rumors of wars," when "nation shall rise against nation, and kingdom against kingdom" (Matt. 24:6–7). On Christmas Day 1832, the Lord revealed to Joseph Smith, "And the time will come that war will be poured out upon all nations" (D&C 87:2).

Although it was fought centuries ago, the final Jaredite battle serves as a type of the warfare and confrontations of the last days, when the earth's inhabitants witness or hear of wars in many lands. The full account of the final battles and wars of the Jaredites covers several chapters in the Book of Mormon (Ether 11, 13–15). The parallels between the Jaredite nation and latter-day peoples are numerous. For example, Jaredite prophets "prophesied of the destruction of that great people except they should repent, and turn unto the Lord, and forsake their murders and wickedness" (Ether 11:1), just as prophets now warn the people of the world to repent and forsake their sins. Jaredite individuals studied "all the arts of war and all the cunning of the world" (Ether 13:16), just as institutions, schools, programs, and manuals are designed to prepare individuals for warfare in our day. Many Jaredite "fair sons and daughters" (this phrase is repeated four times in a single verse) refused to repent of their sins (Ether 13:17), just as many of our own generation prefer wrongdoing over repentance. And Moroni recorded that there was among the Jaredites "all manner of wickedness upon all the face of the land" (Ether 13:26), just as there are all types of iniquity in the world today. Certainly many other parallels could be listed.

Meanwhile, as the wicked are fighting among themselves, the righteous will be preserved by God's power. As 1 Nephi 22:16–17 records: "For the time soon cometh that the fulness of the wrath of God shall be poured out upon all the children of men; for he will not suffer that the wicked shall destroy the righteous. Wherefore, he will preserve the righteous by his power, even if it so be that the fulness of his wrath must come, and the righteous be preserved, even unto the destruction of their enemies by fire. Wherefore, the righteous need not fear; for thus saith the prophet, they shall be saved, even if it so be as by fire."

THE WICKED NATIONS DESTROYED
Isaiah 10:12–19

12 Wherefore it shall come to pass, that when the Lord hath performed his whole work upon mount Zion and on Jerusalem, I will punish the fruit of the stout heart of the king of Assyria, and the glory of his high looks.

13 For he saith, By the strength of my hand I have done it, and by my wisdom; for I am prudent: and I have removed the bounds of the people, and have robbed their treasures, and I have put down the inhabitants like a valiant man:

14 And my hand hath found as a nest the riches of the people: and as one gathereth eggs that are left, have I gathered all the earth; and there was none that moved the wing, or opened the mouth, or peeped.

15 Shall the axe boast itself against him that heweth therewith? or shall the saw magnify itself against him that shaketh it? as if the rod should shake itself against them that lift it up, or as if the staff should lift up itself, as if it were no wood.

16 Therefore shall the Lord, the Lord of hosts, send among his fat ones leanness; and under his glory he shall kindle a burning like the burning of a fire.

17 And the light of Israel shall be for a fire, and his Holy One for a flame: and it shall burn and devour his thorns and his briers in one day;

18 And shall consume the glory of his forest, and of his fruitful field, both soul and body: and they shall be as when a standardbearer fainteth.

19 And the rest of the trees of his forest shall be few, that a child may write them.

The ancient nation of Assyria, with its cruel and bloody leaders and well-disciplined, fierce armies, destroyed other evil nations. The scenario of Assyria and war anticipates the warring nations of our own day and of the future, in their contending for land, power, and riches. Those same evils will be present in our own day, and the thirst for blood will also exist. But just as Assyria, her leaders, and her armies were soon destroyed according to God's plan, so also will the warring nations of the last days be annihilated at the Second Coming. Isaiah's language—*burning of a fire, fire, flame, devour,* and *consume*—applies to both ancient Assyria and the future nations at Christ's coming. Meanwhile, a righteous remnant of Israel will be saved at the last day as they worship at God's temples.[15]

RIGHTEOUS NEPHITES AND LAMANITES ARE SPARED
3 Nephi 10:12–19

12 And it was the more righteous part of the people who were saved, and it was they who received the prophets and stoned them not; and it was they who had not shed the blood of the saints, who were spared—

13 And they were spared and were not sunk and buried up in the earth; and they were not drowned in the depths of the sea; and they were not burned by fire, neither were they fallen upon and crushed to death; and they were not carried away

---

[15] See the commentary on the Restoration, page 25.

in the whirlwind; neither were they overpowered by the vapor of smoke and of darkness.

14 And now, whoso readeth, let him understand; he that hath the scriptures, let him search them, and see and behold if all these deaths and destructions by fire, and by smoke, and by tempests, and by whirlwinds, and by the opening of the earth to receive them, and all these things are not unto the fulfilling of the prophecies of many of the holy prophets.

15 Behold, I say unto you, Yea, many have testified of these things at the coming of Christ, and were slain because they testified of these things.

16 Yea, the prophet Zenos did testify of these things, and also Zenock spake concerning these things, because they testified particularly concerning us, who are the remnant of their seed.

17 Behold, our father Jacob also testified concerning a remnant of the seed of Joseph. And behold, are not we a remnant of the seed of Joseph? And these things which testify of us, are they not written upon the plates of brass which our father Lehi brought out of Jerusalem?

18 And it came to pass that in the ending of the thirty and fourth year, behold, I will show unto you that the people of Nephi who were spared, and also those who had been called Lamanites, who had been spared, did have great favors shown unto them, and great blessings poured out upon their heads, insomuch that soon after the ascension of Christ into heaven he did truly manifest himself unto them—

19 Showing his body unto them, and ministering unto them; and an account of his ministry shall be given hereafter.

Before the Savior's visit to the Nephites at the temple in Bountiful, the land was cleansed of filthiness and corruption as individuals and communities were destroyed. Some were burned or crushed to death; others were buried in the earth or drowned; still others were destroyed by whirlwinds, smoke, and tempests. Only the "more righteous part of the people" (3 Ne. 10:12) were spared during these destructions, and it was to these people that the resurrected Lord appeared and ministered. Not only were the righteous saved from destruction but they were recipients of "great favors" and "great blessings" (3 Ne. 10:18).

Such is a pattern for our own day when God's judgments of destruction are poured out. Most of the righteous will be protected from harm and, perhaps more important, they will find peace and calm in their lives amid hardship. They, like the righteous who gathered at Bountiful, will receive great favors and blessings.

CHRIST'S APPEARANCE AT THE TEMPLE IN BOUNTIFUL
3 Nephi 11:8–12

> 8 And it came to pass, as they understood they cast their eyes up again towards heaven; and behold, they saw a Man descending out of heaven; and he was clothed in a white robe; and he came down and stood in the midst of them; and the eyes of the whole multitude were turned upon him, and they durst not open their mouths, even one to another, and wist not what it meant, for they thought it was an angel that had appeared unto them.

> 9 And it came to pass that he stretched forth his hand and spake unto the people, saying:

> 10 Behold, I am Jesus Christ, whom the prophets testified shall come into the world.

> 11 And behold, I am the light and the life of the world; and I have drunk out of that bitter cup which the Father hath given me, and have glorified the Father in taking upon me the sins of the world, in the which I have suffered the will of the Father in all things from the beginning.

> 12 And it came to pass that when Jesus had spoken these words the whole multitude fell to the earth; for they remembered that it had been prophesied among them that Christ should show himself unto them after his ascension into heaven.

There are many common points between the events set forth in 3 Nephi 8–11 and the events connected with Christ's second coming. For example, on both occasions the wicked are destroyed and Christ descends from heaven. The text states, "They cast their eyes up again towards heaven; and behold, they saw a Man descending out of heaven" (3 Ne. 11:8). Doctrine and Covenants 45:44 describes Christ in the "clouds of heaven": "And then they shall look for me, and, behold, I will come; and they shall see me in the clouds of heaven, clothed with power and great glory; with all the holy angels." At both events Christ wears distinctive clothing: at his appearance in Bountiful he wore a "white robe," and for his second coming he will be clothed in a red robe (Isa. 63:1–3; Rev. 19:13). Many witness these great events. At Bountiful "the eyes of the whole multitude were turned upon him" (3 Ne. 11:8); at his second coming "every eye shall see him, and they also which pierced him" (Rev. 1:7).

THE NEPHITES' ZION
4 Nephi 1:13–18

13 And it came to pass that there was no contention among all the people, in all the land; but there were mighty miracles wrought among the disciples of Jesus.

14 And it came to pass that the seventy and first year passed away, and also the seventy and second year, yea, and in fine, till the seventy and ninth year had passed away; yea, even an hundred years had passed away, and the disciples of Jesus, whom he had chosen, had all gone to the paradise of God, save it were the three who should tarry; and there were other disciples ordained in their stead; and also many of that generation had passed away.

15 And it came to pass that there was no contention in the land, because of the love of God which did dwell in the hearts of the people.

16 And there were no envyings, nor strifes, nor tumults, nor whoredoms, nor lyings, nor murders, nor any manner of lasciviousness; and surely there could not be a happier people among all the people who had been created by the hand of God.

17 There were no robbers, nor murderers, neither were there Lamanites, nor any manner of -ites; but they were in one, the children of Christ, and heirs to the kingdom of God.

18 And how blessed were they! For the Lord did bless them in all their doings; yea, even they were blessed and prospered until an hundred and ten years had passed away; and the first generation from Christ had passed away, and there was no contention in all the land.

This passage from 4 Nephi outlines the peace that existed among the "children of Christ" after Jesus' postresurrection ministry. This specific, historical group of people is a model of a larger assembly who will live in joy during the Millennium, after Jesus' second coming. The millennial Zion, like the Nephites' Zion, will have "no contention, . . . no envyings, nor strifes, nor tumults, nor whoredoms, nor lyings, nor murders, nor any manner of lasciviousness; . . . no robbers, nor murderers, neither . . . any manner of -ites" (4 Ne. 1:15–17). In place of these, there will exist "the love of God" (4 Ne. 1:15), peace, unity, happiness, prosperity, and great blessings (4 Ne. 1:16–18) among the children of Christ.

SOLOMON'S EARTHLY KINGDOM
Psalm 72:1–19

1 Give the king thy judgments, O God, and thy righteousness unto the king's son.

2 He shall judge thy people with righteousness, and thy poor with judgment.

3 The mountains shall bring peace to the people, and the little hills, by righteousness.

4 He shall judge the poor of the people, he shall save the children of the needy, and shall break in pieces the oppressor.

5 They shall fear thee as long as the sun and moon endure, throughout all generations.

6 He shall come down like rain upon the mown grass: as showers that water the earth.

7 In his days shall the righteous flourish; and abundance of peace so long as the moon endureth.

8 He shall have dominion also from sea to sea, and from the river unto the ends of the earth.

9 They that dwell in the wilderness shall bow before him; and his enemies shall lick the dust.

10 The kings of Tarshish and of the isles shall bring presents: the kings of Sheba and Seba shall offer gifts.

11 Yea, all kings shall fall down before him: all nations shall serve him.

12 For he shall deliver the needy when he crieth; the poor also, and him that hath no helper.

13 He shall spare the poor and needy, and shall save the souls of the needy.

14 He shall redeem their soul from deceit and violence: and precious shall their blood be in his sight.

15 And he shall live, and to him shall be given of the gold of Sheba: prayer also shall be made for him continually; and daily shall he be praised.

16 There shall be an handful of corn in the earth upon the top of the mountains; the fruit thereof shall shake like Lebanon: and they of the city shall flourish like grass of the earth.

17 His name shall endure for ever: his name shall be continued as long as the sun: and men shall be blessed in him: all nations shall call him blessed.

18 Blessed be the Lord God, the God of Israel, who only doeth wondrous things.

19 And blessed be his glorious name for ever: and let the whole earth be filled with his glory; Amen, and Amen.

The headnote to Psalm 72 says, "David speaketh of Solomon, who is made a type of Christ." The psalm refers to Solomon as an ideal king who brings perfect judgment and righteousness to all people. The *poor* and the *needy* receive emphasis in this psalm: each of these words appears four times. Certainly the king's special attention is directed to them: "He shall judge the poor of the people, he shall save the children of the needy" (v. 4); "he shall deliver the needy when he crieth; the poor also, and him that hath no helper" (v. 12); "He shall spare the poor and needy, and shall save the souls of the needy" (v. 13). He will not allow injustice or abuse but will "break in pieces the oppressor" (v. 4). During his reign the righteous will flourish, and peace will exist "as long as the moon endureth" (v. 7); he will have "dominion" (v. 8); people will bow to him (v. 9); kings will present him with gifts (vv. 10–11); "all nations shall serve him" (v. 11); and "all nations shall call him blessed" (v. 17). And at last, his "name shall endure for ever: his name shall be continued as long as the sun" (v. 17).

Although it was David's prayer (v. 20) that this psalm of the ideal king speak of Solomon (who did reign in righteousness and power for a time), in actuality the words typify the glorious millennial reign of Jesus Christ, when the Perfect King will fulfill all parts of the psalm, bringing peace, righteousness, and judgment to earth's inhabitants.

SIGNS OF THE FIRST COMING ARE TYPES OF THE SECOND COMING

The portion of the Book of Mormon record that immediately precedes the visit of the resurrected Lord to the Nephites (Hel. 10 through 3 Ne. 11) contains a number of historical events that prefigure, or typify, similar ev̲e̲n̲t̲s̲ ̲t̲h̲a̲t̲ ̲w̲i̲l̲l̲ occur when Jesus returns to the earth. ... ce R. McConkie explained: "It ... 's to learn that the prophecies ... ...adows of similar revelations

[*] E. Dale LeBaron, in his article entitled "The Book of Mormon: The Pattern in Preparing a People to Meet the Savior" (in *Doctrines of the Book of Mormon,* 70–79), has made a careful and accurate study of this subject, listing several examples of historical events from Helaman 10 through 3 Nephi 11 that serve as types of Christ's second coming.

relative to the Second Coming."[17] For example, wars and rumors of wars existed among the Nephites, and they also are among the signs of the times approaching the Second Coming (Hel. 11:1; 3 Ne. 3:4; D&C 45:26, 68; 63:32–33). The willful rebellion of individuals that existed among the Nephites will be found again in the last days (3 Ne. 6:17–18; 7:7; D&C 64:34–36; 112:24–26). Famines and plagues existed among the Nephites and serve as signs of the times (Hel. 10:6; 12:3; D&C 43:25; 84:96–97; 87:6; 45:31). People rejected the Lord's prophets and will do so again (3 Ne. 6:23; 7:14; D&C 1:14; 133:71–72; 135:1–7; 136:35–36). The pride that existed in the church will be found again before Christ comes (3 Ne. 6:11–14; D&C 41:1; 50:2–4; 63:63; 98:19–22). Murders existed then, and they do so now (Hel. 10:18; 11:4; D&C 45:33, 68; 63:33; 130:12).

Many other parallels exist between the period preceding Christ's appearance to the Nephites and the period preceding his second coming. These include the existence of secret combinations (3 Ne. 6:25–30; 7:7–9; 9:9; Moro. 8:34–40; Ether 8:20–25; D&C 38:28; 42:64; 123:13–14), the persecution of the righteous (Alma 1:25–28; 3 Ne. 6:12–13; D&C 99:1; 101:32–38; 123:1–10), earthquakes and great disturbances (3 Ne. 8:6–19; D&C 29:13; 43:18, 25; 45:26, 33, 48; 49:23; 88:88–89), and tempests, thunderings, and lightnings (Hel. 14:23, 26; 3 Ne. 8:5–6; 10:14; D&C 43:20–25; 87:6; 88:88–91).

OTHER TYPES AND SHADOWS

Other historical events foreshadow the great events of the last days. For example, the word *Sabbath* originates from the Hebrew word *shabbat,* which means "to cease" or "to rest"; hence, the scriptures declare that the Sabbath "is a day appointed unto you to rest from your labors" (D&C 59:10); also, "God made the world in six days, and on the seventh day he finished his work" (D&C 77:12). Inasmuch as the Sabbath is a day of rest, joy, peace, and a time to worship the Lord, it seems natural to compare it with the Millennium, the seventh "day" of the earth's "temporal existence" (D&C 77:6) and also a time of peace, joy, and rest. Another example is the destruction of many cities and peoples—Babylon (Isa. 13:6–22; 21:1–10),

---

[17] *Promised Messiah,* 31

Damascus (Isa. 17:1–11), Moab (Isa. 15:1–9), Edom (Isa. 34:1–8; 34:9–15), Judah (Zeph. 1), the Nephite nation (Morm. 6), and Nineveh (Nahum 2)—which is a type of Jesus' judgments upon the world at his coming.

"Come, Lord Jesus"

When most people list the signs of the times, they often think first of those things that are negative and challenging: wars and famines, earthquakes and pestilences, the general and increasing condition of sinfulness in the world. These are important signs heralding the coming of the Lord, as many prophetic witnesses have attested. But the signs of the last days are much more than trial and trouble. The Lord's gifts to the righteous of our time are greater far than his punishments upon those with rebellious hearts.

In the opening lines of his classic novel *A Tale of Two Cities,* Charles Dickens described the time of the French Revolution in language that could also describe our day: "It was the best of times, it was the worst of times, it was the age of wisdom, it was the age of foolishness, it was the epoch of belief, it was the epoch of incredulity, it was the season of Light, it was the season of Darkness, it was the spring of hope, it was the winter of despair, we had everything before us, we had nothing before us." Such are the last days. They are days of trial and days of blessing. During our lifetimes, we will see God sending judgments of punishment upon the wicked. But during the same period he will pour forth great gifts and graces upon the heads of his righteous children.

These are the best of times, and they are the worst of times. These are days of apostasy and days of continuing restoration, days of false priesthoods and days of powerful priesthood keys, days of dreadful plagues and days of spiritual healing, days of drought and famine and days of living water and the bread of life, days of devastating warfare and days when the Prince of Peace reigns in the hearts of the meek. The wicked and unbelieving will see the signs and mock, but the righteous, as children of light, will see them as portents of the coming of their divine Redeemer, Jesus Christ. The unrepentant will eventually mourn their course and its consequences, while the faithful Saints will be filled with gratitude and rejoicing for the loving kindness of their God.

Of course, it is not only the wicked who will suffer from the trials of our times. The righteous, too, will suffer from famine and warfare. They will suffer from many of the evil choices of the wicked, but the righteous have three promises from the Lord:

First, the Lord will provide a measure of protection to those who do his will. They will not be immune to the trials of the day, but they will receive greater blessing and protection than those who choose wickedness.[1]

Second, when the righteous suffer, they may know that "all these things shall give thee experience, and shall be for thy good" (D&C 122:7).

Third, if the righteous die as a result of the perils of the last days, they will go to a place of peace and glory (Rev. 14:13; Alma 14:9–11). Their existence in the spirit world is one of opportunity to continue to serve God and partake of the sweet gifts of his Spirit.

We have set before us two paths: one of faith, obedience, and sacrifice, which will guide our feet through times of trouble and bring us safely to the bright day of Christ's coming; and one of selfishness, doubt, and sin, along which many will walk to the dreadful day of Christ's wrath. That day will surely come. Thus the world rolls through the events leading to disaster for some and supernal blessing for others. Which will it be for us? The paths of choice lie before us.

GIVEN FOR OUR BLESSING

The signs are set, and they are remarkably clear. Some are unique to the last days (the restoration of the gospel, for example, and the moon appearing as blood); others are events or phenomena that have always existed but will occur at an increased rate in the last days (wars or earthquakes, for example). But if we are watching, and if we have the Holy Spirit for our guide, we will recognize the signs for what they are, and we will be blessed.

---

[1] For more details on this promise, see page 351.

Blessing is the Lord's very purpose in giving us the signs. Many of the signs are designed to motivate the wicked to repent if they will. Famines and plagues and earthquakes, by their very nature, engender feelings of fear and weakness and insufficiency. If the wicked will allow those feelings to turn their hearts to God, he will bless them and heal them. But if they will not repent, their eventual destruction will be justified, for they were warned and chose not to hear or obey.

Ezekiel characterized this pattern of warning, possible repentance, and the choice between salvation or destruction when he recorded:

"Again the word of the Lord came unto me, saying,

"Son of man, speak to the children of thy people, and say unto them, When I bring the sword upon a land, if the people of the land take a man of their coasts, and set him for their watchman:

"If when he seeth the sword come upon the land, he blow the trumpet, and warn the people;

"Then whosoever heareth the sound of the trumpet, and taketh not warning; if the sword come, and take him away, his blood shall be upon his own head.

"He heard the sound of the trumpet, and took not warning; his blood shall be upon him. But he that taketh warning shall deliver his soul. . . .

"Therefore, O thou son of man, speak unto the house of Israel; Thus ye speak, saying, If our transgressions and our sins be upon us, and we pine away in them, how should we then live?

"Say unto them, As I live, saith the Lord God, I have no pleasure in the death of the wicked; but that the wicked turn from his way and live: turn ye, turn ye from your evil ways; for why will ye die, O house of Israel? . . .

"Again, when I say unto the wicked, Thou shalt surely die; if he turn from his sin, and do that which is lawful and right;

"If the wicked restore the pledge, give again that he had robbed, walk in the statutes of life, without committing iniquity; he shall surely live, he shall not die.

"None of his sins that he hath committed shall be mentioned unto him: he hath done that which is lawful and right; he shall surely live" (Ezek. 33:1–16).

Of course, the signs of the times are given not only to call the wicked to repentance but also to bless the righteous in several ways:

To warn us that we must be spiritually prepared for the coming of the Lord. We know that we must be pure and holy to greet the Lord. The signs show us that the time is ripening and that we must be ready spiritually.

To warn us that we must be temporally prepared if we hope to be able to meet and endure the trials to come. How can we survive physically in the midst of the disasters coming upon the world? How can we help others to survive? Only by preparing early. The signs remind us that we must do so.

To give us the knowledge we need so we will not be deceived. When some cry, "Lo, here!" and others shout, "Lo, there!" and when some claim Christ has come already and he is in the desert, or others say he has come but is hiding in the secret chambers (JS-M 1:21–22, 25), we can know that their claims are false. The Lord will come in a manner that all will see him, as clearly as the light of the sun comes from the east at dawn (JS-M 1:26; Rev. 1:7), and he will come preceded by his signs.

To give us markers, or signposts, showing us where we are in time relative to the second coming of Christ. If we see truly, we will know which signs have been given (whether in whole or in part) and which remain to be seen.

To serve as a witness of God's plan and his power, bearing testimony through remarkable events that God is in charge of the world and its progress through time. With his power, he will deliver us from the bondage of a wicked world, and he will keep all of his promises.

Each of these purposes is a great blessing to all who will watch for the signs and respond with righteous hearts. Thus, the signs of the times are signals sent from God to his children. Almost all of the signals are visible to many people, particularly if they are paying attention. When we see the signal of the gathering of Israel, for example, as carried out by the missionary work of The Church of Jesus Christ of Latter-day

Saints, we can know that the Lord is performing his work preparatory to his second coming. When we see famines or pestilences, we can know them as signals from God, given to remind us that the Lord will come in glory—and that we need to be ready. When we see the sun darkened, or the nations gathering to battle, or the continuing establishment of Zion, we can know that we are in the last days and that the Lord will indeed come.

INTERPRETING CURRENT EVENTS

How are we to interpret the events around us? When we hear of a devastating earthquake or see the increase of sin in our city or nation, how are we to know whether such events are signs or are simply natural consequences of living in a fallen, mortal world? Nephi counsels us on how to interpret scripture relative to latter-day events:

"I did read many things unto [my people] which were written in the books of Moses; but that I might more fully persuade them to believe in the Lord their Redeemer I did read unto them that which was written by the prophet Isaiah; for I did liken all scriptures unto us, that it might be for our profit and learning. Wherefore I spake unto them, saying: Hear ye the words of the prophet, . . . which were written unto all the house of Israel, and liken them unto yourselves" (1 Ne. 19:23–24).

"And now I write some of the words of Isaiah, that whoso of my people shall see these words may lift up their hearts and rejoice for all men. Now these are the words, and ye may liken them unto you and unto all men" (2 Ne. 11:8).

Nephi teaches that all people can benefit from the words of Isaiah by applying those words to themselves, even if they were not the immediate and direct audience Isaiah was addressing. If we do so, we will find meaning and blessing for ourselves; the Holy Ghost will teach us important truths and give us vital direction if we read the scriptures with an eye to their specific meanings for us.

It may be that we can apply a similar rule to an understanding of the signs of the times as they relate to current events. When we see the gospel being preached in many lands, of course we can know that that is a fulfillment of prophecy that the gospel word must go forth before the Lord will return. When we see Saints gathering to the temple, we can know that the Lord's word is being fulfilled in the last days, and we can recognize it as one of the signs of the times. But how are we to view the many earthquakes or wars or famines? It seems that we can "liken" those signs "unto us." We can know that the Lord promised such things as part of the experience of the last days, and when we see them in our time, we can know that the Lord is sending a signal to those "which have eyes to see" (Ezek. 12:2) that his work is progressing and that the time of his coming approaches.

Even though there have been earthquakes and wars and famines almost from the beginning of time, they apparently will increase in number in the last times, and thus they are given as some of the signs of those times. When we see these conditions in the world, the prophets seem to be saying, we may know that the last days are upon us— and we may properly accept all wars and earthquakes and famines and plagues in our dispensation as signs of the last times.

"Ye say that ye know that the end of the world cometh; . . .

"And in this ye say truly, for so it is; but these things which I have told you shall not pass away until all shall be fulfilled. . . .

"And I [the Lord] said unto them [my disciples]:

"Be not troubled, for, when all these things shall come to pass, ye may know that the promises which have been made unto you shall be fulfilled. . . .

"Ye look and behold the fig-trees, and ye see them with your eyes, and ye say when they begin to shoot forth, and their leaves are yet tender, that summer is now nigh at hand;

"Even so it shall be in that day when they shall see all these things, then shall they know that the hour is nigh.

"And it shall come to pass that he that feareth me shall be looking forth for the great day of the Lord to come, even for the signs of the coming of the Son of Man. . . .

"And then they shall look for me, and, behold, I will come; and they shall see me in the clouds of heaven, clothed with power and great glory; with all the holy angels; and he that watches not for me shall be cut off" (D&C 45:22–44).

Even though the signs have been given to help us watch for the Lord's coming, we must ever be cautious, both in interpreting scripture (which must always be done with the help of the Holy Ghost and living prophets) and in interpreting the events of our time.

"PLANTING CHERRY TREES"

It appears from the signs that the coming of the Lord is drawing near. But he has not revealed the day or the hour, the month or the year—or even the decade or century. So we watch in a spirit of readiness, preparing both spiritually and temporally. We resist the temptation to become unbalanced in our interest in the signs of the times—after all, the signs are not the gospel in its entirety; they are only one part of the gospel. And we live our lives as best we can, rearing our children in faith, loving our grandchildren, continuing with necessary temporal labors, and seeking to build Zion. In 1950 Elder Richard L. Evans gave some helpful counsel that is still timely:

"We must have faith in the future regardless of the ultimate eventualities. One of the greatest calamities in this world would be the calamity of sitting down and waiting for calamities. We must not let the things we can't do keep us from doing the things we can do. We must not let remote possibilities or even imminent probabilities keep us from moving forward with all earnestness and all effort.

"I should like to say to the young people of this generation that they too must have faith in the future. In spite of all the uncertainties, they must go forward and prepare themselves as best they can for all the problems and opportunities of life. Whatever may come here or hereafter, the future will always be better for those who are best prepared.

"No generation has ever lived without facing uncertainty. If those who faced the uncertainties of ten or twenty-five or fifty years ago had sat by and waited for what seemed to them to be imminent calamities, we should not have had the able and ready and well-qualified men that we have today, and that we need and shall need in the next generation.

"So I say to these youth of ours: go forth and live your lives with humility, with gratitude, with repentance, keeping the commandments of God and having faith in the future and preparing yourselves for the future, as the Church itself continues its building. There is nothing to lose by having faith in the future, but there is much to lose by not preparing for the future. . . .

"I recall a reported statement, attributed, as I remember it, to President Wilford Woodruff. Some of the brethren of his time are said to have approached him (they had their troubles also) and to have inquired of him as to when he felt the end would be—when would be the coming of the Master? These, I think, are not his exact words, but they convey the spirit of his reported reply: 'I would live as if it were to be tomorrow—but I am still planting cherry trees!' I think we may well take this as a page for our own book and live as if the end might be tomorrow—and still plant cherry trees! In worrying about things that are beyond our reach, we should not overlook our opportunities with our own families and friends; in worrying about possible eventualities we should not neglect the things that need to be done here and now, and that are within our reach; the things for which we are immediately responsible; we should not neglect [our] present opportunities and obligations.

"I should like to close with a statement of William Allen White: 'I am not afraid of tomorrow, for I have seen yesterday, and I love today.'"[2]

With such an attitude we watch and wait, knowing that "blessed are all they that wait" for the Lord (Isa. 30:18).

"These sayings are faithful and true," the angel said to John the Revelator of his vision of the last days, "and the Lord God of the holy prophets sent his angel to shew unto his servants the things which must shortly be done. Behold, I come quickly. . . . He that is unjust, let him be unjust still: and he which is filthy, let him be filthy still: and he that is righteous, let him be righteous still: and he that is holy, let him be holy still. And, behold, I come quickly; and my reward is with me, to give every man according as his work shall be. . . . He which testifieth these things saith, Surely I come quickly" (Rev. 22:6–7, 11–12, 20).

With that apostle, in trust and hopeful anticipation, we join our voices and say, "Even so, come, Lord Jesus" (Rev. 22:20).

---

[2] Conference Report, Apr. 1950, 105–6.

THE MILLENNIUM AND BEYOND

The Millennium is that glorious season of a thousand years that immediately follows the second coming of Christ. It is a time of peace, happiness, and glory. Following is a summary, taken primarily from the scriptures, of the circumstances of the great Millennium to come.

EVENTS THAT WILL PREPARE THE EARTH FOR THE MILLENNIUM

1. When the Lord comes, every corruptible thing will be consumed, the elements will "melt with fervent heat," and the works of the world will be burned up (2 Pet. 3:10–12; D&C 101:24–25).

2. After the earth is cleansed by burning, the Lord will bring "new heavens and a new earth" (2 Pet. 3:10–13; Isa. 65:17); in fact, the Lord has proclaimed that "old things shall pass away, and all things become new" (D&C 63:49).

3. The Lord will separate the righteous from the wicked (D&C 63:54). The righteous will remain on the earth for the Millennium, whereas the wicked will be destroyed by burning (Mal. 4:1; D&C 29:9; 64:23–24; 133:63–64).

4. The Lord will make a full end of all nations (D&C 87:6).

5. The Lord will bring the city of Enoch back to earth, there to dwell in Zion (Moses 7:62–64)

6. The wicked will remain in the spirit world until after the Millennium has ended (D&C 88:101; Rev. 20:5).

PHYSICAL CONDITIONS OF THE EARTH IN THE MILLENNIUM

1. "In the beginning of the seventh thousand years . . . the Lord God [will] sanctify the earth" (D&C 77:12).

2. The mountains and valleys will be made smooth (D&C 133:22).

3. The land will all be brought into one continent, "like as it was in the days before it was divided" (D&C 133:23–24).

4. "The earth shall be transfigured" (D&C 63:20–21).

5. "The earth will be renewed and receive its paradisiacal glory" (A of F 1:10), becoming like the Garden of Eden (Ezek. 36:35). Like the Garden of Eden, the earth will be devoid of thorns and thistles (Gen. 3:18).

6. The earth will rest for a thousand years (Moses 7:64).

7. The enmity between animals will cease (Isa. 11:6–7; 65:25; D&C 101:26).

8. The enmity between animals and man will cease (Isa. 11:6, 8; D&C 101:26).

9. The curse between the serpent and the seed of the woman will be removed (Gen. 3:15; Isa. 11:8).

10. Man's perfect dominion over the animals will be restored (Gen. 1:28; Isa. 11:6).

11. People will enjoy the fruits of their labors (Isa. 65:21–23; D&C 101:101).

12. Time will be no longer (D&C 84:100; 88:110).

CONDITIONS OF THOSE WHO DWELL ON THE EARTH IN THE MILLENNIUM

1. Children will grow up and grow old (D&C 63:51).

2. People will die only after they reach a hundred years old (Isa. 65:20), and then they will "be changed in the twinkling of an eye" to a glorious state (D&C 43:32; 63:51; 101:30–31).

3. There will be no death as we know it: "there shall be no sorrow because there is no death" (D&C 101:29).

4. It will be a state of gladness, rejoicing, and joy; "and the voice of weeping shall be no more heard in her, nor the voice of crying" (Isa. 65:18–19).

5. Those who are resurrected will dwell in the New Jerusalem (D&C 63:49).

6. Family history and temple work will be accelerated, without the obstacles we now know.[1]

SPIRITUAL BLESSINGS OF THOSE WHO DWELL ON THE EARTH IN THE MILLENNIUM

1. Satan will be bound by the power of God (Rev. 20:1–3; see also D&C 43:31; 45:55; 88:110), leaving him "no place in the hearts of the children of men" and "no power over [their] hearts" (D&C 45:55; 1 Ne. 22:26; see also 2 Ne. 30:18; D&C 101:28). Satan will also have no power "because of the righteousness of [the] people" (1 Ne. 22:26).

2. Children will "grow up without sin unto salvation" (D&C 45:58).

3. The Lord's glory will dwell on the earth, that all may see it (Isa. 35:2; D&C 84:101; 101:25).

4. The entire earth will be as a temple, which God calls "my holy mountain" (Isa. 65:25).

5. The Lord himself will dwell "with men on earth" (D&C 29:11; see also Zech. 2:10; D&C 84:101; 133:25).

6. "The earth shall be full of the knowledge of the Lord" (Isa. 11:9; Hab. 2:14; 2 Ne. 30:15); everyone will know the Lord (Jer. 31:34; D&C 84:98).

7. Eventually, all will come to worship the Lord (Isa. 66:23).

8. All things will be revealed to the children of men (2 Ne. 30:16–18; D&C 101:32–34).

9. Man's every request of the Lord will be granted (D&C 101:27), surely because no one will ask amiss (James 4:3; 2 Ne. 4:35).

10. The prayer of one's heart will be answered even before it is uttered (Isa. 65:24).

---

[1] Smith, *Doctrines of Salvation,* 2:251–52.

SINNERS AND THOSE WHO ARE NOT MEMBERS OF CHRIST'S CHURCH IN THE MILLENNIUM

1. At least for a time, there will be some on earth who are not members of Christ's church during the Millennium.[2]

2. At least for a time, there will be some who worship other gods (Mic. 4:5; Zech. 14:16–19).

3. "There will be wicked men on the earth during the thousand years. The heathen nations who will not come up to worship will be visited with the judgments of God and must eventually be destroyed from the earth."[3]

4. At least for a time, there will be those who are called "sinners" (Isa. 65:20). Perhaps their destiny is the same as that of the heathen nations described above.[4]

SOCIAL CONDITIONS IN THE MILLENNIUM

1. After the cleansing fire that precedes the Millennium, only righteous people will remain on the earth, for "the wicked shall not stand" (D&C 29:11).

2. All enmity among mankind will cease (D&C 101:26).

3. The Millennium will be a time of peace, with no war anywhere (Isa. 2:4; Mic. 4:3).

4. The Lord will keep the people of the earth safe from harm (Hos. 2:18; Mic. 4:4).

---

[2] Smith, *Doctrines of Salvation,* 1:86–87; 3:63–64.

[3] *Teachings of the Prophet Joseph Smith,* 268. The footnote to this statement in *Teachings* gives the following clarification by Joseph Fielding Smith: "The Prophet's statement that there will be wicked men on the earth during the Millennium has caused considerable confusion in the minds of many who have read in the Scripture in many places that when Christ comes the earth shall be cleansed from its wickedness, and that the wicked shall not stand, but shall be consumed. See D&C 5:18–19, 29:8–10, 101:23–25; Isaiah 24:1–3; Malachi 4:1. The evil-minded inhabitants, those 'who love and make a lie' and are guilty of all manner of corruption, will be consumed and pass away when Christ comes. In using the term 'wicked men' in this instruction at the home of Judge Adams, the Prophet did so in the same sense in which the Lord uses it in the eighty-fourth section of the Doctrine and Covenants, 49–53. The Lord in this scripture speaks of those who have not received the Gospel as being under the bondage of sin, and hence 'wicked.' However, many of these people are honorable, clean living men, but they have not embraced the Gospel. The inhabitants of the terrestrial order will remain on the earth during the Millennium, and this class are without the Gospel ordinances. See D&C 76:73–76."

[4] For further clarification of the word *sinner* in Isa. 65:20, see note 2, above. See also Parry, Parry, and Peterson, *Understanding Isaiah,* 578–79.

5. The Lord will give the people "a pure language" (Zeph. 3:9).

6. The people will come to a true unity (Zeph. 3:9; D&C 84:98).

POLITICAL CONDITIONS IN THE MILLENNIUM

1. The Lord will reign over the earth as king (Dan. 7:13–14; D&C 38:21; 133:25; A of F 10).

2. Jesus Christ will be our lawgiver (D&C 38:22; 45:59).

3. The Saints will rule with him (Dan. 7:27; Rev. 5:10; Rev. 20:4, 6; D&C 43:29).

4. Christ and the resurrected Saints will probably not dwell upon the earth continually during the thousand years.[5]

5. There will be two world capitals, Zion and Jerusalem (Isa. 2:3).

CONDITIONS AT THE END OF THE MILLENNIUM

1. When the thousand years are over, men will "again begin to deny their God" (D&C 29:22).

2. Satan will be loosed to reign for a "little season" (Rev. 20:3, 7; D&C 43:31).

3. Satan will go forth again to "deceive the nations" (Rev. 20:8).

4. Satan will gather his armies (the hosts of hell) to fight against Michael and his armies (the hosts of heaven) (D&C 88:111–13). The number of Satan's followers will be "as the sand of the sea" (Rev. 20:8). In the "battle of the great God," Satan and his armies will surround the Saints and "the beloved city," but "fire [will come] down from God out of heaven, and [devour] them" (D&C 88:114; Rev. 20:9).

5. The devil will be cast into "the lake of fire and brimstone," where he "shall be tormented day and night for ever and ever" (Rev. 20:10).

6. The remaining dead will all be resurrected (D&C 29:26–28).

7. The family of man will be judged, to receive a blessing or a cursing (Rev. 20:11–15; 21:7–8; D&C 29:26–28).

8. "And the end shall come, and the heaven and the earth shall be consumed and pass away" (D&C 29:23).

---

[5] *Teachings of the Prophet Joseph Smith,* 268.

THE CELESTIAL WORLD

1. A celestial glory will be established on the earth; it is called "a new heaven and a new earth." The celestialized earth will have no sea (Rev. 21:1; D&C 29:23–24).

2. The earth will be "crowned with glory" and "sanctified" (D&C 88:19, 26).

3. The righteous will inherit the glorified earth (D&C 88:26).

4. God himself will dwell with mankind on the celestialized earth (Rev. 21:3; D&C 88:19).

5. "There shall be no more death, neither sorrow, nor crying, neither shall there be any more pain: for the former things are passed away" (Rev. 21:4).

6 Those in the celestial world will "inherit all things" and will be called the sons and daughters of God (Rev. 21:7).

7. The celestial city of New Jerusalem is glorious beyond description, a place of eternal treasures and heavenly delights (Rev. 21:9–27; 22:1–15).

THE PROPHETS SPEAK ON PREPAREDNESS IN THE LAST DAYS

The prophets have given consistent guidance on preparing ourselves for the Second Coming and for the judgments of the last days. To be spiritually prepared, they tell us, we must repent, be obedient, be humble and prayerful, be united, and live as Saints of God. To be temporally prepared, we need to get out of debt; store a year's supply of food, clothing, and, where possible, fuel; and learn to be self-sufficient.

KEYS TO BEING SPIRITUALLY PREPARED

JOSEPH SMITH

"When I contemplate the rapidity with which the great and glorious day of the coming of the Son of Man advances, when He shall come to receive His Saints unto Himself, where they shall dwell in His presence, and be crowned with glory and immortality; when I consider that soon the heavens are to be shaken, and the earth tremble and reel to and fro; and that the heavens are to be unfolded as a scroll when it is rolled up; and that every mountain and island are to flee away, I cry out in my heart, What manner of persons ought we to be in all holy conversation and godliness!" (*History of the Church,* 1:442).

"If the Church with one united effort perform their duties; if they do this, the work shall be complete—if they do not this in all humility, making preparation from this time forth, like Joseph in Egypt, laying up store against the time of famine, every man having his tent, his horses, his chariots, his armory, his cattle, his family, and his whole substance in readiness against the time when it shall be said: To your tents, O Israel! Let not this be noised abroad; let every heart beat in silence, and every mouth be shut" (*History of the Church,* 2:145).

Brigham Young

"While six-tenths or three-fourths of this people will keep the commandments of God, the curse and judgments of the Almighty will never come upon them, though we will have trials of various kinds, and the elements to contend with—natural and spiritual elements" (*Journal of Discourses,* 10:335–36).

John Taylor

"In relation to events that will yet take place, and the kind of trials, troubles, and sufferings which we shall have to cope with, it is to me a matter of very little moment. These things are in the hands of God. He dictates the affairs of the human family, and directs and controls our affairs; and the great thing that we, as a people, have to do is to seek after and cleave unto our God, to be in close affinity with him, and to seek for his guidance, and his blessing and Holy Spirit to lead and guide us in the right path. Then it matters not what it is nor who it is that we have to contend with, God will give us strength according to our day" (*Gospel Kingdom,* 349).

Wilford Woodruff

"Can you tell me where the people are who will be shielded and protected from these great calamities and judgments which are even now at our door? I'll tell you. The priesthood of God who honor their priesthood and who are worthy of their blessings are the only ones who shall have this safety and protection. They are the only mortal beings. No other people have a right to be shielded from these judgments. They are at our very doors; not even this people will escape them entirely" (Gates, "Temple Workers' Excursion," 512).

"I want the Latter-day Saints to stop murmuring and complaining at the providence of God. Trust in God. Do your duty. Remember your prayers. Get faith in the Lord, and take hold and build up Zion. All will be right. The Lord is going to visit His people, and He is going to cut His work short in righteousness, lest no flesh should be saved. I say to you, watch the signs of the times, and prepare yourselves for that which is to come" ("Discourse by President Wilford Woodruff," 796–97).

"Those who have got oil in their lamps, are men who live their religion, pay their tithing, pay their debts, keep the commandments of God, and do not blaspheme his name; men and women who will not sell their birthright for a mess of pottage or for a little gold or silver; these are those that will be valiant in the testimony of Jesus Christ" (*Journal of Discourses,* 21:126).

"Will he [Jesus] receive us to himself? Are we prepared for his coming and kingdom and the fulness thereof, unless we are sanctified, and lay aside sin, and do right? No. We must sanctify ourselves, and keep the commandments of God, and do those things that are required at our hands, before we can be prepared for the coming of the Great Bridegroom" (*Journal of Discourses,* 2:202).

LORENZO SNOW

"We should understand that the Lord has provided, when the days of trouble come upon the nations, a place for you and me, and we will be preserved as Noah was preserved, not in an ark, but we will be preserved by going into these principles of union by which we can accomplish the work of the Lord and surround ourselves with those things that will preserve us from the difficulties that are now coming upon the world, the judgments of the Lord" (Conference Report, Oct. 1900, 4–5).

"There is rapidly coming something that will try you, perhaps as you have never been tried before. All, however, that is necessary for us to do now is to see where our faults and weaknesses lie, if we have any. If we have been unfaithful in the past, let us renew our covenants with God and determine, by fasting and prayer, that we will get forgiveness of our sins, that the Spirit of the Almighty may rest upon us, that peradventure we may escape those powerful temptations that are approaching. The cloud is gathering in blackness. . . . Therefore, take warning" ("Discourse," 762–63).

JOSEPH F. SMITH

"We believe that . . . severe, natural calamities are visited upon men by the Lord for the good of his children, to quicken their devotion to others, and to bring out their better natures, that they may love and serve him. We believe, further, that they are the heralds and tokens of his final judgment, and the schoolmasters to teach the people to prepare themselves by righteous living for the coming of the Savior to reign upon the earth, when every knee shall bow and every tongue confess that Jesus is the Christ. If these lessons are impressed upon us and upon the people of our country, the anguish, and the loss of life and toil, sad, great and horrifying as they were, will not have been endured in vain" (*Gospel Doctrine,* 55).

"Unless the Latter-day Saints will live their religion, keep their covenants with God and their brethren, honor the priesthood which they bear, and try faithfully to bring themselves into subjection to the laws of God, they will be the first to fall beneath the judgments of the Almighty, for his judgments will begin at his own house" (Conference Report, Apr. 1880, 96).

GEORGE ALBERT SMITH

"In our day we are warned, in a revelation to the Prophet Joseph Smith, that unless we are more righteous than those who are receiving destruction at the present time in many parts of the world, we, too, must lose our birthright and our opportunity and be destroyed here in the flesh. We will not be justified by saying we are living as well as other people. That is not sufficient, my brethren. We have a special destiny if we live for it. That destiny is to live here upon this earth when it becomes the Celestial Kingdom, where God our Heavenly Father and His Son Jesus Christ will be our King and our Lawgiver" (Conference Report, Oct. 1943, 45).

"He [the Lord] has told us in great plainness that the world will be in distress, that there will be warfare from one end of the world to the other, that the wicked shall slay the wicked and that peace shall be taken from the earth. And He has said, too, that the only place where there will be safety will be in Zion. Will we make this Zion? Will we keep it to be Zion, because Zion means the pure in heart?" (Conference Report, Oct. 1941, 99).

JOSEPH FIELDING SMITH

"We shall not escape [the judgments] unless we repent, turn to the Lord, honor our Priesthood and our membership in this Church, and be true and faithful to our covenants" (Conference Report, Apr. 1937, 62).

SPENCER W. KIMBALL

"In the parable, oil can be purchased at the market. In our lives the oil of preparedness is accumulated drop by drop in righteous living. Attendance at sacrament meetings adds oil to our lamps, drop by drop over the years. Fasting, family prayer, home teaching, control of bodily appetites, preaching the gospel, studying the scriptures—each act of dedication and obedience is a drop added to our store. Deeds of kindness, payment of offerings and tithes, chaste thoughts and actions, marriage in the covenant for eternity—these, too, contribute importantly to the oil with which we can at midnight refuel our exhausted lamps" (*Faith Precedes the Miracle,* 256).

EZRA TAFT BENSON

"Heed the Lord's counsel to the Saints of this dispensation: 'Prepare yourselves for the great day of the Lord' (D&C 133:10).

"This preparation must consist of more than just casual membership in the Church. You must learn to be guided by personal revelation and the counsel of the living prophet so you will not be deceived" (*New Era,* May 1982, 50).

HOWARD W. HUNTER

"Jesus taught his disciples to watch and pray; however, he taught them that prayerful watching does not require sleepless anxiety and preoccupation with the future, but rather the quiet, steady attention to present duties" (Conference Report, Apr. 1974, 23).

MELVIN J. BALLARD

"These are the last days spoken of by the prophets of old. These are the signs. Oh, Latter-day Saints, let us, though we be in Zion, be not asleep, for this is the day when no man can be at peace, nor shall we remain at peace in sin or in transgression; for everything will be shaken that is not built upon righteousness, and every man, whether in Zion or elsewhere, who does not keep the commandments of God, shall be shaken and shall fall, and shall feel the chastening hand of the Almighty" (Conference Report, Oct. 1923, 32).

M. RUSSELL BALLARD

"The prophecies of the last days lead me to believe that the intensity of the battle for the souls of men will increase and the risks will become greater as we draw closer to the second coming of the Lord.

"Preparing ourselves and our families for the challenges of the coming years will require us to replace fear with faith. We must be able to overcome the fear of enemies who oppose and threaten us. The Lord has said, 'Fear not, little flock; do good; let earth and hell combine against you, for if ye are built upon my rock, they cannot prevail' (D&C 6:34)" (Conference Report, Oct. 1989, 43).

CHARLES A. CALLIS

"To men and likewise to nations the promises and threatenings of God are always conditional. In the wisdom and goodness of God good behavior, sorrowful repentance and conversion can stay the approach of judgment, or at least secure a respite. People are given time by the Almighty to return to him through repentance. There is forgiveness with Him. Thus the Lord turns aside his judgments for a while at least. Nineveh's people were rescued. They were granted an extension of time. Judgments are conditional. The people themselves are responsible for the calamities that befall them, but when they repent and turn unto the Lord, he hears their prayers" (Conference Report, Oct. 1938, 23).

GEORGE Q. CANNON

"All can embrace righteousness; all can forsake iniquity; all can turn to the Lord. And those who will not but will continue to practice iniquity, I tell you, as a servant of God, they will be destroyed, whether they be "Mormons" or non-"Mormons." Those who wish to have themselves and their posterity perpetuated in the earth must practice righteousness, for righteousness alone will save the people from the calamities that are coming upon the earth" ("Mormonism Inculcates Purity," 24).

NEAL A. MAXWELL

"In our striving to be prepared, therefore, let us be careful to rely on parents, priesthood, and principles—and on scriptures, and temples, and leaders who lead—to see us through. Let us not mistake program scaffolding for substance" (Conference Report, Oct. 1982, 98).

BRUCE R. McCONKIE

"The Second Coming is a day of judgment, a day of rewards, a day of vengeance for the wicked, a day of glory and honor for the righteous. It is a day for which all men prepare by the lives that they live. Those who live as becometh saints shall be as their Lord; those who walk in carnal paths shall be cast out" (*Mortal Messiah,* 3:51).

DELBERT L. STAPLEY

"Let us be sure we thoroughly understand the most important things we can do to prepare ourselves for our Lord's second coming to earth and, by our obedience and faithfulness, escape his punishment. . . . We must set our lives and homes in order. This means a searching of our souls, an admittance of wrongdoing, and repentance where needed. It means keeping all of God's commandments. It means loving our neighbor. It means living an exemplary life. It means being good husbands and wives. It means teaching and training our children in the ways of righteousness. It means being honest in all our doings, in business and at home. It means spreading the gospel of Jesus Christ to all the peoples of the world" (Conference Report, Oct. 1975, 71).

JOSEPH B. WIRTHLIN

"Mortality is fleeting. We all have much to accomplish in preparation to meet Him.

"As Latter-day Saints, 'we believe all things, we hope all things. . . . If there is anything virtuous, lovely, or of good report or praiseworthy, we seek after these things.' [Articles of Faith 1:13.] What do we believe that will motivate us to move forward? What do we hope for? What are the virtuous, lovely, or praiseworthy things we should seek after? I believe we should strive to develop within ourselves the traits of the character of the Savior" (Conference Report, Oct. 1998, 31).

KEYS TO BEING TEMPORALLY PREPARED

WILFORD WOODRUFF

"The Lord is not going to disappoint either Babylon or Zion, with regard to famine, pestilence, earthquake or storms, he is not going to disappoint anybody with regard to any of these things, they are at the doors. . . . Lay up your wheat and other provisions against a day of need, for the day will come when they will be wanted, and no mistake about it. We shall want bread, and the Gentiles will want bread, and if we are wise we shall have something to feed them and ourselves when famine comes" (*Journal of Discourses,* 18:121–22).

"We have got either to make ourselves self-sustaining, or we shall have to go without a good many things that we now regard as almost indispensable for our welfare and comfort, for there is not a man who believes in the revelations of God but what believes the day is at hand when there will be trouble among the nations of the earth, when great Babylon will come in remembrance before God, and his judgments will visit the nations. When that day comes, if Zion has food and raiment and the comforts of life she must produce them, and there must be a beginning to these things" (*Journal of Discourses,* 16:33).

HAROLD B. LEE

"We have never laid down an exact formula for what anybody should store, and let me just make this comment: Perhaps if we think not in terms of a year's supply of what we ordinarily would use, and think more in terms of what it would take to keep us alive in case we didn't have anything else to eat, that last would be very easy to put in storage for a year . . . just enough to keep us alive if we didn't have anything else to eat. We wouldn't get fat on it, but we would live, and if you think in terms of that kind of annual storage rather than a whole year's supply of everything that you are accustomed to eat which, in most cases, is utterly impossible for the average family, I think we will come nearer to what President Clark advised us way back in 1937" (Welfare Conference Report, 1 Oct. 1966, typescript).

SPENCER W. KIMBALL

"Some have become casual about keeping up their year's supply of commodities. . . .

"Should evil times come, many might wish they had filled all their fruit bottles and cultivated a garden in their backyards and planted a few fruit trees and berry bushes and provided for their own commodity needs.

"The Lord planned that we would be independent of every creature" (Conference Report, Oct. 1974, 6).

"In the twenty-fourth chapter of Matthew, the Lord speaks there of hard times, difficult times, more difficult than anything we have ever dreamed of. There will be famines and there will be sickness and drought. There will be many, many problems come, the like of which [World War II] was nothing. So the thing to do is for every mother and her husband to talk about saving a little something for a future that could be disastrous to their own families" (Manchester England Area Conference Report, June 1976, 23).

EZRA TAFT BENSON

"What can we do to prepare for what may lie ahead? Answers to this question have been repeated to our people many times, over the years. Here are some of them:

"1. Get out of debt and live within your income.

"2. Save what you can from your income.

"3. Store at least one year's supply of food, clothing, and other household necessities.

"4. Pay your tithes and offerings.

"5. Support the welfare plan" (*"Pay Thy Debt and Live,"* 11).

"Family preparedness has been a long-established welfare principle. It is even more urgent today.

"I ask you earnestly, have you provided for your family a year's supply of food, clothing, and, where possible, fuel? The revelation to produce and store food may be as essential to our temporal welfare today as boarding the ark was to the people in the days of Noah" (*Ensign,* Nov. 1987, 49).

"Our bishops storehouses are not intended to stock enough commodities to care for all the members of the Church. Storehouses are only established to care for the poor and the needy. For this reason, members of the Church have been instructed to personally store a year's supply of food, clothing, and, where possible, fuel. By following this counsel, most members will be prepared and able to care for themselves and their family members, and be able to share with others as may be needed" (*Ensign,* May 1977, 82).

"You do not need to go into debt . . . to obtain a year's supply. Plan to build up your food supply just as you would a savings account. Save a little for storage each pay-check. Can or bottle fruit and vegetables from your gardens and orchards. Learn how to preserve food through drying and possibly freezing. Make your storage a part of your budget. Store seeds and have sufficient tools on hand to do the job. If you are saving and planning for a second car or a TV set or some item which merely adds to your comfort or pleasure, you may need to change your priorities. We urge you to do this prayerfully and *do it now"* (*Ensign,* Nov. 1980, 33).

"A man should not only be prepared to protect himself physically, but he should also have on hand sufficient supplies to sustain himself and his family in an emergency. For many years the leaders of the Mormon Church have recommended, with instructions, that every family have on hand at least a year's supply of basic food, clothing, fuel (where possible), and provisions for shelter. This has been most helpful to families suffering temporary reverses. It can and will be useful in many circumstances in the days ahead. We also need to get out of financial bondage, to be debt free" (*God, Family, Country,* 331).

GEORGE Q. CANNON

"Do not forget . . . the teachings you have heard and which have been repeated in our hearing for so many years; I refer to the saving and storing of grain; for the day will come when you will see the wisdom of doing so, and when many of you will doubtless wish you had profited by it. For I tell you that wars and desolation will cover the land, just as prophets have declared they would; and these are coming, coming, coming, as plainly and as surely as the light comes in the morning before the sun rises above the summit of yonder mountains, and before we see his rays" (*Journal of Discourses,* 25:260).

J. REUBEN CLARK JR.

"When we really get into hard times, where food is scarce or there is none at all, and so with clothing and shelter, money may be no good for there may be nothing to buy, and you cannot eat money, you cannot get enough of it together to burn to keep you warm, and you cannot wear it" (in "Blessings Promised for Carrying on Welfare Program," 4).

MARION G. ROMNEY

"It is important for us to have, as we have been counseled, a year's supply of food and clothing, and where possible, fuel. We have also been counseled that we should have a reserve of cash to meet emergencies and to carry adequate health, home, and life insurance. Personal and family preparedness, however, is much broader than these tangibles. It must include proper attitudes, a willingness to forego luxuries, prayerful consideration of all major purchases, and learning to live within our means" ("Principles of Temporal Salvation," 6).

"It may be that some time in the future we will survive or starve on what we can produce ourselves" (Conference Report, Apr. 1974, 179).

"We will see the day when we will live on what we produce" (Conference Report, Apr. 1975, 165).

ERASTUS SNOW

"[The Lord] designs his people to prepare while there is time, and while he gives them bread to sustain themselves. But if that time should come suddenly upon us in our present condition, who would be prepared for it? If the news was to reach us that Babylon was really going down, that a general war had overtaken her, causing distress of nations, and the closing up of her manufactories, and the struggle between capital and labor were again renewed, causing domestic and national trouble, and as a consequence we found our foreign supplies cut off, how many would begin to pray that Babylon might be spared a little longer?" (*Journal of Discourses,* 19:181–82).

FIRST PRESIDENCY: SPENCER W. KIMBALL, N. ELDON TANNER, AND MARION G. ROMNEY

"Maintain a year's supply of food for your family. Use prudence and seek reliable information on what and how to store, and observe local laws and ordinances in storage procedures" (Circular Letter, to All Members of the Church, 16 Dec. 1974).

FIRST PRESIDENCY: EZRA TAFT BENSON, GORDON B. HINCKLEY, AND THOMAS S. MONSON

"Speculation engenders fear and can cause members to become caught up in emergency preparedness efforts that are not only costly but go beyond the basics consistently taught. . . .

" . . . We suggest that members concentrate on essential foods that sustain life [for one year] . . . grains, legumes, cooking oil, powdered milk, salt, sugar or honey, and water. The decision to do more than this rests with the individual" (First Presidency Letter, 24 June 1988).

PARABLES OF THE LAST DAYS AND THE SECOND COMING

Parable of the tares: JST Matt. 13:22–29; 35–41; D&C 38:12; 86:1–11; *Teachings,* 97–98, 100–101

Parable of the mustard seed: Matt. 13:31–32; *Teachings,* 98

Parable of the woman with leaven: Matt. 13:33; *Teachings,* 100

Parable of the treasure hid in a field: Matt. 13:44; *Teachings,* 101

Parable of the pearl of great price: Matt. 13:45–46; *Teachings,* 101–2

Parable of the fishing net: JST Matt. 13:48–51; *Teachings,* 102

Parable of the laborers in the vineyard: Matt. 20:1–16

Parable of the wicked husbandmen: JST Matt. 21:33–44; Mark 12:1–12; Luke 20:9–18

Parable of the wedding feast: Matt. 22:1–14; D&C 58:8–11; 65:3; *Teachings,* 52

Parable of the fig tree: Matt. 24:32–33; Mark 13:28–32; Luke 21:29–33; D&C 35:15–16

Parable of the ten virgins: Matt. 25:1–13; D&C 45:56–57; 63:54; 133:10–11; *Teachings,* 36

Parable of the talents: Matt. 25:14–30; Luke 19:11–27; *Teachings,* 68

Parable of the great supper: Luke 14:12–24

Parable of the unjust judge: Luke 18:1–8; cf. D&C 101:81–92

Parable of the kingdoms: D&C 88:51–61, 74

Parable of the redemption of Zion: D&C 101:43–62

Parable of the gathering of eagles: JST Matt. 1:27

—⟨⟩—

APPENDIX 4

REPRESENTATIVE TEXTS ON THE LAST DAYS AND THE SECOND COMING

The following scriptural passages pertain to the last days, the signs of the times, the Second Coming, or the Millennium. These passages are listed sequentially, beginning with the books of the Old Testament, followed by those in the New Testament, the Book of Mormon, the Doctrine and Covenants, and finally the Pearl of Great Price. Although this list is somewhat comprehensive, it is not completely so, and thus should be viewed as representative of the scriptural texts on these topics. Parallel verses (Isaiah 2:2–4 = Micah 4:1–3) are included only once.

Genesis 19:24–28. The destruction of Sodom and Gomorrah is a type of the last days' destruction

Ezra 1:2–5. The return of the exiled Jews to Judah is a type of their latter-day return

Psalm 9:1–20. The Lord judges the world in righteousness and dwells in Zion

Psalm 47:1–9. Sing praises to the Lord, who is the King of all the earth

Psalm 48:1–14. Zion is the joy of the whole earth

Psalm 50:1–6. The Lord comes with devouring fire

Psalm 53:6. Gathered Israel rejoices

Psalm 67:1–7. The Lord governs all people, and they praise his name

Psalm 69:32–36. God saves Zion, and they that love his name dwell in Zion

Psalm 72:1–20. Solomon's reign anticipates Christ's

Psalm 76:1–12. The Lord judges the earth and saves the meek

Psalm 82:1–8. The Lord arises and judges the earth

Psalm 85:6–13. Truth springs out of the earth

Psalm 87:1–7. The Lord loves Zion

Psalm 93:1–5. The Lord reigns and is clothed with majesty

Psalm 96:1–13. Let all be joyful, for the Lord cometh

Psalm 97:1–12. The Lord destroys the wicked with fire

Psalm 98:1–9. Praise the Lord, for he comes to judge the earth

Psalm 99:1–9. The Lord is great in Zion; worship him at his holy hill

Psalm 102:13–22. The Lord rebuilds Zion and appears in glory

Psalm 110:1–7. The Lord's day of wrath

Psalm 129:1–8. Those who hate Zion are confounded

Psalm 132:1–18. The Lord desires Zion for his habitation

Isaiah 2:1–5. The mountain (temple) of the Lord

Isaiah 2:10–22. The day of Jehovah

Isaiah 3:13–4:1. Judgment against the daughters of Zion

Isaiah 4:2–6. Those who escape the judgments of God are cleansed

Isaiah 5:26–30. An ensign to the nations

Isaiah 9:3–7. The Messiah, the Son, is the New King

Isaiah 10:12–19. God destroys Assyria, a type of the destruction at the Second Coming

Isaiah 10:20–27. The remnant of Israel returns

Isaiah 11:6–9. Glorious conditions of the Millennium

Isaiah 11:10–16. An ensign gathers Israel

Isaiah 12:1–6. Israel's millennial song of salvation

Isaiah 13:1–5. The Lord of armies calls forth his hosts

Isaiah 13:6–22. Judgment on Babylon: the wicked are punished at the Second Coming

Isaiah 14:1–3. Israel is gathered, chosen of God, and rests from sorrow

Isaiah 15:1–9. God's judgment on Moab is a type of his judgments on the wicked at his coming

Isaiah 17:1–11. God's judgment on Damascus is a type of his judgments on the wicked at his coming

Isaiah 18:1–7. The Lord's messengers take the gospel to the world

Isaiah 19:1–25. Prophecy concerning Egypt's devastation and ultimate return to the Lord

Isaiah 21:1–10. Prophecy of judgment against Babylon

Isaiah 24:1–12. The world changes the ordinance and breaks the covenant

Isaiah 24:13–16. A righteous remnant rejoices

Isaiah 25:6–12. The Lord prepares a feast for the righteous

Isaiah 26:1–6. A song about a "strong city" and the "lofty city"

Isaiah 26:7–18. A prayer about the Lord's judgments

Isaiah 26:19–21. The Lord responds to Israel's prayer and promises the resurrection

Isaiah 27:1–13. Israel is gathered in the last days

Isaiah JST 29:11–26 = King James Version 29:11–14. The Book of Mormon is a marvelous work and a wonder

Isaiah JST 29:27–32 = King James Version 29:15–24. The meek rejoice in the Book of Mormon

Isaiah 30:18–26. Zion is restored in Jerusalem

Isaiah 30:27–33. The Lord burns the wicked at his second coming

Isaiah 31:1–9. Divine protection for Zion and Jerusalem

Isaiah 32:1–8. Results of the reign of Jesus, our King

Isaiah 32:9–20. Destruction for the wicked, peace for the righteous

Isaiah 33:7–14. The wicked are burned at Christ's second coming

Isaiah 33:18–24. Restoration of Zion

Isaiah 34:1–8. A day of wrath upon Edom (the world)

Isaiah 34:9–15. Edom (the world) is burned

Isaiah 34:16–17. Those written in the book of the Lord receive the land

Isaiah 35:1–10. Latter-day Israel rejoices and blossoms as a rose

Isaiah 40:9–11. The Lord comes like a shepherd

Isaiah 43:1–7. Prophecy of redemption

Isaiah 43:8–13. We witness that Jehovah is God

Isaiah 44:1–8. Israel receives a multitude of blessings in the last days

Isaiah 44:21–23. The Lord redeems Israel

Isaiah 47:1–15. Babylon is destroyed

Isaiah 48:20–22. Song of the flight from Babylon

Isaiah 49:8–12. Israel's return in the last days

Isaiah 49:13–21. The Lord comforts his returning children

Isaiah 49:22–26. Gentiles shall assist returning Israel

Isaiah 51:17–23. The cup of God's wrath on Jerusalem

Isaiah 52:1–12. Deliverance to captive Israel

Isaiah 54:1–3. Zion is established

Isaiah 54:11–17. New Jerusalem is established

Isaiah 55:12–13. Israel returns with joy

Isaiah 56:1–8. Gentiles are welcomed to the covenant

Isaiah 59:15b–21. Salvation for the righteous, vengeance for the wicked

Isaiah 60:1–22. Glory of New Jerusalem

Isaiah 61:4–9. Blessings to restored Israel

Isaiah 61:10–11. A psalm of rejoicing—the marriage of the bride and bridegroom

Isaiah 62:1–12. Blessings for Zion

Isaiah 63:1–6. The Lord's vengeance in the Second Coming

Isaiah 65:17–25. Millennial earth

Isaiah 66:1–6. Righteous are justified, the wicked punished

Isaiah 66:7–14a. Blessings to Zion

Isaiah 66:14b–18a. The Lord returns in power and glory

Isaiah 66:18b–21. Gathering from all nations

Isaiah 66:22–24. Blessings of the Millennial Day

Jeremiah 3:12–22. Judah and Israel return to the Lord

Jeremiah 16:14–21. The Lord gathers Israel

Jeremiah 23:3–8. The Lord gathers Israel

Jeremiah 30:1–24. The Lord hath a controversy with the nations

Jeremiah 31:1–40. The Lord gathers Israel and rules over them

Jeremiah 33:1–26. The Lord gathers Israel and cleanses them

Jeremiah 46:27–28. The Lord gathers Israel and saves them

Jeremiah 50:19–20, 33–34. The Lord gathers Israel

Ezekiel 11:17–21. The Lord gathers Israel, and they keep his ordinances

Ezekiel 16:60–63. The Lord remembers his covenant with Jerusalem

Ezekiel 20:34–44. The Lord gathers Israel, and they serve him

Ezekiel 28:25–26. The Lord gathers Israel, and they dwell in their land

Ezekiel 34:11–31. The Lord gathers his sheep, and he shepherds them

Ezekiel 36:1–38. The Lord gathers Israel and cleanses them

Ezekiel 37:15–28. Israel is gathered by the Book of Mormon; they are cleansed

Ezekiel 38–39:16. Gog and Magog

Ezekiel 39:17–21. The supper of the great God

Ezekiel 39:22–29. The house of Israel knows God

Ezekiel 40:1–42:20. The future temple, its measurements and description

Ezekiel 43:1–27. The temple in action; offerings and holy days; the priesthood

Ezekiel 47:1–12. Waters flow from the temple and heal the Dead Sea

Ezekiel 48:1–35. Israel is apportioned land, the name of the city is "The Lord is there"

Daniel 2:26–45. God establishes his kingdom which shall never be destroyed

Daniel 7:9–27. Adam-ondi-Ahman

Daniel 8:17–26. A king persecutes the holy people

Daniel 10:14–21. Daniel is shown the last days

Daniel 12:1–13. Michael delivers Israel

Hosea 1:7, 10–11. Israel is saved

Hosea 2:14–23. Israel is God's people

Hosea 3:3–5. Israel returns and seeks the Lord

Hosea 14:1–9. Israel returns to God

Joel 1:1–12; 2:3–11. The locusts, or the invading army

Joel 1:13–20; 2:12–17. Repent, and call a solemn assembly

Joel 2:1–2. A description of the day of the Lord

Joel 2:18–27. A vision regarding Zion

Joel 2:28–32. The outpouring of the Spirit

Joel 3:1–14. Nations gather in the valley of Jehoshaphat

Joel 3:15–21. The Lord dwells in Zion, and Jerusalem becomes holy

Amos 5:18–20. The day of the Lord is darkness for the wicked

Amos 9:11–15. The Lord gathers Israel, and they build their waste cities

Obadiah 1:15–21. Deliverance is on Mount Zion

Micah 2:12–13. The Lord gathers Israel

Micah 4:1–13. The Lord's temple is established; the Lord reigns in Zion

Micah 5:7–15. Israel prevails among the nations

Micah 7:1–20. The Lord has mercy on Israel in the last days

Nahum 1:1–15. The Lord comes with fire, vengeance, and mercy

Nahum 2:1–13. The destruction of Nineveh is a type of the destruction at the Second Coming

Zephaniah 1:1–18. The destruction of Judah is a type of the Second Coming

Zephaniah 3:1–8. God pours his indignation on the nations

Zephaniah 3:9–13. The Lord gives his people a pure language

Zephaniah 3:14–20. The Lord reigns; his people are praised among all peoples

Zechariah 2:1–13. The Lord gathers Judah and dwells among his people

Zechariah 3:8–10. Iniquity is removed in one day

Zechariah 4:11–14. Two prophets in Jerusalem

Zechariah 8:1–23. Christ dwells in Jerusalem; Israel and Judah are gathered and blessed

Zechariah 10:6–12. The Lord gathers Judah and Joseph from all parts of the world

Zechariah 12:1–12. All nations gather against Jerusalem; the Lord defends his people

Zechariah 13:1–9. Judah is cleansed and recognizes the Messiah

Zechariah 14:1–21. The Messiah leads Israel to victory

Malachi 3:1–18. A messenger prepares the way for the Lord; the sons of Levi make an offering to the Lord. See also 3 Ne. 24:1–8; D&C 128:24

Malachi 4:1–6. Fire burns the wicked; Elijah returns before the Second Coming. See also D&C 2:1–3; 3 Ne. 25:5–6; D&C 128:17–18

JST Matthew 1:27. Parable of the gathering of eagles

JST Matthew 13:22–29, 35–41. Parable of the tares. See also D&C 38:12; 86:1–11

Matthew 13:31–32. Parable of the mustard seed

Matthew 13:33. Parable of the woman with leaven

Matthew 13:44. Parable of the treasure hid in a field

Matthew 13:45–46. Parable of the pearl of great price

JST Matthew 13:48–51. Parable of the fishing net

Matthew 16:1–4. Some cannot interpret the signs of the times

Matthew 16:27. Christ comes in glory

Matthew 20:1–16. Parable of the laborers in the vineyard

JST Matthew 21:33–44. Parable of the wicked husbandmen. See also Mark 12:1–12; Luke 20:9–18

Matthew 22:1–14. Parable of the wedding feast. See also D&C 58:8–11; 65:3

Matthew 1:1–35. A catalog of the signs of the times. See also JS–M 1:1–40

Matthew 24:36–39. Noah and the Flood are a type of the last days

Matthew 24:37–51. Be on the alert because the day and the hour are unknown. See also JS–M 1:41–56

Matthew 25:1–13. Parable of the ten virgins. See also D&C 45:56–57; 63:54; 133:10–11

Matthew 25:14–30. Parable of the talents

Matthew 25:31–46. Christ pronounces judgment at his second coming

Matthew 26:64. Christ comes in power

Mark 14:62. Christ comes with clouds of glory

Luke 12:35–48. Be prepared for Christ's coming

Luke 14:12–24. Parable of the great supper

Luke 17:28–37. The coming of Christ is similar to the destruction of Sodom

Luke 18:1–8. Parable of the unjust judge. See also D&C 101:81–92

Luke 19:11–27. Parable of the talents

Luke 21:20–28. A catalog of the signs of the times

Acts 1:6–11. Disciples ask when the kingdom of Israel is to be restored

Acts 2:1–4. Pentecost is a type of the latter-day outpouring of the Spirit

Acts 3:19–26. The restoration of all things

1 Corinthians 1:7–8. The Saints are to be blameless when Christ comes

1 Corinthians 15:23–28. The order of the resurrection at Christ's coming

Ephesians 1:9–12. The restoration of gospel

Colossians 3:1–4. The righteous appear with Christ at his coming

1 Thessalonians 2:19. The righteous appear with Christ at his coming

1 Thessalonians 3:13. The righteous appear with Christ at his coming

1 Thessalonians 4:13–18. The Saints meet Christ in the air at his coming

1 Thessalonians 5:1–11. The Saints watch for Christ's coming

2 Thessalonians 1:5–12. Christ punishes the wicked at his coming

2 Thessalonians 2:1–12. The Lord destroys evil at his coming

1 Timothy 4:1–4. Some depart from the faith in the last days

2 Timothy 3:1–7. The divers iniquities of the people in the last days

2 Timothy 4:1–8. Jesus judges the world at his coming

James 5:7–11. The Saints patiently wait for Jesus' coming

2 Peter 3:3–9. Some scoff at the signs of the times

2 Peter 3:10–18. The day of the Lord comes as a thief

1 John 2:15–23. Antichrists appear

Jude 1:14–25. The Lord comes with his Saints; a list of sins that exist in the last days

Revelation 1:7. Every eye sees Christ

Revelation 6:12–17. Opening of the sixth seal: warning voices

Revelation 7:1–8. Sealing of the 144,000 during the sixth seal

Revelation 8:1–5. Silence in heaven; angels prepare to sound their trumpets

Revelation 8:6–13. The first four trumpets bring judgments

Revelation 9:1–12. The first woe: the fifth angel blows his trumpet and brings judgments

Revelation 9:13–21. The second woe: the sixth angel sounds and brings judgments

Revelation 11:1–14. Two prophets prophesy, work miracles, and are killed

Revelation 11:15–19. The seventh trumpet sounds, and twenty-four elders worship God

Revelation 13:1–10. A beast rises from the sea

Revelation 13:11–18. A beast rises from the earth

Revelation 14:1–5. The Lamb and his 144,000

Revelation 14:6–13. Three angels of judgment

Revelation 14:14–20. Three angels of earth's harvest

Revelation 15:1–8. Seven angels with seven plagues

Revelation 16:1–21. Seven angels with the bowls of God's wrath

Revelation 17:1–6. Babylon, the mother of harlots

Revelation 17:7–18. Symbolism of the woman and the beast

Revelation 18:1–24. The fall of Babylon

Revelation 19:1–10. Victory songs in heaven

Revelation 19:11–16. The Lord on a white horse

Revelation 19:17–21. The supper of the great God

Revelation 20:1–6. The Lord's thousand-year reign

Revelation 20:7–10. Satan is loosed

Revelation 20:11–15. The last judgment

Revelation 21:1–8. New heaven and new earth

Revelation 21:9–27; 22:1–5. City of New Jerusalem

Revelation 22:6–21. "Surely I come quickly"

1 Nephi 10:14. The house of Israel is gathered

1 Nephi 13:5–9. The great and abominable church

1 Nephi 14:8–17. The Lamb's Church and the abominable church

1 Nephi 15:12–20. The restoration of the house of Israel

1 Nephi 19:15–17. The Lord gathers the house of Israel

1 Nephi 22:6–12. The Gentiles and the gathering of Israel

1 Nephi 22:13–24. God preserves his Saints and destroys the churches of the world

1 Nephi 22:24–26. Satan has no power during the Millennium

2 Nephi 3:6–15. Joseph the latter-day seer

2 Nephi 6:6–18. The role of the Gentiles in Israel's gathering

2 Nephi 10:7–19. Joseph is restored to his land of promise

2 Nephi 25:9–11. Judah is restored to Jerusalem

2 Nephi 25:17–18. Lord restores his people the second time

2 Nephi 26:14–19. The Book of Mormon speaks from the dust

2 Nephi 27:1–5. Iniquity in the last days

2 Nephi 27:6–20. The Book of Mormon is a sealed book

2 Nephi 27:21–35. The Restoration is a marvelous work and a wonder

2 Nephi 28:1–10. False churches teach incorrect doctrines

2 Nephi 28:11–19. Pride, false churches, and wickedness

2 Nephi 28:20–25. Some say, "All is well in Zion"

2 Nephi 28:26–32. Woes against the wicked

2 Nephi 29:1–10. Some oppose the Book of Mormon

2 Nephi 30:3–8. The Book of Mormon gathers people to Christ

2 Nephi 30:9–10. God judges with righteousness

2 Nephi 30:11–18. All things are revealed during the Millennium

Jacob 5:29–32. The latter-day restoration

Jacob 5:52–77. Zenos and Israel's gathering

3 Nephi 1:4–10. Those who denied the signs of Christ's first coming typify those who deny the signs of his second coming

3 Nephi 5:23–26. The seed of Joseph knows the Redeemer

3 Nephi 8–11. The signs of Christ's first coming are types of the signs that precede his second coming

3 Nephi 10:12–19. Righteous Nephites and Lamanites are spared during the destruction: a type for the righteous of the last days

3 Nephi 11:8–12. Christ's appearance at the temple in Bountiful is a type of his appearance to the righteous at his second coming

3 Nephi 16:6–15. The gospel goes to the Gentiles and then to the Jews

3 Nephi 20:10–22. God's covenant with Israel; the New Jerusalem is built

3 Nephi 20:25–46. The gathering of Israel

3 Nephi 21:1–7. The Book of Mormon comes forth

3 Nephi 21:8–11. A prophecy concerning Joseph Smith

3 Nephi 21:12–21. God executes vengeance upon the wicked

3 Nephi 21:22–29. New Jerusalem is established

3 Nephi 22:1–17. Jesus quotes Isaiah on the gathering of Israel

3 Nephi 26:3–5. Jesus comes in glory

3 Nephi 29:1–2. The Book of Mormon is a sign of the latter-day gathering

3 Nephi 30:1–2. Gentiles are commanded to repent and turn to Christ

4 Nephi 1:13–18. The Nephites' Zion prefigures the millennial Zion

Mormon 5:12–14. Jews begin to believe in Jesus

Mormon 6. God's judgments on the Nephite nation are a type of his judgments on the wicked at his coming

Mormon 7:1–10. Mormon's words to Latter-day Israel

Mormon 8:26–41. Signs, conditions, and wickedness in the last days

Mormon 9:1–6. The Lord's coming is a day of visitation and judgment

Mormon 9:7–26. Revelations and miracles in the last days

Ether 2:7–12. America is a land of promise

Ether 4:1–19. Sealed records are revealed

Ether 13:1–12. The New Jerusalem

Ether 15:1–3. Jaredite warfare is a type of the wars of the last days

Doctrine and Covenants 1:1–5. A voice of warning to all people

Doctrine and Covenants 1:9–17. God's wrath is poured out upon the wicked

Doctrine and Covenants 1:34–36. The Lord comes down in judgment upon the world

Doctrine and Covenants 2:1–3. Elijah is revealed before Christ comes

Doctrine and Covenants 5:19–20. A desolating scourge goes forth

Doctrine and Covenants 13:1. The sons of Levi make an offering

Doctrine and Covenants 27:5–15. Christ drinks of the fruit of the vine; gird up your loins to prepare for the evil day

Doctrine and Covenants 29:1–8. The gathering of the elect

Doctrine and Covenants 29:9–13. Christ burns the proud and the wicked at his second coming

Doctrine and Covenants 29:14–21. A catalog of the signs of the times

Doctrine and Covenants 29:22–25. The earth passes away after the Millennium

Doctrine and Covenants 29:26–29. The resurrection and the judgment

Doctrine and Covenants 33:1–16. It is the eleventh hour, the field is white

Doctrine and Covenants 33:17–18. Be prepared, for the Bridegroom cometh

Doctrine and Covenants 34:5–12. Declare repentance; prepare for the Second Coming

Doctrine and Covenants 35:15–16. The meek look for Christ's coming

Doctrine and Covenants 35:20–21. The elect will not be asleep when Christ comes

Doctrine and Covenants 35:24–27. Zion rejoices and flourishes

Doctrine and Covenants 36:8. The Lord comes suddenly to his temple

Doctrine and Covenants 38:11–12. Angels are ready to reap the earth

Doctrine and Covenants 39:16–24. Laborers cry repentance, preparing the way for Christ's coming

Doctrine and Covenants 42:35. The New Jerusalem is revealed

Doctrine and Covenants 43:17–28. God and his servants lift the voice of warning to prepare for Christ's coming

Doctrine and Covenants 43:29–33. The Millennium comes

Doctrine and Covenants 45:16–23. Christ's coming fulfills his promises

Doctrine and Covenants 45:24–33. Times of the Gentiles, wars, love waxes cold, earthquakes

Doctrine and Covenants 45:34–43. Christ fulfills his promises, signs in heaven and earth, blood and fire, sun darkened, moon turns to blood, stars fall, the gathering

Doctrine and Covenants 45:44–46. The Second Coming and the resurrection

Doctrine and Covenants 45:47–54. Christ appears to the Jews

Doctrine and Covenants 45:55–59. Satan is bound; Christ rules as king

Doctrine and Covenants 45:62–75. A description of the New Jerusalem

Doctrine and Covenants 49:6–8. No one knows the exact time of Christ's coming

Doctrine and Covenants 49:22–28. Be not deceived; Zion flourishes before Christ comes

Doctrine and Covenants 56:1–2. The Lord's day is a day of wrath

Doctrine and Covenants 56:16–19. Lord judges the wicked at his coming

Doctrine and Covenants 57:1–7. Independence, Missouri, is the center place of Zion

Doctrine and Covenants 58:6–7. Laying the foundation of Zion

Doctrine and Covenants 58:8–13. The marriage of the Lord

Doctrine and Covenants 61:4–5. Calamities and disasters are on the waters

Doctrine and Covenants 61:14–24. No flesh is safe upon the waters

Doctrine and Covenants 61:38–39. Saints look forward to Christ's coming

Doctrine and Covenants 63:1–6. The day of wrath upon the wicked

Doctrine and Covenants 63:24–31. The Saints assemble in Zion

Doctrine and Covenants 63:32–35. There are wars on the earth, but the Saints escape

Doctrine and Covenants 63:36–37. The Saints warn their neighbors

Doctrine and Covenants 63:39–48. The Saints give money to Zion

Doctrine and Covenants 63:49–54. Resurrection of the Saints at Christ's coming and during the Millennium

Doctrine and Covenants 63:57–60. This is a day of warning

Doctrine and Covenants 64:23–25. He that is tithed shall not be burned at Christ's coming

Doctrine and Covenants 64:37–43. Zion shall flourish

Doctrine and Covenants 65:1–6. The kingdom of God prepares the Saints for Christ's coming

Doctrine and Covenants 76:63. Righteous people accompany Christ at his coming

Doctrine and Covenants 77:6–7. The book of seven seals

Doctrine and Covenants 77:8. Four angels have power to save and destroy

Doctrine and Covenants 77:11. The 144,000 high priests

Doctrine and Covenants 77:12–14. The time of Christ's coming

Doctrine and Covenants 77:15. Two prophets in Jerusalem

Doctrine and Covenants 82:14. Zion increases in beauty and holiness

Doctrine and Covenants 84:1–5. The New Jerusalem and its temple

Doctrine and Covenants 84:92–97. The wicked receive plagues and curses

Doctrine and Covenants 84:98–102. A new song for the Millennium

Doctrine and Covenants 84:114–120. God's servants warn the people of coming desolation

Doctrine and Covenants 86:1–11. The meaning of the parable of the wheat and the tares

Doctrine and Covenants 87:2–8. Wars and signs of the times

Doctrine and Covenants 88:51–61. Parable of the kingdoms

Doctrine and Covenants 88:81–85. Lift the warning voice so that some may escape God's wrath

Doctrine and Covenants 88:86–93. Men, angels, and signs warn earth's inhabitants of Christ's coming

Doctrine and Covenants 88:94–107. Great events accompany seven trumpet blasts

Doctrine and Covenants 88:108–115. Seven angels blast their trumpets again; Satan is bound

Doctrine and Covenants 88:126. Pray always, that we may not faint while waiting for Christ's coming

Doctrine and Covenants 89:4. Evil designs of conspiring men in the last days

Doctrine and Covenants 90:8–11. The gospel is preached to the house of Israel and the Gentiles in many languages

Doctrine and Covenants 97:10–28. A temple is built in Zion; Zion escapes God's judgments if obedient

Doctrine and Covenants 99:5. The Lord comes quickly in judgment

Doctrine and Covenants 100:13–17. Zion is chastened and then redeemed

Doctrine and Covenants 101:9–12. The day of wrath upon the nations

Doctrine and Covenants 101:13–22. The Saints come to Zion with song

Doctrine and Covenants 101:23–25. All corruptible things are consumed

Doctrine and Covenants 101:26–34. During the Millennium all things are revealed

Doctrine and Covenants 101:43–62. Parable of the redemption of Zion

Doctrine and Covenants 101:63–75. The gathering to Zion is not in haste

Doctrine and Covenants 103:11–28. The redemption of Zion comes by power

Doctrine and Covenants 105:1–5. Zion is built on the law of the celestial kingdom

Doctrine and Covenants 105:9–41. The redemption of Zion comes; certain conditions are met among the Saints

Doctrine and Covenants 106:4–5. The day of the Lord does not come as a thief to the children of light

Doctrine and Covenants 107:53–57. The ancient gathering at Adam-ondi-Ahman is a type of the future gathering at Adam-ondi-Ahman

Doctrine and Covenants 109:38–46. Judgments are sent upon the wicked

Doctrine and Covenants 109:58–69. God's servants gather Jacob and Judah to Zion

Doctrine and Covenants 110:11, 13–16. Moses restores the keys for the gathering of Israel; Elijah comes to the earth; the day of the Lord is near

Doctrine and Covenants 112:1–9. The Twelve raise the warning voice to the world

Doctrine and Covenants 112:23–26. A day of wrath and burning

Doctrine and Covenants 113:7–10. "Put on thy strength, O Zion"

Doctrine and Covenants 115:5–6. The stakes of Zion are a refuge from the storm

Doctrine and Covenants 116. Adam-ondi-Ahman

Doctrine and Covenants 124:25–42. Latter-day temples

Doctrine and Covenants 128:24. The sons of Levi offer an offering of righteousness

Doctrine and Covenants 130:1. When Christ appears, we see him as he is

Doctrine and Covenants 130:14–17. The time of Christ's coming is unknown

Doctrine and Covenants 133:1–15. Go out of Babylon and prepare for the Second Coming

Doctrine and Covenants 133:16–20. The Bridegroom comes

Doctrine and Covenants 133:21–25. The Lord stands in the midst of his people

Doctrine and Covenants 133:26–35. People in the north countries

Doctrine and Covenants 133:36–56. Items regarding Christ's second coming

Doctrine and Covenants 133:63–74. The wicked are destroyed

Moses 7:62–64. The New Jerusalem

Moses 7:65–67. Signs of the last days

SOURCES CONSULTED

The Anchor Bible Dictionary. 6 vols. Edited by David N. Freedman. New York: Doubleday, 1992.

Andrus, Hyrum L. *Doctrinal Themes of the Doctrine and Covenants* (a series of lectures presented at the BYU–Ogden Adult Education Center, autumn quarter, 1957). Provo: Brigham Young University Press, 1964.

Ballard, M. Russell. *Our Search for Happiness: An Invitation to Understand The Church of Jesus Christ of Latter-day Saints.* Salt Lake City: Deseret Book, 1993.

———. Conference Report, October 1984, 17–20.

———. Conference Report, October 1989, 41–44.

———. *Ensign,* November 1992, 33–33.

———. *Ensign,* December 1996, 56–61.

———. "When Shall These Things Be?" In *Brigham Young University Speeches, 1995–96.* Provo, Utah: Brigham Young University, 1996.

Ballard, Melvin J. Conference Report, October 1923, 28–33.

Bennett, William J. *The Death of Outrage: Bill Clinton and the Assault on American Ideals.* New York: Free Press, 1998.

———. *The Index of Leading Cultural Indicators.* New York: Simon and Schuster, 1994.

Benson, Ezra Taft. *Come unto Christ.* Salt Lake City: Deseret Book, 1983.

———. *God, Family, Country: Our Three Great Loyalties.* Salt Lake City: Deseret Book, 1974.

———. *Labor of Love.* Salt Lake City: Deseret Book, 1989.

————. *A Witness and a Warning.* Salt Lake City: Deseret Book, 1988.

————. Conference Report, April 1950, 71–79.

————. Conference Report, April 1969, 10–15.

————. Conference Report, April 1987, 107–8.

————. Conference Report, October 1987, 101–4.

————. Conference Report, October 1988, 101–4.

————. Conference Report, April 1989, 3–7.

————. *Ensign,* December 1976, 67–72.

————. *Ensign,* May 1977, 82–84.

————. *Ensign,* November 1980, 32–34.

————. *Ensign,* March 1986, 3–5.

————. *Ensign,* November 1986, 4–7; 78–80.

————. *Ensign,* November 1987, 48–51.

————. *A Four-Fold Hope.* Brigham Young University Speeches of the Year, 24 May 1961. Provo, Utah: Brigham Young University, 1962.

————. *"Pay Thy Debt and Live . . . "* Brigham Young University Speeches of the Year, 28 February 1962. Provo, Utah: Brigham Young University, 1962.

————. *Vietnam—Victory or Surrender.* Brigham Young University Speeches of the Year, 6 May 1969. Provo, Utah: Brigham Young University, 1969.

————. "The Constitution—A Heavenly Banner." In *Brigham Young University Devotional and Fireside Speeches, 1986–87.* Provo, Utah: Brigham Young University, 1987.

————. "Five Marks of the Divinity of Jesus Christ." *New Era,* December 1980, 44–50.

————. "Jesus Christ—Gifts and Expectations." In *Brigham Young University Speeches of the Year, 1974.* Provo, Utah: Brigham Young University, 1975.

————. "Prepare Yourself for the Great Day of the Lord." *New Era,* May 1982, 44–50.

Benson, Ezra Taft, Gordon B. Hinckley, and Thomas S. Monson. First Presidency Letter, 24 June 1988. "Blessings Promised for Carrying On Welfare Program." *Church News,* 21 November 1953.

Bork, Robert H. *Slouching towards Gomorrah: Modern Liberalism and American Decline.* New York: Harper Collins, 1996.

Brown, Francis, S. R. Driver, and Charles A. Briggs. *A Hebrew and English Lexicon of the Old Testament.* Trans. Edward Robinson. Oxford: Clarendon, 1977.

Brown, Hugh B. Conference Report, April 1965, 39–44.

Callis, Charles A. Conference Report, October 1938, 22–25.

Cannon, George Q. "Mormonism Inculcates Purity." *Deseret Evening News* 33 (27 January 1900): 24.

Carnegie Commission on Preventing Deadly Conflict. Prologue to *Preventing Deadly Conflict: Final Report.* New York: Carnegie Commission on Preventing Deadly Conflict, 1998. This publication can be found on the Internet at www.ccpdc.org/pubs/rept97.

Clark, James R. *Messages of the First Presidency of The Church of Jesus Christ of Latter-day Saints.* 6 vols. Salt Lake City: Bookcraft, 1965–75.

Clark, J. Reuben, Jr. Conference Report, April 1944, 110–16.

———. In "Blessings Promised for Carrying On Welfare Program." *Church News.* 21 November 1953.

Dahl, Larry E., and Donald Q. Cannon, eds. *The Teachings of Joseph Smith: First President of the Church of Jesus Christ of Latter-day Saints.* Salt Lake City: Bookcraft, 1997.

Deseret News 1993–1994 Church Almanac. Salt Lake City: Deseret News, 1992.

Doxey, Roy W. *The Doctrine and Covenants and the Future.* Rev. ed. Salt Lake City: Deseret Book, 1972.

———. *Prophecies and Prophetic Promises.* Salt Lake City: Deseret Book, 1970.

Draper, Richard D. *Opening the Seven Seals: The Vision of John the Revelator.* Salt Lake City: Deseret Book, 1991.

Dyer, Alvin R. *The Refiner's Fire: Historical Highlights of Missouri.* Salt Lake City: Bookcraft, 1960.

Edersheim, Alfred. *The Temple: Its Ministry and Services.* Peabody, Mass.: Hendrickson, 1994.

Ehat, Andrew F., and Lyndon W. Cook, eds. *The Words of Joseph Smith.* Provo, Utah: Brigham Young University Religious Studies Center, 1980.

Encyclopaedia Britannica. 23 vols. London: William Benton, 1962.

Evans, Richard L. Conference Report, April 1950, 102–6.

Eyring, Henry B. *Ensign,* November 1989, 11–13.

Faust, James E. *Ensign,* April 1994, 6–10.

Fay, Sidney Bradshaw. *The Origins of the World War.* New York: Macmillan, 1948.

Gates, Susa Young. "The Temple Workers' Excursion." *Young Woman's Journal* 5 (August 1894): 505–16.

Good News Bible: The Bible in Today's English Version. New York: American Bible Society, 1976.

Grant, Heber J. "The Dedicatory Prayer in the Hawaiian Temple" [27 November 1919]. *Improvement Era,* February 1920, 281–88.

Haight, David B. Conference Report, April 1973, 82–85.

Hales, Robert D. *Ensign,* May 1986, 28–30.

———. "Freedom and Personal Liberty." In *Brigham Young University Speeches of the Year, 1975,* Provo, Utah: Brigham Young University, 1976.

Harrington, Wilfrid J. *Revelation.* Collegeville, Minn.: Liturgical Press, 1993.

Hersey, John. *Hiroshima.* New York: Bantam Books, 1975.

Hinckley, Gordon B. Conference Report, October 1969, 113–16.

———. Conference Report, October 1995, 92–96.

———. *Ensign,* May 1982, 44–46.

———. *Ensign,* November 1989, 51–54.

———. *Ensign,* November 1991, 52–59.

———. *Ensign,* November 1993, 54–60.

————. *Lest We Forget.* Brigham Young University Speeches of the Year, 10 November 1970. Provo, Utah: Brigham Young University, 1971.

————. *The Loneliness of Leadership.* Brigham Young University Speeches of the Year, 4 November 1969. Provo, Utah. Brigham Young University, 1970.

————."'We Need Not Fear His Coming.'" In *1979 Devotional Speeches of the Year.* Provo, Utah: Brigham Young University, 1980.

Holy Bible. Authorized King James Version. Salt Lake City: The Church of Jesus Christ of Latter-day Saints, 1979.

Holy Bible. Revised Standard Version. New York: Nelson, 1946, 1952.

Horton, George A., Jr. "Knowing the Calamity." In *The Doctrine and Covenants.* Edited by Robert L. Millet and Kent P. Jackson. Vol. 1 of *Studies in Scripture.* Sandy, Utah: Randall Book, 1985.

Hunter, Howard W. Conference Report, April 1974, 21–25.

————. *Ensign,* October 1993, 70–73.

Hymns of The Church of Jesus Christ of Latter-day Saints. Salt Lake City: The Church of Jesus Christ of Latter-day Saints, 1985.

The Interpreter's Bible. 12 vols. New York: Abingdon, 1951–57.

Jackson, Kent P. *From Apostasy to Restoration.* Salt Lake City: Deseret Book, 1996.

————. "The Lord Is There (Ezekiel 37–48)." In *The Old Testament: 1 Kings to Malachi.* Edited by Kent P. Jackson and Robert L. Millet. Vol. 4 of *Studies in Scripture.* Salt Lake City: Deseret Book, 1993.

————. "Prophecies of the Last Days in the Doctrine and Covenants and the Pearl of Great Price." In *The Heavens Are Open: The 1992 Sperry Symposium on the Doctrine and Covenants and Church History.* Salt Lake City: Deseret Book, 1993.

Jerusalem Bible. Reader's Edition. Garden City, N. Y: Doubleday, 1968.

Johnson, Clark V. "My Disciples Shall Stand in Holy Places: Jesus Christ in the Twenty-First Century." In *The Heavens Are Open: The 1992 Sperry Symposium on the Doctrine and Covenants and Church History*. Salt Lake City: Deseret Book, 1993.

Journal of Discourses. 26 vols. London: Latter-day Saints' Book Depot, 1854–86.

Keown, Gerald L., Pamela J. Scalise, and Thomas G. Smothers. *Jeremiah 26–52*. Vol. 27 of *Word Biblical Commentary*. Dallas: Word Books, 1995.

Kimball, Spencer W. *Faith Precedes the Miracle*. Salt Lake City: Deseret Book, 1972.

———. *The Miracle of Forgiveness*. Salt Lake City: Bookcraft, 1969.

———. Conference Report, October 1961, 29–34.

———. Conference Report, October 1965, 65–72.

———. Conference Report, April 1972, 25–29.

———. Conference Report, October 1974, 4–10.

———. *Ensign,* October 1974, 3–14.

———. *Ensign,* June 1976, 3–6.

———. *Ensign,* November 1977, 76–79.

———. *Ensign,* May 1978, 79–81.

———. *Ensign,* November 1982, 4–6.

———. Manchester England Area Conference Report, June 1976, 22–24.

———. São Paulo Brazil Area Conference Report, February–March 1975, 72–73.

———. Seoul Korea Area Conference Report, August 1975, 59–61.

———. "Absolute Truth." In *Brigham Young University Devotional Speeches, 1977*. Provo, Utah: Brigham Young University, 1978.

Kimball, Spencer W., N. Eldon Tanner, and Marion G. Romney. Circular Letter to All Members of the Church, 16 December 1974.

King, Arthur Henry. *The Abundance of Heart*. Salt Lake City: Bookcraft, 1986.

Koehler, Ludwig, and Walter Baumgartner. *Lexicon in Veteris Testamenti Libros*. Leiden: Brill, 1953.

LeBaron, E. Dale. "The Book of Mormon: The Pattern in Preparing a People to Meet the Savior." In *Doctrines of the Book of Mormon: 1991 Sperry Symposium.* Edited by Bruce A. Van Orden and Brent L. Top. Salt Lake City: Deseret Book, 1992.

Lee, Harold B. *Decisions for Successful Living.* Salt Lake City: Deseret Book, 1973.

———. *Stand Ye in Holy Places.* Salt Lake City: Deseret Book, 1974.

———. Conference Report, April 1948, 52–58.

———. Conference Report, October 1968, 59–62.

———. Conference Report, October 1972, 123–31.

———. *Ensign,* November 1971, 14–17.

———. *Ensign,* December 1971, 28–32.

———. *Ensign,* July 1973, 2–6.

———. "A Stake Is Born." *Millennial Star* 122 (May 1960): 188–94.

———. "Using the Scriptures in Our Church Assignments." *Improvement Era* 72 (January 1969): 12–14.

Ludlow, Daniel H. *A Companion to Your Study of the Doctrine and Covenants.* 2 vols. Salt Lake City: Deseret Book, 1978.

Ludlow, Victor L. *Isaiah: Prophet, Seer, and Poet.* Salt Lake City: Deseret Book, 1982.

———. *Principles and Practices of the Restored Gospel.* Salt Lake City: Deseret Book, 1992.

Lund, Gerald N. "Things Which Must Shortly Come to Pass." In *Acts to Revelation.* Edited by Robert L. Millet. Vol. 6 of *Studies in Scripture.* Salt Lake City: Deseret Book, 1987.

Lundquist, John M. "What Is a Temple? A Preliminary Typology." In *Temples of the Ancient World: Ritual and Symbolism.* Edited by Donald W. Parry. Salt Lake City: Deseret Book and FARMS, 1994.

Maxwell, Neal A. *Even As I Am.* Salt Lake City: Deseret Book, 1982.

———. *Deposition of a Disciple.* Salt Lake City: Deseret Book, 1976.

———. *Notwithstanding My Weakness.* Salt Lake City: Deseret Book, 1981.

————. *A Time to Choose.* Salt Lake City: Deseret Book, 1972.

————. *Wherefore, Ye Must Press Forward.* Salt Lake City: Deseret Book, 1977.

————. Conference Report, October 1980, 16–19.

————. Conference Report, October 1982, 95–99.

————. *Ensign,* November 1981, 8–10.

————. *Ensign,* May 1987, 70–72.

————. *Ensign,* May 1988, 7–9.

McConkie, Bruce R. *Doctrinal New Testament Commentary.* 3 vols. Salt Lake City: Bookcraft, 1965–73.

————. *The Millennial Messiah.* Salt Lake City: Deseret Book, 1982.

————. *The Mortal Messiah.* 4 vols. Salt Lake City: Deseret Book, 1979–81.

————. *A New Witness for the Articles of Faith.* Salt Lake City: Deseret Book, 1985.

————. *The Promised Messiah.* Salt Lake City: Deseret Book, 1978.

————. Conference Report, April 1979, 130–33.

————. *Ensign,* February 1985, 72–74.

————. Mexico City Mexico Area Conference Report, Aug. 1972, 41–46.

McConkie, Joseph Fielding. "False Christs." In *Watch and Be Ready: Preparing for the Second Coming of the Lord.* Salt Lake City: Deseret Book, 1994.

————. "Joseph Smith As Found in Ancient Manuscripts." In *Isaiah and the Prophets: Inspired Voices from the Old Testament.* Edited by Monte S. Nyman. Provo, Utah: Brigham Young University Religious Studies Center, 1984.

McConkie, Joseph Fielding, Robert L. Millet, and Brent L. Top. *Doctrinal Commentary on the Book of Mormon.* Vol. 4. Salt Lake City: Bookcraft, 1992.

McConkie, Joseph Fielding, and Donald W. Parry. *A Guide to Scriptural Symbols.* Salt Lake City: Bookcraft, 1990.

Metzger, Bruce M. *Breaking the Code: Understanding the Book of Revelation.* Nashville: Abingdon Press, 1993.

Millet, Robert L. "Life in the Millennium." In *Watch and Be Ready: Preparing for the Second Coming of the Lord.* Salt Lake City: Deseret Book, 1994.

———. "Quest for the City of God: The Doctrine of Zion in Modern Revelation." In *Doctrines for Exaltation: The 1989 Sperry Symposium on the Doctrine and Covenants.* Salt Lake City: Deseret Book, 1989.

Millet, Robert L., and Joseph Fielding McConkie. *Our Destiny: The Call and Election of the House of Israel.* Salt Lake City: Bookcraft, 1993.

"Modern Prophecy and Its Fulfilment." *Millennial Star* 27 (25 March 1865): 184–90.

Monson, Thomas S. "In Quest of the Abundant Life." *Ensign,* March 1988, 2–5.

Mounce, Robert H. *The Book of Revelation.* Grand Rapids: Eerdmans, 1977.

Nelson, Russell M. Conference Report, October 1986, 84–89.

———. *Ensign,* November 1991, 59–61.

The New Bible Commentary. Edited by Francis Davidson. Grand Rapids: Eerdmans, 1953.

New Bible Dictionary. Edited by J. D. Douglas. Leicester, England: InterVarsity, 1988.

New English Bible. Oxford: Oxford University Press, 1961.

Nibley, Hugh. *Approaching Zion.* Salt Lake City: Deseret Book and FARMS, 1989.

Nyman, Monte S. "Abinadi's Commentary on Isaiah." In *The Book of Mormon: Mosiah, Salvation Only through Christ.* Edited by Monte S. Nyman and Charles D. Tate Jr. Provo: BYU Religious Studies Center, 1991.

———. "The Second Gathering of the Literal Seed." In *Doctrines for Exaltation: The 1989 Sperry Symposium on the Doctrine and Covenants,* 186–200. Salt Lake City: Deseret Book, 1989.

Nyman, Monte S., and Charles D. Tate, Jr., eds. *The Book of Mormon: First Nephi, the Doctrinal Foundation.* Salt Lake City: Bookcraft, 1988.

Oaks, Dallin H. *The Pure in Heart.* Salt Lake City: Bookcraft, 1988.

———. *Ensign,* May 1996, 71–73.

Ostler, Craig J. "Isaiah's Voice on the Promised Millennium." In *Voices of Old Testament Prophets: The 26th Annual Sidney B. Sperry Symposium.* Salt Lake City: Deseret Book, 1997.

Otten, Leaun G., and C. Max Caldwell. *Sacred Truths of the Doctrine and Covenants.* 2 vols. Salt Lake City: Deseret Book, 1983.

Packer, Boyd K. Conference Report, October 1975, 145–49.

———. Conference Report, October 1992, 98–102.

Parry, Donald W. "Ritual Anointing with Olive Oil." In *The Allegory of the Olive Tree: The Olive, the Bible, and Jacob 5.* Edited by Stephen D. Ricks and John W. Welch. Salt Lake City and Provo: Deseret Book and FARMS, 1994.

Parry, Donald W., Jay A. Parry, and Tina M. Peterson. *Understanding Isaiah.* Salt Lake City: Deseret Book, 1998.

Parry, Jay A., and Larry E. Morris. *The Mormon Book of Lists.* Salt Lake City: Bookcraft, 1987.

Parry, Jay A., and Donald W. Parry. *Understanding the Book of Revelation.* Salt Lake City: Deseret Book, 1998.

———. "The Temple in Heaven: Its Description and Significance." In *Temples of the Ancient World: Ritual and Symbolism.* Edited by Donald W. Parry. Salt Lake City and Provo: Deseret Book and FARMS, 1994.

Parsons, Robert E. "The Great and Abominable Church." In *1 Nephi to Alma 29.* Edited by Kent P. Jackson. Vol. 7 of *Studies in Scripture.* Salt Lake City: Deseret Book, 1987.

Penrose, Charles W. "The Second Advent." *Millennial Star* 21 (10 September 1859): 581–84.

Petersen, Mark E. *The Great Prologue.* Salt Lake City: Deseret Book, 1975.

———. "The Great Prologue." In *Brigham Young University Speeches of the Year,* 1974. Provo, Utah: Brigham Young University Press, 1975.

———. "Homecoming to Palestine." *Church News,* 9 March 1968, 16.

———. *Our Divine Destiny.* Brigham Young University Speeches of the Year, 20 February 1968. Provo, Utah: Brigham Young University Press, 1968.

Pratt, Orson. *Divine Authenticity of the Book of Mormon,* nos. 5, 6. Liverpool: R. James, 1851.

———. *Orson Pratt's Works.* Vol. 2 of *Important Works in Mormon History.* Orem, Utah: Grandin Book, 1990.

Pratt, Parley P. *A Voice of Warning.* Salt Lake City: The Church of Jesus Christ of Latter-day Saints, 1950.

Richards, Franklin D. *A Compendium of the Doctrines of the Gospel.* Rev. ed. Salt Lake City: The Deseret News, 1925.

Roberts, B. H. *New Witnesses for God.* 3 vols. Salt Lake City: Deseret News, 1911.

———. *Comprehensive History of the Church of Jesus Christ of Latter-day Saints, Century One.* 6 vols. Salt Lake City: Deseret Book, 1930.

———. *The Missouri Persecutions.* Salt Lake City: Bookcraft, 1965.

———. *Outlines of Ecclesiastical History.* Salt Lake City: George Q. Cannon and Sons, 1895.

Robinson, Stephen E. "Early Christianity and 1 Nephi 13–14." In *1 Nephi to Alma 29.* Edited by Kent P. Jackson. Vol. 7 of *Studies in Scripture.* Salt Lake City: Deseret Book, 1987.

Romney, Marion G. Conference Report, April 1950, 83–88.

———. Conference Report, April 1958, 125–29.

———. Conference Report, April 1963, 74–78.

———. Conference Report, October 1966, 53–54.

———. Conference Report, April 1974, 176–80.

———. Conference Report, April 1975, 164–66.

———. Conference Report, April 1977, 73–77.

————. "A Glorious Promise." *Ensign,* January 1981, 2–3.

————. "'If Ye Are Prepared Ye Shall Not Fear.'" *Ensign,* July 1981, 3–5.

————. "Principles of Temporal Salvation." *Ensign,* April 1981, 3–7.

Schell, Jonathan. *The Fate of the Earth.* New York: Knopf, 1982.

Schick, Eduard. *The Revelation of St. John.* New York: Herder and Herder, 1971.

Smith, George Albert. Conference Report, October 1941, 96–102.

————. Conference Report, October 1943, 42–47.

————. "New Year's Greeting." *Millennial Star* 83 (6 January 1921): 1–3.

Smith, Hyrum M., and Janne M. Sjodahl. *Doctrine and Covenants Commentary.* Salt Lake City: Deseret Book, 1972.

Smith, Joseph. *History of The Church of Jesus Christ of Latter-day Saints.* Edited by B. H. Roberts. 2d ed. rev. 7 vols. Salt Lake City: The Church of Jesus Christ of Latter-day Saints, 1932–51.

————. *Teachings of the Prophet Joseph Smith.* Selected by Joseph Fielding Smith. Salt Lake City: Deseret Book, 1976.

Smith, Joseph F. Conference Report, April 1880, 95–96.

————. *Gospel Doctrine.* 5th ed. Salt Lake City: Deseret Book, 1977.

————. "The Lesson in Natural Calamities." *Improvement Era* 9 (June 1906): 651–54.

Smith, Joseph Fielding. *Answers to Gospel Questions.* Compiled by Joseph Fielding Smith Jr. 5 vols. Salt Lake City: Deseret Book, 1993.

————. *Church History and Modern Revelation.* 2 vols. Salt Lake City: Council of the Twelve Apostles of the Church of Jesus Christ of Latter-day Saints, 1946–49.

————. *Doctrines of Salvation.* Compiled by Bruce R. McConkie. 3 vols. Salt Lake City: Bookcraft, 1954–66.

————. *Elijah the Prophet and His Mission.* Salt Lake City: Deseret Book, 1957.

————. *Progress of Man*. Salt Lake City: The Genealogical Society of Utah, 1936.

————. *The Restoration of All Things*. Salt Lake City: Deseret Book, 1945.

————. *The Way to Perfection*. Salt Lake City: The Genealogical Society of Utah, 1949.

————. Conference Report, April 1911, 124–26.

————. Conference Report, April 1937, 58–62.

————. Conference Report, April 1951, 57–59.

————. "What the Century Has Brought." *Utah Genealogical and Historical Magazine* 14 (January 1923): 1–18.

————. "The Mission of Ephraim." *Utah Genealogical and Historical Magazine* 21 (January 1930): 1–5.

————. "Prophecy and the Scriptures." *Church News,* 23 July 1952, 5, 14.

Snow, Lorenzo. Conference Report, October 1900, 1–5.

————. "Discourse" [delivered by President Lorenzo Snow, Logan, Utah, 6 May 1889]. *Deseret Weekly News* 38 (8 June 1889): 762–64.

Sperry, Sidney B. *The Voice of Israel's Prophets: A Latter-day Saint Interpretation of the Major and Minor Prophets of the Old Testament*. Salt Lake City: Deseret Book, 1965.

Stapley, Delbert L. Conference Report, October 1955, 13–16.

————. Conference Report, October 1971, 101–5.

————. Conference Report, October 1975, 70–73.

————. *Ensign,* November 1975, 47–49.

"Statistical Report, 1998." *Ensign,* May 1999, 22.

Strong, James. *The Exhaustive Concordance of the Bible*. Nashville: Abingdon, 1890.

Talmage, James E. *The Great Apostasy: Considered in the Light of Spiritual and Secular History*. Salt Lake City: Deseret Book, 1968.

————. Conference Report, October 1930, 70–75.

Tanner, N. Eldon. Conference Report, October 1968, 46–51.

Taylor, John. *Gospel Kingdom*. Selected by G. Homer Durham. Salt Lake City: Bookcraft, 1987.

Taylor, John, George Q. Cannon, and Joseph F. Smith. "An Epistle of the First Presidency." *Millennial Star* 49 (9 May 1887): 289–301.

Theological Dictionary of the New Testament. Edited by Gerhard Kittel and Gerhard Friedrich. Grand Rapids: Eerdmans, 1964–76.

Thomas, M. Catherine. "Jacob's Allegory: The Mystery of Christ." In *Allegory of the Olive Tree: The Olive, the Bible, and Jacob 5.* Edited by Stephen D. Ricks and John W. Welch. Salt Lake City: Deseret Book and FARMS, 1994.

Time Almanac 1999. Edited by Borgna Brunner. Boston: Information Please LLC, 1999.

Turner, Rodney. "The Two Davids." In *A Witness of Jesus Christ: The 1989 Sperry Symposium on the Old Testament.* Edited by Richard D. Draper. Salt Lake City: Deseret Book, 1990.

Walvoord, John F. *The Revelation of Jesus Christ: A Commentary.* London: Marshall, Morgan, and Scott, 1966.

Webster, Noah. *An American Dictionary of the English Language.* 2 vols. New York: S. Converse, 1828. Reprint. Facsimile first edition. San Francisco: Foundation for American Christian Education, 1967.

Wells, Daniel H. "Editorial." *Millennial Star* 27 (25 March 1865): 186–87.

Young, Brigham. *Discourses of Brigham Young.* Selected by (as *Gospel Kingdom,* by John Taylor) John A. Widtsoe. Salt Lake City: Deseret Book, 1941.

Whitney, Orson F. *Saturday Night Thoughts: A Series of Dissertations on Spiritual, Historical, and Philosophical Themes.* Salt Lake City: Deseret News, 1927.

———. Conference Report, October 1920, 30–36.

Widtsoe, John A. *Evidences and Reconciliations.* Arranged by G. Homer Durham. 3 vols. in 1. Salt Lake City: Bookcraft, 1960.

Williams, Clyde J., comp. *The Teachings of Harold B. Lee.* Salt Lake City: Bookcraft, 1996.

Wirthlin, Joseph B. Conference Report, October 1998, 30–34.

Woodruff, Wilford. "Discourse by President Wilford Woodruff." *Millennial Star* 51 (16 December 1889): 785–88.

———. "Discourse by President Wilford Woodruff." *Millennial Star* 53 (14 December 1891): 780–82, 794–97.

———. "Discourse by President Wilford Woodruff." *Millennial Star* 56 (9 April 1894): 225–29.

———. "Epistle of Elder Woodruff." *Millennial Star* 41 (21 April 1879): 241–46.

Woods, Fred E. "The Waters Which Make Glad the City of God: The Water Motif of Ezekiel 47:1–12." In *A Witness of Jesus Christ: The 1989 Sperry Symposium on the Old Testament.* Edited by Richard D. Draper. Salt Lake City: Deseret Book, 1990.

World Almanac and Book of Facts, 1992. New York: Pharos Books, 1991.

Young, Brigham, *Discourses of Brigham Young.* Selected by John A. Widtsoe. Salt Lake City: Deseret Book, 1941.

Young, Brigham, Heber C. Kimball, and Willard Richards. "Fifth General Epistle." *Millennial Star* 13 (15 July 1851): 209–16.

———. "Ninth General Epistle." *Millennial Star* 15 (9 July 1853): 436–41.

SCRIPTURE INDEX

SUBJECT INDEX

—∿∿∿—

Aaronic Priesthood, 32. *See also* Priesthood
Abaddon, 253–54
Abinadi, 435
Abomination of desolation, 268, 324, 355
Abominations, 290–92
Abortion, 220
Abraham: promises to, 50–51, 61, 85–86, 150; land symbolic of covenant with, 114; as type of God, 436
Adam (Michael): prophesies of end of earth, 3; attends to Joseph Smith, 40; calls council at Adam-ondi-Ahman, 401–7, 441–42
Adam-ondi-Ahman: great council at, 385, 401–7; early council at, 441–42
Africa, 250
African–Americans, 248–49
Ahriman, 276
Air, plague upon, 343–44
Allied and Associated Powers, 246
Alma, 238, 324
America: is prepared for Restoration, 29n, 286; as land of New Jerusalem, 155, 157, 191, 282
American Civil War: prophecy concerning, 171, 244–48; blacks fighting in, 248–49
Amos, 324, 414–15
Ancient of Days, 401–7. *See also* Adam
Andrus, Hyrum, 249–50
Angel(s): destroying, to pour out judgments, 11; assist in Restoration, 39–41, 185; are part of righteousness sweeping the earth, 186; loose Satan upon the earth, 252–54; bound, are released, 259, 262; reveal fall of Babylon, 300, 307; to warn of God's judgments, 326, 329–30; seven, with plagues, 330–35; help with harvest of righteous and wicked, 360–65; prepare for Second Coming, 383; do not know time of Second Coming,

388; accompany Christ at Second Coming, 423
Anthon, Charles, 37–38
Antichrist, 211–14
Apollyon, 253–54
Apostasy: great, 28–29, 286; inclusiveness of, 30–31; in last days, 201–3; symbols of, 288–89
Apostles, Twelve, will judge house of Israel, 413, 425–26
Armageddon: battle of, 260, 264–73, 295; explanation of, by Parley P. Pratt, 274–76; commentary on, 276–79
Armor of God, 393
Asaph, 427
Asia, 250
Assyria, 324, 347, 447–48
Atonement: reminders of, 364–65, 420–22; unites righteous with Christ, 430–33
Azal, 143

Babylon: meaning of, 94, 283–84; in last days, 213; relates to secret combinations, 226; as mother of harlots, 285–92; has worldly power, 293–96; Saints to flee, 296–300; description of fall of, 300–307; commentary on fall of, 307–18; receives judgments of God, 324
Ballard, M. Russell: on hope, 15; on world missionary effort, 60, 69–70; on deception, 210; on love waxing cold, 221; on acceleration of disasters, 322–23; on time of Second Coming, 387–88; on preparing for last days, 476
Ballard, Melvin J., 476
Baptism, 436
Beast(s): mark of, 91, 290–91, 339; from bottomless pit, 134, 137; as antichrist, 213–14; as part of satanic trinity, 276; as scarlet colored, 289; has power

[5 4 3]